THE ARAB AMERICANS
A History

THE ARAB AMERICANS
A History

GREGORY ORFALEA

OLIVE
BRANCH
PRESS

An imprint of Interlink Publishing Group, Inc.
www.interlinkbooks.com

For Matthew, Andrew, and Luke—
unending love

First published in 2006 by

OLIVE BRANCH PRESS
An imprint of Interlink Publishing Group, Inc.
46 Crosby Street, Northampton, Massachusetts 01060
www.interlinkbooks.com

Library of Congress Cataloging-in-Publication Data
Orfalea, Gregory, 1949–
The Arab Americans : a history / by Gregory Orfalea.
p. cm.
"Some of this book was published in 1988, in different form, under the
title Before the flames, by the University of Texas Press"—T.p. verso.
Includes bibliographical references and index.
ISBN 1-56656-644-4
ISBN 1-56656-597-9 (pbk.)
1. Arab Americans—History. 2. Arab Americans—Social conditions.
3. Orfalea, Gregory, 1949—Travel—United States. 4. United
States—Description and travel. 5. Arab Americans—Biography. I. Orfalea,
Gregory, 1949– Before the flames. II. Title.
E184.A65O738 2005
305.892'7073'09—dc22
2005002841

Front cover photograph: Kamel and Matilda Awad, with their children, from left: Joe, Rose, and Eddie
(infant) at Coney Island, NY, in the '30s
Back cover photographs courtesy of Mel Rosenthal, from the exhibit "The Arab Americans":
left: Palestinian woman at a Brooklyn Heights peace march, September 16, 2001;
right: Palestinian girl on rollerblades, Bay Ridge, Brooklyn 1998

Printed and bound in the United States of America

To request our complete 40-page full-color catalog, please call us toll free at
1-800-238-LINK, visit our website at **www.interlinkbooks.com,** or write to
Interlink Publishing
46 Crosby Street, Northampton, MA 01060
e-mail: info@interlinkbooks.com

CONTENTS

PREFACE

I once thought—hoped actually—I would never address this subject again. But history has a way of grabbing a writer—and a community—by the neck with challenges and trials no one could ever have imagined. Oh for the days when we were invisible!

I have always had an instinct about danger—mysterious, but one that has been proved accurate enough times to make me take it seriously. The Arab-American community is in danger, from within and without. A few people hide among us who harbor hatreds that no one can fathom. At the same time, the society-at-large, fueled by decades of stereotyping of Arabs and by the atrocities of 9/11, seems prepared to pounce, should any more significant terrorism erupt on US soil. The vast majority of Arab Americans, who are a rather patriotic ethnic group at core, may pay worse than ever for the isolated newcomer's limitless sense of wrong. Lest anyone think I exaggerate, consider that a member of the Bush-appointed US Civil Rights Commission during a 2002 hearing in Detroit predicted that Arab Americans would be rounded up in camps in the event of a new terrorist attack.

It was with this in mind that I returned to the history of my community, to reinterpret, reconsider, expand: to hold it up as talisman and warning. This history of Arab Americans is both more political and more literary than my early book (1988), in which political concerns were embedded almost imperceptively in the narrative. But the past two decades are the most political, by far, in the Arab-American community's history, and a literary renaissance, if not *naissance*, is unfurling by the day. I now confront the growing spotlight on the community and weight on its shoulders, culminating in the horrifying events of September 11, 2001, and the subsequent and troubling Patriot Act, which hovers over us still.

Writing history while it is intensely in the making is a challenge, to say the least. Not a day went by when something on the front page (or further back) of the newspaper begged entrance to the new book. I had to be selective, of course, trying to divine what events and personalities best stand for the Arab-American saga. That story, once tangential to the wars of the Middle East, is, like the wars themselves, front and center in our country's fate. The earlier book did not have to face this extraordinary and perilous moment in history, on which the future not only of our country, but the world, may hang. The complex range of the Arab-American component to the post-9/11 world can be seen in these two surprising anomalies: there was an Arab-American fighter for bin Laden, and there is now an Arab American at the head of all US forces in Iraq (General John Abizaid). To further demonstrate the topsy-turvy changes in the community, in twenty years Iraqi Americans have gone from casting votes of virtually no weight here, to being voters whose votes are front page news—for candidates in Iraq!

I note with sadness the prescience of the last line of the preface to the first book, which observed that "the fallout of America's Middle East policy draws ever closer to these shores." Perhaps the United States was always at the center of gravity of this conflict and never knew it until now, if indeed we know it now. I suppose I sensed that the American-backed Israeli invasion of Lebanon in 1982, which took close to 20,000 civilian lives and ended with spectacular massacres in Palestinian camps, was going to hurt us. How, I did not know and did not want to speculate. The terrorist attack on US Marines in Beirut in 1983, from which many have dated the downward spiral of fundamentalism in the area, seemed a stiff enough warning that we were not in tune with justice and there were people ready to use extreme, violent means to tell us so.

No one could possibly anticipate the monstrosity of September 11. But I have to say I found myself nodding, grimly, at bin Laden's taped message on the eve of the November 2004 US presidential election, in which he speaks of first conceiving of an attack on the "towers of America… as I watched the destroyed towers in Lebanon" in 1982.[1] It gave me a visceral shock to recall that, standing in the Beirut ruins of Fakhani, where an Israeli bombardment had taken out a six-story building, I had written, in the first book: "What would happen if the World Trade Center were hit this way in New York, or the Daily Planet building in Los Angeles? What would the world say? What would it do?"[2] Well, the world said and did one thing; our democratically elected president did another.

It goes without saying that nothing justifies the virulent hatred and destruction of the terrorist attacks on New York and Washington, DC. But our Pontius Pilate hand-wringing concerning the effects of militant Zionism and Christian evangelism on the Holy Land has placed us in an untenable situation—we try to boost democracy in the very Arab world in which our client state makes a mockery of it, at least as far as the Palestinians are concerned. As the first President Bush noted, this cannot stand; either we fix the problem, which we have had a large hand in creating, or the fury of radical Islam will continue to haunt us.

Fixing the Palestine–Israel problem, as 9/11 Commissioner John Lehman has suggested, is a *sine qua non* for snuffing the oxygen of Islamist terror, but not far behind is attention to the widening gap between the rich and the poor worldwide (it cannot help that half of all US foreign aid goes to two countries—Egypt and Israel); cancelling American aid to dictatorial regimes in the Middle East; and the moral imperative to help the Iraqis get back on their feet. With all due respect to our soldiers, our current military involvement appears more counterproductive on this account by the day. Our very presence incites. As General Abizaid himself has said,[3] getting the water, electricity, and roads in working order is a far more important task than the report of guns whose exercise gives us, at best, questionable returns. Political economist Hilton Root has put the trouble with US foreign policy even more succinctly: "humiliation." The humiliation at the bottom of our policies that we have either refused or don't care to see comes back to haunt us.

I have tried to piece together suggestions from the Arab-American community about how we might extricate ourselves from the grim cul-de-sac our country finds itself in, and record as honestly as I could both the community's disgust with terror as an approach to perceived injustice and its attempt to navigate as Americans in a decidedly paranoid atmosphere.

This book is new. Even the earlier material about the history of the early Syrian immigration to and settlement in America has been cut, updated, and rewritten in parts with new research and interviews. Underpinning *The Arab Americans* are interviews I conducted with 140 Arab Americans spanning a period of a quarter century, including second interviews separated sometimes by many years.

"The Political Awakening" (Chapter 6) has an interesting history in itself. The chapter looked at the major Arab-American organizations that grew into being after the 1967 war, and the University of Texas cut it entirely, saying it was "too political." I restore much of it now as it offers an unusual glimpse of something not often discussed: how American Middle East policy is shaped on Capitol Hill. For a time, a weak but nascent Arab-American lobby battled it out with quirky foreign-policy aides who were bombarded at the same time by the Israel lobby. What struck me when I first blew dust off this lost chapter was how current the debate still is, for example, over settlements. The chapter gives an up-close look at the first (and last) time Congress tried to cut aid to Israel over the West Bank and Gaza settlements, through Senator Adlai Stevenson, who paid for his ill-fated effort with his career.

Chapter 8, "Stumbling Toward Peace," follows the roller-coaster ride the community took along with the Middle East in what appeared to be a peace breakthrough in Madrid and Oslo, then the precipitous decline in that process after the assassination of Rabin, the hopelessly over-billed and over-rushed Camp David talks at the tail end of the Clinton era, and the rise of Ariel Sharon to power in Israel. Here, too, I look at the alarming spikes in hate crimes against Arab Americans and those who look like them during the 1991 Gulf war and after the Oklahoma City bombing. Stereotyping in the media, film, books, advertisements, and so forth, grew exponentially in this period and is responsible in part for the unleashing of a subliminal hatred or fear of the Arab in US society.

To draw attention to "American fear" in the subtitle to Chapter 9 ("After the Flames") may be misleading, because there is also a lot of American kindness after 9/11 that I have tried to represent. But the violent, at times Orwellian, backlash some in the community have had to endure is recorded, along with the strange tentacles of the Patriot Act. I look at the new demographic patterns and their implications. For example, the community, for a long time 90 percent Christian, is now about 75 percent Christian, 25 percent Muslim.

The two community portraits in Chapter 10, Detroit and Washington, DC, are deeply concerned with 9/11 and how it has affected the community, from the singing of the Star Spangled Banner at the Comerica Park baseball stadium in Detroit by an Arab-American Muslim woman, to seven Arab Americans' narration of "that black day" in the US capital. I do not hide my own.

Even a few years before my first book was published, I had dropped out of political activism on behalf of the community. I have written elsewhere about this, but suffice to say here work in that vineyard is relentlessly punishing. It is shocking to the system and the heart to see how thoroughly Arab and Arab-American leaders can subvert, muscle out, and otherwise screw each other. The instincts of a "street fighter," as one Arab-American leader described the requirement of success in American politics, I'm afraid I lacked. Though like Nikos Kazantzakis I tried to fuse the man of action with the man of contemplation, ultimately, like him, I ended up giving myself over to trying to understand as a writer what forms there were in the swirling dust and smoke, and where they were headed. Edward Said's exemplary life as both brilliant literary critic and engaged revolutionary stands so tall to all of us who loved him, but even Edward, I think, would have admitted his own life ultimately stood with the power of the pen.

This book is not about Middle East policy, per se; it does recount in several ways the Sisyphean attempt by one community to try and help, however much it has all seemed a crying in the wilderness. After the death of Arafat in 2005, there seemed hope that negotiations between Palestinians and Israeils would get back on track and that, wonder of wonders, Ariel Sharon might be preparing Israelis for a substantial evacuation of settlements on the West Bank after removing those in Gaza. I am not so cynical as to foreclose even a Sharon changing course in old age; as the great short story writer Grace Paley intimates, our lives have to leave room for enormous changes at the last moment.

Changes here abound. The Arab–American community is now an estimated three million vs. two million in 1988; immigration and population statistics in the earlier material have been updated. In some cases, where it would be awkward not to note the death of someone I had once interviewed, I have done so. Stylistically, I have let much of the treatment of the early years stand. I hope returning to the topic as a more seasoned writer will afford a new richness. I continue to believe history and personal search for identity and meaning can be interwoven to profit. History need not be a dry recitation of dates and facts, but something alive. This subject—of an often marginalized if not suppressed ethnic community suddenly coming to stark light—lent itself peculiarly to that theory.

I want to thank several people who have encouraged me to address this subject through the lens of the past two decades or helped along the way: Dr. Michael Suleiman, above all, for a careful reading of the text; Pablo Medina and Albert Mokhiber; likewise, my astute editor Pam Thompson and the remarkable Interlink staff, including Juliana Spear, Hilary Plum, Moira Megargee, Brenda Eaton, Kerry Jackson, and Jenny Morgan; Rose Orfalea, Mark Orfalea, Grace Hamilton, Marvin Wingfield, a font of information at the ADC, truly its institutional memory; Helen Hatab Samhan, Sabeen Altaf, and George Selim at AAI, dedicated and cheerful researchers; tireless Sasha Ross at the Palestine Center; my colleagues at Pitzer College, especially our dean, Alan Jones, Lissa Peterson, Ami Mezahav, Andre Wakefield, Nigel Boyle, and Al Wachtel; Mona Hamoui, Khalil Jahshan, Mary Rose Oakar, Leila al-Qatami; Brigette Anouti at ACCESS; Anan Ameri, Sarah Blannett and Devon Akmon at the Arab American National Museum; Kareem Shora, Christopher Bentley at the US Citzens and Immigration Service, Joseph Jacobs, Robert Fogarty for printing some of this in *Antioch Review*, Joan Mandell, Nina Dodge, Jeff Dosik at Ellis Island, Mike Sarafa, Jeff Baloutine, Gary Awad, George and Nora Hanna, Nisreen Malhis, Jean Abinader, Patricia Sarrafian Ward, Sharif Elmusa, Jim Zogby, Nathalie Handal, Max Holland, Christopher Dickey, and always Naomi Shihab Nye. I hold in grateful memory the beautiful poet and critic Susan Atefat-Peckham; she left this world too soon.

The American Middle East Peace Research Institute in Cambridge, Massachusetts, was generous with the original grant that launched my research; their original board members—the late Hisham Sharabi, Walid Khalidi, and especially the late Edward W. Said—gave me a great vote of faith. Interlink's visionary and tireless publisher Michel Moushabeck deserves special thanks. He is a living example of courage. Thanks, as always, to my wife Eileen, who wielded a lilting knife; her comments, encouragement, and love are my great gift. Our boys, too—Matthew, Andrew, and Luke—sparked my interest in the project even as they did school papers on the Patriot Act, 9/11, and being half Arab, half Irish American. We have had many lively dinner discussions about the topics in this book, and they have helped shape my thinking.

Through the years, I have been humbled by people who saw my earlier work as a kind of cultural lodestone for the community at a time when so much about it was quieted, if not twisted of any semblance of reality. Many outside the community said it opened a window for them not just on a people, but on a problem. I hope I can call on the patience of readers again and pray I have not betrayed their faith by venturing into somewhat different waters by grace of Interlink in this new book. Apologies, dear reader, for a book a little heavier to the touch.

INTRODUCTION

Los Angeles is my hometown, a real place—contrary to myths fueled by Brahmins from the East. I was born within a mile of Angel's Flight downtown and grew up in Anaheim and Tarzana. On our block we were one of two Arab families, two Jewish, two Irish, and one Italian, for good measure. Between the Jewish and Arab families, who faced each other, footballs were fired in the street.

In the fifties nearly everyone in Los Angeles was building gardens and "landscaping," as it was called—dry lots dissolved into green oases. At night thousands of snails would ooze from the soil to feed on the tender shoots of dichondra, a ground cover with thin round leaves about the size of collar buttons. It did not wear well, this dichondra, through baseball games of "pepper" on the lawn and the hordes of feeding snails.

While tending dichondra and hedges and birds-of-paradise, somehow the Rototiller that gave us bloody knuckles and tore up the soil also crushed, if we weren't careful, the newly planted mint. The Arabs call mint *na̓naʿ*. As a child I repeated the double negative over and over: *na̓naʿ*, *na̓naʿ*. And delicious mint with olive oil and raw lamb entered the nose, then the mouth. To call a favorite vegetable of an entire people by a negative was like saying no to all you loved and thereby expecting it to increase. Such was life. My mother's mother, who watched two brothers starve to death in the Lebanon mountain range during World War I, used to say, "Can't be no worse!" The shish kebab can't be no worse, the health of her favorite son can't be no worse, the flowers of her acacia tree can't be no worse.

Early lesson: the mint in America was also subject to a stray Rototiller (and flagstone and fancy cement borders). But a negative was a positive and a positive a negative. What you loved most "can't be no worse." Why? I wanted to learn about the world of such a strange language that called mint *na̓naʿ* and why everyone was sad when *na'na'* was clipped halfway down the redolent leaf—like a butch haircut—by the new machine.

So, lost mint could be a reason for this book.

So could the blind great-grandfather who put his hands on my face when I was nine. I felt the trembling as if his hands had brought my heart into my face, and felt its beat there, right on the cheeks. His hands were veined ridges; his whitened blue eyes searched the ceiling of his small apartment out back of Great-Uncle Mike's house. They say Great-Jaddu (great-grandfather) Malouf liked me. What could be read from a nose that wasn't big yet, from a voice that was blessedly idiotic like the voices of all children reverent before the aged? Could he tell that I was afraid of him? I was afraid he would die in front of me, having heard he was close to 100. Or worse, that he would poke my eye out while searching my face for a clue to who I was. But they said, "This one likes stories." I was also the first grandson—the first born in California, with no stain of Ellis Island, or Atlantic Avenue in Brooklyn, or New York's Washington Street, an enclave in the New World where Arabs first peddled goods, worked in sweatshops, lived in tenements, and hung their own signs on stores. Needless to say, no stain of the tormenting Old World, either. There was no empty praise for the Old Country in my family; they feared it like a harpoon that was still seeking them out fifty years later with its sorrow.

Number two reason to write this book: fear that forced me forward into what I feared—my own people's past. To see and not be blind in the seeing.

Reasons mount without my knowing it. There were grand arguments on the porch of my grandparents in Pasadena into the hot night, and shouts amid the snapping of aces on mosaic tables made of cedar, cherry, mahogany, olive. They were playing whist, or *basra*. And of course *tawila*, or backgammon. Grandfather Awad, who directly descended from what is believed to be the first Arab immigrant family to the United States, in 1878, cries out, "Nasser will take what he must take! Give me a glass water, Matile!"

"Nasser will take the Suez Canal and sit on his people another one hundred years," spits 'Ammu (uncle) Mike. "Get me a glass '*araq*, Wardi!"

"Nasser go to the Roosian," quietly says 'Ammu Assad. "Get me cup coffee, Noor."

All the while overseeing this card game on the packed porch and the debate over the fate of the Arab world is Great-Thatee (great-grandmother to us, but more correctly in Arabic, *sitt*), smoking her *arjila*. It was an evening after the Orthodox Easter, so small bags of sweetened barley and anise seeds and sugared almonds lay strewn on the porch floor. I loved to hear the bubbles of Great-Thatee's hubble-bubble! She never argued, only pulled on the hose tip of the olivewood water pipe and emitted a smoke pure and clean from the rubber tube. No, this was not hashish (though later I found out that Grandfather had set burning marijuana leaves under his nose in the thirties to break up congestion from his emphysema). Great-Thatee, who was almost six feet tall and had a marvelous swirl of black-and-white hair like the topping of a licorice birthday cake, was smoking a small overturned cup of tobacco. It was a clean smoke, I was told. She was a clean woman. I think the two sons she lost in the Lebanon mountains were bubbles in the glass belly of the *arjila*. She was playing with them, I am sure. But this was not something I thought then. Only later, at the end of a long journey seeking the heritage of Arab Americans.

The book, the search, was to be a tribute to the four grandparents—Kamel and Matile Awad, Aref and Nazera Orfalea—and all the immigrants like them who went on to spawn three million Americans of Arab descent. I was proud of their idiosyncrasies and courage, their foolhardiness and *joie de vivre*. They, like other immigrants, had added their color to America, but the color was known by so few. They kept it to themselves.

Kamel Awad (Coney Island photo) lifts the apricot, which has the shape and feel in miniature of the torso of a beautiful woman. The color of the apricot skin is the color of a blush. He lifts it one day when I am about to enter teenage

Matilda Awad (right) and Wardi Malouf hold hands in Brooklyn, 1928. (Gary Awad)

years and says, "Look how the birds have eaten this side." The pit had been pecked. But he turns it. And the other side is smooth, curved, delectable, and sensuous. "This side is why I came to America."

As I grew, I began to find more of the savaged side of the apricot. And my search had to tell of it.

The old ones took me by the jugular, with love. Very few had told their stories, except in passing. Like the "Poor and Burning Arab" in the short story of that title by William Saroyan, they too often sat drinking their bitter demitasses, silent, communicating for hours this way, dusting off the lint from the pant leg and then one day dying. They were too involved with dissolving into America, disappearing, sinking like old coffee into the new soil. The Arabs are connectors of people, bridges, but they are also great hiders, vanishers. There is something savage they wish to forget. Instead of popping from the lamp of Aladdin, they jumped in willingly and stoppered it with the cork of America, because in America they could be what they are best—stubbornly, beautifully individual and lovers of family—without having to deal with the contest of nations on their native soil. But try as they might to avoid it, the oppressive present so far away somehow found them—in a headline, in news of a death, in a crumpled letter.

"Mad Ireland hurt you into poetry," Auden said of Yeats. Say that Mad Lebanon hurt me into this history. For Lebanon substitute as well Syria, Palestine—the entire Arab world hurts one into leaving, and penning some explanation of the reasons to come to America, to try to find a place, even in the snow, to plant a fig tree. I find myself thinking of the uncanny 100-foot-long glass-encased planter that architect Karin Rihbany of West Roxbury, Massachusetts, made in his solarium home. It is filled, behind snow heaps up to the windows, with figs.

And what of the pain of the splinter state that has never quite "taken" or been absorbed into the Middle East as it persists in twisting and turning in the wound it originally made? In a way the Israelis have played a role the Greco-Egyptian poet C. P. Cavafy presents in his famous poem "Expecting the Barbarians." A decadent, bejewelled, flatulent Roman society awaits the barbarians with fear and expectation. But they do not come. The last two lines read: "And now what shall become of us without any barbarians? Those people were a kind of solution." The air in the Arab world today is still thick with the odor of decay, and the "civilized" Israelis have brought neither themselves nor the Arabs any solution. As for the good taxpaying Arab Americans, they bear as much responsibility as anyone for the chaos in the lands of their origin. Therein the dilemma.

Three events influenced my decision to write this book.

June 5, 1967, was the date of my high school graduation. On that glistening day, a day of Disneyland and pool, of hot dogs and stolen beers, my family was entertaining the graduating class. As boys and girls danced liberation from the Sisters of St. Louis and the order of Carmelite Fathers, my father's ears were glued to an intercom speaker on the wall in the breakfast room. It was a radio report. The rock music out back gave way as I stared at his forlorn face. Mother, serving selflessly, as always, plates of ham and sliced beef, stopped to regard him. Israel had invaded three Arab countries—Syria, Egypt, and Jordan—and had destroyed the entire Egyptian Air Force on the ground. Father's face continued to lose its color. I graduated from more than high school that day.

Two years later, I published an article arguing the case for Palestinian rights in Georgetown University's student newspaper. Those were days when mentioning "Palestinians" could engender complete blankness or hateful stares. My article was based on notes from a class taught by John Ruedy and from George Antonius' seminal study *The Arab Awakening*. Original it was not. Two letters to the editor intimated that I must be a Nazi. One of the respondents was a local head of the Jewish Defense League (JDL). At the time I was stunned—I had always had Jewish friends—and I withdrew from further criticism of Israel in public for what I thought would be an indefinite period.

The third and most important event of all was a trip with Grandfather Awad to the lands of his birth, particularly Arbeen, Syria, a little apricot and olive farming village four miles east of Damascus.

The material for this book gathered like tumbleweed for over two decades. It was on the first trip to ancestral lands, with a relative who had left 50 years earlier, that I began to learn that we Arabs and Arab Americans are both responsible for and in some ways indict the other. Each questions the other's priorities. I found the blood bond that was previously invisible. Sometimes it is tight and sometimes it is loose. But it is there.

It began to nag me that there were no available volumes about Arab Americans. We have all reveled in *Roots* and the search for black identity by such writers as Toni Morrison, Gwendolyn Brooks, Alice Walker, and John Edgar Wideman. The search for "Jewish identity" is in some ways synonymous with contemporary America's own self-searching. It is not an exaggeration to say that the history of the American novel since World War II is the history of the alienated Jewish intellectual struggling with the universe to wring from it some drop of meaning. The names are myriad—Bellow, Malamud, Singer, Shaw, Heller, Roth. I took to heart much of their work—at times profound, at times wrangled, but always robust. The Holocaust had become a literary touchstone of Western life pained by existence. I felt it. But I wondered if there were touchstones peculiar to my own background.

There were portrayals of Chinese, Japanese, Irish, Hispanic immigrant experiences, and a surge of work on Native Americans. There were many treatments of Italian American life, from mafia to sainthood. Even the Armenians, one-fourth the size of the Arab population in America, were captured in the classic *Passage to Ararat* by Michael Arlen, as well as the more recent *Burning Tigris* by Peter Balakian. Had the Arabs fallen into the black hole of Atlantic Avenue?

The Arab Americans' silence about their past contributed to the general silence. But other reasons—spurred by events in the 1970s—became evident. The Arabs' unique and unpleasant status of becoming, since the oil embargo of 1973, "the last ethnic group safe to hate in America" (Nicholas Von Hoffman) had something to do with the general disregard and reinforced Arab-American reticence. Of course, after 2001, reticence was a luxury few Arab Americans could achieve.

Some voices have told part of the story that I cannot. Many dissertations on Arab-American communities and history have languished and died a quick, inauspicious death in the card catalogues of academia. One such is the fine, detailed 1961 Ph.D. dissertation of Adele Younis, finally published in 1995 as *The Coming of the Arabic-Speaking Peoples to the United States*. I am indebted to the sociologists Philip and Joseph Kayal's *The Syrian-Lebanese in America: A Study in Religious Assimilation*. It is a well-researched, if somewhat repetitive, treatment of the largest—though not only—Arab-American population. The Kayals are most interested in how the Eastern Christian's trappings of religion began to disappear in the US, particularly those of the Melkite and Maronites rites. (The Kayals are themselves Melkites.) *Becoming American*, by Alixa Naff, concentrates on early Syrian life, stopping at 1939; her main interest is with the Syrian peddler. The best-written book on the subject, however, is long out of print and outdated: Philip K. Hitti's *The Syrians in America* (1924).

I am also grateful for the anthologizing work done by Barbara Aswad (*Arabic-Speaking Communities in American Cities*) and the brothers Nabeel and Sameer Abraham (*Arabs in the New World*; *Arab Detroit*), Detroiters who concentrate on Detroit, and whose essay collections have gathered essential data on a community that, for some reason, has never been designated as a minority by the US Census Bureau. Diverse, excellent anthologies edited by Eric Hooglund for the American-Arab Anti-Discrimination Committee (ADC) (*Taking Root*) and for the Smithsonian Institution Press (*Crossing the Waters*). Michael Suleiman's keen scholarship and massive bibliographical work on the community have been a boon to everyone.

I am not writing a detached history. This is the result of a personal quest, a realization that took root in me slowly that I was not one, but two, and that the heritage of my people was simply not known and was often distorted in the United States. This seemed a dangerous mix, given the nature of US politics and the implication, particularly since 1967, that I was descended from a people considered to be an enemy of America, though indeed until 1991 we were not actually at war with any Arab country. In some ways, the Arab Americans live the oddest double life of any ethnic group. I wanted to chart how we dealt with it—radical disavowals and radical assertions of heritage and everything in between—up to the ringing of Beirut by a wall of fire on their television sets in 1982, to September 11, and beyond.

Who were we to deserve this? Who were we not to deserve it? Who, indeed, were we? Suddenly, strange purple *kufiyas* were in fashion during the siege of Beirut, and women wore them on the boulevards of Washington, DC, as scarves. They seemed like pelts. Hummus, the erstwhile spread that Arabs made of chickpeas, was called "Israeli dip" in the Farmers' Market near Beverly Hills.

Who were we? Internationalists, or burrowing lemmings? Exemplary Americans by virtue of what we did and confronted, or merely good Americans by virtue of what we avoided? What made a Philip Habib come out of retirement to negotiate cease-fires in Lebanon and risk a third heart attack? What made Najeeb Halaby, former president of Pan Am and head of the FAA under President John F. Kennedy, assume the post of chairman at Beirut's American University just when the country was being torn asunder by Israel, Syria, and fifty factions? What made Helen Thomas, the chief and touted veteran UPI White House correspondent, eat her evening meals at Mama Ayesha's Calvert Cafe, a restaurant in Washington, DC, owned by an old family of Palestinians from Jerusalem?

What made me, a teacher of English and literature, find myself in a decade moving from the classroom in a little California college surrounded by bougainvillea to Washington, DC, to become the first full-time Arab–American lobbyist and, finally, to Beirut, where I would be offered a "job" with the Palestine Liberation Organization? What made me stand before the flames? To see what faces were in them and try to hear what they were saying? The answer lies in a long history, and it began for me in a journey to the oldest city on earth.

—ONE—

GENERATIONS REUNITE
IN ARBEEN, SYRIA

When a life-changing telephone call comes, the phone rings as it does any other time. Before I get to that, I must say what I was doing on my first job out of college. At $60 a week, I wrote about ten obituaries a day for the *Northern Virginia Sun*—roughly a dollar an obit. I was hungry in more ways than one.

A morning exchange with the funeral directors would go something like this:

"Eaves Funeral Home" (tone reverent, calm).

"Hello, Mr. Eaves, this is the *Sun.* Anything today?"

"No, nothing today!" the voice sang at the recognition of an accomplice.

Or: "Bingham Funeral Home."

"Hello, Mr. Bingham. Got anything today?"

"Well, young fellow, I got a Rotarian for you. I got a lovely little lady from the D.A.R., and, by gosh, you've got yourself a general with four stars and a biography already written by the bereaved."

The voice on the phone was light and snowy.

"Boy, this is your Jaddu." It was Grandfather Kamel.

"I don't believe it."

"You better. It cost me lotta money to call you."

"Okay, I believe it. Are you all right?"

"Never been better. Boy, what are you doin' next week?"

"Working."

"What you do for work?"

"I write about dead people."

"Dead beeple?" The voice began to laugh with a wheeze. "How 'bout you come write about live beeple."

"What do you mean, Jaddu?"

"Boy, you comin' with me and Matile and Rosie, you mother, and Gary, you uncle, to Damascus."

I let the line talk to itself in a sound that is a little like scratching

1

the head, a little like the heart being perforated.

"Boy, you comin' to al-Sham. You know what al-Sham is? Damascus. I bought you ticket today. We goin' back to where I was born. You can get ready?"

"Jaddu, I don't believe it."

"Boy, you betta believe it."

"What should I do with my job?"

"You betta quit that job. Bring some clothes to wear and clothes to give. I'm talking about the boor beeple over there. I'm talking about Arbeen!"

Arbeen. It clanged a bell inside me.

"We leave one week. To Baris. Then we all meet there and go to Beirut. Then the *bilad* (home country)."

Grandfather's cockeyed alliteration told me: he had chosen two of his children, his wife, and his eldest grandchild to rendezvouz in Paris from where we would fly to Beirut and drive over the Lebanon mountains to the dusty village of his birth.

I hung up, dazed. Kamel Awad had been back to see his five brothers and one sister in Arbeen only once since emigrating to the United States in 1920. Except for one brother, Issa, none of his immediate family had ever been to America, and except for his wife, Matile, none of his family in America had ever seen the Old Country. The Awads had moved from Brooklyn after World War II to settle in the hot dry climate of the West because of Jaddu's emphysema. For a time, they had tried to sell their Corday handbags—an embroidered bag popular during the war because of the scarcity of canvas and leather (used up by the military)—in Florida. But in the words of Grandmother Matile, "Florida was no good, honey, because they don't wanna buy handbags; they only want the sunshine. In California, they want handbags and sunshine."

Kamel Awad (center) in Arbeen, Syria, with four brothers—Tawfiq, Amin, Abdu, and Salim. (Gary Awad)

Pasadena, California, was good to the Awads of Arbeen. As a boy I would climb up to the roof of Grandfather's handbag shop on Colorado Boulevard where folding chairs had been placed for the family to look out on the Rose Parade on New Year's Day. When we got bored by the overwhelming smell of a million chrysanthemums, the cousins would sneak down into the musty old store and play blindman's buff among the display cases. Many a New Year's was rung in with us hiding, muffling laughter behind naked mannequins.

Corday handbags faded as an item of demand, and by the mid-fifties Grandfather had opened a small contracting firm of twenty sewing machines to produce women's ready-to-wear dresses and sportswear. Soon nearly all of the Awads and Orfaleas had plunged into some form of "rag" business; for Jaddu it meant 25 more years in a sweatshop. He added his own special touch to garments with the embroidery machine; even after his retirement, he was the only one to use it.

I think at an early age I developed a hunger for beauty against the backdrop of greasy, sweating sewing machines and the hum of the cutter's blade. After my father had launched his own venture as a garment manufacturer with an orange dickey, I was exposed early on to the bustling, at times manic, at times alluring, world of fashion. As a boy I worked summers picking orders, boxing dresses, and sweeping dust, thread, and cloth piping from the long factory aisles. If I was overawed by the sleek turns of models, I was also never far away from the oilcan on a Singer, the steam of a presser, and the electric flash of Mexicans traveling through fields of cloth with their foot-long blades.

No one would have guessed among us cousins that bundling chunks of dresses for sewing at Jaddu's factory would contribute to a success that would prompt him in old age to invite one of us to the land of his birth, a place that had come down to us in stories and myth. I was the lucky one. The pilgrimage to Arbeen meant that we would take boxes of clothes for our poor relatives instead of sending them, as we had each Christmas, with a prayer that they would arrive in Syria and not the Bermuda Triangle. Arbeen—with its olive and apricot orchards and fields of *ful* (fava beans)—was distinguished by little, other than it was home to what was assumed by scholars to be the first Arab immigrant family to America—the Arbeelys. Family folklore linked us with them (Mother's birth certificate listed her as an Arbeely). The 1972 journey would somehow relink a century of wandering. I was excited, nervous, even afraid—the feeling a plug must have when it is about to enter a socket and light up a million phone calls under the ocean. How many loves and tragedies would this late-20th-century hookup with our Syrian origin start?

In 1878, Dr. Joseph Awad Arbeely, a native of Arbeen, packed up his wife and six sons and came to America. Dr. Arbeely was not the typical Syrian peasant; he was president of a college in Syria and came to America for freedom and opportunity. It has also been said that he was soured by internecine warfare in his own land and had witnessed and miraculously escaped the massacres by the Druze in 1860.

Arbeen, once a small farming village, is today a mixed Muslim and Christian suburb of 100,000 four miles east of Damascus. In 1860, the uprising of the Druze, a schismatic sect of Islam, caused 5,000 deaths in the Damascus area. Arbeely fled with his family to Beirut, but eighteen years later he dared to cross as many seas as he had to to get to America.

An article in the *New York Daily Tribune* on June 20, 1881, painted a picture of the strange new arrivals in Manhattan and hinted that already the Arbeely sons were divesting themselves of things Arab:

> Yusif Arbeely, who with his wife and six sons came to this country from Damascus, Syria in August, 1878, arrived in this city recently from Tennessee with his son, Nageeb. The father is about sixty years old and has many of the characteristics of his race. He still adheres to the dress of his native country. He wore yesterday a shirt made of purple silk striped with yellow, a fancy scarf about his waist, baggy trousers buttoned at the ankle, and a red cloth conically shaped hat called a *tarboosh*. Nageeb and his brothers have only retained the red cloth cap. Both sons and father have dark olive complections [sic], black eyes and black crisp hair and beards. Nageeb, who is very handsome, appears to be thirty, although he said he was only nineteen. The Arbeely family enjoys the distinction of being the only Syrian family that has ever come to this country.

Joseph, the father, crisp hair and all, described his reasons for coming to America:

> I left my relatives and friends behind because I desired freedom of speech and action and education advantages for my children. In coming here I have escaped the disadvantages of a retrograding civilization and a tyrannical government and have found all that I came in search of. My friends were greatly surprised at me. It was an experiment, but it has proved successful. You ask me why more of my countrymen do not come. There are two things in the way. One is that the Turkish government is opposed to emigration from the country, not only discouraging it, but taking measures against it; the other is that correct ideas of your great institutions here have not been spread among the people.

Whatever the image of America in the Arab world—a universally good one until recent years—125 years after Arbeely's "experiment," there were an estimated three million Americans of Arab descent. Democracy suited them well, freedom better. If there were incorrect ideas as the lands of their birth receded, gained independence, then became embroiled in an endless series of wars that slowly implicated the new land of their choosing, those misconceptions were at least as much American as Arab.

Nageeb Arbeely, Joseph's eldest son, became the examining doctor on Ellis Island for the Arab immigrants. Another son, Ibrahim, later ministered to Theodore Roosevelt in Washington, DC. And we were to travel back to Arbeen, the source of the westward Arab stream, to discover the life they left. Our lives were to be put in stark relief. I gave notice on the death desk in Arlington. My editor said, "Don't get caught in a war."

At Orly Airport in Paris, Jaddu—a peppery, squat charmer with twinkling brown eyes—toted a respirator around with him like a poodle. We were delayed there for hours waiting for a connecting flight and Jaddu, breathing heavily, smiled like the Buddha. He'd take a few hits of oxygen and ask for an El Producto cigar.

"Matile, why you give me this stuff? I wanna good smoke."

"Sorry, my honey," Grandmother said, wagging the oxygen hose at him. "You gotta be strong for the *bilad*."

He flirted with the stewardesses on the flight and made sure to tell them all that he was taking his family to Syria, the land of his birth, for the first time.

Over the Aegean, a fire ignited in one of the plane's engines and the Boeing 707 was forced to drop nearly all its fuel into the sea. The plane made an emergency landing in Athens. By this time Jaddu's brow was knitted in folds like a stack of Oriental carpets. He was losing energy and began to wonder aloud if we were doomed never to see the *bilad* together, and that he would die a half-step short in Greece, the country that had the bad taste to put ladles of oil on stuffed grape leaves instead of the saving potion of lemon juice. To die among greasy grape leaves! This would be a bad fate. It was late at night in the Athens airport and the passengers were sleeping on their duffle bags. Not Jaddu. He lit an El Producto.

"Boy, if I go, why not with something in my mouth besides that damn hose?" he pronounced. "If I go, I go up in smoke, not air conditioning."

Finally the plane was repaired and refueled and, a day after leaving the United States, our expectant group opened the drapes of the plane window to see land coming at us like a green squall. It was Lebanon, and dawn. The sun caromed off the plane's silver wings and hurt our tired eyes. In an instant we came to life at the sound of the cockpit's announcement to fasten seatbelts, *défense de fumer*, prepare to land in Beirut. We hid the cigars from Jaddu even though the lesson had come at me: if you are in this Arab clan you make a negative to print a positive. You smoke like an ocean liner stack in order to breathe well, your lungs billowing. You have emphysema, but you unfurl your lungs like a flag of your joys and agonies and wave it, coughs and all, to the homeland.

Approaching Beirut is like approaching a wall in Paradise. The beaches rush at you, then the boulevards and *suqs* (marketplaces) and apartments and houses of limestone. Then the wall of green—the Lebanon mountains. In many ways the Beirut coast resembles that of Santa Barbara—both cities are set on the only stretch of coastal land, on the American Pacific and the eastern Mediterranean, respectively, that runs East–West instead of North–South. The land indents for Beirut and Santa Barbara. It allows the sun to follow a methodical path across the horizon; in Beirut and Santa Barbara you always face the sun. Both cities, known for their lush acacias, eucalyptus, palms, and pines, rest in front of abrupt geologic surges. But the mountains in Lebanon are higher than California's Santa Inez range.

We alighted in the strength of dawn. The roads in from the airport were baking and dust climbed over the taxi in a dawn wind.

We had had too many cartons of clothes for the Arbeen people, and the Lebanese customs officer was about to chalk up a hefty overweight fee. Jaddu slipped him a picture of Ulysses S. Grant. The official touched the black patent leather border of his officer's green felt cap, flipped the bill over to see if it had a back, stared beyond his shoes to make sure no ant was looking, and, without lifting his head, said, *Ahlan wa sahlan, ya akhi* (Welcome, my brother).

We were shooed through the line into a taxi where a man with one gold front tooth opened the door and gave the same greeting to us.

We drove through the quiet streets. This was 6 AM, Sunday. No one was anywhere near the green ocean. I felt weightless. A light breeze rippled dusty palms along the beach. The eyes of the shops were closed with corrugated iron lids—so many garages snoozing. After we splashed our faces with cold water at the hotel, something changed. The heat felt clearer.

The Mediterranean Sea was not to be ours that first day because of construction along the shore in front of the hotel. We could only regard Mare Nostrum through a tangle of barbed wire. It was not an auspicious start, to see a captive sea, but we made little thought of that. This was, after all, the Promised Land. It was the land my grandparents cursed and praised daily; never an olive dropped into the mouth without someone saying, "They have olives like that every day in the *bilad*."

It is worth emphasizing here that *bilad* does not connote a certain country—Syria, Lebanon, Egypt—but rather a whole milieu, a world that to me as a child festooned the imagination with pomegranates and figs as in my grandparents' backyard. The *bilad* meant the Origin Point, a secret place where we all came from, God's arms. To go to the *bilad* had nothing to do with wrapping oneself in a flag. More to do with thyme—on the hands, in the fields, and bitter enough to curl the tongue. Thyme and time. Both were your birthright and you would possess both if you returned there. Political accusations could be thrown out against any one Arab government or all of them as a whole. But the *bilad* was different. The *bilad* was the magic coat we carried in our hearts. Jaddu was opening the sleeves for us so we would not be cold in America again.

The first morning in Beirut we enjoyed a breakfast at our hotel on the Corniche, the northwest corner of the city that juts over the sea. Waiters put out dishes of *labani* (a thickened yogurt spread with oil, with mint dashed on top), piles of Arabic bread, dishes of apricot jam, and cups of Nescafé. Only Jaddu ordered the watery earth that is Arabic coffee. It took the rest of us a while to warm up to it at every meal. By the end of the summer our tongues were well burned. To this day I can drink the hottest substances without a flinch. Some lands give you a birthmark; others give you a burnt mark.

To have Arab food in the morning in public was new to me, my uncle, and Mother. Breakfast is the most private of meals, and Arab food was a private food for us in America. Here all was public. The waiters smiled; their gold teeth shone in the sun, all the more for the gaps surrounding them.

Jaddu did not want us to fall for the Western lures of Beirut until we had seen Syria, his world. Within a day he was ordering a taxi driver to take us to Damascus 60 miles away up over Lebanon's mountains. A special stand downtown was the place to wait for an al-Sham (Damascus) taxi. A driver called out as we approached: Al-Sham! Al-Sham! It sounded like a poignant, declarative, unembroidered statement that he was ashamed. But no. He was just eager for the 25 dollars to take a carload to Damascus.

None of us was prepared for the driver's madcap style over the mountains—gunning the gas around blind corners and passing vehicles on same. More than once Mother would bark, ʿ*Ala mahlak!* (colloquial for "Take it easy"). It was our introduction to the land of no lanes and few stoplights, where every turn is Mr. Toad's Wild Ride.

The drive in the mountains was gorgeous, the summer air fragrant with the smell of acacias and pepper trees—exactly the trees in my grandparents' yard in Pasadena. But now a whole country! As we ascended we passed old limestone houses notched in the mountains, mules and sheep hardly acknowledging our presence on the road. At Shatturah we stopped to sample rolled Arabic bread wrapping sugared laban, a special sweet of the area.

The road was clear through the mountains, though twisted. There were no roadblocks of Syrian soldiers, the PLO, Phalangists, Israelis, or Hezbollah. It was one of the last years that ancient road from Beirut to Damascus was open to the traveler, three years before the Lebanese Civil War erupted. Over the mountains into the Biqaᶜ Valley, Lebanon's breadbasket, a vendor of cherries caught our eyes. It was here that Mother climbed right out of her body.

We were eating the cherries and spitting out the pits, looking out over a grove of cherry and olive trees. On the other side of the road swayed a wheat field, the breeze brushing the wheat back and forth in the mild heat. Jaddu kept saying, "Watch for the worm, boy." We ate avidly, though the cherries were warm and bland. The taxi driver ate his in the car; we saw an arching of pits come out his window, some tapping against the old Mercedes. The Middle East is filled with old Mercedes and fruit pits.

Mother heard something. None of us heard it, but she did. She said it was a flute. We went on nibbling the cherries, trying to absorb the fact that this was actually Lebanon and not the canyon road to Dead End Beach in California. Mother stopped eating and turned her head toward the wheat field. A dragonfly buzzed over the ruts in the road. Mother let it pass and walked across to the wheat field and disappeared. After a while we ran across and looked. Through the strands of wheat we saw a distant green upland and two figures facing each other. One was Mother, beautiful, in a long, persimmon-colored dress; the other was the figure of a shepherd with a *kufiya* over his head, playing on a crooked wooden flute. The tones were low, sonorous, and almost swallowed by the swishing wheat.

Perhaps the shepherd was entranced: Arab women did not usually dress so formally in the countryside and Mother was fluent in Arabic. For her part, she stood motionless. He would stop, shrug his shoulders. She gestured with her hands for him to continue.

Suddenly the shepherd boy responded to a distant figure who appeared to be shouting at him. No doubt it was his father. The boy was neglecting his flock of sheep. Green-carpeted hills beyond the wheat shone like satin. The shepherd bowed, picked his tunic up from the ground, and ran off. Mother came back entranced: "I felt like I was Ruth in the Bible listening to Boaz."

"Did you speak to him?" we asked.

"Yes."

"Was he surprised?"

"He said he didn't know there were people in America who spoke Arabic."

"What was he playing?"

"Some Arab tunes on his flute. But he kept apologizing, saying he had a real copper flute at home and this one was only for when he was with the sheep. He said it was broken."

And then her eyes teared up. "He wanted to give me the flute. But I refused."

"You refused?" My uncle and I were furious. It would have been a fine keepsake.

"But that is okay. His music went right in." And she thumped her heart, said "Hurry." It was time to go, and all piled in the taxi and left the shepherd looking back in the wheat.

Later, a boy waved what looked like a green fan at us alongside the road and made the taxi stop. He was selling fresh stalks of chickpeas whose kernels were green and crisp. They were a common snack that summer. I had never seen chickpeas "in the raw"; in hummus, yes; in yellow soft beans, yes. But not like this. They made all of us sneeze, as if we had an allergy to the way they really were.

At the Syrian–Lebanese border we went through the first of many tie-ups with passport checks. Since Lebanon became a free country in 1943 and Syria in 1946, ambassadors have not been exchanged between the two countries. The border, the distinction, has been kept purposely vague by a larger and stronger Syria, and the passage of nationals between the two countries was always easy.

The taxi driver dickered for two hours with the Syrian border police, finally getting our passports stamped with a visa. We were to find out over the summer that as American travelers in Damascus we were unique. In five weeks I saw only a sprinkling of European tourists and never met one other American in the ancient city's bazaars, cafés, and hotels.

The only distinguishing geography between Lebanon and Syria is a short rise of dry hills covered with scrub brush. Quickly the road descends into semi-arid desert. There, on the road to Damascus, Saul of Tarsus was thrown off his feet by a bolt of lightning. The distance from the border to the capital city of Syria is short— twenty miles— but for us it was too short. We wanted to savor the approach that took us along a surprising slit of green that became the Barada, or "ice-cold," River. Few cities, according to Philip Hitti, have as much reason to be thankful to a river as Damascus has. In the 9th century BCE, Naaman, the Syrian general, questioned whether there were any waters in Israel to match the Abana (Barada) (2 Kings 5:12), and poets in 700 CE praised the cold river as creating an earthly paradise. Traveling the road where persecutors are made saints, you want to linger. I looked up at the sky. No lightning bolt for me!

More palms out of the desert crust. The Barada deepens, its banks grow. The white dust on the western approach to Damascus seems to come into molecular collection little by little—a donkey, its driver with a brocade white cap, a telephone pole, another, a vendor of wild berry juice lifting the ladle from his shoulder, buildings shaped from limestone. And then the throng! The incredible stir of humanity in the world's oldest continuously inhabited city (3,500 years) raced between honking donkeys and Mercedes.

Our hotel—the Samiramis—had not yet been rebuilt and modernized. For years it was the only hotel in the center square of Damascus. It was a landmark for Grandfather, who was a personal friend of the owner. In 1977, the Hotel Samiramis was stormed by then-Iraqi-based terrorists led by Abu Nidal, and the owner was shot to death in the scuffle. This was the same Abu Nidal who haunted PLO Chairman Yasir Arafat for a decade, killing PLO moderates throughout Europe and the Middle East in an effort to stop compromise with Israel. Abu Nidal later held court in Syria and Libya, still shadowing Arafat and even targeting Americans, before he died in Iraq in 2002 by gunfire (though ruled a suicide, it is widely believed the arch-terrorist was killed by the security forces of Saddam Hussein). But that summer the Samiramis was our haven, and we checked in, to the hugs of the owner and his family.

Jaddu collapsed in the hotel room, asking for his respirator. We gave him a few hits and then he bubbled, "Nobody accept any invitation to stay with relatives. We stay here at Samiramis."

"Why?" we asked.

"If you stay with one relative, the others will take offense. Then you never get rid of them. They will pull you apart."

Within minutes, bursting into the room were two cousins from Arbeen who had heard from the hotel owner that we had arrived. They were to be our closest companions for the rest of the trip, and they were irrepressible.

Sami Awad Hanna[1] pulled Grandfather up from the bed with one strong jerk and squeezed him with authority and love. Sami, about 30 then, was tanned as shoe leather (that's what we called pressed apricot, "shoe leather," or qamar al-din). His agate brown eyes went across the room, his finger pointing to each head in mental notes, kissing this cousin, that one. He had the short, abrupt movements of a soldier and we were not surprised to learn that he was a captain in the Syrian army. He spoke a halting English and tended to be quiet unless addressed.

His brother, the other emissary from Arbeen, was a little ball of fire. If Sami contained his warmth like a generator, Adeeb Awad Hanna spewed it forth like a conical firework. An Arab leprechaun with green eyes and a smile as wide as the Cheshire cat, Adeeb had a spirit that was formidable. When he smiled his teeth spread like an accordion and his nose picked up as if it had been darned and pulled by the God of Mischief. Adeeb became my fast favorite. When introduced, he held me by the shoulders and looked up, his eyes beaming. "Greek!" he pronounced.

Adeeb danced over the bare floor of the hotel room. He slipped on a fallen bedspread, laughed, embraced my mother, asked my uncle Gary what was on our tape recorder. He pressed it, and Arabic tunes came out. Adeeb snapped his fingers and danced around in a circle in the small space, churning his hands alongside like gears.

"Boy," Jaddu wiped his brow from the heat—there was no air conditioning. "You do not know what you in for tonight."

He was right.

Later, Adeeb and Sami arrived with a large deputation of cousins and flagged three taxis out in front of the Samiramis in the crowded square. Damascene men rushed by, arm in arm, lecturing the air, heading home after a day's work.

Time condensed into an amber gel—everything slowed as the taxis moved northeast out of the city on the road toward Homs. The taxis moved in amber. A wave of a seller of charred ears of corn was as if in a slowed movie projector. In the dimming light a sign flickered: *Arbin.* It was the French spelling of the little village's name. Our turn was executed soundlessly and Syrian dust billowed around the cabs like clouds. We passed a small open market, a cobbler nailing shoes, another standing and watching the road. Slowly, from the cumulus on earth, the children emerged and clustered alongside the taxis. From out of the old, whitewashed clay walls they came. Their faces were beam points of color in the amber. Soon, it was as if the children had inhaled all the dust and dispelled the darkness; they were oozing from the crevices of the village, smiling, shouting. Outside the glass of my window one fellow was waving his hand as if to say: Do Not Forget Me in This Crowd You Are About to See!

The taxis were forced to halt by children jumping on the hoods and on their tops. We watched feet dangle into the windows, brown-skinned lads making faces upside down. By now there were over a hundred children surrounding the three vehicles. Our driver began to curse and Jaddu told him to shut his mouth.

"Me shut my mouth? Who do you think you are?"

"I am Kamel Awad from America!"

"And I am Muhammad Izzedine from the moon."

"Do you like it on the moon?"

"My brother, the moon is a civil place compared to this hellhole of your relatives."

We stepped out into the amber. The children swarmed around Jaddu. His face and name were a legend in Arbeen. He was the only one of his generation to leave the village for Damascus, not to mention America (though there he had taken one brother, Issa). Five brothers and one sister still lived in Arbeen. They had stayed working the apricot groves and the bean farms and tending the flocks of sheep.

The adults of the village lagged back, letting the children carry the first wave of their excitement. Children spun around Gary and me, but they stood back from Mother. Was she an "artiste" (Syrian parlance for actress, singer, but also a woman of the night)? Their own mothers wore heavy black dresses, with white scarfs over their heads; their skin was wrinkled and toughened by the hard life of the soil. No one believed that this finely dressed woman was my mother. They held back from her smile and persimmon dress as if from a flame.

"*Ya dini*" (literally, "my religion"), Mother said, lifting a little girl in her pink pinafore to ask her name. "Noora!" she squeaked. Mother sang the first verse of an Arab song to her. And it was as if the flame had turned into a pond. The children mobbed her.

Meanwhile I had noticed a taller fellow inching toward me—someone about my height and age and coloring, with well-combed dark hair, high cheekbones, and dark eyes. For a second I had the weird sensation of a shadow approaching.

"Greek, I am... your cousin, George." Every word had been carefully prepared.

We embraced, kissed on both cheeks as is the custom. My hands were used to the texture of cloth after a boyhood working in a dress manufacturing plant; I felt the polished cotton of his shirt pull over his shoulders. Something strange went through me. I stood back. He was wearing my shirt!

It was a dark paisley-print sport shirt sent in one of the boxes of clothes marked for the Old Country at Christmas. In that instant, I experienced a kind of vertigo. The 10,000 miles from Los Angeles to Damascus shrank to the foot of Syrian earth between us. This was one of those rare moments outside of lovemaking when a person feels his whole being transformed into another. I looked at George. A dab of shyness went over his chiseled face. The shirt fit him perfectly. He was to enter engineering school at the University of Damascus in the fall, but he still helped his father, Selim, till the soil and pick the apricots. If it had been Jaddu's brother Selim who had decided to leave the land of his birth and step on the gangplank to America, I would have been George; he would have been me. At that moment, as I was feeling the paisley pattern along the shoulder blades of my cousin, the Arab past made a direct, electric current into my life. I was no longer a resistor, an inert listener to tales, an intellectualizer. But for a small twist of fate I would be the one worrying about induction into the Syrian army. I would have been the one to risk his life on the Golan Heights. I would have been the one to sleep with three other brothers in one room and use a toilet that was a gaping hole in the floor. And George would have enjoyed a car of his own at sixteen, and diving into Californian swimming pools, perhaps with the luxury of conscientious objection against the

Vietnam War. There are no conscientious objectors to military service in the Middle East. Unless you flee your country.

George and I walked arm-in-arm, as Syrians do, through the flowering mob of children. Soon my grandfather's five brothers and one sister, Shahda, came to greet us. The brothers were ʿAbdu, Tawfiq, George, Selim, and Amin. Only Issa, who had come with Kamel to America, was missing. He had died in Pasadena some years back, shortly after placing his last bet on the dogs at Santa Anita.

The first thing that struck me—besides the midnight blue pantaloons of the men and their shirts tied at the neck with strings and the rilled, leathered skin of these farmers—was the fact that Jaddu had the only brown eyes of the bunch. They were all either blue- or green-eyed, with cheeks of bronze, a handsome tribe. Jaddu's puckish, shining, dark eyes were the exception in his village family, and I pondered that the dominant gene, surrounded by dominating recessives, had been the one to cast his fate to the wind.

Were the Crusaders of the 11th century responsible for these twinkling blue and green eyes in the largely Christian village of Arbeen? It seemed possible. There are many fair Muslims, as well.

We were swept by the crowd into the courtyard of Amin. Slow-minded or troubled by ill-hearing, Amin had ten children then and by now has eleven. Early on we noticed that he had difficulty with his speech. He had eyes as blue as the height of noon, a chin with white hair bristles, and a balding head with white hair flying up as if about to jump before falling out. Though he was the youngest, Amin looked like the oldest of the brothers. There were rumors of brain damage at birth. When Jaddu had left Arbeen in 1920 he was told by his mother: "Don't you ever forget your brother Amin." It was to Amin's family that most of the boxes of clothes were routed; he was the poorest of the farmers of the village.

The crowd had forced us to the head of Amin's courtyard where there were chairs set out for us, Jaddu to be at center. All eyes were on us on the porch. The buzzing and rumble that had grown from the road to here began to simmer down. There is nothing wrong for one to feel at least once in a lifetime like a king or queen. This we all felt. Gary and Mother were speechless before the crowd. What had we done to deserve this red-carpet treatment? We had done nothing but be Americans and come back to see them. Far from distrusting us, they were spellbound, by our fine clothes and—who knows?—sheen of prosperous innocence. Syria then had been billed as one of the United States' enemies (after September 11, Syria willingly aided the United States with the richest intelligence on al-Qaeda of any Middle Eastern country).[2] If policymakers had been present that day in Arbeen when children sang through the trellises for the Americans, they would not have been able to fit Syria into a box marked "demon."

The rumbling of the crowd compressed itself, waiting. Perhaps they wanted to see if we would metamorphize into F-4 Phantoms!

Grandfather Kamel stood up, all pockets of his lungs called into action. He raised a glass of 'araq from his squat boxer's frame and shouted: "I bring you your cousins from America!"

He may as well have stripped naked. They went crazy. He introduced each one of us, but they did not clap; they instead sang a folk song on each introduction. It was as if each one of us was a pause between verses of a song. Arbeen brims in my ears and heart as a place where song was talk. This should not have been a surprise, though. The first words of a song were found in Syria on clay tablets dated 1400 BCE.

Soon the children were singing to one another. The boys hung on one white wrought-iron trellis and the girls on the opposite one. They alternated verses, singing to each other. *Al nin nin nin ni! Al nin nin nin ni!* The feeling was that of being inside a nickelodeon. *Frak il habayeb rah genini!* (Staying apart from loved ones drives me crazy!) Whether the boys and girls sang separately by intention, I do not know. But it made for a wondrous syncopation. Staged, I would call it the Almond Opera, because these children's faces—bright, teeth yellower than American kids' but spread wide and gleeful—appeared as singing almonds.

We were given a tour of Amin's house, though there were only two rooms to see. How he fit ten children in there no one really found out.

Adeeb, the lawyer-firework, leapt up at a pause and saluted Jaddu with a poetic speech that found him flinging his fingers out and back as if he were directing an orchestra of himself. And then, just when Adeeb seemed finished, he would point toward heaven with a diminutive digit, smile slyly, pull back the flesh around his eyes, and fling out a song.

This speechifying and songmaking and poetry shooting (*zajal* is a tradition where one poet jerks up and tries to out-metaphorize the other) went on for over two hours. Then preparations were begun to slaughter a sheep.

Throat slit, the animal dug its hooves into the soil and kicked the basin a young cousin had put out to catch the blood. The basin hit a little girl in the shins; she screamed and wanted her mama. The mama came and retrieved the basin, putting it under the spurting neck. The boy, embarrassed but game, pushed the sheep's head to the ground over the basin and kept looking up at us in case we would like to take a picture of the pouring blood. Mother gasped and went back to the porch. She stuck to vegetables that night.

I searched for a place to put an olive pit and one cousin put out his hand, took the pit, and hurled it over a wall onto the street.

Others wolfed down pieces of cheese we handed over our backs, spinach pies, hot shish kebab. It was an eerie thing to eat with so many people staring over your shoulder. It put a knot in the stomach. For a second I thought of the debaucheries of the Roman senators, who threw legs of chicken over their heads to the dogs or eunuchs.

After dinner we were taken for a tour of the barnyard where there were milk cows, a few chickens, and goats. A donkey stood off in the corner, chewing gristle. Adeeb grabbed Gary and jumped on, cranking the thing's tail as if it were a Model T. The children laughed; Mother said, *Haram al-himar*, a lovely alliterative inversion that means "the poor ass."

Back at Amin's, the *'araq* was poured. When I was a child it was a thing of marvel to watch an aunt pour water into *'araq*, a clear liquor much stronger and stiffer than anisette but with that licorice flavor, and turn it white as milk. It was a delicate chemistry akin to the priest turning water into wine, and wine into blood. Of course, in the Catholic mass the wine never really turned to blood; it still tasted like sweet wine, which made the mystery all the more mental and strange. I tended to identify Father's family (the Catholic one) with unprovable miracles, whereas Mother's side (Orthodox) found miracles a daily occurrence, as easy as tipping a jug of water and creating a spool of cloud that whitened the glass!

So it has been all my life—the Eastern Orthodox side giving me palpable mysteries, earthen wonders, the Roman Catholic side bequeathing an Intellectual God, a God of Abstract Belief and Complex Theology. In the Catholic church, when you are married you go up an aisle and back, once. In the Orthodox, you go around in circles, endlessly, with your crown tied to your betrothed's crown. As an Orthodox, you either get very dizzy or you lose your bride! A God of Blurred Distinctions versus a God of Infinitesimal Distinctions. St. John Chrysostom versus Aquinas. But anyone can drink a glass of *'araq*; it just so happened that in my family the Orthodox side liked it and the Catholic side did not.

We were on an island in the desert that is Damascus of the Barada and al-Awaj rivers. And our cousins in Arbeen could not stop praising the night. Cousin George held the *darabukka* (bongo) and another readied the eggplant-shaped guitar, or *'ud*. They were poised.

"Oof oof ooooooooooof!"

This was not someone getting his toes stepped on or lifting a crate of soda bottles with a herniated disc. This was a singer telling the crowd that he was clearing his throat and ready to belt one out. It is the singer's way of telling everyone to stop talking and listen.

"Ooooooooooof!"

A head that looked as if it was going to burst from pressure of too much blood was quieting the crowd. It was Nassif, of the House of Daoud. His lungs spread like a bellows, and many nights to come were hushed by his "Oofing."

I want to linger a bit on the phenomenology of Oof. Like Aretha Franklin or Otis Redding stretching a note out a capella at the beginning of a soul song, the audience punctuates each end of the long note pulled like an eel from the lung with a *Ya Allah*, or *Aywah* (yes), or suchlike. It is the equivalent of "Amen, brother," "Tell it like it is," or "Don't you know I know you know I know?" Oofing is a way of speaking for the audience, of collecting their pains and loves into one big blasting voice. But the key to Oof is the relishing of the approach pattern, the runway.

There is another way to Oof at an Arab night festivity. And that is stretching out the word *layl* (night). For a people whose days are relentlessly subjected to the sun, the nights take on deified, quenching proportions to the Arabs. Night is all, philosophically, musically, and literally. Above us was no roof. The hovels of Arbeen did most of the entertaining in the courtyards outdoors.

Both Oof and *layl* may seem like ends in themselves, but they are not. After many Oofs and *layls*, the singer will trigger in the collective memory of the crowd the first words of a song and everyone will join in, clapping, the *darabukka* slapped forcefully, the swollen *'ud* plucked.

Mother rose. Rose rose.

She began to dance, kneading the air as an Arab woman does, her hands twirling around some invisible rope. The dignity of her unmoving but smiling head captured all. Her eyes filled with the *layl* of the song. The crowd of cousins and villagers whooped, the teenage boys craned their necks, the old women delighted, the embroidery of their bosoms heaving. I was relieved she stood up. I was afraid to say something; my Arabic was poor. Let her speak for us with her dance, we of the first and second generations who didn't know how to address the villagers.

She danced in front of her father, in front of the myriad cousins who had heard of her as Rose, the only daughter of Kamel from America. Slowly she pocketed the whole village without closing her hands.

A cock of the rooster flew up onto the long run of tables. It was Adeeb. Everyone laughed and held their breath and plates. What a sight—little Adeeb three feet higher than Mother, who continued for a while, then faded back into the porch, clapping for him. He strutted. He pronounced. He glided. He exuded. Not a pro like Nassif, Adeeb used his lawyer's eloquence and sly eyes and accordionlike teeth to make the most of his song. He was adept at punctuating words; in fact, I saw a small slingshot of saliva fly out of his mouth over the table at the word for bread, *khubz*.

The music intensified. George's hands turned beet red from pounding the *darabukka*. From the street through the courtyard door stumbled the Ashishi. Music to him was like catnip to the cat. (When riding his favorite jackass, the man had the habit of telling the animal to stop by saying *"Hish! Hish!"* He also once shouted at a runaway horse, *"Hashashu!* [Stop him!]." Thus the nickname.) The Ashishi had just finished sweeping the dust off icons at the Orthodox church in town. He had kicked a can or two, cracked a few green chick-peas between his teeth, and, no doubt, downed a bottle of *ʿaraq*. He was the custodian of the church and his face was red with tincture of alcohol.

The music, which had stopped at his entrance, immediately whipped itself into a fever when the Ashishi began fondling his stomach and dancing around in a Sufic trance. From his mouth sprang verses of an ancient Arab folk song celebrating the nine months of pregnancy. Each verse is a month; each verse the pillow got lower in the Ashishi's robe, until, vibrating like a drunken cobra, he shrieked, gave up the spirit, and pulled the pillow from his stomach like a disgorged rabbit.

The crowd revolved like a joyous wheel of fortune, spontaneous song and dance and poetry and mime erupted from one cousin to the next. My uncle Gary had acquitted himself well with a toast to the cousins, "May you live as long as you want, but never want as long as you live," given deftly in Arabic but stolen from Abbott and Costello. He poked me in the ribs at the delirious applause. Grandmother gave her timeless "God bless you and keep you safe" toast with a glass of red wine she took for her anemia. "Can't be no worse," she commented later on the content of her toast. When the invisible wheel turned to me, I was shaking. It came in the form of a bowl of loquats and a bottle of *ʿaraq*.

For every loquat I ate, Adeeb poured a glass of *ʿaraq*. Claps at each toss, huzzah, pandemonium. I stood to give an invocation in pidgin Arabic:

> Brothers and sisters, the heart is a Hindu apricot.
> The night is like the heart.
> The heart is like an airplane.
> The airplane is like the wind.
> Awad and Orfalea came from America
> To see your faces like roses.
> Your beautiful faces.
> Your faces turn our hearts to butter
> And our heads to *ʿaraq*.

George promptly put a hole in his *darabukka* and had to borrow a new one. The music hit a quick fever pitch. Pulled by the singing and rhythmic clapping of the crowd, and by Adeeb's urgent hand, I got up to dance.

All spun round. "Abu Ali! Abu Ali!" Adeeb shouted. This was some Islamic folk warrior known for his bravery and thick moustache. Remarkably, I managed not to fall over, but bowed to all, blew a few kisses, sat down. Fifteen minutes went by. I rushed blindly to the toilet, which was nothing but a cotton curtain hiding a hole in the tiled floor. It was there that I deposited the whirling minaret and church steeple, the snide days of youth, the *mishmish Hindi* (loquat), and the *ʿaraq*.

I awoke in the night. I was lying down on a cot indoors. An old man whispered in the darkness, his hand rubbing my stomach in calm circles. A tight pain gripped me there. Over the distant roars, the voice took command. The old man's face bent into the moonlight. It was ʿAbdu, oldest of Jaddu's brothers, the father of Adeeb. The moon made a rim of light on his *kufiya*. Slowly, the pain subsided under the swirl of a weathered hand. I put my hand on his. It felt like the bark of a pepper tree. The pain was over. ʿAbdu knew, for he stopped praying, pulled a blanket to my chin, and went back to the crowd.

Since our summer in Arbeen I have been a believer of quiet miracles in the face of innumerable furies. ʿAbdu's cure was the first of three miracles that summer of 1972.

Damascus is so old that its famous seven gates, or *babs*, to the city, built in ancient Roman times, are considered relatively new structures.

The sites that our relatives from Arbeen found most important were: St. Paul's Sanctuary, the grand Omayyad mosque, and a Palestinian refugee camp on the outskirts of the city. Because most of the Arbeenians were Christian (about 90 percent of Syria's eighteen million people are Muslim; 10 percent are Christian, a one-third loss of the Christian population since that visit; there are about 5,000 Syrian Jews), the site of St. Paul's escape near Bab Kisan was very important to them.

Damascus became the first place Saul tested his new name, Paul, and his new faith, preaching in the synagogue. Some of the Jews did not trust him and plotted to kill him. But his disciples put him in a basket and lowered him over the wall of the city, and he escaped to Jerusalem.

Adeeb took us to a sanctuary that had been built on the site of Paul's late-night basket ride, which even marked the window from which Paul was supposedly lowered. In earlier days, a church had been there and then a mosque. The present chapel was built in 1941; since 1964 the boys' orphanage next door has been run by Melkite Catholics.

Inside the chapel the air was cool, the limestone blocks shielding worshippers from the Damascene heat. Above two small altars are marble carvings, one of St. Paul's vision, the other of his midnight ride in the basket. A monk gave us a prayer in a pamphlet, to be recited in St. Paul's Sanctuary, which ensured the faithful of 300 days' indulgence by decree of Pope Pius X. In pre-Vatican II parlance this meant that if you were going to purgatory after death to atone for a few sins, you'd get 300 days cut from your sentence. The Catholic church has since stopped the practice of indulgences. We said the prayer anyway; you never know what another pontiff will decree.

Then we headed to the grandest of all Damascene structures: the Omayyad mosque.

The Omayyad mosaic depicts, well, everything. It runs 100 feet high and 50 feet long—an entire high wall. The tiles sparkle gold-green and blue. In it, the pageant of humanity from the Garden of Eden flowed through the waters of the Nile and Barada to Damascus and beyond. It is not, however, a panoply of famous warriors or historical figures. The Palestinian geographer Maqdisi visited Damascus in 985 and described the Omayyad mosque mosaic as "bearing representations of trees and towns and displaying inscriptions, all the ultimate in beauty, elegance, and artistry. Hardly a known tree or town does not figure on the walls." Not wars, but nature and civilization adorn the mosaic.

At the center of the courtyard gurgles a fountain whose water is an exotic turquoise, as if a secret pipe had tapped the South Seas under the desert. Raucous Damascene streets and marketplaces surround the mosque; stand anywhere in the Omayyad courtyard and you hear only the gurgle of water. It is transfixing. It has the stilling effect of a bowl of roses put in the center of a Quaker prayer meeting. It turns the spirit to a river, its natural state (what is the body, 90 percent water, but a red delta of veins and arteries?).

It was in this inner sanctum of the mosque that we discovered a dome within the dome: a sarcophagus styled like a Romanesque church in which it is said St. John the Baptist's head is buried. Thus, Christianity is contained within Islam. The great precursor of Christ, John the Baptist, was ordered decapitated in a rage by Herod, the King of Judah; the head was served up to him on a platter by Salome. The head is cradled like a talisman inside the grand mosque of Damascus. Still, it gave us an odd feeling, if for no other reason but that it seems gruesome to imagine a head revered by itself anywhere.

On the way out, Adeeb gave us some history of the mosque. It was built in 705 by al-Walid, the grandson of Muʿawiyah, who started the epochal Omayyad caliphate in Damascus, which shifted the center of Islam from the Arabian peninsula to Syria.

Muʾawiyah himself, after Mohammed and Umar, has been called

one of the ablest men in the history of the Arabs. Under him, Islam, according to Philip Hitti, "breathed more of the Mediterranean and less of the desert." He was quite tolerant of Christians and Jews; Christians were placed in charge of the Islamic state's treasury, and the poet laureate of the empire, al-Akhtal, was likewise a Christian. Mu'awiyah had his detractors, among them the traditional northern Arabians (thus he wooed the southern Arabians). He is reputed to have once said, "I apply not my lash where my tongue suffices, nor my sword where my whip is enough. And if there be one hair binding me to my fellow men I let it not break. If they pull I loosen, and if they loosen, I pull."

The Omayyad caliphate reached its peak in one generation; after the demise of al-Walid, eight caliphs followed, one worse than the other. Signs of affluence and decadence pulled the regime down— slaves multiplied, concubines flourished, wine poured in enlarged goblets. It was to have a fate similar to Beirut's so many centuries later, but not until one of the caliphs indulged himself swimming in a pool of wine, gulping enough of it to lower its surface. This same scoundrel committed an extraordinary sacrilege. He took target practice with bow and arrows at an opened volume of the Qu'ran![3]

It wasn't long before I became enchanted with a deaf girl of the village. During the opening night festivities, her struggle to greet Jaddu (she was one of Amin's daughters) brought the only quiet interlude of the night.

"She is very beautiful," Adeeb said to me as the crowd hushed at her purposeful push to the porch. "Her name is Fayzi."

She dressed like none of the young women in the village, even then. A shapely figure, she had on Western women's slacks and a shiny midnight blue synthetic blouse that matched the dark blue of her eyes, which had flecks of brown in them. A loving smile lit her pale cheeks. She hugged Jaddu forcefully as if he would help her. She held out dead batteries and a bad hearing aid in an open palm, as if they were betrayers. Her words were an urgent, garbled telegram.

Jaddu began to cry. That set off Mother and Grandmother. The seed was planted there for Fayzi's coming to America; but no one knew then that the doctors across the sea could offer no more help for her problem than could the Syrian doctors. She had a neurological loss; no operation could fix it.

There was a christening and then a funeral in Arbeen that summer. For the first, Fayzi dressed luminously in white lace—it was her newest brother's baptism. At that event, I realized the close-knit weave that celebration and violence can have in the Middle East.

The boy was named for Grandfather Kamel. He was Amin's latest child; Mother became his godmother. The *khuri*, or Orthodox priest, came to Amin's house. He had the longest hair of anyone in the village and tied it in a ponytail. Hundreds of the villagers turned out for the evening baptism. All were given candles and the priest took the baby in his hands, candles afire surrounding. He plunged the child into a basin of water, baptising him by immersion in the Orthodox tradition. Just when everyone thought the boy was drowning, the *khuri* pulled him up with hairy forearms. Little Kamel's mouth was as wide as a sea bass; he dripped a trail of water and seemed to say in his surprise, "Who is this lunatic? Get me a towel!"

The villagers crowded around, joking in the steamy air made hotter by the candles. The priest did not hesitate to punctuate his incantations over the sopping child with curses to the crowd. "I have baptized you with the water of life—shut up everyone!—and with this miracle you have entered God's chosen kingdom—please harness your tongues—and hereby do offer you eternal—damn the country of everyone of you—eternal life, for the power of God is greater than you, greater than all the hatred in the world."

We were sitting at the sparkling dinner tables laid end to end when it happened. In the midst of the low roar of guests' talk and the clinking of glasses and plates, I heard the report of a revolver from the far end of the tables. I jerked my head and focused on a dull-looking, fat man in khaki clothes being shoved by a woman, looking as if he had been slapped. By the expressions of the women around him and their intense downward stares, it was obvious someone had been hit, and hit low.

The man had earlier saluted his Bacchus by shooting the pistol into the air above our heads, a feat guaranteed to land a bullet or two in someone's *araq*, if not skull. Luckily, no one had been hurt. But now something else had happened. Extreme efforts were being made to spare the American visitors alarm or contact with the injured. But out of the corner of my eye I saw a little girl about five years old being whisked away through the crowd. There was blood on her leg. She had been hit by shrapnel flying up from the cement floor torn by the bullet.

The singing and eating went on. Jaddu held up a piece of cheese, unaware of what had happened. It was as if the crowd's voices had risen to cover the tragedy. Mother, who had heard something, accepted the explanation that it was a popgun. I glanced over my shoulder, unable to locate the injured girl or trail of blood. The fat man whose gun had done it all went on eating. His careless approach to praise had brought suffering. I was angry that he wasn't expelled immediately from the table, accident or not. I was livid that everyone seemed to sweep the little girl's bloody limb under the table.

Soon desserts came, and I was assured by Adeeb that it was nothing, her foot was bandaged. But to me, the table had become a world, the world, where beauty and suffering were as tightly woven together as reeds in a basket. Which reed is the tragic one, which the comic? It is hard to tell. In Arbeen that night I sensed a predilection for taking violence in stride in the midst of happiness that was both awesome and disturbing. I was not so sure it was peculiar to Arabs or to villagers. Modern life is lived at fever pitch, risks inherent at every turn.

Later in the week an old man of the village died and we went to his funeral.

At the hand-dug grave on the outskirts of town, the procession stopped. A boy of fifteen recited a poem to his departed grandfather after the wood casket was set in the hole. It was this young poet, and not the *khuri*, who had the last say. His words brought tears from relatives and friends; they seemed to sob in tune with the rhythms of the poem. Finally, three eggs were placed in the grave. Sustenance in the afterlife.

The next day Adeeb fished us from the Samiramis to take a walk to the Suq al-Hamidiyah, the great bazaar darkened by a crude roof of corrugated metal slats in the center of Damascus. Adeeb was nervous, excited. He had news. Three Japanese commandos had sprayed machine-gun fire at Lydda Airport in Tel Aviv, killing 25 people and wounding 78. Two of the commandos had committed suicide; one was captured.

"You see!" Adeeb pronounced. "The whole world is on our side!"

I did not share his leap in logic—the world was certainly not represented by a few crazed gunmen, nor, for that matter, was the Palestinian cause. There was a note of desperation behind Adeeb's glee. After all, Syria had fought in and lost two wars with Israel and was sliding toward a third.

I knew only the rudiments of the Arab–Israeli conflict then. (I am not so sure learning its complexities is edifying.) But a decade later as I was touring the refugee camps and PLO installations in Beirut and southern Lebanon, the collection of international idealists and malcontents struck me as a foreboding motley. In its hunger for comradeship against oppression, the PLO appeared to have let in inauthentic elements that infected the organization with the nihilism surrounding a "hopeless cause," rather than the cool-headedness of an idea whose day had come.

Our side? We did not want our relatives hurt by Israel or anyone else. But the Japanese commando raid left us cold. The duality of being an Arab American became starker that day.

Reaching the Suq al-Hamidiyah, we saw the white holes in metal slats above our heads where musket shots had pierced through in the Arab revolt against the Turks during World War I. More holes were added during the Syrian rebellion against the French, who finally pulled out in 1946 when Syria became independent. Some holes were larger than others—perhaps bullets from new battles had followed old bullets. The Suq's ceiling was a constellation of war.

One Arab merchant began to barter over a table of *kufiyas*. He asked for fifty lira ($10).

"Uncle, I give you twenty-five lira; it is, after all, very wrinkled."

"My brother, do you know the more wrinkles the more distinguished? Forty-five lira."

"Uncle, what is this spot here? It must be an ash from someone's *arjila*. Thirty lira."

"My dear brother, no one is smoking the *arjila* within two blocks. This is a collector's item. The brown spot marks the signature of the craftsman. Forty lira."

"Oh my uncle, the gentleman in the next stall is selling *kufiyas* for ten lira and throwing the *'iqal* (ropelike fastener) in for free. Thirty-five."

"Little brother, the jackass that you call a gentleman in the next stall is selling *kufiyas* made of the great false fiber of the West. This *kufiya* is cotton. And I will throw in an *'iqal*. Thirty-eight lira."

"Most gracious uncle, your work is the best in the Suq al-Hamidiyah. Your coffee is also the most delicious, and your hospitality is second to none. Thirty-six lira."

"Young brother, all my life I have wanted to go to America and meet the cheapest people on earth. Thirty-seven lira and sold."

After the strange news about the Japanese commandos and the gunshot at the christening, we were in need of another miracle. And we got it—deep in the eastern Syrian desert at a convent called Sidnaya. Where the lame are made to walk and the blind to see.

Over the years, I have retained a skepticism about "big" miracles. If Jonah was swallowed by the whale, I tend to think he did not take weekend accommodations but was regurgitated as a bad meal. If the Red Sea was parted by Moses, no doubt it was also parted by the winds of the imagination. The miracles I hold to are the infinitesimal ones, occurrences that may not defy science but certainly defy probability.

Sidnaya in the eastern Syrian desert is the Eastern Orthodox's Fatima and Lourdes, though a much older site than either. Not commonly known in the West, Sidnaya is far out in a vast sand. Its altar is covered with crutches of the lame who were cured.

Approaching Sidnaya along the sand-strewn road in a desert struck white by the sun, the feeling is of a mirage. The convent appears to be carved out of a limestone escarpment. A few old limestone block houses of the village stand below it, vibrating in the heat. Approaching Sidnaya cars miraculously disappear. We were the only vehicle for miles. We found ourselves stuck behind a donkey loaded with lettuce for the convent, led by bridle by a man who looked a hundred years old.

"Sidnaya" derives from Aramaic, the language Christ spoke, still spoken in a few villages near the miraculous site—Maloula, Gabaadine, and Bakhaa. It means "Our Lady," but also "hunting places." The history of the convent at Sidnaya dates back to 547 CE and Justinian I, emperor of Byzantium, who was to bestow on the empire an advanced and tolerant legal system. Justinian was traversing the desert of Syria on his way to attack the Persians when his troops camped, thirsty beyond measure since their last water had been drawn in Damascus, roughly twenty-five miles west. The emperor spotted a gazelle and gave chase up a rocky hill until it halted at a spring of sweet water. On the escarpment Justinian watched as the gazelle transfigured into an icon of the Blessed Mother, blazing with light. According to the story, a white hand came out of the icon gesturing toward the kingly hunter and the icon said, "No, thou shall not kill me, Justinian. But thou shalt build for me a church here on this hill." Both the vision and the gazelle then vanished.[4]

On the request of the abbess to a Greek monk living in Jerusalem, one of the four original icons painted by St. Luke the Evangelist came to rest at Sidnaya many years after Justinian. In the Syrian desert, the monk was attacked by jackals and wolves and highwaymen, but each time he repelled them with the elevation of the miraculous icon of St. Luke.

We stopped the taxis at the base of a long staircase of stone, and walked up it, zig-zagging past the ass with the lettuce. The driver did not care. He knew we would wait for him for lunch. A young nun greeted us at the massive door to the convent. Through a colonnade a larger nun, older, came out of the shadows. She stopped about forty feet from our group.

"Ya tiqburni!" Grandmother Matile sang. (This is impossible to translate; the literal meaning is "Bury me!")

"Matile, may God be praised!" the abbess sang back.

The abbess and Grandmother ran into each other's arms and romped around in a circle like schoolgirls. We were bewildered. Jaddu thought his wife was laying it on a little thick for a complete stranger.

But this was no stranger. And here is the first part of the miracle of Sidnaya: The abbess and Grandmother had been childhood friends 200 miles to the west in another country, the mountains of Lebanon. They had not seen each other for 56 years—since 1916. Not since World War I.

Suddenly Matile Malouf Awad's piety in Pasadena with candles floating in oil never extinguished in front of her miniature icons and holy cards of the Blessed Mother made sense. She had always been the one in our family with a special religious—even mystical—

touch. Here she was exclaiming "Bury me!" at various octaves to an abbess who looked like she had just seen Justinian. The two of them could have been gazelles.

Grandmother dropped to her knees to kiss the ring of the abbess. But the abbess would have nothing of it, and bent to the floor as had Matile. She kissed Matile's ring. I think they could have kept on this way for another 50 years, up and down like two jack-in-the-boxes. We followed the two of them; the tall abbess's arm on Matile's shoulder, little Grandmother sliding her short, sturdy legs forward at the speed of delight.

"Gary," I said. "Do you have anything you want cured? I think we are in a privileged position. Why don't you ask for more hair?"

"Why don't you ask for less? Or a nose job?"

"But a cure. We have to be sick."

"The next time we fall in love we have to come to Sidnaya."

After a meal with the nuns Grandmother strode with determination to the chapel. It was a place she was born for, a place in which she totally belonged. Here was her chest-of-drawers small altar at home burgeoned to the size of grandeur. All in the care of her old friend.

Above the altar hung hundreds of crutches like sleeping bats. In the sanctuary a strange, compacted light glistened like ice. Thousands of jewels were piled in heaps above the tabernacle in an alcove sheathed in satin. As we approached the communion rail Grandmother dropped to her knees. Jaddu standing behind her. He was never a religious man, preferring to read the newspaper on Sunday.

As if in a trance, Matile stood, a woman possessed by a kind of love no one knows anymore. She went under the railing, never taking her eyes off the altar. Halfway toward it she stopped, crossed herself, still whispering private prayers to the Virgin, slipped off her wedding ring, and left it among the countless jewels at the altar of Sidnaya.

Jaddu shook his head, still standing outside the sanctuary.

Matile prayed for some minutes more, crossed herself, turned, and never looked back. Her finger was as bare as 50 years before when Kamel had stolen her at age fifteen from her family house in Brooklyn before they married on the run. It was as bare as the day in Lebanon during the Great War when her mother announced that the second of two brothers had starved to death. It was as bare as the Syrian desert where Justinian saw the gazelle linger by a spring. As bare as the room of an anchorite.

It was a custom, we were told later, for pilgrims to Sidnaya to leave jewelry, and millions of dollars' worth of wedding rings, necklaces, lovers' pendants, brooches, and earrings rest there in the desert, guarded only by a colony of nuns. Yet no one ever stole even a ring from the altar.

Thus concluded the second miracle of the summer of 1972.

The third and last miracle of the trip occurred a few days later. I had been asked by my bedridden grandmother on the other side of my family back home to visit the town of her birth in Lebanon—Zahle. It is on the eastern side of the mountains descending into the Biqa⁣ᶜ Valley. She was certain I would like it.

Crossing the border late in the day, we arrived in Zahle by nightfall and checked into the Hotel D'Amerique. We could hear the rush of a river across the way, the one that flows straight down a hill through the center of Zahle. But we were too tired to explore the town and took two rooms, grandparents and Mother in one, Gary and I in the other.

At about 2 AM, there was a knock at the door. Gary went to look. A yellow light from one naked bulb in the corridor stole into the room and I tried to bury my eyes in the pillow. But it was useless. I got up and went to the door. There was a dark figure of a man in an overcoat.

"Don't you know your own father?" the shadow demanded.

My mind was blank. My father was supposed to be in New York City on a business trip. He could not come with us.

The figure moved into the yellow light. I leapt at him. Gary later said I flew across a space of about ten feet, which could be a record for the standing broad jump, not bad for being half-asleep.

If I was tired, Father was goggle-eyed. He had been without sleep for 48 hours, ever since leaving the United States to seek us out, not knowing just where we'd be. No problem. Only the whole of Syria and Lebanon to search through.

He had been lonely.

Some, when lonely, go to a show, or two shows; some go to a bar, or a nightclub; some hire a lady of the night. Some drop pills or make long-distance telephone calls. Some read pulp novels or Nobel Prize-winning novels. And some visit Times Square. Father found himself on business, alone in New York City, and he bought a ticket to Damascus.

Problems: for one, no one on the Orfalea side of my family speaks good Arabic. Father was no exception. Problem two—he had never been to the Middle East, and since World War II he had not been to Europe. Problem three—we were three weeks into the trip; for all he knew we could have checked out of the Samiramis long ago and, in fact, had. In short, he had done something very crazy. But he was always a master of surprise, and this was to be his grandest.

He motioned me to be silent. Gary went and knocked on the grandparents' door, stood back, and told Mother there was a message for her. Mother is adept at hyperventilation and when she saw the moustachioed man with the overcoat now draped over an arm she did a good rendition of the Hyperventilation Nocturne, orchestrated by the Lebanese crickets and Barduni River.

"Easy, Rose, easy."

"A-Aref, A-Aref, A-Aref!"

I'll put the curtain down on that scene.

The owners of the D'Amerique awoke in all the commotion and were amazed at the night visitor's arrival. They turned the entire kitchen and food cache over to us, eliciting a promise to get the whole story in the morning.

It went like this: Father had fired a salesman who had stolen samples of dresses he was marketing in New York. His spirits were down. And he missed the family. He purchased a ticket to Damascus, via Paris, just as we had done. After one more day in New York's garment district, he hopped to Kennedy Airport, then to Paris, where he bought a bottle of Chanel No. 5 at the duty-free shop, then to Beirut, then to Damascus by the wild ride over the Lebanon mountains. Syria had been the birthplace of his father, Aref Isper Orfalea, Sr., too (at Homs). But his motive for travel was not roots; it was flowers. He had come not for history, but for history's bloom—his own family.

Arriving at the Samiramis he was stunned that we were not there, and collapsed on a sofa in the lobby, chain-smoking Marlboros. Bread and cheese offered by a waiter did no good. Father figured he had blown three summers' vacation money. We were not globe-trotters. A big trip for us during my childhood was hauling off to Lake Tahoe or the lower Sierra Nevadas. Father glanced out the window; there were very few women in Damascus square, and the ones who were there dressed in long robes with scarfs over the heads. There was no way to write this one off as a business trip. Damascus was not a place to sell miniskirts or granny dresses.

The owner took pity on him. He brought over the telephone number of Adeeb, and one ʿId al-Annouf, who was married to Adeeb's sister, Suad. ʿId knew English better than the Arbeenians, having served with the British army in Syria as a telegrapher during World War II. Father gained his first speck of hope hearing ʿId's voice over the crackling telephone line, dialed at an old-style black metal phone. ʿId had a high laugh.

Soon Adeeb and ʿId—at six feet one inches, one tall Arab among us Lilliputians—arrived at the hotel. ʿId lifted Father off the ground like a brown bear. Adeeb pranced around, tickled that Aref had come all the way from the United States on an impulse.

"Where are they?" Father asked, adjusting his thick-lensed glasses, looking at a map.

"They are in Zahle," said ʿId.

"You mean I missed them by only one day?"

"Yes."

"How do we get there?"

"Tomorrow," said Adeeb. "We can take taxi."

"But they might leave for Beirut by then. I have to go tonight."

ʿId and Adeeb looked at each other, the giant and the gnome.

"We're with you," ʿId said, and Adeeb nodded quickly.

"What about work?"

"Work? I will call Suad. She will tell work that we are on an important commando mission in Lebanon!" ʿId's brown eyes blazed, and his big hands lifted above his head.

So the three of them got a fast taxi and drove out of Syria around midnight. Here was Father passing through the land of his ancestors as if it were so much flotsam to get where he really had to go.

When they made it to Zahle, it was so late that all the shops and restaurants were closed. One by one they woke up people at the hotels along the Barduni, asking for the Awad or Orfalea families. There was only one hotel left at the end of the line. Utterly exhausted, ready to give into sleep after the depressing trip, father dropped his hand down on a desk bell at the D'Amerique, rousing a young man named Said.

"Yes, we have a Kamel Awad here. Two rooms."

ʿId and Adeeb punched Aref and beamed with stifled glee.

In our nightclothes we heard the story in the hotel kitchen until dawn. Then we slept and heard the story again.

Father joined us to tour Zahle, the town in which his peddler mother, Nazera, had been born in 1886.

The Barduni River is a legend. Crystal and cold, it speeds down the mountain and is indeed Zahle's main road. Cafés and restaurants snuggle along the river as it descends through the mountain town in small falls and cascades. We ate lunch at one that served endless dishes of *mazza* (hors d'oeuvres), including *tabbouli* (parsley and bulgur salad), *baba ghannuj* (eggplant dip), and hummus, but also lamb brain and spinal cord (a white, rubbery string). We inhaled the pure Zahlewean air, a refuge for asthmatics throughout the Arab world.

Zahle's roads are pitched, winding. The main street sported Jabaly's theater. The owner stood on the steps in a three-piece suit, checking his gold fob watch. I asked if he knew a Jabaly family that had spawned a Nazera Jabaly a century before; she was among the first thousand women immigrants from the Arab world, and she was my grandmother. He said the woman was his aunt!

I have mentioned three miracles. There were also three warning signals that something malignant lurked in the fragile societal body of Lebanon, even in this boom year for tourism in 1972. The first warning was in Zahle; it was during a meal served by a great-aunt, another relative of Nazera.

The aunt took us on a tour of Nazera's house of birth. She barged in with no deference to the Muslim couple's small abode. At the age of 87, Nazera could still remember the poplar leaves outside her window in Zahle three continents and eighty of those years away. There they were, swishing in the Zahlewean breeze.

Later, the aunt, a gruff woman with thick calves, put a gigantic spread of food out for us. As she pointed an upturned palm for us to sit, eat, she turned around and faced a twelve-year-old-maid. "Go sleep on the floor in the kitchen, you little dog!" she spat out. With one sentence, she had turned our appetites sour. Mother—for the second time—could not eat.

Nazera Jabaly Orfalea as air raid block warden for her street in Cleveland, Ohio, during WWII.

Chances are the maid was a Palestinian girl from one of the camps near Baalbek in the Biqa' Valley. The little girl actually went and lay down on the stone floor with only a tattered throw rug underneath.

Later, we traveled to another mountain village, Mhciti (also Shreen), near Bikfaya, where Grandmother Matile had been born. She went on foot to her ancestral home, which overlooked the blue mountains. There relatives presented her with a 13th-century axe with curved blade that had been left by the Crusaders. Matile had no use for axes; she gave it to her daughter. For years it hung above a wet-bar in our California family home alongside a painting of Hank Aaron.

Adeeb roused us earlier than usual, banging at our door at Samiramis.

"Today we go to Palestinian camp. *Yallah.*"

Yallah is the Arabic version of *andele*, *vite*, and *pronto*. It is almost synonymous with the desire to go; few go slowly.

Father had been received in Arbeen and Damascus as a hero, a kind of Humphrey Bogart figure. But before we once again slid into the night gaieties, Adeeb wanted us to see Yarmouk, the Palestinian camp on the outskirts of Damascus harboring about 20,000 refugees. We were game.

We traveled along a whitewashed adobe wall east of the city as if to go to Sidnaya. But this was not miracle day. Nor were we following a road to Palmyra, where in the eastern Syrian desert stands the largest spread of Roman ruins outside Italy. We followed a wall that turned to contemporary ruins. These were the ruins of the Palestinians. The inhabitants of the pock-marked labyrinth of walls and shacks had lived in the camp for a quarter-century at that point. (Now, a half-century.)

In some ways, the hovels were not much different from the village of Arbeen. The quarters were more squashed, if that were possible, and the walls to the tiny dwellings in more disrepair. But my first thought was that the Palestinians in Syria were living on a par with the peasant farmers who were our Syrian relatives.

But the air was different; there was a nip of hostility from the start. Gary immediately disappeared on the backstreets of the camp with his Minolta camera. Faces of people peeling onions or lounging in broken chairs turned and watched him silently make his way into the children-strewn street.

We had a number of Syrians with us, translating, including Adeeb and Sami. I noticed a man in his fifties who was brushing an old horse. As we began talking, a crowd of about twenty gathered around to listen. I asked the man where he was from.

"Sarafand, in Palestine," he said, still brushing dust off the horse. Sarafand is on the coast, south of Haifa.

He had been in the Syrian camp since 1948 when his family fled Palestine in the war that eventually led to the creation of Israel and uprooted 750,000 indigenous Palestinian Arabs.

I asked if he had sunk some roots in his 25 years in Syria.

"I cannot grow even vegetables here—there is no land for it," he spoke calmly, but distinctly. "The land is Syrian government land. I used to have 100 dunams (25 acres) of land in Sarafand and farmed it. Now, like everyone else, I take any work I can get—shine shoes, sell Chiclets, work in restaurants, or do nothing and live on nothing."

The man adjusted his white cotton cap, shifted his head upward, and stopped working on the horse. The horse neighed softly, picking up a hoof. His raw skin showed in patches; the hide had fallen out from some disease.

He said, "I want to die in my homeland."

He pointed to a series of walls down across the road from the camp. "It is the Jewish cemetery here," he said, with no particular expression.

The third unlikely neighbor in this triangle of tragedy—in addition to Palestinian refugees and Jewish dead—was a series of scattered cardboard boxes in a field past the camp. Crude holes for windows had been cut in the large boxes, as if they were playthings of a giant's children. I guessed they might be domiciles of gypsies or of Bedouins. No. They were the dwellings of Syrian refugees from the Golan Heights, captured by Israel in the 1967 June war. It is a fact that the Syrian refugees were living in even worse conditions—at least in 1972—than their Palestinian counterparts. It may have had something to do with their more recent refugee status—only five years out of their homes.

On one Palestinian roof was planted a tall, dusty juniper in sod. It stood proudly against the bleached hovels and the dry sky. It was only pale green but it was alive, and it was more important to that refugee than connection with the news. That dusty juniper spoke of a modest hope amid all the bitter reasons to despair or hate.

As for the Syrians from the Golan Heights, it was still a shock to see them living literally in refuse in their own homeland, five years or not. It gave an inkling—with no substantiation other than the scattered boxes for homes—that Syria would deal as severely with its people, and perhaps more so, as with Israelis or the Palestinians.

One of the Golanis was stirring a brazier of coals. His face was leathered by sadness. It resembled beef jerky: thin, lined, dark reddish brown. There was no spice in it, though. His wife, robed in black even in the hot sun, held an infant. His boys played in the dry lot around them, kicking tumbleweed with a stick. He offered us coffee.

Suddenly we heard a shout. It came from the Palestinian camp, which, in back of the Golani boxes, looked like a real town. We realized that Gary had not come with us and rushed back. Sure enough, Gary was being chased by a mob led by a woman who was shouting "Devil! Devil!" We hopped out of the taxis. She grabbed her large breast, pushing it up with her hand, incensed at the sight of us: "Get out of here you American Jews! Get out of here right now!" The woman's wrath communicated itself to a growing crowd of about a hundred.

"What did you do?"

"Nothing," Gary said. "I took some pictures."

Adeeb offered, "She thinks you took a picture of her breast feeding."

"I took a picture of a crowd of people."

"Look at them. They want to lynch us. That gal probably has her breast photographed by every UPI and AP cameraman east of New York. But she doesn't expect it from us."

It was too late to clarify, to tell them we really were Arab Americans, that not all Americans were against them, nor, for that matter were all Jews. The husbands were getting angry, the children expectant of violence. Sami and Adeeb took one look at the breast-feeding woman's toothless anger and raised stick and said, "Yallah. We go back to Arbeen."

Father, who was still fatigued from his long trip, was most shaken. He mumbled, staring out the window, "Terrible. Look what we have done." He wasn't talking about the snapshot. For an instant our Arab heritage was obliterated.

Gary sheepishly wound the film in his Minolta. Something in that woman snapped today, I thought. If we had cameras, we were Americans, and if we were Americans, we were Jews. And the enemy. She had had enough, for that day, and probably for her life. I'm not sure it would have made a difference if we had convinced her we were Arabs. Our clothes were too shiny, and our curiosity too detached.

Beirut awaited. Its grand hotels, casino, decadent nightlife, sparkling forbidden beaches, and beggars. A Palestinian poet puts it more bluntly: "Beirut is a rat where a car runs on artificial turf / off a cliff."[5]

Speaking of cliffs, they seem to get steeper going west over the mountains toward Beirut. From high up, Beirut appears a far-off island, a flat intricacy of the sea. How free the road was driving down the mountains to Lebanon's capital! And how treacherous. How unfree it became—blocked by armies and militias—and how treacherous. Guardrails cross the road today, but never ran along the sheer drop, and still don't. Peacetime or wartime, no one will ever be protected from falling in Lebanon.

Driving into Beirut was an exhilarating recognition: familiar trademarks of the West were everywhere. Coke bottles tipped to a Bedouin's mouth, script in Arabic, skyscrapers, tall cranes, luxury hotels that had given the city its nickname, "the Paris of the Middle East." As we turned the roundabout in the center of the city, I caught sight of the second warning of the impending cataclysm in Lebanon.

A legless man straddled, with his stumps, the center divider of the roundabout, putting his hat out to both incoming and outgoing traffic of the capital. He was a startling unofficial greeter. He saluted those who dropped a lira or two into his hat and smiled broadly under his black-and-white *kufiya*. Like some kind of traffic signal the beggar's hat—it was Western—went back and forth to leaving and arriving cars. Behind him towered the Phoenicia Hotel and the Holiday Inn. The latter, nearing completion, would have three years of bustling life until it was completely gutted in the civil war. The large gap between rich and poor in Lebanon told its grim story in the legless man of the roundabout. It was not easy to forget the little maid forced to sleep on the floor in Zahle or this cripple in the capital in spite of the ensuing excitement.

We pulled up to the esplanade in front of the Phoenicia Hotel. Ice-cold air conditioning hit us on entering, glass doors opened by velvet-gloved Lebanese and Palestinians. The grandparents and parents checked in, and from their sweeping window looking out on the Beirut port they could see the elegant old St. Georges Hotel resting on the waterfront like a golden galleon. The St. Georges was then the favorite of journalists; later the war made them take cover in the nondescript Commodore Hotel downtown. Below stood the fake Doric columns of the esplanade. No one could foresee in that splendid view that those columns would tumble, and the glass of every window in the Phoenicia shatter, and the St. Georges turn into a haven for rats, drug pushers, and people with bodies to dispose of. That was three years down the road yet, the Battle of the Hotels.

Gary and I wanted to be in the heart of the city, so we found a little pension, the Salaam House, in the Hamra district. It had only three floors and we stayed on the top one in a room freshly painted gray.

I remember parting the small curtain of the window in the pension shower in the mornings, looking out through the steam of hot water and seeing a woman flattening *safiha* (meat pies) with her hands on a stove across the way. The streets of Beirut are narrow, and the love, death, and food of one's neighbors are not more than an arm's stretch across the alley. I inhaled. The air was blessed.

We soon made friends with a dark beauty, Hind, the daughter of the Salaam House's owner, and her blonde, rather feline Lebanese friend, Cynthia. They became our constant companions.

I see a tableau of the porch at the Salaam House, whose name is scripted in turquoise on the white stucco; the wrought-iron balconies and lattices are also turquoise. It is a small peacock, this pension! On the porch is the old Iraqi diplomat taking his morning tea.

"So, you work for an oil company, Gary?" Hind says, pulling her shiny, straight dark hair over a shoulder before pouring coffee and hot cream for him.

"Yes."

"But you have come to the wrong country. You must go to the Gulf to discover oil. Here we only have olive oil."

"My company doesn't have Middle Eastern oil. Only in the North Sea near Britain do we have concessions overseas. It's mostly domestic."

"So you will never live abroad," her eyes shone. "What a pity. You better find an Arab girl while you can, rather than those spoiled American women."

"Someone who can really pour the hot cream," I offered.

"Precisely," Hind smiles, and puts a plate of olives in front of us.

The Iraqi diplomat takes this all in with a gold-toothed smile. Then comes the fine figure of Cynthia up the steps.

"Babe! I want you to meet two Americans."

Cynthia does not shake a hand, but curls hers and lays it limply in mine.

"You are not American; you are Arab, aren't you?"

"Arab Americans. And you don't look Arab yourself."

"My father was British, but my mother..."

"Her mother, *yi!*" Hind adds, holding a hand up.

"My mother is Lebanese to the bone."

"You have more freckles than an Irish colleen."

"My father dropped them into the yogurt," she spreads her teeth, neatly gapped in front.

Gold bracelets of both young women tinkle in a kind of harmony as we pass dishes and eat. The Iraqi diplomat has read his paper five times over, twice right to left, twice left to right, once up and down.

"America I don't like," Babe pouts.

"Why?"

"Americans are chameleons. They don't know who they are. They are gruff and arrogant people, and childish, too."

"Would you like to join us for a movie?"

"Americans think the whole world revolves around their little finger."

"We could go to dinner, too."

"Americans are presumptuous."

"I understand you have a lot of cats."

"Twelve."

"Who will watch them while you're gone?"

"My dog. And Mother. Americans are so practical."

We later saw *Husbands* with French and Arabic subtitles; it was drastically cut. Babe pointed to the screen and whispered, "You see how nasty your American men are to their women? Going all the way to London to cheat on them."

"Americans are so impractical."

We had a fine time with Hind and Babe that summer. But Babe never stopped criticizing America, its men, its foreign policy, its mores, and its boorishness. She did, however, like American soft drinks.

During our Beirut stay, we ran into a number of American friends. Walking down the shopping district of Hamra, we bumped into Khalil Hakim, who had studied with Gary at the University of Chicago. Khalil was now manager of the Libby Foods plant in Beirut; food chemistry was his specialty. He took us on a tour of the plant and showed how ptomaine poisoning was prevented in the preservation of canned goods.

Khalil drove us to his family home near Damour; it was made of the traditional limestone. He warned us on the way that trouble was brewing in Lebanon. Neighborhoods had to pay extortion money to civil authorities in order to get sewage and telephone lines, which were months, years, in the waiting. The Muslims, he contended, had little to show for themselves, and their areas were always the ones slowest to be upgraded by the Maronite-dominated government. He said the regime of President Suleiman Franjiyah was thoroughly corrupt.

"In Chicago I was very interested in the Middle East crisis. But since 1967 our people have had so many setbacks. The disunities have crippled us, and I believe we have made some big blunders. I've lost my sympathy."

He was to lose more. The Libby plant was destroyed during the civil war in 1975 and Khalil would flee to Athens, and then to Saudi Arabia. It would be another forced exile for him—he was born a Palestinian in Jerusalem.

Life went on as usual in Beirut. One night we cooked out with the girls from the Salaam House. I gave Cynthia a 10-pound note and asked her to buy some hot dogs, kerosene, and buns. She bought caviar and expensive cheese. ("I hate those crass materialists!") We hired a cab driver for 25 pounds to take us to a free beach just under the casino's snapping red lights in east Beirut (I do not remember anyone then actually referring to "east" or "west" Beirut). He pronounced he would get up at 1:30 AM to come and get us and promptly fell asleep by the side of the road, mouth gaping against the car window.

Soon we were rolling away from the glowing coals on the cold sand. Babe murmured with a voice that resembled Lauren Bacall's. We tried to roll away from the casino marquee, but there was no escaping; its periodic flashes turned the whole beach pink.

A few nights later, we four took Adeeb, who had come to visit from Damascus, on a beach walk at Summerland, south of Beirut. It was there that the third warning came.

Just as Babe reiterated she couldn't put all her eggs in a foreign basket, Adeeb called out, "There's someone with Gary."

Four dark neolithic figures approached, sloshing in the tide. Two were Hind and Gary. The other two were Lebanese soldiers in fatigues, automatic rifles slung over their shoulders. The beach, they barked at us, was under heavy guard against a sea commando raid by the Israelis, and what in hell were we doing on it, particularly with these American girls. One soldier poked Babe in the arm and accused her of being an Israeli spy. Babe, who had the misfortune of being light of skin and hair, was speechless. Adeeb fumed. Clarence Darrow couldn't have done a better job.

"You idiots! These women are Lebanese, not Americans. These men are not Arabs, but Americans. And I am a Syrian, you dopes. Not even in Syria do we have such ridiculous surveillance. How dare you! I am a lawyer in Damascus."

The elder of the two soldiers, a corporal, started examining Babe and Hind's bodies with a flashlight, first the face, then the breasts, and then the legs. Babe told them we were lovers who had come to the beach to kiss.

"No," the corporal said, dropping his cigarette. "You came out of the sea as spies."

Babe took over from Adeeb and lambasted them in the filthiest

Arabic I have ever heard. They were finally convinced. No foreigner could curse like that.

Though the country was not exactly at ease, even then, it was not reassuring how quickly those Lebanese soldiers substituted appearance for reality, how fast they mistook their own for an enemy. Lebanon's history as a bridge between two worlds—East and West— had made for a spirit of internationalism. But in Babe's fears, and in the soldiers' paranoia, I sensed a counterstrain of xenophobia, a repugnance for outsiders. Which strain would win?

"It may have been that day at the Palestinian camp outside Damascus." Father was speaking from his hospital bed at the American University of Beirut hospital. His ulcer was bleeding. He had complained of pain in his stomach ever since the little riot at Yarmouk. Jaddu, too, did a stint at the same hospital when his emphysema acted up. But the look on my father's face mirrored a strange torment; it was not unlike the paleness I saw when his ear was glued to the radio report of war in 1967 back home in Los Angeles. It was strange; his family was so Americanized. He was born in Cleveland, played high school football, grew up to be a respected leader in the West Coast garment industry, moving easily among the Jews, Arabs, and hurried racks of clothes. He was a paratrooper attached to the 82nd Airborne during World War II and helped liberate the Provence town of Draguignan. He was as American as anyone can get, yet there was something in his face that needed answering.

Shortly thereafter, the parents left for the States; the grandparents stayed on.

Though it took some convincing, Hind and Cynthia accompanied us for a day trip to southern Lebanon. It was known then as Fatahland.

The road south of Beirut grew weeds; it was lined by a listless stand of eucalyptus. Before long it became a mirage of dust. The first check point, at Sidon, was manned by Lebanese soldiers (in ensuing years it would be manned in turn by United Nations forces, the PLO, the Israeli army, the Shiʿite militia Amal, and Hezbollah). From Sidon south the taxi driver we'd hired began eating red pistachios fervently, piling up the shells on the front seat. A soldier at Tyre told us we had to proceed at our own risk in the next 25 miles to the southern border. The area was almost entirely under the control of Palestinian guerrillas (and today Hezbollah). The taxi driver took his stand at Tyre: no farther. He reached for a fresh bag of pistachios.

Silently, we walked down the mosaic-tiled road amid columns of Roman ruins. Closer to the Tyre port there were older ruins—4,000 years old—of the Phoenicians. We looked down the shore. A silver wing of land glinted in the sun: Israel.

Passing Palestinian refugee camps on the way back to Beirut outside Tyre and Sidon, the Lebanese women scoffed at our dismay. The cabbie was now smoking. The women said we were idealists. The Palestinians, recently kicked out of Jordan (1970), were already espousing Lebanon as the main staging ground for attacks on Israel and were already treating people in the south like dirt.

"Mark my words," Hind said. "No good will come of this."

We countered that it would be good for Lebanon to show compassion if it was to expect it itself. The presence of half a million Palestinian refugees in Lebanon (grown from the original 150,000 in 1948) cried out for a more lasting solution. Such a large group of homeless needed a home, as did the Jews who fled the terror of Nazi Germany. The natural solution was some part of historic Palestine as a state for the Palestinians.

Hind shook her head, "Is Lebanon only a floor mat?"

Adeeb in Damascus had said of the PLO, "The guerrillas are men without a country. Such men have nothing to lose."

I am not so sure about that now.

Just before leaving Beirut, we went to visit the caves at Jaita. Inside the caves the air was cool. Stalactites dropped in spears as old as the earth. Stalagmites had formed below them, yearning upward at a most patient rate. In the smaller caverns, the golden formation of sand met and made pillars. Pipe organs. Faces of struggling men. Women with huge breasts. A horse rider. A lonely child. They were all there under the earth at Jaita in mute forms of sandstone. The farther we went down from the light of day, the deeper our own heartbeats seemed to pound. Finally, we stopped. A subterranean river was below, sloshing. Maybe by such a canal the damned could be taken from hell.

Back in Damascus, a meeting was arranged for me with President Hafez al-Assad's press secretary, a Syrian administrator for UNWRA (United Nations Works and Relief Agency), and a Palestinian spokesman, originally from Jerusalem. A surprise in the small group of journalists there was Otis Chandler, then publisher of the *Los Angeles Times*, my hometown paper.

Much of the meeting was predictable, some ironic, and some prophetic. The press secretary emphasized that the Arabs were not against the Jews, but against the expansionism of Israel. Syria was against the Rogers Plan (an earlier version of the Reagan plan, which would have attached the West Bank to Jordan). Syria was "against any project which does not come from the Palestinian people themselves." (Ensuing years proved the irony in that statement. In 1976 Syria stopped the PLO in Beirut and in 1983 expelled Arafat and his forces from Tripoli.)

The Syrian spokesman was irritated by "a lot of rumors in the West that Syria is torturing Jews and violating some Jewish ladies. We have opened our Jewish Quarter in Damascus to visitors who can speak with Jewish professionals, doctors, traders," he declared. "Did you know the largest department store in Damascus is owned by a Jew? That we have thirty Jewish students at the University of Damascus?" We had visited the Jewish Quarter ourselves and found it clean and quiet.

The press secretary uttered an angry clarion: "Let the battle cover the whole Arab nation. Let the battle continue. Unless we make of Palestine another Vietnam, American public opinion will care less about us." One breath had him washing his hands of America, the other hankering after American opinion.

I left the meeting troubled and went out into the Damascene streets. It was late afternoon. An assault of smells distracted me—rosewater, crushed berries, bitter coffee grinds. An old man poured purple berry juice from a jug balanced on his shoulder into a cup for a peasant. I walked past a sherbet seller fashioning a cone of the only flavor in the city—pistachio. Ma‘zahr, or orange water, was in the sherbet and almost made me sick, for by now I could sniff it on any sweet. Fruit stands hung with oranges and grapefruit like groups of women with their heads turned. Damascene workers lingered, broke their arm-in-arm stride, threw a few piastres down, drank a glass of juice, and continued on, pointing to heaven.

I came to the Street of Gold, and Wahib Awad Hanna's little gold cubicle. (Wahib was one of eight children of ‘Ammu Selim, another of Jaddu's brothers. George Hanna of the paisley shirt was a younger brother of Wahib.) Wahib of the upturned jaw smiled while hammering medals of the Blessed Mother and miniature embossings of Qu‘ranic suras. Sweat dripped from his forehead. He was tired of staring at gold with a hot needle. He motioned through the window for me to kill an hour in the Suq al-Hamidiya and come back; then we would leave.

I went back into the lengthening shadows of the city of my ancestors. The streets were thickening with workers on their way home from the cotton mills, from the new ambitious highway projects, from markets and bread ovens, from the stores that sold everything from frankincense to orange water. The people's faces were leather, oiled by sweat. They seemed to seethe with a collective need through the streets. Their quickly moving loins and mouths showed life and ideas running through their systems like precious water dissipated all too soon in the heat.

The muezzin pierced the golden air with a call to prayer. Some of the crowd bent right where they stood; most hurried, as if to blur their bodies before the sight of God.

In front of the suq, I stopped to buy a glass of berry juice. My eyes fell absently on a little girl who had pieces of dried lamb on her bottom lip. She was in the center of the street, not more than four years old. She flickered among the spokes of bicycles, through the striding legs of workers and students, behind burdened donkeys and carts, and past the wheels of cars. She seemed to be looking for something. No adults were attached to her.

Why, of all the people on earth, had we found ourselves enemies of these?

She was so young, but in the ancient sun she seemed already turned to sedimentary rock. Her legs were bruised and her brow dirtied. Her eyes, though, burned a little amber behind a vagrant whisp of hair.

I followed her a while and then realized she was going nowhere, would never go anywhere. She was a spoke of the street. She would know little and want little, and perhaps have a husband one day who would die at war with a country my taxes kept unyielding. Or with my own.

But she was my own.

A hand gripped my bicep.

"You...were lost?" Wahib asked in quiet English.

"What can we do for that girl?" I asked, turning back. But she had disappeared in the street.

A timeless time came to an end.

Wahib put a medal he had made around my neck—the gold Blessed Mother. I looked one last time at the faces of Arbeen—and for a second wished Jaddu had never left. There was Shahda, his one sister, the marvelous rills of time on her face. She was trembling. Great Uncle Tawfiq: handsome, sunburned forehead, sad. And Great-Uncle Selim and his moon-round face. There was little Great-Uncle ᶜAbdu, who had cured me with the swirl of his ancient hands. There was Adeeb, this wide smile furled like a ship at anchor. He was silent. ᶜId—the tall, giant bear. And the children, one after the other, bestowing kisses like flowers on our skin. Fayzi held me tightly. Her little sister, Nora, who had followed Jaddu so closely the whole summer, even helping him with his oxygen. And then George Hanna, who was wearing in farewell the paisley shirt again.

Over the next decade news from Arbeen was scarce. Letters were rare. The ones I sent—including a long poem to the villagers—were never answered. Yet somehow word came. During the 1973 war, Wahib, the goldsmith who rescued me from a feeling of despair on the Damascene street, was killed with his twin infant daughters and two others when a Syrian army transport truck plowed into his car in a freak accident. Old ᶜAbdu died a natural death, as did Shahda. An

Israeli bomb fell on ʿAbduʾs farm during the war but did not go off due to his heavily irrigated fields. The children found it in the mud. Adeeb and Sami married in their late thirties, as is common in our family.

A tie across the globe had been made, however bad connections were through the mail. Fayzi did come to America, though her sojourn was difficult. Accompanying her was little Nora of the pink pinafore. A sought-after seamstress, Fayzi returned to Syria before Nora, who went quickly to the head of her class in English and became a fast fan of the Los Angeles Dodgers. She returned to Syria after ten years in America in 1984, marrying her cousin, George Hanna of the paisley shirt. (They finally settled in Los Angeles, and have two fine children, Selim and Amy.)

But flying back over the Atlantic in 1972, Wahib's medal touching my breastbone, I looked below for a long time. The water was a dark gray-blue, like a restless hide of some animal never satisfied. In America we are all bitten by the independence bug; in Syria and Lebanon that summer I had felt a glorious communion that does not extinguish personality but blends it. The blending, the warmth, is all-important, and, one sensed, the roles fairly set. I wanted to stay but knew I could not, that somehow I did not quite fit, though I had never felt more at home in my life. Then I thought that, paradoxically, if Jaddu had not had the courage to leave at the century's beginning, the power of that reunion and kinship might never have happened.

On the hide of that watery blue beast, Jaddu came in 1920 in a ship seeking a better life; the hive of Damascus had been stifling in some way. No doubt that was the other side of such warmth. I imagined the great ocean liners and steamers, the barges filled with immigrants from the Old World in the hold, so many nets of sardines, so many catches from oppression, neglect, and poverty. They were the Irish in mid-19th century with no potatoes; the Italians with blistered vines; the Jews with scars of pogroms; and after them, the Greeks and Slavs and Russians fleeing bloody revolutions.

But there were also Arabs—a trickle at mid-century that grew after 1890 and reached a yearly peak at World War I of about 10,000. They came from the destitute Syrian province of the old Ottoman Turkey, and the Lebanon mountains in that province. I saw them below creating the waves of the great blue animal that led to America; they, too, had the mighty No! in their eyes, seeking a Yes.

I wanted to find out why they came, these Syrians, Lebanese, but was also curious about those from other Arab countries, such as Egypt, Yemen, Palestine, Iraq. I wanted to trace where they settled, the lives they lived in the New World, the dilemmas they faced, the contributions they had made to America. Finally, I wanted to try to do something to right the political wrongs by which our relatives and their people suffered and for which, partly, we were responsible. On my return I began gathering information, in an informal and then increasingly formalized way, about the history of Americans of Arab descent. I had no notion, looking out on the Atlantic that day, that my search would lead me back to Beirut once again.

If I needed a final push, it came on a dark night in a hospital on October 4, 1974. From the day of our return from the triumphant reunion in Syria, Jaddu's health deteriorated. In two years, he was on his deathbed in Pasadena, breathing fast, oxygen tubes in his nose and a mask over his mouth. Crosstown that very night, in another hospital, was Nazera Jabaly Orfalea, Father's mother, the one who came from Zahle. She had just passed away at 88. Kamel had always said, "When the old lady goes, then it will be time for me." Nazera and he had been close friends cross the marriage, both cut from the same tough immigrant cloth. Kamel did not know, however, that she had just died, nor even that she was hospitalized.

Members of the family took turns standing watch through the night. At one point, I was in Jaddu's room with a cousin and a brother.

He struggled for air. It seemed he had struggled for air most of his life. This was a man who, in a sense, had introduced me to myself, or at least had shined a light on a dark, submerged chunk of the soul I had hardly known existed. He had, by taking me to Arbeen, passed a baton. He did not guarantee that it would be clean, or light, or without smudges of blood.

"Jaddu," I suddenly touched his chest. "I know you cannot speak. But I must ask you something, and if you answer yes, raise your left hand. Otherwise, raise nothing. Do you think life is good?"

Seconds became years. My brother and cousin were transfixed watching the motionless man on the hospital bed. Though in a coma, he raised his left hand slowly—intravenous needles and all—then dropped it. Five hours later, he was dead.

– TWO –

SEEDS TO THE WIND: THE FIRST WAVE OF ARAB IMMIGRATION (1878–1924)

Scouts, navigators, translators, Eastern rite missionaries, escaped slaves, and camel corps trainers: these first explorers of the New World from Arab lands found America as exotic as did any Western visitor the Orient. On his deathbed, my grandfather from Syria had proclaimed that life was good; his predecessors daring the Atlantic westward would have also said: life is wild, lonely, and short.

The Arabs were to come in groups and sizable numbers only after the emigration of the Joseph Awad Arbeely family in 1878 from grandfather's village of Arbeen, Syria. By contrast, the first gathering of Jews in the New World were the 23 who landed in New Amsterdam (New York City) in 1654, about 200 years before the first documented lone Arab settler. But history flares with a few daring Arab soldiers-of-fortune who traveled by force of will (or forced will) across the Atlantic—in Arabic, "The Sea of Darkness"—before any thought of settlement.

THE STUFF OF MYTHS: ARAB ADVENTURERS IN THE NEW WORLD

Grandfather Awad arrived in New York City from Arbeen in 1920 aboard a tramp steamer. He could never have known that a much earlier notch may have been made on American stone by sailors from Lebanon before the time of Christ. They were a people for whom a sea horizon was as enticing and capable of mirage as a desert. They were the Phoenicians.

In New Hampshire's Pattee's Caves and on hewn stones in southern Pennsylvania near Mechanicsburg are strange inscriptions that have led at least one historian to conclude that the Phoenicians landed in America between 480 and 146 BCE, long before Columbus or the Vikings. The ancient cities of Phoenicia—Tyre, Sidon, Berytus—are part of the modern state of Lebanon. Whether these inscriptions in stone in rural America—ciphers of the world's oldest alphabet—were carved by some overzealous Lebanese eager to establish a patrimony beyond the smoldering ruins of modern Lebanon, or were indeed the markings of history's first crew team, is left to speculation.[1]

Fascinating recent evidence has been unearthed of an ancient North African—and particularly Libyan—presence in the American Southwest. There archaeologists with no knowledge of Arabic or ancient tongues as late as 1962 found indecipherable petroglyphs and labeled them "Great Basin curvilinear." But in 1980 the linguist and fossil expert Barry Fell revealed that an inscription on rock in the Valley of Fire, Nevada, was written in ancient Kufic Arabic and spelled a man's name, Hamid (or tranquil). Fell also found striking similarities between southwestern Indian pueblo and pre-Islamic Tunisian and Libyan architecture, pottery, and dress. Among many other petroglyphs unlocked was an exhortation not to offend Baal written in ancient Numidian (North African) script and dated 650 BCE. According to Fell, these ancient Libyans of the western American high desert did not come just to explore; glyphs of alphabet and math lessons show they were teaching their young.[2]

The Columbian era is lit by some Arab torches. Columbus' monumental voyage may have been inspired by an escapade of eight Arab sailors who took a ship from Lisbon before Columbus and landed in South America. The Arab geographer al-Idrisi documents the voyage of the eight Arabs, but historians discount the claim that they inspired Columbus to try to reach the East by sailing west. Nevertheless, a visitor at the 500th anniversary of Columbus' birth in Italy found a copy of al-Idrisi's account among Columbus' belongings on display.[3]

In 1492, Columbus did choose as his primary translator a Spanish Arab, or Moor, converted to Christianity after the fall of Granada, which had been ruled by the Arabs for 600 years. His Christian name was Louis de Torre and he was in all likelihood the first man of Islamic culture to set foot on North America. He was of no use in speaking to the American Indians, though he would have been useful in speaking to East Indians.

Morocco—linked by Gibraltar to Arab Spain—was to have a special relationship with the New World and, later the birth of the United States of America. In 1528, a former slave from Morocco named Zammouri guided a Spanish expedition into Florida. In 1539, a Moroccan Arab named Estaphan (Istefan) was picked as a guide to Fra Marcos de Niza, a Franciscan sent by the viceroy of New Spain to explore the Southwest. Estaphan was killed by a Navajo arrow before he could get back to tell the Spaniards about the cactus. There are records as early as 1717 of Arabic-speaking black slaves who would not eat pork. Finally, Morocco—under Mohammed III—granted free passage to all American ships in 1777, thus becoming the first country in the world to officially recognize the independence of the United States. A "Treaty of Friendship" between Morocco and the United States was drawn up and signed in 1787 by Mohammed III and George Washington.[4]

In spite of Morocco's contribution in scouts and diplomacy, North African Arabs were not to contribute much to the large First Wave migration from Arab lands to America (it was over 95 percent Syrian–Lebanese–Palestinian). But one North Carolina family, the Wahabs, claim to trace their ancestry in America back to an Algerian shipwreck in 1779. During the American Revolution the Continental Congress negotiated with Algeria to stock horses for Washington's depleted cavalry. A ship carrying the horses hit a reef southwest of Cape Hatteras and some of the men and horses swam to shore. Today there is a cemetery on Ocracoke Island, North Carolina, with the name Wahab (in Arabic, giver of strengths or talents) carved on gravestones dating back to the early 19th century.[5]

Evidence from 1790 supports the possibility of Arab adventurers and traders settling early in the Carolinas. In the House Assembly of the state of South Carolina, a distinction was made between Moors and blacks, that is, "sundry Moors, Subjects of the Emperor of Morocco," were to be tried according to laws for South Carolina citizens and not under the codes for black slaves. A century later, however, Syrians were forbidden to vote in many states as part of the "yellow race" and did not get a definitive court ruling on their right of franchise until 1915. This chronic question of what color hole to fit the Arab in only compounded the identity crisis of a people who had been dominated by the Turks for 500 years and had difficulty showing fealty outside their own village.

Another early trade agreement, such as the one with Morocco, that brought contact but not settlement between the new American nation and the Arabs was the arrival of an Omani cargo ship in New York harbor in 1840. The rotund commander of the *Sultana* did not care to market oil or base rights; he certainly had no idea of the value of Oman's Strait of Hormoz to oil tankers a century later. He probably wanted a square meal and fresh water. After 87 days at sea, the 350-ton *Sultana* and its crew caused a stir during their three-month stay in New York. Its commander was "a small, slightly corpulent, bearded Arab gentleman, to whom all paid deference. His complexion was tawny, his eyes were black and piercing. . . . About his person hung an air of natural dignity. To the surprise of gaping port officials, he addressed them in tolerable English."[6] This was Ahmad bin Naaman, and his English should have been no surprise since the British had been in Muscat and Oman for a century. Today the Omani commander's portrait hangs in New York City Hall.

There is recent evidence of a Jermiah Mahomet settling before the Civil War in Frederick, Maryland, where he raised horses and worked in real estate.[7] But the two most celebrated "first" immigrants from the Arab world dying on American soil were not recorded until 1854 and 1856. One was a Bible student who died young in Brooklyn; the other was a camel driver who lived to a ripe old age in Quartzsite, Arizona. One wanted to return to Lebanon (or Syria, as the Ottoman Turkish vilayet was called); the other did not. One was a Christian, the other a Muslim. Their stories encapsulate the solitary lives of the first Arab sojourners in America. With them, an era both begins and ends.

If it wasn't for Palestine, a Lebanese—and a Maronite at that— would not have been singled out by Philip Hitti as the first official immigrant in America from Arab lands. If it wasn't for the magnetic pull of the Holy Land on tourists from America, Antonios Bishallany would never have made it to Boston harbor in 1854. Bishallany was a dragoman, a tour guide, in Palestine.

Born in Salima, a small village of olive trees and pines in the mountain district of Metn in Lebanon in 1827, Bishallany had a simple childhood of tending to olive trees and the family vineyards. The limestone-bricked house of his family had been theirs for over a century. What pushed him to notch his name in history was a combination of family tragedy, personal pluck, and a burning desire to expand his learning.

At age 10, Bishallany was uprooted with his family from their home in the pastoral mountains after their vineyards were burned to the ground by marauders. They moved to a town outside Beirut, but in two years his father died and Bishallany became the family breadwinner. He developed a taste for travel while in the employ of the Italian consul in Beirut, who took him as his valet to such Mediterranean ports as Smyrna and Algiers.

At 23, Bishallany—typically enough for Lebanese—wanted to be his own boss and started as an independent interpreter and guide for tourists to the Holy Land. He provided his clients with tents, food, maps, and itineraries and accompanied them through Syria, Palestine, and Egypt. He must have been quite an entrepreneur; though his Italian was good, his English was poor. Nevertheless, one New Yorker recorded his first impressions of Bishallany in Beirut: an energetic, good-natured young man unconcerned about payment—"All that he would demand was a letter of recommendation."[8]

Two years later, in 1854, the New York businessman found a young man wearing the *tarbush*, or fez, entering his office. Bishallany had sold everything he owned for $300 and had sailed for America, landing in Boston after a two-month voyage. He immediately went to New York, met with former clients he had guided around the Holy Sepulcher, Mount Sinai, and the like, and finally settled in with a wealthy Fifth Avenue family as a butler. The housewife of the family would earn his obsessive thanks for taking care of him when tuberculosis struck all too soon.

Soon Bishallany was exchanging Arabic lessons for English lessons and "the light was never put off in his chamber before midnight."[9] But in his first American winter, he displayed signs of the illness that would eventually be fatal, and by the summer of 1855 he was taken by his New York benefactor to the summer resort of Richfield Springs, which reminded Bishallany of Lebanon. In the autumn he entered Amenia Seminary School in Duchess County, New York, but began coughing fitfully as winter set in. The principal loved the young man's zeal to learn, particularly his repeated desire to return to Lebanon and help his country. Afraid that Bishallany would be made the butt of schoolboy jokes, the principal found the opposite—the other students competed for his attention: "The chap was extremely polite, sociable, simple-hearted, excellent in conversation and wit, and to the extent that the most brutal student could not keep from being attracted to him."[10]

He complained in a letter to his family in Lebanon that doctors refused to "phlebotize" him, because bloodletting "is not practiced in this country." He quoted from a poèm of homesickness, said he had no money to bequeath to them—all had been spent on medicine and education—and that he purposely left off dating the letter because "I am cognizant of the time the Lord will send for me."

By fall of 1856, Bishallany was dead. He was buried in the Greenwood Cemetery in Brooklyn, the symbols of the lion, serpent, and lamb carved in the gravestone of lot 181. For one who coughed practically from the day he arrived in America, he was remarkably serene at the end, ready to leave "this transient world." Forty years later, Brooklyn and New York City would be the centerpoint of Arab settlement in the New World.

Bishallany made his stand in America, though short, by the grace of a Yankee merchant. His Muslim counterpart, however, owed his American sojourn to the Confederate president. It was Jefferson Davis who thought of a scheme for a camel highway in the American Southwest.

While Bishallany was in New York in 1855, Davis—as secretary of war—assigned a US Army major and Navy lieutenant to round up camels in the Middle East. They traveled to Cairo and Smyrna and other ports to barter for creatures durable in hot waterless climes. The first trip, in 1856, brought back 32 adult camels, two calves born aboard ship, two Turks, and three Arab camel drivers, one of whom was called a "Bedouin-and-Camel medicine man" (the American

Indian shaman's role appropriated easily to other "savages"). One of the Arabs was Hadji Ali, then 28, nicknamed "Hi Jolly" and referred to as "the happy little Turk." Since the Arabs had been under the yoke of Ottoman Turkey since the 16th century, the misnomer was probably not a happy one for Hadji Ali. Westerners commonly blurred (and still do) the ethnically different Semitic Arabs with the Indo-European Turks. In fact, it was not until 1899—twenty years after their immigration stream started—that Syrian immigrants gained a separate classification from "Turk in Asia" at Ellis Island. The identity problems common to all immigrants were compounded for the Arabs in the United States: first they were taken as Turks; then Syrians became Lebanese; Lebanese hid behind "Phoenician"; and today Arabs are often mistaken for Iranians. Hadji Ali would not be the first Arab American for whom the question "Who am I?" was a particularly piercing one.

In 1857, an Army engineer, Edward F. Beale, set out on orders to blaze a camel trail from Port Defiance near Goliad, Texas, across the northern deserts of New Mexico and Arizona to the Colorado River bordering California. California had recently entered the Union, and Jefferson Davis wanted to connect to it at once. Hadji Ali and the camel trainers went on strike early in the journey; in fact, they never left Camp Verde near San Antonio. It seems they had not been paid in six months. Beale wrote Washington that something was amiss and wondered why the government was delinquent in paying the camel tenders. He regretted not having them on his trip with the camels, for they were "the only men in America who understand them."[11] The American Civil War broke out two years after the desert expedition ended, and Jefferson Davis had more to tend to than blazing trails in sand. He became the first and last president of the Confederate States of America.

Other obstacles presented themselves. With the coming of the railroad in the Southwest, camel traffic, as well as horse and muletrain traffic, was made obsolete. Six native trainers weren't sufficient to deal with the camels. There also grew a belligerence between camels and men, mules and horses. Contrary to Beale's initial ecstasy, the camels had trouble with surfaces that were more gravel than sand: "Their soft-padded feet were literally cut to pieces by the dry, rocky ground of the Southwest."[12] In 1866, the War Department sold 66 camels to Bethel Coopwood of San Antonio, Texas, for 31 dollars a head. Some would later turn up in parks or circuses, or hitched to a rancher's buckboard. The camel was woven into the folklore of the Southwest as a ghoulish figure that could appear out of the desert, stir up trouble, and vanish.[13]

Hadji Ali prospected for gold awhile and then settled into a job as a scout for the US Army. In a move that prefigured name changes

Joseph Lupus (on left, middle row), an immigrant from Dibel, Lebanon, mans the engine of the Denver–Rio Grande railroad in 1912 at Helper, Utah. (Carmen & Joseph Awad)

at Ellis Island, Ali became a US citizen in 1880 at Tucson under the name Philip Tedro. Shortly thereafter he married Gertrude Serna; they quickly had two daughters. But "Hi Jolly" was called by the desert more than married life and he returned to prospecting in 1889 in Quartzsite, about a hundred miles west of Phoenix. It was there in the Arizona desert that the first Muslim immigrant in America died in 1903, unknown by 5,551 fellow Syrians who arrived in America that year escaping deprivation.

"Hi Jolly" was the last of the era of solitary adventurers who dared the Sea of Darkness from the Arab world to get to America. He became something of a legend in Arizona and was cared for in his old age by ranchers and prospectors, who appreciated "his gentle nature, his personal integrity and his unfailing kindness to animals and to his fellow man."[14] Whether or not he practiced Islam is unknown. His name suggests that he had been a "Haj," one who had done his duty by visiting Mecca. His final Mecca was in a land just as hot, but profane.

Both Bishallany and Ali were enshrined for their pioneer roles in American history. The Lebanese student's home in Salima was made a national museum by Lebanese President Suleiman Franjiyah in 1971. "Hi Jolly" received his accolade in the New World. In 1935, the Arizona Department of Highways erected a pyramid on Ali's grave, topped with a copper camel.

THE WITHERED CEDAR: WHY THE ARABS LEFT SYRIA AND LEBANON

It was appropriate that a highway department memorialized Hadji Ali. Wanderlust has never been foreign to the peoples of historic Syria, Lebanon, and Palestine. From earliest times, the long, blue arm of the Mediterranean pulled the inhabitants of its eastern shore to the West; they followed not only the setting sun but also native impulses ranging from intrepidness to trade. Those longboat strokers—the Phoenicians—established early colonies in North Africa (at Carthage), in Sicily, and in southern Spain, selling among other things a purple dye made from the murex mollusk that would become the color of nobility in ancient Rome. The ancient Hebrews migrated from Palestine to Egypt to Europe. The Roman poet Juvenal complained about Syrian immigration to Rome, saying the Orontes River (of Damascus) was flowing into the Tiber. In 1283, the first and one of the largest emigrations of Maronite Catholics from Lebanon occurred when they escaped Mamluk oppression by fleeing to the island of Cyprus. Mongol and Tatar hordes from Asia, and periodic political and religious upheavals, only encouraged the native love of wandering that flowed in the Levantine's veins from earliest times. Facing deserts or mountains to the east, they chose the sea.[15]

Longstanding contact with Western powers through trade and conquest—as well as their geographic given as the crossroads of East and West—made the historic Syrians often oscillate between xenophilia and xenophobia, two opposed cultural urges that played themselves out over the centuries in a hospitable internationalism, as well as a distrust of invaders. Except for the classical Omayyad caliphate centered in Damascus in the seventh and eighth centuries, Syria—and its Lebanon province in particular—was never militarily powerful or able to defend itself against outside, predatory forces. These realms were caught between conflicting forces, for instance, the Mongols and the Seljuks; the Turks and the French and English; and, in the case of Palestine, British and Jewish colonizers.

What were the causes that propelled emigration from the Arab world to the United States, which began in the 1870s, crested at World War I, and was halted by immigration laws by 1924? The answer has been the subject of much controversy, ranging from economic venturesomeness posited by Alixa Naff to Philip and Joseph Kayal's emphasis on a desire to flee sectarian and political conflict. Salom Rizk, one of the few early Syrian immigrants to chronicle his passage to and experience in the United States, cites visitations in his village of ʿAyn Arab by "two kinds of plagues: one of locusts, the other of men."[16] The men were, specifically, tax collectors and conscriptors for military service from the Turkish capital.

The political economist Charles Issawi sees Arab immigration to the New World as being sparked by the following: "tensions accompanying economic and social transformation; the imposition of conscription; the spread of foreign education; the improvement of transportion; and the massacres of 1860."[17] Most certainly, a growing population caused by the advent of better hygiene and a scarcity of cultivable land—particularly in the Lebanon mountains—was an important factor, as well as periodic famines, insect blights, and droughts that, among other things, wrecked the crucial sericulture, or silkworm production, that was a staple of the Lebanese economy in the 19th century.

But some are quick to point out that the protected *mutasarrif* of Lebanon—granted some autonomy after the massacres of 1860—was relatively tranquil in the last decades of the 19th century. While the initial and immediate spur for the trickle of Arab immigrants that boarded European steamers to America may have been no more spectacular than the desire for adventure and prosperity (rumors of "streets of gold" in America were as tempting to the Arab peasantry, who formed 90 percent of the First Wave immigration, as they were to the Irish, the Italians, and others), Naff's assertion that "no memorable political or economic event unleashed Syrian migration to the United States" strikes one as interpretive of the skin of history, rather than its underlying currents. Naff, for instance, barely mentions the Druze-Maronite massacres and is strangely silent about what to many Syrian immigrants is the most traumatic collective experience (whether firsthand or through relatives): starvation in World War I. It is almost as if Naff's central thesis—that Syrians were the most quickly assimilating of ethnic groups in America—must hinge on less than traumatic reasons for coming to the country in the first place, as opposed to say, Eastern European Jewish immigrants, who fled pogroms and were imbued with a strong ethnic identity that played itself out obsessively in literature and politics. (She also dismisses the many firsthand accounts of trauma at the hands of the Turks, tax collectors, or war as calculated *modus operandi* of early immigrants to ingratiate themselves with their fellow Americans by earning asylum as any other "troubled masses" would.)

If one is looking solely at the first clusters of Arabs who came to Ellis Island in the 1880s, the motivations of those I have interviewed ratify the thesis of the age-old Levantine wanderer looking for a new market. But statistics show that in 1914, the first year of World War I, more Syrians came to America than in the whole period of 1869 to 1895. If the first courageous, plucky few set off to get sick in steerage for opportunity, it is just as certain that those who followed them shortly had more licking at their heels than the desire for a dollar. And though studies have shown at least a quarter of Syrians returned to their homeland after coming to America—and more wanted to—

few stayed there. After World War I, Lebanon was in wreckage, Syria and Palestine embroiled in growing battles for independence from European mandate powers. In short, there was little to go back to. If they migrated first in fairly venturesome spirits, after the "war to end all wars" they stayed here because the bridge behind them was cut and left burning.

In fact, the spur to original Syrian migration was multitudinous, and grew more and more complex as the century waned and World War I approached. As Irving Howe has said in his massive study of East European Jewish immigration, *World of Our Fathers*, "to separate for any but analytical reasons, the most exalted notions for the migration from the most self-centered is probably a mistake." My own studies indicate five areas of importance, some neglected and some oft-cited: the wooing and salubrious role of American missionaries in Syria; the shattering of the religious mosaic in 1860; economic uncertainties exacerbated by overpopulation and the land squeeze; the death throes of the Ottoman Turkish empire and ensuing lawlessness, taxation, and conscription; and the starvation of one-quarter of Lebanon's population during the Great War. In particular, I want to dwell on the last reason because no one since Philip Hitti in 1924 has done so—at least in book form—and because my informants in the Arab-American community repeatedly and obsessively referred to it.

American Missionaries Preach to the Converted

One of the reasons Arabs chose to emigrate to America in the 19th century owes itself to a religious oddity: American Christians proselytized the original Christians of the Holy Land. Of course, in Greater Syria and environs, Islam was dominant, but in the area where missionaries concentrated—Lebanon and parts of Palestine— well over half the population was already Christian.

The early New England evangelists were filled with zeal, adventure, goodwill, and a pinch of arrogance. Whatever they guessed were the needs of Christians surrounded by heathens, or heathens surrounded by a need for meaning (i.e., schools and medical supplies), they guessed right and by the mid-19th century earned for themselves "an inestimable position in the hearts and minds of the Syrian people."[18] They did not, however, effect a mad dash to Protestantism; few converts were made. The Maronite Catholic hierarchy saw to that.[19]

The center of a haystack would hardly seem like the place to hatch a plan to spread the Gospel in the land where it was first spoken, but so it was. In 1806, a group of students at Williams College in Massachusetts took refuge from a storm in a haystack. Perhaps the storm intensified their fervency for the woes of other lands; in any case, by the time they emerged, they had crystallized a plan—not unlike an early Peace Corps but with religion as the zinger—that they would present to the faculty of Andover Theological Seminary four years later: to minister to the Levant.

The first two young ministers licensed to serve in the Holy Land from the new Comissioners for Foreign Missions were Pliny Fisk and Levi Parsons, formally appointed in 1819. In a sermon that he gave on October 31 in Old South Church in Boston, Fisk touted an item of some commercial value: Bibles. He spoke of the eastern Mediterranean as a "radiating point" into the Far East for tons of the religious books. The Syrian archbishop of Jerusalem was having trouble obtaining printed Bibles in Arabic, having been turned away in both Rome and Paris, with only minor success in Britain.[20] And so with a little American ingenuity, Fisk stunned his listeners with his goal to explore the Holy Land, replete with salable Arabic Bibles. It was with the assumption of backwardness and its offense to "Christian sensibilities" that the Foreign Missions gave final instructions to Fisk and the other departing evangelists:

> From the heights of the Holy Land and from Zion, you will take an extended view of the widespread desolations and variegated scenes presenting themselves on every side to Christian sensibilities... The two grand inquiries ever present in your minds will be What good can be done? and by what means?[21]

The directive betrayed an indecisiveness as to the mission in Lebanon and Palestine. The comissioners did not tell Fisk to ask the natives what they wanted; they postulated a kind of solipsistic internality once they touched down on Sacred (but backward) Ground. It is as if the purpose of the mission were an existential awe and self-questioning. The Middle East had Othello; it did not need Hamlet.

As for the "Mohammedans" (an inaccurate appellation for Muslims that prevailed for centuries in the West), no doubt the first American missionaries contained in their intellectual grab bag the knowledge that Dante had stuffed Mohammed in the eighth of nine circles in Hell and in the ninth of ten Bolgias, there to wallow in his own filth right on the edge of Lucifer's stronghold. The great figures of Islam, such as Avicenna, Averroes, and Saladin, though admired by Dante, are still unsaved, and, as Edward Said points out, "condemned, however lightly, to Hell [the first circle of the Inferno]."[22]

The Stockbridge Indians gave Levi Parsons a donation of $5.87, two gold ornaments, several ornamental baskets, and a pocket lantern inscribed, "This is to illuminate the streets of Jerusalem."[23] If the American Indians—so recently colonized and subjugated—had discovered that Jerusalem's streets needed lighting, those streets must be dark indeed.

Parsons and Fisk both died young—after three and seven years, respectively—in the mission service, Parsons buried in Bethlehem, Fisk in Beirut. But they had established Beirut as the center of American missions in the Near East. Adele Younis described their zeal and later that of William Goodell (the three were all born in 1792) as the overseas afterglow of the spirited American Revolution:

> The young [evangelists] exemplified their times: their intellectual endeavors were intertwined with firm moral and spiritual sensibilities. This manifest restlessness drew attention to the Americans who became known as a "nation of doers." It seemed strange to the Arabs that so much apparently selfless effort had no ulterior motives.[24]

Three positive contributions were made by the Americans in early-19th-century Syria, which at that time included modern Lebanon and most of modern Israel. They helped to stimulate the Arab printing presses, which effected a renaissance in public reading. They established schools, which dotted the mountains. Last, they introduced medical help to a province of the Ottoman Empire that the Turks had all but abandoned for social services.

In a way, the Europeans gave the Americans a special "in." After the Druze–Christian massacres of 1860, French links with the Maronites were tightened, as were British links with the Druze. Therefore, the American missionaries, considered unbiased, were sought after by both sides. It was to their credit that the missionaries, for the most part, did not take flee in the 1860 bloodshed. The home of the Reverend and Mrs. Simon Calhoun became a sanctuary for both sides, with Maronites, Orthodox, and Druze women storing their jewelry, money, and clothes with them, so that "these missionaries who had been before cursed and excommunicated by the Maronite patriarch, bishops and priests as 'incarnate devils' now held in trust without receipt all the wealth of both Christians and Druzes."[25] In the midst of the massacre at Deir al-Qammar, Calhoun kept his head. He steered clear of condemning the Druze as a people: "It may seem strange to you, but so it is that we have moved from place to place without fear, through the midst of the Druze. They never offered an insult, and permitted us to protect the Maronites and their property without a word of objection." Calhoun's counsel could echo tragically through a century of Western mishandling of the Middle East: "I urged all to wait patiently in hope that all grievances will be redressed in due time."[26]

It would be wrong to infer that the Arabs themselves stood by stiffly as the slaughter took place. Many helped with humanitarian deeds; one, the Algerian ʿAbd al-Kadir, took Syrian Christians into his home during the massacre in Damascus and was rewarded for his valor by a present of two gold-mounted pistols from American

President James Buchanan (just as his own country was about to plunge into civil war). ʿAbd al-Kadir wrote many tracts, as a Muslim, against the massacre, "as contrary to Islam and the Quʿran, and these were widely distributed."[27] The leader of the Druze, Said Jumblat, protected Christian merchants with whom he had close ties at Deir al-Qammar.[28]

Immersion in the life of a troubled country was not without pitfall for Americans. Dr. Cornelius Van Dyck, who liked to dress in an Arab ʿaba as he ministered to the wounded—and who spoke perfect Arabic—was almost executed as a Christian Arab. A Druze interceded, shouting, "This is Hakim [wise one] Van Dyck!" Years later, Van Dyck saved the would-be executioner's life in his hospital.[29] The disturbances of 1860 in Syria brought in $150,000 in world relief—one-quarter of it from the United States—for 26,000 refugees. Henry Jessup, a missionary for over three decades in Syria, published 30 letters in the *New York Herald* describing the catastrophe in which 20,000 were killed and serene villages, such as Zahle, were reduced to cinders. Daniel Bliss, the founder of the American University of Beirut, later figured that "the events of 1860 were a

On January 15, 1927, the New Syria Party held this banquet in Detroit in honor of Shakib Arslan, the leader of the Druze revolt against the French. (Robert Khouri)

kind of mental earthquake that shook the people out of a self-satisfied lethargy and made them long to know more of the world outside Syria."[30]

Certainly the selflessness of medical missionaries like Calhoun, Van Dyck, and George Post made for gratitude. The founder of the first cooperative hospital in America (in Elk City, Oklahoma), a Syrian named Dr. Michael Shadid, made explicit his indebtedness to the example of an American surgeon at the time: "And here. . .[in Beirut] was Dr. George Post, famed throughout Syria for his skill and almost miraculous surgery, the man who became my ideal, inspiring me with a burning determination to become a doctor, to go out to little villages like Judeidet and heal the sick."[31] One Christian woman in New York City spoke of the Americans as "God-sent to our country. They took care of our eyes and hair." A Druze businessman in New York called them "angels in our land."[32] An Orthodox woman in Pasadena, California, related that so salubrious was the example of the Presbyterian missionaries to her husband in Syria that he stubbornly refused to go to the Orthodox church, preferring the Presbyterians, who also gave him and his wife the necessary support to get through the Great Depression in New York.[33] In an atmosphere of crimped financial opportunity, overpopulation, and growing turmoil, the Americans gave the Syrians an example of a better world. It is one of history's tragic ironies that when the Americans arrived in Lebanon a century later they did so not with doctors or missionaries but with guns.

The Religious Mosaic Shatters

Most historians place the origin of Lebanon's civil war in the inequities fashioned into the Lebanese constitution when the country became free in 1943. Maronite Catholics, whose only large numbers in the Arab world are in Lebanon, were given predominance in the parliament and were guaranteed the presidency. Others date the problem back to 1932—the last time a nationwide census was taken in Lebanon—when somewhat suspicious polling gave the Maronites the largest segment of the various confessional groups that made up the country.[34] Nevertheless, the most striking early example of intersectarian strife was the 1860 massacres. It is simply incorrect to say that Lebanon's problems—massive as they are—are "centuries" old. At most, they are a century and a half old and coincide with full-scale European power intervention that wrested some control over the Lebanon mountains from the Ottomans, ensuring it a measure of autonomy, however fragile and fractious.

Maronites and Druze hold at least two things in common: both are special offshoots of their respective religions (the Maronites have their own Catholic rite, which uses Aramaic, the language of Christ); Druze are a schismatic Muslim sect believing in reincarnation, who do not have imams or mosques. Both share the Lebanon mountains as a chief ancestral homeland.[35] The Maronite monks fled to the Lebanon mountains from Syria in the 7th century after repression, not by Muslims but Byzantine Christians under Justinian II. The Druze were a heretical sect of Islam founded by the Shi'ite Caliph Hakim in the 10th century. Forced out of Egypt, they took refuge— as did so many other splinter groups—in the backbone of the Lebanon mountains, specifically the southern part, the Shuf.

Relations between Druze and Maronites were amicable for the better part of a millennium, up to the 19th century. The Druze actually helped the Maronites many times: "Throughout their history, especially in their dealings with their sometimes zealous Maronite vassals, the Druze have displayed a tolerance toward other religions that is scarcely characteristic of the cradle of revealed religion and fanaticism that is the Middle East."[36] Indeed, in the 16th century, two Maronite patriarchs, chased by their own Maronite brethren from the Qadisha Valley, hid in caves until given asylum in the homes of Druze amirs in the Shuf. If anything, Maronite expansion and prosperity were the result of a Druze "open-door policy" toward Maronite developers for 200 years. The Druze amir Fakreddine admired the hard-working Maronites of the northern ranges and openly invited them to clear land in the south where Druze and Shi'ites predominated. If the land was cultivated for ten years, it was given to the Maronites in ownership.

But by the early 19th century, an old Lebanese cycle began to turn again: generosity (or laxity) to outsiders gets out of control, tightens abruptly, and xenophilia turns to xenophobia. The Maronites began pushing for political power commensurate with economic successes. By now the Maronites had virtually surrounded the Druze in the mountains, with the latter losing ground in the Shuf. The Maronite population was growing and hunger for more land added to rising tensions. One Englishman, who lived among the Druze for a decade between 1840 and 1850, found the Maronite style in Deir al-Qammar obnoxious. Colonel Charles Churchill reported opulent Maronite estates: "Their leading men amassed riches. They kept studs, their wives and daughters were apparelled in silks and satins and blazed with jewelry. The few Druzes who still inhabited the town were reduced to insignificance as hewers of wood and drawers of water."[37]

Riots occurred in 1820 and 1840. But the tinder for the worst explosion occurred in an argument over a chicken between two Maronite and Druze boys in Beir Meri and erupted into a gangfight that killed more Druze than Christians.[38] The backlash was extreme. The Maronites were not prepared to meet the more disciplined and smoldering Druze fighting forces. The Druze struck at Deir al-Qammar in May 1860, flaying the Maronite abbott alive and poleaxing 20 monks. In a bloody 22 days, 7,771 Christians were murdered, 360 villages destroyed, 560 churches ruined, 43 monasteries burned, and 28 schools leveled.[39] By the end of the year 20,000 Christians had been killed, including 5,500 as far away as Damascus. Many Druze perished as well. As for the ruling Turks, they gave Christians asylum, only to disarm them and turn them out to face their oppressors.

The 1860 slaughter was to have repercussions far into the 20th century. According to an informant, when Maronite Phalangists inserted themselves deeply into Druze territory in the wake of Israel's 1982 invasion of Lebanon, Dr. Samir Geagea, head of a Phalange unit, was asked by Druze notables what he was doing there, to which he replied, "I am returning to you the visit you paid to us in 1860." Killings followed. And Deir al-Qammar was blocked by the Druze for ten days with no water or food entering for its 30,000 residents. Memories die hard in Lebanon. Historians agree that because of the Druze–Christian disturbances, 1840–1860 were the two darkest decades in Syria since the Ottoman Turks captured the area in the 16th century. According to Albert Hourani, they also caused an unusual relief effort: "Money given in Europe and America for the victims of the Lebanese Civil War of 1860... provided one of the first examples of international charity."[40]

After witnessing and miraculously escaping the massacres in Damascus, Dr. Joseph Arbeely took his family to Beirut for an eighteen-year stretch, finally deciding to leave the Middle East altogether "for the progress of my children." An Orthodox, he resisted the urgings of the Russian consul in Beirut to go to Russia; he selected America. Arbeely had been imbued with a love for learning from his earliest days when he walked from Arbeen to Damascus to school "until the Patriarch recognized his literacy in an age of darkness when reading and writing was limited to three percent of the population."[41] He learned medicine under an American medical missionary named Boldine, and he collaborated with Dr. Cornelius Van Dyck on a Bible translation into Arabic.

Arbeely was not alone in specifically mentioning the horror of the massacres as propelling him westward. Another survivor, who settled in Pittsburgh, said:

> The Druze and Mohammedan Syrians, backed up and helped by the Turks, themselves attacked us. For three days the men and women of our village fought back. My husband shot and killed two of them and I was loading the guns. They killed a good many of our neighbors before we fled. I had six young children by that

time but I was determined that if I ever got the chance to leave this place I would do so.[42]

Though there was no real intersectarian fighting in Syria and Lebanon from 1861 to World War I, to suggest that such a bloodbath as occurred in 1860 did not have psychological aftershocks would be disingenuous. If a physical wall was not erected between Druze and Maronites in the mountains, a psychological one was erected by the disturbances and has never really been torn down, as more recent skirmishes attest. That being said, what could explain the lag time of twenty years from the massacres until the largely Christian Arab emigration began? There are reasons beyond the oft-cited quest for a better living that historians seem not to have detected, at least in the context of the massacres themselves.

First, emigration from Syria did begin after the massacres, but to Egypt rather than America. The boat fare was cheaper, and Egypt was an Arab country where the language was Arabic and the milieu familiar—and, at least for a while, more free. Educated Syrians also wanted to help the Khedive, the ruler of Egypt, with his new water projects attendant to the opening of the Suez Canal in 1869. Jessup mentions at least a thousand Syrian "refugees" leaving for Alexandria, Egypt, in the wake of the 1860 massacres in Damascus. By 1907, emigrant Syrians in Egypt possessed 10 percent of that country's total wealth and numbered 30,000.

Second, historians have disregarded what was going on in America and Europe at the time. In 1860, the United States was hardly an inviting nation—it was in the throes of its own Civil War, which lasted five more years. As for Europe, troubles erupted in the Franco–Prussian War in 1871.

Third, confirmation that America could be a place to make a real living— as opposed to providing a temporary escape—only came when stories filtered back from the international trade expositions starting in 1876. This activated US steamship promotion in Syrian ports.

Fourth, Syrians had some reasons to believe that justice might finally issue forth from Constantinople, the seat of the Ottoman sultan. In 1856, the Sublime Porte announced that a Muslim could convert to Christianity without being put to death. Though shocked by the massacres, many Syrians took hope when 4,800 Druze were found guilty. But Turkish authorities dragged their feet and eventually shut their eyes. Only 48 were sentenced to death, 11 to life imprisonment; most of these never served their sentences.

Three Syrian memoirists who emigrated from the Lebanon mountains to America at the turn of the century discussed intersectarian tension. Each dealt with it differently, each showing a distinct strand in the weave that made a Syrian emigrant.

George A. Hamid was a circus owner who might have rivaled the Ringling Brothers in the 1940s in the United States. He was a legendary tumbler who had performed in the Wild West shows of Buffalo Bill with Annie Oakley; he once said, "In my early showdays, 'Arab' and 'acrobat' were synonymous." Hamid, who claimed to have tumbled through a thousand cities and "thumped the dirt of almost every hamlet in America," came from Broumana, Lebanon, to the States in 1906.

Hamid describes an incident that took place in his village when he was seven, when the Muslim and Christian communities almost took each other to the sword over a broken *braak* (actually *ibriq*, a water jug). A Muslim girl pushed him as they struggled to fill their jugs at a well, making his jug crack on the ground. Hamid head-butted her and stole her jug. Within the hour a Muslim group of fifteen men with clubs were shouting outside Hamid's home. The circus owner's description of the confrontation between his father and the Muslims is both a testimony to the typical First Wave Christian's stereotyping of Muslim violence ("As killing was a fairly common practice over there with wholesale massacre no rarity, and these were Mohammedans to boot, I knew that this mob might really mean business") and a salute to his father's diplomatic acrobatics, which averted a disaster:

> I stood up, slowly. "Father, I—" I began.
> "Silence!" he roared.
> He turned to the Mohammedans.
> "Neighbors," he said. (Holy smoke! calling them neighbors? What if my father had possessed plaguing power, there would be no Mohammedans left in the world!) "Good neighbors," he went on, "I can plainly see that my cur of a son has done you an unforgivable injustice. But I, his father, demand the privilege of killing him..."
> Then—crash!—I was on the floor. Pain lashed through me and I was jarred by two heavy kicks. The last sounds I heard were the satisfied jeers of the Mohammedans.[43]

The ardor of Hamid's father in portraying the anger Muslims felt helped defuse the situation—once again, the Levantine use of mask, of theater in this case, deflected tempers that had a habit of igniting too much too soon, before suddenly disappearing.

Salom Rizk, chosen by *Reader's Digest* in the 1940s to lecture across America as the quintessential American immigrant, describes the anomalous fate of one in Syria whose religion could not be pinned down. Nursed at the nipple of the three monotheisms (he claimed to have no mother), Rizk was a man set apart from a society that lived by sectarian divisions:

In Syria there is a saying that he who drinks the milk of a cow becomes like a cow. I had drunk the milk of Christians, so I should become a Christian. But I had also drunk the milk of a Mohammedan. Would that make me a Mohammedan? No. What was I, then? I was a child of Shaitan, the devil. Who else but the devil would inspire the milk of mortal enemies, of people of whom God disapproved? I was terrible. I would turn out to be a monster. I must be avoided.[44]

A number of immigrants, however, testified that nursing at multisectarian breasts was not a problem and, in fact, common, especially for orphans. Assad Roum, from Arbeen, Syria, for instance, found it unproblematic to take his half-sister to Muslim women for suckling.[45]

This dialectic of the "stranger," and its implications for the Arab-American character, finds another striking expression in the memoirs of the Reverend Abraham Rihbany, whose articulate account of his emigration from Syria to the United States found its way onto the pages of the *Atlantic Monthly* in 1913. Rihbany makes no bones about it:

Assad Roum and pregnant wife, Nora, en route in 1937 on the Esperia Genova from Arbeen, Syria, to Brooklyn. (Elsie Roum)

clannishness was a staple of Syrian life. His birth in the town of El-Schweir is seen as a blessing, not because of his beautiful brown eyes but because the fighting strength of the Rihbanys was increased by one male member in its struggle with the rival clan in the town, the Jirdaks. (Both clans were Christian.) Rihbany castigates the Hatfield–McCoy syndrome in the Lebanon mountains. In describing his family's fate, however, when they moved to the Druze-dominated Shuf town of Betater, Rihbany unwittingly stumbled on what I take to be a ruling disposition that emigrants took west from Syria, namely, the safety of the stranger:

Betater was inhabited by Christians and Druses, who were in the majority and the ruling class, and some Mohammedans. The Christians represented the Greek Orthodox, Greek Catholic (Melkites) and Maronite churches. As usual, they lived at war with one another and united as "Christians" only when attacked by the Druses. The clannish feuds also existed within the various sects. We, however, were "strangers," and, having no clan of our own in the town, were immune from attacks by any and all of the clans because of our weakness. "Thou shalt not oppress a stranger" is a command which is universally observed in Syria.[46]

The Rihbanys were treated well in the town and escaped cross fires because they were new and unknown. The Orthodox welcomed them, but so did the Druze. When a five-year-old Rihbany died, nearly the entire clan of Druze notables showed up to pay respects— an unusual number—largely because the Rihbanys were "sideless" by nature of their strange new presence in town.

Rihbany happened onto something. Syrians had the oldest history on earth as their heritage, historical roots so deep it is a wonder they did not find the earth's molten core. But in the 19th century, they began taking care of strangers. And then in growing waves of tumult, they became strangers themselves.

Economic Gyrations, the Land Squeeze, and Overpopulation

After a century of chaos and decay, Syria and particularly Lebanon began to achieve some measure of economic well-being in the latter part of the 19th century, spurred by the unprecedented onrush of European ships calling at Levantine ports after the European powers intervened forcefully in the disturbances of 1860. There is no doubt that the Syrian peasant, stirred by the progress that had trickled down to his hamlet, wanted more than a trickle and began reading the literature of steamship companies with avidity.

Steam navigation in the Mediterranean began to make European traders a regular sight at the Levantine ports. In 1840, two lines, British and Austrian, had regular services to Syria; by 1914 nine lines had regular services to Syria on a weekly to monthly basis. In the 1830s, total shipping into Beirut was 50,000 tons; by 1886 it had risen to over 600,000 tons.[47] The building of a modern port in Beirut by the French in 1880–1895 nearly tripled that figure by 1910.

With the establishment of the first silk-reeling factory in Shimlan, Lebanon, in 1846 (by an Englishman), the centuries-old native silk-weaving industry increased. By mid-century, one-quarter of all exports from Lebanon were silk. By 1857, the British consul in Palestine put the number of Jaffa oranges exported at six million; increased quantities of Syrian barley and hard wheat—used for beer and dough—were sold abroad. By 1911, an average of 20,000 tons of soap was being manufactured, with centers in Nablus and Jaffa. Tobacco was grown for export in Palestine, the Biqa^c Valley, and near Latakia, though checked in 1860 by a Turkish government monopoly, which in 1884 transferred rights to a European consortium.

Much cultivation, however, continued on an age-old subsistence basis, peasants working for landlords to produce grapes, lemons, pistachio nuts, figs, almonds, and melons, as well as maize, lentils, chickpeas, beans, rice, and sesame. The traditionally strong Syrian cotton crop, however, was threatened by competition from Egyptian and American cotton and was crippled by a bad drought in the years 1889–1892.

Other factors made the economic prosperity less than uniform or salutary. The opening of the Suez Canal in 1869 diverted some of the transit traffic to the East that would ordinarily have stopped for overload transport on the Syrian coast. Steamships going through the Black Sea had a similar effect. Also, high Turkish taxation on loom industries and the lack of tariffs to protect against the onslaught of cheaply priced machine-made goods slipping in from Europe hurt the traditionally strong Syrian cloth industry. Perhaps the most serious blow to the native Syrian economy in the midst of this whirlwind of trade, however, was the silkworm blight of 1865–1871, which hit sericulture production just as it was beginning to prosper. Though partly aided by the importation of silkworm eggs from France, the production of Syrian silk never really recovered; by the early 1920s, it was down 85 percent from late-19th-century figures.

Better medicine—once again introduced by American doctors—sharply reduced epidemics and, coupled with a virtual elimination of famine, brought the Syrian population to double from the 1830s to 1890 (from an estimated 1.3 million to 2.7 million). Beirut's population increased from 10,000 in the 1830s to 150,000–200,000 by 1914; Tripoli, from 15,000 to 50,000.[48] This overpopulation, especially in the Lebanon mountains, which had little arable land, began to squeeze peasants, whose holdings were already small. Fathers who would normally divide their land with their sons were having more children than could make a living on the diminishing parcels. Many immigrants and their descendants pointed to this land squeeze, ratifying the opinion of Abdeen Jabara, whose family came from the Biqa^c Valley of Lebanon, that there was no more land to divide.[49]

The Lebanon mountain area was relatively tranquil for the rest of the century after the massacres ("Happy was he who had a goat's resting place in Lebanon" the saying went). The surrounding areas did not share in this peace, however, and were more exposed to Ottoman policies, which grew increasingly oppressive nearing World

War I. But even the Lebanon mountains weren't devoid of the restive. Najib Saliba notes:

> The situation was not totally satisfactory because Mount Lebanon was cut off from its fertile hinterland, the Biqaᶜ plain, as well as the plains of Sidon and Tyre. Its territory was largely mountainous and little suitable for agriculture. With a high birth rate, little farming and virtually no industry, emigration served as a safety valve for what might otherwise have been an explosive situation.[50]

As Hitti put it, "Women were more prolific than soil" in Lebanon, and the cramped conditions made people hanker for a journey and a change. J. M. "Maroun" Haggar, the nonagenarian founder of Haggar Slacks in Dallas, mentioned that there was "nothing to do" in his hometown of Jazzine, Lebanon, which he left in 1906. "We were starving to death," he said.[51]

Many immigrants from this period cited heavy and arbitrary taxation as a prime reason why they sailed out of Beirut to the New World, a stimulus not unlike that which drove the American colonies to revolt from Great Britain. The American novelist Vance Bourjaily recalled anecdotes of his grandmother from Kabb Elias in the Biqaᶜ Valley:

> My grandmother spoke with a great deal of animosity of the Turks and particularly their tax-collecting methods...Stories about how her family outwitted them by hiding their assets when they got word from the next village that Turkish tax collectors were there. Sometimes her brothers would get in caves out in the hills and throw rocks at the tax collectors on their horses, try and scare them. I guess some would get hit on the head with the flat side of swords.[52]

Albert Rashid, one of the last surviving original store owners on Atlantic Avenue in Brooklyn, put it this way: "There was no fairness, no humanity shown by the Turks toward the population. Turkish taxmen came and assessed our land as owing 100 bushels of wheat; because of drought, we couldn't get that, so they took our family reserve and left us hungry."[53] Rashid emigrated in 1920 from Marjayoun in southern Lebanon.

In addition to contact with American missionaries, European traders, and European officials who "protected" the mountains after the 1860 massacres, a prime stimulant to Syrian emigration was the praise heaped on the United States by those who exhibited wares at the international trade expositions and came back to Syria selling America as one big Suq al-Hamidiyah, the great Damascus bazaar. The first of these to attract Arab exhibitors opened in 1876 as the Centennial Exposition in Philadelphia. Tunisia, Egypt, and the Ottoman Empire exhibited everything from cotton to coffee.

At his Atlantic Avenue Tire & Battery service station on Atlantic Avenue, Brooklyn, in 1929, Michael Malouf (left) works with his father, Abraham (right) and two friends. (Albert and Nancy Malouf)

Religious items from Palestine were especially sought by Americans: rosaries, olivewood carvings of the Star of Bethlehem, crosses labeled "Made in Jerusalem." The Syrians also vended ceramic vases, gold filigree jewels, and amber "worry beads." The Tunisian cafe served Arab coffee for 25 cents a cup, and spices, nuts, and perfume of attar of rose made one visitor catch "delicious whiffs of... the sweet, stimulating perfume which must be the breath of the Orient... a faint, intoxicating aroma."[54]

One commentator thought the huge Carthaginian mosaic of a lion attacking a horse was the best artwork of the entire exhibition. Others must have thought so, too, and a wire screen had to be put around it after vandals began stealing its tiles for souvenirs. A Moroccan kiosk was transported for the exhibition intact and displayed arts and crafts. Americans could smoke waterpipes at cafes. The Arabs and Turks, who won 129 awards, sent 1,600 individuals and firms, more than any other exhibitors except the British and the United States itself. Immigration records show that eight Syrians emigrated to the United States the year of the Philadelphia fair; some had undoubtedly decided to stay on.

The other important international fairs were in Chicago (1893) and St. Louis (1906)—in my travels I happened upon the long bar from the Chicago fair, now in a skid row dive in New Jersey. J. M. "Maroun" Haggar arrived in St. Louis just after the fair there. St. Louis at the time was the wholesale dry goods capital of America and the source of supply for many of the earliest Syrian peddlers in the Midwest, including Haggar, who went on to found a $300 million clothing business.

The Hard Hand of the Turkish Sultan

If the Lebanese "cedar" began to be cramped at the roots by overpopulation, the spirit of the people also began to wither throughout Greater Syria from the policies of an increasingly worried Ottoman sultan. Taxation, lawlessness, crop snatching, and conscription combined with fear of revolt that was brewing in Syria and broke out in World War I in the Hejaz region of Saudi Arabia. As Sir John Glubb, commander of the Arab Legion for seventeen years, once wrote, "from first to last, 1517 to 1917, the Ottomans had never been able to feel much sympathy for their Arabic-speaking peoples."[55]

If there were authorities for wheat tax—too many of them— there were none for arresting a highwayman who had knocked a brother cold and snatched his purse. From the time of the Druze massacres, the Sublime Porte—ordered by the British and French— withdrew most of its security forces from the Lebanon mountain area, leaving it underpoliced and exposed to lawlessness and domestic violence. Justice in such circumstances was piecemeal at best and nonexistent at worst. One Lebanese immigrant who settled in Los Angeles as a successful realtor reported that after he had accidentally dealt a mortal wound to a friend while cutting tobacco with a large shearing blade, a policeman on horseback from Beirut came up the mountain and surreptitiously arrested him. Though it saved him from an imminent lynching, he feared for his twelve-year-old life, since they were heading for Tahdin prison in Beirut, a place few came out of alive. The officer was finally "bought off" by relatives who got him drunk at a cafe and helped release his young prisoner.[56]

As for court trials for civil disputes, the results were hardly edifying. A Lebanese immigrant from Duma near Tripoli—an accountant who later met with Harry Truman about the establishment of the State of Israel—fingered corruption in the Turkish court as the main reason his father brought his family to the New World. Simon Rihbany's father had been educated by American missionaries in Tripoli and was imbued with ideas of democracy. In a court trial over inheritance of property after Simon's grandfather died, the Turks were evidently conniving to snatch the land:

> Right in the middle of hearing in Tripoli my father, seventeen
> years old—already cultured in the American tradition and English

justice in Egypt—just blurted out, "They're lying!" Because you know, we Rihbany people are very free in our opinions and very honest... It was true. A wealthy, powerful man could bend the law. It was not government by law, but by individuals. And it has been the same thing in Lebanon all along.[57]

Though the Rihbanys won the case, the father "was disgusted. He came to his uncle and mother and said, 'I want to leave this country and go to the land of justice.'" Within a few months he sailed from Beirut to Marseilles to Philadelphia. It was 1891.

Given the sense of injustice and brewing hunger for independence, it is no surprise that few Arabs wanted to serve in the Turkish army. Although protected from conscription until 1908, after that, Christian subjects, too, were forced into the army. Some tried to buy their way out. But many served. The mortality rate of Arab soldiers in the Turkish army was high: of 240,000 conscripts, 40,000 were killed, many of them thrown into the front lines of battle in World War I; 150,000 Arab conscripts deserted. Albert Rashid's brother would dress on the streets of Marjayoun as a woman to avoid the draft, until he could stand it no longer and took twelve-year-old Albert with him to America.

The Turks' reaction to resistance by Arab subjects was hardly soft; they did, however, make attempts to borrow money from Germany to upgrade services in the Syrian province. But it was too late. By 1913, one observer found Turkey wanting any government or institutions and its leaders suicidal:

> It [Syria] is a land which might have become the wealthiest in Asia if natural forces at work had been allowed free play. But they have been paralyzed systematically by the masters of the country, who are the Turks, and whose steady aim has been to drain the land of its resources and use them for their State.[58]

On May 6, 1916, fourteen Christian and Muslim Syrians were hanged in Beirut and seven in Damascus by the panicking Turkish government. Both Lebanon and Syria today commemorate this event and named each site "Martyrs' Square." Under the swaying shadow of hanging men, many made plans to leave the country as soon as they could. Some participated in the open rebellion. The owner of an engineering and construction company in Los Angeles, who grew up in Brooklyn, recalled that his father fled the country after strangling a Turkish officer.[59]

A. Ruppin estimates that in the 30 years leading up to World War I the population of the Lebanon province was reduced by one-fourth, due to 100,000 emigrants. Although records are not reliable due to Syrians being lumped together with Greeks, Armenians, and others under the "Turkey in Asia" category before 1899, Saliba estimated that 5,000 Syrians had reached the United States by the turn of the century. The increasingly forlorn Levantines also went to Africa, Latin America, and Canada. By 1901 there were 4,000 Syrians in Australia and by 1903 there were 1,000 in Canada. In Latin America, particularly, the *qashsha* (peddler's bag)-carrying Syrians would rise not only to commercial prominence, as they did in the United States, but also to political prominence.

A last insult by the Turks to the growing sophistication of the Syrians was suppression of the free press. In collaboration with some conservative church authorities, the iron hand of Sultan Abdul Hamid II (1876–1909) repressed the publishing ferment in 1880. Thousands of books were burned or buried in the ground to keep inspectors away; writers were fined, expelled, or imprisoned.[60] The Syrian intellectuals who could get away took refuge at first in Cairo and have dominated the Egyptian press ever since. Others went to America and effected a literary revolution in Arab letters through Kahlil Gibran's touted Pen League. One poet who took flight from Zahle to Rio de Janeiro, Fawzi al-Malouf, died young there, an Arab Keats. He wrote, "O wings of the imagination, mightiest of wings against whom the winds break their back." In World War I, it was Lebanon whose back was broken.

Lebanon Starves

The traumatic event that shadows the collective mind of the original Syrian immigrants is the starvation that gripped Lebanon during World War I. Records show that the peak years of First Wave Syrians arriving in America were 1913 and 1914—9,210 and 9,023 immigrants, respectively.

Ironically, the cause of the starvation was not primarily the Turks. The Allied fleets—British and French—blockaded the coasts of Syria and Lebanon from the time the Ottoman Turks entered the war on the side of the German Kaiser. These Allied ships prevented any food from entering Syrian ports to relieve the already overtaxed domestic farmers, whose small crops were being confiscated by Turkish battalions. For four years, there was virtually no food imported into Syria; the mountain range—which endures heavy snows in winter—was hit the hardest. Though a quarter of the population had already left the mountains, at the height of the blockade most were too poor or too weak to move very far. Original immigrants I have interviewed talk of eating lemon and orange peelings from garbage heaps; one woman said they picked up horse dung, washed it, and ate the remaining hay. People lay dying in their mountain hovels or on the street. Some murdered for a piece of bread, or were murdered. Others charged murderous prices, and it was not uncommon to see

Lebanese mountain elites exchanging fine jewelry and china for a few sheaves of wheat.

Salom Rizk watched refugees from World War I pour over the Lebanon hills: "They told of a salt shortage so severe that the women walked long, weary miles to the sea with jugs on their heads to get sea water, only to have the soldiers make a brutal sport out of shooting the vessels from their heads."[61] One of the women Rizk may have seen shunting back and forth across the mountain searching for food and water was Mary Kfouri Malouf. Her father was the mayor of the mountain village of Shreen. During the war he sold his property to feed the poor, but he died in the midst of the war. Mary, his daughter, then began an ordeal to feed her four children. One of them was my grandmother. Over the years she related to me a series of stories of uncanny pathos. From them a picture can be drawn of a dark and snowy mountain, wolves waiting to devour humans, who themselves were hunting for food:

> My mother used to leave for us one loaf of bread, for me and my two brothers, Wadi° and Taniyus. They were smaller and I used to take care of them. I used to give them small pieces of bread like this, about two or three inches, that's all—a day. That loaf of bread has to last us for three days until mama comes back....
>
> At that time I run to the little store in my country up the block. I said, "Please, *Allah yikhalliki* [May God preserve you]! Please give me a loaf of bread. When my mother comes she will pay you for it." The woman said, "Go ahead, you! Your mother die now. She's not living any more. Go on. Get out!" She chased me away. She don't give me no money for the bread. We go around begging for a piece of bread from the people.
>
> So I came, we sit—I never forget that as long as I live. Me and my kid brothers were sitting at the edge of the door, crying, hungry. If we stay that night without food I am sure, I am very sure, we die. So we were sitting down like that and I saw my mother coming down on the street. We stopped crying, calling her, "Mama! Mama!" She had some *°adas* [lentils]. She boiled them and gave us some soup because our stomach is dry. Because we don't eat for three days. She boiled the *qamh* [gram kernels], the hummus, and the *°adas.* I told her the story about the lady who don't give us a piece of bread. "*Ya-haram* [what a shame]!" my mother said.
>
> Again she buys stuff and she goes back. She went to stay up the hill, waiting for somebody to go by so she could go to Zahle. She can't go back by herself because the robber come, hit them, and kill them. And the wolf eat them if they walking by themselves. One boy up the hill, he went with his blanket on his

back. My mother saw him on the road, dead, laying in the street. From hunger on the way to Zahle.

In the end my mother said, "I am very tired. I'm gonna take you to Zahle with me and I work over there. We try and do something to support you." So we took a little room in Zahle. Mother left us to come back ʿa biladna [to our country, or village] to buy stuff to go back to Zahle. We have nothing to eat. We go around; nobody give us nothing. Taniyus die from hunger. My mother, when she came back, "Wiynu akhuki [Where's your brother]?" Qult, "Mat" [I said, "He died"]. Sarit tibki, haram [She started to cry, sad to say].

She left us there in one room and goes back and forth. She said, "Maybe there you feel better." A couple of weeks after, the other one die—Wadiʿ.

So she said, "No more. Let's go back to our country." So we came back—one-day walk. My mother and Mike [a brother] still go back and forth to Zahle. One day I see a truck coming, picking up people from the street, dying. Just like you were hauling boxes of cabbages, dirty clothes, or dirt. They pick up the person and throw him in the truck. I was small, you know. I said I'm gonna walk after them and see what they gonna do with those people. I followed them maybe two, three blocks. They have a hole over there and they dump the truck just like you dumping dirt, and they cover them. That's all. No priest. No nothing. They throw them down. I was maybe six or seven. That's all.

One time couple of doors up the hill, I see a lady. She was digging a hole under the tree. I was watching her. She go in the house; she take her son, put him in the hole, and cover him. Right in front of her house under the tree.

Her family sustained two more deaths related to the war and the lawlessness of the mountains. Her mother's brother was robbed on the road to Zahle, beaten severely on the head. He barely made it home. His wife opened the door, he walked into the house, and he dropped dead. Grandmother's oldest brother, Milhem, was mortally wounded when Turkish soldiers shot at his horse-drawn wagon:

When the war is finished, my brother came back from Baalbek sick. When he walks, he walks backward. Brain injury. He told my mother, "When I was coming here the soldiers were marching in and the horse got scared and started running." He was sitting in a tunbur, a wagon, and it started running with the horse down the hill. He fell with the horse and the wagon on the cemetery. Right on the cemetery. That's why he hurt his head.[62]

It was morbidly fitting that Mil-hem Malouf died from striking his head on a grave-stone, for that is what Lebanon became in World War I, a giant gravestone, whose inscription would be written by expatriate poets and by the coloni-zing French, who took over the country.

About the Holocaust of World War II, when six million Jews died (one-quarter of world Jewry), much has been written—so much that the black event itself

A starving mother and her two children huddle near a makeshift cross in front of their hut during the famine that gripped Lebanon in WWI. (Al-Akhlaq, 1922)

almost loses its bottomless horror in the churning of movies, novels, television series, memorials, and panels on the Nazi death camps. Of Lebanon, where it has been estimated that at least 100,000 people starved to death during World War I (a quarter of the population), there has been a deathly silence. It is like a blank spot in history. Part of the reason for this is that little has been told: the emigrant Lebanese–Syrians affected a uniquely evasionary character about the subject with outsiders. Most of the first-person eyewitness sources of the mass starvation are in Arabic. Only small bits of these invaluable stories have been translated into English. Of the "many moving accounts" Saliba notes about the famine, he points out four, all of which are written in Arabic and none of which has been translated—not even a sentence—into English. This appears to have been a classic case of "avoidance syndrome" in the emigrant community. During the war, only one source, the 1916 special issue of *Al-Funun* dedicated to the starvation in Syria (written by the Lebanese émigré poet Nasib Arida), was published in New York, and I believe it, too, remains untranslated.

By 1916 fatherless and motherless children strayed into the desert to be picked up by Bedouins. The Druze population of the Shuf stumbled toward Houran and the Golan Heights in southern Syria. Hitti quotes an eyewitness report by a professor at the American University of Beirut:

> Those who did not flee to the interior in quest of sustenance joined the ever-increasing horde of beggars in the city. Among the beggars were those with enough energy to roam the street and knock at doors, ransack garbage heaps or seek carcasses. Others would lie down on the street sides, with outstretched arms, emaciated bodies and weakening voices. Still others, including infants, could speak only through their eyes.... By 1918 the entire lower class of society had been virtually wiped out.

Hitti himself concluded that, in Lebanon's case, the evidence showed "a deliberate effort to starve and decimate the people."[63]

Complicating an already horrid situation, in which typhoid, malaria, dysentery, bubonic plague, and yellow fever were breaking out, a dark cloud "veiled the sun" over the Syrian countryside in the spring of 1915, stripping whatever fruit trees were bearing. The calamities in Syria during World War I began to resemble the biblical landscape of Job. It is appropriate that one of the most eloquent recountings of this catastrophe should come from one of America's largest potato growers. Born in 1902, Amean Haddad, who sold the Safeway Markets firm about half of its spring potatoes, survived the worst of the famine in the mountains during the war. His parents had left him behind in their flight to America, and Haddad weathered the brunt of the bad years virtually alone, in his early teens:

> We had peaches, apricots, vegetables, just about to be picked. And when the locusts came they wiped everything out. You would see the stems of a tree peeled. They have eaten the skin. And you see the trees, instead of being green, they have turned white. All you saw under the plum tree was the pits. It was not only bad; it was a sight you will never forget. You are hungry and here is an animal who came over and ate what you could have lived on. That was what disturbed me. Why did the *jarad*, the locust, come and eat all our food? Our grain, our wheat, barley, corn, vegetables, our plums—everything. Why?

Since the Turks provided no help, makeshift relief efforts by civilians were all people could rely on. Haddad described them:

> You would be walking on the street and you would see a body lying on the ground. And you would get to it, nod, just a dead body. And that happened many, many times in a day. A friend of

mine, Tawfiq Filfli, my age, volunteered with me—there was no law and order—to make a stretcher out of two long pieces of wood. We made it like a step ladder. We carried those dead people way out away from town. Because nobody would come. And many people caught their disease but we didn't. And we were the ones who carried them. He took one end, I took the other. They didn't weigh very much because they died from hunger.[64]

Yellow fever, *al-hawa al-asfar*, was cited by Haddad as the second-largest cause of death in Syria at the time.

At war's end, my grandmother's brother Michael Malouf witnessed a most bizarre thing. In a town near Zahle, named Riyeh, the Germans and Turks had hidden armaments and bombs underground. "They had a city on top and a city on the bottom," said Mike Malouf. Wheat and oats from the surrounding villages were stored there, all confiscated by the Germans and Turks. Above the munitions dump and cache was a field of wheat and oats. The English, pressing their advantage, began bombing Riyeh:

I was right on a big field over there. I was walking; all of a sudden I see something in the air and a big bomb dropped. And you should see the fire that started. And then the soldiers running away all over the place. But the people—it was killing them left and right. What happened then—ammunition is for nothing. Take what you want. Guns. Everything you need. You want gold. You want money? Free-for-all. If you were lucky, you survived. If not, you get your head blown off...

There was one lady there, she had two boys with her. She saw the wheat was about forty, fifty feet high in the air. The wheat, piled up outside. She wanted to start picking the wheat, taking the wheat. All of a sudden the bomb hit her, took her head completely off. So one of the boys starts crying and hollering, "I want my mother's head! I want my mother's head."[65]

The woman had apparently nudged a live bomb dropped by the British, or one of the explosives hidden by the Turks and Germans.

As if the Deity himself had gone crazy at the war's devastation, a severe earthquake hit the Lebanon mountains on Armistice Day, November 11, 1918. Pete Nosser, a retired businessman in Vicksburg, Mississippi, remembered that the tremor came while he was working in the almond grove in his village of Shekarn: "I could see the bucket of syrup [*dibs kharrub*] shaking. I looked up at the tent— it was shaking. I looked over at the houses and they shook like the trees. An American Arab who had come back to our village shouted at us, 'Get out of your houses! This is an earthquake!' We didn't even know the word."[66]

Lebanon had lost half of its population to famine and emigration. Is it any wonder that it would fare so poorly in the dice game of nations, that it would so easily fall prey to the avaricious, both inside and outside? Luckily, the emigrants did not forget the suffering of those they had left behind. If they tried to sweep the tragedy under the carpet of prosperity, Syrian émigrés still sent over $259 million from the four corners of the globe to Lebanon during World War I.

Certainly, the refugee problem was not born in Lebanon with the Palestinians in 1948. Besides the Lebanese themselves, thousands of Armenian refugees came into Lebanon from the Turkish domain during the war. (The Armenians had been subjected to genocide at the hands of the Turks, losing one million people.) Thirty thousand refugees lived in tents in and around Beirut during the war. Many villages and cities were emptied. By the end of the war, ancient towns that had been lived in for thousands of years were ghost towns. The coastal town of Batroun went from a prewar population of 5,000 to 2,000 by war's end. From Sidon south, American records showed that, of 77,000 inhabitants, 33,000 had died in four years of war. Mirroring the ruined mountains, over one-quarter of the dwellings in southern Lebanon were wrecked. Of the survivors in the south, about 40 percent were paupers. There were 2,600 orphans in the south alone.

Sixty-eight percent of the early Syrian emigrants were male, a majority unmarried and in their twenties. Of those that were married, only 12 percent brought their families to America in the First Wave, from 1878 to 1924. As one commentator put it, "many villages lost their young blood and became shelters for senior citizens."[67] By war's end, one village in the mountains, Bayt al-Shibab, or "Home of Youth," was transformed in parlance to Bayt al-Ajazah, or "Home of the Elderly." Palestine, too, lost many to emigration. Jewish Palestinians were reduced by one-third of their prewar total though Jewish immigration to the country rose sharply under the British Mandate.

What all this foretold for the future of Syria—and especially for its Lebanon sector—was not difficult to surmise. With the brain drain to Egypt, Boston, and New York, and the large size of migration from the worker-peasant class, the few men of means and education who did stay had a virtual lock on power. And it is these men—the Franjiyahs, Gemayels, Chamouns, Jumblatts, Salaams, Karamis—who became the warlords of contemporary Lebanon. It does not seem unlikely that if they could not rid themselves of the habit of exceptional blood feuds it was because of their initial status as the kingfish in an abandoned sea.

Who Am I? The Syrians Dock in America

Assad Roum stood on Ellis Island in 1939, nineteen years after he had first come ashore at the famous immigration processing center in America. He was now a citizen, recently married in Syria, and had established an embroidery and Corday handbag manufacturing business in Brooklyn. He waited in the mist that day for his new bride to arrive. But when Nora Roum docked from her month-long voyage across the sea, pregnant, Assad barely had a chance to embrace her near the traditional "Kissing Pole" on the island. Immigration authorities detained her for several months in the hospital ward there; for Nora had trachoma, the dreaded eye disease that sent so many immigrants—Syrians included—back to the homeland with no chance of becoming American. Nora gave birth to the Roums' first child on Ellis Island. When she was approved as an immigrant and could go to the mainland of New York to join her husband, she was so ecstatic that she convinced Assad to name their infant daughter Elsie, after Ellis Island itself.[68]

More than half the current US population can trace its heritage through Ellis Island; more than half have relatives who staggered through the doors of the great emporium with its chandeliers and magnificent steeples across the water from the Statue of Liberty. In the period 1880–1924, sixteen million of the world's destitute (or 60 percent of the 27 million immigrants to America at this time) were processed at the little islet made from the landfill of the New York subway. Among them was the vast majority of 150,000 Syrians, including Assad Roum.

Essa Boghdan runs the tool-and-die machine at his factory in Brooklyn in the 1920s. (Elsie Roum)

For a long time, Ellis Island was in ruins. Shut down by the Immigration Service in 1952, by which time airplanes had replaced boats as primary conduit to freedom, Ellis Island became a hangout for daring teenagers, who would motorboat over from Jersey or Battery Park. It fell prey to mice, vandals, and, in 1976, the National Park Service, which took tourists through a mist of ghosts and huge empty halls with walls of peeling paint, rusty pipes, cobwebs. Old files and medical equipment are still there. One old wheelchair in the tent of a spider web has wooden footrests. It took $162 million to restore the once majestic first home of so many whose hearts quickened at the sight of America and who, in fact, laid the foundation of the America we have today. The newly restored Ellis Island Museum opened its doors in 1990.

A Park Service tour guide at Ellis Island started his hour-long discourse about immigrants with an anecdote of Golda Meir's father, who escaped a pogrom in Russia. The moving story was followed by a less interesting one about an immigrant from Barbados; three stirring references to Jewish immigrants were sandwiched in with mention of German, Irish, Italian, Greek, African, Chinese, Polish, Japanese, even Cambodian immigrants. But when told that by 1924 at least 150,000 Syrians had immigrated to America, the guide drew a blank. For me, it was a disconsolate note, as I listened to the ghosts of the Syrians, nauseated as so many were from the seas, try to spell out their names in English, or be turned away because of trachoma, or wander wide-eyed into the cacophonous corridors filled daily with up to 15,000 ragged but hopeful immigrants from around the world. They seemed as unknown in the late 20th century as they were a century back, when they were miscalled "Turks" and listed as such until 1899—a humiliating reference given the fact that most were Christian and had sacrificed so much to get away from Ottoman Turkish rule. Perhaps it was at Ellis Island that their identity crisis in America would begin, where Yaccoub quickly became Jacobs, and first names became last.

The Syrian did not easily fit into a race pigeon hole. A September 3, 1909, *New York Times* editorial rang out, "Is the Turk a White Man?" Salloum Mokarzel retorted, asking if it was fair to consider every Turkish subject a Turk. In 1914, a South Carolina judge complicated matters: Syrians were "free whites," but not "that particular free white person" Congress had in mind for citizenship in 1790, namely, those of European descent. This racist conclusion was overturned the next year by the Dillingham Report of the Immigration Commission, which explained that "physically the modern Syrian is of mixed Syrian, Arabian, and even Jewish blood." But the matter never completely submerged. In the 1920s, a candidate for local office in Birmingham, Alabama, not only eschewed the Negro vote, but also spat out, "The Greek and Syrian should also be disqualified. I DON'T WANT THEIR VOTE." As late as 1923, the Syrian's nationality was being challenged by the same South Carolina judge as "Asian," namely anywhere east of the Persian Gulf. Someone evidently showed him a map.[69]

Perhaps it was due, too, to the fact that they were among the last in line of an immigrant surge that crested at the turn of the century and was shut down by law in 1924. Though by 1913 nearly 10,000 Syrians were leaving ships at American ports a year, they were but a drop in the bucket and a late drop at that. The largest single ethnic group in America—the Germans—had begun to immigrate as far back as 1710, and by 1900 German Americans numbered five million, accounting for a quarter of the population of America's largest fourteen cities. By the time of the first Syrian immigrant family to American in 1878, there were already 200,000 German Jews in the country. Nine thousand American Jews fought in the American Civil War at a time when "Hi Jolly" and Antonios Bishallany were just about the only Syrians in the United States. Syrian immigration at its peak between 1900 and 1914 was only 7 percent as large as Jewish immigration at the time. In the first decade of the 20th century, the Syrians ranked 25 of 39 immigrant nationalities.[70] Yet the Syrians came to America at such a pace that they alarmed the Ottomans and other authorities, who felt the very schools the Americans had set up for them would be emptied. By 1924, many of them were.

The Syrians at the end of the 19th century moved by donkeyback or a three-day foot trip to the harbors—Beirut, Tripoli, Haifa, and Jaffa. There they encountered eager steamship merchants, as well as a whole class of hucksters ("sharpers" poet Amin Rihani called them), who would do everything from bribing Ottoman officials for *tadhkaras* (passports) to securing $30–$50 tickets for the short dinghy voyage to the steamer as well as the long overseas journey. All this was done for a price, of course, and middlemen made quite a profit. But the Syrians paid for their blankets and ferries, ready to take what would be the longest sea voyage anyone took east-to-west to America. Three bribes were not uncommon to receive the necessary endorsements to get on the ship in Beirut—a half *madjidy* (or Turkish dollar) to passport officials, another 50 cents to an inspector of the rowboat between wharf and steamer, and yet another 50 cents to the final inspector at the steamship's gangplank. As the Reverend Abraham Rihbany said after running this gauntlet at the end of a tiring trek, "We left our mother country with nothing but curses for her Government on our lips."

The ship ride across the old sea was "unfriendly," and Rihbany tried to sleep on crates filled with quacking ducks: "Other human beings joined us in that locality, and we all lay piled on top of that heap of freight across one another's bodies much like the neglected wounded in a great battle." An argument broke out between a Syrian in the "duck apartment" and an Egyptian woman:

> *Lawajh Allah* (for the face of God), said the kind-hearted Damascene, and squeezed himself a few inches to one side. In an instant, the wrathful Egyptian wedged herself in, squirmed round until she secured the proper leverage, and then kicked mightily with both feet, pushed the beneficent Damascene clear out of the wave-washed deck.

In Marseilles, Rihbany saw electric lights for the first time in his 24 years, as well as his first train. Marseilles unveiled the last Sirens for the Syrian peasant before he braved the Sea of Darkness to America. The port seethed with hawkers of everything from Western clothes to sex. Some Syrians ran hostelries and guided the weary Levantines, giving them directions and lodging for the nights they must wait. Rihbany bought a Western bowler hat, flinging his Oriental fez hat aside; it gave "a distinctly Occidental sensation...stiff and ill-fitting."[71] Another immigrant through Marseilles from Zahle remembered meeting a merchant marine uncle who threw his newly purchased British safari hat into the sea, saying no one in America wore them.[72]

Amin Rihani, the poet who came to the United States in 1888 from Freiyka, Lebanon, compared the cramped lodgings in steerage to Lebanon's sericulture: "I peeped into a little room, a dingy smelling box, which had in it six berths placed across and above each other like the shelves of the reed manchons we build for our silkworms at home." In his sardonic novel of the Syrian immigrant experience, *The Book of Khalid* (1911)—the only of its kind—Rihani called the pathway of the immigrant a virtual "Via Dolorosa" with the Stations of the Cross in Beirut, Marseilles, and Ellis Island.[73]

Salom Rizk remembered a cabin mate who "would dangle a rosary from the porthole when the seas were rough," and how, when he once left the porthole open after quieting a storm with a medallion of St. Christopher, a huge wave washed in and flooded the cabin. Two angry stewards mopped up the mess and threw the medallion into the sea.[74]

Syrians and other immigrants went through the "boiling down" effect of steerage, and got their first taste—though a foul one—of life in a democracy, where accidents of race, class, privilege, and religion in the Old Country were steamed into a common "new man," linked by little more than the desire of a whiff of clear air, a foot on terra firma. Arab refugees from Jerusalem bartered crosses of olivewood for an extra cup of clear water. Tarbushes of the proud were tossed around like so many insignificant footballs, battered, lost at sea. How bizarre it must have been to be suddenly a minority as a Muslim, now among a horde of Christians and Jews. One Christian immigrant—who translated poetry by Kahlil Gibran—recalled being helped with food and comforting words by a Muslim on his journey across the sea.[75] The enmities of sectarianism drained off in the sea and the agony of adjusting to a new country. At least they had Arabic—treasured tongue—in common.

Some avoided danger more threatening than the sharpers of Marseilles. Said Hanna, a Syrian immigrant from Damascus, told a story of initial frustration when he had arrived in Marseilles too late to catch his ship, which was to link up in Southampton, England, with a huge new oceanliner bound for New York. But when the Titanic sank at sea, he counted himself a lucky man and never again worried about being late.[76] Actually, of the 1,500 people who died on the Titanic, 126 were Arabs, mostly in steerage. At least 29 Arabs survived; one, Anna Yousef, settled in Michigan.

The "Island of Tears" awaited them in New York as they entered the misty harbor, passing the great statue holding a flame surrounded by wire. "Tears" because, of the sixteen million immigrants who arrived in this period at Ellis Island, two million never got out of its examination rooms, except to be sent home because of disease, mostly trachoma. Actually, those who arrived before 1893 were processed at Castle Garden, attached to Battery Park by landfill. It was there that in 1877 seven Algerians who had escaped prison in French Guiana had been "exiled" by the mayor of Wilmington, Delaware, where they had been arrested as vagrants: "The men are quiet and very attentive to their religious duties. They go to the northeast side of the building four times a day and quietly perform their devotions, at the same time 'looking toward Mecca.' They are all somewhat proficient in the French language."[77]

But Ellis Island was the site of entry for most Syrians (some came through Pawtucket in Rhode Island, Philadelphia, or New Orleans). Woozy, disoriented by raucous shouts in five different languages to go "Forward! Quickly!," they found themselves herded into the throng in probably the largest building any of them had ever entered. They had to traverse three stations of doctors, the first of whom pulled out an average of one in six immigrants marked for further checking by crayon or chalk: H for heart, K for hernia, Sc for scalp, and X if the immigrants were suspected of being insane or mentally retarded. At Station Two, the immigrants had to walk up a long flight of stairs; if they hobbled, they were chalked. Surviving that, they were checked for communicable disease. Leprosy? A scalp disease called favus? Syphilis? (The latter had entered Lebanon for the first time when the French came into the country in 1861, bringing with them the "Franji sore.") The final, most dreaded stage of this gauntlet was the trachoma check. It was here that Brooklynite Sadie Stonbely from Aleppo, Syria, was poked so badly in the eye during the examination that she had bad vision in her left eye for the rest of her life.[78] In spite of these pitfalls, according to one Syrian immigrant, Ellis Island was fondly called *bayt al-hurriya* (the house of freedom).[79]

An American senator aided an early Syrian constituent from Worcester, Massachusetts, whose two boys were being held at Ellis Island because they had trachoma. He telegraphed President Theodore Roosevelt to "prevent an outrage which will dishonor the country and create a foul blot on the American flag." Roosevelt responded quickly, and soon the boys were allowed to join their mother. Years later, Roosevelt visited Worcester himself and discovered that the boys' eyes had been damaged by the glare of sea water, not trachoma.[80]

Arriving indigent, or penniless, could keep an immigrant mired on Ellis Island. One man who escaped a Turkish pogrom against Armenians in Tripoli, Lebanon, at the turn of the century by disguising himself (with the help of Muslim friends) in Muslim clothes ("He had to step over dead people, the ground wasn't showing") had sons already in America when he arrived at Ellis Island. They worried that he had no money to show immigration officials. And they hatched a scheme:

> The story—it's a secret but I'll tell you now. It's too late; everybody's dead. My brother went and bought a box of candy and he lined the bottom of it with gold pieces, and he put the candy on top. And he went to the boat dock, down in the pier. Downstairs they sell fish, they sell, you know, nibbles, things like that. My brother bought a lot of things there and put them in a basket (with the candy and gold). My father was standing up on the boat. And he told my father in Armenian, "Take the box of candy and leave everything else to anybody who wants it. Just take the candy and go to your room. You'll find out why I sent it up there." When he went he found, sure enough, I don't know how many pieces of gold. Because when he comes at Ellis Island they've got to show a certain amount of gold to come in here, that you were well enough to take care of yourself.[81]

By 1907, the Syrian Ladies' Aid Society was in full force helping Syrians acclimate themselves to New York once they got through the Ellis Island checks. Many emigrants spoke with warmth and appreciation about Dr. Nageeb Arbeely, who was chief Arabic examiner in the early years on the Island, as well as his brother, Dr. Ibrahim Arbeely, who published an English–Arabic grammar for the immigrants in 1896. Relatives gathered at the famous "Kissing Pole" to greet the newly processed arrival with anxiety and ecstasy before the new would-be American from Syria crossed the lapping waters of the Narrows and caught a first sight of that huge zither—the Brooklyn Bridge.

Life on Washington Street

By 1900, over half the Syrians in America lived in New York City, most of these squashed in with the "shanty" Irish near the wharf on the Lower West Side on Washington Street. There they set up coffeehouses, bazaars, weaving factories, and groceries in direct contradistinction to more-established inhabitants of the area: the bankers of Wall Street, who viewed them with much curiosity.

Washington Street—the closest thing to a Little Sicily the Arabs ever had in America—was alive from dawn to dusk with noisy, guttural shouts, price bartering (there was no fixed price in an Arab marketplace, as if commodities only take on value in the give-and-take of human personality). Odors of anisette and *arjila* smoke rose into a street already heavy with fumes of coal and gas from lamps and heating furnaces. A café owner poured Turkish coffee at the noon hour, and the demitasses clattered at the passing of a horse-drawn carriage, a Syrian boy with a heap of linens in a satchel ready to go out door-to-door. Peddlers fanned out from the mother colony on Washington Street, supplied with notions, linens, and silks hauled in their *qashsha*, or little wooden or leather cases. They loved to be outdoors "smelling air," as Rihbany put it, and, as Naff has shown, peddling in strange streets across the land was a good, open-air class-room for learning English.

Syrians in Manhattan and New Jersey resurrected their silk industry, which had been throttled by blight in the homeland. By 1924, there were 25 Syrian silk factories in Paterson and West Hoboken. The federal Industrial Commission quoted a New Jersey proprietor referring to the Syrians' "instinct for weaving silk"; he preferred their work to those of the Italians or Armenians. Hitti described the kimono industry in New York—35 manufacturers on Washington Street—as being exclusively in the hands of the Syrians, and almost all the Madeira lace outlets were owned by them. Nevertheless, their chief competitors, the Jews, owned 241 garment factories by 1885, or 97 percent of all such factories. Still, half the sweaters made in New York were made by the early Syrians. The N. P. and J. Trabulsi Co. was called the "king" of the woolen knits. F. A. Kalil, on Broadway, won a national competition to use "Red Grange" on a sweater.[82] Though few ventured into subterranean mines or worked in blast furnaces, the Syrians endured their sweatshops for a foothold in America.

From dawn until late into the night, a seamstress bent over her Singer sewing machine, pulling its black wheel down like a maid drawing water. Spools of thread twirled and slid under the

"The Syrian Colony, Washington Street" was drawn by W. Bengough at the turn
of the century. The drawing hangs in the Museum of the City of New York.
(Courtesy of Museum of City of New York)

needleworker's jabbing spindle. Steam hissed off the pressers. Helping
her husband in a shop as well as peddling on the street, the Syrian
woman probably never saw the white of the silk or linen she spun and
stitched because the turn-of-the-century gas lanterns cast a yellowish
tint on everything. One Lebanese woman related how she juggled the
two worlds—children and work—with literally every limb:

> I used to work for the people my mother worked for. I used to
> work day and night. When I get my son, Joe, I put him in the
> carriage. When he cry, I shake the carriage with my feet and work
> with my hands. I used to work for Barsa and Mrs. Stonbely. I sleep
> a little. I put the work next to my bed. Then I get up quick. I said,
> people gonna come tomorrow morning, got to work. I work very
> very hard in my life to raise my kids.

To her, there was little chance to even walk the bazaars of
Washington Street: "I don't know the difference. I'm workin'. When
the baby small, I put him on the fire escape outside. When he start

moving, I put him inside. I never go anywhere. Only on Sunday I take them in my hand, go to church, and come back. That's all."[83]

But there was pride, too, in the craftsmanship of clothes, rugs, fabrics. One Syrian needleworker on Washington Street told a haunting story, which jumped unconsciously from Aleppo to Pennsylvania, linked by the struggle for life represented to her by the loom:

> My father-in-law used to go to the Aleppo cemetery—they used to tell us that—to weave some design. He used the cemetery wall to put [hold] his loom. I know my cousin used to have next door to our home a loom factory. . . . My son was in Korea and he was wounded. In Valley Forge Hospital he used the loom to exercise his arm because he was shot in the neck and his arms were paralyzed. For a whole year in Valley Forge Hospital he used that loom and he made a rug for me.[84]

Though the patriarch had the bark in the Syrian family, anyone who spent more then three days in an early Syrian home knew that the wife and mother had the bite. Though not "liberated" in the modern sense of having choices, the Syrian mother, as peddler, needleworker, or shopkeeper, achieved, by dint of her forceful labors and strong good sense, the power in the Syrian home. William Peter Blatty makes this heroic, dominant role clear in the memoirs of his peddler-mother, *Which Way to Mecca, Jack* and *I'll Tell Them I Remember You*. Novelist Vance Bourjaily called his immigrant grandmother from Kabb Elias "the total strength in my life," a woman of "incredible character and vision." She had come to America in 1894, leaving a wastrel husband behind, supporting her children while making beds and cooking at a boarding house for Syrian mill workers in Lawrence, Massachusetts.[85] Liberation was work and sacrifice, the two words virtually synonymous. If anything, the dominant role of the Syrian mother was diluted somewhat when the firstborn generation became mothers themselves and scarcely worked outside the home.

Pay for garment workers was abysmally low, hovering around $10 a week, and women usually got half that. Peddlers often did better, earning between $200 and $1,500 a year:

> They began coming in small groups in the garb of mendicants. They wore red fezzes, short open jackets, short baggy blue trousers to the calves of the legs and ill-fitting shoes. As soon as they had passed the immigration authorities they would at once go out into the street to ply their trade. At the end of the first day in America the whining Maronite would have added five dollars to his hoard, while the Irish or German immigrant would be bustling about trying to find work to enable him to earn a dollar.[86]

The peddler from Washington Street became an emissary from the exotic land and, at the same time, an American entrepreneur in the making. He even helped the American export trade. When World War I cut Latin America off from European trade, the Syrian peddler—supplied by the Syrian-owned warehouses in New York of the Bardawill, Jabara, Tadross, Ackary, Sleiman, and Atiyeh families— fanned out to South America, where Syrian emigrants provided necessary rest stops: "The Syrian merchant in every country of South America, Asia and Africa, and Australia thus became the distributor of the products of the United States."[87]

Though Syrian hardihood and venturesomeness were generally acclaimed, the land of the free was far from accepting the "colorations" the gene pool was undergoing with massive immigration. In 1882, the Chinese Exclusion Act barred Chinese immigration. In 1899, the Associated Charities of Boston reported its opinion that "next to the Chinese, who can never in any real sense be American, [the Syrians] are the most foreign of all foreigners." Stereotypes such as these filtered into US textbooks. As late as 1990, one historian quotes uncritically anthropologist Edward Hall's claims that sniffing is part and parcel of what it means to be an Arab:

> Arabs constantly breathe on people while they talk… To the Arab, good smells are pleasing and a way of being intimate with each other. To smell one's friend is not only nice but desirable, for to deny him your breath is to act ashamed… When couples are being matched for marriage, the man's go-between will sometimes ask to smell the girl."[88]

One need not deny the olfactory sense to see this assessment as downright bizarre.

In 1902, Senator Henry Cabot Lodge tried to ramrod a halt to all immigration, which was vetoed by President Theodore Roosevelt. That same year descriptions of "Oriental warfare" filled New York papers when a police roughing up of five Syrians at 70 Washington Street turned into a melee, with one Syrian described as a "giant" who could hold nine men on his shoulders. The image of the Syrian colossus (in contrast to the cartoon "vermin" image of Yasir Arafat seventy years later) was exploited when a murder on Washington Street made front-page news, the headline October 29, 1905, reading in the *New York Herald*: "FACTIONAL WAR IS WAGED BETWEEN SYRIANS OF NEW YORK CITY. CUTTING AND SHOOTING. BROTHER AGAINST BROTHER, VILLAGERS AGAINST VILLAGERS, AND OLD FRIENDS ARE PARTING. VOICE OF WOMEN HEARD." The *New York Times* on October 24 spoke of "wild-eyed Syrians [showing] the glint of steel in two hundred swarthy hands." The cause of the scuffle? Typically enough, religion: a disagreement over the merits of the Syrian Orthodox bishop. The press overreaction contrasted with a more sober report by Lucius Miller: "In his love of law and order the Syrian cannot be excelled.... The universal testimony of the police authorities is that there is no more peaceful and law-abiding race in New York City."[89]

Though they were often co-religionists, a more chronic, low-level trouble occurred between the cedar green and the shamrock green— the Syrians and the Irish. The Industrial Commission Report on Immigration said, "The Syrian in New York has housed himself in the tenements of the old First Ward from which he displaced an undesirable Irish population, the remnant of which torments him." Settlers from that period report many kinds of harassment: a Syrian peddler woman had her *qashsha* lifted out of her hands by a taunting Irish window washer letting down a hook;[90] the owner of the Courtland Hotel on Washington Street remembered that on Halloween the Irish "fill up stockings with flour and go and beat the Orientals with it."[91] (Another woman remembered a Cockney Englishwoman shouting over a Brooklyn fence of grape leaves after witnessing the Syrian neighbors beating raw lamb in a *zidra*, or stone bowl, outdoors for *kibba naya*: "Cannibals! Uneducated people!"[92]) The Irish-Syrian tiffs declined when intermarriages occurred—for the rare times when they ventured out of their own community in wedlock, the Syrians preferred the Irish. The whole era takes on a mirthful cast when one knows that the closest confidant and trainer of the top Arab-American boxer, middleweight contender Mustapha Hamsho, was an Irishman.

It is hard to believe today, when Arabs are represented in film and theater as little more than terrorists or rich philanderers, that the early Syrians were the subject of a very popular Broadway play in 1919, *Anna Ascends*. The heroine was a Syrian waitress named Anna, working at a Washington Street coffeehouse run by the worldly-wise proprietor, Said Coury. Playwright Henry Chapman Ford, who had been mesmerized by Anna Ayyoub, a Syrian waitress in the Boston Beach Street colony, spoke of a Syrian family he had known in Washington, DC, in 1912: "Their family life, their clean way of living impressed me and I decided that the Americanization of such a race was a big factor in making the 'melting pot' one of the greatest nations of history." Ford went on:

> I figured here is a people who could read and write probably 6,000 years before the northern 'blue eyes.' Here is a race who had a fine culture along with the great Egyptian dynasties, and as criminology seems to be a statistical fad at the present writing, here are a people who have less, en ratio, in prisons, than any other in the world. Hence, I figured, why not write a Syrian drama, a virgin field, anent the Syrians?[93]

The play did not do for a bar what O'Neill's *The Iceman Cometh* did, nor did it capture the pathos and music of ghetto life as did *Fiddler on the Roof*. Neither high tragedy nor robust musical, *Anna Ascends* owed more to the light comedy intrigue of Noel Coward and the unabashed energy of George M. Cohan. Anna herself is a study in the Syrian working-class girl on Washington Street: "She carries a two-gallon olive oil can in each arm. Strings of garlic are around her neck. A small pocket dictionary is under the pit of her left arm and a sheet of paper with an order written on it in Syrian is in her mouth. In her blouse pocket is an American flag."[94]

Whatever good intentions Ford had, his play connected Anna's attractiveness to her ability to "ascend" the social ladder and hide her Syrian past. The Syrians, like Anna, were ready to ascend, too, virtually from the day they stepped off the boat at Ellis Island. If a name was to be sacrificed, more power to the new name. Only decades later would the dropping of Arabic names cause one Arab-American poet to lament:

> ... even my father lost his, went from
> Hussein Hamode Subh' to Sam Hamod.
> There is something lost in the blood,
> something lost down to the bone
> in these small changes. A man in a
> dark blue suit at Ellis Island says, with
> tiredness and authority, "You only need two
> names in America" and suddenly—as cleanly as
> the air—you've lost your name.[95]

But as the Reverend Rihbany had shown, there was convenience in being "the stranger," even to one's own people.

Peddlers and Factory Workers

The one-time mayor of St. Paul, Minnesota, is not recognizably Syrian. His name is George Latimer, but his mother was named Nassar, and her father was a Syrian peddler moving a cart of notions back and forth along the railroad tracks of Poughkeepsie, New York. On a summer day in 1983, Grandson George shook his head, jumped down the steps of his modest home, and drove off to see about lower-income housing, better plumbing, and preservation of the heritage of Swedes.[96]

When America listens to its favorite disc jockey it is listening to the son of an early Syrian peddler. Casey Kasem noted that his Druze father, Amin, left al-Moukhtara in Mount Lebanon in 1895, peddling up through South America and Mexico before dipping his body in the Rio Grande to become "an old olive-skinned wetback." Kasem remembered with fondness a figure from his Detroit childhood, "a Druze man who was always neat, clean-shaven, who made such a good reputation downtown in every Detroit office building carrying his little case as a peddler up until ten, fifteen years ago."[97] Half a century after the peddler era, the man struck Kasem as a cipher of lost times.

The Syrian peddlers went everywhere—from Washington Street in New York City they fanned up toward Utica and Buffalo; from New Orleans they peddled in Mississippi, Louisiana, and Texas; along the Rio Grande olive-skinned "wetbacks" at the turn of the century peddled in border towns (one family rivaled Haggar slacks in El Paso—the Farah slack people whose founder was, yes, a peddler); they peddled out across the Midwest to Indiana, Iowa, the Dakotas; they peddled, shouting, "Buy sumthin', ya ladies—cheap!" by the shores of the Pacific.

Essa Lupus, First Wave immigrant from Dihel, Lebanon, comes home after a day's work at the steel mill in Orem, Utah, in 1943. (Carmen and Joseph Awad)

Before parcel post, and J. C. Penney stores, the car and bus and subway, the Syrian peddler took to the American farmwife, factory worker wife, and country squire wife an invaluable item—the marketplace. The marketplace—the *suq*—in one little *qashsha* (from the corruption of the Spanish word *caia*). It usually contained dry goods: notions of thread, ribbons, handkerchiefs, laces, underwear, garters, suspenders. A hook to lure the interest of the woman who might otherwise be afraid of this character with the dark hair, baggy pants, and sunburned grin was a special satchel of items fresh from the Holy Land (no matter that often these crucifixes, rosaries, and Orthodox icons were manufactured in the Japan of its day—New York—they were holy). One fourteen-year-old boy from Karhoon, Lebanon, peddling in Worcester, Massachusetts, was nicknamed by customers, Jerusalem.[98] As Naff points out, rosaries were often displayed on a stick (to heighten the drama) or arranged on an arm like spaghetti straps on an alluring dress. Thus did the holy take on the touch of the sensual. To the Iowa farm wife, whose husband spent his day covering himself with dust and wallow and corn, this Syrian visitor, however odd, was welcome. And she bought—to the tune of a $60-million business for the Syrians by 1910.

For the peddler, hoisting his 50-to-200-pound packs or carrying the notions cases was a way to overcome isolation in his new land. It allowed him to literally walk out into America, without the tedious, sometimes humiliating attempts to adapt to American behavior in a fixed setting. Others peddled: German Jews, Irish, Swedes. But apparently the early Syrian took particular pride in it as if it defined his intrepidness. Too, it seems the Syrian was adaptable to both rural and city markets. He thrived on the empty spaces, once again that blessed stranger.

The highways in Sioux Falls, South Dakota, owe their origin to a Muslim construction company owner who came from Karhoon, Lebanon, in 1878 and peddled. Ali Ahmed al-Oodie had also sunk his stakes as any pioneer, homesteading in the Black Hills.[99] Down South, along the rural stretches of the Mississippi River, the father of the man with the longest service in the Mississippi legislature peddled at the turn-of-the-century: "He bought in Vicksburg what he could carry on his back, 'cause he walked in the beginning, went through the countryside. Then as he was able he got a horse and buggy, then a wagon. He became a merchant with a store in Hermanville, then a store eventually in Vicksburg." Above the store was the home, "very Lebanese in feel" with arches and off-white, buff brick, and porches looking out over the river—the manse of a peddler from destitution.[100]

It was backbreaking work on the road, where the Syrian's biggest enemies were the cold and exposure without a roof. On the road for up to six months (others peddled for a few weeks at a time, some were only day peddlers), they had to do everything possible in cold weather to keep from freezing to death. Still, there are tales of women's frozen skirts cutting their ankles, of blackened frostbitten faces, and of men sleeping in buggies who froze to death by morning.[101] One horrid night a Syrian shepherding a woman married to a fellow villager in Lebanon was caught out in the cold and stole into a small building:

> I opened my kashshi and I used a scissors....under the frame of the window, it opened, and we entered. We saw two cases in which they put the coffins. I told her that this room had two beds, one for her and one for me. From our fatigue and the darkness, we did not see the graves....Then the moon came out. The woman looked outside and cried out..."We are sleeping in a mausoleum and the dead are beneath us in the boxes." And she leaped out of the shed and I after her.[102]

Inevitably there were cultural misunderstandings. Given a room for the night, an anxious shaking Muslim peddler seized the beard of his Norwegian host in Sioux Falls, South Dakota, and kissed it, a gesture of reverence or request in the Arab world. The Norwegian began strangling him until he was rescued by his companion, who had been waiting out on the road.[103] Disaster was usually warded off by an explanation and a great deal of nervous laughter. Humor was the Syrian's key to the heart of America. It is no mistake that three of the most accomplished actors of Lebanese origin were comedians—Danny Thomas, Jamie Farr, and Vic Tayback. Their ancestors peddled, and peddling was the longest and hardest burlesque stage in any town.

The average per capita income for an American in 1910 was $382. For the Syrian, it was three times that, at least $1,000 per annum. This annual salary was four times that of the American farmer, slightly less than twice the income of a factory worker, a coal miner, or a salesman in a shop. In short, for the immigrant considered by one report to be, besides the Chinese, "the most foreign of all foreigners," it was not a bad showing.

It was also a testimony to how the Syrians had made American self-reliance their own. A former American ambassador to Morocco remembered his father from ʿAyn Arab peddling "socks and shoes and Levis and tablecloths" to the farms around Cedar Rapids, Iowa, which he "bartered for food [until he] got enough food to start selling." The diplomat recalled: "The one thing we were always taught by my father was never to work for anybody else. Just be responsible for your own destiny and not live under anyone else's leash." These Emersonian lessons, however, did not preclude a shrewd understanding of customer and "niche" market:

> [As a youth] I would hit the road with my dad, mainly just for company for him. At this time he was peddling rugs out of his truck to the farmers and eventually to the Catholic church. He was selling almost exclusively to the Catholic priests because they were the only ones who could afford an Oriental rug.[104]

While it is safe to say that a sizable number of pioneer Syrians peddled, by no means did all or even a majority do so for their first work. Some thought the work was beneath them (particularly those who were educated in the Old Country). Others preferred the less risky and soon-to-be more profitable line of supplier, the storekeeper who stocked the peddler. It was an inevitable step up for a peddler, too, to open his dry goods store in Cleveland, or Cedar Rapids, or Detroit. For many, factories near the port of embarkation in America lured them with the prospect of quick cash.[105]

Take the case of a rousing, raisin-faced gentleman in a cardigan sweater whose laugh was that of a jaybird. Before he became "Taxi Joe," Elias Joseph went straight into the woolen mills of Woonsocket, Rhode Island. In 1912 at Ellis Island, "we land nine o'clock in the morning; like I tell you, six o'clock I went to work." Soon he was involved in a fight with a fellow steam-powered loom worker who needled him about his origins:

> I work nights. Ten cents an hour. I want you to get this down because it's how it's happened and what's happened. I went to work—only word I say, "No." That's the only word. Third night I was working and the boss came and make me clean up the machine. Another fellow sits next to me; he keeps pestering me. He says "Are you Greek?" "No." "Are you Syrian?" "No." "Are you French?" "No." "Are you English?" "No." "Romanian?" "No." "Bulgarian?" "No." "No?" "No, no, no." "Spanish?" "No." "American?" "No." And after, I get so mad I say to him, "You go ahead till you die," in Arabic, "I'm not going to answer you no more." I get up and I let him have it—one over the head. I says, "I'm dying to have somebody to talk to. And you pestered me for two hours and you wouldn't talk to me."

Taxi Joe found new work at Woonsocket Dye, where other Syrians worked. The superintendent of the factory taught him how to mix the base (vicerol) for the dye for a raise from 10 cents to 12½ cents an hour, the wage everyone else was making (Syrians comprised one of the cheapest labor pools at the time). "If I know what I know today," he said, reflecting on the pittance he thought bounty then, "I would have make him pay me, you know what I mean? But I don't know nothing. I can't even read or write or even talk."[106] After a stint with the US Army in World War I, Joseph returned to Woonsocket and purchased the first "closed car," a Ford, in the town. It was called a "limousine." Joseph became "Taxi Joe," Woonsocket's first taxi driver, and, at last, his own man.

Many Syrians worked in the New England cloth mills in Lawrence and Fall River, Massachusetts, at the time wool and cotton centers of the world. A retired lieutenant colonel in the US Air Force, Edward Abdullah, recalled taking his father's lunch to him at one of Fall River's cotton mills:

> I would run home when school let out at 11:30, get something to eat and take my father's pail to him, usually something like lentil soup and a kind of Lebanese goulash made from lamb, rice, and peas. The mill sold milk to the workers. But nine times out of ten—I remember this well—he would save the milk for me and I would drink it walking back to school. Going into the mill was like walking into an oven. It was 110 degrees in summer! And the steam, which was to keep the threads from snapping, and the noise … the vibration of those looms! My generation, the first-generation Americans, vowed we would never go to work in the mills.[107]

In Maine, most Syrians worked in the factories, in the sardine cannery of Eastport and the woolen mills in such places as Dexter, Madison, and Vassleborough. By 1915, Waterville had the largest Syrian population in the state, brushing up against French Canadians who had immigrated to the town during the same period and constituted the largest ethnic group in the city. The two groups, predictably, fought in the factories under the eyes of the Yankee owners.[108]

One of the centers of America's industrial boom at the turn of the century, Detroit—destined to become the city with the largest Arab-American population—had 50 Lebanese Christians, mostly single men, in town by 1900. Just sixteen years later, according to archives at the Henry Ford Museum, there were 555 Syrian men working at the Ford car plants, a sizable amount even for the tail end of the so-called peddler era.[109] In short, though the Syrian liked to be his own boss, what he was most after was a steady job. Family waited back home for his remission. If Ford rang the whistle more than the lonely road, so be it. He would take Ford.

Among the Syrian factory workers who eschewed the peddler path was one Nathra Nader, who arrived in Newark, New Jersey, in 1912 from Zahle. But his experience was short-lived. He worked one year in a machine shop there and later said, "I see how factories work."[110] The man was the father of Ralph Nader, America's leading consumer advocate, about whom columnist Michael Kinsley has said, "No living American is responsible for more concrete improvement in the society we actually live in than Ralph Nader."

Some like Nathra Nader fled abysmal factory conditions and took to the open road. A retired civil servant in San Francisco remembered that his father had come in 1906 from Homs, Syria, through Ellis Island, only to be lured to a shoe factory in Montreal. But after he contracted what was then called "miner's consumption," or silicosis, from leather dust, he journeyed to Hosmar in the Canadian Rockies, where "it was high and dry. I think my parents were the only people of Arab heritage in that region. They sold in the mining camps, rented a horse and buggy, and peddled merchandise. The miners would pay in gold coins."[111] He did quite well, regained his health, and moved to Vancouver.

Similarly, George Milkie, who had come from Bishmizeen al-Kura, Lebanon, in 1913, quit work in a steel mill in Seattle to offer residents of the foggy northwestern town a different kind of notion—fresh fish from a basket! Milkie then graduated from basket to horse-drawn buggy to Model T Ford to a refrigerated truck.[112]

Some bypassed peddling, shopkeeping, and the factories to get right into the marrow of America—banking. George Faour, along with his brothers Daniel and Dominic, started the first Syrian-owned bank in the United States in Manhattan on Washington Street in

1891. Among the earliest Syrian arrivals to Boston, in the 1880s, the Faour brothers made their money in linen. According to a Syrian associate of theirs who worked at Chase Manhattan Bank, the Faours—who were the main lenders to "Little Syria" in New York during its first difficult years—had slept in the basement of a store on Washington Street, subsisting for days on a diet of bananas and bread. Though the richest of the early Syrians, the Faours lost $1 million in the Depression, and George died alone in a boarding house.

The Chase Manhattan associate originally emigrated from Egypt in 1913 because of "a lot of talk of war" and Italian and Turkish skirmishes. George Fauty's grandparents had come earlier, in 1905, through Pawtucket, Rhode Island. His father "couldn't get himself" to work in the silk mills in Pawtucket. Being educated he struck out for Manhattan, enrolling son George in P.S. 20 on Albany Street, nesting in the Syrian enclave on Washington and West streets. Both parents worked in a crowded apartment of three rooms with four children and two adults. In a year they had moved to a cold-water flat in Brooklyn, where "a quarter in a box gave you enough gas for a while and then when we'd see the gas going down, you put another quarter, and that keeps you going. In other words, you were never billed. You paid right on the spot." Fauty worked through high school for "pin money." He quit, though, and found a job with the Daniel Reeve chain store where a checker didn't have an adding machine. He totaled figures "on a paper bag." A supervisor took a liking to this "excellent mathmetician" and got him an interview at Chase Manhattan, where he got a job at the age of sixteen and never left. It was 1922.

Fauty had to leap one barrier before he was hired:

> They didn't hire Jews in those days. That was a mustn't. And the personnel director told me, "You go to your parish. I want a letter from the priest of your parish." My father took me to the Reverend Basil Kherbawi, who was pastor of Saint Nicholas Cathedral and a graduate of Columbia University. He prepared a letter for me: my father handed him a dollar.

Being Syrian may not have been much of a help, either:

> A cousin of Eddie Baloutine's used to sell ties. He couldn't get a job anywhere because he was a foreigner. And everytime I would see him down in that area in the street selling ties he would ask, "How in the hell did you get a job in the bank? I can't understand it!"... My thinking was older. I never said anything to anybody and they believed [that he was an American WASP]. Due to the fact that I completed high school and spoke well. And on my application I never said I was born in Cairo, Egypt. I said I was born in Brooklyn, New York. I was aggressive. I told you I was well read. No one ever questioned it.[113]

Others entered WASP America through manufacturing: the Merhiges with silks in Brooklyn, the Bardwills of Manhattan with linens and silks. Some started making items other than cloth. The father of Joseph Jacobs, owner of Jacobs Engineering, had a US monopoly on straight-razor manufacturing in Brooklyn when during World War I Americans could not get German imported razors.

The peddler began to fade by 1910 with the influx of new inventions, such as the car, bus, and subway, and the entry of the Sears mail order catalog and Woolworth's five-and-dime stores. He had, however, entered America's literary imagination. A short-story writer in 1912 dealt with the Syrian honorifically in "The Peddler." A children's author recalled youthful days in *The Laugh Peddler*, in which a bronzed-faced Yusuf Hanna, burdened with heavy bags, saves the life of a boy drowning in a Minnesota river.[114] Memory of the Syrian peddler also inspired the character of Ali Hakim in the musical *Oklahoma!*

Perhaps no better tribute to the Syrian peddlers can be found than in their own words, their own tales. As a boy, I listened to the stories of my paternal grandmother, Nazera Jabaly Orfalea, for days under a grape-leaf trellis, alongside a dollhouse in her Los Angeles backyard. In 1893, she was one of the first thousand Syrian women in America and peddled her notions all over the eastern seaboard as a young girl before being caught in matrimony by a Syrian linen store owner in Cleveland, though she did everything to avoid surrendering her independence. She kept a journal—the only one extant by a woman Syrian peddler, to my knowledge. When I asked

Zachary Mafrige with his son, Stevens, in their delivery car, a stripped down 1912 Model Ford, 1915, Texas. (Courtesy of the Institute of Texan Cultures)

how she managed to offer holy water from her notions case, she proudly proclaimed, "Why, I blessed it myself!"[115]

Family and Religion

The early Syrian's family was the fountain of life from which everyone drank. Perhaps too much, as one can sometimes drink water in enough great gulps to become dizzy. The Syrian love of family is not unique; the Italians, the Jews, the Irish, and other ethnic groups try to hold fast to family ties in the age of the pill and divorce. But for Arab Americans, family has always been especially valued, to the point that the quest for self often begins and ends in family. In many ways, the family is the self, the self by itself a highly foreign, existential concept, only a puff of air. Family life is a vindication of the multiplicity of existence and in it the lessons and responsibilities of life are learned deeply, or not at all. The paradox of the gregariousness of the Arab American is that it is rooted in ancestral isolation—the isolation of Druze and Christian Lebanese mountaineers, and the more ancient confrontation with empty space that the desert presented the Arab. The isolation of minorities in the system of Ottoman Turkey made for a fragmented society but for families woven as tightly as a prize carpet.

Families worked hard together, pitching in every available limb. On Sunday, after church, the Washington Street Syrians would amble uptown to take the children for a walk through Central Park. There they marveled at an alcove of green they identified with Lebanon, and a 224-ton obelisk called Cleopatra's Needle, donated to the United States by the Khedive of Egypt in 1881 to better US–Egyptian ties. Today the hieroglyphs of the 3,500-year-old obelisk have been virtually rubbed out by the smoke and smog of New York factories and autos, making it as mysterious today as was the arrival of Syrians a century ago.

At first too small in number to warrant parishes of their own rites, Syrians welcomed the arrival of the first Melkite priest in 1889, the first Maronite priest in 1891, and the first (non-Russian) Orthodox priest in 1896. Before they set to work founding their own missions and churches, Protestant and Roman Catholic churches serviced them. (Louise Houghton listed ten Roman Catholic churches with large Syrian congregations and eighteen Protestant churches with Syrian pastors in 1911.)

Though the Melkites were the first to minister to their own, in 1890—when the very old St. Peter's Church in Manhattan became known as a "Syrian Catholic Church"—their first original mission was established in Chicago in 1893, and the first Melkite church built from the ground up was in Lawrence, Massachusetts, in 1902. The Maronites administered to their group at a Catholic church in

Manhattan in 1890 and set up three of their own churches in Boston, Philadelphia, and St. Louis in 1897. The first Syrian Greek Orthodox parish was begun at 77 Washington Street in Manhattan in 1896, with a second in Brooklyn in 1902. Thus, by 1890, there was one church for each of the Melkite, Maronite, and Syrian Orthodox communities in Manhattan.

The Reverend Basil Kherbawi, an Orthodox priest, was the first cleric to document the numbers of Eastern churches in America. In 1913, Kherbawi found 16 Melkite parish churches in operation, 16 Maronite churches, and 18 Eastern Orthodox (which often included in their congregations Ukranians, Slavs, and Russians). By 1924, Philip Hitti counted 33 Maronite churches, 22 Orthodox churches, and 21 Melkite. Though these figures are not solid because on occasion a mission community without its own structure was counted as a "church," the evidence indicates that among the First Wave Syrian immigrants Maronites were the largest and most organized group. Today, however, the Antiochian Orthodox archdiocese far outdistances the Maronites and Melkites in both churches (159) and communicants (400,000, a four-fold increase from 1988 to 2005). Five of the earliest Melkite churches were closed due to declining membership and assimilation into both the Roman Catholic community and the Orthodox. Other Christian sects, such as the Iraqi Chaldeans, the Egyptian Copts and the Syrian ("Jacobite") Orthodox came much later (see Appendix 5).

The existence of an early Melkite church in Rugby, North Dakota, had been lost to history until recently. Rugby was founded by Syrian immigrants from Forzol and Zahle in 1897, scarcely a decade after North Dakota had joined the Union. They were mostly farmers taking advantage of the Homestead Act, including Father Seraphim Roumie, who sold his own claim for $400 to help build the Melkite church there in 1903. But in 1911, a severe famine hit the area, and a fire destroyed the church; the Melkite Syrians of Rugby disappeared, leaving the place a virtual ghost town.[116]

Though there would be no Arab mosques in America until the late 1920s, Houghton listed nine Muslim "religious bodies," three Druze and one Shiʿite community in Sioux City, Iowa, by 1911. (It is interesting that the well-known sociologist did not incorporate "Shiʿite" into "Muslim.") Though there were about 75 Eastern rite churches in the United States by 1924, more than half were in the east, and, as Naff has said, most of the western Syrian immigrants went without their own churches for a generation.

Today the only remaining evidence of the early Washington Street community—save two prosperous stores of the Awns and Jabbours, which cater to Wall Street—are two churches, St. George's Melkite and St. Joseph's Maronite, both established in 1915. Perhaps it was fitting. As the Kayal brothers have noted, "The Syrians do not regard 'place' as the root of their community identification. Rather, they prefer to utilize the primordial ties of blood and faith."[117]

For baptism, the Eastern rite churches would immerse the infant in a large basin of water rather than sprinkle the baby as the Roman Catholics do. For funerals, the community would gather, as in the Old Country, for "a meal of mercy" (wake) that would often separate female from male mourners, the former dressing in black and wailing over the casket. But nothing moved the early Syrians—and later ones—more than a wedding.

As they have from time immemorial, weddings hold out the hope, at least symbolically, of rectifying conflict, or reconciling antipathies, and many of the early Syrians and their Arab-American progeny reveled in stories of ceremonial harmony. A Maronite priest later serving in Youngstown, Ohio, elatedly told how at his grandmother's marriage in Mount Lebanon the neighboring Druze had an important role: "When she was married they put her on a wild white stallion and the Druze attended and they were burning incense. They had two men holding the stallion down as they led her in a procession from her village to her husband's village."[118] The "enemy" Druze literally delivered the Maronite bride to her husband.

In America, weddings may have lacked white horses, and in the early days they were often held in the immigrant's parlor. But with the growth of the churches the splendor of an Eastern wedding rite unfolded here. The Orthodox wedding, in particular, stood out for its beauty, grace, and solemnity. Golden crowns connected by a sash of silk were placed on the bride and bridegroom's heads. During the priest's blessings the couple would join hands with the wedding party, moving in a circle in the sanctuary. Not a few times the silk band between crowns got tangled. A further mixup sometimes occurred in the complex activities of the priest canting in ever louder decibles, "The handmaiden of God, Elizabeth, is wedded to the servant of God, Joseph, in the name of the Father and of the Son and of the Holy Spirit," as well as touching one spouse's crown to the other's forehead four times. In the confusing repetitions, Elizabeth could easily become the servant of God and Joseph, the handmaiden.

At the sumptuous wedding feast, a lace sack of almonds was placed along with sweetened *qamh* (barley) and *zibib* (raisins) near each guest's placesetting. Much dancing and singing ensued. Mary Macron described the wedding feast vividly:

> The women... vied with each other to compose beautiful chants. Rhyming and lilting, laughter and joy were captured on a golden chain of words ending in the pealing, exultant cry of the *zaghrut*, *La la la la lu lullu li-'ayshah!* "To life," they sang. "To life!" An

Arab wedding was not just a family event, a community occasion, and a weekend of festivities. It was, rather, a command performance. Everyone had to sing, everyone had to dance.[119]

With the ratio of men to women at least four or five to one in the First Wave, it was natural that many Syrian men went back to Syria to find wives. Over a quarter of the early immigrants did return to Syria, many to effect a match begun via the mail, though few stayed in the Old Country. Some, out of sheer loneliness and the sparse crop of Syrian women, married outside the community, though by 1910 only 6 percent of Syrian children were the products of a mixed marriage. The figure rose to 8 percent in 1920, and has steadily increased since. (In fact, a study based on the 1990 US Census showed over 80 percent of US-born Arab Americans had non-Arab spouses, an intermarriage rate much higher than other non-European ethnicities. This was especially true for Syrian and Lebanese Americans. For those of partial Arab ethnicity, fully 96 percent marry outside the Arab community. Obviously the fear factor since 9/11 has only intensified this extraordinary trend toward assimilation; in fact this ethnic identity may very well be in an advanced stage of disappearance.)[120] Results in early days were often problematic: in 1928, the editor of the *Syrian World* said that many of 125 Druze who had married American women had become divorced.[121]

Clearly, though, the risks were worth taking since, especially for a Syrian male, as one author intimates, being single was "both unnatural and deplorable."[122] A March 5, 1899, article in the New York-based Arabic paper *Al-Hoda* put it bluntly:

> Bachelors value money lightly; they squander it in clubs, theaters, and houses of ill repute. All of these places are traps for immigrants in a foreign land. A man who marries and has a family is respected, responsible, and motivated to save. Therefore, men should marry, not at an early age but between the ages of 22 and 30, and their mates should be chosen not for their wealth but for their education. Such wives will create enduring happiness.

Some First Wavers waited many decades before returning to the Old Country to choose a bride. The wife of one tearfully told a touching story one spring when her husband, then 82, was in the hospital with a stroke. Nicholas Bitar, born in 1900, was a kind of legend to the villagers of Bazbina, Lebanon, which is located in the Akkar, the northeastern corner of the country. At the age of eight, before World War I, in conditions where food was getting scarce, the boy Nicholas had a hunger to learn. He would go from town to town in the Akkar trading his food allowance to teachers for lessons. This continued into the war, when he in essence traded the last of his food to unemployed teachers, who were starving. He went to Tripoli by donkey and traded the animal for books. Bitar came to the United States after the war, and soon found himself ministering not as a priest, but as a doctor to the Syrians in Pittsburgh who worked in the steel mills and peddled razor blades. For decades his story became a way of punishing indolent children in Bazbina to the effect that "there's a man from here who sold his own meals to get an education and now he's a doctor in America."

Nelly Bitar grew up hearing these stories of Nicholas. When she was only 11, Dr. Bitar revisited Bazbina and met her. They were cousins through her mother (whose maiden name changed from Bitar to Khouri when her father became a priest) and he asked her what she would like as a present. "*Chocolat*," she said in French. He replied, "All I have is chewing gum. Take that." Then Bitar leaned and whispered to her mother, "Take care of this one—she's a beauty."

During a 1950 reunion, Bitar came back to Bazbina and was stunned by the dark-haired, green-eyed Nelly Abdo. But he didn't remember her from his former trip. As Nelly put it, "I remembered him, however. He said, 'I used to have black hair but now it is gray.' I said, 'It hasn't changed so much.' He was surprised that I would be able to compare what he had looked like then with now. He sat by me after that, and said that I was a rose in a field of daisies."

A year later, at 50, Bitar took his nineteen-year-old bride on a strenuous honeymoon up in the Lebanese mountains to Bhamdoun. They toured Beirut and the Biqaᶜ Valley and even then Bitar was pointing out to Nelly the tragic overspill from the Palestine war. She remembered him saying, "If they don't put these differences aside and help the Palestinians in the camps, those damn rich Arabs, a bloodbath will take place." She said, "It sent shivers down my spine. He worked from day one, 1948 and the war, sending clothes to the old country and the refugees."[123]

Romantic as is the Bitar story, it was education, not beauty, and industriousness, not pleasure, that were most attractive to early Syrians in marriage. This is no better represented than in the store ledgers of Johnny Nosser of Vicksburg, Mississippi, which show that he took one day off to marry in 1925, and the next day was back at the register.

Marriage, religion, and a profit mixed hilariously in the life of a grandfather of an early immigrant to high-altitude Penasco, New Mexico. Pete Sahd, born in 1911 in Roumieh, Lebanon, told the story about his ancestor, Abdo Yussef, who came to Las Vegas, New Mexico, in 1892: "He sent back to Lebanon for a picture of his wife. When it arrived in Vegas, someone else received it and promptly sold it for $50.00. He claimed the photograph was the Virgin Mary, the patron saint of Lebanon."[124]

In Bazbina, Lebanon, Dr. Nicholas H. Bitar of Pittsburgh marries his hometown sweetheart, Nelly Abdou, on July 22, 1951, before bringing her to his new home in the United States. (Nelly Bitar)

Syrian Doughboys

Though the leader of the immigrant communities was usually a priest, Washington Street's first "defender of the peddlers" was a Syrian bricklayer. Genial, college educated, Musa Daoud was described as "strong as a titan" in warding off a gang attack on a Syrian peddler (*New York Times*, 4 June 1894). A helper of Dr. Nageeb Arbeely on Ellis Island, Daoud often welcomed new arrivals in his apartment on Washington Street, where they marveled at his library.

But the Syrians' view of politics was at best skeptical. In 1924, Hitti declared, "The Syrian cuts no figure in the political life of his nation." Much of their traditional shyness toward the halls of politics stemmed from their experience under the Ottomans; for centuries the Syrians had had no experience with representative government and had been conditioned to distrust the authority of pashas, caliphs, and garrison heads of the Sublime Porte, who could tax them severely or draft them into wars in which they had no stake.

Fifteen thousand Syrians—or 7 percent of the entire community—served as doughboys for Uncle Sam, many registering without waiting for the draft, eager to get some licks in on behalf of their new freedom and against their former Ottoman oppressors. Hitti found that in the long lists of pro-German, pro-Turk sympathizers supplied by the US government after four years of war, there was not one Syrian to be found. Their fervency was marked. In Portland, Maine, all the Syrian youth in the town (fifteen) volunteered before the draft was called. A world's record—2,805 rivets hammered into a steel ship in only nine hours—was set by a Quincy, Massachusetts, plant gang whose foreman was a Syrian. The *Boston Herald* editorialized, "There are no better Americans these days than Charlie Mulham and his fellow Syrians."[125]

Michael Suleiman has translated from Arabic part of a book on Syrian participation in World War I, *The Syrian Soldier in Three Wars* (1919), in which Lt. Gabriel Ward highlights his own activities serving in the Spanish–American War, fighting guerrillas in the Philippines, and serving in the Great War in Europe. With the American flag as a frontispiece, the book recorded "pride in serving his new country and heaps praise upon his fellow Syrians who also joined the US armed forces."[126]

A fig picker ("Eat dead figs—the best thing for your heart!") from al-Ma'r-rah, Syria, who emigrated because he did not want to serve in the Turkish army fought for the United States in Europe. Before the Armistice and his relaxed encampment underneath the Eiffel Tower, he had a harrowing experience with a fellow Syrian-American doughboy:

> I was friendly with one fella, they call him Deeb. He was just like a brother. When we went to the front line he was under a shell and all of a sudden the poor fella go down. "*Lakin* [but], come on, Deeb, you gonna die there, come on!" I tried to help him. I held him a little bit, and a little bit, and after that I said, "Well, I can't help you no more." We promised each other no matter what happened to us we gonna stick together. But when you are there you fight for yourself. You don't care for your father or mother or sister or brother. So I left him and I didn't see him no m-o-o-r-e! [sings in dirge].[127]

But one of the most vivid accounts by a doughboy from the Levant was that of Ashad Hawie. A member of the famed 42nd "Rainbow Division," 167th Alabama Infantry Regiment, he was probably the most decorated Syrian in the war. Hawie compared the forced march of Christmas 1917, when many of his fellows were barefoot, to his ancestral homeland: "When we reached our halting point in the valley of the Marne after six days on the march, my own feet were swollen and bloody, though snow and low temperatures were not new to one reared in the Hills of Lebanon." Finally, when he was sleeping, exhausted, standing up in a trench, "a yellow flare from the German line" exploded in a "flash brighter than sunshine." It was gas, chemical warfare introduced into the human race, and Hawie's first battle.

Later, in July 1918, he received the Croix de Guerre from the French when, on the Nevers-Sedan road, he captured a German quartermaster sergeant, who carried instructions from the High Command for a resupply of munitions; Hawie also successfully led a grenade counterattack on the elite Prussian Guard. He fought at the ferocious Battle of Verdun, in which more than half his company were killed. But he had to pull up more courage than he thought he had for the pivotal Argonne Meuse battle, often called "the death blow to the German Army." Facing the famous "Kreimhilde Stellung," the Germans' intricate trench system, Hawie's Rainbow Division was trapped in the Argonne woods, facing a machine gun nest. Six messengers were sent out in desperation—all were killed. Hawie volunteered to be the seventh. After crawling to the machine gun nest where four Germans were firing away, he tossed in three Mills hand grenades. Gen. John Pershing pinned the Distinguished Service Cross on Hawie's chest, saying, "Young man, to my mind you are the greatest type of American citizen. You have won your citizenship, not by the scratch of a pen in a quiet court office, but grappled it from the mouth of a cannon."

Hawie was wounded five hours before the Armistice was signed November 11, 1918, after sparing the life of one German soldier who had fired on his group from a house showing a white flag. Hawie told his surprised fellows, "This is a Christian army. Unnecessary slaughter is not Christian. We must teach the Hun they must not kill."[128] Hawie evidently did not know that the army had plenty of Jews and some Muslims in it, too. Hawie's fate took an especially pathetic turn, however, when he returned from the war to find that his mentally disturbed brother was on trial for murder. Largely because of Hawie's public speaking and war record, the brother was spared execution.

During the Great War, the American Syrians purchased "much above their proportionate quota" of liberty bonds, according to Salloum Mokarzel. In the Fourth Liberty Loan campaign alone, 4,800 Syrians from the New York area, roughly 64 percent of the population there, bought $1.2 million worth of war bonds. They had also established Red Cross and Boy Scout chapters in numerous cities. But the final coup for the newcomers who shouldered the rifle for America came when they captured the silver medal for second prize in the 1918 Fourth of July parade down Wall Street. It must have weighed on some of the Syrians leaning out of a brownstone window to watch their float pass how strange it all was. To be in America, winning prizes celebrating freedom and the end of a war that had stripped one's homeland of its trees, food, and people. To be in America, with shreds of free press confetti matting one's hair, to be happy, foolish even, dancing the *dabka* on the float among this symphony of strangers moving down Wall Street—but knowing that others in the Lebanon mountains had so recently been eating dung as they starved.

One exhausted American doughboy recently returned from the French front was probably not among the revelers. Soon to become the guiding critical force behind the cluster of Syrian émigré poets in New York City, later the biographer of Kahlil Gibran, and as he neared the age of 100 a candidate for the Nobel Prize in Literature, he wrote a poem about the terrors of war and the cost of the famine in Lebanon. Memorized by students throughout the Arab world, the poem remains virtually unknown to his fellow Americans. Here is part of "My Brother" by Mikhail Naimy:

> Brother, if after the war a soldier comes home
> And throws his tired body into the arms of friends,
> Do not hope on your return for friends.
> Hunger struck down all to whom we might whisper our pain.
> Brother, if the farmer returns to till his land,
> And after long exile rebuilds a shack which cannon had wrecked,
> The waterwheels have dried up
> And the foes have left no seedling except the scattered corpses.[129]

Strangers among Strangers: The Early Muslims

There is a legend about a Muslim settling in America before "Hi Jolly": In the early 16th century, an Egyptian named Nosreddine came to nestle in the Catskills of New York where he fell in love with Lotwana, the daughter of a Mohawk chief. Dutchmen bet Nosreddine that he could not win her heart; the game Muslim lost the bet and, frustrated, strangled Lotwana. For this, he was burned at the stake.[130]

Legends aside, most Syrian Muslims—who made up less than ten percent of the First Wave migration—began coming to America about twenty years after the Christian migration started in the 1880s. (A few Yemenis managed to slip through the Suez Canal in 1869 to head to America.) Some Muslims peddled, as did the other Syrians, but many were attracted to the great booming midwestern factories of steel, tin, automobiles, and trains in cities such as Pittsburgh, New Castle (Pennsylvania), Detroit, and Michigan City (Indiana). Not a few were attracted by the Homestead Act to the midwestern heartland, taking up farming as they had done in Syria. New York civil rights lawyer Abdeen Jabara traces his heritage back to a maternal grandfather, who came in 1898 from Musda Bulheist in Lebanon's fertile Biqa' Valley on the promise of free land: "He landed in Mexico, having heard that they were giving land away in the

A Muslim immigrant in the early 1900s, with Ellis Island in the background
(From Augustus Sherman Collection of Statue of Liberty National
Museum and Ellis Island Immigration Museum)

Ninety-five-year-old Jora Sallie sits on her front steps in 1985 near her daughter, both members of the New Castle, Pennsylvania, Muslim community. (Anthony Toth)

United States, up in the northern part of the United States. He rode in a wagon from Mexico to North Dakota where he got 160 acres of land if he would agree to farm it."[131]

Jabara's father followed the other major trend of the early Muslims—the lure of quick riches that has played its rhythms to the poor of the world since the beginning of the smokestack age. Sam Jabara arrived in New York in 1920 with a piece of paper that said, "Boyne City, Michigan"—240 miles north of Detroit. Thus he bypassed the auto factories where many fellow Muslims were employed to work in lumber camps, livery stables, and a tannery factory where he was injured by acid. The ruination of the father's lungs by chemicals influenced the political activism of his son in later years.

Perhaps it was shyness about religion and the fear of quoting from the Bible, rather than the Qu^{c}ran, to eager housewives that turned the Muslims more quickly from peddling to factories and farms. Hearing that America was the "land of unbelief," no doubt, kept Muslim Syrians from migrating in groups until the turn of the century. As an elderly Muslim woman put it,

> In 1885, my father planned to accompany some Christian friends to America. He bought the ticket and boarded the boat. Shortly before sailing he asked the captain whether America had mosques. Told that it had none, he feared America was *bilad kufr*, a land of unbelief. He immediately got off the boat.[132]

Four early Muslim settlements lay claim to the honor of being the first to build a mosque in America—Detroit, Michigan City (Indiana), Ross (North Dakota), and Cedar Rapids (Iowa). Abdo Elkholy, a historian of early Muslim Syrians, says the first mosque built in America was in Highland Park, Michigan, in 1919. But it was dismantled within five years and is now a church. Other historians refer to the founding of Islamic associations in Highland Park in 1919 and in downtown Detroit in 1922. A dome was put atop a rented building in 1924 in Michigan City, Indiana, according to the son of one of the mosque's founders, Hossein Ayad. "You could tell it was a religious building," said Abe Ayad. It fell prey to urban renewal in the late 1960s and had been "misused" for years: "They tore the rugs up for prayer when there was a wedding or funeral. These are violations of the sanctuary, things you would not find in a mosque in the Middle East. The mosque is for prayer, and prayer alone."[133]

It seems likely that the first structure built solely to be used as a mosque was in Ross, North Dakota, in 1929. One hundred Syrians comprised the isolated community of farmers and peddlers in Ross in 1900, but it took 30 years to build a crude building that resembled a large, sunken duck blind. The Cedar Rapids community was the first to build a mosque with minaret and dome from scratch in 1935. Rebuilt with a minaret from which one can see the Quaker Oats Company's giant grain silos, it is probably the oldest surviving mosque in America.

Lured by General Motors and Ford to Detroit, US Steel to Pittsburgh, box factories and Willis Auto to Toledo, or the loom industries in Quincy, Massachusetts, the Muslim Syrians also found themselves working on train cars in Michigan City, Indiana. Many of the first mass-produced autos were built by the early Syrian Muslims. So were the elegant, velvet-lined Pullman cars in Michigan City. It was not a little ironic, inasmuch as these modes of transportation were scarcely evident in the land of their birth. So numerous were these workers at one plant that when Muslims celebrated ʿId al-Fitr after fasting for the 30 days of Ramadan, Pullman National had to shut down.

A former director of the Islamic Center in Washington, DC— founded by Palestinian Muslim Joseph Howar in 1949—recalled his imam father's work founding the mosque in Michigan City and one in Gary, Indiana, where the Muslims worked in the steel blast furnaces. It was at the Gary house of worship that the son found his father shot to death one day; he memorialized it in a powerful poem.[134] In the early years imams were hard to come by. After Abude Habhab wrote repeatedly to Egypt in the 1920s requesting an imam, he finally received a positive answer. Hitching up his horses, he went down to the train station at Gary and waited, but no Arab imam emerged. A Hindu figure clad in white approached him, though. He spoke no Arabic and little English. Habhab and the man ended up communicating through the Qu'ran. This was the Sufi Bengali, famed among the early Syrian Muslims as their first official imam from the Old Country—even if it was India. He traveled widely over the Midwest, settling in Chicago. His book in English, *The Life of Mohammed*, was widely read by Syrian Muslim children in the United States.[135]

Druze, who took to peddling even less than did other Muslims, set up colonies in Appalachia where their mountain hardihood could be tested, and as early as 1908 they could be found in numbers in Seattle, Washington. Some Druze peddlers made it to California, too; the oldest living original Druze immigrant there, Albert Kirwan, arrived in California in 1911 and worked as a tailor in West Covina for eighty years. Amil Shab, who arrived in Detroit after World War I, later settled in California, running a ten-acre citrus orchard. For him it was a replacement for the famine in Lebanon: "All my six brothers, my mother and father died of starvation and illnesses in one year. I lived off berries, cactus, and weeds."[136] A sizable number of Muslim Palestinians settled in Chicago in the early part of the century, working the stockyards and setting up grocery stores.

The difficulty of identifying people of Syrian descent was often compounded when they turned out to be Muslim. A New Mexico family from Zahle named Hind, who raised sheep, were thought to be Hindus and were derogatorily called "Turco" and "Gypsy."[137] An old Ross, North Dakota, farmer described his transformation from "Syrian" to "Finlander," which, to the surrounding Scandinavians, was appropriately remote. The same farmer told of cooperation in the old days between Muslim and Christian Syrians, facilitated no doubt by a mutual lack of clergy. Their beliefs blended into an elemental monotheism:

> God is one that raises the sun and the moon. Isn't that right? I couldn't interpret it but put your fingers on it, see. Who let your fingernail grow? The one above, the good Lord. But they carry it too far—put Christ ahead of God. Number one is number one. We used to have Tom Danz and Abdullah Danz who were Christians, and they felt the same way and associated with the Muslims. When we were at an evening [affair], the Christians and Muslims all together *nil'ab waraq* [play cards], cuss like hell. But there's no need for partiality.[138]

The Syrian peddler-turned-farmer worked the hard soil as if the earth were a loom, stretching his seed along an invisible warp. But the Dakota Muslims generated their oddities. One of them was Joe Albert, who gained local fame as a bear wrestler. When the community was subjected to the Dust Bowl drought of the 1930s, a locust plague, and a horde of "army worms" that ate through fenceposts, many began to leave. But those who stayed witnessed something of a miracle at the hands of the visting imam from India:

> Remember that Bengali? They hadn't had rain here for weeks and everything was dry and dusty. He told us—this missionary from India—to come to church [i.e., the makeshift mosque], and we were going to get rain. He fascinated the heck out of me. And he prayed. There wasn't a cloud in the sky. And Ahmed Abdullah went home in a car and had a wreck with it on account of the storm. Half their chickens were drowned. I never forgot that. He preached at the theater, too. Either he had the weather checked way from Washington all the way down, or something.[139]

Christian, Druze, or Muslim, by the mid-1920s, most of the Syrians knew that, come hell or high water—like the Jewish tailor, the Irish pub owner, and the Japanese farmer—they were here in America to stay.

–THREE–

TRANSPLANTING THE FIG TREE: THE FIRST GENERATION ON AMERICAN SOIL (1924–1947)

B ecause of the restrictive quotas of 1924 and the worldwide financial depression, Syrian immigration to the United States was only a trickle between the two World Wars. From 1920 to 1930 only 8,253 Arabs entered the country, 2,933 of them Palestinians. From 1930 to 1940, the foreign-born Syrian population here actually declined, though entering Palestinians doubled (2,933 to 7,047), due to disturbances with Zionist settlers and the British in Palestine.

THE DEPRESSION AND THE SYRIAN AMERICANS

Among those inter-war immigrants was Sam Kanaan, whose father had come to Boston from Lebanon in 1888, returning to die during World War I. His young son witnessed cannibalism in Tripoli during the famine. Kanaan, told that he could pass as a US citizen if he fetched his father's papers from a trunk, took a steamer to Providence, Rhode Island, in 1928. He couldn't have come at a worse time. The country was sliding toward the Depression, and, as if by cruel reminder that the heyday of quick money and prosperity for the Lebanese peddler and entrepreneur was over, it was given to Kanaan to care for the poet Kahlil Gibran, who was dying of alcoholism:

> No work. I used to go to nightclub. I met Gibran. Well, he was a great guy. But the time I came people know Arabic. And he talk to me and the people play cards. He don't play no cards. He like a drink. He said to me, "Sit down here, you come from our country. Tell me, what's this and that." Twelve o'clock. One o'clock, everybody go home. And then the guy who own the club, he say, "Take him home." He used to live on Tyler; I live on Hudson Street. So I take him home. Too many times. He gave me a picture [of the Good Shepherd].

Kanaan described the food lines and lack of heat in Boston:

But I come in 1928… Can't get no job, no nothing. We used to stay by line about a mile. A lawyer, a doctor, in a line till we have coffee and a doughnut. Many times we get to end of line, no more left. Because there's too many in line. I have a hard time. We sleep in a room. Get up in the morning, water frozen in the pipe. We sleep in room, no heat, no nothing. We only get papers from the street to burn them up in the stove. And warm them up.[1]

Kanaan went back to Lebanon in 1933 because of pneumonia; a doctor had recommended a dry climate—Kanaan thought of California but felt it was better to go where his family was. The problem of employment, however, was the same as when he had left. There was simply not enough farmland for the extended family—when they did farm, it was only for two or three months. Kanaan also mentioned troubles with the French. When the American consulate called on him in 1936 in his village and said he had 24 hours to get back to the United States or lose his citizenship—in spite of an American accusation that he was a spy affiliated with a leftist "club" (the anti-French Kataʿib)—Kanaan came back. There was work in the United States. And in a quintessentially Lebanese statement, he exhorted, "Don't ever sit down and cry if you can move."

A Palestinian from Taybe who arrived in Providence in 1926 had quite a different depression story. Educated by American Quaker schools in Palestine, Shukri Khouri became a lawyer in the United States and was befriended by the Massachusetts state treasurer, Charles F. Hurley, who later became governor. Khouri helped in his election campaign and by the mid-thirties was appointed by Hurley to be assistant liquidation counsel for the state. At the same time that a Palestinian American was liquidating US banks in Boston for the governor, the British were liquidating the last sustained Palestinian resistance to their rule, during the general strike and revolt of 1936–1939. Khouri spoke out in an interview in 1937 with the *Worcester Telegraph*. When asked if he was attacked for views critical of Zionist aims in his homeland, he responded, breathing heavily after a long illness in his home in Chevy Chase, Maryland: "They didn't give me threats. I gave them threats!" There was hell to pay in the garment factories, however: "I attacked the senatorial committee that was sent from here to study the question of Zionism in Palestine. In fact, I accused them of being prejudiced, biased. That is what the Zionists resented so much. They were cutting [firing] Arab workers in their factories. Yes, our girls were working in dresses."[2]

Many among the most prosperous Syrians in America went broke. The millionaire Faour brothers—the first bankers from the community—lost a million dollars, lost their beautiful homes on Shore Road in Brooklyn, and went out of business. Others among the wealthier Syrians managed to hold on and even to help the American community at large during the hard times. Iser Tibshareny, for instance, had established in 1927 one of the first real estate and investment firms in central Arizona (many Lebanese peddlers had been attracted to Arizona in the 1890s mining boom). In the 1930s, when the town of Mesa was suffering from the Depression, Tibshareny showed "resourcefulness and humanness" in the way he handled commercial tenants. Instead of evicting them because of their inability to pay rent, he devised a lease plan, in which tenants paid a percentage of their income. According to one sociologist, "the plan helped soften the Depression blow and kept several merchants from leaving the area."[3] There were others who actually improved, testing their mettle against the hammer of pain and want. George Fauty, the immigrant from Egypt who worked his way up through Chase Manhattan Bank, found himself making $2,100 a year when the average was between $1,200 and $1,500 during the Depression. "I was very fortunate," he recalled, wiping the sweat off his head in a Brooklyn summer. "Like I say, I must be cloaked with the Holy Spirit."[4]

Others took advantage of the desperate climate to speculate and boldly advance a business interest. As the following story of a Brooklyn chauffeur who had started his own auto shop demonstrates, investments could be had in the worst areas of town during the Depression, with a kiss, a prayer, and not a little graft:

> I was just working. In the Depression, where there's no money, nothing.... So I went to New York—over there you could do anything and get away with it as long as you paid graft. I saw a Jewish fellow over there, Leon. I said, "Leon" (he was in with the politicians), "we have to pass those plans. What are we going to do to build the building? Because you gotta be 200 feet away from the church, school, or hospital in order to have gas tanks. What do you think it will cost me to have plans approved?" He says, "Five hundred dollars under the table." I said, "Okay, you go ahead." He went ahead and he got everything stamped approved. We went ahead with the building.

In addition to the courthouse across the street, there was also an Elks Club that operated as a speakeasy on Saturday nights. The Syrian went to his garage one night and found a mob:

> I can't believe it. I can't even go in the garage. Cars all over the street. All blocked up. Big Cadillacs, limousines, chauffeur driven, and everything else, from one street to another. The whole street is blocked. I took an ice pick! I took an ice pick and I just walked like this—you can't believe it—to all the tires! You could hear the air![5]

The ice-pick caper was just one example of the toughness, even meanness, that it took to navigate a successful business during the

Depression. But the auto shop owner—who had experienced starvation in Lebanon during the First World War—was not going to disappear from his spot on the earth now, not in Brooklyn. Here the law—malleable as it was—was on his side.

The tough grew soft befriending another Syrian—this one from outside Damascus—whose business in Brooklyn, Pyramid Embroidery, went bankrupt:

> People selling apple on the street. We couldn't do anything; we have to cover up and feed the family. Really, sometimes we haven't got a nickel to go on the subway. This was worse than the war for couple years. So we ask him [foreclosure broker], "If you are Christian, or not Christian, if you believe in God, we are a family of four brother and one sister. We got seven kids in the family. Just think twice before you do anything like that." He stopped. We asked him if he wanna sell the house, maybe we try to sell it to somebody to, you know, support us with the money. He was asking $15,000 for the house. We went down to Mike Malouf. He bought the house for us. Those days he have a good garage, have business, gasolines, sell tires. He make quite a lot.[6]

The Syrians' attitude toward President Franklin Roosevelt was universally good. Independent and entrepreneurial as they were, they admired his compassion for the downtrodden and his extended hand to the immigrant. Taxi Joe (Elias Joseph) of Woonsocket, Rhode Island, called Roosevelt "the father of our country" and contrasted him to Hoover: "He [Hoover] used to tell the people, 'If you wanna go back to your country, we'll pay your fare and put you on a boat.' Well, the people decided to go back. So Roosevelt took over. He says, 'Well, I need those people. Don't send them back! I want everybody to live.'"[7]

It was actually during the Depression that Maroun Haggar from Jazzine watched his fledgling pants business begin to grow. By 1929, the year of the crash, Haggar had 6,000 feet of floor space and employed 250 people in what was then called the Dallas Pant Manufacturing Company. Even as the country was barely beginning to recover, in June 1933 Haggar organized a "Prosperity Picnic," marching his employees down Main Street in Dallas singing, "Happy Days Are Here Again." In the midst of fifteen million unemployed nationwide, Haggar—later called by some the "General Patton of pants"—was hiring.[8]

A general storekeeper in Vicksburg, Mississippi, had more difficulty than Hagger in the Depression, though he offered everything from pants to river paddles. But he appreciated Americans' generosity and returned it. Native of Shekarn, Lebanon, Johnny Nosser pointed a finger skyward:

J. M. (Maroun) Haggar, Sr., at his desk in 1926 in the Sante Fe building in Dallas, Texas, where he started the Haggar men's slacks manufacturing firm. (The Haggar Company; courtesy of the University of Texas Institute of Texan Cultures)

The groceries in the store belong to the wholesaler, don't belong to me. I didn't have anything left. That's the history of the Depression for me. And many others like me. I was going to quit. I went to that wholesaler (I owed him $1,575). I said, "Mr. Luston, I'm going to quit before I eat all what you got in there, and they belong to you." He said, "Forget about it. John, you've been my good friend since 1924. You been a good customer. You been paying bills every time it's due. Where you wanna go? What you wanna do? Sleep on the street? You better stay where you are... Forget about this money you owe me at the present time." And sometimes I have two and a half, three dollars I'll pay on that bill. Oh God! I paid all that money to that man and we stayed in business and by 1939, everything in the store was mine. Faith in God get you on your feet! Friends![9]

Stores were sacred to the Syrians; the loss of them, or threat of loss, was a blow akin to sacrilege, though most were plucky enough to pick themselves up and start over again. One granddaughter of a Lebanese immigrant woman who ran a speakeasy during the Depression in Schenectady, New York, readily admitted that her favorite memory of childhood was time spent at "Nana's store." The grandmother herself clung to the place long after it had stopped turning a profit.

As Faith Latimer, daughter of the former Arab-American mayor of St. Paul, Minnesota, described it:

For years my father and uncles had been exasperated with Nana for not selling and "getting out of there." Nana and Grampa were getting older, robberies were becoming more frequent (it was ridiculously dangerous), and they could get along without the income. I am unclear why Nana resisted giving the store up for as long as she did. Was she afraid of leisure time, the way many old people are, who are used to hard work? Did she fear financial insecurity?[10]

The Syrians in America feared it, yes, especially after their initial financial successes in the New World peddling, weaving, selling over a counter. In October 1931, *Miraat al-Gharb*, the Arabic émigré newspaper published in New York, editorialized feverishly for a national Syrian relief committee—not for Lebanon and famine—but for the US Syrians in the Depression. Typically, the emphasis was on self-help, not welfare. The Syrian Ladies' Aid Society of New York City was distributing food and money to especially hard-hit Syrian families in the city. Benefits were given where oudists strummed and Syrian chanteuses sang to raise money. An organization of people from Aleppo—al-Kalemat—gave $1,291 from a benefit to the Aid Society. St. Nicholas' Young Men's Society gave half the proceeds of a *hafla*, or party, on October 17, 1931, to victims of the Depression.[11]

More was lost besides businesses. A surprisingly successful Melkite school in Rhode Island—the first in America—which had as many as 156 students enrolled to learn Arabic, closed down in 1934 after thirteen years of operation, a victim of the Great Depression.[12] The hard times effectively quashed what inclination there was in the first native-born generation to learn Arabic. It was difficult enough to eke out a paltry living from the unregenerate edifice of English-speaking America in broken English; it was impossible to do it in Arabic. Jobs were found by English. To Sam Kanaan—who wrote a memoir in meticulous Arabic script—writing Arabic in America was "like pissing in the wind."

America, however, took some solace at the onset of the Depression from poems by Mikhail Naimy. The very few he did in English were published in the *New York Times*.[13] In one of its last editorials, the *Syrian World* noted that national governments were having trouble "balancing their budgets," as were large corporations. But editor Salloum Mokarzel's greatest sadness was saved for "the most pathetic case... that of the small man, the one who through systematic savings and self-denials accumulated a small capital with which to open a shop, a store, or some other industrial undertaking." Out of work, he is "in a position of utter helplessness, for he is neither fit by training nor capable by former connections to find other means of earning a livelihood.... The Syrians fall mostly into the latter category."[14]

Thrift and "mutual helpfulness" might ease the small Syrian businessman's woes, but Mokarzel knew what he was talking about. In 1932, after seven years of publication, he printed the last issue of the *Syrian World*. With it passed the only nationwide vessel in English of the early Syrian intelligentsia, an inculcator of roots, a symbol of unity across all the Arabic journals whose points of view were scattered on Druze, Maronite, and Orthodox compasses. In many ways, the *Syrian World's* death was also the death of pan–Syrian-American culture. The Depression took away the cornerstone of ethnic pride. Once again, the Syrians were left to their own gregarious, protective, culturally solitudinous selves.

WORLD WAR II

Aref Orfalea, eighteen, was dreaming on the porch of his Cleveland, Ohio, home in 1942. The war had begun in Europe and he was restless, feeling his school days useless. Recently, he had fallen asleep in a movie theater and had slept soundly through both features into the night, managing—in his dreamy, slumped state—to avoid the detection of even the popcorn clean-up. He was rescued from his slumber by his mother, a former peddler from Zahle. Perhaps if she hadn't come he would have, like Rip Van Winkle, slept through the war. Aref left high school, as did so many young American boys, to test his courage in the crucible of battle. Hitler's Germany had to be stopped. And Aref's older brother had already joined the army and was stationed in Burma. No one ever likes being left behind by siblings—even if the destination is a kind of hell.

Aref would find himself jumping out of an airplane over Draguignan, in the controversial subsidiary D-Day landing in southern France called Operation DRAGOON. A prefatory night jump, Aref would say 40 years later, was the most terrifying experience of his life. Though ground resistance was surprisingly light (DRAGOON would be dubbed "the Champagne Campaign"), Aref strained himself carrying a 75-pound

Aref Orfalea of Cleveland, OH (right) with GI friend Billy Vance shortly after World War II. (Rose Orfalea)

radio over the Maritime Alps into Italy, sloshing through mud and cold. Later, attached to James Gavin's 82nd Airborne, Aref's 551st Parachute Infantry Battalion sustained 84 percent casualties (only 110 of 643 walked out) at the brutal Battle of the Bulge. At least 100 of the unit were killed, some fallen on the snow-packed earth or earlier hit in midair. Others, wounded, froze to death in Belgium's bad winter. Aref's own feet froze and threatened to become gangrenous. He was evacuated stateside, twenty years old. The war came to a close over the radio in his Camp Carson, Colorado, hospital room. Long after he died, 56 years later, the 551st received the Presidential Unit Citation from President Clinton for its extraordinary ordeal and heroism.

Because ethnic records were not kept, and since there were few Arab-American VFW groups (the John Gantus VFW in Los Angeles is still active), it is difficult to ascertain exact numbers. But it is a reasonable estimate that at least 30,000 GIs of Arab lineage fought for this country against the Axis powers. Judging by isolated records, it is likely that a greater percentage enlisted than in World War I—in one small Catholic parish in Woonsocket, Rhode Island, from 25 Syrian families, 29 more served, including nine sets of brothers.[15]

In fact, America's first World War II flying ace was Col. James Jabara. A native of Wichita, Kansas, and of Lebanese background, Jabara would later shoot down fifteen Russian MIGS in the Korean War to extend his top "ace" status into the 1950s (an "ace" is a pilot who downs more than five enemy aircraft). Jabara was virtually unknown by the Syrian community in the United States until his name was flashed across banner headlines in the *New York Times*. He was awarded two Distinguished Flying Crosses, and in 1950 he was named by the Air Force Association as its most distinguished aviator.[16]

Other young Syrians destined for fame aided the war effort in unusual ways. A young officer out of Dallas, Texas, where his father ran an interior decorating service in the Neiman-Marcus Building, was Najeeb Halaby. At Langley Air Force Base, Halaby became one of the first Americans to test the jet. These sound-barrier breakers that went to Mach I were very unstable in those days. A number of P-51s and P-46s lost their tails in dives, which caused the latter to be nicknamed "The Widowmaker."

Among the pilots Halaby instructed in the YP-59A, a new and ultimately unusable jet, was the American legend Charles Lindbergh. It was a humbling moment for the young Halaby to run his boyhood hero of the solo *Spirit of St. Louis* flight across the Atlantic into the grim, supersonic jet age. Lindbergh was filled with mixed emotions, too; he had not been a fan of America's entry into the war. He had been, in fact, an isolationist and pacifist, who was disliked by Roosevelt. But Halaby called Lindbergh, "an echo of Da Vinci."

In January 1952, Maj. James Jabara (center) explains to Capt. Eddie Rickenbacker (left) and Gen. Hoyt B. Vandenberg how he shot down six Russian MIGs over Korea. (Federation Herald, and Immigration History Research Center)

Halaby almost lost his life when testing a captured Messerschmidt near Newark. It was one of the few planes capable of reaching 500 mph in level flight, and he had a premonition of disaster on entering the cockpit and not being able to read the German panels. The brakes were terrible and the steering was "as agile as a Panzer tank." He lined up on a runway notorious for crashes, pointing straight at the city of Newark. Soon he was close to stalling out right over downtown Newark:

> Suddenly it hit me: on a German airplane, that tab switch had to be reversed. Instead of pushing forward to get the nose down, maybe it should be pulled back—the exact opposite from the American tab controls. I pressed the tab switch back instead of forward and the nose obediently came down a split second before I would have stalled out.[17]

Halaby's glorious moment as an aviator, however, came just before the end of the war in the Lockheed Shooting Star, the nation's first operational jet fighter. On May 1, 1945, Halaby took off from Muroc AFB, California, and arrived five hours and forty minutes later in Patuxent, Maryland—the first transcontinental jet flight in US history. He had become a Lindbergh of the shock wave, a soloist of the American land mass, rather than the cold, dark Atlantic on which his forebears had come in ships. Perhaps it was emblematic that now the firstborn generation Syrians were in the United States not only to stay but also to lead.

Leadership could take odd forms. Pvt. William Ezzy, a Syrian GI, took experience gained working in textiles with the Maloufs of Salt Lake City and led with needle and thread:

> When we were in Kiska [Alaska] we had to detonate a lot of
> unexploded bombs; because of the tundra, they didn't detonate.
> And many times with the demolition squads the shrapnel would
> fly up. We lived in tents. And as I was the only one on the island
> with a fabric background I had to go around and patch the tents…
> I got the name of Omar the Tentmaker.

One of the more down-to-earth memoirs of combat was written by Lt. Louis LaHood of Peoria, Illinois. He flew thirty combat missions—five over Berlin—in the bombardment that "softened up" the German war machine before the Normandy landing in June 1944. None of his crew was hurt in these missions, and he later received the Distinguished Flying Cross.[18] LaHood's log descriptions of thirty B-17 bomber missions over Germany, France, and Belgium testify to both the steely detachment and the nervousness that come into the mind of a bomber pilot dropping so many thousand pounds of destruction:

> Berlin again! Guess Doolittle wants the place blown off the map.
> But I wish he'd come along with us some time. Instead of sitting
> on his fanny and telling all the people that he bombed Tokyo,
> Rome and now Berlin…This was the third raid to Berlin in four
> days. I was so damned tired that I couldn't fly formation over
> fifteen minutes at a time. I thought my arms were going to fall off
> a couple of times (Mission #12, Berlin, March 9).
>
> This Cherbourg is a flak house if I ever saw one. In about two
> minutes they had hit about seven engines and one boy got a direct
> hit and went down out of control. Nobody got out of the ship and
> he hit the ground going straight down! Our ship had several holes
> in the wings, fuselage, and a tail. Nobody dropped their bombs on
> target. I feel like an old man at 25 (Mission #29, Dessau, May 27).[19]

Back at home, the Syrians worried and prayed like other American families that their children would come through the terrors of battle safely. A Syrian Red Cross drive was held on February 13, 1944, at the St. George Hotel. A fourth War Bonds drive of the Syrian–Lebanese–Palestinian Committee (interesting that by then the Syrian identity was now splayed to include separate Lebanese and Palestinian identities) was aiming for a $2 million goal. Apparently, the community in Brooklyn had already raised millions for the war effort and was complimented officially by the Treasury Department. George Hamid, the circus impresario and owner of Atlantic City's Million-Dollar Pier and Steel Pier, raised $300,000 as chairman of the Army–Navy Emergency Relief Society from the theater industry alone. He was also appointed by the Navy Relief Society to be general chairman of outdoor amusements.

First Lt. Louis LaHood of Peoria, Illinois, pilot of the B-17 Flying Fortress
"Black Magic," lost a propeller after a bombing raid over Schweinfurt, Germany,
March 24, 1944. (Louis LaHood)

One Syrian community published a regular magazine about happenings on the home and war fronts that was sent to GIs around the globe. Published privately in Brooklyn, *Greetings from Home* was put out irregularly in 1944 and 1945; issues are still cached in musty trunks by ex-GIs from Brooklyn. It tells of a "One Man Service Center" on 293 Henry Street in downtown Brooklyn, and of Michael Shaheen, whose café-store on Atlantic Avenue was a meeting place for draft inductees before the war. Shaheen and his wife kept up a steady correspondence with their "Write-a-Letter Club" to the GIs, out of their store filled with the odors of Arabic coffee and *baqlawa*, the diamond-shaped sweet.

Gloria Amoury's efforts—probably the best in the publication— culminated in a long poem that fronted the Christmas 1944 edition sent overseas. Unabashedly sentimental—and not a little warning that Penelope was being wooed ("Fresh roses from a suitor fat and gray")—the poem contains stock figures from a Syrian family home in America that would touch the right chords of GIs with that heritage: "It's Christmas in a Brooklyn home. / The soft Turkish rugs muffle the sound of the restless feet."

Sally Mansour and Selma Daas penned an endearing satire on Arabic accents that would remind GIs of their older generation back home in a "Dear Fuad" letter. An excerpt:

> How you like this new work you doing? To me it sound a little danger, Fuad, but of course, I don't tell Mama that. You remember how she always afraid when you drive our automobile—how I'm going tell her now you driving ten-ton truck? Dinchu worry about it, baby. I tell her is only—*shu ismuh* [what's his name]— jeep.... Don't forget wear your raincoat and rubbers whens rain.

Some of the more interesting reading in *Greetings* was provided by GIs in the field. Cpl. Thomas Hattab wrote from a South Pacific battle zone about first donning his helmet, "M-l, Helmet, Steel": "All was Stygian darkness. I lifted it up, and staring back at me were two burning eyes peering from a cavernous pit. I put it away for the rest of that trip. The shock was too great."

Although the Syrian community did not have celebrated conscientious objectors, at least one chap, whose relatives came from Kabb Elias in Lebanon, entered war, as did Hemingway before him, as an ambulance driver and came away with conclusions about modern warfare as dreadful and perhaps even more nihilistic than Papa Hemingway's. Vance Bourjaily's first novel, *The End of My Life*, was published in 1947, a year before his friend Norman Mailer, published his own landmark first novel, *The Naked and the Dead*. Mailer's antagonist, Croft, slogs through the fetid swamps of the Pacific campaign against the Japanese. Joseph Heller satirized the bombing mission of American forces over Italy in *Catch-22*; *The Young Lions* by Irwin Shaw dealt with the European front. But Bourjaily chose Syria and Lebanon as his war setting because he had gone there with the Ambulance Corps.

Bourjaily treats the Middle East with empathy, sometimes awe, though he is never patronizing. About Beirut's poorer sections he says:

> Most of them were Moslems back in there, and in there were their stores, their restaurants, their coffee shops. It was Hell's Kitchen, the Lower East Side, the heart of the city. There were stories of soldiers who had gone into the district and never come back: others of those who had crawled back, robbed and beaten.

Bourjaily characterizes the Arabic-speaking people that the hero, Skinner, and his company meet as "warm people, with a long tradition of hospitality. They offer enmity where enmity is offered them; they respond to friendliness with friendliness; they are, except when angered, or when one tampers with their customs or ceremonies, humorous, humble and wise."[20]

One of Skinner's best friends on his grim adventure is Benny, a Jewish American who is altogether immersed in the concept of a Jewish state brewing in Palestine:

> Benny is a lonely guy. All evangelists are lonely; everyone who believes something as zealously as Benny believes is shutting off parts of himself from other human beings. And, since the people who share the belief are similarly cut off, he needs people who will respect without agreeing or disagreeing; people whose minds work differently, who like him without reference to his central belief.[21]

Bourjaily finds war absurd but natural. The ending of his novel is even darker than that of *Catch-22*. Yossarian had a life raft at least; Skinner has only a cell to which he walks, "impatiently," after a nurse he has taken to the front is killed by a shell. It would be wrong to identify Bourjaily's vision as the "Arab-American" response to World War II though it is the only World War II novel set in the Middle East. But in its vision of the war as evidence of the chaos of being, in its refusal to see the war nationalistically, it has the internationalism that marks great novels, and also reflects something ancient in the Syrian consciousness. It is also one of the few novels on American bookshelves that does not paint the Arab world on a moral level lower than our own.

Making a Name: First-Generation Notables

The generation of Syrian Americans who were the first to be born on American soil were growing up in the 1920s when US courts were finally determining that Syrians were not Chinese (and that Chinese were not subhuman). This first generation came of age during the Depression and World War II—many of them fought for the United States in the battles for Europe and Japan. It was for this generation, too—perhaps the most Americanized of all—that Arabic was a tongue whispered in warmth or shouted when a glass was broken at the dinner table. It was not the language that made friends or secured work, and it certainly was not useful in assembling a field rifle in the army. In many ways, the first generation—now senior citizens—was the most assimilated of all. They embraced the Kiwanis, Rotary Clubs, Masonic orders, PTAs. They were full-fledged members of their church boards and helped enhance the reputation of their mosques. They held fast to the Eastern religious life of their ancestors.

I interviewed many first-generation Syrian and Lebanese Americans but was intrigued by the emergent notables of that group. They were the ones who, in fact, put the name "Syrian" or "Lebanese" into the American vocabulary before there was much consciousness at all of the Arab world other than as a place of sand, strife, and belly dancers. In some ways, since their efforts at Americanization were at the highest levels of society and their chosen fields, the images they projected were as determinate, and probably more so, of American perception of Syrian values and beliefs as those of the rank-and-file themselves. Lacking unity and punch in groups, each notable or celebrity carried a lot of ethnic weight. Some were conscious of it, some not, some quite willing to utilize it for gain, some for philanthropy, and some tried their best to disregard it.

Danny Thomas' home hangs over the San Diego Freeway from a craggy point in Beverly Hills. On the other side of the freeway a flowered hillside hides Los Angeles' largest dumpsite. When I was younger, Thomas' was a home that people would point out to me—"There's Uncle Tannous." Of course. Uncle Tannous was Hans Conried on *Make Room for Daddy*, the family television series that lasted eleven years and went into at least nine seasons of reruns. Danny Thomas was his fictional nephew. I wanted to find the real Uncle Tannous. And on a spring day in 1983 I did.[22]

Villa Rosa's wrought-iron front gate opened with an electrical command from inside the house. The noisy Open Sesame barely gave enough time to note the Latin inscription of the coat of arms: *Beatus qui intelligit cur natus sit*. Blessed is he who understands why he was born. On either side of the gate as I entered were lighted kerosene lanterns. Behind, cars with passengers holding Hollywood maps idled, like sharks circling a diver whose air hose is conspicuously tangled.

The front doors had knockers of the theatrical comic face. A maid opened a door for me as I rapped with the face of laughter. I was taken to a huge den with a circular card table ladened with cups of cigarettes and nuts. As I sat down, I became aware of piped-in music; for the duration of our interview mild tunes filtered behind us.

I somehow expected Danny Thomas to be in a bathrobe, as "Daddy" on a Saturday morning, holding a cup of coffee (Maxwell House, Brim). Instead, a man wearing jeans, a western belt with large buckle, a demure sportshirt, and a two-day growth of beard almost stumbled into the room. He was about 5' 11", slender, and looped a large cigar through his fingers. He dabbed it gently into an oblong copper ashtray to break the beginning of an ash. As he came over to shake hands, squinting his warm eyes through glasses, the famed hooked nose seemed to measure me. My impulse was to squawk: "Welcome, Uncle Tannous!" I felt at home in the clasp of Amos Jacobs of Toledo who grew up in an impoverished family of nine children, raised, in fact, by his aunt and uncle. Amos created a stage name from the names of his oldest brother (Danny) and youngest brother (Thomas). The fusion made him his brothers' keeper.

It was the infant Danny—Amos Jacobs' brother—who was responsible in a way for St. Jude's Children's Hospital being built. A few months old, little Danny was bitten in his crib by a rat and later went into convulsions. (The Jacobs family lived over a pool hall then.) The actor's mother, who had the proverbial Lebanese immigrant mother's devotion to the Blessed Mother (Adhra'), on her knees in prayer promised that if her child was saved she would beg alms for a year for the poor. He was, and she did.

There was the sense about Danny Thomas, even at age 68, that he didn't quite believe the opulence that surrounded him. I found him quite serious in our conversation, cracking few jokes, and vulnerable, even anguished. Arab Americans who don't know each other often introduce the topic of Lebanon as if it were still a resort. Strangers, all the Lebanese diaspora are travel agents for a place that they know has been completely riddled by violence. "I never saw such civilization in my life as they got in Lebanon," he intoned, taking his seat at the card table trimmed with Arabic calligraphy. He took not one pine nut or cigarette the whole time.

In Beirut, gorgeous women lying on the hulls of the speedboats in their bikinis and the great French Casino du Liban is the biggest gambling casino in the world—it's all marble. It's marvelous... I went in 1962; God, they went crazy. They went nuts. Oh! *Allah yarhamu* [God rest his soul], Emil Bustani was my host. He was to be the next president, but he died in a plane crash in the Mediterranean. His bones are still down there; they never retrieved them. Anyway, when I went up to Bsharri they had big signs in Arabic and English, *Bsharri Welcomes Her Son.* It was just beautiful.

Thomas sprinkled Arabic throughout our conversation in an accent not different from any of my relatives. Unlike Yiddish, however, Arabic isn't familiar to Americans. "My vocabulary in Arabic is not small," he asserted; he used it for Arab crowds.

Born in 1915 in Deerfield, Michigan, Amos Jacobs was the son of Shadid Ya'qub of Bsharri, who came to the United States in 1901 after witnessing Ottoman Turk atrocities. Ya'qub eventually ended up in Toledo because many Maronite Bsharraniyah were there—the colony was founded by an M. H. Nassar, who, according to Thomas, "had a dry goods store and also a produce stand. He used to grubstake those guys who would come."

And where did Danny Thomas get the inspiration for Uncle Tannous? Thomas smiled and blew a thin stream of smoke upward: "That's my uncle Tony—Taniyus in Arabic. Funny man, oh, yeah. Beautiful man. Great sense of humor; he loved to laugh." Uncle Tony ran a boardinghouse and cafe in Toledo and actually raised the waif Amos Jacobs.

Like so many Syrians coming over in the First Wave immigration, Thomas' maternal grandfather was turned back at Marseilles because of trachoma. At Ellis Island, his father had to make sense of his name in a hurry. It went from Ya'qub to Jacobs in the flash of a hand. "My mother," Thomas said, "is Tawq and father's family is actually Karuz. They're both prominent families. They've had members in parliament since they had a parliament in Lebanon. Habib Karuz just retired as minister of tourism. Gibran Tawq is in the parliament now—a handsome boy, a bright boy. I think he'll make president one day."

"But what of Ya'qub?" I asked.

"We stopped with one of the grandfathers called Ya'qub. You know, every other generation used to take the name of the great-grandfather and delete the word *ibn*, for some reason. Actually, by this time our family should have been Boulos, because he's the last great-grandfather that I know about."

I was getting dizzy—Karuz, Boulos, Ya'qub, Jacobs, and now Thomas. Which was it?

"Well, it's *ibn, ibn, ibn,* that's all," Thomas retorted, as if that made perfect sense. "Hell, my uncle Tony was known as 'Stambuli' because his father was the first ever to go to Istanbul. Ibn Stambuli. So when he came to this country he was Ibn Stambuli and va-va-voom—they forgot the ibn and he became Stambuli. My father's name in Bsharri was actually Abou Miflih. Miflih was the first born. Dad named us all with the Arabic phonetic 'Meem'—"Miflih, Milhim, Majid, Mufrij, and Mizyid."

"How did you go from Mizyid to Amos Jacobs?" I asked, reeling.

"My American name was Amos Jacobs," Thomas said without a pause. "Amos Joseph Alfonso Jacobs."

"Your father changed it."

"He didn't change anything. We were all born here."

"But his last name… "

"His name is Shadid Ya'qub—Shadid Karuz Gemayel Ya'qub. *Ibn, ibn, ibn, ibn!* Ya'qub was out of the Bible—Jacob. They just translated it. Yousef is Joseph. Taniyus is Anthony."

Mixed with the muzak, I could almost hear "Who's on first, What's on second, and I-Don't-Know's on third."

Thomas spoke fondly of his father, a peddler who sold his wares from farmhouse to farmhouse. "He was smart," he smiled. "He didn't carry it on his back. He put it in a cart." When I mentioned the story of my grandmother Nazera blessing her own water to sell as Holy Water, he sang out, in Arabic: "*Ya 'ayni! Ya akhi!* [My eye! My brother!]."

At times, Thomas was accused of being chauvinistic toward Lebanon and ignoring other Arab states and causes. But he poked fun at those who forget that everyone was once called Syrian: "Funny, we all say, even staunchly, 'We're Lebanese! We're Lebanese! Remember that.' And then, 'Pass the Syrian bread, give me the Syrian cheese!'"

In 1974, Thomas made his second trip to Lebanon just before the country descended into a savage civil war. He did a benefit for the al-Salib al-Ahmar (Red Cross) for Madame Franjiyah, the president's wife. A cover photo from *Middle East* was framed on the wall of his study. I asked him what had changed between the 1962 and 1974 trips in Lebanon.

"They were building more," he mused, then halted, perhaps thinking of the incipient destruction. "Also, I noticed that the refugee situation was closer to the city now, on the ride from the airport, whereas before they were on the sides of the roads. I really felt for them and so did all of our people. They entertained us—the various dancers and singers were Palestinians in all the places we went to. We slipped 'em a few hundred dollars, couple hundred here, couple hundred there. We had to look like the land of milk and honey!"

I brought up an incident my father had told me about at a convention in Ohio years back where a cousin of ours, Henry George, had witnessed a Maronite priest stand up and attack Danny Thomas. He remembered it immediately, "Youngstown," he mused, his chin wrinkling. "That was the Syrian–Lebanese situation. We established ALSAC (American Lebanese–Syrian Associated Charities) in 1957. It has to be 1958. I knew there were the people who were die-hard Lebanese—some in the eastern states refused to join ALSAC because the word 'Syrian' was in it. So I was bringing that point up, 'Don't forget. We were all Syrians when they came here. There was no Lebanon.' And this priest jumped up. Oh, he was livid. It was the very beginning of my speech and it loused up everything. But we finally won him back."

I wondered what the priest's name was. Thomas demurred: "He died. *Allah yarhamu, dashshiruh* [God rest his soul, let him be]."

The idea of starting a hospital for children with so-called incurable diseases is a bit of folktale among Hollywood philanthropists and among certain Arab Americans, as well. Thomas described it many times. In 1940 he was working a supper club called the Club Morocco in Detroit, where he had just met and married Rosemarie Mantell, an Italian American singer. A baby was on the way (Marlo Thomas), and the fledgling showman was struggling to buy groceries, enough so that his wife suggested he go into the grocery business. During a time filled with "an agony of indecision," something happened. He described it in a publication of Norman Vincent Peale's: "On Tuesday night a man came into the Club Morocco. He was celebrating something. His pockets were filled with little cards that he was handing out to people as he tried to tell them about an incredible thing that had just happened to him."[23] The man's wife had been miraculously cured of cancer. The next day Thomas went to church and when he reached into his pocket to make a donation, he found the card of St. Jude, patron saint of the hopeless, or "The Forgotten Saint." It was then he promised that if St. Jude "would help me find some clear course in my life" he would build him a shrine. His career took off, but it wasn't until the 1950s in New York that he had a dream that reminded him of his promise: a boy injured in a car accident who bled to death with people looking on. It took ten years to raise the money but St. Jude's Children's Research Hospital opened its doors in 1963.

It was in raising the money that Thomas learned some hard facts about the Lebanese–Syrians in the United States. A few helped out enormously. Thomas credits Mike Tamer of Indianapolis as the guiding force of ALSAC. Al Joseph helped in Chicago. "But we couldn't get the masses," Thomas admitted. "We could only get those that understood what we were trying to do. I went all over the country. I said, by our deeds we are going to resurrect the dead of our grandfathers and grandmothers who came here and fought language and customs barriers. They died and are buried in western cemeteries in a land strange to them. They came here and made possible our birth in the United States and educated us and many of us have succeeded. We're denying our heritage by allowing them to die and never to be known. 'By our deeds they shall be known.' In

Arabic, I said, '*Mnerfa al-mawta min al-qabr* [We can raise the dead from the tomb]!' Well, they starting firing salutes to me in New Jersey, New York, going crazy. God—the Messiah had come! I said to Mike Tamer, 'This is it, pal, this is beautiful. This is gonna really go.' Two weeks after I left they forgot I was there."

The experience left Thomas with this sober conclusion, "On an individual basis many people of our heritage have contributed much to their own community, their state, and even to the country. On a cooperative basis, taking in the entire population they have done nothing. I tried with ALSAC to make them all come in and say, 'This great institution of pediatric research is ours.' I still do it in spite of them. It is being done in their name." St. Jude's $400 million budget is funded by corporations and a few dedicated philanthropists, many Arab American, those with names like Joseph, Jamail, Coury, Maykel, Ayoub, Harris, Haggar, Othman, Maloof, and Karam. No child pays for treatment at St. Jude's. The hospital is free.

Thomas's first tips in comedy came from watching Abe Reynolds, a Yiddish comic, play a burlesque in Toledo at which Thomas sold soda pop. "Reynolds," he recalled, "was a funny man, never said hell or damn on the stage, sang parodies, and told stories apropos the song he was going to sing, which was a kind of modus operandi for me, which I don't do anymore. I mean, parodies. The ethnic comics were prevalent in those days—the Italian, the Irish, what they called 'the Southern Negro,' of course the Yiddish—and they were funny. They were funny making fun of themselves, which I think all minorities have to learn to do in order to survive. You make fun of the tragedy at hand." Which Thomas did, calling his 1951 sheet music booklet of songs "The Wailing Lebanese."

Rosemarie Thomas interrupted us, questioning why her husband had placed a map of Lebanon where he did. "I didn't want to lose it, sweetheart," he responded. "And I know we'll lose it." She showed him a few custom-made shirts and Thomas nodded amiably, cigar poised, but balked. "Those aren't my fronts!" his voice raised with alarm. Rose left, mumbling something about the collars.

We discussed the nature of comedy and comedians Danny had known through the years. "We have a rule of thumb," he nodded. "Show me a man in trouble and I'll show you a funny man. Not catastrophic trouble. But trouble. Charlie Chaplin was a great exponent of that. People have to relate to you. They can associate their problem with yours and you kind of solve theirs. And you laugh as you go." He went down a list of the greats. W. C. Fields—"An angry man." Edgar Buchanan—"Master of the slow burn. The slow burn was a big part of my career. When I did the flat tire and no jack stories. Slow burn. Anticipation, which is never as good or bad as consummation when your mind conjures up oh so much more than what's there at the end."

Rosemarie Thomas entered again with her husband's shirts, some of whose collars were frayed and needed mending. The comedian and his wife discussed the size of the collars in what seemed to be an old duet of, well, trouble. Finally Thomas said, "Honey, you gonna barge in and out like this all day?" Rosemarie said she had a lot of work to do. "Oh, my goodness, you're a busy lady," he flipped his eyebrows up, shaking his head. "She's so efficient, my wife. Drives me crazy. Can't stand efficient people. I'm a procrastinator. I don't do it until it has to be done."

Danny Thomas was accused by some Arab Americans of being "soft" on Israel, of not standing up for the suffering in the Arab world. In 1982, Thomas did get involved narrating a film called *To Lebanon with Love* by George Otis of High Adventure Ministry, an evangelist who operated out of southern Lebanon in collusion with Israel and its proxy army there then under Maj. Saad Haddad. It backfired. Thomas was stunned at the furor it caused. A woman in Los Angeles wrote a letter accusing him of being against his heritage, and the then director of the American-Arab Anti-Discrimination Committee, James Zogby, wrote a letter to him that Thomas called "scathing."

One year later, Danny Thomas was on stage for the ADC and others at the Kennedy Center as MC of a symphony concert for the victims of the war. He read excerpts of poems by Kahlil Gibran. During our interview, he expressed many views on Israel's invasion of Lebanon, the Sabra and Shatila massacres, the PLO, Yasir Arafat, the Phalange, but he literally begged me not to print them, standing up at one point and exclaiming, "Don't you know? My horror is that I can't take sides!" He meant that he couldn't compromise his efforts on behalf of the children at St. Jude's.

Thomas said, "We all did things on the quiet… spoke up for Lebanon, for its sovereignty. We are still doing it; President Reagan has been a friend." As for hopeless causes, he agreed that the Palestinians were the primary ones in the Middle East: "Every night on my knees I pray for them. They gotta give 'em a country, where they can govern themselves."

Danny Thomas returned to stories. "Like my son says to me, 'Dad, all the stories you tell about the old days with your parents and your uncle and your aunt and the tough times and the fun times. What am I gonna tell my kids? I was born in Beverly Hills? My parents got me a brand new car when I was sixteen?' I said, 'What do you want from me? Tell them about their grandfather!'"

This one popped out a laugh. And, as if on cue, Thomas went into Uncle Tannousism playing two voices: "To him everything in Lebanon was greater than here. 'Oh, we got dat deere. We got better.' 'You play golf?' 'Whaddya mean, sure I blay.' 'What do you shoot?' 'Whaddya mean what do I shoot?' 'You good?' 'Yeah, very good. We

Danny Thomas, circa 1976 (Aramco World Magazine).

got over there golf.' 'What do you shoot—in the 70s?' He said, 'More!' '80s?' 'More!' He got up to 120. Thought that the higher the score the better. 'More!' *Kull shay* (everything) over there bigger. The watermelon is that big, and the grapes are like that, a woman's shoulder couldn't come in the door. Everything was larger than life. And the water was ice cold, you couldn't put your finger in it for ten seconds, which was true back then. Everything he says is true." Perhaps there is more truth to an Uncle Tannous than a Danny Thomas. Perhaps our fictions define us.

If laughs rode on the stories told by Danny Thomas, it may not be too much to say that the state of the nation rode on the stories written—sometimes ten a day—by Helen Thomas (no relation), White House correspondent for more than half a century with United Press International, an icon to American journalists, the young and seasoned alike.

Hired by UPI in the days of Franklin Roosevelt, Helen Thomas was often the first to ask a question during presidential press conferences (AP and UPI alternate the privilege), and always, due to seniority, she was the last to speak: "Thank you, Mr. President." Presidents from Camelot to Contragate have often cringed as she stood, dark hair closely coifed, coal-black eyes steady on her notes, a nasal voice cutting through the room. Sam Donaldson of ABC News said of her, "I think she's the best. A lot of us have learned how to ask questions from watching Helen. I'm pretty well able to hold my own... to get the attention of the White House. But when push comes to shove, I defer to Helen."[24]

As a straight news journalist, she was one of the best, acknowledged by many milestones and awards: the first woman to be named White House bureau chief for a major wire service; the first woman officer of the National Press Club; the first woman admitted to Washington's prestigious Gridiron Club; and the first woman recipient (in 1984) of the National Press Club's Fourth Estate Award (Theodore White, James Reston, Eric Sevareid, and Walter Cronkite have preceded her). Helen Thomas is polite, cogent, direct. No embellishment, rather concision. She has, in fact, asked for only one word to be etched on her tombstone, "Why?" A reporter in the afterlife, no doubt.

As for her background, she does little to hide her relishing of it. Jackie Kennedy Onassis once called Thomas and her then AP rival Fran Lewine the "harpies," and thought they were of Spanish descent. Thomas set her straight—they were Arab and Jewish, respectively. She eats most evenings at Mama Ayesha's Calvert Café, a quaint little Middle Eastern restaurant next to a bus rest stop run by Palestinian immigrants from Jerusalem who came to Washington, DC, in 1950 during the Second Wave of Arab-American immigration. She had a special affection for Ayesha Howar, the ancient founder of the Calvert Café, whom she affectionately called "my second mother." Ayesha often read Helen's fortune in an overturned coffee cup's grounds and "her predictions often hit the bull's eye."

No doubt the eyebrows of Mama Ayesha raised in 1983, when Helen stood up to ask the first question of President Ronald Reagan about vigilante activity by Jewish settlers against Arabs on the West Bank. It caught Reagan off-guard. He had not heard about these shootings, he said. The admission made headlines. Twenty years later, on January 9, 2003, Helen Thomas challenged George W. Bush's White House spokesman Ari Fleischer, "You said the President deplored the taking of innocent lives. Does that apply to all innocent lives in the world?" Fleischer responded, "I refer specifically to a horrible terrorist attack on Tel Aviv." Helen replied in her blistering follow-up, "Why does he want to drop bombs on innocent Iraqis?"

Since Ayesha was born in Jerusalem, and since the Calvert Street Café hosted Helen's wedding reception, it seemed natural to conduct our interview at Mama Ayesha's, where Arabic music clomped a *darabukka* and clinked castanets in the background, and Mama herself hunched over the phone as if waiting for a call from God. Helen suggested the place, in fact. It is right down the street from her condominium. She came with a friend, Joanie Rashid, the daughter of a director of St. Jude's Hospital, Bud Rashid.

Helen greeted me, eyes warm as the strongest Arabic coffee, teeth stained by the same. She asked me—good reporter switching the interview around—about myself and the book. As she motioned to the

Ayesha Howar (right) at her Calvert Café with Helen Thomas, circa 1970s (Harry Naltchayan)

waiter for *mazza*, she asserted that on Middle East issues "Eisenhower showed more courage than any president. In the end none of them have been able to call a spade a spade."[25] It reminded me of a remark made by the chief aide to the House Foreign Affairs Subcommittee on the Middle East in the midst of the invasion of Lebanon in 1982. When asked what would move the House to cut arms to stop the invasion, Mike Van Dusen said, "Concentration camps for the Palestinians." "There's your lead for the book," Helen lit up.

Helen Thomas was born in Winchester, Kentucky, on August 4, 1920, to Mary and George Thomas, Lebanese immigrants of a Tripoli shipbuilding family. After working as a peddler, her father moved the family to Detroit in 1924 and opened a little grocery store. Of her Detroit neighborhood in the 1920s of Germans and Italians, with blacks in an outer ring, she said, "My first awareness of being different was in kindergarten where everyone was blonde and blue-eyed. I felt I was dropped from another planet. They wanted to make you feel you weren't 'American.' It was only after World War II that Americans discovered there were 'people' living elsewhere."

"We were called 'garlic eaters,'" she smiled, tasting some Syrian bread and eggplant dip. With such a big brood of nine kids, eating was "a convivial sport." She laughed, reminiscing, "We were alive! Every dinner table was a mass argument. We played off each other, fed off each other. Big families are a brawl. We brought our interests from all over town and the country. It was inspirational. But by the time nine kids were there it was kind of out of hand..."

For her parents, as for many immigrants, "education was the Holy Grail." Helen was enjoined to achieve—she wasn't pressured to marry as a young woman. (Helen married at 51 to AP rival correspondent Doug Cornell.) Whether or not it was the shipbuilding and seafaring heritage of her Tripolitan ancestors, "freedom for us was far more than for most Arab-American families," she asserted. So Helen took a burning desire to make something of her life to Wayne State University, with a decision to pursue journalism.

From the early years in Detroit's Arab community she also took two other things: a sensitivity for the outcast, the one without a voice, and a sense of the sacredness of life. When I asked her for her favorite "Arab" gesture she responded by raising her hands upward, eyes in supplication to the ceiling of Mama Ayesha's. Throughout the interview, Helen Thomas would punctuate remarks with a *nashkur Allah*, thanks to God. "God is running through everything all the time in Arab parlance," she smiled. She remembered her mother's *quna* (icon) fronted by a burning wick floating on oil as a guiding light of her childhood.

She admitted that when she was called "foreigner" in Detroit schools she came home crying: "But you stayed the course. You had your life. I was made aware of prejudice at an early age, which I never forgot all my life and that's why I'm a liberal. I was hardly mutilated, but I was deeply impressed. I spent the rest of my life fighting discrimination."

In 1942, during the war, Helen traveled to the nation's capital seeking her fortune. Her first job was hostessing at a restaurant; then she landed copy girl work at the now defunct *Washington Daily News* for $17 a week. After a year fetching coffee for other reporters she was laid off, a blow that almost propelled her back to Detroit. "Who the hell wants to get dismissed?" she asked. "But every knock is a boost. They did me a big favor, as far as I'm concerned."

They certainly did. Soon she joined United Press (now UPI) for $24 a week and for twelve years rose before the sun at 5:30 AM to fill the Washington news ticker with stories and to do local radio. Fifty years later, the "super ego" of the White House press corps, according to *New York Times* correspondent Steve Weiser, Helen was still getting to work earlier than anyone, usually about 7:30 AM.

Helen Thomas' first glimpse inside the White House was at the 1944 Christmas party by invitation of Franklin and Eleanor Roosevelt. "The presidency awed me, but presidents do not." She told one reporter, "I think that presidents certainly have the toughest job in the world, but I don't have a bit of sympathy for them. They asked for it to the tune of millions of dollars, and to the pain of their families and their friends. So I think it's toe-to-toe. Presidents should know when they get into the White House that they have to be accountable."[26]

Helen's favorite White House was the Kennedys'. She makes it clear in her autobiography that she had an eye for the inseam of Camelot, a way of picking out the hidden tension between Jackie and Jack. When John Kennedy, Jr., was born, Helen caught JFK by the sleeve and asked him if he wanted his son to grow up to be president. The president paused and said, "I just want him to be all right." One of her favorite JFK insights is: "If we cannot end our differences, we can at least make the world safe for diversity." When he died the victim of a crazed assassin in Dallas, his UPI shadow mourned: "I don't think anything in my years at the White House can compare to the death of Kennedy. I still feel the pain of his death ... like a death in the family, a personal loss."[27]

Helen remembered a luncheon in the Blue Room of the Johnson White House during the Vietnam War when the black singer Eartha Kitt shocked everyone by standing up and crying out, "You send the best of this country off to be shot and maimed. They rebel in the street. They will take pot... and they will get high. They don't want to go to school because they're going to be snatched off from their mothers to be shot in Vietnam." Helen called it "one of the most dramatic moments I have ever observed in the White House."[28]

Nixon was a reporter's president. His darkness made glistening news. Helen devoted the largest section in her book to him. Helen saw it all, reporting as the government unraveled and official after official resigned or was fired. She followed Nixon to the Middle East, where she found it a tremendous irony that several million Egyptians danced for him while several million Americans were holding their noses. Just before the end in July 1974, when Helen checked into a motel in Laguna Beach, California, near the summer home of Nixon, the owner said, "This is your last trip, isn't it?" She thought to herself in Arabic, *Maktub*, "It is written."

Helen sat back from reminiscing, and ordered a *baqlawa*.

Mama Ayesha roused herself from her meal and phone: "*Salamtik* [your health], ya Helen!"

"I come here for comfort and good luck," she winked at me.

"Remember when you screaming?" Mama seemed caught in a private reverie.

"She reads my cup," Helen said.

"I have no family, Mama continued. "Everybody dead. You family is your father and mother. When they die, it's over."

"You love your family, don't you?" Helen asked.

"Not now! You know what they did to me?" Mama deferred from explaining further and the waiters dispersed.

Helen met Mama Ayesha in 1950 and they became fast friends. She has visited Mama's home—"It's on a beautiful site in Jerusalem on the Mount of Olives." The blatant American siding with Israel, she admitted, pained her: "In 1967, after the Six-Day War, they were dancing the *Hava Nagila* in front of the White House, and I must say I mourned the Arabs who died and who lost their country."

We all went into the night of the West Bank of the Calvert Street Bridge. The next day, Helen would rise for the president; I would rise for her; Mama would rise to cook for all.

"Everybody in America is my child!" proclaimed Mama Ayesha Howar when I returned to interview her two years later.[29]

"Ahlan!" Mama greeted me, lifting her head like a Galapagos tortoise; she hardly ever moved from her maroon Naugahyde booth in back of the Calvert Café, telephone always at her side. Looking at her with her white hair in pigtails, I slid back in memory to my student days at Georgetown twenty years before when a waiter named Mahmoud, who resembled Humphrey Bogart, would dance around the tables balancing *'araq* in a glass on his head.

Most assume that Ayesha never married, but she wasted no time dispelling that rumor. She was married to a Shafiq Koutana in Jerusalem when she was 21, but he had divorced her in the Muslim way: "He went to the Muslim law, the Sharia, and said, 'I have no wife,' and I wasn't his wife anymore after one year." Koutana refused to come with her to America, living in her house on the Mount of Olives with another wife. Mama never went back to see it. He paid her a visit 25 years later in Washington, but she wasn't too impressed. Shortly after arriving in the United States, Ayesha married a second time—to a Palestinian American veteran of World War I named Issa Abraham. When he died in 1956 he was buried in Arlington National Cemetery. "They made twelve shots and they gave me the flag."

Mama motioned to a waiter to bring demitasses of Turkish coffee and told me about her life before leaving Palestine. During the famine that hit the Levant at the time, Mama remembered, people would be lucky to eat orange peels, "Everybody they go to the grave and come back." Cholera broke out and killed her mother. "Every day 30 to 40 people dead," she said. When asked why the Palestinians didn't revolt against the Turks at this time, she said, "They had no food to move. Everybody stay home."

In the interwar years, Mama raised pigs, making a thousand pounds of pork a week for the British, as well as providing vegetables. The British liked her, "I worked with the British nurses at the hospital. I go buy them every vegetable, everything they ask for. They teach me how to cook English food. I know how to cook it better than the English people!"

Helen Thomas, ever present in the evenings, brought some birthday cake over to Mama, who greeted her, "*Salamtik*, ya Helen!"

In the 1940s Mama was an honored ally of the British—they would take her in their limousines on her rounds to gather food supplies to Sarafand, Ramle, Lydda. "Just like I am the King!" she smiled. "Nobody else, only me, because I am honest with the British." But she remembered the bombing of the King David Hotel by Menachem Begin's Irgun and the death of a cousin: "Joe Howar's brother was killed there. They brought a bomb in a can where they put the milk, throw the can on the floor, and it blow up." She heard the explosion: "I think it was awful. Do you think it was right? That's why I came here. I get tired of seeing these things. When the British gone, I get lost. I missed them a lot. If you want to write a history about me, you'll find it in the British Army."

She went for a time with the British Lincoln Regiment to Jordan, but she was in Jerusalem when the war broke out between the Jewish settlers and the Arab Palestinians. She was just up the road when the massacre at Deir Yassin, also by Begin's Irgun, happened: "We have some relatives murdered there from my home town. You know what they did? The women with the pregnant they cut them and take the baby outside in the woods. One woman came, she cry for her daughter and they kill her and put her with her daughter.

Wallah [by God], the Palestinians suffer a lot." A nephew of Mama's later related to me that his wife's family—the Zahrans—had 45 people killed at Deir Yassin. His wife's father, Juma Zahran, had lost his first wife, three daughters, and a son; the man now lives in Amman, Jordan, one of the last survivors of Deir Yassin.

Mama described the exodus of Palestinians to surrounding Arab countries, but she thought "the Arab world sold Palestine. I got sick. I wanted to leave." Her cousin Jimmy Howar met her at the train station in New York in 1950, but in Washington she got lost: "I went for the first time to the streetcar. They go round and round and round. I can't speak well and one man came, asked, 'Where you going?' and I said, 'To my cousin's on First-a Street.' He let me out there."

In 1960, she started the Calvert Café. "I am the cook, the cash register, the waiter—I am everything!" she crowed, clearly speaking in the historical present tense, since she rarely moved from her telephone-on-chair. A nephew of hers, Abdullah, came to join us and suggested it was time to call Jerusalem. Each night, Mama called her relatives halfway around the world. When she finished, I asked her if she'd like to return. "I want to see my house again…. Maybe I go. Who knows? If it's no trouble I will go. I don't want trouble because I had enough."

What was Mama Ayesha's solution to the Middle East problem? Ever the entrepreneur, she thought a profit motive could help: "Well, it's better for the Jews to be together with the Arabs because they make money. This way they can go to the Arab world and make business. Now they can't go anywhere. The Arab Jews, they are better off than other Jews [from Europe]. Those [Ashkenazim] will never forget the problem. They scared. They think the Arab is like a snake biting. They're wrong. The Arab people are nice people. There's no sense to say—I don't want you. This is your hometown. You will come here and we will live together. Like America."

In 1993, over 90 years old, Mama Ayesha Howar died in Washington, far from Jerusalem, but close to a phone.

For a time, only one American was father of a queen—Najeeb Halaby. His daughter, Queen Noor of the Hashemite Kingdom of Jordan, was the fourth wife of King Hussein. In many ways, the tall, handsome Halaby, in his seventies, set up the unlikely match, striking up a friendship with Hussein years earlier. They were both avid airmen.

Both men headed entities imperiled by the Arab–Israeli conflict. Hussein's Jordan fought four wars with the Jewish state since 1948, when Najeeb Halaby was working under Secretary James Forrestal at the US Department of Defense. Halaby was chairman emeritus of the American University of Beirut and tried, after taking the reins of the embattled school in 1983, to stem the loss of faculty and students in the midst of relentless violence. It was not easy. Shortly after Halaby took over, his hand-picked president, fellow Californian Malcolm Kerr, was shot in the head by a Lebanese gunman.

But the tragedy did not stop Halaby. How do you stop a man propelled by his past? How do you stop the man who test-piloted America's first jets during World War II, coached Charles Lindbergh in one, and set an aviation record for the first transcontinental solo jet flight across the United States? This is an informed daredevil, Stanford and Yale educated. This is also the man who was head of Pan Am Airlines when the first hijacking of a jumbo 747 occurred in 1970. The hijacker was a Palestinian commando. An Arab American faced off with an Arab. The result was a blown-up plane.

Najeeb Halaby was thought by many in the Arab-American community to have "shirked" his origins. Speaking with him in his modest condominium in Washington, DC, revealed that nothing could have been further from the truth. Sky blue—that was the color of Najeeb Halaby's eyes. But the nose was certainly not Semitic and neither was the height. He revealed himself confidently, in measured cadence, letting the concern come through his voice in careful dropperfuls of emotion. There'd been a fire on the first floor. Unperturbed, Halaby steered through the maze of workers and seated me in front of—a crackling fireplace! This was a man who took danger in stride. Fire last time did not mean fire the next.

Halaby was gifted with a bi-ethnic heritage. His mother was of Scots–English background (and was still going strong at 96). His father, Najeeb Senior, came to the United States from Zahle, Lebanon (the family originated in Aleppo, which in Arabic is Halab). He arrived in steerage at Ellis Island in 1900 and, at age twelve, began peddling along the eastern seaboard with copperware, jewelry, rugs, and damask.

The elder Halaby was a particularly good hawker of exotic wares. As his son once wrote, "I think he could have sold Stars of David in the middle of Baghdad."[30] Some of the more intrepid peddlers found their way to wealthy Americans—Halaby heard about Bar Harbor, Maine, a summering ground for the rich where he met Mrs. Grover Cleveland, whom he charmed and who supplied him with the letters of introduction that launched his career.

By 1912, the man from Zahle hightailed it to Dallas where, he had heard, wealth came in the form of cotton and oil. It wasn't long before he had married Laura Wilkins, daughter of a Confederate soldier from Tennessee, and the two put together the venerable Halaby Galleries, which lasted through the 1920s as a sought-after interior decorator on the top two floors of the Neiman-Marcus building. Najeeb's shrewdness with sales linked with Laura's

Christian Science reliance on rationality and control. Their work space came by way of an invitation from Stanley Marcus. As the son would put it later, "An Arab and Jew working together in a temple of luxury trade a half century ago!"

Halaby's own description of his father is not unlike that of many original immigrant Syrians who "made it" in the United States:

> My father was a handsome man, just under six feet, and very attractive to the ladies. Toward me, his only child, he vacillated between penitentiary discipline and a marshmallow permissiveness. He could be very sweet, generous, compassionate, and sentimental. He also occasionally beat the hell out of me. He was loving and very emotional, with a short-fused temper and tremendous pride in his Arab heritage. Unlike many Syrians, Lebanese, and others from the Middle East, he refused to change his name or pretend to be anything he wasn't. To my later regret, we never spoke Arabic at mealtime, as did many Arab Americans, but I did pick up a few epithets in the old man's native tongue.[31]

The elder Halaby did much to assimilate as fast as possible. He broke the racial prohibitions against Arabs, Armenians, Jews, and African Americans at the Dallas Athletic Club where he entered with full privileges. No doubt his wife's strength and "uncompromising nature," as well as her beauty, helped. As coffee arrived in care of his second wife, Allison, Najeeb drew a psychological portrait of his father vis-a-vis his own development:

> That first generation of the immigrant Arabs really wanted to be 100 percent American and changed their names and their religions even. They wanted to be in the Rotary and the Shriners and the country club. And they wanted to arrive socially, politically, professionally. And so when you're raised in that kind of atmosphere, you wanted to be all-American. Yet… I've found in going back to Syria or Lebanon, through the food, the atmosphere, the air, the sights, sounds, you feel a root that just comes without logic or intellectual activity. It just is down inside you.[32]

Interest in public service involving work under four presidents (Truman, Eisenhower, Kennedy, and Johnson) stirred in Halaby at an early age. Halaby credited his parents' "high priority in the budget for education" for this concern for public service, but also the Christian Science that obsessed his mother, took over his father, and was pressed into him.

"The Arab has quite an affinity for the other dispossessed, disinherited," he said thoughtfully, folding his fingers into each other. "Because he's had that. He came to this country as a minority. He's remained a minority. Though some travel with the hot shots, the rich

Najeeb Halaby (right) receives a handshake from President John F. Kennedy at the White House after Halaby's 1961 swearing-in ceremony as head of the Federal Aviation Administration, as his mother, Laura, watched. (Alexa Halaby)

set, and forget the minorities, others have said, well my God, but for the grace of good fortune, there go I. I could still be peddling my wares in a cart. I find people like [Ralph] Nader and [James] Abourezk are dramatic examples of champions of the powerless."

Underdog advocate at the beginning of his law practice, Halaby worked for the Legal Aid Clinic in the Watts area of Los Angeles. He called himself "an FDR Democrat" who was not always popular with his own family in his adoption of liberal causes (his mother voted for Nixon, even though Kennedy had appointed her son FAA head).

One of the things that bothered Halaby about his father was his attitude toward the Jews:

> It was partly based upon competition in business and professional life, partly based on envy of commercial and social success, and partly wanting to distance himself from an unpopular minority, one even more unpopular than [Syrians] themselves. [By meeting many Jewish law students] I pretty much rid myself of the feeling that my father had about Jews as an ethnic-religious group. But the great equalizer was World War II. It made us all feel we were equal.

The elder Halaby died when his only son was twelve and had recently experienced the pain of his parents' divorce. As with Danny Thomas and others I interviewed, it wasn't just poverty that spurred the great ones to excel, but poverty of parental attention, or abundance cut tragically short.

Internationalism became second nature to Najeeb Junior because his folks took him every summer to Europe and the Middle East on antique furniture and rug hunting trips for their gallery in Dallas. His childhood was filled with horizons few children see. It fed his love for air travel, and his sense of social mission led him in the war effort to pioneer the testing of the new jets, including his then-secret cross-continental solo flight that took 5 hours, 45 minutes, far better than the standard DC3's 22 hours. It did not go into the record books until years later because of its secrecy. Halaby called the experience "ethereal, a unique sight to fly over the Rockies and over the desert. Before that, you had to go through the valleys, and suddenly now you just overfly everything!"

He nudged the cookie plate toward me—the unflappable Arab host. In 1948 Halaby went to work for Secretary of Defense James Forrestal. He remarked about that, "It was considered kind of risky of Forrestal to appoint an Arab American in a very sensitive job—international security affairs." From there he became one of the civilians who helped put NATO together and became first chairman of its Military Production and Supply Board.

Halaby tangentially touched a Middle East fiasco in the making. Forrestal was soon to become one of the first—and certainly one of the most tragic—targets of Zionist apologists frantic about the creation of a Jewish state in Palestine. Forrestal was, in a word, not for it. Halaby's immediate superior was Robert Blum, a Jewish American assistant secretary for international affairs. Forrestal, as Halaby remembered it, had made a pack of enemies, even before the Israel issue hit him in the ribs, including Truman and J. Edgar Hoover. Then Forrestal ran into the juggernaut that was Zionism in 1948. The defense secretary worried that the creation of Israel would lose America more friends than it would gain. He commissioned the respected publisher of the *Louisville Courier-Journal*, Mark Ethridge, to study the impact a major Middle East conflict would have on US access to oil and on US security. Ethridge reported that the military would be in serious trouble in the event of a cataclysm there.

Truman received the report. Halaby recalled, "Forrestal was damned by the Jews for pursuing the American strategic interests rather forcibly. Some of his Jewish friends in New York portrayed him in caricature in newspapers as anti-Semitic." Forrestal ended up jumping to his death from a twelfth-story window at Bethesda Naval Hospital. By then, Truman had ignored the Joint Chiefs and carried the US vote "Yea" for an independent Jewish state in Palestine.

Halaby reflected on the mood in the United States at the time: "That was the peak of sympathy for the Jewish people. There wasn't much understanding of Zionism as distinguished from Judaism. The issue was really a homeland for the homeless Jews, and the Zionists were active, but nobody was really aware of it. There is still a deep, wide sympathy for the Jews who suffered in the Holocaust. You might say justice for a few Jews is an injustice for a few Arabs in the total world scene. And we've never gotten that thing balanced." For Halaby, the dispossession of the Palestinians is "a major unfinished business of the American conscience."

"It's total hypocrisy to send $10 million a day for a bullyboy like [Ariel] Sharon to occupy Lebanon and repress West Bankers." He opened his hands now and leaned forward, "I mean that's contrary to everything we ever believed, taught, lived. We can't live with that. And yet we can't quite deal with it, either."

Appointment by newly elected President Kennedy to head the Federal Aviation Administration was a unique honor for Halaby: "That was a thrill in the sense that it was the first time anyone of Arab-American background had ever had a presidential appointment," he smiled. JFK, Halaby said, would not have let the Middle East crisis sit on the back burner, exploding at will while the United States looked on powerless. He believed that Kennedy would have tackled the problem at the root: "Because he really resented overpressuring and because he really wasn't as dependent upon Jewish [campaign] money as some have been. On the other hand, Johnson was considerably more influenceable." It was under President Johnson that large-scale arms shipments from the United States to Israel began.

One horrible Labor Day weekend in 1970, a Connecticut state trooper fetched Halaby from his cottage on Fisher's Island off New London, where he had stowed away with his family. Soon he was reading a coded message from Pan Am in London—AFTER DEPARTURE AMSTERDAM FLIGHT 93/06 SEP SUFFERED 9052 REPEAT 9052. That number was the code for hijacking. Two men armed with revolvers and hand grenades commandeered the flight en route to New York. The gunmen were from the Popular Front for the Liberation of Palestine (PFLP). The "unfinished business" of Palestine, as Halaby called it, had turned grim. The hijacking era had begun, and it had begun on an Arab American's watch.

The event shook him up: "It was ironical: the loss of the first jumbo jet in flames [in Cairo] set by the craziest of the homeless, frustrated Palestinians, who missed their assigned Israeli target and hit an airline headed by an Arab-American aviator who had labored long to help get recognition of the rights of the Palestinian people—and in my father's homeland, too!"[33]

But Halaby admitted to me that he had been "under wraps" concerning opinions on the Middle East issue while serving at Pan Am and with the FAA, roughly a period from 1960 to 1972. Only by the 1973 October War was he free to speak out. In fact, the day of the massive airlift of US armaments that rescued the Israeli Army from defeat by the Egyptians, who had just about recaptured the Sinai, Halaby was waiting for an audience with King Faisal of Saudi Arabia. "The airlift," he recounted, "was outrageous to me. I resented the outcome of the 1967 war, but I wasn't really emotionally involved in it. It seemed to me to involve Egypt and Syria more than Lebanon. From 1973 on I have gotten emotionally, actively involved."

I asked him for specifics. He had individually lobbied certain policy makers and congressmen. Halaby was in the Senate gallery the day of the vote on shipping AWACS to Saudi Arabia. Sen. John Glenn, an ill-fated 1984 presidential candidate for the Democratic nomination, was a personal friend who stymied him by "going back and forth" on Middle East issues. George Shultz, the secretary of state, was a Bohemian Club campmate of Halaby's in 1982 during the siege of Beirut. Shultz asked him for ideas for US action. Shortly after the unveiling of the Reagan Peace Plan, Halaby shook hands in a White House receiving line with Shultz and the secretary said, "Well, did you see your hand-tracks in that speech?" There were elements of Halaby's notes in the plan. He has had his effect. He felt it "justifies not being a joiner."

Halaby thought most Arab Americans wouldn't buy the "whole Arab cause," and that their political groups live in an illusion: "Well, [most Arab Americans] don't want to be identified with the total Arab cause or Arafat or Hafez al-Assad. They say 'I'm a Syrian

Queen Noor of Jordan in the 1980s.

American or a Lebanese American, or Palestinian American. Why should I take all of the burden of the mythical Arab nation on my back?' There isn't any such thing as the 'Arab Nation.' The Arab cause is too diverse and inconsistent, so to hell with all that." He stood, pacing, reading notes for some meeting. "Arab Americans don't want to get spread too thin. They might give some money anonymously to ADC and NAAA [National Association of Arab Americans], but they're not going to go to Congress on behalf of an association. And finally—why let yourself be a target? Do things anonymously, quietly."

Najeeb Halaby picked up photos of two grandsons (two grand-daughters came later) as I rose to leave. It was obvious he was proud of them and even somewhat beguiled by the extraordinary windfall and drama of the marriage between a Princeton co-ed, whose grand-father was a Syro-Lebanese peddler, and an Arab king.

As for Queen Noor, she later assessed her relationship with her father as "extremely difficult," and though she "loved and admired" him, she confessed that he was "beset with financial problems, a troubled marriage, and the added pressure of being an oddity in WASP Washington."[34]

Vance Bourjaily was hunting coyotes with a shotgun the day I pulled into Iowa City, Iowa. His tall wife, Tina, a weathered woman with a sunburned face and eyes fiery blue as black opals drove me through their 500-acre farm in a Jeep, bouncing over ruts, pointing out the carcasses of dead sheep. Four sheep had been attacked by coyotes the night before, and their entrails were pulled out of their stomachs. "Well, it's the tastiest for them," said Tina, though the coyotes would eat the meat later. The stench of the decaying bodies, meshed by flies, was ungodly. I opened up three gates for us before two figures approached in the distance, one tall, one short, shotguns slung over their shoulders like the crossbars of a crucifix.

Vance Bourjaily is one of America's preeminent novelists. Once friends with Norman Mailer, Bourjaily and the storied Mailer diverged in their careers, the latter to stardom and six wives and the former to a life of teaching at the famed University of Iowa Writer's Workshop, thirteen critically acclaimed but not altogether profitable books, and two wives.

The short Bourjaily and his tall son, Philip, threw their guns in the Jeep and we headed for the farmhouse. Philip's eyes were heated blue, too; Vance's blue, less fiery, but large with contained mirth and some pathos. At the farmhouse on Redbird Farm, Bourjaily got out cold bottled beer, a relief on the hot summer day, and showed me around. On the walls of the disheveled, earthy place were mementos of nearly four decades of marriage and writing. A birthday gift of "The More Fool" from his daughter, Robin, with a photo of Vance, legs up, pouring himself a beer. The poem reads: "Nor ever shall / Until I die / For the longer I live / The More Fool am I." A large crew oar (his son's) above a painting by Tobias Schneebaum, an abstract of a mannish figure torn, in conflict, circling strokes of his own flailing arms. The man has a doglike head. "It's an in-transition house," Bourjaily grinned, spreading crows-feet, though they'd lived there for nearly twenty years.

As we sat to chat, a dog named Moss fell asleep between us. Bourjaily fondled a kitten as he talked, beer in his other hand. Vance Bourjaily is one of the only serious American novelists of Lebanese heritage to make a name for himself in fiction. (William Peter Blatty made more money with demonic potboilers.) He welcomed the chance to reminisce about his father, Monsour Bourjaily, known to the world as Monte, who, among other things, had earned a high living at one time with United Features Syndicate as the ghostwriter of Eleanor Roosevelt's daily column, "My Day." He also probed his ancestral past.

His father, whom he has described as a "round-armed, fluent and persuasive man, with irresistible brown eyes behind business-like glasses,"[35] was born in Kabb Elias, Lebanon, in 1894 and was brought to America by his mother at age five. The reason appeared to be a bad marriage. Her husband was a cousin known as a big drinker who, when drunk, exhibited feats of strength: "His favorite was to lie down on his back, have one great fat man stand on his stomach and one on each shoulder, and then raise himself up. Six hundred pounds of fat men with him. Apparently he did that once too often and tore himself up inside and died."[36]

Before that happened, Vance's grandmother had had enough of his "kick[ing] her around" and stole off one night over the mountains to Beirut, hiding in a cave with her son, Monsour, watching her husband ride by on horseback searching for them. They went through Marseilles—where the Arabic name was given a French lilt by a French official—and on to Ellis Island. In the United States, the grandmother settled in the Syrian colony of Lawrence, Massachusetts, working in a boarding house for Syrian mill workers, cooking, making beds, cleaning up. She had also taken up her *qashsha* and peddled linens, enough to put her son through high school and to save for return passage to Lebanon.

As I heard this story, I marveled at how similar it was to that of Kahlil Gibran's mother, whose father was an imprisoned dissolute. Or, for that matter, my own grandmother, Nazera, whose abusive father immigrated after his wife abruptly deserted the family, dying in Brazil. The shattering of marriages was not a common theme in early Syrian immigration, but perhaps it was good for fomenting in the progeny the desire to write. Bourjaily's grandmother had "incredible character and vision" and made an enormous impact on his life. He remembered living with her in the house when growing up, listening to her tales.

As for his father, who married a farm-girl journalist, Barbara Webb, there is deep respect, love, and some puzzlement. In an *Esquire* piece entitled "My Father's Life," Bourjaily recalled the days when he was a titan heading United Features Syndicate, friends with Eleanor Roosevelt and other New York mandarins, as well as days when he fell from grace.

Monte Bourjaily launched syndicated comic strips, including Al Capp's "L'il Abner." But he also took a big risk cashing in his UFS stock for three-quarters of a million dollars, for he lost most of it with a picture magazine that anticipated the great success of *Life* and a humor magazine, *Judge*, the comic book before its time. By 1940, he was broke; his son described the pathos with a scene of his overqualified father slipping blotting paper into a pair of expensive wingtips where the soles had worn through as he worked on a dock: "He is explaining to me, this morning, in his residential hotel room, that his job involves bossing longshoremen, overseeing the opening of bales of unsold comic books which have been returned by the wholesalers. The books must have their covers returned by the wholesalers. The books must have their covers cut off so as to be exported as bulk paper, not resold as some kind of reading matter. The irony there, given the choices my father made, is thicker than those British soles are thin."

After serving as an aide to Gen. John Pershing in World War I, Monte Bourjaily hit the pinnacle of journalism, threw it (and two wives) away, and ended up scratching a living in small-town papers. Years later, in 1976, Vance received a letter from a friend of his father from high school years in Syracuse, now 83, who reassured the writer that Monsour "had a peculiar habit of hitching up his pants—and he had an infectious laugh..." His father by then was 82, in Florida, slipping in his treasured English, Arabic creeping into his weakening voice. Vance concluded his touching memoir, "It's okay. Dad. You and mother gave so many of those words to me."[37]

Dislocation marked the early years of the author-son's life. Born in Cleveland in 1922 (where his parents were both writing for the *Cleveland Plain Dealer*), he was soon moved to Syracuse, then New York, and took long trips overseas. Bourjaily glibly recalled seeing a young girl in England expose her female parts under a bathing suit to him when he was only five, and a friend of his mother's trying to fondle him on board ship back to America. Discovered, she grew hysterical and tried to pitch him out a porthole. Vance's mother rescued him. His mother ordered the children to drink wine instead of water, which she thought was contaminated. Before grammar school, Vance Bourjaily figured he had learned some lessons about "sex and violence and a taste for booze."

By age seven, little Vance had penned his first poem, "The Dance of the Fireflies," where the fireflies outlast a battle with beetles. By ten he fancied himself something of a young playwright and took on the role of Puck in *A Midsummer Night's Dream*. He was twelve when his parents divorced, and he was sent to boarding schools in three different states, a grim time that he developed into his novel *Confessions of a Spent Youth* (1960).

Bourjaily went to Bowdoin College in Maine, near where his father was editing the *Bangor Daily News*. At nineteen, he volunteered to join the American Field Service as an ambulance driver in World War II and was stationed in Lebanon as well as Italy. The seeds of this experience went into *Confessions* and his first novel, *The End of My Life* (1946). That book's last scene, where an ambulance driver's girlfriend is killed by strafing at the front while he is trying to woo her, was drawn from real life, except the real girl was not fired upon: "Fiction, I was to learn, may be the art of telling what never happened, or of telling what damn-well-did, but often it comes out of the masochistic mysteries of might-have-been."[38]

Though his father admired his novels, he was sometimes embarrassed by their sexual frankness. To Monsour, a writer was measured best by, said Vance, "whether you're in the newspaper. You're page one; that's better than anything else." But Vance's career took off on what looked like a rocket in wartime and just after when "book publishing boomed along with the cannons"; the wisdom went, "If he can spell his name the same way twice, give him an advance."[39] After inspecting a sheaf of his poems and plays, the legendary Scribner's editor Maxwell Perkins gave him an advance of $750 to write a novel. He was, at the time, just returning from Osaka, Japan, where he had been sent after being drafted in 1944 into the real live army, only to watch over the ruins of a defeated nation.

Perkins helped him give his rough novel a beginning and an end, things Bourjaily learned to appreciate in fiction. *The End of My Life* was followed by another with Scribner's, *The Hound of Earth*, about a man who deserts his work on the Manhattan Project after witnessing the devastation of Hiroshima. Soon after Scribner's faded for a while from the publishing scene, Bourjaily had an eight-book contract with Dial Press, which sustained him for twenty years until he completed *A Game Men Play* (1980).

What a different world it was then for the promising but untutored young author when advances were given to writers on raw talent. In the competitive climate today one must be a star, or languish for decades sitting on moldy manuscripts. As he told me, he thought my generation of writers was hampered by excessive scholarly inspection of the theories of writing: "Your new generation of writers knows a hell of a lot about writing novels. You haven't had a chance to catch up technically with what you can do unless it's matching what you know about it. And it makes it difficult." When he started out, he knew nothing about Henry James' theories of fiction—getting them second-hand through his idols Hemingway and Fitzgerald—and wrote purely from instinct, as did Mailer, Bellow, Shaw, and others at the time.

In 1946, he married Tina Yensen, a beautiful young horsewoman, who was working at the state department. In New York he fell in with the crowd of exciting postwar authors—Mailer, Bellow, Capote, Shaw, Miller. A critic, Jack Aldridge, gave his already out-of-print *The End of My Life* a boost in *After the Lost Generation*, favorably comparing its

Novelist Vance Bourjaily at Redbird Farm, Iowa City, Iowa, July 1983
(Gregory Orfalea)

treatment of the "loss of youth in war" to *This Side of Paradise* and *A Farewell to Arms*.

Bourjaily edited a literary magazine, *Discovery*, which published early pieces for the New York crowd, including Mailer's "The Dead Gook" and Styron's "Long March." Closest to Norman Mailer, with whom he and Tina shared "a belief in the transcendental necessity of parties," Bourjaily proudly noted that at his best party James Jones met Montgomery Clift and picked him for the lead role in *From Here to Eternity*. Bourjaily swapped his manuscript of *The Hound of Earth* for Mailer's *Barbary Shore*, each giving the other needed critical suggestions for revision. They lived near each other in Mexico City for a time and often went to bullfights together, following the Hemingway trail.

Bourjaily combined some short pieces ("Quincy at Yale" and "The Fractional Man" were published in the *New Yorker*) into *Confessions of a Spent Youth*, his only novel to have an Arab-American protagonist. In it, Quincy visits his ancestral village of Kabb Elias. A quarter-Welsh and half-Lebanese, he says, "The largest fraction I was brought up not so much to conceal as to ignore." He broods on his movement in America through a "fluid society [with] no community of moral belief" and contrasts himself to his Old World relatives as "uselessly complicated and discontent as they were simple and steadfast and proud."[40] Quincy's at first comical, then insistent attempt to mask as an Arab leaves him lost. An Arab-American critic has written cogently about *Confessions*: "For Quincy, to pose as Arab may well be a way of simultaneously approaching and keeping at arm's length his earliest memories of home and connection to others. To decry the consequences of emigration may well be to lament his premature passage into loneliness."[41]

By 1979, Bourjaily had left Iowa for the University of Arizona; in 1985 he took the job as head of the writing program at Louisiana State University. Bourjaily's wandering, troubled, outsider heroes had finally injected themselves into his professional life. Today he lives with his second wife and young son in Florida.

I wondered why he had written only one of his books from the point of view of a hero of Arab origin, especially when some of his literary associates, such as Mailer and Bellow and Roth, had milked their Jewish heritage quite strongly. To do that, he felt, an author "would have to have been a kid who was brought up in an Arabic-speaking ghetto, or working-class neighborhood, who is really confined in folk ways, in customs. These have to be the tensions of his boyhood and adolescence. They certainly weren't for me." He thought Saroyan had done this admirably for Armenians, where "the ethnic community is seen as confining, restricting, but perhaps if you get wounded, you go back to it to get bandaged. But the felonious American immigrant novel would be my father's novel, not mine."

His grandmother from Lebanon, however, had appeared in fictitious form in *Confessions*; she was "the total strength in my life," he said.

His father's sensitivity to being of Arab background forced him to distance himself from it, particularly when he wanted to move up in American society, and probably imbued in his son a similar distancing. "Whatever it was in the Lebanese boyhood and adolescence which Irish kids teased him about—being dark, big nose, not speaking English very good, poverty—he didn't want to be tarred with it," Bourjaily said. Though raised Eastern Orthodox himself, Monte Bourjaily went to the Roman Catholic Church. Yet he didn't completely sever his ties to the Syrians. He was friends with composer Anis Foulihan. Vance remembered as a boy frequenting the legendary Sheik Restaurant (once on Washington Street), when it was in Brooklyn, and meeting Salloum Mokarzel, the editor of the *Syrian World*, whom Monte admired. He recalled Mokarzel: "He looked like Adolph Menjou, with black moustache, urbane, spoke unaccented English, and had pretty daughters. I was sorry they weren't a little younger! Mokarzel was a sophisticated man with something of a magnetic personality which could draw back temporarily to the Lebanese community people like my father."

But the estrangement from the renowned Mailer flickered through when I asked if it ever bothered him that, as accomplished a novelist as he is, he had never been on the Johnny Carson or Merv Griffin shows. "Oh sure," he smiled. "We all want success in its various guises, and one of them is to be a public figure. But it's hard for me." A short man who speaks in almost a whisper, he indicated he hadn't had the ability to be a self-publicist, such as Mailer and Capote. "If I could have done it, I probably would have," he said.

The death of President Kennedy was a turning point for him as a writer and citizen. "I felt very strongly that there had been a kind of rebirth of hope in the country with Kennedy," he said. "There was a tremendous identification on the part of guys my age. He was the best of us. So when he was killed it was like—they got us." One of Bourjaily's most praised novels is *The Man Who Knew Kennedy*.

Bourjaily wanted to stretch a bit on the hot summer day and suggested we take our beers and some cheese and crackers to his study in an old abandoned school-house on their property up the road. There he got out some old photographs of writer friends, including one of him riding an elephant in a South Carolina parade with poet James Dickey. Another was of Ralph Ellison and his wife, one of Kurt Vonnegut and him in Biafra. A pile of books on the floor, reaching up over his head, were authored by his former students, including John Irving.

I opened the subject of the Middle East with the pacifist author. The invasion of Lebanon had shaken him, he admitted: "What I felt was, the poor, fucking Palestinians, and I didn't mean the PLO. I meant those miserable Palestinian old men and women and children who live in refugee camps and have all their lives, who are pawns in a game the PLO, Syria, Lebanon, and Israel don't give a damn about. They're suffering human beings. And that's where my heart was."

Bourjaily ran his gnarled hand over a bronzed dome and short, graying hair: "My emotions about that part of the world are enormously complicated. It has to start back 45 years ago to an enormous sympathy with the Jews. A lot of the reason I went to World War II was because of what Hitler was doing to the Jews. I got to what was then Palestine. I had family feeling for the people I was seeing in Lebanon, but I also was very enthusiastic about what the Jews were doing on the kibbutzim. I went down on a leave and helped them harvest the wheat on a kibbutz. I took the naive view, I suppose, that we were all so much together. If you were anti-Semitic, it meant you were anti-Jewish and anti-Arab, too."

In some ways, he chuckled, his deepest sympathies were for the people in the middle—"the poor goddamn British policemen getting shot at by both sides!" But the "first flaw in my admiration and support for the Jews," he thought, was the terrorism of Begin's Irgun. He had not, however, ever heard of the massacre at Deir Yassin. Though the Jews in Israel seemed to him "better disciplined, more rational," than the Arabs, "my adherence to their [Israel's] side probably grew gradually weaker through the years so that I was ready to lose a lot of it when they invaded Lebanon. When that happened, they lost me."

Knowing of the tremendous commercial success of a book that chronicled the heroic independence of Israel, *Exodus*, I wondered what prevented a similar book for the Palestinian diaspora experience? Bourjaily thought there was a reason. He referred to a candid speech given fifteen years ago at the Iowa Workshop by an editor from New York, who said that in the publishing business the rule of thumb is, if you sell New York, you sell the country. In New York, according to the editor, 90 percent of hardcover buyers are Jews. Such a book on the Palestinians would turn them off. And the Arab-American readership in the United States, the novelist believed, isn't significant. But Bourjaily did not discount that such a book could be written and with merit: "I think if you were to take the plight of the Palestinians—and I think it's one of great dignity—you would have to make that shift in focus from partisanship to symbolic condition. The reader would have to say, yes, we're all refugees in some sense or another, in this world."

He gazed out the hazy window of the old schoolhouse writer's loft, where he and Tina had slept in a bunk: "I am neither wealthy nor well known. Perhaps fulfilled."

—FOUR—

THE PALESTINE DEBACLE: THE SECOND WAVE OF ARAB IMMIGRATION (1948–1966)

Alfred Farradj, a Californian with water combed into his silver hair, ran a typewriter and office machine store in Berkeley for more than two decades. He loved the San Francisco Bay area, its lush, blue inlets, its Golden Gate Bridge, the freedom that blows in with the breeze or hippies. People were good to his family and it prospered. So much so that Alfred Farradj was sure he could get me a good discount on a new typewriter. Other than Detroit, the Bay City appears to be the Palestinians' favorite in the United States. The old Chinese groceries in San Francisco are now owned largely by Palestinians. When a new Palestinian arrival is greeted on the streets of San Francisco, he isn't asked, "How are you?" but rather, "*Wayn fatah?*"—"Where are you opening?"

Over lunch with a view of the water, Alfred sat back, wiped his mouth, and said, "I felt more a foreigner in Jerusalem than in San Francisco." But Alfred Farradj was born in Jerusalem. He did not leave it because he wanted to. In 1946, Farradj was a 26-year-old accountant working for Freeman Company, a British-owned distributor of Morris cars. His father ran a candle shop in the old city of Jerusalem. Alfred looked up from his desk one day to hear a grim report: Menachem Begin's gang, the Irgun, had blown up the King David Hotel. Alfred's brother, Ibrahim Farradj, who was working for the Palestine government at British headquarters there, was killed in the explosion, along with 87 other mostly civilian British and Arabs and 15 Jews.

Two years later, in 1948, full-scale war broke out between the Zionist forces and the indigenous Palestinian Arabs, poorly reinforced—if that is the word at all—by a ragtag collection of Arab forces. On November 29 of the previous year, the UN General Assembly had voted for a partitioned state in Palestine—one part Jewish, one part Arab—and by May 15, 1948, the British pulled out. On that day, Alfred Farradj became—without knowing it—a refugee.

He was hurried off by friends to Bethlehem:

> It was three months before my parents knew if I was alive or dead.
> I finally made it by foot—it took hours because every time there
> was fighting we had to detour. I stayed with my aunt, who was
> alone and hard of hearing. Eight hundred bombs they said fell that
> night on Jerusalem and the doors would fly open. I took her
> downstairs. At my parents so many bombs fell that the room was
> covered with black dust.[1]

Shortly afterward, Farradj went to Amman, Jordan, as one of
about 750,000 native Palestinians (of 1.3 million) displaced by Israel's
war for independence. By 1968, he would finally come to the United
States to settle, one of 802,827 Arabs listed as immigrants to the
country between 1948 and 2003 (133,929 came from Palestine or
Jordan—almost all of them Palestinian). Because many Palestinians
came to America from countries of first refuge, such as Syria and
Lebanon, it's probably safe to estimate that at least one-fourth of the
post–1948 immigration was Palestinian, leaving us today with about
250,000 Palestinian Americans.[2] That figure, about 5 percent of the
total Palestinian diaspora worldwide (excluding those who live in
Israel, the West Bank, and Gaza) is 29 percent of the number of
original Palestinian refugees. The fact that a sizable group of those
refugees emigrated to the country that most supported the forces
that evicted them is perhaps one of the strangest paradoxes in US
immigration history (see Appendixes).

Though US immigration statistics list only 4,385 strictly
"Palestinian" immigrants from 1948 to 1966, tens of thousands more
immigrated from other lands of first refuge. The routes they took
were as various as the sea lanes and air lanes of the vagabond world
they entered. Some came directly from the newly created Israel—
where the remaining Arab population often lived in degraded,
second-class citizenship. Some came after spending time in exile or
in camps in Egypt, Jordan, Lebanon, Iraq, Syria, and the Jordanian-
occupied West Bank. Some, like Alfred Farradj, came after they were
fed up with the pain of working in Arab countries and seeing their
homeland being eaten up little by little with no Arab army able to
stop it. Some, like Columbia University professor and literary critic
Edward Said and Georgetown University professor Hisham Sharabi,
were stranded in America, enrolled in universities and unable to
return to Palestine because of war.

The Second Wave of Arab immigration to America—45,201—
dominated by the debacle of Palestine, also included the beginning
of what would be called the "brain drain" from newly independent
Arab states, such as Egypt, Syria, Iraq, Jordan, and the North African
Arab countries. Some were dissatisfied with the series of coups that

occurred frequently in these new states, some wanted a better standard of living, and some were political exiles from intra-Arab squabbles and the Arab-Israeli conflict.

Much distinguishes the Palestinian and other Arab immigrants in the Second Wave from their forebears who charted the path to America in the First Wave. Economic concern, the search for a better livelihood, was the primary reason most early Syrians came to the United States, with political deterioration and warfare a secondary reason. These factors were reversed for the Second Wave Arabs, who, arriving in the United States after 1948, would not have come if it hadn't been for upheaval. Unlike the First Wavers, many were refugees and exiles who had lost a land that was not to be regained and would be transformed beyond recognition.

Unlike the early Syrians—who were 90 percent Christians—the Second Wave Arab immigrants were 60 percent Muslim. They arrived more by plane than boat and tended to be in much better financial position than were the early turn-of-the-century Arabs. They were better educated than the earlier group, whose members were overwhelmingly illiterate before coming to the United States. This combination of distinctive differences between the Second Wave and the First Wave kept the two communities for many years separate and distinct, until the cataclysmic wars of 1967, 1973, and particularly 1982, drew them into a unique political cohesion, however ephemeral. On the one hand, the Second Wave Arab Americans had every reason to be even more grateful to the United States than did the previous group. Since many were exiles from war and political upheaval, the United States provided for them a secure haven. Their superior education and skills might be assumed to have helped them adapt to the sophisticated post-World War II American society more quickly than did their peddler and factory laborer forebears.

But this was not necessarily so, for a number of reasons. First, the very skills they carried with them to the New World on 707s, which initially slid them into US society more easily, also gave them access to social structures that required them to hide their views. Because 60 percent were Muslim, many were more spiritually alienated than the First Wavers. Third, as Palestinians—drawn by US freedom—they were concomitantly repelled by US policies, and this made for extremely torn feelings, ambiguities not as marked in the earlier immigrants and their progeny. Fourth, whereas early Arab immigrants and their offspring shared in the wholesale adaptation to the mores of America—wanted them, gloried in them—because in most cases they had come from lands where national independence was still unmet, the Second Wavers kept "their bags packed" much longer than had earlier immigrants. Fifth, the alienation the Second Wavers carried with them into US society was not alleviated much by interaction with the earlier Syro–Lebanese immigrants, whose status was sunk deep into America by this point; in any case, they did not want to be reminded that the Middle East was once again smoldering. In short, First Wave and Second Wave immigrants did not socialize much, though they might attend the same churches and mosques. Hisham Sharabi described, for instance, meeting an old Lebanese family descended from the turn-of-the century immigrants in Chicago at the time of the Palestine war: "Arab Americans had no status, no entity, no consciousness, no existence whatsoever. We once were invited to a Lebanese home. Politically they had no consciousness whatsoever. They didn't even bring the subject up."[3]

SYRIAN AMERICANS REACT TO THE BREWING PALESTINE CONFLICT

Contrary to the benumbed Lebanese the student Sharabi met in Chicago in 1947 who had no notion—or didn't let on if they had—that Palestine was in the process of being excised from the Arab world, there were attempts by Syrian Americans from an early date to speak out on the issue in US forums. The attempts were certainly not the result of mass galvanization. They were not nearly as organized and fervent as those of US Zionist institutions. They were isolated blips on a dark screen, warnings that went unheeded or unheard.

In 1927, *Al-Bayan*, the Druze journal in New York, dealt with a US congressman's suggestion to issue coins and postage stamps commemorating the Zionist "rule" in Palestine. *Al-Bayan* believed that Palestine was certainly "rich" enough in "historical facts" of its own. A little disdain is couched in the journal's injunction to native Palestinians "to rally to the defense of their rights so that the Zionists may not monopolize the offices and resources of the country head and tail."[4]

No doubt the worst riots to date in the growing abrasiveness of Jewish colonists and Palestinian Arabs—those in August 1929 in Hebron—spurred the 1929 debate between Syrian-American novelist and poet Amin Rihani and M. Weisgal. It was during the bloody confrontations of 1929 (of 250 Arabs and Jews killed, 64 were non-Zionist religious Jews in Hebron) that a young Alfred Farradj first heard Arabs shout, "Down with Balfour!" He also remembered "some [Arab] sympathy for the [Jewish] Hebronites. In fact, there were Arabs who smuggled some people out of Hebron to spare them from the massacres."[5]

A nearly forgotten chapter in the battle for Palestine—the 1936 Gandhi-like, nonviolent six-month general strike by the Palestinian Arabs—was recalled by many Second and Third Wave immigrants. Naim Halabi, born in 1900 in Jaffa, had a mixed reaction to it: "It was terrible. You couldn't find anything to eat. You have to smuggle things from place to place. All the boats were on strike. Only government officials used to work. But during this period Jews took advantage of the situation and built a port in Tel Aviv."[6] It was a strike that cut across all classes. According to Shukri Khouri from Taybe, whose father fought for the United States in the First World War, "a strike of the automobiles" was monitored by a Mr. Dajani of the national bank in Palestine. "There was no driving," said Khouri. "Naturally, anybody who operated his car did so against the desire of a coalition headed by Dajani."[7] Alfred Farradj remembered, "There was nothing to do for all the Arabs. You couldn't go to your business or your school. Prices dropped to nothing. Twenty-five eggs for a shilling. Lamb for 25 cents a pound. Women went door to door begging for money for vegetables they were selling. It wasn't a wholehearted feeling about the strike."

Economic pressures finally were too great for the people, and the very group that had started the strike—the Arab Higher Committee— called it off (at the urging of three Arab kings who cautioned reliance on "our friend," Britain).

Within a year, open Arab rebellion against the partition of Palestine reached its peak, and the members of the Arab Higher Committee were exiled by the British to the Seychelles Islands. Alfred Farradj recalled with some irony that upon returning from exile one of the leaders, "Khalidi [mayor of Jerusalem] gave stamps to us children at school from the Seychelles."

Palestinians still contemplate that remarkable six-month experience in nonviolence. A 1980s immigrant from Ramallah, in the West Bank, to Washington, DC, who had been imprisoned by the Israelis, called the 1936 event "an exception of the time" under an occupation authority that was actually trying to get out itself. "Nowadays if you strike for one day, the occupation [forces] will come and get welding machines, hacksaws to force open the stores," he said. "There's no chance for that kind of long-term thing. Also, for the shopkeepers themselves, they can't win, because if you strike you're going to get it from the Israelis, if you don't get it from the Palestinians themselves."[8] In spite of such understandable skepticism, the concept of nonviolent resistance resurfaced on the West Bank a half century after the brave, ill-fated experience in 1936.[9]

With the back of the Palestinian Arab resistance broken in 1939, and the increasingly listless British resistance to Zionist gun-running and emigration, by the mid-1940s it appeared that a bloodbath was inevitable. The US Arab voices were few. The only groups that had existed from the early 1930s were the so-called regional Syrian-Lebanese Federations—Eastern, Midwest, Southern—which were largely social in function. They had resisted national unification, as well, and hence were no match for the highly organized American

Zionists who had, as early as 1922, elicited congressional backing for what the Balfour Declaration in 1917 had called a "national home" for the Jews in Palestine.

But some isolated Arab Americans decided to play catch-up. In the mid-1940s, the community was called to testify before Congress on the question of Palestine. This was a first, and the community elected Philip K. Hitti, the eminent historian from Princeton, to deliver testimony. Hitti minced no words in his statement before the Foreign Affairs Committee of the House of Representatives on February 15, 1944: "From the Arab point of view political Zionism is an exotic movement, internationally financed, artificially stimulated, and holds no hope of ultimate or permanent success." Hitti reminded congressmen that the last attempt to construct an alien state in the Holy Land—the Crusaders'—lasted less than 50 years. Hitti traced uniform Muslim opposition to the idea of a Jewish state that had grown to a fever pitch in states fighting British colonialism, such as India. But this opposition "does not spell anti-Semitism," Hitti emphasized. "Of all the major peoples of the world, the Arabs perhaps come nearest to being free from race prejudice."

Sympathy with the Jewish plight in Germany was strong among the Arabs, Hitti confirmed, but the idea of a state that would exclude 90 percent of the indigenous inhabitants was odd to them. Hitti then made an offer to persecuted Jewry that directly challenged the US government's moralisms over Palestine—why not open US soil to Jewish immigration? "They [the Arabs] fail to understand why the American legislators, so solicitous for the welfare of European Jews, should not lift the bars of immigration and admit Jewish refugees, millions of whom could be settled on the unoccupied plains of Arizona or Texas. This certainly falls within their jurisdiction."

It has often been said that the creation of Israel was acquiesced to by a US government adamantly opposed to unlocking the immigration door it had opened so generously at the turn of the century, to German Jews, Polish Jews, Italians, Irish, and, of course, Syrians, as well as many others. Hitti's suggestion to use Arizona and Texas stuck in the craw of representatives from those regions, no doubt. Hitti's unsettling offer was quickly muffled and forgotten.

Hitti continued his tireless work as the decade moved toward all-out war in Palestine, but to no avail. Records show that the Maronite academician met with Muslim and Jewish groups in October 1944 for reconciliation strategies. He helped found in the waning hours of the year the Institute for Arab American Affairs (IAAA) in New York City and testified on its behalf before the Anglo-American Committee on Palestine in 1946.

Sidestepping the inevitable fracas over membership, IAAA tried to disseminate its publications among US policymakers. One interesting booklet, *Arabic-Speaking Americans* (1946), written by Habib Katibah and Farhat Ziadeh, was the first attempt since Hitti's own *The Syrians in America* (1924) to translate the community to the American public at large. The book had a unique organization: it cataloged and described Arab Americans by profession from kimono and negligee manufacturers to artists and musical composers like the then-popular Anis Foulihan. It was also the first known organization that referred to a distinctly "Arabic-speaking American" community, as opposed to Syrian-American or Lebanese-American. It was not until the late 1970s that the appellation "Arab American" would begin to be used by the community at large, and even then not widely until the 1990s.

American Middle East policy, which during World War I Seth Tillman found to be "ambivalent," by World War II was clearly "contradictory."[10] During the 1944 presidential campaign, President Roosevelt personally endorsed unrestricted Jewish immigration to Palestine and the establishment of a "Jewish commonwealth." His wife, Eleanor, was even more fervent for such goals. Yet, in 1945, Roosevelt met with King Abd al-Aziz of Saudi Arabia on the USS *Quincy* in the Suez Canal, later reassuring him in a letter that the United States would "take no action... which might prove hostile to the Arab people."

Though Roosevelt had met with top Zionist leaders, such as Rabbi Stephen Wise, the closest that Arab Americans came to his administration was a meeting with his secretary of state, Cordell Hull, in the early 1940s. According to Shukri Khouri, he, George Kheirallah, Faris Malouf (a First Wave immigrant peddler who became a prominent Boston lawyer), and Dr. Fuad Shatara met with Hull and a Jewish delegation, with both sides presenting their views.

After Roosevelt's death in 1945, the Zionist leaders in America jumped on Give 'Em Hell Harry Truman as soon as he was in the saddle. After some initial reservations, he gave them heaven. At a key meeting in 1948, recalling the long efforts of Zionist leader Chaim Weizmann on behalf of persecuted world Jewry—and the inability of Weizmann to secure a meeting with Truman at the zero hour— Eddie Jacobson, a former partner in a men's clothing store with Truman in Kansas City, broke into tears. Those could be called the most weighted tears in post–World War II American history. Truman, at first piqued, scheduled a meeting with Weizmann. The rest, as they say, is history.

Before the fateful hour in 1948 the Syrian Americans did not meet with Truman. In 1946, Truman told American diplomats serving in the Arab world, "I have to answer to hundreds of thousands anxious for the success of Zionism; I do not have hundreds of thousands of Arabs among my constituents."[11] In fact, there were

October 3, 1951: President Harry S. Truman meets representatives of Arab-American organizations. (UPI/Bettmann Newsphotos)

approximately a half-million Americans of Arab descent at the time. They would wait three years for their first official meeting with a US president. In 1951—after the Federation of Syrian-Lebanese Clubs finally achieved national unity (it was short-lived)—a visibly uncomfortable Truman met with a federation delegation. He gave them ten minutes.[12]

IMMIGRANTS FROM A LOST PALESTINE

Many Palestinian Americans who survived the 1948 full-scale war that created Israel speak of it with bitterness, incredulity, sorrow. But none I met had lived through quite so much as Naim Halabi, 83 when I interviewed him in northern California, and none managed to match, in spite of such dislocations, his magnetic serenity. With a head of hair white as a swan's wing and white moustache to match, the handsome Halabi, though a latecomer to these shores, declared the US Constitution to be "a second Bible." A brother of his named Abraham was nicknamed "Abraham Lincoln" when young. Halabi visited America briefly in 1937, after the break-up of the nonviolent general strike in Palestine, in which he had played a part. He lived through the evacuation of his native Jaffa by the Turks in World War I (French warships were shelling the coast), though he said, "One noble thing about it—not a single house was looted or touched [by the Turks]." Halabi, who was an English teacher, tennis coach, and importer of India tires from Scotland in prewar Palestine, was critical of British double-dealings and Arab lack of cooperation with the British mandate commissions: "This was one of the stumbling blocks. Until now we say no, no, no. We are not taking things positively, you see, and so we make mistakes. It's a weakness on the part of the Arabs." Halabi, who counseled Zionists "to look far to the distant future, not only the present, and see they are living in an ocean of Arabs and they have to befriend them, not subdue or degrade them," also had advice for Yasir Arafat: "Yasir, don't stick to arms and ammunitions. You have tried it and you have failed." This Halabi, who was raising the five children of his sister in 1948 after their father died (they all came to America), who was asked by Sabra (native-born) Jews to hide them should the war turn against them, who saw parts of bodies fly by after an Arab coffeehouse was blown up across from his building on Ben Yehuda Street, whose building itself was exploded, spoke with a fixation of homes stripped in Jerusalem by the insurgents:

> For centuries we have cultivated the land, we built homes. Jerusalem, Ramallah, Beit Jala, Jaffa—all built of solid stones, not bricks or cement... I went on Thursday morning on the fifteenth of May downtown to the garage. I took the rotor arm from our car and put it in my pocket... On Monday morning I saw our car on the main street [looted], people looting other houses. I put sand sacks on the windows of our home. The Jews of Jerusalem had gotten short of food. So they went after food when the war broke out. They took all the food from the [Arab] houses [in Jerusalem]. Then they took mattresses and covers. Rugs, every home had several rugs. They exchanged them with America to get ammunition. They started to loot everything—pianos, furniture, everything, everything! On Saturday when they left their synagogues they used to come in scores to the houses, break in and take things. After a few days they put us in a [military] zone. Architects would take what we use and their doctors what they use from clinics. Even they took the wire, cable from the roads. They took shutters, window shutters, because they are wooden. They used to come up to basins which are fixed into the walls, or washtubs, or water heaters, see. Once I stood in front of a [Israeli] tractor and said, "I can't move from here until you go. This is part of the house. It's not movable." It was difficult to

oppose them, and in the end, they took everything.[13]

Under the new Israeli rule, Halabi suddenly could not find work. He was refused an import license. A fellow Mason would not let him sell gasoline because he was an Arab. After scratching a living with a small clothing shop, he went with his family to Jordanian-occupied East Jerusalem in 1956. In 1958, he left for Lebanon. In 1977, after living through the worst years of the civil war in Beirut, he finally emigrated to the United States, and San Francisco. His favorite home after losing so many homes? "Where there is peace."

I sought out a number of Second Wave Palestinian immigrants in the United States who had long since taken citizenship and rooted, however precariously, in American society after their abrupt exile from an ancient, heretofore holy, land. Many had tales of woe concerning al-Nakba ("The Catastrophe," as the Palestinian Arabs call Israel's war of independence). Among the most interesting of these were Aziz Shihab of Dallas, Texas; Edward Said of New York City; Hisham Sharabi of Washington, DC; and Nabila Cronfel of Houston, Texas.

It is not often that one is introduced to someone via a poem. But an esteemed poet from San Antonio, Texas, captures her father in love with figs, "ripe tokens / ... of a world that was always his own." I count myself a lucky friend of Naomi Shihab Nye. Given the chance to scout out the exact declination and shade afforded by her father's fig tree, I did not resist. The tree is in the middle of Dallas, a city not known for anything as viable as figs but rather typified by freeways and long, dry expanses filled by shopping centers on the ground and Texas storms in the sky. His fig is a particularly tall tree, as if given freer rein than most. There is another one in the front yard. But the one in the backyard was Aziz Shihab's pride, and he filed through the branches of fig as if going through the years of his life.

Shihab is a native of Sinjil in the West Bank, a Muslim whose father had had four wives. He had spent the dark days of the 1948 conflict working as a newspaperman only to discover in the disengagement agreements between Israel and Jordan that the Jordanian chief negotiator cared more about spit-shined shoes than the details of the treaty he was to sign. Shihab would become one of the only Americans of Arab background—and certainly the only Palestinian—to be an editor on a major US daily newspaper. His work with the city desk of the *Dallas Morning News* was shifted in 1983 to special sections. It was easier, less strenuous work, welcome since his heart attack in 1978. If there were political motivations, Aziz did not know about them.

Shihab took me for a midnight stroll of two miles in a lawn-green, quiet night, lifting his walking stick on each stride and placing it ahead of himself in military style. This was a man who craved ritual, not for official sake, but for the sake of personal meaning. A short man, but with strong legs, his taciturn demeanor flew into a squawking laugh if the right chord was hit. He pointed out who lived where on the block, and it struck me that few people who live in large cities would bother to identify their neighbors. Aziz also lifted the cane to demonstrate distances, to refer to where one building once was and is no longer in the incessant building passion of Dallas. Perhaps, too, he was doing something he would do if in Jerusalem, which he has revisited on occasion to see his nonegenarian mother, Khadra, who lived until her 1992 death in Sinjil, 25 miles to the northeast. The original family home in Jerusalem is now occupied by an Israeli rabbinical school.[14]

Born in 1927, Aziz Shihab spent much of his youth in Jerusalem away from Sinjil and in a boarding school because of his father's wives. "Whenever I came home it was a good deal of tension between wives," he said.[15] They all lived in the same compound with a courtyard; Aziz' mother was the first wife and she was the last survivor of them. Aziz' father worked for the British when they held the Palestine Mandate, with the department of roads, smoothing potholes and putting in directional signs. Aziz himself would bicycle and walk these roads, such as the one from Jerusalem to Ramallah, during the general strike of 1936 in which Palestinians protested British occupation and Zionist immigration.

But he was young at that time. By 1948, however, he was 21 and teaching in a school in Jerusalem. Like many Palestinians in America, he could recall little emnity between Arabs and Jews in Palestine on a person-to-person level: "In fact, a lot of our neighbors were Jews and I never felt any tension. I personally did not realize this was a Jew or this an Arab. In fact, I remember my father going to the Jewish doctors when he had eye trouble and I did not distinguish between Arabs and Jews."

He witnessed many battles of the 1948 war, including the collapse of the old Jewish part of Jerusalem. His view of the Arab forces was dim: "The Jews were very organized and knew exactly what they were doing and the Arab army came in—they didn't really know what they were there for. It was very obvious. They were not organized; their leadership was pretty strange, pretty poor. When you have five Israelis who were organized with a goal against even one hundred Arabs who didn't really know what they were there for— that's why the big defeat."

As for the British: "I remember specifically one incident walking in Jerusalem with a fez on, kind of bourgeois and I was pretty happy," he said. "I was cool, putting it on the corner of my head. A soldier came and kicked it off my head and said, 'You are nothing but an Arab.' We didn't have a great deal of luck."

After the smoke cleared in 1948, West Jerusalem was captured by the forces of the Haganah and the Irgun, and Aziz's family gave up their house and moved to Sinjil, on the road to Nablus. Aziz commuted to East Jerusalem to work at a radio station as a broadcaster and then assumed duties as, of all things, the censorship director for the press office of the Jordanian army. He became close to the Jordanian governor of Jerusalem, with whom he worked until leaving the area for the United States. What he witnessed, however, during the disengagement talks was less than edifying and remained riveted in his memory 40 years later halfway around the world—in particular, a phone call from Moshe Dayan.

The commanding officer of Jordan's army was away from his desk one day when the phone rang. Aziz picked it up and discovered Moshe Dayan on the line, a leader of the Jewish victors with whom, certainly, no one on the Jordan side was supposed to be talking. When Aziz's boss found out, "he was very upset [and] wanted me to never mention it again to anyone, and that shook me up. Because I thought Moshe Dayan was a great enemy and the war was going on and people were killed. What's he talking to Moshe Dayan for? I didn't know what was going on."

When there was a cease-fire, and the sides had agreed through intermediaries to hold a disengagement meeting and sign a truce agreement, Moshe Dayan represented the Israeli side in Jerusalem, and Aziz's boss represented the Arab side. "He was so concerned that his shoes were shined and suit was pressed," Aziz recalled with bile in his voice. "I couldn't believe it. And I mentioned, you know, that's not important. We are going to decide the fate of so many people. His concern was for the cane that he carried, that the brass was shined, his shoes shined, his pants were perfectly ironed. And when we got there Moshe Dayan looked like a bum." There was also some difficulty over reading maps: "It was puzzling to me that the Jordanian officers really didn't even know how to read a map. They didn't know the difference... this is why, I think, once the truce was signed, villages were divided right down the middle. They didn't know the difference. Israel was playing games with them. So they were good people, but not battle-type people. They didn't know much about Palestine and I don't think they cared much for Palestinians."

Being a second-class citizen under the Jordanians made him itch to leave: "I wanted to get out of there and the best way to get out was to go to school." At first he made arrangements for the Jordanian government to pay for university education for him in the States, but "they never pursued it; they never paid anything." He was accepted by Washington University in St. Louis and was soon on "an old beat-up-looking ship" sailing through the Mediterranean from Beirut to Marseilles to Ellis Island, then in its last years of operation. "I was glad to get out, with the intention of staying out as long as the situation [in Palestine] was what it was," he declared.

He debarked in New York in 1950 from a Greek ship, after having thrown all his shoes overboard except the ones he was wearing. He vowed to buy all new shoes in America. Aziz described his arrival, which just happened to coincide with the mayhem of a Columbus Day parade:

> I had the phone number of somebody who was a Palestinian to call and he wanted me to come to his home. "If you come here don't talk, don't mention the Jews because I have Jews who are guests in my home." So I never did go. I stayed in a hotel and the very next morning there was the Columbus Day parade. I couldn't believe the number of people, all the strange silliness in the streets of New York. It was just overwhelming. The parade went right in front of the hotel and it was just far too many people. I can't remember the name of the hotel; there were Arabs, and I started talking to them. A lot of them were Palestinian merchants who came here to get rich. And I did not know if they were living in the hotel or just congregating in it. But they knew I had just come from [Palestine] and they were asking how the situation was. I told them a few things about it. But they really seemed interested mostly in a story than anything else. You know you take a Jew in this country—even now if he has never been there he talks about Israel like his home. Even those people [Palestinian Arabs] who came from there—there was nothing special.

Aziz married Miriam Allwardt of St. Louis and finished college at Washington University. By 1956 and the Suez crisis he had taken American citizenship. His experience as a journalist in Jerusalem and his fluency in English landed him work in the 1950s with the *St. Louis Globe Democrat*. He was enthusiastic in those years for the Arab cause and gave liberally of his time to lecture clubs and organizations about the Palestinians. And it hurt him:

> I was speaking a lot and I spoke to a group in St. Louis where there was a man named Morton May, who was president of May Company department stores and obviously a Zionist. From what I understood later, he made a call to the newspaper. They came and told me, "You can't do that." I said, "Why can't I do that in my own town?" "Well," they said, "you can't go around attacking the Jews." I said I wasn't attacking the Jews, I was attacking the Zionists and Israel. "Well," they said, "Morton May is one of our biggest advertisers." He owned

Famous Stores in St. Louis. [And he had told them], "You tell him he just can't do that." Later they fired me, I think because of that.

The newspaper guild, however, stood by Shihab; he was an active member, a shop steward. Their pressure kept him on the paper for a while, but he was demoted from the editorial department to circulation, which he knew nothing about. "They were trying to force me to quit, which I finally did, and they paid me severance pay," he said. In his judgment, the May fiasco was the cause. There was no bitterness in Aziz Shihab's voice, but a sternness, a recounting of facts however unpleasant by a seasoned journalist, though in this case the injustice had been done to him as an American by an American.

At this point Aziz and Miriam packed up their belongings and two children, Naomi and Adlai (named after the two-time losing Democratic presidential candidate Adlai Stevenson), and went to Kansas City, where he and his wife had first met. They stayed some peaceful years there until something got under Aziz's skin—he was offered a chance to edit a newspaper in Jerusalem in 1966 and he took it. The Shihab family left, however, on the eve of the June War of 1967 in which Israel captured the West Bank and, with it, Shihab's village of Sinjil. They had been tipped off by an American friend at the United Nations five days before the lightning-quick war commenced.

For seven years, Aziz worked for the San Antonio, Texas, daily. In 1975 he moved to Dallas to assume a job on the city desk of the *Dallas Morning News*. I wondered if after the 1967 invasion he felt as compelled to speak before American groups as he had after 1948:

> When I came back I did the same thing but not to the same extent. I spoke again and became known through the newspaper. I was president of a [newly formed] American Arab Club in San Antonio and we would meet at the university there and invite speakers. But I realized two things. One, the American audiences really didn't care for the hard facts. After your speech you are leaving [and] somebody would ask you the most strange questions. "Oh, you came from Jerusalem, so you are a Jew." After you spend an hour speaking to them! So you know they are not listening. The second thing was the Arab members of the club—50–60 altogether—were just another Arab world, so divided, fighting each other. I am more disappointed in the Arab world and the Arabs than I am disappointed in the United States.

Battles—not with the Zionists—but with the Arab community in Dallas helped sour Shihab, no doubt. Because of his unusual position as an editor of a major daily, and because the community often felt it was alone and unheard, Shihab was particularly deluged everytime Israel bombed South Lebanon or started a new settlement on the West Bank.

Even at the celebration for the groundbreaking of a mosque in Dallas, a fight broke out, Aziz said, and the police were called: "It's pathetic." For him the fact of internecine Arab strife had taken on the size of myth, of quandary in his mind, something mysterious that— if answered—would unlock so much in Aziz's world: "I hope that someday I will know the answer to why the Arabs cannot unite and like each other. When I see an Arab I don't care whether I have never met him; I have a strong feeling for him. But you listen to them for ten minutes and you don't want to see them again. I don't know what it is. I don't know if it's our history of being occupied by other people that divided us. I don't know if it's our mentality, because we certainly have a lot of love. But why we don't direct the love to each other I don't know."

About the Israeli invasion of Lebanon in 1982—one that galvanized the community more than any other event since 1948— did it stir the toughened sensibilities of Shihab? He said, matter-of-factly, "I am not surprised at anything the Israelis do. I am not surprised that they want to expand and kick out all the Arabs from there. That's been their policy since they were created. So when the Arabs come and scream... so what? What's new about it?" But as an American, had his cynicism taken over completely? Was there nothing as a private citizen he felt compelled to do to help the fate of those he left behind? "I believe the pendulum turns," he said. "How it's going to happen, I don't know."

At this point we went into the kitchen and Miriam Shihab sat down with us. She was dressed in a kind of folk dress whose ethnic origin could not be determined—some fanciful breed of angel, no doubt. It looked to be a self-made dress and she is a self-made person. She smiled and said that her daughter is more devoted to the "Arab cause" now than her husband. I couldn't resist asking her if there were adjustments marrying a Muslim Arab, and a Palestinian for that matter, after growing up Protestant in St. Louis.

"Of course, you know there would be," her blue-gray eyes flashed. "After we had two children one of their teachers came to our house and said, 'Oh we just think you made the most wonderful adjustment.' I said, 'What's that? What are you talking about? What's so special? You know, we just got along because we are happy to get along. He's different; I'm different—okay. No big deal. You don't think of it as adjusting—you just do it!'"

But after the coffee was poured, Miriam Shihab let her hair down and recalled some humorous contrasts about this new man from the Levant: "He was old country first. Don't wear sleeveless dresses, don't wear shorts, don't speak to another man on the street even if you work with him or know him very well! Return a wedding present from a boyfriend with a note—'We don't want your wedding present'—and things like that were a little hard to do!" She looked over at Aziz, who sat motionless, brows perennially pursed, but with the habit of giving his wife her say. "Now he has adjusted and he wears shorts and I can almost dress as I please. I can speak to almost anybody—not quite! You know, he gets mad, but I do what I please more or less. Perhaps as we get older I notice the differences more—maybe the first blush of infatuation goes away and you think, 'What am I doing?' If your children are gone and then there's only two of you, you think, why do I have to take this all my life? I want my freedom!" She said the last with mock excitement that almost pulled her over a synthesized inner brink.

"We are lucky," Miriam concluded, recovering from her doubt. "A lot of people don't make it to 54 years of marriage." As for mixed marriages between an American and foreign-born spouse of a different culture, "I don't advise it for anybody. I always tell people don't do it unless you find you can't function or get along without each other."

They took me to an Arab market in Dallas filled with sacks of thyme, cardamom, sweet basil, and other herbs and spices that always thrust me back onto a porch in my past. We stopped at a very small new café run by Lebanese expatriates come since the civil war. Aziz wanted to patronize them and help them get started and wasn't much interested in their politics—though a cross tattoo inked into the owner's skin showed him to be a Christian. Finally, we returned to their modest home with the immodest fig trees. A ladder stood inside the one out back, though it was a month to go before August would fatten the sweet, pliant fruit. I imagined Aziz standing on that ladder at night, testing the softness of the figs far from Jerusalem.

Until his untimely death in 2004, Edward Said's life embodied many contradictions. In a country where English professors are largely conservative in both habit and politics—given more to tweeds than flak jackets—Said, as an author, television commentator, and sought-after speaker, represented Palestinians and the PLO. He came from a blue-stripe, preppy, educational background (Princeton, Harvard) and yet was close to Yasir Arafat. (Later, he became one of Arafat's strongest critics.) Said lived in New York City, the cradle of American Zionism, and yet was the leading Palestinian-American critic of Zionism. Famous as a Middle East thinker, he was one of the foremost literary critics of our time whose initial academic work dealt with Joseph Conrad. His life was fundamentally given to seeking justice for Palestinian Arabs, yet he counted few Arabs as his closest friends. His father was an American GI in World War I; he was a major critic of US military policy.

In truth Said's worlds—literary and political—were always interlinked. The foundation of his literary criticism assumed a political and moral commitment. After his first writings on Conrad and a book exploring how and why novelists "begin" their stories, Said wrote a quartet of seminal books concerning the Middle East (*Orientalism*, *The Question of Palestine*, *Covering Islam*, and *After the Last Sky*). Said hatched a new trend in contemporary literary criticism: engaging, committed, politically sophisticated, and skeptical. He espoused "secular criticism" and aimed a broadside volley at the New Critics of the 1950s who had dominated American approaches to literature for three decades:

> But it is no accident that the emergence of so narrowly defined a philosophy of pure textuality and critical noninterference has coincided with the ascendancy of Reaganism, or for that matter with a new cold war, increased militarism and defense spending, and a massive turn to the right on matters touching the economy, social services, and organized labor.... A precious jargon has grown up, and its formidable complexities obscure social realities that, strange though it may seem, encourage a scholarship of 'modes of excellence' very far removed from daily life in an age of declining American power. Criticism can no longer cooperate in or pretend to ignore this enterprise.[16]

Ivory tower, this philosophy of criticism is not. His office was in a brick tower, actually, on the second floor of Columbia's administration building, just above the university's president.

It was a cold October day when I got off the bus at the 116th Street entrance to Columbia University and walked across the green of the venerable school on the upper West Side. In many ways, the setting fit Said—the walls of ivy and peace on the outskirts of destitute Harlem.

Said's shirt was a mauve grid—the effect was proper but somewhat contrary, even melancholic. He appeared ten years younger than his age, except for strands of gray in the coal-black hair along his ears. His eyes shone like coal; he had a puckish, dimpled smile and a boyish but resonant voice. For one of such pronounced, even famously controversial opinions, I found him at times self-deprecating and impatient with renown. In his Byzantine sentences, he was above all kind and even whimsical in his recollections of early days in Palestine, where he was born in 1935.

Conrad seemed a good boat in which to launch. I wondered if he noticed something of the *Heart of Darkness* in Beirut. "No, no," he reached for the professorial pipe and wandered around the desk looking for tobacco. "I mean, my interest in Conrad is really because it strikes me that he wrote from a point of view that resembles my own experiences. He was born in one society and wrote in another and wrote about a third one. The dislocation and peculiar angle of vision, and then the difficulty of sort of getting it right in a language

Edward W. Said addresses the 1985 ADC convention (Doug Roberts)

that was always trying to write about a reality slipping away, is what struck me."[17]

Said was aware of a dislocation in his life "at the very beginning." He was an Arab going to an English school, a Christian in a Muslim society. Even his Episcopal faith put him outside the larger Christian minorities. "Let's say I was never completely at one with the culture or society of which I was a part," he said. "There was always a part of me that wasn't there." Later, he put this plaintively in a memoir written in the fever of discovering he now lived with a death-dealing illness, "The overwhelming sensation I had was of always being out of place. Thus it took me about fifty years to become accustomed to, or, more exactly, to feel less uncomfortable with, 'Edward,' a foolishly English name yoked forcibly to the unmistakably Arabic family name Said."[18]

Said's father ran the family business in Jerusalem, the Palestine Educational Foundation, the largest vendor of books and magazines in Palestine at the time. After founding it at the turn of the century, Wadie Said later branched out to publishing and marketing office machinery and Arabic typewriters. In Cairo, part of the family business thrived even more than in Jerusalem. But in 1911, Wadie left Palestine because the Ottoman Turks were about to draft him into the army to fight in Bulgaria. He was one of the few First Wave Palestinians to join their Syrian brothers in coming to America.

The son's eyes sparkled when recalling that his father had enlisted in the US Army in World War I, like others, ready to fight for democracy but not for autocracy with the Turks. Edward recalled with some mirth Wadie's trip across the ocean to the United States. It had been a story told often in Said households in Jerusalem, Cairo, and Lebanon:

> He went from Palestine to Port Said and Alexandria, was stuck there a while, then spent some time in Southampton, England. He worked his way across the ocean as a waiter. He was very seasick. He used to wait on tables and then go and throw up in the galley. And the story he liked to tell a lot was that a purser asked, "Have you ever been on ship before?" And he said, "Yes." And the purser said, "All right, the first thing I want you to do is clean the portholes." My father didn't have any idea what the portholes were, so he cleaned everything but the portholes!

Wadie jumped ship in New York City—getting on a streetcar with a friend and not coming back. "He qualified for illegal entry," Said recalled, bemused.

The "typical self-made man who credited America with a lot of his business know-how," Said's father ran a successful paint company in Cleveland for a number of years and studied at night at Case Western Reserve to become a lawyer. But the pressure on him to take care of his family back in Jerusalem was too great. He returned in 1920, married a woman who was half-Lebanese in Nazareth in 1932, and though he kept his citizenship papers, only returned to the United States briefly in 1951 to escort Edward to school.

Edward Said remembered the partitioning of Jerusalem into zones; when he was a schoolboy at St. George's High School, "you couldn't cross from one zone to another without a pass to go to school. There was a lot of worry about going to the wrong kind of theater—a Jewish one, or an Arab one." The reason was simple: movie theaters were blown up. As for classmates who were on the other side, Said recalled a Jewish boy named David Ezra: "One felt some kind of tension. I liked him. We were friendly."

Before the end, Said had many wonderful times in Palestine, which he recounted to me. His "fondest memory," however, was not an event but a condition, being "always surrounded by a large number of family members, cousins, aunts, uncles, and so forth. And not only in Jerusalem, because my mother's family lived in Ramallah and Jaffa and Haifa." Nowadays, that closeness, he admitted, was lost: "What really happened after was a tremendous dispersal."

He especially liked day trips to Safed as a boy, and going up to Tiberias along the Sea of Galilee to swim and have a picnic. One of the Galilean villages he recalled was Tubrah, where you could buy roasted corn-on-the-cob from carriage vendors, black ears of fresh corn: "That's a very important early memory that I have," he said wistfully, looking over his shoulder out the window that showed the cold university green. "The last time I was at that shore was almost 40 years ago."

What brought the scholar, finally, to America was very unscholarly activity—he was kicked out of a prep school in Cairo for bad behavior. The boy had gone to Cairo with his family after the 1948 war. Said explained his fall from academic grace at Victoria College Prep:

> The atmosphere at school—all the students were essentially Arab and all the teachers English—was charged. I thought the British—though of generally high caliber—were essentially hostile, for reasons that had to do with British imperialism. There's a certain kind of condescension. The relationship between teachers and students was adversarial. So I was kind of a ringleader... And we would insult them openly, in Arabic, which they didn't understand. I feel that it was sort of a good thing that I left in that way rather than doing what a lot of my classmates did, which was finish the school. I didn't get a school certificate. A lot of my clever classmates went to Oxford and Cambridge, but I came to the United States.

Another run-in with the British, one that, according to Said, "seems to have made the most impression on me when I was a kid in Cairo," resulted in his being ejected by the secretary of the posh al-Jazirah Country Club. Said's family, being upper class, were allowable members, but when Edward strolled across one of the club's greens at dusk one day, a Mr. Pilly stopped him and told him to get out. "You're an Arab and we don't allow Arabs here," the secretary said. "This was one of the first indications in my life of the importance of race over class," he reflected, one cinder of anger remaining in his voice.

Said was allowed back in Victoria Prep on probation, but he left anyway. And through a friend of his father who was at the American University of Cairo, he was accepted at a prep school in Connecticut. In 1951, together with parents, Said voyaged across the seas. They went back, leaving him alone in America, as his father had been 40 years before.

Said credited his early years in the United States for creating his Palestinian consciousness, "because from the moment I arrived, really, until now, one is always aware of the tremendous interest in Israel which bears on you as a Palestinian and as an Arab." Like many Arab-American youth, he was called camel trader, rug dealer, and the like and was "singled out for especially unfair treatment in various ways" but nothing as severe as a beating. "No, I was always too big and strong," he laughed. "No, I never had that experience in my life."

He was a humanities major at Princeton, finishing in three years of independent study. He did not study with Philip Hitti there or delve academically into Middle Eastern affairs at all. In fact, Said knew little about Arabic poetry; educated at British schools, he was more versed in European literature and had to study his Arabic at home with tutors. Living in Cairo had sparked an interest in opera and theater. He remembered seeing Gilbert playing *Hamlet* in Cairo in 1944.

During the Suez War of 1956, which took place during his last year in college, Said began to test an appetite for the Middle East fray, publishing an article in the *Princeton Tiger* about the war. It was mixed with a few tentative speeches on campus and elsewhere. He did have friends who were becoming politically active back in the Middle East, people he visited on summer vacations, particularly in Lebanon, where his father had moved after the nationalization of various industries in Egypt by Gamal Abdul Nasser. Said's father believed that his American citizenship wouldn't help him anymore in Egypt. Ironically, Abdul Nasser espoused political policies that Said agreed with. More ironic and sad, although Wadie Said loved Lebanon and especially the mountain town of Dhour el Schweir where the family would summer, when he died a threat forced the family out of the place. Said recalled, "Almost his dying breath [in 1971] was 'Bury me in Dhour el Schweir.' But we were unable to buy the lot because we were considered outsiders. My mother wanted to build a little memorial, just a slab with a small park around it. A quiet place. I was on sabbatical in Lebanon in 1972–73 and I went up to negotiate. You had to buy a graveyard plot—we finally settled on a Catholic graveyard. And then we got threatening phone calls: 'If you build anything here, we'll blow it up.' So that was the first indication, already in early 1973, of bad feelings between the various communities. Perhaps it was that my father was Palestinian. I don't know."[19]

By the time he received his doctorate from Harvard in the early

1960s, Edward Said knew he was staying in the United States. The June War of 1967 was an important date in his evolving self-consciousness as a Palestinian. "I felt a complete collapse of expectation," he exclaimed, tapping the pipe on an ashtray. "I mean, one thought that there would at least be a fight."

He called a leave year at the University of Illinois in 1967 "the worst year of my life." Three things combined in this period of "tremendous upheaval" in his personal life: "The shock at the actual quick results of the war, the hostility and tremendous pressure I felt from the surroundings, and my own trauma, which was independent of that."

Shortly thereafter what became the germ of the classic *Orientalism* was solicited by an old friend, Ibrahim Abu-Lughod. The two scholars had been students together at Princeton (Abu-Lughod was a graduate student) and Ibrahim asked Edward for an article for an anthology he was editing on the Arab–Israeli crisis. Said wrote "The Arab Portrayed," his inaugural effort in how the West perceived the East.

The phone rang. It was a friend from Yale University discussing a speech Said had just given, which had stirred up a furor among some anti-Palestinian students. The friend read him an article written for the Yale student newspaper by Jonathan Kessler, a staff member of the American Israel Public Affairs Committee (AIPAC). Said's eyebrows hiked upward and he smiled puckishly. "Read this," Said thrust the article over his desk to me.

I read out loud, "Said is a master propagandist. He takes in much of his audience because much of his propaganda doesn't come across as propaganda." "He says that what I say is 'accurate but not true.'" Said grinned. We both agreed that was an interesting concept. I asked him if he'd ever been physically assaulted during his numerous talks around the country.

"I've been threatened a lot," he began to reload his pipe. "But that [Yale] audience wasn't hostile. The speech was given in a chapel; it was jam-packed, hundreds of people, and I got a standing ovation. Generally speaking, I think, with one exception that I can remember in ten years, when there was a lot of screaming and shouting and interrupting at the University of Miami, most of what I've done has been reasonably well received."

One professor at Wake Forest University whom I had talked with told me that when Said was there for a talk he was tersely introduced by the English Department chairman, who then left the room, giving the impression that establishment departments aren't that crazy about him and his controversial opinions.

"I don't think that's entirely accurate," he insisted. "There are two aspects to my work that are difficult for some people. One is that my literary work, strictly speaking, is what I have called 'oppositional.' It goes against some of the currents in the academic study of literature. But it's still considered too establishment in the sense that I teach at a big university, tend to be characterized, foolishly, as a kind of academic 'star' of some sort. You know, I've done the Gauss Lectures at Princeton—all that kind of stuff. There's that side to it. Within the establishment I'm considered a kind of sport. But then unlike anyone roughly in my comparable position, I have this other political side that is difficult for a lot of people to deal with. Now I don't blame them. I mean, I find it difficult myself. Only rarely do I feel that I'm paying a price for my political views, however. It's not something that I am forced to confront every day, mainly because what I teach really has very little to do with my active political involvement. And I make a point—rightly or wrongly—never to teach anything to do with the Middle East although I've had opportunities to do that."

His work, since *Orientalism*, had "more and more converged on political issues in the study of culture." He examined literary paradigms to show "there's always been a political undercurrent within literature in this country; first, there was the battle against Stalinism and then there was McCarthyism, then Vietnam. But there's a deliberate, very powerful current trying to extricate literature, culture generally, from the overtly political. I think it's a misreading. I mean that in itself is a political gesture and more and more people are aware of that. It had to do with the way certain writers are studied. In my field for example—modern literature—the tremendous emphasis upon people like Wordsworth and Keats in the Romantic period to the exclusion of Shelley is a part of this attempt to deal with people who are not only nonpolitical, but antipolitical. Wordsworth and Coleridge, in particular, turned their backs on the French Revolution, became more conservative, and so on. The ethos of romantic scholarship has a lot to do with that. A lot of my work in modern literature has to do with reestablishing those connections which have been suppressed."

We came back to a suppression more immediate and violent: that of Palestinian nationalism by Israel's invasion of Beirut and expulsion of the PLO from Beirut in 1982. What was Said's reaction? "Helplessness, outrage," he said quickly in a voice sharpened to precision point. "My entire family was there for that. And my wife's family was there, too. It's a sense of outrage and anger and a very powerful sense of injustice and isolation. You know, a lot of people support the Palestinians, but the fact is in the Arab world what's happened is the continuing isolation of the Palestinian movement."

The eloquent man began to unravel. "You know, there are certain things that defy understanding. One of them is how can you drive a people off its land and say that it didn't happen, or in some way justify it, or in some way pretend that it's their fault for having been there in the first place. All that sort of argument. Another is how you explain the continued victimization of those people after you've done that—killing them, calling them terrorists, colonizing what's left of them, subjugating them, oppressing them in the worst possible way. How do you account for the fact that, even as this is taking place, the people who are doing it get credit for being democratic, lovable people?"

Said felt "denial formation" was the most accurate psychoanalytic description of how the Arabs looked at Palestinians now: "You say, 'This isn't happening, or in some way it's good for them or it's good for us.' All the attempt to deny that these quite acute sufferings are in fact taking place. That's the only way I can explain it."

At the time, for Said the real solution was "a Palestinian state, I think, in some measure federated with Jordan"—somewhat akin to the Reagan plan. "I think that would make a great deal of sense," Said continued. But after the failure of the Oslo peace process in the 1990s and a deeply influential trip to South Africa, Said rejected the once vaunted two-state solution and returned to the idealism of his youth and the notion of one binational state where Arabs and Jews would live together as equals, not only before the law but in practice. As he put it in a landmark 2001 essay, "Separation can't work in so tiny a land, any more than apartheid did."[20]

Even after the assassinations of PLO moderates like Issam Sartawi, Fahd Kawasmeh, and Said Hammami, Said still could say, "I do believe in reconciliation. I do think it's possible. I shudder to think of a state of conflict that is going to endure, because it seems to me that the stakes rise, positions harden, and the outcome is likely to be even more violent than anything we've seen."

Turning to Arab-American culture, I wondered if Edward Said felt an Arab-American *Exodus* or *Fiddler on the Roof* was in the making. "I don't know," he pondered carefully. "I'm not sure that in this culture you can have one frankly." He continued: "Sociologically there aren't enough—or there isn't a tradition yet of Arab Americans who write, who are involved in the arts. Second, it's not perceived as particularly important. You know, maybe there are other issues that are more important, like surviving, maintaining your identity, and so on. And don't forget the problem with language. For most of us, language is not something that's easily taken over. It requires an almost sublime act of arrogance to say that I'm going to do something of this sort. But the question is, can you make an impression in the face of the dominant culture? I think the dominant culture in terms of the imagination is largely Jewish. You know, there's a lot of very important work in its own terms. Not only in its own terms, but in absolute terms, very good cultural discourse in essays or fiction and so on. And in that, the Arab American simply plays a very tiny, marginal, unimportant role."

As for shortcomings in the Arab-American community at large and a prognosis for the future, Said felt two fundamentally opposed currents—nostalgia among recent arrivals from the Middle East and assimilation urges—still skewered the community: "The main problem is the inability of the Arab American to make the two stay together in order to create a mode which is Arab American, which isn't laughable and bumbling and halfhearted. You know, Danny Thomas is an example of that, a kind of folkloric, ethnic, self-neutralizing kind of thing. The prognosis can't be worse than that; it has to be better. What forms it will take is hard to tell. I think there is now developing a mode which is Arab American which has its own idioms with some logic... It's very much in a gestating stage."

I could not resist the final question to which everything, ultimately, must move in his mind as a Palestinian exile and an American. If there were a Palestinian state, would he return there?

"I'm fully of two minds," he said earnestly. "In other words, on the one hand I would say yes, I would like to do that. But I'm also committed by force of habit to a sense of exile and rootlessness. New York, I think, enhances that."

Some years after this interview, I encountered my mentor, his shrunken body ravaged by a decade-long battle with leukemia, at a 2003 ADC convention in Washington, DC. He had entered quietly, taking a position in the back of a huge auditorium with the multitudes standing, a worn bookbag over his gaunt arm. I touched his arm, as he stared at the speaker far off. He recoiled, full of nervousness—at least this is what I wanted to believe —not seeing me. It was a most tragic last encounter, except for the fact that with me was our eldest son, Matthew, who witnessed one of the great men of our time speak for the last time with signature passion and compassion. "He was wonderful," said Matt, who picked out a teeshirt of Arabic calligraphy and wore it all over the country, especially wherever there was a basketball court.

You didn't expect Hisham Sharabi to tell you he had a maid in his aristocratic family home in Jaffa, a German Jewish woman whom he loved, who adjusted his starched white shirt on his graduation from grammar school with a fond exhortation, "Der blousa must be this way." You laughed. And Sharabi barely let one corner of his stony mouth crinkle.

He was a short man, utterly serious, on whose taciturn face a smile seemed never to have passed. His wit came in a syringe-full of acid and he had been known to make mincemeat of formidable thinkers with his cutting analyses.

Sharabi was an institution. Author of numerous textbooks on the Arab world and a stunning memoir in Arabic that he refused to have translated into English, co-founder of Georgetown's unique Contemporary Arab Studies Program and the Arab American Cultural Foundation, Sharabi was the dean of committed Palestinian intellectuals in this country. Like Edward Said, however, his academic training was not in Middle East studies or Arabic but, in his case, philosophy.

With a calm born of absolute skepticism, Sharabi folded his hands and told me he was quite ready to leave the United States at any time up until the mid-1970s: "I was, psychologically speaking, always ready and packed to go back. I never really unpacked until December 1975 when the war in Lebanon made it clear to me that I couldn't go back home. Even to Lebanon."[21]

Sharabi called Lebanon "a second home" because his mother's family came from Tripoli, and the Jaffa brood would often summer in Aley in the Lebanese mountains. Sharabi also went to high school in Beirut and then attended the American University of Beirut. Thus, the expulsion of the PLO and Palestinians in general from Lebanon after Israel's invasion made Sharabi say, "I've lost two homelands, so to speak."

Sharabi had brothers and sisters in Syria, Jordan, and Saudi Arabia. But Jaffa was the origin point, famous for its oranges, which he noted "are still called Jaffa oranges in London and Germany and France where they are being exported by Israel. These orchards, which have surrounded the town, were for generations Arab owned, run by Arabs. Now they are owned and run by Jews, but they've been paying Arab workers."

Sharabi's sternness may have resulted from his growing up fast. He was sent away to boarding school at the age of seven, to the Quaker school in Ramallah. His memories of Jaffa, therefore, are not voluminous; the section of town he was born in, Mashia, is now totally razed to the ground. When he would come home from school he loved to take in a film at the Alhambra cinema in Jaffa, which is still standing. And summer vacations were a dream of blue sea at his grandfather's place in Acre in the northern tip of Palestine. There he would swim and fish with his cousins. In fact, at his office at Georgetown University there were only three photos on the walls— of Acre, "because they bring me back to my boyhood."

One of Sharabi's favorite activities as a boy—bizarre enough— was visiting cemeteries: "We used to love cemeteries, for some reason. Because in Acre on the Feast Days people would go out and visit their dead and take food just to make a picnic out of it, slipping around the graves. My family never did it because I don't think we had so many dead there."

As Sharabi ticked off the key dates of the conflict from the

Balfour Declaration (1917) to the present, he said, "The Palestinian struggle against Jewish colonization of Palestine is one of the most determined and certainly the longest in history of any colonial situation. Three generations have been living this nightmare."

For Sharabi, one of the dominant impressions of his early years was a train robbery, not by western outlaws, but of the Palestine Railroad by Irgun terrorists. He was eight years old: "It must have been '37, or '36. The train goes out from Jaffa, from the center of town, through Tel Aviv to Lydda. And then from there to Haifa. When we got to Tel Aviv we were ambushed and they tried to kill the driver of the first engine to derail the whole train. But apparently they didn't succeed in doing that. They kept shooting at the passenger cars and I remember my mother covering me with her body on the floor. Everybody yelling and shouting. That is probably my only memory of being in a state of danger, directly exposed to Jewish terrorist attack."

When the Haganah and Irgun irregulars attacked Jaffa, Sharabi's mother was at his grandfather's home in Acre. His brother and father fled Jaffa to Nablus, where his father's family came from, thence to Amman, Jordan. His mother and her family ended up in Beirut. In essence, the Israeli war of independence split the Sharabi family in two.

The bewildered, pained graduate student Sharabi faced the strange city of Chicago during the dispossession. It was winter: "I didn't dare go outside at all, since as soon as I stepped out the door an icy wind blasted against me, my nose turned to ice, and my ears felt like they would freeze and break off. Ah, for my homeland! Its blue sky, its good air and warm sun!"[22] He was 21 and, like Edward Said, he was invited to speak on Palestine to various student clubs. The first talk was packed with interested students. He was surprised to find that everyone was Jewish, including two fellow residents of his international house: "They were not hostile to me. But [other] Americans were not interested in the problem. They were Jewish and their concerns were totally different from the ordinary American. Nothing in my environment moved at all on this issue except American Jews and, of course, the American press. I used to buy the New York Times every day at 11 AM when it arrived by plane. I sat and read the unfolding of the catastrophe. It was very hard, I must admit. Very hard and alone."

In 1979, defying hardliners, Sharabi, along with Farhat Ziadeh, spoke at the New Outlook Conference in Washington, DC, arranged by a humanist, dovish Israeli journal. Still, he told me that Israel's current path was a "defiance of everything that makes up history." He went on: "This colonization is unique in many respects. In the first place, it occurs at a time when the entire region has been decolonized. It's a movement in reverse. It comes at a time when the colonial world has collapsed everywhere in the world. They simply have come too late to that part of the world... I don't think Israel has a future as a colonial society. The Jews have a future, but not as colonists, not as a racist, superior, dominating power. This is a phase that will pass."

As for the Arabs, "the infrastructure of a modem society is already being formed. And when that society is completed it will be like Hong Kong or Taiwan confronting China."

Although he was raised a Sunni Muslim, in his teens the religion fell away from Sharabi's life: "My grandmother was very devout. I would hear the Qu'ran constantly, I'd see everybody praying five times a day. They tried to send me to get religious instruction as a little boy, during the summer, in the neighboring mosque. But somehow it didn't catch."

"What today would you bow your head to?" I asked. "What system, or collection of absolutes?"

"None whatsoever," came the reply. "I have become through the years more and more relativistic. My approach is certainly very tolerant, but on the whole, skeptical of absolutes. Truth, with a capital T, good with a capital G."

Sharabi felt that for successful Arab Americans, "those who make it, one of the first reactions is to get out of it, to disassociate themselves—they want nothing to do with the community. It's like the opposite of the Jews. When the Jew becomes wealthy and socially prominent, he becomes correspondingly responsible for the community."

A silence surrounded Hisham Sharabi, repelling some, attracting others. Yet my strongest memory of him is his chairing a meeting of West Bank notables from all factions, whom he had gathered in Washington, DC, in an emergency conference in November of 1982, just after the Sabra and Shatila massacres. The meeting was predictably raucous, and a PLO representative in the room apparently exercised a veto on the large delegation. Sharabi—after hours of argument—finally rose, drew all eyes, gave a speech filled with subtle rebuke that, once again, the Palestinians were missing the boat due to technicalities and fear. He then left the room.

Sharabi confessed in his memoirs, still largely untranslated from Arabic, that while he found American grad students in Chicago filled with a "spirit of commitment and sense of responsibility" a fellow Arab student was "always ready to put his books aside if he had an opportunity to drink a cup of coffee with a girl." Absent a stern "outside authority" such as a father or professor, "a chaotic tendency would take its place and it made him shirk responsibility and seek pleasure." Never one to shy from self-criticism or criticism of the culture he came from, in the last two years of his life, he finally went back home to live—not in Palestine, but close to it, in Beirut, near his daughters Nadia and Leila. He lamented, "How Time defeats us! We grow old, yet our hearts remain as they have always been."[23]

In the dead of winter, in January 2005, Hisham Sharabi died of cancer in Beirut at 77.[24] If not Palestine, at least he had palms and the sea and his beauties nearby. From my perch in California looking out at the snowy San Bernadinos, I see him smile. Such sternness, such a smile!

The Second Wave Palestinian sorrows tend to be elegies over a lost world. They may be indignant as Said's, foreboding and melanchoic as Sharabi's, but underneath most testimony is a thick layer of skepticism and disillusionment, such as mirrored by Aziz Shihab. Some Second Wave Palestinians emigrated later than 1948 after fleeing to neighboring Arab countries. They often are very successful and tempered by unsavory, or disappointing, experiences in the Arab host countries, which—except for Jordan—did not grant Palestinians citizenship and kept them at a political arm's length and in pariahdom. One such Second Waver is Nabila Cronfel, a beauteous, lithe director of a fashionable high-rise apartment condominium in Houston, who came to the United States from Damascus in 1960.

It took 25 years in America for Nabila's father to try the impossible: a Disneyland-like replication of the Cronfel home in Jerusalem, but in Laredo, Texas. In 1975 (the year before he died), Elias Cronfel purchased the biggest house in Laredo, a historic landmark in town, as a birthday present for his wife, Aimee. The structure was in a shambles, a real fixer-upper, and, as it turned out, no Cronfel ever lived there. In 1983, a private school leased it. But Elias had been attracted to it because it was made of limestone—a traditional building block of Palestinian houses—and he told his wife, "I want to return you to Jerusalem!" Nabila lifted the lids of her olive green eyes and smiled, "It was totally impractical, the big old Salinas House. But he did it."[25]

In Jerusalem before 1948, Elias Cronfel was a prosperous importer of English linens and men's clothes. He owned the city's Spinney Building and did a lot of business with the British. His respected opinion was sought after by one of the many international committees that toured Palestine. As for the 1947 partition of Palestine into two states—not accepted by most Arabs—Elias Cronfel thought it was all right.

But squads of the Irgun and the Stern Gang were shooting up the Arab sectors of Jerusalem from armored cars. Nabila said, "The terrorists came driving down our peaceful residential street shooting and the maid fell on two children, my brothers." The violence of 1947 was to her mother "the last straw," and by 1948, as full-scale war broke out, the Cronfels left Jerusalem for Syria. They left all their possessions—Bohemian crystal, silver from China, Bombay beveled glass, rare mahogany pieces, clothes, photos of relatives. They also abandoned some of the choicest property in Jerusalem near the King David Hotel, which today houses Israeli government buildings. The only member of the family to return was Nabila's sister—in 1967. "She was cursed by Israeli residents," Nabila said ruefully.

Damascus was not much more hospitable in those early, trying, chaotic years of putting things together after the tragedy than it is today to Palestinians, official jargon to the contrary. Nabila was born there in 1954, but by 1960, Elias had decided to take the whole family to the United States. As with the First Wave immigrants, they took a boat and got seasick.

They arrived in New York City, but quickly made their way southwest to the border town of Laredo where two Cronfel brothers had gone in the 1930s, coming up at that time from Honduras. "If I put myself in my parents' position, it is hardship," Nabila said in her scratchy voice, a contrast to the gentle beauty of her face. "My mother knew no English or Spanish. My father was in his fifties and to start all over is not easy with four kids. He took nothing for granted, coming out of the hardships in the Middle East war. And mother was an independent woman."

There was a small community of Arabs at the time in Laredo. Elias slowly expanded from a dry goods store selling women's lingerie to an electronics shop. Soon he was trading with Mexico over the border and his company registered at one time one of the highest volumes of US–Mexican trade on record. But as the peso was devalued and the recessions of the late 1970s hit, the Cronfel family business was also hit. In 1983, unemployment in Laredo was a whopping 27 percent. One by one the Cronfels followed Nabila to Houston where there is a sizable and prominent community of about 20,000 Arab Americans. It is growing with Third Wave immigrants, quite a few from Lebanon, and wealthy Syrians who are "not too happy with what's going on" in the Assad regime. The Saudis who come often to Houston do not stay. "They like it too much back there!" Nabila confirmed. (Well, yes and no. The trickle of Saudi immigrants to the United States the year I met Nabila Cronfel (170) increased fourfold by 2003, to 737. The number of a plane.)

One final glimpse of the old family home in Palestine years into exile has tempted more than one Palestinian American, often with children born in America tagging along in bewilderment. Hisham Sharabi returned in 1993 for a British documentary; it was a bittersweet encounter. In 1982, Aziz Shihab, swallowing a nitroglycerin pill for his heart, returned with his poet daughter Naomi to the home they lost in Jerusalem in 1948. There was a toothless broom-maker still selling brooms in the neighborhood—Naomi wrote a powerful poem about him—but most everything else had changed. The large Shihab home was now a dormitory for rabbinical students. The man who cheerily answered the door told them in a thick Brooklyn accent, "It's really fantastic being a settler—now I know how the pilgrims felt." Hearing that an Arab family had lived there, the settler was confused, thinking that the property must have been sold to the rabbi. "We never sold it," Aziz shook his head. The young settler put out an awkward hand, apologized, and disappeared.[26]

For George Bisharat, the situation evoked complete denial. A law professor at Hastings College in San Francisco, Bisharat took his own family in 2000 to inspect the home his grandfather had built in 1926 in Jerusalem, dubbed then "Villa Harun ar-Rashid" in honor of the great Caliph of the Golden Age of Islam. Handed over by the British to the Haganah after the smoke cleared in 1948, the Villa was subdivided into flats. Israeli Prime Minister Golda Meir herself had lived in the upper flat in the 1960s. Meir, who once had the gall to assert that the Palestinian people did not exist, made, according to Bisharat, a valiant attempt to sandblast the name "Villa Harun ar-Rashid" off the property. It was not entirely successful. Bisharat spotted the name in vague markings in the tile. In an earlier visit by himself in 1977, Bisharat discovered a retired Israeli Supreme Court justice and his wife living in the Villa. They flatly denied that the Bisharats had ever lived there. In 2000 there was an American from New York who proudly said the Villa was included on walking tours of Jerusalem. He repeated, "a half-dozen times," says Bisharat, that "the family never lived here" and genially sported a newspaper article that proved it.

Bisharat stood out in the streets with his little son and daughter and wife and cried. Some 10,000 homes in West Jerusalem were looted and seized in the months before the war between Israel and the Arab states in 1948, his grandfather's one of them. He now has a thick file of attempts by the Bisharat family to recover Villa Harun ar-Rashid, none of which have worked or even been acknowledged. But he writes, "We have not disappeared, nor have we forgotten, our existence a reminder that one people's liberation was founded on another's dispossession... Recently I found my daughter lingering over photos of my father as a boy in his Jerusalem home. I know now that she and my son both are heirs to the truth about Villa Harun ar-Rashid."[27]

OTHER SECOND WAVE IMMIGRANTS FROM ARAB REGIMES

The Second Wave of Palestinians, Egyptians, Iraqis, Syrians, Lebanese, Yemenis, and others was a small one, about 80,000 immigrants in nineteen years. Aside from Palestinians, the rest constituted new immigrants from countries just emerging into independence and going through growing pains that included revolution, purges, redistribution of wealth, corruption, and megalomania. The largest portion of these immigrants were Egyptian (about 20,000).

Shahdan El Shazly, born in Cairo in a 1944 into a military family, was a Sophia Loren lookalike and a successful investment advisor in San Francisco. She did not come to the United States for political reasons. In fact, at the time of her immigration —1960—her father was one of President Nasser's confidants. El Shazly fell in love with a

Chinese American from Chinatown, San Francisco. The boil of cultures from the Middle East, the Far East, and the Far West of the California coast cooled into an earthy mix in El Shazly. She became Egypt's first woman paratrooper. Her father led Egypt's forces to the turning-point crossing of the Suez Canal in 1973, and became an Egyptian hero after this credible military showing against the heretofore invincible Israelis paved the way for the Sinai disengagement and the Camp David Accords.

Egypt's first woman paratrooper, Shahdan El Shazly, boards a plane for a jump in July, 1960; El Shazly is now an investment advisor in San Francisco. (Shahdan El Shazly)

But the general believed that Anwar Sadat, president of Egypt, had botched directives to the general staff during the war, compromising field positions that could have ensured, if not victory, better cards at the bargaining table. His *Crossing of the Suez* was banned in Egypt and caused El Shazly to be deported. While ambassador to Portugal, El Shazly was exiled because of his criticism of the Camp David agreement. He later resided in Algiers. His daughter went to an Arab-American convention in Washington, DC, with a petition to Hosni Mubarak on behalf of her father. Shahdan was suave, svelte, with hair in a modest Afro and glistening dark eyes and wide smile that spoke of someone who by her own admission "has never had an identity crisis."[28]

She was Egypt's first woman paratrooper; years later she was one of the first women in San Francisco to make a mark in the investment business. And though meeting Frank Chinn in London when she was seventeen was a turning point in her life and propelled her to America and San Francisco's Chinese community, she admitted that the idea of equality of sexes in America had appealed to her before that: "I think I thought about it [leaving Egypt] long before that... I was fascinated mostly with the freedom that I thought then women had." But she continued, taking a drag from her cigarette, "Of course at the time I was very young—freedom to me was chewing gum and smoking and wearing pants!"

Freedom was barely what she got in her whirlwind romance and marriage. An international businessman, Chinn took Shahdan to California, then Hawaii and Southeast Asia. By the time she was 21, she had two children. But perhaps, as she later felt, she was spared psychological burdens: "I often thought about getting married young and what that means. I think it's not all bad as so many people say because the twenties are a very turbulent time and when you've married, they're not, because you are too busy—shopping, cooking, taking care of the kids—to worry about your identity."

Even in the leading liberal city in the United States, there were indications that she had not landed in a complete feminist utopia. One day she and another woman investor found themselves at a meeting at the all-male University Club, where they were told they couldn't take the regular elevator because "sometimes there are men with no clothes." They ended up riding the service elevator to the meeting. But she wasn't resentful: "I was happy to be one of only two women in the group."

Lack of identity crisis, she confirmed, came from having "a strong family and an extended family." The many-layered Egyptian past contributed to a sense of belonging, of a wisdom chain, whereas "America really has no history." She said with disdain, "You take a kid here and the furthest he will remember is maybe his grandfather." For her, 5,000 years of culture comes bursting into the consciousness of the Egyptian through proverbs, things not told in school, but known through family and tale. One of her favorite proverbs was, "A child in a mother's eye is a gazelle."

El Shazly's own children, born American, have given her cause to reflect on Egyptian and American approaches to modern troubles. One boy at fifteen had difficulty with his mother's divorce. He had been to private school in England and starred for its soccer team. Coming back to San Francisco he had to enroll in a public school where gang wars prevailed. He refused. It caused a family ruckus. Her ex-husband recommended that the boy go to jail as a wayward child. Her current husband recommended a psychiatrist. But for Shahdan, there was a warmer way, and she pinpointed it in an Arab proverb, "Take the child as big as his brains." The English of it would be, "Take him at his own level." "It's very American to go to a psychiatrist because if you're not achieving there's something wrong with you," she said. She rode the waves of her son's agonies and doubts and he turned out fine.

Ultimately, though she is happy in America, she misses "a sense of permanence which I have never felt in this country." In Egypt there is timelessness: "People don't move; people don't change jobs; people don't change addresses. I mean I go back to Egypt and it's the same. Twenty years later, for example, I find that the man at the club who is the porter is the same man. I find the same waiters there. I go to my old school and all the teachers that were there when I was a child are still there. At the Ministry of Information where I worked one summer in high school I go back now and the elevator man is the same, the department is the same."

El Shazly says the thought of growing old in the United States distresses her. I asked her why. She said: "For the elderly, it's a terrible society, I think. Old people here—there's no respect for old people. There's natural respect that we have for our elders in the Arab world; it doesn't exist here. I am constantly amazed and appalled at the people that put their parents away in these institutions. I can't imagine an Arab woman alive and well putting her mother away, or an Arab man for that matter." I informed her that indeed the first Arab-American rest home had been opened in 1983 in Brooklyn, the community's oldest colony. It was not being patronized hugely, but a few elders were being admitted. "That's the Americanization, isn't it?" she exclaimed.

At this point, El Shazly's tall, blond second husband strolled into the hotel room. When asked what it was like being married to an Egyptian American, he said, "I grew up in a middle-class family where I was taught rules. You abide by these rules and you'll succeed. [She] has an orientation that's much broader, much more worldly and isn't driven to success. She understands life; it's not just her as an individual. All Egyptians I've met through her have a broader and deeper understanding of life. They discuss life all the time, and philosophy and history and politics. They're discussing life and we're discussing the mechanics of living. How do you work, how is your job, how do you commute, what your kids are doing. Tax shelters. But these people are in the life of living, instead of the life of working. They've been in touch with a few millenniums, and Americans just can't even come close to that. I can't."

Shahdan remembered the 1948 war; only a child, she hid with her grandmother in Cairo in bomb shelters during the Israeli raids. Her father was a general who fought in the 1948 war, as he had against Rommel in World War II, during which, after getting orders to withdraw, he had gotten a reputation of intrepidness and fortitude by staying behind and destroying all the Egyptian materiel before Rommel could seize it.

In 1967, General El Shazly was the only Egyptian general to actually get inside Israel, Shahdan said. "He was also the only Egyptian general who came back with his troops and his equipment intact," she continued. A Douglas MacArthur-type figure, her father kept running into the politicians head-on. When he retreated with his troops in the 1967 debacle, he did not get into a Jeep or convoy; he walked through the desert with his troops all the way to Cairo. His men respected him immensely.

Inevitably, the conversation turned toward Anwar Sadat and her father's falling out with him after Camp David. What did Shahdan feel, as an American, about Sadat's bold move to Jerusalem in 1977?

"I truly believed when Sadat first started that he was going to drag everybody to the brink and then change his mind and prove to the world that, you see, it is the Israelis [who are the problem], not the Egyptians. I never believed he would sign [a treaty]. And when he went to Jerusalem I said, 'Son of a bitch, he's going to get the Nobel Peace Prize.' But I never really thought he would sign. After he signed and things continued [to get worse] I thought he was duped. Now I'm beginning to believe that he really knew what he was doing; he didn't care. He wanted to do something in his lifetime and let somebody else worry about implications."

Camp David, to her, was responsible for the conflagrations in Lebanon and the West Bank because it took Egypt out of the equation. But I wanted to know what use had it been for Egypt to fight four wars to no avail. The military struggles seemed pointless.

"Quite the opposite," she countered. "Because the 1973 war made it imperative for the Israelis and the Americans to stop this because the 1973 war was too close for comfort. No longer can they [the Israelis] be considered invincible and no longer can they say a war would not work. If it wasn't for Sadat, the 1973 war would have worked. This has been validated by a lot of people in Egypt, the high command, Mohammed Heikal. Nobody said Sadat was right and El Shazly was wrong."

A Syrian Second Waver who landed in Rhode Island in 1952 lived among factory workers, old textile weavers, and dyers. For Father Abdulahad Doumato, a retired priest in the Jacobite rite of the Eastern Orthodoxy—an obscure sect that has about 20,000 adherents in the United States—ministry was his life. He saw holy oil emerge miraculously from the cement altar of the Jacobite, or Syrian Orthodox, churches along the border of Syria and Turkey.

Holed up in a small, board-framed house in Central Falls, Rhode

Island, Father Doumato was repeatedly victimized by crime. Thieves once stole the chalice off the altar of St. Ephraim's, the church of which he had been the pastor. Thieves also pilfered some gold pens he had on his desk at home. Crime has made quite a different America for this kind, warm, but sad priest than the one that greeted him in the early 1950s. He believes in holy olive oil miracles; he cannot believe the rise in crime.

When asked if he would have come to the United States knowing what he knows now, the priest—a US citizen for almost 40 years—said, "No."

"I thought America was the best country," Father Doumato told me on a dreary March day in the living room of his home, with his old, blind father rocking nearby and a younger, bearded priest from a neighborhood parish. "I mean, how can you find freedom outside America? That's what I used to think, and I came and I saw it that way and was never sorry. I was happy with my neighbors, with my fellow man, my parishioners. I never had any hardship—never. I was well respected. But things happen that I don't like. I still believe in the American way, the Americans as Christian people. But there are newcomers. If they want the country to go bigger and larger and more active, they are supposed to police it better."[29]

There are eighteen Jacobite Syrian Orthodox churches in the United States, but only sixteen priests. The shortage of "Syriani" priests is so acute that in 2004 a non-priest monk had to be recruited from Syria to take over St. Ephraim's. The main distinguishing factor between them and the mainstream Antiochian Orthodox is that for their mass the Syrian Orthodox use Syriac, which is similar to Aramaic, Jesus Christ's tongue. In fact, Father Doumato translated the Lord's Prayer into Aramaic, which today is only spoken in three Syrian villages. The translated Lord's Prayer flows in a script less curved and scimitarlike than Arabic; Aramaic seems to be a cross between Arabic and Hebrew. It bends to the left in straight, diagonal tails, as if in an unvarying wind.

During the troubled years leading to the war at the turn of the century, Syrian Orthodox moved down from Turkey into Syria proper and Lebanon, most to the section of Jazireh in Syria, where 100,000 are said to live. After World War II more moved to Lebanon, which today has about 2,000 Jacobite families. But since the Lebanon civil war, the Jacobites have been on the move again, this time to the New World. People like Father Doumato had made the beachhead in America. For years St. Ephraim's had only 40 families; after the Lebanese civil war, that number grew to 100.

The Syrian Orthodox—united with neither Rome nor Byzantium—came to America, according to Doumato, because of "persecution and hardship." Like all minorities, the more minority you are, the more isolated and suspect you are.

"Among the three or four million Syriani in Turkey today, they never identify themselves as Turks," he said. "They never accept it, even on paper." He noted that once when he was a citizen of Turkey they labeled him as Syrian Orthodox. In Syria, they accept it more; in Lebanon they accept it probably because many Lebanese are Christian. He told with enthusiasm about a meeting of the Jacobite Orthodox patriarch in Jazireh with the top Muslim imam of the area: The imam said, "Sayadna, your eminence, we are welcoming you warmly because we are of the same blood. We lived for generations as Christians; that's what our forefathers told us. But they were cowards; they accepted [to be] Muslim. You are stronger; you stay with your faith."

Father Doumato said that the Christians there call the Muslim Arabs *tayo*, a Syriac word that emphasizes their Christian roots. He spread his hands and told with animation stories of Syrian Orthodox finding fellows of their small sect as far out in the desert as Palmyra. "On paper, they say they are Syrian Arabs, but deep down they say, 'We are Syriani.' They keep the faith and religion first."

I mentioned Sidnaya, the miracle site out in the Syrian desert, which we had visited in 1972, and Father Doumato nodded knowingly, though Sidnaya was *Rum* (Antiochian Orthodox) and there were miraculous sites particular to the Jacobite in Kamisne, near Turkey. His eyes widened: "Back there it's a different life. Here they believe by material things and the dollar. There they believe by faith. In our churches, near the border of Turkey, in Kamisne, still until today every once in a while oil comes from either the altar or the wall or part of the church. So many people—Christian and non-Christian—and the government, went and examined these places. There is nothing wrong with it. Just miracle. *Zayt*, olive oil. Some from icons, some from the ground, some from the wall, mostly around the altar area. It's amazing."

Father Doumato was convinced that back in time I was Syrian Orthodox because of my last name. He told me a story about Orfa, or Urfa, which is in Turkish Armenia. He said the king there (Apgar) wrote the only extant letter to Jesus Christ, asking him to visit his city to cure him of some skin disease. A native saint, Ephraim, born in Sabeen in the Syrian district, because of persecution moved to Urfa, where he taught and became a famous preacher. He died in Urfa, which is still largely Armenian Catholic and Syrian Orthodox Christian.

Father Doumato brought his four children and wife to the United States in 1952 to be a pastor to the Central Falls church, which had been built in the 1920s. He was chosen and he chose to come. He was glad because the education in America, he felt, would be better for his children. But he missed the tightly knit family he left in Syria. "The whole world's changed today," he said. "We used to keep the family together. I was just telling some people, you go to Damascus or Aleppo or Homs on this narrow road; you see those Orfali families! Five, six, ten houses. Not like that here. They live two-, three-story houses, each one different, but they don't talk to each other."

Father Doumato lived for years in America before his church and home were broken into in 1983. The drunken vandals even started a fire in the sacristy after taking the chalice and smashing the organ. What really burned inside him was the lackadaisical police. He saw a hit-and-run accident in front of the church one day; the driver was drunk. The police came and Father Doumato shouted to them to pursue him. The police didn't give chase, just wrote up a report. Doumato wondered whose car it was. They shrugged their shoulders—stolen by some Italian from Providence. "They don't care," Doumato sighed. "If they rob you, or they kill you here, they come, just take note."

It was a common phenomenon—an original immigrant who probably had little English badgered later on by more recent immigrants who don't know any English. But Father Doumato did not have the leavening ingredient of the First Wave immigrants who had to live with terrible prejudice because of their foreignness. He arrived in America at the peak of its prosperity and stature in the world, the 1950s. He was educated, too, and knew some English. The descent into crime of the modern American megalopolis was more precipitous an adjustment for him, perhaps, than for older folk who had done the hard-knock factory work or peddling when Syrians were considered Chinese.

But they were dying out. And Father Doumato was tipping past middle age, with fewer miles to go before he slept. The new immigrant speaking Spanish, lighting his cigarette on the corner in loneliness or anger, spoke eloquently of a tougher reality than the Syrian Orthodox could comprehend. In their despair, perhaps, he and the Puerto Ricans shared more than he thought.

—FIVE—

THE THIRD WAVE: WEST BANK CAPTURED, LEBANON TORN ASUNDER, IRAQ WARS WITH IRAN, KUWAIT, AND THE US (1967–2005)

Why would the period from 1967 to 2003 be considered a distinct Third Wave of Arab immigration to the United States? It is true that the 757,626 Arab immigrants who came during these years shared much with those who came from 1948 to 1966. The largest segment of Third Wavers were probably Palestinian, though they may have come to the United States through Jordan, Syria, Lebanon, and Persian Gulf countries. The 121,737 listed under "Jordan" alone are mostly Palestinian. Many Third Wavers were professionals like the Second Wavers; if anything, that trend intensified. Naff documents that between 1965 and 1976, 15 percent of Arab immigrants to the United States were professional and technical workers, once again mostly Palestinian. On September 16, 1983, *Middle East International* reported that half of all Arab science and engineering Ph.D.s had left the Arab world.

But the question remains: what differentiates Third Wavers from Second Wavers? First, and most obvious, the Third Wave is thirteen times larger than the Second, due to a great extent to the loosening of US immigration restrictions in 1965. Second, the Third Wave was fleeing not only intensified Israeli aggression but also intra-Arab warfare on a scale not seen since the mid-19th century. Those Iraqis, Lebanese, and Syrians, for instance, were not just leaving situations that had been shaken by change of rule, or new economic structures, as in Nasser's Egypt. They were leaving societies wracked by abysmal violence. The two US invasions of Iraq only added to the turmoil.

After the Palestinians—whose absence was beginning to make certain West Bank towns, such as Ramallah, resemble homes for the aged just like those left by famine-stricken Lebanese during World War I—the contemporary Lebanese constituted the second-largest group of Arab immigrants from the Third Wave. The intolerable barbarism of the civil war and Israel's 1982 invasion brought 119,562 new Lebanese immigrants to America since the war's inception in 1975. Iraqis began for the first time to come to the United States in sizable numbers (108,144 since 1967); some of this influx was due to professionals who did not want to throw their lives away fighting a meaningless war of attrition with Khomeini's Iran, a war that in a decade caused over a million deaths. Many Iraqis also fled hardships ensuing from the United States' reversal of Iraq's invasion of Kuwait and the imposition of harsh UN sanctions in the 1990s against the regime of Saddam Hussein. In fact, in the dozen years between the first American invasion of Iraq in 1991 and the second invasion that toppled Hussein in 2003, 53,388 Iraqis immigrated to the United States. Syria, whose prospering economy was beginning to plunge by the mid-1980s, contributed sizable numbers to the Third Wave immigrants (71,033 since 1967), some disillusioned by corruption or the occasional brutality of the Assad regime, whose crushing of Islamic fundamentalist rebels at Hama in 1982 caused the death of 20,000 civilians.

Third, one cannot discount the rise of Islamic fundamentalism throughout the Middle East as fueling the Third Wave immigration by Christian Arabs (though at least 60 percent of Third Wavers are Muslim). The Christian population of Palestine (including East Jerusalem, the West Bank, and Gaza), for example, which used to be 15 to 20 percent is today under 2 percent. Since 1944, Jerusalem's Christian population alone has been cut by two-thirds (10,900 today). Certain Christian sects, such as the Iraqi Chaldeans and Egyptian Copts, felt increasingly isolated in their societies, and with beachheads already established by a handful of earlier immigrants to America, they began coming in larger numbers. The Chaldean community in Detroit, for instance, grew from 3,000 in 1960 to 80,000 in 2003. Egyptians immigrating from 1967 to 2003 number 129,518, many of them Copts.

In sum, the Third Wave Arab immigrants carried a greater burden of internecine conflict than did previous waves, and hence they would tend to be less likely than previous groups to consider going home. (It should be no surprise that new immigration from the Arab world to the United States dropped precipitously after September 11, 2001.) The Third Wave immigrants, partly because so many were highly educated Palestinians, also felt a greater drive to participate in the new Arab-American political groups that grew in the wake of the 1967 June War. Third Wave Palestinians, with the homeland still fresh in their minds, were ready to be foot soldiers in the tedious, frustrating task of lobbying US policy makers, unlike First or Second Wavers who could either be cynical or despairing and in any event tended to be isolated chiefs. More angry with the US, the Third Wave paradoxically made more enthusiastic participants in American life. With a kind of crude symmetry, the number of Palestinians coming to America increased as the number of American-financed Israeli settlements increased on the West Bank and in Gaza, occupied since the 1967 June War. It was as if America were paying these immigrants to relocate away from Israel, giving Israel a free hand with expropriated land.

The children of Third Wave immigrants, and their children, have a markedly different experience adjusting to American mores. In a mid-1990s study of Dearborn Arab-American teens, one sociologist noted the greater weight of change on the girls:

> The essence of being Arab was most sharply expressed by the behavior of the females… The Arab-American girls are the only ones who seem to feel more tension between the two pertinent forces. They feel pressure to act honorably, yet are lured by the perceived autonomy possessed by "American girls."[1]

In fact, the study shows one boy breaking down and crying when told his sister is dating an "American"; in another case, a Muslim father proudly announced he is the only one who can kiss his daughter—on the forehead.

A study of Arab Canadian youth in Edmonton, Alberta, found that 86 percent of male teens identify more as "Arab" than "Canadian" (however only 64 percent of female teens clung to their "Arab" roots more than Canadian identity). And while most felt familial closeness, support, and Arab hospitality as pluses, 30 percent of the teen girls tried to hide their origins (only 10 percent of males did). This was not a post–September 11 survey, though it did take place after the 1991 Gulf war.[2]

IRAQIS, YEMENIS, AND EGYPTIAN COPTS

Aside from the Palestinians and Lebanese, wracked, it seemed, by interminable conflict, burgeoning communities of Iraqi Chaldeans in Detroit, Egyptian Copts in places like Jersey City, New Jersey, and Yemenis in Detroit factories and on California farms represented unique immigrant experiences in America, with wide swings of the pendulum between the urge to stay in the United States and the desire to return to impoverished or chaotic origins.

Chances are that lunch salad purchased on a noon break in Detroit is served up by a Chaldean immigrant from Telkaif, in northern Iraq just outside the ancient ruins of Nineveh. Chaldean Catholics, who have escaped turmoil and the expropriation of private property in their native land own about 1,500 "party stores" (beer, wine, and liquor stores), small markets, and supermarkets in Detroit. The community's swift growth proved once again that one nation's war is another nation's cheap sandwich.

The Chaldeans are a fiercely proud people who trace their Christianity back to St. Paul's missionary journey to what was then Assyria and Babylon. There are 150,000 Chaldeans in the United

States, most in Detroit, with smaller groups in Chicago and in San Diego and Turlock, California. In 1889, probably seeking the Trade Exhibition, the first Chaldean arrived in the United States and settled in Philadelphia, through he later went back to Telkaif. Chaldeans began to gather in groups in Detroit around 1910, taking up work peddling and in the new car factories. Their motives were primarily economic. The Second Wave Chaldean immigrants in the wake of World War II were largely part of the brain drain and came from major Iraqi cities like Baghdad. But after 1965, the loosening of immigration restrictions by the United States, and the ascension in 1968 of the socialist Ba'ath Party in Iraq, Chaldeans began coming directly from Telkaif in greater numbers.

Like the Jacobites, the Chaldeans use Syriac, an Aramaic language, in their liturgy. A few members of the Chaldean community prefer an age-old allegiance to an early church heretic, Nestorius, who differed from Rome on several doctrinal issues. Nestorians, also called the Church of the East in the United States, live mostly in Chicago. To further complicate matters, these Nestorians are sometimes included in yet a different Eastern Christian sect called the Assyrians, who number approximately 300,000 in the United States, and include people from Iran and Armenia, as well as Syria, Lebanon, and Iraq. Assyrian Christians can be Catholic, Orthodox, or Protestant; their Aramaic is accented somewhat differently from Chaldeans. Interestingly, at a 2003 conference in Iraq after the fall of Saddam Hussein, Chaldeans and Assyrians agreed to start using the phrase Chaldo-Assyrian in referring to themselves.[3]

As with other Third Wavers, the Chaldeans had overtly political reasons for leaving the Arab world. In their case, the strife between the Iraqi government and the ethnic Kurds in northern Iraq spilled over into Telkaif. Many Chaldeans testify that they were subject to discrimination by Muslim Arabs of Iraq. Moreover, Telkaif was considered a backwater village scorned by most Iraqis: "In fact, the term 'Telkefee' was used in Baghdad as a term of derision, applied to anyone from the Mosul region, and indicated an ignorant, small town hick, a term somewhat akin to the American term, 'hillbilly.'"[4]

Even more recent Iraqi immigrants than the Chaldeans have been Muslims fleeing the constant carnage of the Iran–Iraq War and the two US wars against Iraq. Few families were not hit by at least one casualty in the seemingly endless plagues of war that have affected the country. Since 1967, at least 108,144 Iraqis have left their land and have found shelter in the United States. One of these is a university professor of pharmacology in Houston who otherwise describes himself as a "sedentary" man.

Karim Alkadhi, born in Iraq in 1938, felt strongly that life in Iraq, even under Saddam, was more lucrative, served as a better medium in which to raise children than the drug-riddled United States, and generally not as lonely as America. Yet in 1980 he brought his young family—wife and two children—to Houston, where he taught at the University of Houston. "To be very frank," he told me, "there were some things done in preparation for the Iran–Iraq war we didn't like. All the foreign wives, for instance, should apply for Iraqi citizenship, said the government. I asked why." He never got a satisfactory answer. "I served five years in Iraq… it was time to move on."[5]

Alkadhi described his attachment to Iraq, nevertheless, still as "very strong." His son, Isam, and daughter, Rheim ("desert gazelle"), both know Arabic—though it was learned on the road in Libya. "In terms of money, we were doing better in Iraq," he admitted. "I didn't come to the United States for dollars that grew on trees." But it is in discussing politics and the question of freedom of expression that Alkadhi revealed the subliminal stimulus for emigration: "The leaders in the Middle East—they are hell. You can say as much as you like here. I think that's good. What counts is that I can criticize anyone without endangering my life or my freedom. If you didn't criticize the government in Iraq, you were all right."

In many other ways the Alkadhis were "very happy in Baghdad," where, Alkadhi said, "we had the best of both worlds"—Western lifestyle and goods and Middle Eastern closeness and family orientation. "Baghdad was booming," he said. "Money was flowing out the ears from agriculture and oil revenues. Thousands of Iraqis were taking vacations in Europe—even small shopkeepers were splurging." Before the Iraq wars, the government was liberal in allowing hard currency out of the country—up to $3,300 per person. When the war with Iran began in 1980, this was greatly reduced.

At first, Alkadhi thought the war was launched out of "personal animosity," but as it dragged on he came to the realization that "it was going to be a war whether Iraq had attacked or not." Khomeini's agents had exploded a number of Iraqi installations over the border in the months before the war. "If Iran wanted to make peace it would have sued for peace," Alkahdi said. "Khomeini obviously wanted to take Iraq, or put in his own lackeys."

"It would probably be better for my kids to grow up in Iraq," he felt. "There you don't have to worry about peer pressure and drugs. There are plenty of cousins there to play with. Individualism here and its attending psychic disorders you don't find there. Schools conform to procedure—the school is boss there. There is no conflict, for instance, about prayer in the classroom. If you are non-Muslim, you just leave the class at prayer time."

A secularist, Alkadhi does not think fundamentalism would take hold in Iraq: "On the whole, Iraqis are not very religious, really. There are three or four breweries in Iraq for beer and that's not enough to fill demand. They import it." And the disunity of his homeland didn't help. "I felt the Arab world becoming so tattered," he sighed. Yet Alkhadi said this long before the US invasion had brought to Iraq the sort of chaos and internecine struggles Saddam had kept a tight lid on; now Islamic fundamentalism was in the ascendant, an irony Alkadhi later noted.

Recent Iraqi immigrants tend to be more sanguine about America than Alkadhi and tell stunning tales about a quarter-century of violence and fear that plagued Iraq. One day in 1991, Basim al-Khafaji was speaking about the Saddam Hussein regime in his kitchen at home while his wife held their infant son. "Don't talk so loud!" his wife hushed him. "When it gets that bad," al-Khafaji noted, "that you can't speak in front of your one-year-old, well, the heck with it!"[6] He and his family immigrated in 1993 to Cincinnati, where he did his medical residency, and finally to Detroit.

Al-Khafaji's English has no accent, the result of living in England as a boy, and it has helped him in the post-9/11 world. Still, he fondly remembers his years living in Najaf, a surprisingly multicultural world. "Because the city houses a Muslim shrine [Khomeini had lived in exile there], Najaf has lots of people from different backgrounds who are descendants of scholars who came there and settled from Afghanistan, Iran, Lebanon, Pakistan." He played soccer, rode his bike, prayed once a week at "the beautiful shrine" at Najaf with its sparkling mosaics and gold dome. The souk "was like a mall."

The ascent of Saddam Hussein to power had an immediate effect on his boyhood classroom. Within a year of the start of the Iran–Iraq War (1980), "out of 25 of my classmates, 12 were gone." They weren't drafted. Najaf is a Shiʿite town; Saddam was obsessed with Shiʿites being a "fifth column" in Iraq—hadn't they led a revolution in Iran? al-Khafaji's classmates and their families were expelled over the border to Iran or jailed. His justification was that they were of Iranian descent, which was totally untrue in many cases. Many were merchants and their homes and cars were confiscated.

"And those were the lucky ones," said his friend, Zuhair Allebban, who came to the United States in 1976. Director of cardiology research and drug testing at St. John's Hospital in Detroit, Zuhair told an apochryphal story—well-known throughout Iraq—about Saddam's speeches. They were covered on the nightly news, and schoolchildren were required to comment on them the next day. Some teachers quizzed the children, not about the content of Saddam's speeches, but about the reaction of their parents to the speeches. After one boy confessed that his father had spit at the television, the man was executed. In this way, Allebban intimated, Iraq's own children become a network of spies.[7] When asked if

Kenan Makiya's bestselling *Republic of Fear* exaggerated the situation, al-Khafaji thought it was an "underestimate of what went on."

During the Iran–Iraq War, al-Khafaji saw "columns and columns of coffins" coming to Najaf for Shi'ite burial. Saddam used Shi'ites more or less as cannon fodder, with whole brigades of them going to fight in the South, while his own Sunnis were put into intelligence or to the rear with the high command. As the coffin trains approached, the Iraqi flags would be removed and a common blanket put on them so that Iran could not detect how many casualties they were exacting.

"You engulf and digest it," said al-Khafaji, "and you recognize— it's evil all round. It was a senseless war, a senseless loss of life, and it went on and on." A strong, dark, soft-spoken man with glasses, he blinked several times and shook his head.

Saddam ruled by fear and bribes. At one point during the war with Iraq, he offered $100 to $200 to anyone who would build a mosque in Iraq; mosques built during this time aimed to co-opt fundamentalists and spy on pious Muslims. This went on during the sanctions period after the 1991 Gulf war. Those structures remained after Saddam's fall, and, al-Khafaji noted, they have become the seedbed of the rebellion against the fledgling democratic government. Both men called the insurgents "Wahhabis," after the early brand of Muslim fundamentalism in 19th-century Saudi Arabia. "I know a Shi'a who converted to the Wahhabis," said al-Khafaji. "His mother was so sad."

Hardly a family in Iraq did not know death during the Iran–Iraq War, and al-Khafaji was no exception—his aunt's husband, a tank commander, was "blown to pieces in the South." He also lost several friends. He described a high desertion rate in the Army, which took a half million dead—"You could bribe anybody in the Army at that time." What Iraq called POWs in Iran, Zuhair said, were hundreds of thousands of soldiers who deserted.

Basim al-Khafaji had hopes when the war with Iran ended in 1988 that things would improve, but Saddam's impulsive invasion of Kuwait settled that. After his residency at the University of Cincinnati, he and his family settled in Detroit in 1996. Why? "Well, you miss your bread, for one," his eyes gleamed behind the glasses. Though Detroit was as close to a souk as he was going to get in America, al-Khafaji still longed to return to Iraq someday and make a contribution. He wasn't deluded about the magnitude of the problems. In 2005, after having toured Syria, Iran, Saudi Arabia, and Jordan, his assessment was grim: "The regimes in all these countries need to go. These are not regimes that can survive. There is an utter lack of respect on every level—the governments toward the people, the people toward the governments, the people toward each other. We have to respect humankind. As Imam

Ali said, 'Every human being is your brother in faith or in humanity.' That's the bottom line."

Is it hard being away from an Islamic society? "Quite the contrary," said al-Khafaji. "I saw no Islam there," he retorted. "Islam is here! In the United States! I went to the Middle East, I saw Muslims, but no Islam. I came to America and I saw Islam, no Muslims." The pathologist spoke with revulsion about viewing a "huge palace in Mecca" for royalty across from a corner of the sacred Ka'baa, while nearby sprawled the hovels of peasants and the street poor, people you never hear about in Saudi Arabia.

Al-Khafaji's advice to George W. Bush concerning the besieged democratic experiment in Iraq: "It's easy for me to say as I am living in air conditioning in America, but I do think the Iraqis can do it themselves. We have a willingness and determination to do it. How can you ask a young fellow from Texas who has never seen the country, stuck in a piece of metal in 140-degree heat, to establish democracy in Iraq? You're asking too much of him. Hand it over to the Iraqis as soon as you can. Whenever the Iraqis tell you, do it."

Both Basim and Zuhair bemoaned the shorthand in the press which pits Shi'ite against Sunni in Iraq. "I challenge you to find a pure Shi'a or Sunni," al-Khafaji stated. "This so-called split between the sects is new." They reeled off many examples of intermarriage between Sunni and Shi'a and even noted that Saddam Hussein's name is Shi'ite in origin. They felt that the two communities mix well in America. They both agonized over the misconceptions about Islam and Shi'ism, in particular, in the West. About the rite of Ashura, al-Khafaji insisted, "Scholars such as Sistani have begged people not to hit their heads with a blade or chains with glass on their chests, that this is not a good idea and that they should do nothing in Ashura to harm themselves. It is an antiquated custom." Al-Khafaji mentioned that Imam Hussein, whose assassination in 680 CE sparked Shi'ism, was a "Christ-like figure. You cannot but shed tears hearing his story. Even Gandhi said his role model was Imam Hussein." They quoted the holy man with obvious reverence through a proverb passed on from his grandfather, the prophet Mohammed, "Wherever you see evil, stop it with your hand. If that is not possible, use your tongue. If not that, at least keep it at bay in your heart."

Post-September 11, America has given both men pause. Basim al-Khafaji admitted that his habit of browsing libraries has been curtailed due to the Patriot Act's surveillance of patrons, "Now I ask myself: Do I really want to do this?" This practice reminds him of nothing so much as the burning of Khomeini's books in Najaf at the beginning of the Iran–Iraq War.

As for Dr. Zuhair Allebban, he admitted "some apprehension" in initial conversations with strangers in America because of his accent, and he wasn't pleased when both his wife and daughter were pulled off a plane in England for questioning in July 2004 on their way to Detroit. Still, he loved to tell the story of when he first came to the United States in 1976. He had been told that Americans eat dogs. "I went to a Sambo's in New York," he smiled. "I was worried. I was very careful. And there on the menu was a hot dog. 'Boy,' I said to myself, 'they really do eat dogs!' I didn't eat meat for two weeks!"

A friend of the two Shi'ites, pharmacist Mustafa Alsamarae is a Sunni with no love for the Saddam regime, who arrived in America in 1994 "seeking safety for my family."[8] During his five years of service in the Iran–Iraq War, Alsamarae tended to the wounded, "I remember one soldier, so brave, a big wound in his chest. 'I feel cold,' he said to me. I took off my jacket and covered him. And then he died." Mustafa also saw a soldier commit suicide and another executed near Basra. With barely a breather between that devastating encounter with Iran and the invasion of Kuwait, Alsamarae confided, "It's painful. I saw my country collapse in one day because of the wrong decision of Saddam. What, am I supposed to give him applause? I was serving as a pharmacist in the south of Iraq after the Gulf war had stopped, and a UN official came up and asked me what I needed. At the time I was angry at both sides and replied, 'What do I need? 'You destroy my country and now you ask me what I need?' We had a shortage of medicine and drugs throughout the 1990s."

Alsamarae spoke with some pain about the daily life with four children under UN sanctions after the first Gulf war: "Everytime I go out, I ask myself, will I find milk for my kids?" He saw widespread malnutrition and many cancer patients, noting that the US used uranium for bombs that could penetrate tanks: "In 1995, I lost my 35-year-old cousin, who died of leukemia in a matter of days."

Like his Shi'ite friends, Alsamarae recalled better days of intermingling between Shi'ite and Sunni, as well as Christians, in Iraq. "When I hear about the Sunni [insurgents] bombing a church in Iraq now, I can't understand it," he said. Unlike Allebban and al-Khafaji, however, Alsamarae felt that the Muslim sects and Christians did not mix well in Detroit. The $10 million huge mosque (newly minted in 2005) on Ford Road, the American Muslim Center, was 95 percent Shi'ite, and Imam Qazwini, despite his attempts, had not been successful in wooing Sunnis to it.

Unlike al-Khafaji, Alsamarae has no desire to return to Iraq: "I believe the better future for my family is in the United States. It went from bad to worse there. I don't think there is hope for democracy there—it will take a long, long time. It took this country 300 years. We had our own civil war here, don't forget. Iraq will need time to grow up."

Still, Alsamarae, a gentle man with kind eyes, bristles at some of the misconceptions in the American media about Arabs: "They always talk about 'sleeping cells' [sic] here. No one gives us a statistic about how many Iraqi soldiers have died alongside Americans. Many Iraqi Americans have died as interpreters [during the second American invasion of Iraq]. We have funerals for them in our mosque here in Detroit." He mentions an Iraqi-American soldier, whose name has been withheld, who was present during Saddam Hussein's capture.

The attacks of September 11 shook him to the core: "I was so scared. I expected at my pharmacy anyone would attack me at any moment. They could retaliate against my wife going to the market, my kids."

About the current situation in Iraq, "It's a mess—we are not achieving anything but bloodshed. We cannot solve this problem with the military. We need a political process. The mistakes our military makes encourage people to be out of the law." At the same time, Alsamarae scoffs at the sentence of one insurgent with rocket-propelled grenades (RPGs) at his home—10 years. "It's not enough punishment to root out this problem," he said.

That night in August 2005, the three Iraqis and I attended a special event at the new mosque on Ford Road called "Enough is Enough!" Six young Muslims, including Zuhair's daughter, Emann, a Fulbright scholar, spoke on a panel about how to counteract stereotypes about Islam, part of a nationwide effort in the wake of the July subway and bus bombings in London.[9] "I go online and I let them know I am hurt when you call my faith a faith of violence," said Ahmed Nasir, a computer programmer. The speakers all stressed the importance of informing Americans at large about Islam. "Being informed in these times is not just a responsibility," said Jim Jouney, a pharmacist. "It is a duty." At the same time, a reporter for the *Detroit Free Press*, David Crumm, asked, "Why is it that when there is violence in Ireland, we don't ask Irish-Americans for comment. But when there is any violence in Iraq, our community here is questioned." The audience, split between women on the left and men on the right, seemed to agree.

As Mustapha and I walked out, I asked about the Muslim call to prayer. "In Hamtramck, where the majority of the population is Pakistani, the local government allowed it," he said. "But not here. To have it five times a day would disturb the neighbors." Into the night surrounded by Ford, the chirr of crickets, and accelerating cars, we disappeared.

Near the Detroit River and the Chrysler and Ford motor factories, and a fair distance from the suburban Iraqi Chaldeans and even Dearborn's Iraqis, is an entirely different group of recent Arab immigrants to the United States: the Yemenis. Yemen occupies the mountainous southern and southwest corners of the Arabian peninsula. A sprinkling of seafaring Yemenis came to the United States after the opening of the Suez Canal in 1869. Of the 36,170 Yemenis listed as immigrants from 1948–2003, most journeyed to the United States after the 1968 civil war that created two Yemens, which were subsequently reunited in 1991. Some Yemeni immigrants to the United States actually came through Vietnam, where they worked as watchmen in warehouses, in shops, and on the docks. Though there it was easier to get a visa without being literate, they left Vietnam during the war against the French.[10] They followed various pathways to jobs—over 500,000 to Saudi Arabia and three Gulf states in the oil boom. In the United States they found work in car factories in Detroit, on farms in California's San Joaquin Valley, as well as in foundries in Buffalo, New York, and Canton, Ohio.

There really is no Arab immigrant group comparable to the Yemenis, 90 percent of whom are unaccompanied young males, semi-literate or illiterate, with little knowledge of English. Uniquely, most Yemenis, even thirty years after their migration commenced, have not taken root here. Most shuttle back and forth on jumbo planes to Yemen, buying homes back there with money earned here. In short, the Yemenis—with some exceptions—constitute the most definitely "Arab" of any migrating group from the Arab world over this century, and may be considered as a group more temporary workers than immigrants. Their presence in the Detroit area, especially in the Southend of Dearborn, is the most concentrated of any Arab population in the United States. Only Atlantic Avenue in Brooklyn rivals the bazaar that sports myriad Arab signs and shops down Dearborn's Dix Avenue.

The Yemenis of Detroit have been closely studied by sociologists and anthropologists, most notably Nabeel Abraham of Henry Ford Community College. In 1983, Abraham found that 1,000–5,000 Yemeni workers constituted up to 15 percent of Chrysler's Hamtramck plant (known as "Dodge Main"). Scrambling for work when the car factories closed, many Yemenis could be found busing tables, washing dishes, and even manning cargo ships. One estimate found fully 20 percent of seafarers on the Great Lakes to be the dark-skinned, lithe, Arabic-speaking Yemenis.[11]

Though as late as 1959 most of the Muslim-dominated Southend of Dearborn was Lebanese, the steady influx of Yemenis assured that community dominance there, where by the late 1970s 2,000–3,000 Yemenis were living and working. Dix Avenue is peopled with Yemenis hanging out at myriad coffeehouses, playing cards, gossiping, preparing to go to work. Over half the stores in the Southend are now owned by Yemenis, a telling pattern of the belated pull of American soil. So heavy was the Yemeni influence becoming in the Southend that the old Lebanese mosque built in the 1930s on Dix Avenue had its control wrested by a fervent Yemeni religious sheikh in 1976.[12]

It may be a bit of a surprise to discover that, for a time when they were split, the large majority (70 to 80 percent) of Yemenis coming to America emigrated from capitalist Yemen and not the communist regime of southern Yemen. The few hundred from southern Yemen, though, were far more educated and urbane than their northern counterparts. Many emigrants came from a hot spot along the two Yemens' border. A city called Ash-Shaar, just over the border in northern Yemen, contributed more to Yemeni emigration than any other town.

In return for a little "coffee money" (*qahwa*), native Yemeni lenders (*wakil al-mughtaribin*) will finance everything from the rural immigrant's plane tickets to subsequent construction of the addition of a bedroom to his Yemeni home. This "coffee money" is a service that takes the place of interest, forbidden in Islam. So important is the *wakil*, a latter-day "sharper," in this migration pattern that the laborer's paycheck money is sent to him before it is distributed to the immigrant's family in Yemen.

The key indicator of Yemeni loyalty is the amount of money sent back home. It appears that Yemeni salaries in Detroit range from around $10,000 to $15,000, and that it is not uncommon to find auto workers remitting two-thirds of these amounts to family back home. The extent of the Yemenis' patriotism in the midst of the hustle of modern America—their own hustle included—was seen when the president of Dodge Main UAW Local 3 tried to coax the Yemenis to settle their families in Detroit. He offered six-month leaves (two months higher than the norm) to any Yemeni who would go back to Yemen and retrieve his family for relocation in Detroit. Even seven years later, no one had taken Joe Davis up on his offer.

The clash of cultures elicits some interesting social phenomena among the Yemenis. Involvement with drugs, alcohol, women, and gambling among Yemeni youths caused some to be dubbed *ta`ishin* ("the frivolous ones"), whose rough equivalent in English would be "slackers." Vagrants and those stricken with alcoholism who walk Dix Avenue and do not work are called *bumin* (bums). These are all ostracized by the immigrant community, unless they meet their share of home remittances through work. Work forgives a litany of vices to the Yemenis as, indeed, it does with many Americans.

Except for the stray youth seen taking his blonde girlfriend to the movies, interaction between Yemenis and the host society is probably the most restricted of any Arab immigrant group. In the 1976 Detroit municipal elections, for instance, though several Arab-American candidates sought the support of Yemeni citizens, those few who had the vote didn't use it. Though Yemenis belong to the labor unions, they look dimly on strikes and refuse to participate. (In the California farmlands, few Yemenis joined the Chavez union.) Indeed, in the early 1970s, the Detroit's plan to raze much of the Southend of Dearborn where so many Yemenis live met with little resistance. For the most part, the Yemenis are content to replicate their village structures in their coffeehouses (villagers tend to stick to patronizing the coffeehouses of other co-villagers in Yemen, not co-neighborhood dwellers in the United States).[13]

As for the Egyptian Copts, whose Christianity dates back to St. Mark the Evangelist's trip to Alexandria in 62 CE, they began arriving in the United States in significant numbers in the mid-1960s. The first two Coptic churches were established in New Jersey and California. There are now nine Coptic churches in America, and about 50,000 Copts. The largest community is nestled in Jersey City, New Jersey, where Copts own grocery stores and work in factories.[14]

THIRD WAVE PALESTINIANS AND LEBANESE

Based on the 2000 US Census, the three top states of settlement for the estimated 250,000 Palestinian Americans are California (20 percent), Illinois (10 percent), and Florida (8 percent). Although there are large communities of Palestinian-Americans in Detroit and Los Angeles, research shows up to 15 percent of Third Wave Palestinian immigration to the United States has been to Chicago, where they have congregated on the poor southwest side of the Windy City. Like Mexicans before them, Palestinians have been a "convenient barrier population" between blacks and whites in Chicago, many working for low wages ($1,200/month on average) as shopkeepers and clerks. Fully 70 percent feel overall neighborhood conditions—crimes, gangs, drugs—are bad. Substance abuse and gambling addictions are not uncommon.[15] As is always the case, addiction and crime follow class, not race.

When I was growing up in Los Angeles, the only newspaper that serviced the Arab-American community there was the *Star News* edited by Henry Awad. After it went under in the early 1960s, Palestinian Joseph Haiek started the *News Circle*, which gradually worked its way to normal column justification, grammar, and spelling. Today it is a readable, interesting monthly magazine with full-color covers, the only one of its kind in the United States.

A short, genial man with a grin that offsets his balding pate, Joe Haiek welcomed me in the midst of a translation job the office was doing for some company. The *News Circle* survives by using family employees—the time-honored way for the small immigrant businessman. Translation for companies and a new publication dealing with auctions help him pay his bills—barely. Getting people to pay for the magazine is a perennial problem (Haiek offers wealthy

Arab Americans the front cover photograph and lead story for $2,000, a kind of vanity press feature to pay for the bulk of the issue).

At the outbreak of the 1948 war, Haiek was at the Salesian Catholic High School in Jerusalem: "We saw some fighting around the school, and the occupation, but we were not harmed."[16] Being in Jerusalem he also heard about the massacre at Deir Yassin nearby, but his family did not flee, except to cross the city to the Jordanian-administered East Side.

I asked Joe if his own personal advancement continued after Israel was established. Sitting in front of an open window through which the rush of freeway cars could be heard, he shook his head: "No. When you are under occupation, you will be a robot. Try to go up in other circles and you can't, because why would they let an Arab occupy that place when an Israeli can? It's impossible. So you have to be on your own or you have to submit to whatever is there." We discussed the case of Fouzi al-Asmar in Ramle, whom Joe knew from boyhood days. Al-Asmar couldn't get schooling in his chosen field, electrical engineering: "It became apparent to me that not only newspaper advertisements, but also most other things in this country, apart from laws and taxes, were not for Arabs."[17] After serving some time in prison for activism, al-Asmar came to America in the early 1970s.

Joe Haiek got along for awhile in just about the only field Arabs could eke out a minor living—services. He bought and sold American-made tractors that Israeli farmers weren't using. He'd recycle used ones to Arab farmers who still had a shred of land left in Israel (most was expropriated) or were tenant farmers. He also did unsalaried work helping to manage a plot of land for the Latin patriarch near Jerusalem, which supported vineyards and hay. He was also involved wih the Terra Sancta Club, an organization of Christian lay people in Jerusalem, and cut his journalistic teeth putting out its newsletter.

I wondered what it would be like to grow up as a Christian playing in the very paths Christ walked: "This question—I call it 'the American question,' because they feel it so important where Christ went. We are walking all our lives the way Christ went, day in, day out, including His cross on our back. The life of the Palestinian people is a continuous crucifixion!" He brightened, relishing the phrase, "Crucifixion, not only from the Israelis, but also from world politics and our Arab brothers. They all can arrange to cut the Palestinians out of their system."

Haiek first got his notion to leave the land of his birth during the 1956 Suez War when Egypt was vanquished: "*Khalas*, I thought, it is finished." It took him "ten minutes" to make up his mind to leave what he felt was a losing cause for his people, and eleven years to finally go. He arrived in Los Angeles with his family in 1967 just after the June War. "We had to go through the hardship of changing language, being new here, can't find jobs," he related. Though there were a few family members here already, he believed that "family is not enough because there is a social life around you."

Why Los Angeles? For him, "LA had the same weather as Palestine. When we came in September the smog was at its peak, but we didn't feel it. We went through that." Before long he was working at Northrop—a maker, ironically enough, of jet fighters that the United States sent to Israel. He found himself in an assembly line. Language was a steady block on the job, then and now. "I am with you here 30 years and with broken English, a heavy accent!" he said, chagrined. He told a story about being laid off and not being trusted because of his English: "There was a lady who was polite to my face but would tell my supervisor, 'Don't send Joe to bring blueprints, I can hardly understand him!' She was very pretty. Many around her just wanted to sleep with her. Once when she was alone I told her a joke. She started laughing. And I said, 'This is what really amazes me. How come you understand my jokes, but you can't understand the number of the blueprint...?'"

He was excited about my wanderings to collect material on the community: "If nobody write about them, it means they are nothing. How can you fulfill the needs of the community when they are nothing? What puts them up? Not their Cadillacs, not their $6,000 ring, not their perfumes or a limousine."

The wonderful frustration of Haiek turns to a kind of melancholy in a younger Palestinian immigrant to the United States. One would think that Bassam Idais would be fiery in his anger. But he, too, had been through his own baptism of loss and now appears to be in the United States—in San Antonio, Texas—to stay, in spite of being knifed while working at a family icehouse one dreary, hot night.

Having been born into part of the Holy Land already under foreign occupation in 1954—Sinjil on the West Bank—Idais was too young to have been scarred by the jolt of 1948. He remembered occasional radio broadcasts from Egypt and Jordan during those early years with exhortations to throw the Israelis into the sea and wild claims of impending victory, but he didn't see any real violence until the 1967 June War:

> I was in school at the time. Officials began running and saying, "Close the school! Get out!" We left the school and my family saw the jet fighters all over there and we slept in shelters. "Don't sleep in the house or try to go outside in the field or under a tree—stay inside." We kept listening to the radio and from the way they were talking the Arabs were victorious. "We knocked down twenty, fifty planes!" Within twelve hours a few guys came from a town close to Ramallah

and said the Israeli soldiers are already inside Jerusalem and had taken over the whole of it and were driving toward Ramallah...The Israelis were getting closer and closer to Sinjil and we just raised those white flags. There was no defense at all.[18]

At first there were no arrests by the occupying army. But after two weeks the Israelis began calling on young people to see if they had any connection with the PLO or were hiding weapons. Bassam's father was jailed twice because he was accused of having guns. "My dad never carried a gun," Idais said, looking around the green backyard of his cousin in America. "He was a policeman during the Jordanian rule, but he never had a gun." The pressure, he said, never let up until his own departure six years later.

And so, faced with a situation he had come to find "intolerable," Bassam Idais, who hadn't enough money "to go to a café and drink a Coke," decided to leave in 1973. The only available jobs under the Israelis were waiting tables in restaurants or manual labor in construction. He had tried to work for the Israeli government for one week, planting trees on Temple Mount in Jerusalem for two dollars a day. "There was no future," he said glumly. "They treated you like slaves."

Sinjil was a town of about 4,000 people in 1967. Today, according to Idais, most of its young people have left, leaving 3,000 aging residents. All 27 of his high-school classmates are now in the United States. His aging father, however, went back to live in Sinjil.

On one trip back, Bassam was, typically, detained for six hours, enduring a strip search and stiff interrogation. "They even offered me a job one time, saying 'What do you do in the United States? How much do you make? We are willing to pay you more. If you make a thousand dollars, we'll pay you two thousand,'" Bassam related about the Israeli agents. "You want me to work against my people?" he shot back. Clearly, they wanted him as a spy and grilled him for information about the PLO.

Wasn't there a real irony in migrating to the country that funds the one expropriating the Palestinian West Bank day by day? Don't the immigrants think about this? "They think about it," Idais admitted. "But they have no choice. Where can they go? We're hoping that one of these days there'll be peace and a Palestinian state. We're not so happy here. I mean, I would rather live in my country. I don't care how good life is here or the schooling or the job."

Bassam has known loss in war. During the 1967 conflict, a close friend's father was killed on the border of Lebanon. The friend joined the PLO. "A lot of people joined the PLO right away during that war," he stated. "Sons and brothers of the dead joined the PLO immediately."

A stabbing at work—inflicted by a crazed Vietnam vet who

thought Bassam was Vietnamese—will sober a man. It certainly brought home to him the feeling that "you're not safe in America. Since then I just hate to walk into a convenience store," he admitted. "I hate to see somebody carrying knives. It just scares me. You know, in Sinjil there is war all the time, but people are friendly. A lot of people leave their houses unlocked, even now. They can go anywhere. They don't have any bother that somebody will rob them or hold them up or rape them. You never heard of such a word as 'rape' before, back home. They have a manner, a pride, morals—all kinds of good things— even if they're poor they're happy with what they have." It was a dramatic irony, and one I would hear from a number of Palestinian immigrants to America—the peace of the United States contained threats that the war of the Middle East didn't.

The topic of prejudice came up. An accounting major, Bassam had applied in several market chains, such as Seven Eleven and HEB markets to be an auditor or accountant. He believed he was rejected because of his accent, even though he had more schooling than one person hired (who had only a high school diploma). More specifically, he has encountered the inevitable discomfort some Jewish Americans have in facing a recent Palestinian immigrant:

> One time a man at Foley's at Northstar Mall where we were shopping noticed me speaking to a friend in Arabic and he asked, "Are you from Israel?" I said, "I'm from Palestine." He looked at me and said, "There's no Palestine. It's Israel now." I said, "No. It's still Palestine." He didn't like that. He said, "Why don't you say Israel?" "It's not Israel," I responded. "It was the West Bank of the Jordan under the Jordanian government!" He was angry, looking around; I think he was scared, too. Every time we see him, he'd go to the other way. But we're not criminals here.

For Diana Sahwani, life in Israel as an Arab was a "suffocation; it's a kind of death."[19] Living there for her was like living "in a big prison." Though about 20 percent of Israel is Arab (1.3 million of 6.8 million Israelis), there is almost a total dependency on the Jewish sector economically. On the list of Israeli municipal improvement priorities, the Arab neighborhoods are at the bottom. The once-proud Arab sector of Haifa has declined, and though there has been some restoration of old homes in the Wadi Nisnas sector, progress is slow. Tax money by the locals too often goes elsewhere.

As she talked, Diana would barely move a muscle in her near perfect, ivory face. She admitted she had had any spontaneity drained out of her by the time she was a teenager. "Growing up in Israel was so frustrating," she said, touching a hand to her swept-back black hair. "There is no falling in love—feelings did not exist in an extremely conservative Arab subculture. Emotions were like a disease. If you don't have any you're much better off, because this way, you keep your family name unblemished."

Dr. Suheir Daoud, who in 2002 became the first Israeli Arab woman to earn a doctoral degree in political science (from Hebrew University), disagreed. "I experienced totally the opposite," said Daoud, who, together with her Israeli Arab husband Wadie, has a little son.[20] Rather than decrying the decrepit quality of Wadi Nisnas, the Pomona College professor said she enjoyed getting falafel there with her family.

I asked Diana Sahwani to explain her own complicated feelings further. Slowly she opened up about the separateness of Jews and Arabs in Israel, and the identity crisis of Israeli Arabs who stayed behind, thinking they would hold stubbornly to what was theirs, only to be engulfed by the expanding tentacles of the Jewish state that all too often isolated rather than embraced them. Even today, Dr. Daoud admitted, 51 Arab villages in Israel are not recognized by the State—most are Bedouin—and do not receive basic services like electricity and water.

At the same time, the life expectancy of Israeli Arabs is higher than neighboring Arab countries (74.6 years for men, 77.9 years for women), three years higher than in Lebanon, five years higher than in Syria, nine years higher than in Egypt.[21] And what is the picture economically for an Israeli Arab? Certainly it is improved over the 58-year-history of the state of Israel, and it is often better than for his Arab counterpart. But it is still woefully below that of the state's Jewish citizens. The Israeli Arab's per capita income is a little more than half that of his Jewish counterpart. The appraised value of an Arab home is 60 percent that of the average Jewish home, though almost all (92 percent) of Arabs own their home; only 69 percent of Jews do. Evidently, Arabs will not let go those old buildings, the last hint of ownership of the land itself.

At the time I interviewed Diana Sahwani—in the eighties—she confessed to wanting to be a writer, but picked engineering where "no emotions were involved." At the time, she worked at an aircraft company on a missile program in Wichita, Kansas. But by 2005, Suheir Daoud pointed out that literature by Israeli Arabs was flourishing (she herself had published a collection of short stories), the number of Arabic newspapers in the Jewish state had nearly doubled between 1982 and 2002 (from 37 to 60), and that the rate of kindergarten and preschool attendance for Israeli Arabs is six times higher than in Egypt and three times higher than in Jordan. Still, she noted, the rate of Israeli Jews attending universities is twice that of Israeli Arabs (24 percent to 11 percent).

In the political world, still constricted for Israeli Arabs, especially since the second Intifada in 2000, there had been some progress— and some nagging practices that smacked of racism. Until 1984, Arabs could not legally form their own political parties; most had to settle for the marginal Israeli Communist Party. But today there are several secular and even Islamic parties founded by Arabs in Israel. In 1999, the first Arab woman was elected to the Knesset (though the percentage of Israeli Arab women elected in municipal races in 1998 was only 0.6 percent, compared to 15 percent for their Jewish women counterparts).[22] Still, the humiliation Diana Sahwani spoke of when she had to show her ID card at agencies, on street corners, to policemen who stopped her for traffic tickets, to cash checks, is still there—and that includes "nationality" on the ID card listed as "Arab" or "Jew," rather than "Israeli." And worse—there is a number code which indicates if one is an Arab.

When she got her U.S. green card in 1980, Diana Sahwani was asked her nationality. "I refused to put 'Israeli' because Israel doesn't call Arabs Israelis, but Arabs," she explained. "The immigration officer said, 'Arab is not a nation, and Palestine doesn't exist.' He was right, of course. So I suggested 'stateless.' It was accepted and that was recorded under my nationality."

Suheir Daoud pointed out, "We [Israeli Arabs] have been fighting in the last 15 years to be acknowledged as a national minority and to be called 'Palestinian.'" But a fight is not a reality; if Dr. Daoud takes the U.S. green card, she may be faced with the same dilemma—that same blank space for nationality—as Ms. Sahwani.

The Lebanese of the Third Wave came to America for drastically different reasons than did those who braved the first steamship trails to Ellis Island. Their country was torn asunder, from without and from within. The largest subset of the three million Arab Americans is that of Lebanese background (34 percent); most of these are descendents of First Wave immigrants. Of the 135,350 who have come here since 1967, 122,262 Lebanese have come since the civil war commenced in 1975. Each violent spasm in a country where central government's role in public life was for two decades practically nonexistent caused new immigrants. According to Tony Khater—who came to the United States in 1972 due to "economic suffocation"—if not for the rich, the poor, and the stubborn, over 75 percent of Lebanon would have left the country by now.

Self-described as "hyper," my friend Tony had a difficult time sitting still. Typically, he liked to visit for a coffee (coffee, in Tony's parlance, is a solid—you "take a coffee" and thereby have life in all its grounds). First, he would pour himself a glass of water from the tap, then have the coffee, chatter about the latest flare-up in Lebanon (his parents still lived in Beirut), and then abruptly stand up and say it was time to leave.

Just after he took work at ADC, Tony received word from Beirut that his older sister, Samia, had died of a rare blood disease. He flew home in the war-weary atmosphere to mourn for her with his parents. Another sister, Ehsan, froze in the middle of the streets one day during the civil war, caught by gunfire, and suffered shellshock for a year afterward. His father, a retired soldier in the Lebanese army, had been hit in the streets by a stray bullet. After months of huddling in Tony's Washington apartment, Ehsan ventured out to the new world to get work at Blackie's House of Beef as a hat-check girl. His brother, Bassam, worked in an optometrist's shop. For a while, Tony worked in the Arab-American groups, especially adept at community organizing and linkage with other ethnic and special interest groups. On many occasions, however, Tony bemoaned that he was making a living off the suffering of his country and longed to leave the political groups. After securing his green card he left ADC and NAAA and entered law school at Georgetown University. His father admonished over a crackling long-distance phone call from Beirut to his 32-year-old son, "Tony, do me a favor—try and enroll for once in the marriage school!" Ultimately, he became a lawyer, a public defender in Washington, DC.

"Immigration has always been a sort of safety valve for Lebanon," Tony explained. "Lebanon is one of the most densely populated countries in the world. University graduates were on the increase there in the late 1960s and early 1970s, and they had no job prospects. Hence they turned to the United States, to Latin America, Africa, and Australia."[23]

Tony estimated that most Maronite youth fought for the Phalange during the civil war in Lebanon, and if they didn't their sympathy was still deep. He chose not to fight as a Maronite. But here he suffered:

> I mean, your country is your point of reference and when it is being displaced, phased off the map, you feel it. It was like hearing the news that a mother or father was dying of cancer and you are unable to go back. We lost touch with my parents for a few months in 1976. Then I heard they needed money. I tried to get them some—all I had, 200 dollars—but the bank told me it would have to send the money to Damascus where they would have to pick it up. It was ridiculous. They wouldn't have done it. I later heard that my father was prepared with lots of food stored up. A bomb hit the apartment where we lived. My mother told me all the canned food spilled on the floor, sardines, tuna, you name it. She was happy it did not hit the other side of the kitchen where the new refrigerator was!
>
> Water—it was hard to get. In wintertime, they collected water on the roof of the building. Bassam would put a hose on the roof down the balcony into a bucket. Then they would go to Baabda—which had a polluted spring—and carry off water in their cars. It was really a hard time.... Walking over to their shelter was in itself

a danger. My father got shot in his side by Palestinians at Tal Zaatar. It was a tough time sleeping.

"And yet you didn't want to fight?" I persisted.

"On whose side to fight?" his voice cracked, and his forehead furrowed. "There's where it was a bit weird. If I knew whose side I wanted to fight on, I would have had less of a problem."

"It wasn't so easy for you to be pro-Phalange?"

"No," he was definite. "The Phalange were suicidal. They were exploding the whole country just to kill an ant."

But what about the tremendous corruption in Lebanese politics that showed the state to be decayed from within, aside from the Palestinian element. "Corruption everyone took for granted," Tony said nonchalantly. "In the elections of 1970 I was paid 50 Lebanese pounds to take my parents to their hometown of Saghbine to vote for a certain list. My first bribe! I liked it."

Tony fondly recalled youthful days walking with his grandfather about fifteen minutes from the store in Marjayoun to a Shi'ite village nearby, Dibin. They had lunch there often and had to cross cemeteries to get there. "There was a *jami'* [mosque] there and they started chanting *Allahu akbar* [God is great]," he recalled with a distant gaze. "It was so pleasant. Until I was seventeen I didn't have any sense of Muslim–Christian conflict in Lebanon. Our school, though mostly Christian, had about one-fourth Muslims, usually rich ones. The two groups fraternized a lot."

Tony Khater took the pledge of allegiance and became an American citizen in 1987, but for many years, 'Ala' Drooby, another Lebanese immigrant from Beirut, did not. A man of few words, a not uncommon minority strain in the Arab character, Drooby sat in his office at the Houston Medical Center, a few strands of hair combed like a median strip over his head. His expression was intense, concentrated, quiet, his demeanor that of a mongoose who has had plenty of run-ins with cobras. I was told by leaders of the Houston community that Drooby was a "must" interview, and not just because he headed the sizable Houston contingent of the Arab American Medical Association. Drooby told it like it was—stripped.

> I left Lebanon on account of three kinds of pollution that I had found there [he stated in rat-a-tat-tat style]. I had said to myself, either love it or leave it. So I left. The three kinds of pollution are social, aesthetic, and acoustic. People were too noisy, radios blaring, car hoots. The lack of respect for the beauty of Lebanon—which, of couse, nobody puts merit in, but there is no merit in disfiguring it. They would cut trees and build ugly buildings. Now let's move to the serious part, namely, the various corruptions that everyone knew

about and seemed to expect to come to an end through some sort of magic. Of course, I don't believe in magic, so I thought that, since we were living in a country that was above all committed to Western ideas, I should raise my family in a Western country. Australia was a good mixture of English and American cultures and habits.[24]

Drooby did not stay in Australia because his American-born daughter had graduated from university and wanted to settle in the land of her birth. She also left Lebanon after an eight-month stint doing social work in 1977 when she realized the hatred "was an irreversible course." His two sons—a physician and a realtor—also came from abroad to the United States the year the whole family decided to transplant to America for good. They followed the route of the daughter, who had tried the hardest to mend Lebanon; America waited at the end of the failed experiment. Now retired, for many years Drooby taught at Baylor College of Medicine and worked at the Texas Medical Center with Vietnam veterans suffering from mental illness.

Though Drooby was lucky enough to take "the good part of Lebanese life" before he got out, the suffering of those he left behind haunted him: "There is no way to quantify the misery of people who have lost their children, their parents, who have been killed for no worthy cause—bystanders. People who were standing in their homes who just got killed. Or people who were standing in front of bakeries who were machine-gunned. And other people preventing the fire department from coming to offer help to burning homes..." His voice trailed off. He was revolted by the massacres at Sabra and Shatila, but even more so that the Lebanese inquest took a year to convene and in the end indicted no one: "Now this is a continuation of what has driven me out. There was no guts to state things black and white. Open television; open radio. Listen, and you will find nothing but wordy statements. Not worthy—wordy—like good old Shakespeare said, nothing but words."

Typically for émigré Lebanese, Drooby spoke as an internationalist: "I have found that human beings behave exactly the same way wherever you are, even if you are in Alaska or Siberia." Iconoclast to the end, Drooby even thought the traditional hospitality of the Lebanese was "a put on." "This cult of 'I can knock at your door and have coffee' is not true," he emphasized. "Coffee was always offered to people who didn't need it. But if someone came and needed less than coffee, he wasn't given coffee or sugar or anything."

I didn't think Drooby was leaning toward accepting American citizenship with these comments and I was right. "I've always said nationalism is the first poison," he put his hand firmly on his desk. "I don't mind becoming a Tierra del Fuegan. I don't care. I would pay my dues. I would limit myself to moral ethics like I've always done. It doesn't matter two hoots what passport I am."

Arab Americans, to Drooby, did not show signs of being able to organize effectively as a political entity: "I think it takes some training. It begins with very rudimentary things, like not being particularly upset at stopping at red lights in the middle of the night. Then there is the constant fear that this political organization might alienate them from their present country or environment." He did not, however, ever experience prejudice, though he had been politically active. On the contrary, he believed that some professional colleagues who had experienced prejudice were to blame themselves: "I think it's exclusively their doing."

Then there's no need for an American-Arab Anti-Discrimination Committee?

"No," he said bluntly. "ADC will not be able to change the behavior of its members, nor the members their own behavior. This is something you cannot get from meetings or reading pamphlets."

"So you are saying discrimination or ill will is caused by the victim, the insecure one who needs an adversary?"

"Yeah. I would like to add to this that, of course, as in clapping, one hand will not do it. There will be certain attitudes waiting to be confirmed in the recipients. In other words, if I go into an environment that is anti-Arab and I confirm their opinion, it will be anti-Arab. But if I disconfirm it, if I know how to disconfirm it, then it will be different. That is a difficult job. It is very unsettling to the people whose attitudes you have disconfirmed. But we will always have prejudice in human nature."

Would Arab culture and mores be something he would want to instill in his children and grandchildren? "No," he said. "I do not need to instill it. It will be witnessed. With my death, it will disappear, because these are modeling things. It's not by precept; it's by example. But even in the Middle East, it's adulterated. There's no such thing as a pure culture; it's all bastardized."

He felt no conflict between being a Muslim and practicing psychiatry; he was, predictably, against all fundamentalism, Christian or Muslim. "From discussing God's fish to discussing God's politics, or His love—it's the same, all of it. You'll find that in African tribes, in Australian aborigines." He had been on a *hajj*, a pilgrimage, to Mecca in 1971, and he said with typical bluntness that it was "just a version of a meditative exercise," and that he had gone out of curiosity. "I don't think that God is better in one geographical spot," he said. He did not think that revolutionary Islam—such as Khomeini's brutal version—was valid: "This is no Islam at all."

Many years later, in early 2005, his voice shaking with Parkinson's disease, ʿAla Drooby spoke with me over the phone from Houston.

Indeed, he had broken down finally and taken US citizenship, just before the catastrophe of September 11, 2001: "There was too much discrimination against people with green cards, and my wife recommended it."[25] Ironically, on the brink of returning to visit Lebanon he was "toying with the idea of staying." Given his extreme discomfort with how life had deteriorated in Beirut, a misery that propelled him to this country 25 years ago, I was shocked. Why? "Well, it's partly loyalty to our first country," he said quietly. But then he admitted, "What is happening here is disgusting. When I came here, I thought it the ideal country, the ideal Constitution, the ideal society. What happened to the Constitution? The Patriot Act! Our foreign policy! Wolfowitz? I would never have believed when I came here that this would happen to America."

—SIX—

THE POLITICAL AWAKENING
(1972–1981)

Before I turn to the tumultuous political events of the 1990s, which threw Arab Americans into a harsh light that only grew more so after September 11, 2001, the political awakening of the community in the 1970s and 1980s provides a revealing distant mirror. The community, and the country as a whole, waded through many trials after the September 11 attack, as well as an incoherent, often self-defeating policy in the Middle East. But how it navigated earlier troubles is instructive. Arab Americans were slow to organize politically. Part of this may have been due to a reluctance to "stand out" in a host society, an attitude that probably dated back to the 500-year experience of subjugation of Arab lands under the Ottoman Turks. This reticence was then abetted by an interregnum of colonial overlords—British, French, Italian—between the world wars of the 20th century.

In the United States, the risks—economic, occupational, political—to the Arab-American community in tackling hostility toward Arabs in general and Israeli suppression of Palestinians in particular were rarely seen as worth taking. This was not helped by an official American policy of supporting Israel no matter what it did to the Arabs or what danger its policies brought to the United States itself. The mind-numbing fractures in Lebanon, the internecine conflicts inside and between autocratic Arab regimes (Iraq vs. Syria, Iraq vs. Kuwait, Sunni vs. Shiʿite Iraqis, Morocco vs. the Polisario, the two Yemens, civil war in Sudan, etc.), not to mention the two wars the United States fought (and is still fighting) in Iraq have made the problem of how to find "common ground" politically with other Arab Americans—on Middle East policy alone—relentlessly challenging.

Nevertheless, after Israel's lightning six-day war in 1967, the community in the United States was galvanized, by fits and starts to be sure, to political action. At the same time, Arab Americans were making strides into the US electoral body politic never before achieved. In the years following 1967, the election and appointment of public officials from the community to high office was a hopeful sign. The year 1972 was a banner one in which the community's first US senator was elected, James Abourezk from South Dakota. In 1974, Philip Habib was appointed assistant secretary of state, largely on the basis of his mediation efforts during the Paris peace talks with the Viet Cong. In 1988, John Sununu, the governor of New Hampshire, became the first President Bush's White House chief of staff. In 2000, Spencer Abraham, former US senator from Michigan, became only the second Arab-American cabinet member as secretary of energy (the first was Health and Human Services Secretary Donna Shalala under President Clinton).

It wasn't until 1972 that Arab Americans had more than one member in the US Congress at a time. In that year, a former aide to Ralph Nader was elected to Congress from Connecticut, Toby Moffett. That same year James Abdnor was elected in South Dakota. In 1976, Mary Rose Oakar (D-OH) and Nick Joe Rahall (D-WV) were elected, the latter the youngest member of the House at the time. In 1980, George Mitchell won the seat of US senator from Maine, filling in the spot vacated by Edmund Muskie. By 2005, there were five members of Congress of Arab extraction, four in the House: Nick Joe Rahall (D-WV), Charles Boustany (R-LA), Ray LaHood (R-IL) and Darryl Issa (R-CA), who led the extraordinary 2003 effort that unseated California Governor Gray Davis in a recall election; John Sununu Jr. (R-NH) was the one US Senator. On domestic issues, Arab Americans are as polar opposite as Rahall and Issa.

It would be impossible to describe the myriad organizations that embraced the world of politics springing up in the Arab-American community since 1967. There are Arab-American Democratic and Republican clubs, Arab-American war veterans associations, political action committees, medical associations, business and trade groups that enter the political fray in one way or the other. There have been dozens if not hundreds of Arab-American organizations local and nationwide, which address the community's concerns on the Middle East, though the life span of such groups is notoriously short. And they are not often well-subscribed while they last. If the community is three million strong today as is often claimed, then the number of Arab Americans who belong to such groups is only about two percent (60,000) of the community. To add to the endemic problem of recruitment, after September 11, many otherwise non-political, philanthropic groups were shut down by the FBI in the general frenzy to stopper anything and everything that might be construed as abetting terrorism. For Arab Americans, that might be anything and everything in which they form association. The climate was disconcerting, to say the least.

Nevertheless, when the smoke of disintegrated or shut-out political efforts cleared, three national membership groups maintained themselves for more than two decades in recent times: the Association of Arab American University Graduates (AAUG), the National Association of Arab Americans (NAAA), and the American-Arab Anti-Discrimination Committee (ADC). By 2003, after merging with NAAA, only the ADC remained. A think tank, the vigorous Arab American Institute (AAI), founded in 1985, added statistical analyses and networking for current and potential Arab-American political leaders.

THE ASSOCIATION OF ARAB AMERICAN UNIVERSITY GRADUATES (AAUG)

In June 1967, just after the Six-Day War began, according to Abdeen Jabara, a handful of Arab Americans, "exceedingly depressed over the events in the Middle East and asking what we could do," met in the home of Rashid Bashur, a renowned professor of medical sociology at the University of Michigan. Also in attendance were Adnan Aswad, Fawzi Najjar, and Jabara himself, who drew up the articles of incorporation. In the fall, the group inaugurated the AAUG in a meeting at the Middle East Studies Association (MESA) convention in Chicago. Forty-four members joined; Abdeen Jabara became first executive secretary.

A year later, AAUG held its first convention in Washington, DC, with noted Palestinian intellectual Fayez Sayegh giving the keynote speech. In 1969, with Ibrahim Abu-Lughod as president, AAUG had its first large convention turnout—600 people—at Northwestern University. Made up largely of migratory Second Wave Palestinian academicians, AAUG acquired a building in Belmont, Massachusetts, that served as the organization's headquarters until its demise in 2000.

Though it was involved in political protests and other such activity, AAUG's primary role was always tapping the sizable brainpower of its members, mostly Second and Third Wave immigrants. It was the first of the major organizations involved in publishing books and a scholarly journal (*Arab Studies Quarterly*, edited by Edward Said and Fouad Moughrabi). At its height, AAUG had about 4,000 dues-paying members, the smallest of the national, nonsectarian Arab-American groups, but for a time it remained the most stable, relying on the analytical capacities of its members rather than responses to the spasmodic upheavals in the Middle East.

Yoked closely to the intellectual and political life in the Arab world (for example, in 1975 AAUG sponsored a Human Resources Development conference in Kuwait), AAUG maintained a strong, consistent criticism of the failings in Arab politics and society. On rare occasions, the NAAA and ADC issued protests of violations of human rights in Arab countries. But the AAUG, which saw itself as a kind of intellectual laboratory for change in the Arab world, bit that difficult bullet often and responsibly, to its credit. AAUG was no friend of monarchs or militant Zionism. It was progressive and secular, though some complained that its arrows were shot from too high in the ivory tower.

Those who grew disgruntled with AAUG's academic perspective left the organization for other paths. It was two AAUGers who helped found the Palestine Human Rights Campaign (PHRC) in 1978— Abdeen Jabara and Jim Zogby. The latter became the first executive director of the new ADC in 1980 and after a bitter clash with ADC-founder James Abourezk started the Arab American Institute (AAI). Sadly, the Arab-American political groups were as fractious as those in the Arab world. There are some things democracy cannot change. Still, the issues were always serious and fraught with personal if not organizational risk. Surveillance of the Arabs in America did not start with September 11. In 1968, AAUG took up the case of three Yemenis who were accused of plotting to assassinate President Nixon (the case was later thrown out of court). A more serious threat to Arab-American civil rights occurred in 1972, when President Nixon initiated Operation Boulder, a little-known directive to the FBI to monitor activities of Arab students and politically active Arab Americans following the killing of eleven Israeli Olympians in Munich.[1] Abdeen Jabara of Detroit, whose phones were tapped, pursued a lawsuit that took over a decade to settle: "You have to understand all this was not only before 9/11, it was before Watergate! We filed with some trepidation, because the FBI was seen at that time as being an agency that could do no wrong."[2]

What was at stake, Jabara said, was "whether or not the FBI may maintain information about a person's non-criminal political activities." Though there have been other suits of the kind—by African Americans, for instance—Jabara contended that this was "probably the most advanced of its kind in the country" at the time. Back in 1983, Jabara showed me a three-drawer file full of cases of Arab Americans who were being watched, tapped, or visited by the FBI. Attendance at a poetry reading, even, could bring one under surveillance, he said. When asked what the chances were that someone who had worked for NAAA or ADC was on the FBI rolls, he said, without hesitation, "Very good."

AAUG's president Cherif Bassiouni wrote Attorney General Kleindeist on October 16, 1972, of Arab-American alarm over a "dragnet investigation based solely upon an individual's national origin." FBI Director L. Patrick Gray (who was to resign over Watergate) denied knowledge of the cases AAUG and the ACLU discussed. He also denied that national origin had anything to do with the investigation, but rather "membership or activity in organizations which have been reliably reported to threaten the internal security of the United States."[3]

Over a decade since the lawsuit, Jabara discovered that the FBI had monitored his telephone conversations in thirteen separate wiretaps and disseminated information on him to seventeen US government agencies and three foreign governments.[4]

One of the most fascinating of AAUG's friends in its early years was Israeli Arab poet Rashid Hussein, who addressed the national convention in 1971. A Jewish friend who drove him to Newark to take out his naturalization papers recounted that Hussein, at first delighted, took the little American flag he had been given and broke it on the way out of city hall.[5] After living for a while with his American Jewish wife in the suburbs of New Jersey, Hussein went to live alone in Manhattan, his final days a kind of "personal holocaust," according to critic Salma Jayyusi. On February 1, 1977, Rashid Hussein was found dead in his apartment in New York, the victim of a fire started by a dropped cigarette. Alcoholism had taken its toll, but more, his homelessness and loneliness. In an ironic cooperative gesture, a synagogue in upper Manhattan arranged for his funeral, which was paid for by the PLO. American journalist I.F. Stone memorialized him: "It seems as if there are forces in Israel which fear the Arab friend more than the Arab terrorist. They broke his heart." The Palestinian poet Mahmoud Darwish wrote a moving elegy to his friend, "On Fifth Avenue He Greeted Me."[6]

Rashid Hussein had had a impossible time trying to square his love of freedom and democracy with America's tolerance of Israeli occupation of Palestinian lands beyond what had been sanctioned in 1948 by the international community. He would have been surprised to learn what the AAUG found out in a 1982 poll conducted by the group's think tank, the Institute for Arab Studies (IAS). The poll, which was conducted by Richard Wirthlin, the chief pollster for the Republican Party and President Ronald Reagan, revealed public attitudes that neither Gallup nor Harris, to that point, had cared to plumb. Among the results of the 67-question telephone survey of 1,020 American adults were the following:

> 76 percent believed that Palestinians should have their own state; Only 29 percent felt that such a state would threaten the security of Israel; 72 percent agreed to a freeze on further Israeli settlements in the occupied territories; and 69 percent felt that Israel had violated the US Arms Export Control Act by misusing American weapons in its invasion of Lebanon.

In 1983, the American Israel Public Affairs Committee (AIPAC) claimed in its McCarthy-like "hit list" of Arab-American organizations, *The Campaign to Discredit Israel*, that AAUG had a $1.4 million budget. It was probably smaller; shortly after it closed its doors in 2000, the disillusion of its founders was universal.

THE NATIONAL ASSOCIATION OF ARAB AMERICANS (NAAA)

It was on a rainy March day in 1979 when a representative from the National Association of Arab Americans met me in the cafeteria of the US Senate to give me information and ended up offering me a job. At the time, I was assistant press secretary to a California senator, one of only three Arab-American aides on Capitol Hill. John Richardson said, "You could do a lot more good if you came and worked for us."

At the time, I hardly knew a thing about the NAAA, the only lobby at this time for Arab Americans. The organization had been founded in 1972 in Washington, DC, by attorney Richard Shadyac, Professor Hisham Shirabi of Georgetown University, and former Army colonel and Nixon aide Peter Tanous, who hoped to transfer the intellectual fervor of AAUG into the political arena.

Richardson described the organization's goals: a separate independent state for Palestinians; a pluralistic, nonsectarian Lebanon out from under the influence of both Israel and Syria. Did the organization lobby in the general framework of acceptance of Israel? He nodded. Coexistence with Israel in its pre-1967 borders or something close to them was agreeable. NAAA supported the Camp David negotiations if the Carter administration could make good its promise to bring legitimate Palestinian representatives into the process, and that meant the PLO. A West Bank–Gaza Palestinian state was the goal.

Abdeen Jabara later contrasted the AAUG and NAAA: "NAAA drew upon a totally different constituency than the AAUG. It was not an émigré organization by and large. It was largely an organization of Americans who were first and second generation, who felt themselves to be good, red-blooded, God-fearing, flag-waving Americans. NAAA aimed at influencing legislators and AAUG ideally aimed at reaching different sectors."[7]

For the first four years of its existence, NAAA was in fact one person—Helen Hage, who worked on a half-time salary. It was Hage who collected the first mailing lists for the one erratic publication (*Voice*) and Hage who began to reach out to the media (Mike Wallace of CBS became a friend).

At first, the organization's intent to be the first Arab-American lobby was bolstered by precious little action due to a minuscule budget and staff. In 1973, James Abourezk, then a first-year US senator, and NAAA founder Richard Shadyac testified against $2.2 million for US arms authorized to bail out Israel in the 1973 October War, in which Egypt and Syria attempted to retake land captured by Israel in 1967. Still, NAAA was not well-known by the community it claimed to serve. If anguish was expressed over the

Israeli occupation, it took place within the framework of the Eastern churches.[8] NAAA held annual conventions, sparsely attended, and in 1976 officers met with President Gerald Ford during one of the periodic "reassessments" of US–Israel policy that always seem to be short-lived.

Though most of the 1970s saw a steady escalation of US arms sales to Israel (France's DeGaulle had stopped selling Israel arms and jets after the 1967 war), NAAA did little downstream lobbying and developed no amendments to foreign aid bills. A few congressmen made isolated attempts, such as William Fulbright (D-AR), Paul Findley (R-IL), Abourezk (D-SD), and David Obey (D-WI). When I came on board after my conversation with Richardson in 1979, I had to find out about Obey's unsuccessful attempt to shave about 10 percent of Israeli aid in 1976 from his own office. Clearly, NAAA was not keeping useful legislative records.

Richardson's hiring in 1977 had been a turning point of sorts. Handsome, friendly, if sometimes stiff, Richardson brought an involved Middle East pedigree. A graduate of Williams College (the school where the first American missionaries had hatched their scheme to preach to the Arabs 150 years before), he later wrote his master's thesis on President Woodrow Wilson's ill-fated King–Crane Commission to Palestine. He had been president of American Near East Refugee Aid (ANERA) for 10 years before registering as NAAA's first lobbyist in 1978 (24 years after AIPAC had registered its first lobbyist). Predictably, reports periodically surfaced in the Arab press that Richardson was a CIA plant, but to me his interest seemed genuine. (Disillusioned when he left the organization four years later, he told me, "I thought twenty years ago that if only enough people knew the facts and if I worked hard enough with them, the situation would get better. It only gets worse.")

But with Richardson on board, in 1978 NAAA began to turn heads. Israel's first invasion of Lebanon, the Camp David accords, and a controversial tripartite jet sale to Egypt, Israel, and Saudi Arabia were all events on which the new lobby cut its not very sharp teeth.

Israel's invasion that year up to the Litani River in response to a PLO attack on a bus in northern Israel killed 1,000 civilians and uprooted 265,000 Palestinians and Lebanese. NAAA issued an early, important Arab-American statement eschewing violence, "Terrorism must be condemned, whether it is conducted by resistance groups or by the forces of a sovereign state."

Israel's test-run for a full-scale invasion four years later drew a unique reaction from NAAA—a lawsuit. The May 11 suit was directed against the state department for not enforcing the Arms Export Control Act (AECA) that forbids US arms recipients from using the weapons for anything but "legitimate self-defense." Even

Secretary of State Cyrus Vance had questioned the "proportionality" of the invasion to the provocation.[9] The suit was withdrawn when Israel pulled back from its neighbor to the north.

While the tripartite jet sale was breaking, Michael Saba, a former NAAA director, had a bizarre experience in the Kafkaesque tradition of Middle East politics while having coffee at the Madison Hotel in Washington, DC. Some men sat in a booth next to him and began talking in Hebrew and English about things that would haunt Saba and activate NAAA for years to come. Stephen Bryen, then a key aide to the Senate Foreign Relations Committee, was speaking with officials from the Israeli embassy. Saba was disturbed by the way the conversation evolved: Though an employee of the US government, Bryen continually referred to the US government as "them" and to Israel as "we" and "us." Bryen talked about holding the West Bank as a "security issue." Saba sat bolt upright when he heard Bryen say, "I have the Pentagon document on the bases, which you are welcome to see."[10] Saba later discovered the document was classified. The conversation turned around the subject of the proposed US arms sales to Egypt, Saudi Arabia, and Israel. Saba got the distinct impression Bryen was coaching the Israelis. He took feverish notes and later gave an affidavit to the FBI about the extraordinary conversation.

Bryen and his mentor, Richard Perle, later turned up in powerful slots at the Pentagon under President Ronald Reagan. (In 2003, Perle was a key voice urging the second President Bush to attack Iraq and even Syria, while Bryen sat on something called the US–China Commission.) Both Bryen and Perle pursued and won policies that hurt trade with Europe and killed Soviet–European cooperation on a gas pipeline, while at the same time gaining Israel easier access to US arms and technology. In April 1980, NAAA filed a Freedom of Information Act (FOIA) request to the Department of Justice, which had squelched a grand jury investigation into the Bryen case. It took three years to elicit 1,000 pages of documents, most of which were rendered incomprehensible by copious deletions. A Court of Appeals ruling on NAAA's suit forced the turnover of more material in 1986; the FBI man who had handled the Bryen file found himself harassed in retirement.[11]

NAAA was quick to claim its first political victory when the tripartite jet sale was passed after acrimonious debate in the Senate on May 15, 1978, but in fact the organization was, at best, a minor player in the drama. The main reason the sale went through was the fierce determination of the Carter administration. White House lobbyists tied the sale to developments in the peace arena with the upcoming Camp David Summit and the need to gain support from Arabs who thought Sadat's going it alone was treasonous.

NAAA's statement the day after the Camp David Accords were signed September 17 was independent and upbeat: "NAAA welcomes the progress toward peace achieved by the Camp David talks hosted by President Carter for Egyptian President Anwar Sadat and Israeli Prime Minister Menachem Begin. President Carter is to be commended for his initiative in the search for Middle East peace." Of course, a stickier wicket than the Sinai remained: "A critical question is whether Israeli intransigence on withdrawal from the West Bank and Gaza Strip in fact changed at Camp David, or was merely repackaged."

On November 6, 1978, Begin's government approved $32.5 million for the construction of 900 new housing units for settlements in occupied territories. Neither Carter, however displeased he was with the apparent betrayal, nor the US Congress saw fit to add any stick to the Camp David carrot. The Arab American community's belief and patience was beginning to fray:

> It is not surprising that Prime Minister Begin—or any other Israeli leader—thinks that he can tell the Administration to go to hell, confident that the cornucopia of American weapons, cash, and political support will pour out unabated. Israeli arrogance toward the United States is not an accident, and the Congress must face up to its responsibility for this state of affairs.[12]

In its lobbying in Congress, and beyond, NAAA grappled with a range of complicated and difficult issues. Some were as old as the racism and stereotyping of the Associated Charities of Boston in 1899, when the organization had declared Syrians to be, next to the Chinese, the "most foreign of all foreigners," or of South Carolina's Judge Smith, who back in 1914 had found Arabs to be free, but not "that particular free white person" who could vote. The racism came with new twists: Now Arab Americans and their ethnicity were skewed in lurid, sensational movies, or defamed when they ran for public office.

Some issues were completely new to the community, such as the incarceration of Sami Esmail. With the Esmail case, Arab Americans had brought home to them that if their opinions on Middle East issues did not get them thrown in jail in America (a freedom not as protected since September 11, 2001), they certainly could in Israel. In October 1978, Esmail, 23, an American student at Michigan State University, was released from a high-security prison in Haifa where he had been jailed for 11 months. On release, Esmail's disturbing remarks were printed in NAAA's *Focus*:

> They wanted me to say that I was a member of a Palestinian organization and had gone to Libya for two-and-a-half or three weeks in August for military training. I told them that was absolute nonsense... They said they were going to use me as an example to

other Arab Americans as well as non-Arab Americans who speak out for the Palestinians....[13]

At the same time, NAAA was trying to reveal not only the possible espionage of Stephen Bryen, but that of Zalmon Shapiro. *Focus* (November 15, 1978) reported a link between a thirteen-year-old unsolved case of missing US government uranium and the production of nuclear weapons by Israel. The first facility from which uranium disappeared—Nuclear Material and Equipment Corporation (NUMEC)—was headed by Zalmon Shapiro. On August 29, NAAA President Hisham Sharabi wrote Secretary of Energy James Schlesinger, calling his attention to Shapiro's role in the uranium diversion and questioning the wisdom of Shapiro's current involvement in government-sponsored high-level nuclear research. Several investigations began, including a year-long Government Accounting Office (GAO) probe. Unfortunately, the GAO's report was blocked from publication by both the FBI and CIA. So much for stopping the proliferation of weapons of mass destruction.

NAAA soon found itself embroiled defending an Arab-American candidate for Congress in California, George Corey, against a smear campaign. His opponent, Leo Holsinger, circulated an article from *Focus* (February 1 1979), which he claimed proved that Corey had ties to "Arab oil interests." Before this, Corey had led two-to-one in the polls. One week after the ethnic issue was raised, Holsinger led Corey by five percent. Corey precinct workers canvassing house-to-house began to encounter prejudicial remarks like "Oh, that's the Arab" and "I understand his wife is a white woman."[14] After losing the March 6 primary, Corey, a lawyer who had been mayor of San Bruno and served in the US Air Force, issued a statement:

> When Mr. Holsinger and his aides publicly question whether or not I support terrorist organizations, or that I am influenced or controlled by foreign political interests as a means of pointing out my ethnic background, a great disservice is done to voters which in no way can be rectified by public disclosures of the truth.[15]

At this time, truthful disclosure was hard to come by concerning the PLO, too, not because the organization had nothing to say of interest to policymakers (an historic acceptance of Israel had begun to be articulated), but because there was an official Kissingerian lock-out of any diplomatic contact with it. NAAA struggled, as much as it could, against the muzzling of the media that was in place. In May 1979, Shafiq al-Hout, a senior PLO official from Beirut, visited the United States, speaking at Princeton and Yale, and to a small enclave at the Middle East Institute in Washington, DC. Few in the American public would know about it, however, because the state department enforced a media blackout on anything al-Hout said. It was an extraordinary infringement of the First Amendment, and the *Washington Post* editorialized against the state department's ban.

Looking less like a revolutionary than an insurance salesman, a balding al-Hout in rumpled business suit was pressed to make a declarative statement for the record (a record wrecked by the publishing ban). He recounted a fifteen-year evolution in PLO policy and said:

> We now focus on 18 percent of the land of original Palestine—the West Bank and Gaza—and proclaim that we shall settle for a Palestinian state on that land. If my father were alive now and knew of these significant concessions the PLO has made over the years, he would take a pistol and shoot me as a traitor![16]

The statement jibed with one Chairman Yasir Arafat had given US Representative Paul Findley (R-IL) the previous year, reported by the daring Associated Press, that the PLO "was willing to renounce and grant de facto recognition to Israel if an independent Palestinian state was established in the West Bank and Gaza with a connecting corridor."[17] Al-Hout's corroboration cried out for publication, though nothing had appeared in the *Washington Post*. The article I wrote for the NAAA's *Focus* was the only news article on al-Hout printed in the United States.

The tendency of Arab-American political groups to splinter and go against each other showed itself during the 1979 NAAA convention, when a board member, Jawad George, worried that the stepping down of President Hisham Sharabi would drain NAAA of Palestinian focus, announced he was forming his own group, the Palestine Congress of North America (it lasted for a few years before sinking). Sharabi went out with class and a cautionary note: "Wild talk may make one feel good, but the price paid for this in political credibility and effectiveness is ruinous. By discipline and self-control, NAAA has, against all subjective and objective odds, succeeded in proving itself a responsible political group."[18]

In my position at the NAAA at the turn of the decade, I began to walk Capitol Hill; an overview of some of the aides and legislators I worked with gives an interesting sense of how powerful the Israel lobby is and how long our current problems have been with us.

Scott Cohen, a pipe-smoking, soft-spoken aide of Senator Charles Percy (R-IL), was intrigued by al-Hout's "quid pro quo" statements but still felt the key to a breakthrough for the Palestinians was unilateral PLO recognition of Israel. (Cohen was prescient; in 1988, at Madrid the PLO did just that, launching the Oslo peace process and bringing Arafat to President Bill Clinton's White House.) On the House side, I visited with an informed and sympathetic Mike

Van Dusen, longtime staff director of the Europe and Middle East Subcommittee, then chaired by Rep. Lee Hamilton (D-IN); he had met al-Hout but was not at liberty to speak about it.

The toughest office then was that of Millicent Fenwick (D-NJ), whose Middle East aide was a one-man cannonade of wrath against the PLO. A former Mideast and Africa reporter for UPI, the aide blinked his eyes nervously, going off on tangents about Arab "radicalism" and "terrorism." He quoted Arafat's loose rhetoric and wondered if he could be trusted. A trading of atrocity stories got us nowhere. He had one interesting idea, though: that the PLO agree to a five-year period of no border incidents or tension in the territories to coax Israel into accepting a separate state. All well and good, but would Israel do the same? When Fenwick retired, her aide surfaced as one of two chief aides to the Senate Foreign Relations Committee.

The administrative assistant to Senator Richard Lugar (R-IN) was a surprise: a congenial, blue-eyed, blond Syrian-American named Mitch Daniels, who said his folks had been promised a horse at his birth by their relatives in Homs. (He would years later surface as the director of the Office of Management and Budget for the second President Bush and in 2004 win the governorship of Indiana.) Lugar was developing an independent voice on the Senate Foreign Relations Committee. Daniels counseled NAAA to concentrate on Lebanon, treat the Palestinian issue with "benign neglect" for a while (as if they hadn't been given enough malignant neglect to fill a century).

At the office of Senator Richard Stone of Florida I met the aide who took over the seat vacated by the notorious Stephen Bryen: Barry Schochet, who promptly poured me a glass of fresh orange juice. One could have worse starts discussing the Middle East. Barry was rational, world-weary in the way those who follow this issue closely become, but not given over completely to despair. Confessing he read *Focus* religiously, Barry said he knew nothing about Arafat's promise to Rep. Findley to recognize Israel in return for the promise of a separate state. "We have the same goals for the area, peace and justice," I said in parting, shaking hands. "Let's work together."

On June 7, former history teacher in the Detroit ghetto and aide to Senator Spark Matsunaga (D-HI) Sid Rosen challenged me right off, "Are you anti-Israel?" I said I wasn't, and that supporting an Israel and a Palestine wasn't mutually exclusive. He wondered what would happen if Israel annexed the West Bank and Gaza, then offered the right of repatriation and compensation to Palestinian refugees all over—wouldn't it be better to have Israelis and Palestinians work together rather than to "ghettoize" them. Rosen had just articulated the concept of the bi-national state Palestinians had wanted since 1948. He smiled: "We should get together. Too bad we have no influence!"

For a short time, NAAA set its sights on a little-known clause in the Export Administration Act (EAA) that would bind the United States to ship its domestic crude oil to one nation alone for fifteen years—Israel. NAAA's new president Joanne McKenna flew in from Cleveland and handed out "ISROIL" pamphlets to commuters in gas lines. Sid Rosen in Matsunaga's office thought the ISROIL issue was small potatoes and urged us to begin to address the West Bank settlements: "Any way your group and the Arabs in the Middle East, of course, can defuse the Israeli barricade mentality it will help peace." But Israel was stepping up its bombing of south Lebanon and that called for immediate attention.

When President George W. Bush enunciated his adminstration's post-9/11 doctrine of "preemption" in justifying the invasions of Afghanistan and Iraq, he was following a path Israel had cut years before. As an Israeli military spokesman said on May 6, 1979, "Israel's policy is to hit anytime and any place to preempt terrorist attacks on Israel." On July 2, Defense Minister Ezer Weizman was quoted in the *New York Times*: "Israel will strike at Palestinian targets in Lebanon anytime it chooses." Any pretense of striking "in retaliation" was dropped. NAAA editorialized: "As usual, most of the dead and wounded are villagers whose only 'crime' was being in the wrong place at the wrong time."[19]

By August 26, NAAA counted 221 Lebanese and Palestinian civilians killed in at least eighteen Israeli preemptive strikes on southern Lebanon. Six attacks alone occurred after the PLO unilaterally announced a moratorium on commando raids from Lebanon. It was as if PLO forbearance egged Israel on—the weaker the doe, the stronger the lion. We did not know it then, but we were witnessing the rehearsal of the 1982 full-scale invasion.

The idea was hatched to dock Israel ten percent of its military aid as a symbolic expression of US disapproval of the preemptive strikes. NAAA took around photographs of the damage and two spent American-manufactured cluster bombs. On September 6, Rep. Pete McCloskey (R-CA) put me on the hot seat, asking that I lobby him in front of three constituents and his strongly Zionist aide, Josh Teitelbaum, who quickly argued Israeli bombardment as self-defense. I countered that international law does not give a nation the right to make preemptive strikes. When Teitlebaum pointed out that PLO raids had been stopped by Israel's bombing, I asked why the bombing continued for two months after a voluntary moratorium on cross-border raids was granted on the request of Austrian Chancellor Bruno Kreisky.

McCloskey carried the ball further, asking Josh what he expected from people who had been locked out of their homes for 31 years. "Josh," he said, "The new preemptive strike policy of Israel is making more commandos by the day. It creates more enemies than it kills." Teitlebaum mentioned Israeli civilian casualties; I noted that, though reprehensible, the numbers were infinitesimal compared to the deaths caused by the air bombardment. McCloskey added, "We don't arm the PLO. We arm Israel and they are misusing our weapons."

But getting others interested was no slam dunk. Arab-American Congressman Toby Moffett (D-CT) felt the aid cut would only get 30 votes and accomplish little more than flushing out Zionist furor. He said he had floated a similar idea five years before and "I haven't heard the end of it from the Israel lobby since."

In the end, no one, not even McCloskey, offered the amendment, but Mary Rose Oakar (D-OH), a Lebanese-American congresswoman, stood on the House floor and cried out:

> Mr. Chairman, listening to the debate concerning this bill, I have been somewhat amazed that no word has been uttered about the unwarranted and apparently illegal use of American weapons in the country of Lebanon that is contributing to the devastation of that poor country. Now, is there no conscience for a country that has always been our ally?[20]

Twenty-four years later, having lost her seat in Congress, Oakar assumed the position of head of the newly merged NAAA and ADC.

On the Senate side, pain surrounding his eyes, Senator Dennis DeConcini (D-AZ) told me he missed Abourezk in the Senate, and that though our ten percent cut amendment had no chance in his august body, there was no reason the state department had to pussyfoot around. A clear-cut determination about violation of American arms law was in order and he would make a call to the state department's Morris Draper on it. Senator Pat Leahy's (D-VT) aide, Bob Paquin, said NAAA was in the right place in the right time organizationally and that we had a drum-tight case on Lebanon with the amendment. An aide to Senator Daniel Inouye (D-HI), Bill Jordan, said in a southern drawl, "Ah told a Jewish friend of mine you watchin' the Holocaust. I can't believe you people who suffered that are doing what you are to southern Lebanon."

Promise dies quickly with things Middle Eastern. An excited aide to Senator Jesse Helms (R-NC), Dick McCormack, had just written the speech of presidential candidate Governor John Connally of Texas backing Palestinian self-determination, a bit of courage rarely seen in presidential politics. Predictably, his stock fell into the basement and Connally faded quicker than an awning in the desert.

At Mark Hatfield's office, aide Jack Robertson said his boss was up-in-arms about Israel of late, partly because Morris Amitay of AIPAC had lied to Hatfield, promising the Oregon Republican he'd get the West Bank settlements stopped in six months. Jack thought it would be a good idea to transfer the $100 million cut from Israel to Lebanon.

On September 25, after the vote to cut aid to Pakistan in an Appropriation Committee mark-up, Hatfield, eyeglasses braced halfway down his nose, looked at a list of preemptive attacks by Israel on Lebanon and said, "We're going to apply all US laws today, aren't we? Depending on the country." Then he proposed his amendment. Astonishingly, the first counter came from none other than DeConcini: "Violating the AECA calls for stopping all arms shipments to a country. We're not going to do that to Israel."

"That's why I'm asking for a symbolic ten percent cut," Hatfield retorted.

DeConcini asked how Israel was to defend itself against the PLO. "Not with cluster bombs, anti-personnel weapons and F-15s used in another country," Hatfield returned quietly. Silence gathered. Sensing a slaughter, Hatfield withdrew his amendment, but said, "Israel's priorities are wrong and we know it. We know why we're enforcing our export law on Pakistan and not Israel. We don't have a Pakistani lobby."

Inouye said cryptically, "All hands are dirty in Lebanon, even American hands."

The Committee's aging, near senile chairman, Warren Magnuson (D–WA), croaked some scripted poppycock, "Israel leads the world in its ability to reclaim water and set up irrigation systems better than ours! And they offered a Marshall Plan for water to the Arabs. It was refused by the Syrians, and do you know why? Because the man who offered it was a Jew!"

I came out of the meeting burning, having misjudged DeConcini, Inouye, and even Hatfield. But Hatfield had not left the battle; he was just choosing better ground. On October 11, 1979, Hatfield stood up in the near-empty well of the full Senate and offered the amendment; this time he didn't withdraw it. It made history—the first time a reduction in aid tied to Israeli policies was to be voted on by the US Senate. His was an impassioned plea that Israel stop its merciless preemptive bombing strikes on southern Lebanon.

The amendment caused an uproar on the Senate floor, which suddenly became flooded with senators rushing to deliver prepared pledges of support for Israel, included Senators Javits, Packwood, Inouye, Mathias, Chaffee, Boschwitz, Stone, Levin, Bradley, and Kennedy. The amendment, they said, would send "the wrong message," that the United States is "no longer in support of Israel and that Israel is fair game (Inouye), that "delicate negotiations" would be upset (Kennedy), or that a ten percent cut would harm Israel's security—"This hits her really in the solar plexus" (Javits).

Few acknowledged Hatfield's cry of conscience when he said, "I suggest that the more bombs Israel drops on southern Lebanon, the more Palestinian terrorists will be created out of that kind of action.

Neither the policy is valid, nor the results something we can ignore."[21] Only two Senators spoke in favor of Hatfield: Adlai Stevenson (D–IL) and James McClure (R–ID). Stevenson said Israel's provocative actions had brought the world to a "nuclear threshold," and he stated, "It is curious how reticent we are to represent ourselves even in such extreme circumstances." He commended Hatfield for his "courage, a quality, I regret to say, not abundant in our politics." The amendment was tabled, 78 to 7. Three lobbyists from AIPAC chuckled in the gallery. Voting against tabling were Senators Bellmon (D–NE), Burdick (D–ND), Gravel (D–AK), Melcher (D–MT), Hatfield, Stevenson, and McClure—all but Stevenson from rural midwestern and western states. The vote cost Gravel his seat in 1980; funds poured into Alaska for his opponent from far-off New York. None of the others lasted much longer in the Senate.

Out of a sense of frustration over Hatfield's defeat, I wrote a paper, which quoted Thoreau, who had refused to pay taxes over the Mexican War a century before, and demonstrated that on average each American taxpayer was offering Israel $37 a year, more than it gave its own government for mass transit ($17), higher education ($32) and urban renewal ($15). NAAA was wary of a tax revolt and did not back it. Edward and Mariam Said, Hisham Sharabi, Abdeen Jabara, and San Franciscan lawyer Anis Shamiyeh joined me in subtracting the figure from our returns for the year. The IRS basically ignored this action.

The year 1980 was a portentous one in the history of Middle East issues on these American shores. For the first—and last—time, the US Senate took on Israeli settlements, but in the zero hour grew frightened, a fear that rippled far into the future, for nothing destroyed the Oslo peace process in the late 1990s as much as the unabated Israeli settlement of occupied territory. The same year, stereotyping of the Arab entered the highest ranks of the US government in Operation ABSCAM, a caper to catch unscrupulous congressmen in which FBI agents dressed as Arab sheikhs offering money for favors. NAAA editorialized, "Lest anyone fail to understand the inherently ugly nature of stereotypes, let him reflect on the impact of an FBI operation that, instead of being called ABSCAM, was instead called JEWSCAM. The outcry would be tremendous and fully justified."[22]

On February 26, 25 Congressmen—2 Jewish Americans among them (Reps. Ted Weiss of New York and Anthony Beilenson of Los Angeles) objected to the FBI's methods, and elicited an apology from Director William Webster, which was also sent to NAAA. Michael Kinsley, then an editorial writer with the *New Republic* (later editor of the *Los Angeles Times* editorial pages), visited NAAA offices and later wrote a stinging indictment of ABSCAM.

But settlements were the big item in 1980—as they would be still 25 years later. The time seemed right to seize the initiative on the heels of Hatfield's attempt to link American aid to objectionable Israeli action. Whereas a Congressman might shy from docking Israel on preemptive strikes on Lebanon due to the PLO guerrilla presence, the problem of settlements, of often armed vigilantes placed at feverish pace among a basically unarmed civilian population, was a compelling one. President Carter had called the settlements "illegal and an obstacle to peace." But no one said it would be easy halting them. Then-presidential candidate Edward Kennedy, otherwise generally a champion of the downtrodden, had in essence ceded the West Bank to Israel when he answered a question on *Meet the Press* in December about settlements, "I don't think we can get into internal matters."

NAAA's editorial, "Settle the Settlements Problem," drove home the message:

> Only the American taxpayer—whose generosity has been unmatched for 32 years—can do it [stop the settlements] with the help of its duly elected representatives. It is time for Congress to take a moral step and replace noise with substance by a cut in aid to Israel equal to Israeli expenditures this fiscal year on settlements in the West Bank and Gaza... Americans will agree with this issue because it makes sense.[23]

When the *Washington Post* and the *New York Times* editorialized on February 12 and 14, respectively, for such action, too, NAAA began to feel it was riding a rare wave. On March 1, 1980, the United Nations Security Council passed a resolution condemning the settlements. Then, within a day of the US vote in support of the resolution, President Carter was visited by a delegation from the American Jewish community. Shortly thereafter, he repudiated the US vote with the weak explanation that there had been a "faulty communication" between Secretary Cyrus Vance and UN Ambassador Donald McHenry.

Meanwhile, as if in defiance of the UN, on March 11, Israel expropriated 1,000 acres of choice land in East Jerusalem at Beit Hanina, most owned by Palestinian Arabs, many of whom were Americans living in Detroit. It posed an uncomfortable dilemma for the state department, for under the Hickenlooper Amendment to the Foreign Assistance Act of 1962, foreign aid is to be suspended to any country seizing control of American-owned property. We flew five of the incensed owners in from Detroit to meet with their representatives, including John Dingell, the state department, and the White House. The state department's legal advisor David Small admitted it was a "unique quandary," but no action was taken to invoke the law.

McCloskey wanted to take the lead in proposing a cut of aid to Israel, perhaps $150 million, the state department's estimate of the cost of the settlements. The results of a poll of his constituents on settlements released in April were startling: 83.5 percent were for a $500 million cut in aid to Israel tied to settlements. In a meeting with constituents in Palo Alto (which contains the whole Stanford University community) only 2 out of 100 opposed the aid cut if Israel persisted settling the territories. Significantly, McCloskey was using a figure three times that of NAAA. During this feverish time, McCloskey's aide Annie McLain related that his new chief of staff, Amber Schultz, described as an admirer of Menachem Begin, was trying everything she could to keep McCloskey from sponsoring the settlements amendment, including, some staffers thought, wooing him.

On April Fool's Day, 1980, NAAA testified for the second time, now before the Senate Foreign Operations subcommittee of the Appropriations Committee. The PHRC also chimed in with a suggested $150 million cut. Chairman Inouye in basso-profundo voice called the testimonies "thought-provoking" and ventured "something may come of it." Inouye was a master of the tantalizing.

Meanwhile, vigilantism on the West Bank was running wild. Two West Bank mayors—Mohammed Milhem of Halhoul and Fahd Kawasmeh of Hebron—were summarily deported by the Israelis for speaking out against the military occupation, acts of collective punishment and a rebuke of the indigenous democratic process. In taking both mayors around Capitol Hill, I found neither radical in any way; both were articulate and genuine in their urging of a two-state solution. Milhem told a group that failure to establish a second state for Palestinians would do more harm to Israel than refusing it (a position even Ariel Sharon was to admit two decades and tens of thousands of deaths later). For his troubles, the genial Fahd Kawasmeh not only never went home to Hebron where his family, he told me, had lived for over a 1,000 years, but in 1984 he was assassinated by Arab rejectionists in Jordan. Two more mayors— Karim Khalaf of Ramallah and Bassam Shakaᶜa of Nablus—were maimed by car bombs detonated by people traced to Begin's cabinet; Shakaᶜa had his legs blown off. On that same day, McCloskey informed NAAA he was readying floor action on settlements.

It was not to be. Morris Draper traveled down the Potomac from the state department to bark McCloskey off the rug, saying a bad loss would "send the wrong signal" to the Israelis, while a victory or large pro-cut vote would upset the proverbial "delicate negotiations" on West Bank autonomy. But the autonomy deadline had come and gone and all but the undertaker could see that Camp David's casket, at least in regards to the Palestinians, was already sunk in the ground. Hamilton arm-twisted McCloskey on the House floor, bizarrely citing some agreement, violated daily, that US aid was not to be used "beyond the green line," blithely ignoring the fact that American funds were easily fungible from one Israeli pocket to the other. McCloskey caved; what was achieved was more talk, a two-hour stingerless colloquy.[24]

We were to have somewhat more luck, but not much more courage, in the Senate.

On June 9, newly appointed Secretary of State Edmund Muskie took the occasion of his first speech to severely criticize settlements. It was getting difficult to ascertain just what the Carter administration's attitude was. First, the backpedaling over the UN vote, then Draper's pressure on McCloskey, and then this curve ball from Muskie. Was it forever all-talk, no-show?

Mike Hathaway with Sen. McClure felt that if NAAA could get Senator Joseph Biden's name on the settlements amendment, "You've won." On June 16, I met Joyce Shub, his tough-nut aide. She shook my hand with three fingers and said, "Yes, the Jewish community is fed up with these settlements. I think if Stevenson sticks to just that $150 million as a cut and contains the argument to that, it's worth voting for." But Gravel's Bill Hoffman warned that AIPAC had called his boss to kill the amendment.

We grew bold and, with two NAAA board members in town from California, took on Alan Cranston (D-CA), whose chief of staff, Jerry Warburg, was a scion of a prominent New York family. So much for California roots. Stanford-educated, the dapper Warburg droned "Israel's security" to any criticism of its behavior. One of our board members got fed up with his evasions and blurted, "Look. I worked for the General Services Administration for twenty years. I love this country. And I am tired of seeing the Levingers and the Kahanes go over there and terrorize Arabs." Warburg stiffened. Later, on the phone, when I pressed him for a personal meeting with Cranston in light of AIPAC's easy access, he said he was going to hang up in three seconds. And he did.

In his office in the US Capitol, Richardson and I met with Adlai Stevenson, the son of the man who exposed the lies of the Soviet Union about missiles in Cuba with one photograph. He sat in silence, rubbing his head, then looked up and said, "We've got to do something." Stevenson had been in touch with Chicago Jewish leaders, whose support he felt he could count on. He set to working on a speech.

On June 17, 1980, Stevenson, who had single-handedly fought to achieve the anti-Arab boycott legislation in the 1970s and received a B'nai B'rith award for it, offered an amendment to cut aid to Israel by $150 million over settlements. In spite of receiving nearly half of US foreign aid, he said, the Begin government "blithely, sometimes insultingly" ignored US policy on settlements. "Massive US aid to a truculent Begin government raises some rather large questions of objectivity—not of me, but of the US government," Stevenson said. He responded to critics, "I am not suggesting coercion. I am not suggesting punishment. I am suggesting that we make it clear that we in the United States will no longer let ourselves be coerced."

The response was a fusillade. Though he criticized the settlements, Frank Church, then chairman of the Senate Foreign Relations Committee, condemned Stevenson's amendment, as did Packwood (R-OR), Javits, Dole (R-KS), and Mathias (R-MD), with shopworn cliches of "upsetting a delicate peace process" (though it no longer existed), or "driving Israel into a corner" (as if the Palestinians hadn't been suffocating in one). The amendment was tabled by Church by a vote of 85–7. Senators backing the lonely Stevenson were Bellmon, Hatfield, McClure, Helms (R-NC), Young (D-ND), and most significantly, Majority Leader Robert Byrd (D-WV), the one remaining member of that group still in the Senate and a ringing critic of our war in Iraq. Not one stood up to say a word in Stevenson's defense. On the other hand, Stone of Florida rose, fuming, planting his hands firmly on his desk, to announce that here and now the Senate was going to put an end to this "rumor" that Senate support for Israel was slipping. So much for Barry Schochet's orange juice.

Stevenson listened to the barrage alone on the Democrat side of the well, turning over his eyeglasses on his mahogany desk. He rubbed his eyes. I noticed AIPAC lobbyists smiling again in the gallery. Another cursed seven votes! What had happened to Biden? Percy? All of Inouye's misgivings did not amount to the proverbial hill of beans.

Unlike with Hatfield's ill-fated amendment, the media picked up Stevenson's effort extensively. It was the lead story on the front page of the *Washington Star* (a daily newspaper that no longer exists). It was picked up by the Associated Press and appeared in the *Washington Post, New York Times, Los Angeles Times, Chicago Tribune, Baltimore Sun, Cleveland Plain-Dealer*, and even Agence France Presse.

Some near Begin gloated over the lopsided vote. Foreign Minister Yitzhak Shamir told the Knesset on June 18 that Stevenson's defeat proved "that the whole world is not against us and that it is worth fighting for our cause." However, on June 20, the Israel daily *Ha'aretz* attached significance to the Stevenson amendment:

> What counts is not the Senate rejection of that motion but the
> very fact that it was introduced by a Senator who has a large Jewish

constituency whose record is not anti-Israel, and that the motion was backed by the Senate Majority Leader. All this only goes to show the extent to which the government of Israel's settlements policy turns US statesmen against it... If kind words prove to be ineffective it should come as no surprise if the number of Senators subscribing to Senator Stevenson's stand would increase... [25]

It was not to happen. Inexperienced, impatient, naïve, NAAA went through one of its many purges, and a settlements amendment was never offered again in the US Congress. An African-American activist told me it took ten years of patient lobbying to achieve sanctions on South Africa, and many years after that to get Nelson Mandela freed. We had to be in it for the long haul, ideally offering the settlements amendment yearly, picking up five more votes here, five more there. Certainly the Israelis have never stopped settling, so the issue didn't go away. But we plain dropped the ball. Our "all or nothing" approach to legislation mirrored an inviolate righteousness that characterized too much of our Arab counterparts dealings with Israel, as well. And, as Mary Rose Oakar intimated years later, the community abandoned Stevenson in his loss. When he then lost his Senate seat and could not gain the governorship of Illinois, it sent a message that Arab Americans were not going to bail you out if you went out on a limb for them. It goes without saying that the monies going into congressional pockets of those uncritical of Israel continued and even intensified.

In the fall of 1980, Dick Shadyac was asked to head an Arab American Re-elect Carter and Mondale Campaign Committee, something of a first. But it wasn't long before it was scotched from within. Giving into pressure, campaign chairman Robert Strauss cut Shadyac and the Arab Americans out. It was embarrassing and insulting. A virtual replay occurred during the 1984 presidential campaign when Walter Mondale, after received four checks of $1,000 each from Chicago Arab Americans, returned them for no specified reason.

Local races were not immune from this kind of thing, either. In 1983, Philadelphia Democratic mayorial candidate Wilson Goode returned $2,725 in contributions to ADC's Philadelphia chapter when Republicans accused him of taking "Arab money." In 1986, Rep. Joseph Kennedy (D-MA) turned back contributions from Massachusetts Arab Americans, thought twice about it, and accepted them back, later apologizing to the national convention of ADC. In that same year, a Maryland candidate for Congress returned $500 to an Arab American constituent. In the 1989 race for New York City's mayor, candidates David Dinkins and Rudy Giuliani were both cool to taking any contributions from the Arab American community, fearing backlash from the city's sizable Jewish community. [26]

Meanwhile, some American Jewish voices were coming out of the closet. In the September 15, 1980, issue of *Newsweek*, Joseph Eger, a world renowned French horn player and conductor of the Symphony for United Nations, compared Menachem Begin to his own father, who had performed the rites for the dead over a daughter who had married a non-Jew: "Just as my father's beliefs unwittingly contributed to the death of a loved one, so is outdated political orthodoxy contributing to the destruction of my own people." In calling for a two-state solution and talks with the PLO, Eger, whose uncle had been president of the Zionist Organization of America (ZOA), said, "We may find, if it isn't too late, that what is good for the Arabs—and all people—is also good for the Jews."[27]

In 1981, NAAA fired its energetic and astute executive director Jean Abinader, and pulled David Sadd off its board to take over. He immediately took me off the lobbying effort; it remained moribund for some time. Soon Sadd, a Navy graduate, was meeting with arms merchants and the Saudis. When lobbying did commence, it wasn't for settlements or Lebanon or human rights, but AWACS, a radar plane, sought by Saudi Arabia from the United States, as well as add-on armaments for its F-15s. I left the organization. I hadn't joined NAAA to help push arms to any country—Israel, Saudi Arabia, or otherwise. It was a sad commentary on the Arab-American lobby that the only substantive thing it successfully allied itself to that passed through Congress were these arms bills.

For the matters that still lay untended deep in the hearts of Arab Americans—the Palestinians and the fate of Lebanon—it was left to

In 1978 an Arab-American delegation, including members of the AAUG and NAAA, meets with President Jimmy Carter during the development of the Camp David Accords. Among those in attendance are Mike Saah, Richard Shadyac, Ralph Nader, Bill Mansour, Michael Suleiman, and Bill Baroody. NAAA's John Richardson sits next to Carter. (Arab American National Museum)

another group to spearhead efforts. While NAAA's officers were fundraising in the Arabian Gulf in the summer of 1982, Israel invaded Lebanon. The new group, the ADC, founded by a US senator, picked up the ball in a very dark hour.

THE AMERICAN-ARAB ANTI-DISCRIMINATION COMMITTEE

In 1978 after quitting the US Senate when his first term was up, calling it a "chickenshit outfit," James Abourezk assumed a role as the premier Arab-American activist. In May 1980, he founded the American-Arab Anti-Discrimination Committee (ADC), modeled, to some extent, on the Anti-Defamation League of B'nai B'rith. Born and raised on the Rosebud Sioux Indian Reservation in South Dakota where his Lebanese-immigrant father ran a general store, Abourezk was a lifelong battler for the downtrodden. He started ADC in the wake of the FBI's sting Operation ABSCAM, calling it "the last straw."

The newest of the Arab-American groups, ADC was soon to become the largest and achieve the most staying power. Due primarily to the indefatigable stomping of the communities by the pugnacious, irrepressible Abourezk, at its height in the wake of Israel's 1982 invasion of Lebanon, ADC had 22,000 members. But twenty years later, in the wake of the September 11 attacks, ADC's membership had shrunk to 5,000, half the total it had in its first year.

Highly visible and dynamic in its early years, ADC would be subjected to attacks that quickly moved from verbal to violent, culminating in the 1982 pipe-bombing of the West Coast office that killed its director, poet and schoolteacher Alex Odeh.

Abourezk himself explained his awakening as an Arab American:

> It probably all started when I made a tour of the Middle East in 1973, my first year [as a senator]. I had a very dramatic experience when I went back to my parents' village in Lebanon, Kfeir, about ten to fifteen miles from the Israeli border. There was a canvas banner put out along the road, right near a bomb crater made by Israeli warplanes. In Arabic it said, "Welcome Sheikh Senator James Abourezk." And in English it said, "Phantom jets made in USA."[28]

Abourezk appointed James Zogby, the PHRC founder, his first executive director. A baseball pitcher in school days, Zogby, like Abourezk, had a penchant for lighting up a fat cigar. He was a study in contrasts. Zogby was a family man and ran the organization like a family. He possessed a gentle voice, but in the early years, he could harangue with the best of them. Politically mercurial, at the start of the 1960s, he was a member of Young Americans for Freedom of Barry Goldwater, and by the end of the decade, he had joined Students for a Democratic Society (SDS) and actively opposed the

Vietnam War. After he was forced to leave the left-leaning ADC in 1984, he formed a think-tank, the Arab American Institute, in part with money raised by a Reagan Republican. He became a familiar figure on television commenting on Middle East issues.

The board of directors Abourezk gathered added stature to ADC that NAAA could never quite achieve. It included five US Congressmen (three African Americans and two Arab Americans), Edward Said, Hisham Sharabi, Noam Chomsky, Henry Schwartz-child, Reverend Jesse Jackson, and Reverend Joseph Lowery. ADC's secularized board appealed to a broader segment of society than NAAA's, which restricted full membership to Arab Americans.

The first two ADC issue papers were written by Jack Shaheen, a media expert at Southern Illinois University, and a pioneer in the field of anti-Arab stereotyping.[29] Zogby himself wrote an intriguing study comparing anti-Semitic cartoons that appeared in Weimar and Nazi Germany and pre-World War I Russian newspapers to cartoons in US newspapers that distorted the Arab image. Two cartoons side by side showed an OPEC Arab pig and a Rothschild pig, 60 years between them.[30] There were dozens of cases of FBI harassment waiting on ADC's doorsteps. A woman in Eden Prairie, Minnesota, was visited by an FBI agent in July 1980 who claimed an anonymous phone caller identified her neighbor Noha Ismail as a "Palestinian terrorist." At first, the FBI was unsure whether Noha was a man or woman. Ismail's neighbor was shocked that the wild speculations about a librarian and respected ten-year resident of the Twin Cities were given serious consideration by the FBI. The *Minneapolis Star Tribune* (November 21, 1980) editorialized about the Ismail case:

> On the surface the methods used in this instance defy comprehension. Asking, in effect, whether a citizen is a terrorist is unlikely to elicit the response that, yes, I am a terrorist or my neighbor is one. On the other hand, if the FBI were merely trying to help Noha Ismail, it chose a strange way of doing so. Whether intended or not, intimidation results.[31]

Perhaps the most politically "hot" and dangerous subject was the Jewish Defense League (JDL). ADC put an early focus on this kooky organization, whose members had done everything from firebombing the office of a New York Jew associated with the Bolshoi ballet (a woman was killed) to shooting up the Dome of the Rock in Jerusalem, killing two Arab civilians. Robert Friedman, a courageous author, shined a hard light on the paramilitary organization and its founder, Rabbi Meir Kahane, in his scathing book, *False Prophet.*

From the beginning, it seemed that the JDL had its eye on ADC, as well. Kahane held a press conference outside the National Press Building in 1980, shortly after Zogby had begun ADC's one-man office there. Announcing his intention to set up a Jewish state in the West Bank, Kahane railed against ADC, calling it a PLO front, and proposed his solution to the West Bank problem: expel its million Arabs.

Between 1979 and 1985, there were six violent incidents against Arab Americans traceable to the JDL. It was a seed-bed of hatred waiting to burgeon beyond the group itself. (About two decades later, in the single year following the events of September 11, 2001, there would be 700 incidents of hate crimes and harassment against Arab Americans—or people thought to be Arab.)

The 1979 firebombing of the offices of the Palestine Human Rights Campaign and Clergy and Laity Concerned in Washington was "approved" by a JDL spokesman, who neither denied nor admitted culpability. Two gasoline bombs containing nails started a fire outside an apartment housing Arizona State University students of Palestinian origin on March 25, 1982. In Brooklyn, on April 6, arsonists set fire to an old and respected Lebanese restaurant, the Tripoli. The place was completely destroyed; one woman was killed and eight injured. A taped caller said the Tripoli was "the underground headquarters of the Palestine Liberation Army." In 1985, several Boston police were seriously injured trying to defuse a pipe bomb planted at the Boston offices of ADC; around the same time, the Washington, DC, offices of ADC were firebombed. The following year its West Coast director was murdered.

Friedman documented the close connection between the JDL and the West Bank settler movement. When cars of three West Bank mayors were booby trapped in 1980, maiming two of them, Kahane and six settlers from Beit El were linked to the assassination attempts. Meanwhile, Kahane openly announced his intention to blow up the al-Aqsa mosque in Jerusalem, the third holiest shrine in Islam. Explosives were found planted there on at least two occasions. Kahane served for a time in the Israeli Knesset before his death at the hands of an Arab assassin in New York.

When my mother worked for a time at the University of Judaism in Beverly Hills, she befriended a faculty member named Yehuda Lev, who had once written, "If the JDL is looking for enemies of the Jewish people to fight, there are millions of them. They are called Arabs..." (*Israel Today*, 1978). When I met Yehuda, an affable man, he had changed his opinion and thought the JDL an aberration. I wonder how he feels today. Not only did Bassam Shaka°a lose his legs and Alex Odeh his life to their violence and creed, but so did Israeli Prime Minister Yitzhak Rabin, who was murdered by a Jewish right-wing extremist, an act that also killed the Oslo peace process.

In 1981, ADC issued a paper, "Harassment of Arab-Americans Visiting Israel and the Occupied Territories." Strip searches at Tel Aviv Airport, interrogations that could last days, surveillance while visiting relatives on the West Bank, long and humiliating security checks at the Allenby Bridge coming from Jordan, arbitrary arrests—they were all taking place regularly, with little complaint from the US Embassy, long before 9/11. One liquor store owner from San Bernadino, California, said he knew three instances of relatives and friends being followed in their cabs, stopped, beaten, and robbed by Israelis shortly after the strip search at the airport. He was certain the muggers had been tipped off by Israel security guards, who had seen their money. An Arab-American senior diplomat with the US state department who lived in Annandale, Virginia, tried to get his father buried in his hometown in the West Bank. The Israelis wouldn't let the corpse go through Tel Aviv because the deceased wasn't Jewish. In a transfer from a metal to a wooden casket over the Allenby Bridge, the Israelis did not let the man's sons handle the body, but did it themselves, crudely and provocatively. The diplomat ended up being strip-searched on the border; one Israeli soldier used the man's nail clipper to clip his own nails!

This was all two decades before an Israeli bulldozer ran over American peace activist Rachel Corrie in the West Bank, killing her, to virtually no protest from her own country. She was not Arab American.

Though it made strong, often fruitless efforts politically, ADC's meat-and-potatoes issues dealt with stereotyping. One of its first campaigns went against a Florida Toyota dealer whose billboards read, "Buy a Toyota! Drive an Arab crazy!" When ADC threatened to take legal action, the dealership withdrew the sign, as well as offensive bumper stickers and television ads.[32]

When a fuel company, Preston of Lowell, Massachusetts, sold a charcoal briquet named SHEEKS, showing in an ad an Arab sheikh being immolated, ADC notified the company of intent to sue. Preston responded on February 11, 1981, with an insulting letter with references to Arab sexual practices, but SHEEKS was soon withdrawn from the market.[33] The Amberly Greeting Card Company stopped printing a postcard—under complaint of Maureen and Mounzer Chaarani of ADC Los Angeles—which extorted, "Fight Oil Prices! Mug an Arab today!"[34]

Even Junior Achievement, Inc., a longstanding group introducing teenagers to the fundamentals of business and manufacturing, was found to have used the convenient stereotype when, it one of its teaching projects, it sported an Arab character in sunglasses and headdress, dubbed DOPEC. JA President Richard Maxwell responded to ADC's protest, "We certainly did not intend any disparaging reference to anyone. Thank you for bringing this to our attention."[35]

The problem could be seen at dictionary level. Both the 1980 *Roget's Thesaurus* and the 1976 *Merriam-Webster Collegiate Thesaurus* persisted in including offensive definitions and synonyms for Arabs.

Roget had as synonyms for "street Arab" "churl, villain, yokel, bumpkin, lout." In a similar defamatory vein, a "Jew" was listed as "cunning, lender, rich, extortioner, heretic." Ottenheimer Publishers responded to ADC's office on July 2, 1981: "The comments in this book (Roget's Thesaurus) concerning ARABS and JEWS will be corrected in the next printing. This information is being passed on to our editorial department and you can be sure that your comments will be noted."

Merriam–Webster, however, held out. Their thesaurus offered synonyms for Arab as "vagabond, clochard, drifter, hobo, tramp, vagrant." The company resisted ADC protests with a series of form letters, until finally Merriam–Webster's president, William Llewellen, wrote defending the "comprehensive" nature of the book and the company's determination not to give into minority group pressures.[36] The synonyms still remain in some recent editions.

ADC officers met with CBS executives in New York and Washington, DC, about their programming, asking why Arabs are featured on television not in simple human roles, but always around war-and-oil-related themes.[37] Following similar protests over ABC's "The Unholy War" and other programs, ADC was visited by a reporter for *TV Guide*. The result was an excellent investigative cover story, in two parts, "Blind Spot in the Middle East: Why You Don't See More Palestinians on TV" (October 24–30, 1981).

Talk show hosts are known for their abrasiveness, but one broadcaster for WJNO-AM in West Palm Beach, Florida, drew flack from ADC for particularly abusive comments about Arabs. To give only one example of Mike Levine's rant (October 9, 1981):

> I know I'm going to sound like a bigot, but try to understand: who are we trying to impress, Arabs? They don't think like people… Are we dealing with people whose mentality praises violence, raises it to an art form? They extol it. They love it. They think in ways we do not understand. They have reasoning processes that have absolutely nothing to do with Western mentality… We can send a message to those goons…They love death, violence…We are dealing with people who are subhuman.[38]

On October 20, Levine suggested that those who think the United States should negotiate with the PLO harbored a "manic cruelty." The station's parent company, Fairbanks Broadcasting, responded to ADC's alarm, saying it was "sorry and not proud to have our Company associated with such comments," promising they would not go on their air waves again.

Even in the legitimate theater, plays were being produced tasteless in their defamation of Arabs, a far cry from the 1919 Broadway production *Anna Ascends*, about a Syrian waitress who falls in love. One was *Oh, Brother!*, a musical produced by an Israeli, Ze'ev Bufman, that opened at Kennedy Center in fall 1981. An attempt to frame the Middle East problem along the lines of Shakespeare's *A Comedy of Errors*, *Oh, Brother!*—supposedly set in post-revolutionary Iran—had pointedly Arab characters. In it, crude and insulting references to Islam abound, and dances satirize the Islamic mode of prayer.[39] A critic for *Jewish Week*, in fact, found the play to contain "shocking insensitivity" and to be "crude and sophomoric." (It was not the first or last time Arab and Jewish Americans would link up to protest anti-Semitism against both Semitic branches).

ADC weighed in on popular music. A popular 45-rpm, "Abu Dhabi," performed by the Nerve, depicted Arab immigrants hoping to become millionaires in the United States. Unable to differentiate between dimes and quarters, they overcharge customers at grocery stores and hope to meet American women who, as the lyrics go, "will wash our clothes while she holds her nose." The listener call-in campaign resulted in the song's distributor, Paid Records, Inc., apologizing to the ADC.[40]

The media were generally supportive of ADC's campaigns. On June 26, 1981, the *Cincinnati Enquirer* editorialized about ADC and anti-Semitism:

> It is possible, the committee fears, that Arabs will be converted into similar objects of opprobrium today—with consequences conceivably as catastrophic. The object lesson ought to be that it is scientifically and morally wrong to ascribe any quality or set of qualities to any race, religion, nationality, or ethnic group. Men and women of all origins deserve to be assessed on their own merits and demerits.

Of course, it was in the realm of politics where stereotyping was potentially the most dangerous. On the positive side, ADC in Michigan succeeded in including "Arabs" as a protected class in new state affirmative action legislation, the first such inclusion in the country. But in the 1981, American Jewish members of ADC informed the organization of a series of "mock" debates being carried out by the Anti-Defamation League of B'nai B'rith in midwestern cities where a "Palestinian supporter of the PLO" in Arab dress debated an Israeli. In one such farce, a "Mr. Fashid" made all kinds of outlandish, even absurd statements such as the Holocaust was a hoax and Palestinians had a claim to the land dating back "a million years." At the debate's end, the headdress was removed to reveal Mr. Fashid as an Egyptian Jewish resident of Detroit and employee of ADL. The hoax drew criticism from the audience; several people left the room. ADC formally protested "the tasteless masquerade" carried on by the ADL.

National officials, as with ABSCAM and the Paul Rand Dixon slur of Ralph Nader as a "dirty Arab," could be tongue-loose when it came to Arabs, and ADC began to call them on the carpet. When Michigan Governor William Milliken linked the economic crisis to "those damn Arabs" in December 1981, his office was flooded with letters. Three days later, Milliken apologized publicly. Chrysler Chairman Lee Iacocca get himself in hot water when he recommended "kicking the hell out of the Arabs." Even New York Governor Mario Cuomo, known for his sympathy for ethnicities and the underprivileged, had to eat some crow when a member of his staff in the 1982 gubernatorial campaign, circulated a cartoon of his opponent, Lewis Lehrman, dressed in Arab garb trying to buy the governor's mansion. It was certainly one of the more unlikely uses of the stereotype—Lehrman was Jewish! ADC Utica (NY) chapter head John Zogby called the cartoon "a gross caricature, conjuring up the image of Shylock."

ADC championed Arab Americans of all religious stripes, including Egyptian Copts. When the Coptic St. Mark's Church in Denver was vandalized in January 1981 (the local media said it was a "hit" against Iran) ADC protested and supported the St. Mark's community. Neglected by the United Farm Workers (UFW) union in California, 6,000 Muslim Yemenis working the San Joaquin farmlands received help when ADC opened a branch offices in Bakersfield and Delano.[41]

The zealous efforts of Abourezk and Zogby began to pay off. By the end of 1982, the national office had a 22-person staff and 10 staffers in seven regional offices. There were 44 functioning chapters. (Today there are 35.) Almost from the beginning, sensing the staying power of Abourezk's commitment, NAAA sought a merger, offering the South Dakotan its presidency on a platter. But the merger did not happen until two decades later, when NAAA was practically dead as an organization anyway.

There were limitations at ADC, too. For one, the rolls were filled with Second and Third Wave Arab Americans—most of them Palestinian and Lebanese. Though more highly motivated and active than the skeptical descendants of First Wavers, they constituted a smaller segment of the Arab American population. For another, as always, events in the Middle East tended to inflate and deflate membership. During the 1982 Israeli invasion of Lebanon, membership ballooned. But it went down sharply with the kidnappings and car bombings that covered the dark, chaotic landscape in Lebanon for the rest of the 1980s, rising somewhat with the early years of the Oslo peace process, then falling precipitously after the horror of September 11. For a while, few Americans of Arab origin raised their heads to do much more than go to work and to the store for groceries.

In an April 1996 protest rally in front of the White House, Rafeef El-Hajj speaks on behalf of a Michigan family who lost two young sons in an Israeli attack that month that killed over 100 refugees sheltering at the United Nations base in Qana, Lebanon. (Arab American National Museum)

—SEVEN—

BACK TO LEBANON

Before the Flames

After I left the NAAA, I spent a month in the spring of 1982 in Lebanon, to find out what had happened in ten years to Beirut, to friends, to family, to the political causes we had begun to champion in the United States.

In an Orange Grove at Tyre

In an orange grove that two months later would be razed, Colonel Azmi Saghiyeh of the PLO administered communion. Under the tight mesh of orange trees, while his soldiers looked on and smoked, Colonel Azmi, the commander of the Tyre pocket, tore morsels from a lamb shank. *Agnus dei, qui tollis peccata mundi...* Lamb of God, who taketh away the sins of the world. His men, in fatigues that blended with the waxy leaves above, brought two large tin platters of rice, pine nuts, and lamb. We—two from America, three from Italy, one from Jamaica—were motioned to a wooden table that recalled my childhood picnics near orange groves in California. The table was not redwood; no sprinklers sprayed delight.

Stopping in front of each guest, Colonel Azmi pulled mutton off the bone and placed a piece of it in our open mouths. Each of us chewed with a strange, stunned smile. The handsome colonel, whose russet-colored hair was cut neatly, did not crack a smile, but his amber eyes shone. For a minute he was Puck, priest, and guerrilla leader. As he stood in front of me I noticed the deep scar on his forehead. It was said he received it in battle with King Hussein's marauding troops in Jordan, 1970. Then—Black September. Now—Orange April, with the heat coming.

"More! More!" the colonel urged us, sitting down, pulling at his bone with his teeth. It was the best rice and lamb I had ever had. The *sunubar* (pine nuts) were plentiful, not like the very few placed in the center of a *kibba* (meatball). As children in America, we would eat each pine nut slowly, the way you would eat three-colored candy corn, slowly, taking each color—yellow, orange, and white—one at a time, until the sweetness was gone. In the orange grove of the revolution along the ancient city of Tyre, pine nuts in rice were plentiful, the air suffused with orange blossoms, and the branches so tightly woven we could not see the sky.

Earlier in the day we had driven on a bridge over the Litani River, in which Palestinian and Lebanese peasant women were washing their clothes and filling their jugs. The Litani empties into the Mediterranean at Tyre, taking one clear blue vein to its god. Most everyone in Lebanon believed the Israelis wanted the Litani. The Israelis had bullets and jets, but not enough water. The Lebanese had water and a beautiful snowy mountain, but no jets. The Palestinians had no jets or water and only slivers of land sucked away from them daily in the West Bank and Gaza. But in Lebanon, at least that April, they still had a few orange groves in which to hide, and wait.

The colonel had said, "No questions until we eat." And so back in his tent after the meal, near a lamp that glowed even in daytime because of the grove's darkness, the questions began. "Against the sea? It is we who are being driven into the sea... tell your Congress... tell your president... the bias in the media... " He went on and on, but the lamb was on my mind, given by three fingers the way an Orthodox priest blesses himself. I could hear the Kalashnikovs of the guerrillas knocking against the trays and glass jug in removing them. Above, the Israeli jets looked for a hole in the orange trees.

This was the communion of those whose cause to live was older than mine and from whose land my family came to America nearly a hundred years ago. This was the communion for those who loved America so much that ideals burst like roses and browned. This was the communion against the F-15 and the Rockeye cluster bomb. This was the communion of those who might have wandered too far to find their heritage. The heritage was oranges and war. Now one seemed to mean the other.

As the Plane Lowered over Cyprus

At Orly Airport in 1972 three generations of Americans from the Levant had smiled. And why not? Damascene and Beiruiti relatives were waiting to celebrate with the Awads and Orfaleas. 1972 had been a "peak" year for Lebanon: tourism was at its highest, commerce and banking were flourishing. The world-famous jazz festival in the Temple of Jupiter at Baalbek was sporting Ella Fitzgerald.

But in 1982 no family was with me, and no smiles on the faces of passengers who lined up for the Beirut connection of Air France from Charles de Gaulle Airport in Paris. The Lebanese, though, seemed more sober than somber. Some women wore designer jeans and coats with fur collars; some men sported Homburgs and leather attache cases. Thick eyeshadow on lovely women hid the shadow of war. They were émigrés heading back to Beirut to see family briefly and then leave again. They were Beirut businessmen who had taken Parisian breathers.

As the plane lowered over Cyprus, the orchid on each empty seat in first class began to move. The empty hangers in the first class closet jostled softly. Most everyone on the flight wore headphones. Still, little by little, the man next to me revealed himself, in a torrent of philosophy that mirrored two Phoenician precursors of the Lebanese: Zeno the Stoic and Epicurus. Later, I was told that people could be very talkative on the Paris–Beirut flight, because once on the ground they had to take care what they say and to whom.

Samir, a Lebanese architect born in Senegal, educated in France and working in Beirut, responded to my compliment that he resembled US Congressman Nick Joe Rahall (D-WV), whose family came from Marjayoun in southern Lebanon. After sharing a thin Davidoff cigar, he gestured with manicured hands, "Listen to me. I make myself whomever people would like me to be. If a Muslim talks to me I answer back in a Muslim accent; if a Christian, in Christian accent—and you learn to know both. If a stranger speaks French, then French; if English, then English. What are nations? What do they matter? Survival is the key. For that, I am nobody, nothing, and yet everybody. Look, the Lebanese are optimists. If I shed tears tonight over one who is killed, tomorrow I'm up selling my fruit on Hamra Street because life goes on. How do you say? *Esperance*. Hope. That's a big word with Lebanese. We have had seven years of violence and I'm still alive. So—why not seven more?"

At this, he lit another thin cigar. "Business and money. Very important here. Business to take our minds off the death, and money to buy security. We make lots of money because there are no taxes, no assessments, no government! *Anarchisme, oui*? Believe me, don't skimp on money while you're here. Take a taxi—a yellow one—from your hotel anywhere. It will cost more—$20 from the airport to Hamra for instance—but you have to spend money for security. That's a very important word here—security."

This fixation with security and the chameleon internationalism is peculiarly Lebanese. Samir compared the Middle East conflict to both theater (America is the producer, Israel the director) and a meal of lamb and salad (Israel, the lamb, eats the salad made of the Arabs, and the United States eats them both).

As we crossed over the silvery water, Beirut harbor grew into the window pane, then the green hills, the limestone houses, and the abrupt mountain covered with April snow. *Lubnan*. Ancient Semitic root-word meaning "white," white as the treasured snowy mountain (*laban*, yogurt in Arabic) where hermits and anchorites and clans of all sorts escaped the plunderers. And developed their own paranoias...

Samir insisted that I take the remaining Davidoff cigars. "I would like to have you to my house, but if you should get blown up by a car bomb, I would never forgive myself," he said.

As we descended from the plane, at the base of the stairs were two Lebanese army soldiers—tall, cheeks sharp and reddened—pointing with M–16 submachine guns to where our feet should walk between them.

Soldiers Get Younger

I had forgotten how young soldiers are. At the airport, two looked like they had just finished playing soccer. Behind them a sea of porters surged forward amid a swell of men in different battle fatigues. My architect friend, Samir, waved good-bye.

We had arrived at dawn ten years ago. Now it was afternoon. In 1972, Jaddu had paid off a few Lebanese custom officials because we had extra boxes of clothing for our poor relatives in Damascus. In 1982, with the risk of smuggled weapons or drugs so much higher, our bags were hardly touched. The customs man didn't even lift his head before waving us on. Most wars make customs agonizing: in Lebanon, customs was simply superfluous. Anarchy had made the term "corruption" quaint.

A timid-looking, navy blue-shirted man in his thirties came up to us and introduced himself: our guide, Mohammed. He had an immediately reassuring voice, a chipmunk-like moustache, and friendly eyes. Later in the week, after a late dinner at the hotel in which he castigated a Finnish photographer for being touchy about Arab men and tried to turn an Indonesian stewardess into a revolutionary, he pulled a revolver from the back of his belt and said, "I am reassuring because of this."

Mohammed helped us with our baggage into a beat-up Mercedes and sheepishly turned his hands upward when the porter stood glaring for a tip. Mohammed did not have any Lebanese pounds, and neither did we. The porter, with a three-day growth of beard, fumed and stared before walking off, pushing his cart abruptly. Was he Lebanese? Our guide was Palestinian. I did not think Mohammed had intentionally slighted the man, who was scraping by like everyone else in Lebanon. (Only the builders and the gunrunners made fortunes off the destruction). There seemed no overt snubbing on our guide's part. And yet...

It took me back a decade to the lunch thrown for us in Zahle in the mountains by the aunt who set a bountiful table—*mazza*, *kibba*, *tabbouli*, *hummus*, *baba ghannuj*, all the sainted foods—and how she had taken our appetites away when she ordered her young Palestinian

maid to sleep on the stone floor. Two perhaps unconscious snubs—
one of a Lebanese by a Palestinian, the other the reverse—were all
too emblematic of the hatred that caused the deaths of 150,000 in a
vicious sixteen-year civil war (or 3.3 percent of the Lebanese
population). Forty different armed militias sprang up, 900,000
Lebanese and Palestinian civilians were made homeless by the
internecine fighting and two Israeli invasions, and at least one-fifth
of the Lebanese (600,000) emigrated to other lands.[1]

We drove up from the airport through three checkpoints—one
Lebanese army, two Syrian—before getting to Palestinian security
just south of Beirut's center. One Syrian soldier asked if we had
"magazines." "That's a new one," Mohammed smirked. "He wants
heroin, money, or guns and says—'Magazines?'"

Traffic thickened as the airport road moved near three large
Palestinian refugee camps—Sabra, Shatila, and Bourj al-Barajneh. It
was 2:30 PM, and already rush hour in Beirut. Most government and
professional offices closed at 2 PM in West Beirut for security reasons.
Still, vendors had a go of it until nightfall, taking their chances. The
contrast of poverty and wealth so pervasive in Beirut ten years earlier
remained. In front of Sabra ran a wall of designer shoes from Paris
and Rome, the vendor sitting beside them on a wooden chair.

We passed open-air shops of chickens and parakeets and
shrieking parrots. Stalls of furniture and small appliances. Alongside a
stall of plucked chickens hanging from hooks were tricycles hanging
from hooks. I thought about the children who would pass by those
bikes, be denied, and not live to ask again.

"You trust me?" Mohammed pulled a Marlboro pack from his
shirt pocket. "That's pretty good for a terrorist!" He offered us
cigarettes. I refused his offer six times on the first day. But in the
Middle East, cigarettes are tantamount to oxygen. One offers
cigarettes the same way you would roll down the window of a car to
give a passenger fresh air or offer a thirsty traveler water.

Finally we had arrived at the Hotel Beau Rivage two blocks
from the Ramlat al-Bayda ("White Sands") beach—a key target, we
were told later, for an Israeli sea assault. It was a fine place, with a
small circular drive underneath shade palms flicking in the breeze, a
doorman, a huge dark-gray lobby where the television is the center
of attention, and a dining room with windows fronting all sides and
an excellent view of the Mediterranean. As I dipped my fork into
lemon-soaked cod, I glimpsed a boy in uniform washing a Syrian
tank as if it were a car.

The Beach of Cans and Bottles
In 1976, US Ambassador Francis Meloy was shot and killed within view
of the Beau Rivage on the beach road. A few blocks south, in the Jnah

section of Beirut, the Iraqi Embassy was blown sky high in December 1981. The building was supposed to be "bomb proof" and its leveling was more than the usual embarrassment to the neutered Lebanese government. Some say the explosion— which killed 60, including the Iraqi ambassador—was an "inside job" by Iraqi dissidents, as the dynamite was planted deep underneath the structure of the building. The Iraqis were so incensed they moved their headquarters to East Beirut in Hazmieh near the presidential estate of Baabda—one of the only areas of Beirut patrolled by Lebanon's own army.

A great story of survival was told about the exploded Iraqi Embassy. A man survived pinned in the rubble for two weeks on some chocolate in a smashed pantry and a trickle of water from a pipe ripped open by the blast. The story seemed quintessentially Lebanese in its absurd, almost heroic determinism. One man survived on chocolate; 60 others perished writing memos or swabbing floors.

I walked along the shore one of the first nights, past kids playing soccer in front of the Syrian tank, past a Palestinian guard near an anti-aircraft gun housed in the bed of a truck. Seven years of war had made Beirut's beach a minefield of trash. Along the seawall ran a strip ten yards across and two feet deep of rusted cans, glass bottles, and empty plastic containers of Sanin and Sohat springwater. Beyond, the old Mediterranean uncoiled. It was not inviting. It was as if the sea were a cobra raising its head, hissing: Stay out.

The soldiers guarding against an Israeli attack that night were not Lebanese, but Palestinian and Syrian. And the sun grew like a tumor in the sky over everyone—uniformed or not. A burning lethal pinkness that made everyone civilian. It was Saturday night. Drivers of souped-up cars gunned their engines along the beach road, spinning out in a frenzy as if they were driving in some final Grand Prix. The drag strip down by Summerland south of the city on the way to Damour (curious—there's a "Summerland" just south of Santa Barbara) had been shut down, so the drag-racers had taken their sport closer to the city. They were not just teenagers, either. It was as if all the tension of Beirut had gathered here, engines roaring. When they died down, the gunshots began.

Enough. I had seen the cans and bottles and disposable diapers of the West pile up at the doorstep of the Orient. I had to get back to the Beau Rivage. The Syrian soldier squinted when I called hello to him, "*Marhaba*," the way you announce yourself in a dark forest if you hear rustling in the underbrush.

Mahmoud Labadi Turned the Car Ignition

... and in the backseat of the yellow Toyota I instinctively turned my head. In the first three months of 1982 at least 126 people were killed in Beirut by car bombs. Turn the key in the ignition and the car blows up. Car bombs were a new twist in the city's string of anarchy and brutality. But the engine roared to a normal start and Labadi, the PLO's spokesman, drove out of the parking lot. No lot attendant was to be found. The minimal security surrounding key PLO offices amazed us throughout the trip. We were not searched once in three weeks. Grace Halsell, a writer I was traveling with, said that in Israel even her lipstick had been searched.

Labadi drove on the left shoulder of the road, in order to make the turn as they do in Greece, and for a second the world was topsy-turvy. We passed by Raousche on the northwest edge of the city, where assorted shops came after the civil war leveled the downtown suqs. Beirut ceaselessly rises from its own ashes. And the poor shopkeepers who had fled the horrid no-man's-land (the Green Line, which ends in the *zaytuna* section near the seashore) had placed their corrugated tin hovels at the very end of the land at Raousche, overlooking a sheer cliff and Pigeon Rocks. Some had fallen off.

To survive one catastrophe in Beirut was child's play. One had to rise up and rise up repeatedly. Labadi pointed to a section of the Raousche market exploded by two car bombs a couple months earlier. Thirty of the ramshackle shops were destroyed as well as sixty parked cars. Unable to depend on the government, or the leftist Lebanese National Movement, or Palestinian groups in the area, the shopkeepers quickly banded together in a committee and in one month's time had rebuilt the torn blocks of the market. The Lebanese are like the Palestinians: slapped down here, they appear there. They are like mercury. Or protoplasm. (Or, a couple decades later, Iraqis? Al-Qaeda?)

Finally, we arrived at a coastal restaurant called the Sultan Ibrahim, which serves a four-inch-long fish of the same name, a delicacy throughout the eastern Mediterranean. Labadi scooped up the silvery fish in his large hands and threw them back into the basin the waiter held out. "Grilled!" he ordered. By the time we sat down, the restaurant was abuzz.

Labadi told us that lunch with visitors was his only vacation. He worked from dawn to way past dusk. What of PLO Chairman Yasir Arafat? "He is a prisoner," he said. "The people at the head of a revolution are the least free." Labadi was sparing when talking about himself. Near 40, he had joined the PLO in 1965 while a university student in Bonn, Germany, a city he "really loved." He had been in the resistance for seventeen years and had seen friends give into despair or disillusionment. "We are a free organization," he said, with head bowed. "People can come and go freely." His voice lowered when speaking of his predecessor, Kamal Nasser, under whom he had worked. "He was shot in the mouth." Labadi dipped a piece of bread into the hummus and chewed slowly.

Nasser had been a much-revered poet of the Palestinians. He was sitting at his desk at home April 10, 1973, when Israeli commandos burst into the room, killing him and two others. One Israeli shot him in the mouth precisely because he was a poet and a legend among Palestinians here and abroad. Another story surrounding Nasser's grisly death was that as a Christian Arab he was shot in the palms, the feet, and the side of his chest.

Labadi steered conversation to the Western media, which he felt had been more sensitive to the Palestinians the past year or two. He had a copy of ABC's "Under the Israeli Thumb" on Betamax, and called *Washington Post* correspondent Ed Cody "a personal friend who has the courage to write what he sees." (Later, Cody would tell me at the Commodore Hotel bar that he was able to report objectively because "I don't care for either side.")

Arts and sports could further world reception of Palestinian rights, Labadi thought. "We need a Palestinian *Exodus*, yes," he nodded, referring to the novel by Leon Uris that sold over twenty million copies by 1967 alone. "But Palestinian directors are not so good as the Egyptians." There is a Palestinian soccer team with a coach named Zhivago, but "it is terrible: they even lost to Yemen. My God, if they lost to Yemen, what would they do in London?"

Yasir Arafatu!

March 30. Squashed into an auditorium in the UNESCO complex facing the painted poster INTERNATIONAL DAY IN SOLIDARITY WITH THE POPULAR UPRISING IN OCCUPIED PALESTINE AND THE GOLAN HEIGHTS. The stage seemed set for a school play. *Julius Caesar*? *Hamlet*? Yasir Arafat as the Dane.

The Lebanese and Palestinian flags draped over long card tables shared the same colors—red, green, and white—except one. The Palestinian added black. A well-ordered Palestinian military band with purple berets and gold braid on their shoulders played bagpipes—an inheritance, no doubt, from the British who had the Palestine Mandate from 1918 to 1948. Quite a contrast, this proper military band, to the security guards in tee-shirts and jeans, their pistols sagging from their belts.

We were addressed by a woman lawyer from France, Frances Weyl, whom Arafat kissed on the forehead as though she were a nun. She was followed by an Algerian representative, who got the best cheer of all. Then came a Greek, an Egyptian (mild applause), a Czech, and a young Japanese man who saluted "Yasir Arafatu!"

A funny thing happened with the representative from Cuba. His Arab translator—prematurely gray, skinny as a rail, wearing thick glasses and thick moustache—was the most dramatic translator I had ever seen. His voice was shrill and weepy at the same time. The

Cuban looked like he had lost his place in his speech. The translator
flew way past the time mark, past the page. The translator-turned-
demagogue. Then the Cuban resumed speaking Spanish, playing
catch up. Who was translating whom? The Cuban sprang his finger
high until his face turned red. He spit. He gripped his paper hard.
Fidel! Bay of Pigs! Freedom! Then came back the translator in
Arabic. The crowd liked the heavy part, which the translator surely
was making heavier. Back and forth, back and forth. But the Cuban
would not be upstaged. He swung his fist, his cowlick quivered, his
chin vibrated with anger. The crowd went wild.

After three hours of speeches even the master of ceremonies was
tired. He sat cross-legged on the floor in front of the podium,
smoking. At just this moment Arafat rose to speak, and the audience
came alive. Huge applause and loud chanting. Arafat, who came
across in English interviews as very mild and soft, had a rousing
masculine voice in Arabic. It took on many timbres: powerful, angry,
but also gentle, prankish, warm. He dipped his head low and smiled,
raising his eyebrows, slowly lifting his right hand, then forcefully
bringing it down.

"Why… why do we only share bad times with the Lebanese?"
he asked the audience, as if sitting in the living room with cousins,
forehead furrowing, voice imploring. "Why never the good? We
want only a path in Lebanon, not a home. I appreciate the Lebanese
people very much because they are suffering very much for the
Palestinians. And still they support us."

At critical junctures in Arafat's speech, a spindly, tan youth called
out "All the fronts!" hurling two lines of spontaneous poetry at
Arafat. It underscored the folk love that Palestinians had for Arafat.
But it also seemed to be a kind of warning to the leader not to
detach himself too much from his people.

When he was done, the crowd applauded and then filed out in
a manner that was surprisingly civil. With all the guns, pistols,
passions and rhetoric—no one was hurt.

Weeds from the Sandbags on Rue UNESCO

The streets of West Beirut were quiet. It was Sunday, and, contrary to
journalistic shorthand, West Beirut was not all Muslim but contained at
least 70,000 Christians. Some were going to the Sts. Peter and Paul
Orthodox Church, others to the Church of the Capuchins, the French-
language Catholic church—both in the Hamra district in the center of
West Beirut. The sun was hot but a cold wind napped at a dusty palm
or two and swayed the fallen telephone wires on Rue UNESCO,
which moved on the concrete like tentacles of a beached squid.

Drained, troubled by the Palestinian Land Day speeches I had
heard the day before, I took a walk alone from Ramlat al-Bayda

along the Corniche Mazraa up to the heart of West Beirut in Hamra. Though it would seem no one would want to advertise political fealty in the hornet's nest of militias and gangs, posters—political and cinematic—were plastered everywhere. In the poster race, President Hafez al-Assad of Syria had the lead, with Kamal Jumblatt, patron saint of Lebanese leftists, a distant second. Jumblatt, well loved by the Lebanese, had been assassinated by the Syrians in 1977. Both dead and a mystic, Jumblatt was relatively safe to advertise. A very tall full-length poster of him hovered like an angel above a Shell gas pump where Rue UNESCO goes into Rue Verdun. A few Assad–Qaddafi posters existed, a yoking of separate portraits of the two—something about as natural as the alliance of Syria and Libya. Here and there a shot of the disappeared Imam Musa Sadr, the "absent" leader of the Lebanese Shi'ites. Surprisingly few posters of Arafat lined the limestone and yellow stucco walls, and hardly any of the president of Lebanon himself, Elias Sarkis.

As for movies, it was just like home: sex and violence. And was as it irony or prophecy that when the first Syrian tank arrived in Beirut in 1976 to police the cease-fire it turned off its engine in the Place des Canons (Place des Martyrs) in front of the Rivoli Theater, whose marquee advertised *Les Divorcees*? For eighteen months of bloodshed in the civil war, this movie played to no one.[2]

On Rue UNESCO three images struck me. The first was a small wooden chair sitting in the middle of the road, with two stones atop a cinder block on its seat and a green plant growing out of the chair's back. Had artifacts become the only soil of Lebanon? Had chairs become road dividers? Then I came across a young boy sitting in a burlap bag begging in the gutter. Cars missed him by inches. Ten years ago there were beggars in Beirut. And there were the lame. A man with no legs had settled himself on a median strip begging with a hat to both incoming and outgoing traffic. Ingenious! This boy was only deeply pathetic. Legless, he seemed the cipher of a whole world. Finally, at a Syrian checkpoint, a kind of mute Lebanese protest. In a pile of sandbags, weeds were growing. The war had gone on that long. There was the tragedy of Beirut and Lebanon, and also its secret answer. Weeds would grow from sand, from the very armrests of guns. Pray the weeds would win.

Return to the Salaam House

In Beirut, perhaps more than in any place in the world, "destruction" and "construction" coexisted and implied each other. Holes of red earth were everywhere ("Hamra" in central West Beirut means "red") and the only thing more pervasive than guns was cinder block. But today was Sunday and the cinder block was mute as so many squared bones.

Rue UNESCO runs into Rue Verdun, then Rue Dunant and Rue du Rome until I arrived in the heart of Hamra—its shops, vendors, and small hotels—piles of its red soil everywhere. City of open wounds. City of lipstick and bomb craters. There it was. Two blocks off Rue Hamra.

The beige stucco and turquoise shutters of Salaam House were filthy and the windows boarded over with plywood. Cardboard boxes, bottles, plastic containers of Sohat water were strewn on its front porch, where the old Iraqi diplomat used to take his tea and recite poetry to us from the Abbasid caliphate of the tenth century.

I asked a boy selling fruit and cigarettes in the street if he knew of the owners, where they were, if they were alive. He went across the street and questioned a neighbor. They spoke in an Arabic too fast for a pilgrim whose hair was whitening at the root. Finally, we mounted the stairs of the hotel from a side entrance. He rang a bell. Ten years fell on the floor like earth. A face in the open door, a dark face with no makeup, hair tucked in a bun, a face above a black dress as if she knew I was coming and wanted to show that the lover of Lebanon was in mourning.

"You've come."

Two young boys clung to her brown calves. "Please come in." The crow's-feet pulled from her eyes as she kissed me on both cheeks, though the rest of her face was brown and smooth. Before I could exclaim what was almost a question—*Hind, you are still alive*—she sat me near a five-foot-long puzzle on a coffee table. "It's a scene of some woods, the kind we used to go to in Lebanon with no fear," she said, looking directly at me. "But I wish there were some running water in this scene!"

Hind asked if I liked Turkish coffee *hilwah* (sweet), *wasat* (medium), or *murra* (bitter). I picked *wasat*; she picked *murra*. Within minutes I realized Hind's courage and bitterness in that city of murderous solitudes. She had married the very son of the old Iraqi diplomat who had sat on the veranda, a Muslim in fact (she is Maronite Catholic). "Be sure I did it before the war [in 1975], for after, to marry an Iraqi here would be impossible," she said, holding onto her screeching younger son. Her husband was gone for months at a time; he worked in the Gulf, as did many Lebanese men, leaving a covey of tough and strained wives behind in the war zone. She worked as a schoolteacher but stayed inside most afternoons and evenings. With the puzzle.

"Since there has been such a 'brain drain' from Lebanon, what is left here is the get-rich-quick people, the *nouveau riche*," Hind said, pouring the thick coffee from a brass pot. "Drugs?" I asked. She flicked her hand upward as if shooing flies: "Drugs? Drugs are too cheap here to make much money. They're making money from building and guns, my dear. As well as protection money. Everyone in West Beirut pays protection money to a different gang. In East Beirut they pay their tax—it's protection money of course—to the Kata'ib. Believe me… there are no jobs here, unless it's building or blowing up buildings."

She turned to the past and smiled: "I remember the marshmallows we cooked till they were black on the beach by the Casino. Oh, those were the best days!"

And what happened to Cynthia, the blonde friend of hers?

"She married an Egyptian. They moved to Hawaii where he teaches. She went the furthest of anyone."

The Israelis Break the Sound Barrier

The nights began to mount like the days. Nights I spent sleepless but exhausted on my hotel bed, the glass door open to the balcony for a night breeze. By 7 PM the sound of cars faded from the road. By 9 PM shots rang out, some distant like termites in the foundation of earth, some close like fireworks. Who was fighting whom was anybody's guess.

But during the day the bustle of the city desperately rebuilding itself dominated. Except for one sound. *Turn your cheek, God.* Two slaps. Sabri Jiryis, director of the PLO Research Center in Beirut, clutched the jiggling tea cups and looked out the window. Shrieks in the street. Rattle of groundfire. As if in control of Time itself, the Israeli Air Force broke the sound barrier. The F-15s struck noon; Israel was Beirut's clock tower. "But they are not quite precise now," said Jiryis, "They do their reconnaissance every day in the past. Now you don't know when or if it's going to be an attack."

Jiryis's *The Arabs in Israel* had been the first book to name the problem of a half million Arabs living inside Israel as a second-class minority. After arrests and harassments by the Israelis he had left his hometown in the Galilee with two suitcases of clothes and a bag of books.

"Actually, the PLO asked me in their Hebrew broadcast to leave Israel and run their Hebrew broadcast from Cairo," he related. "But the moment I went there, Black September happened [the decimation of PLO forces in Jordan]. So the radio station was shut down and I came to Beirut."

Jiryis was a quiet man whose office was meticulously neat. He seemed to hunch over himself, his face pitted and filled with dark birthmarks. His skin had the color of day-old coffee, his suit was immaculate and brown.

Jiryis called his secretary on the intercom and gently asked if the firing we heard was anti-aircraft. He smiled wanly. "Well, some of our people will be happy now to try this new four-barrelled anti-aircraft gun, a Russian one used in the October War," he said.

Is a Palestinian state closer or farther away than ten years ago? "I don't look at it that way," he spoke slowly, carefully. "It's dialectical. But more and more an impression that is almost controlling me is that a Palestinian state won't be made peacefully. I can't believe the Israelis will accept it unless you force it on them."

On April Fool's Day at the Modca Café

Cups clattered, coffee spilled, and faces turned. Car bomb? Stalin Organ? Israeli bum bum? Furrowed heads and tense eyes focused on the boy who knocked over three white café chairs. He picked himself up, sheepishly grinning at the terrified café dwellers, and ran off down Rue Hamra.

At the Lebanese tourist office across from the leading newspaper, *An-Nahar*, I placed a call to Damascus. Two women with blank faces operated the phones in an office with nothing on its walls, not even a picture of fabled Lebanon. The call took 45 minutes to get through and when it did, a snowstorm of static came with it. It was said the line from Beirut to the United States was clearer than to Damascus, only 60 miles away. My cousin Suad began to cry. How am I? How is the family in California? Who has died? Why am I here? When I mentioned the war threat in Beirut she steered the conversation to something else, such as my getting sick on a Hindu apricot in Damascus ten years before. Her children were all grown; her son, Nino, out of college and wanting to study surgery in the United States, but it was so hard to get a visa if you are a Syrian.

Could I help? What was I doing in Beirut? Snowstorm. Before snow completely consumed the Beirut–Damascus line we made a date. I would come to see them in one week, via taxi, over the Lebanese mountains, if such a thing were possible.

Dining with the Revolution

Two days later I visited the family of Kahlil al-Wazir, also known as Abu Jihad, the head of the PLO's military forces and a close aide to Arafat. His younger brother, Zuhair, was president of the General Union of Palestinian Students (GUPS), which oversaw the education of 4,000 Palestinians worldwide in some 37 branches. Their favorite lands to study in were the United States (25 branches of GUPS), the Soviet Union, and Romania. Zuhair, who had studied in Romania, had a medical degree himself and was proud of historical Arab contributions to medicine. He said that medicine and engineering were the most popular fields for Palestinian students abroad and that Palestinians were second only to Americans in the degree of education, by ratio to population, in the world.

The al-Wazir family home in Beirut was a walk-up apartment in a guarded building, to which I was driven in a guarded car. There I was introduced to an old couple in traditional Palestinian dress, the parents of Khalil and Zuhair, whose robes and headdresses formed a sharp contrast to the Western-style dress of their children. They appeared to have stepped out of the past. The mother, large and squat like Zuhair, began to narrate the flight from Ramle in 1948 as if she had been thinking about it forever: "I carried Zuhair and Abu Jihad and one more child for three days from Ramle. We went to Qabab, a wheat village. We were afraid to sleep. We were completely surrounded by Zionists. My girl was so thirsty she almost broke down. Then we reached Salbit, which had a well, and drank and washed our faces. At midnight mortars were thrown around us, but we slept anyway because we thought—if we're going to die, we'll die. The Zionists came and shouted, 'Yalla! Go to Abdullah! [king of Jordan].'"[3]

Suddenly Abu Jihad burst into the room in military fatigues. He was a well-built, slender man of medium height. His movements were determined; he greeted my friend and me and announced, even as he picked up a piece of Arabic bread, "We have confirmed that the Israeli forces are moving into the gap and will invade in 24 to 48 hours. But we are ready for them and will hurt them. As Abu Ammar [Arafat] has said—if they come, they are welcome."

Far from being nervous, he seemed almost relieved, as if the tension of waiting for the attack had finally burst. It stunned me, how easily he hoisted his daughter Hannan on his knee and greeted his family, ready to eat with strangers. Wonder at such collection clashed with fear.

Before leaving I regarded the al-Wazir memorabilia on a table: two brass roosters, a ceramic rabbit, and a tray from Niagara Falls.

In 1988, after the PLO's expulsion from Lebanon, Khalil al-Wazir was assassinated by a seaborne Israeli hit team at his home in Tunisia. I wondered if the Niagara Falls tray survived. I wonder if he said welcome.

Alone at the Syrian Border

For days I tried to find a way to get into Syria to meet my cousins from Arbeen. Unlike ten years before, when visas were routinely given at the border, the war has made transfer into Syria more difficult. And I did not have a visa.

I began counting Syrian checkpoints out of Beirut, over the mountains, through the Biqaᶜ. There were ten. The taxi trip seemed endless, and endlessly tense. The only rest stop was at Shatturah, where we ate some of the famed sweets. I bought some wine and delights for my relatives, who planned to meet me at the border just in case there was a mix-up over a visa. I was sure Adeeb Awad Hanna, my dear leprechaun lawyer cousin, would settle everything.

When the driver let me off at the border customs check, I gave him a phone number to call my relative Suad, Jaddu's niece, to tell her that I was at the border.

The Syrian soldier inside shook his head. Sorry. An American? He gave me a desultory look, as if to say, big deal—we don't give visas here anymore. Another soldier outside said he couldn't do anything either. No one allowed me to call Damascus. I waited for three hours. By 3 PM, the winds of the foothills at the border sent a chill through my bones. People came and went; it was Easter weekend. Two huge busloads with Saudi flags passed by. Mecca was a long way off.

The taxi driver disappeared. None of my relatives came. Hungry and cold, I finally flagged a cabbie with some room to return to Beirut. Months later I discovered that the first driver never called my relatives. And that they had prepared a meal for me that went very cold.

A woman in the back seat with two children was a Palestinian returning to the Sabra refugee camp. The driver inexplicably stopped in Aley in the mountains and left us sitting for an hour and a half in the damp. It was night when we returned. The woman and her children were let out in the darkened dust at the camp. On an impulse, I decided to get off on the coast road and walk back to the hotel, each passing truck from the south roaring by with guerrillas, or frenzied merchants, honking at me. I had never felt more alone.

THE ISRAELI INVASION OF LEBANON

Barely a month after my return to the States, on June 3, 1982, the Israeli ambassador to Britain, Shlomo Argov, was shot in the head by assassins connected to Abu Nidal, a Palestinian version of Osama bin Laden, but more nihilistic, with no pretensions of religion whatsoever. Abu Nidal was an equal opportunity butcher—he killed Israelis and Palestinians alike. Israel had never cared to separate the rejectionist policies of Abu Nidal from those of Yasir Arafat (several of whose associates had been gunned down by Abu Nidal men, too, and who had a contract out for Nidal himself), and thus took advantage of the atrocity in London to launch its much-awaited, full-scale invasion of Lebanon to root out Arafat's PLO. Months later, after over 19,000 people—mostly civilians—lay dead and 30,000 maimed or wounded. From his hospital bed Argov himself chastized Menachem Begin for a disastrous venture, which would become Israel's Vietnam.

For Arab Americans stunned by the invasion, which led to the encirclement and merciless bombardment of Beirut and finally to the massacres at the Sabra and Shatila refugee camps, this became a defining hour: "Lebanon in 1982 was to be the most traumatic experience the community had encountered since the mass starvation in Lebanon in World War I."[4] Arab Americans of every age and background, from Lebanese grandmothers in Pittsburgh to third-generation students at UCLA found themselves signing petitions, lobbying congressmen, attending candlelight vigils, and participating in silent protest meals of *mujaddara*. Everyone, it seemed, had relatives or friends who were being hit by the war in Lebanon. It was from Lebanon, of course, that a majority of Arab Americans hailed; Lebanon, most vulnerable and utterly chaotic in the seventh year of its own civil war, was the ancestral heartland.

American Jews had once watched in agony as the US government blocked American shores to large numbers of Jews fleeing the Nazis. Forty years later, Arab Americans, too, waited for their government to do something as Israel drove harder and harder at Beirut with US weapons. For two-and-a-half months, until he lifted the phone to call Begin on August 4, President Reagan said hardly a word.

It did not help to discover that Secretary of State Alexander Haig as early as January 1982 had given Israeli officials a "green light" to proceed with the invasion and that the United States had secretly bolstered the attack with a massive new infusion of armaments that spring.[5] One such US "smart" bomb destroyed an entire building, killing 100 people in an unsuccessful effort to finish off Arafat. These rather dumb smart bombs seem to have had American tacticians in thrall for two decades; they would be used again with the same hamfisted inaccurate results against Osama bin Laden in Afghanistan and Saddam Hussein in Iraq.

ADC devoted tireless, if unanswered, efforts that summer of 1982 to get US arms shipments to Israel halted until it withdrew from Lebanon. The vehicle was the so-called Rahall Resolution (H.C. Res. 359). Citing "total disregard for US interests," Rep. Nick Joe Rahall agonized, "For the sake of humanity, how far can this whitewash spread? Will Israel stop its maddening surge, already much deeper than originally announced?" But Rahall could only muster 14 of 535 House members to sign his resolution; 7 were African Americans and 5 were not running for reelection. He was not helped by a harsh media attack on his emergency mission with other congressmen to Lebanon; they were dubbed "the Gang of Four" (*New York Post*, July 27, 1982) and "Innocents Abroad" (*Cleveland Plain Dealer*, July 30, 1982). The *Post* was so full of spleen it misidentified Rep. Mervyn Dymally (D-CA) as "an aide to Arafat"!

Many other avenues to halt the slaughter were tried. ADC spearheaded a petition for an arms embargo to Israel and immediate US-PLO talks, which received 37,000 signatures. It contracted with Robert Gray and Company, a public relations firm with close ties to the Reagan administration, to produce five full-page ads protesting the war in 63 US daily newspapers. Five Congressional seminars were sponsored on the Hill with experts on Lebanon, the Palestinians and Israeli war intentions. ADC members daily picketed the Israeli Embassy, while the organization produced a documentary, *Report from Beirut, Summer of 1982*, written by Saul Landau. In an especially moving effort, ADC brought 50 injured Lebanese and Palestinian children to the United States for treatment, while Abourezk toured the country for relief donations with two doctors, one of whom, Chris Giannou, had amputated a thousand limbs in a day in Beirut.

Perhaps the most dramatic confrontation of the war on US shores occurred when Rep. Clement Zablocki (D-WI) said to Begin's face on June 21, "My constituents have told me my hands are as bloody as those of Israeli soldiers." Zablocki, chairman of the House Foreign Affairs Committee, was sure Israel had broken US laws, "There is no doubt in my mind. The law is very clear—it is intended for defense purposes... In the case of Lebanon, Israel went too far" (*Washington Post*, June 22, 1982). At one point, Zablocki was so incensed he suggested, "If we're not going to enforce the Arms Export Control Act, then let's repeal it."[6] Uneasy laughter rippled over the committee room.

Zablocki was in tune with the public. By September, Gallup was registering 50 percent of Americans—including 18 percent of American Jews—in favor of some form of aid curtailment to Israel. These figures were unprecedented. According to an NAAA poll of 83 of 100 Senate offices, 66 percent said their constituent mail was opposed to the invasion. Yet none of this affected the aid flow. In fact, the next year (1983), US aid to Israel increased by $310 million: "It appeared to Arab Americans that Reagan was a silent general in Israel's war."[7]

At the beginning of August, the Israelis had completely encircled Beirut. Visibly moved, John Chancellor of NBC *Nightly News* looked out over the smoking ruins and spoke on August 2:

> What will stick in the mind about yesterday's savage Israeli attack on Beirut is its size and scope. This is one of the world's biggest cities. The area under attack is the length of Manhattan Island below Central Park... The Israeli planes just never stopped coming. Israelis say they were going after military targets with precision... There was also the stench of terror all across the city. Nothing like it has ever happened in this part of the world... What in the world is going on? Israel's security problem on its border is 50 miles to the South. What's an Israeli Army doing here in Beirut?"[8]

Twenty-two years later, Osama bin Laden, in a taped message on the eve of the 2004 Presidential election, would point specifically to this trauma: "The incidents that affected me directly go back to 1982 and afterward, when America allowed Israelis to invade Lebanon with the help of the American Sixth Fleet..." While the Sixth Fleet did not come onto the scene in Lebanon until after a ceasefire, bin

Laden's reference to the falling "towers" of Beirut—and their connection to New York—was unmistakable and eerie: "As I watched the destroyed towers in Lebanon, it occurred to me to punish the unjust the same way."[9]

Stateside, the Israeli Embassy, sensing the American press finally turning against the invasion, released a report "rating" 48 US newspapers and their coverage of the war. Meg Greenfield of the *Washington Post* said the evaluations "not only don't tell the story, they actually distort it."[10] Nevertheless, the *Post* welcomed Jewish leader Michael Berenbaum into their newsroom to observe it and query reporters and editors; no such offer was tendered to the Arab-American community.

The siege of Beirut began to cause some Arabs to draw absurd conclusions. A consul from an Arab embassy in Washington suggested at a café one night that the PLO and Arafat should "commit suicide" in Beirut; it sounded to my ears as a suggestion to fight Israel to the last Lebanese civilian. It was insanity and I told the consul just that. There were squabbles that belied the serious moment. At an ADC dinner on June 26, the heads of ADC and the Palestine Congress of North America (PCNA) locked horns over the fact that no Palestinian flag was displayed along the American and Lebanese flags along the dias. On the positive side, wives of the Arab ambassadors went on a hunger strike in front of the White House in Lafayette Park, a bit of bravery in striking contradistinction to the empty squawking of their husbands. One Arab American from Detroit who joined the strike (and later died from it), Musallem Eadeh, said, "I have seen too many massacres, too much death." The hunger strike, more than anything else, caught the eye of the White House, and after a meeting between the strikers and Nancy Reagan, the horror began, finally, to hit home to the president.

But not with enough force to stop the Sabra and Shatila massacres. On September 16, right-wing Lebanese Phalangists, who had colluded with Israel, were led to the entrance of two large Palestinian refugee camps in southern Beirut by Ariel Sharon's subordinates. Over three days, with machine guns and knives, they murdered close to 1,000 Palestinian civilians. George Will, an American columnist with no special affection for Arabs, compared the slaughter to massacres of Russian and Czech Jews, "The Palestinians have now had their Babi Yar, their Lidice."[11]

The outcry in Israel was immediate and outdistanced anything in the United States. Two ministers in Begin's cabinet resigned in protest. The 700,000-member B'nai B'rith International called the massacres at Sabra and Shatila "a heinous crime," while the streets of Tel Aviv and Jerusalem flooded with hundreds of thousands of protesters. In Israel's darkest hour of shame, its conscience shone. As

Israeli Rabbi David Hartman put it, "If the voice of Isaiah is not heard in the corridors of power, then Israel has itself become a pagan nation."[12]

Though many American Jews were revolted—Rabbi Arthur Hertzberg, for one, called for Begin's immediate resignation—the Conference of the President of Major Jewish Organizations made no statement about the massacres. (Earlier in the summer, on June 24, 385 Bay Area Jewish Americans signed an ad published in the *San Francisco Chronicle* entitled, "Menachem Begin Does Not Speak for Us.") Perhaps sensing he had more of an opening on the Potomac than the Mediterranean, Begin published a full-page ad in the *Washington Post* on September 21, crying "Blood Libel." The ad copy posited a blatant lie: "The civilian population of the camps gave the clear expression of its gratitude for the act of salvation of the IDF (Israel Defense Forces)."

On September 22, eight of the signatories of the ill-fated Rahall Resolution issued a statement, "We must sadly observe that had H.C. Res. 359 been implemented and the full force of the United States been brought to bear, there may not have been a Friday massacre at Sabra and Shatila."

There were some heartening conjunctions of like-minded Arab and Jewish Americans during the invasion of Lebanon. At ADC's fifth and last Congressional seminar September 23, two distinguished American Jews appeared, I.F. Stone and Joseph Eger. The world-renowned French hornist and symphony director, Eger spoke movingly of reconciliation between the two branches of the Semitic tree:

> I can't believe that Jews are basically predators or annexationists. They are simply people who believe, because of their fear and insecurity, that only military policies will provide the deeply yearned-for peace. Those policies have not worked; they are not working. Not for Israel, nor for the Diaspora... It is time for change.[13]

The goodwill of these sentiments was marred later at an interdenominational memorial service for the victims of Sabra and Shatila. When I.F. Stone publicly castigated the Phalange, the Lebanese ambassador bolted from the platform of speakers and shouted an ethnic slur. It was tremendously embarrassing to those in the audience who understood the Arabic and knew the eminent Stone and his solid principles. It was also a crooked reminder of how thin was the "alliance in infamy" that Sharon had concocted with the Phalangists.

For his costly, and ultimately useless destruction in Lebanon, Sharon was later chastized by the Kahane Commission in Israel, removed from his cabinet post, and sent into political exile, rehabilitated only in recent years as—unthinkable as it would have seemed in 1982—Israel's prime minister. He had a like-minded US president in the saddle, a believer in striking back at all costs, and the equally counterproductive phenomenon of Palestinian children strapped with explosives killing themselves in gatherings of civilians.

But in 1982, for Arab Americans, what could not be denied was that the Lebanese themselves had carried the guns and knives into the camps and did the killing at Sabra and Shatila. In the worst hour of the war, Arabs were killing Arabs, and Christian Arabs yet, against Muslim Arabs. It was nothing short of a sacrilege to the mostly Christian Arab-American population and precipitated in itself a decline in Arab-American involvement in the Middle East conflict.

ALL FALL DOWN

How did the people I had so recently visited in Lebanon fare when the bombs fell? Col. Azmi Saghiyeh committed a spectacular suicide when, holed up in Sidon with Israelis he had taken prisoner, he was surrounded by Israeli forces, who refused to allow him passage to Beirut. He exploded a grenade, killing himself and the prisoners. The PLO spokesman Mahmoud Labadi left Arafat and joined the forces of the Abu Musa faction, which, with Syrian troops, laid siege to Arafat in Tripoli. The wife of Sabri Jiryis was killed during the bombardment of Beirut, and many of his priceless historical records were taken by Israeli troops. George Azar, an Arab-American photographer I had spent time with in Beirut, returned to the States looking for negatives of photographs he had taken of the war for *Newsweek*; the magazine refused to release them to him. Suhayla, a Shiʿite woman I'd met, watched the seige of Beirut on television in Saudi Arabia. Youmna, a friend of the Salaam House's Hind, managed to escape to Cyprus, where she married her American beau among Greek ruins in the middle of the war, and later emigrated with him to Washington, DC.

Jack Dagilitis, a longtime American resident of Beirut who had hosted me during my visit, suddenly appeared in my ADC office that summer. He recounted that Americans were included among those who had been drinking their own urine at the height of the seige, which had cut off the water supply. He had been elected by an expatriate group to journey to Washington to plead with US officials to do something. May Sayegh, head of a Palestinian women's union, who cooked a supper for me in Beirut, called late that terrible summer to say she had evacuated with the PLO (which went into exile in Tunisia). She was in Washington, DC, anonymously, to visit two children schooling in America. She could not meet me but wanted to hear my voice. "We are dispersed to the ends of the earth," she sobbed.

The 1982 invasion of Lebanon spurred an unprecedented Arab American political activism, but that declined precipitously after the shocking massacre of Palestinians at Sabra and Shatila by right-wing Lebanese Christians, the confusing turning on Arafat by the Syrians at Tripoli, which seemed to mimic Israel's own seige of Beirut, and the extraordinary terrorism and kidnapping of Americans and other Westerners that erupted from often faceless quarters.

After a little more than two years of activism on behalf of the community and its concerns, I took stock before leaving the field. The failure of the Hatfield and Stevenson amendments in the two years leading up to the invasion of Lebanon may have emboldened Israel to the notion that no amount of bombardment of Lebanon or settling of the West Bank would cause a loss of US money. No doubt that conclusion remains. Though Israel finally withdrew from Lebanon in 2000, periodic bombings still occur, and the growth of settlements continue today. They never stopped throughout the entire Oslo peace process in the 1990s, and they continued in 2003–2004, as Israel erected its version of the Berlin Wall to American peeps and gasps and open wallet.

Unlike Jim Zogby, who became the closest thing to a "professional Arab American" the community had, Abourezk's involvement, like that of many others, lessened after the Lebanon war. In the late 1980s, he left Washington for his native South Dakota, returning to Rapid City to practice law for those he had served long ago—Native Americans. Though ex-officio head of the organization for some time, by the mid-1990s he had left the ADC board of directors. Only in 2003, disturbed by the ramifications of the Patriot Act, did Abourezk re-join the ADC board. The need was great, but the task immense; ADC's and NAAA's combined membership (10,000) was down to less than half ADC's own rolls at the highwater mark in 1983.

Khalil Jahshan, who directed both NAAA and ADC at various times in the lean years of the late 1980s and 1990s, speaks of the elusive "60,000," what he calls the "true constituency" of Arab-American political efforts—in short, the community's politically interested and active faithful.[14] And that 60,000, Jahshan reminds, is often in the process of being re-won, because "We have lost it several times." Even at 60,000, that is only 2 percent of the community. Contrast that with the US membership of B'nai B'rith alone (200,000 in 2005), or 5 percent of the community. Another indicator of the difference: According to Stephen Isaacs, within several days of the October 1973 War, American Jews raised $100 million for Israel; at the height of the 1982 Lebanon War, ADC's Save Lebanon raised $250,000. It was generous by Arab-American standards, but it was no match.

U.S. Department of Justice

United States Attorney
Eastern District of Michigan

---

211 W. Fort Street   **AUSA Robert Cares**
Suite 2000   *Telephone: (313)226-9736*
Detroit, Michigan 48226   *Facsimile: (313)226-2372*

November 26, 2001

Dearborn, MI 48126

Dear

    As you know, law enforcement officers and federal agents have been acquiring information that may be helpful in determining the persons responsible for the September 11th attacks on the World Trade Center and the Pentagon. Furthermore, they are pursuing all leads that may assist in preventing any further attacks. I am asking that you assist us in this important investigation.

    Your name was brought to our attention because, among other things, you came to Michigan on a visa from a country where there are groups that support, advocate, or finance international terrorism. **We have no reason to believe that you are, in any way, associated with terrorist activities.** Nevertheless, you may know something that could be helpful in our efforts. In fact, it is quite possible that you have information that may seem irrelevant to you but which may help us piece together this puzzle.

    Please contact my office to set up an interview at a location, date, and time that is convenient for you. During this interview, you will be asked questions that could reasonably assist in the efforts to learn about those who support, commit, or associate with persons who commit terrorism.

    While this interview is voluntary, it is crucial that the investigation be broad based and thorough, and the interview is important to achieve that goal. We need to hear from you as soon as possible - **by December 4.** Please call my office at (313) 226-9665 between 9:00 a.m. and 5:00 p.m. any day, including Saturday and Sunday. We will work with you to accommodate your schedule.

Yours truly,

JEFFREY COLLINS
United States Attorney

ROBERT P. CARES
Assistant United States Attorney

*The case of the "LA 8" in the late eighties, and subsequent Anti-Terrorist Act of 1996, prefigured the sweeping curtailment of civil liberties after the September 11 terrorist attacks on the United States. Here is an example of the USA Patriot Act in action: a US Attorney letter to an Arab-American resident of Dearborn, MI, requesting an FBI interview because "you came to Michigan on a visa from a country where there are groups that support, advocate, or finance international terrrorism." (*Arab American National Museum)

264

–EIGHT–

STUMBLING TOWARD PEACE
(1984–2000)

THE CASES OF ALEX ODEH AND THE LA 8

In the wake of disillusionment following the Lebanon War, two incidents in Los Angeles in the mid-1980s would rock the community nationwide. One was the assassination of an Arab-American leader—the first in the community's history. It had a sizable chilling effect on the community's activism. The other were the arrests of seven Arab nationals and one Kenyan on charges of espousing "world Communism." The case of what came to be known as "The LA 8," was a harbinger of unprecedented clamps on civil liberties after the attacks of September 11.

In a tragic assault that still simmers under the surface of the Arab-American community twenty years later—the case is still open—on October 11, 1985, the West Coast director of ADC opened the door to his Santa Ana office and was killed by a pipe bomb explosion, the result of a trip-wire device. Several others were injured and the building sustained massive damage. Alex Odeh, 44, the father of three young girls, taught at a local community college. He had made the mistake of calling for talks with the PLO on a radio program the night before (his condemnation of the Achille Lauro hijacking, however, was not broadcast). Born in Jifna, Palestine, he became a US citizen in 1977. In Los Angeles, Irv Rubin, the Jewish Defense League's head, who had been arrested by then 36 times, said that he "shed no tears" and that Odeh "got what he deserved."

Within a year, the FBI indicated that four suspects, all with dual Israeli-American citizenship and all members of the Jewish Defense League (JDL), had fled the United States and were living in the West Bank settlement of Kiryat Arba. Israel rejected repeated attempts at cooperation or extradition. Finally, in 1991, one of the suspects, Robert Manning, was arrested by the Israelis, extradited in 1993 and, in 1994, sentenced to life in prison without parole for another murder—the mail bomb killing of Patricia Wilkerson.[1] In 1994,

Manning's wife died in an Israeli jail before extradition. After years of prodding by the ADC, in 1996, the FBI issued a $1 million reward for information leading to the arrest of the killers of Alex Odeh. Alongside the FBI's Top 10 Most Wanted for Los Angeles website, Odeh is listed as one of three key victims for which it is "seeking information."

A memorial statue to Alex Odeh was erected in front of the Santa Ana library in 1994, but in 1997 it was vandalized. In 1998, a detective novel loosely based on the Odeh killing was published: *Raising the Dead* by Roger Simon. A reviewer said, "Simon demonstrates shrewdly that the road to fascism is paved by people who never question anything, including themselves... Moses Wine doesn't crack the case until he dons Arab garb, a kind of Jewish *Black Like Me*. Predictably, he feels the sting of prejudice."[2]

In December 2001, the FBI arrested two men in Los Angeles it suspected of planning attacks against Muslim and Arab-American organizations in the United States: Irv Rubin, chairman of the JDL, and JDL member Earl Krueger. Many in the Arab American community suspected that they were involved in the Alex Odeh case, as well. Rubin was said to have committed suicide in his jail cell in Los Angeles in 2002.

Less troubling than the Odeh case, but with greater civil liberty ramifications, the matter of the LA 8, too, remains unresolved. On January 26, 1987, FBI and INS agents in Los Angeles arrested six Palestinians and a Kenyan, seeking to deport them under provisions of a long discredited and soon-to-be repealed McCarran–Walter Act of 1952, itself created at the height of the "Red scare" during the McCarthy era. One week later, another Palestinian was arrested. The eight were charged with belonging to a terrorist organization (the Popular Front for the Liberation of Palestine, or PFLP) that advocated the "doctrines of world communism." For a time, the LA 8 were held in maximum security cells.

Although the PFLP conducted airplane hijackings in the 1970s, in the sixteen-year history of the LA 8 case, the US government has never demonstrated that the eight suspects were ever involved with such activity, nor that they have been guilty of any unlawful or violent act. They all denied PFLP membership. Instead, the matter at hand has been "guilt by association," a canard used liberally under the terms of the Patriot Act after September 11 to incarcerate, arrest, or deport people as various as the head of a charity and a college student.

Within two months of their arrest, FBI director William Webster admitted to Congress that the eight "had not been found to have engaged themselves in terrorist activity."[3] Yet the case went on and on, including four trips to the appeals court and a review by the Supreme Court that generated watershed rulings supporting citizens' First Amendment rights. Comparing the LA 8 action with FBI zealousness to shut down an American-based El Salvador solidarity committee, two authors said, "the FBI's preoccupation with political activity, in particular with statements critical of the US government and its foreign allies, overwhelmed any investigative interest in uncovering evidence of violent crimes."[4]

Indeed, language in the FBI case against the LA 8 rang similar to that used in COINTELPRO, the agency's discredited attempt to harass and curtail anti-Vietnam war protests in the 1960s and 1970s. What really was at stake here were the LA 8's alleged political activities on behalf of the PFLP, activities that had not led to the deportation of supporters of the Nicaraguan Contras, the Afghan mujaheddin, or various anti-Castro groups, all of which had used violence to obtain their goals. In January 1994, a district court in Los Angeles ruled that the LA 8 had been selectively targeted for deportation and blocked their expulsion from the country on First Amendment grounds. A US Court of Appeals upheld the ruling a year later, citing the need for a "principle of tolerance for different voices" in times of crisis, pointing out excesses toward foreigners as far back as 1798 and in the Palmer Raids of the first "Red scare" in 1919–1920.

There appears to have been preparation by the justice department shortly before the arrest of the LA 8 for rounding up people whose political activities were undesirable, whether they were a physical threat or not. In November 1986, two months before the LA 8 were put behind bars, an Alien Border Control Committee at the justice department circulated a document entitled, "Alien Terrorists and Undesirables: A Contingency Plan." The plan proposed building a detention camp in a remote area of Louisiana to hold such "undesirables" until they could be expelled. To top things off, the Arab-American mayor of Oakdale told ABC's *Nightline* it would be "good for business"![5]

Whatever its artful dodge of a title (which smacked of control of Mexicans along the porous southern border), the Alien Border Control Committee listed students from Arab countries whose visas had expired and identified certain countries, all Arab, as being likely origins of terrorist aliens.[6] It was just this Louisiana concentration camp that Reps. Mary Rose Oakar and Nick Joe Rahall called into question face to face with the FBI in the late 1980s, and it is apparently a camp that one member of the US Civil Rights Commission believed in 2002 Arab Americans might be scurried to if there were another terrorist attack like September 11.

In 1986, FBI agents produced a 1,300-page report on the PFLP's "support activities" in Los Angeles, all of which were lawful and nonviolent. It tracked distribution of the group's literature "with an intensity usually reserved for shipments of illegal drugs."[7] One of the eight, Ayman Obeid, was accused of was carrying an anti-American slogan while protesting Israel's invasion of Lebanon.

In 1987, the ADC (and other Arab American, Irish, and immigrant rights' groups) sued the federal government over its surveillance and the sequestering of the LA 8 (*Arab American Anti-Discrimination Committee vs. Meese*, and later *vs. Reno*). The government's mammoth 10,000-page defense of the LA 8 arrests pointed to, among other events, three dinner dances held by Palestinian Americans in southern California. These *haflis*, hundreds if not thousands of which are held across the country each year, raised money for charities. Judge Stephen Wilson in his landmark 1989 rulings two years after the LA 8 were arrested found FBI agents woefully remiss for their misunderstanding or misidentifying of legitimate fundraisers for legitimate charities. He pointed out the government itself had noted as legitimate a fundraiser that it later used as evidence for deportation.

In February 1999, in a "stunning reversal," (Cole's and Dempsey's words) the Supreme Court ruled that Congress had stripped it of power to review selective enforcement of immigration laws. The Court basically said the LA 8 had no right to object to deportations if they belonged to terrorist organizations. In essence, the decision left all immigrants to the United States who did not have citizenship with no First Amendment rights to political expression or activity. It was a set-up for the Patriot Act. It was no surprise, then, that after September 11, Muslims were rounded up by the thousands and questioned, some held in detention for months or even years.

THE COLEICO DOLL AND THE FIRST INTIFADA

Leaving no doubt that long before September 11 Arabs were seen in the culture as inescapably brutal, one of the largest toy manufacturers in the United States, Coleico Industries, created a "Nomad" doll in its "Enemies of Rambo" series. This doll was dressed in traditional Arab clothes and described in its packaging as "a marauding Bedouin," a "heartless terrorist," and the leader of "a band of cutthroats and thieves." Rambo himself looked like a nice guy by comparison.

During the Christmas 1986 season, ADC joined peace organizations opposed to war toys to oppose in particular this Coleico doll. Demonstrations were held at toy stores as shoppers filled their carts; Coleico was bombarded by letters and phone calls from Arab Americans and others amazed that such a thing could be peddled on the occasion of the birth of the Prince of Peace (who was, after all, a Semite and may have worn clothes not dissimilar to the Enemy of Rambo).

It worked. Coleico pulled its TV ads for the Nomad doll and ultimately took it off the market. It was the first time ever that a manufacturer of war toys deleted an item because of public pressure.

In that same year, Elektra Records put out a song by The Cure, a popular British rock group, called "Killing an Arab." The song was not as horrid as its title indicated; in fact, the lyrics were based on incidents in Albert Camus's classic novel, *The Stranger*, and were not defamatory toward Arabs. Camus himself, of course, was born and raised among Arabs in Algeria and was sympathetic to the Algerian revolution against France. Unfortunately, some American disc jockeys took what was manifestly an anti-prejudice song and played off and even harped on the title in anti-Arab comments. The Cure itself was alarmed when it got wind of what was happening. The music group sent a letter to hundreds of rock radio stations nationwide asking that "Killing an Arab" not be played. A press conference was held in January 1987 in which The Cure's manager Chris Parry expressed dismay at how the song's intent had been twisted. Parry also announced an agreement with Electra Records and ADC that put a sticker on one million albums, audio cassettes, compact disks, and videocassettes that said "Killing an Arab" is "a song which decries the existence of all prejudice and consequent violence. The Cure condemns its use in furthering anti-Arab feeling."

What had started with a skewing of artistic intention ended up a national lesson in racial sensitivity concerning Arabs. The *coup de grace* was The Cure's August 11, 1987 benefit, concert at New York's Ritz, which raised $35,000 to benefit Palestinian and Lebanese orphans. It was a deft turnaround.

Among the many movies that fed the Arab stereotype released in the 1980s in the run up to the first Palestinian intifada and first US invasion of Arab countries (Kuwait and Iraq), one that stood out as particularly offensive was *Ishtar*, which starred Warren Beatty and Dustin Hoffman, two otherwise politically sensitive, and in the case of Beatty, outspoken actors. Though ADC went to the pre-release screening, it was too late to affect script changes; the film came out in spring 1987. Among the objectionable contents in the film were an injunction to "go act Arab" (con people), a cheating Arab cabbie, a beautiful Arab girl (Isabelle Adjani) who plainly admits, "Western culture is superior," and offensive song lyrics, such as those in "I Look to Mecca," which kicks around the Muslim prayer. Film historian and critic Jack Shaheen also noted that during the filming in Morocco the same day Israeli planes bombed Tunisia next door, an interviewer asked Dustin Hoffman if he felt in any danger. "[Only] when you can't make it to the bathroom," Hoffman sighed.[8]

One week before the release date, ADC jumped into the breach and contacted 150 film critics and brought their attention to negative distortions about Arab culture and behavior that ran throughout the film. The film was panned by most critics, and not just for its crassness about race. One of the first times the Arab-American community actively questioned a major motion picture's objectionable content, the *Ishtar* campaign itself received heavy media interest, including a feature on *Entertainment Tonight*.

As for fiction, the 1984 appearance of a Leon Uris novel, *The Haj*, did not signal any intellectual growth on the author's part. If possible, it is even more biased than *Exodus*, which in 1958 set a novelistic blueprint for how to frame the Superman Israeli vs. the abject, undependable, hopelessly unstable Arab. Thirty years after its appearance, *Exodus*, with its repetitive use of "a quarter of a million kill-crazy Arabs at your throats," had sold twenty million copies worldwide, a veritable foreign policy *Uncle Tom's Cabin* (except Uncle Tom was nicer). In *The Haj*, Uris upped the ante; he let an Arab stereotype himself: "We do not have leave to love one another and we have long ago lost the ability. It was so written 1,200 years earlier. Hate is our overpowering legacy."[9] Several Arab-American groups protested *The Haj*'s gross racism. Its sales did not match those of *Exodus* and it was almost universally panned. At this time Casey Kasem gave a breakthrough speech against the long line of Arab stereotyping in the film industry directly to a board of the directors of the Screen Actors Guild (SAG). He asked the Guild to make a general statement to its members to try harder to provide balance in dealing with Arabs as characters or Middle Eastern themes. Was the public—and the industry—becoming more savvy, or was it too late?

A doll, a song, a movie, a novel. William Blake wrote in "The Foundation of Empire," "Empire follows art." Even bad art, one must add; in the case of American Middle East policy and the myths on which it has rested, extremely bad art has foreshadowed extremely bad policy. In any event, with US public opinion hardened by such trash to the point of indifference or fear or revulsion (kidnappings and car bombings during the mid-1980s in Lebanon, mindless retaliations for the siege of Beirut, did not help matters), in an atmosphere in which Reagan was facing off with Andropov and later Gorbachav missile-to-missile in Europe, fearing their cause had been completely forgotten or derided, in the face of continued Israeli repression, the Palestinians revolted with stones.

Arab Americans were drawn into the fray, quite literally, when fourteen-year-old Amjad Jibril, an American citizen, was shot and killed by the IDF on the West Bank at the peak of the revolt. The ADC accompanied two of his cousins stateside to the state department and demanded an investigation into the murder. Steadily the body count rose, mostly of stone-throwing youth. In the period of the first intifada (1987–1993), about 1,100 Palestinian civilians were killed (one-quarter children) and 100 Israelis (6 children). About 850 homes sheltering 3,000 people were bulldozed or sealed, and 50,000 Palestinians thrown in prison, some subjected to grotesque conditions and held without charges or trial. Several spectacular massacres occurred, including that of seven Palestinian unarmed workers picking olives in a grove and later twenty Palestinians at the Temple Mount in Jerusalem near the Muslim holy site of the al-Aqsa mosque. The Israeli government alleged that the soldiers were protecting Jews as they worshipped at the Wailing Wall. But a CBS *60 Minutes* report demonstrated conclusively that the Palestinians began throwing stones only after the IDF soldiers fired indiscriminately into the crowd, and that no Jewish worshipers were in the area at the time. Several dozen Israeli soldiers were court-martialed for their brutality, but no one above the level of major. Certainly not Col. Yehuda Meir "who had ordered soldiers to break the legs and arms of Palestinians" throwing stones, nor "shoot and cry" Gen. Amram Mitzna.[10]

Unique demonstrations stateside were held in solidarity with the intifada and its comparative restraint. In San Francisco, the Palestine Aid Society sent messages to the Israeli soldier asking him to desist and otherwise play golf, that were tied to balloons and released over Golden Gate Park and San Francisco Bay. The Council of the Presidents of National Arab American Organizations took part in a symbolic dumping of food in front of the Israeli Embassy in Washington, DC, to protest Israel's effort to crush the uprising by starving it out with a food blockade. Also in Washington, under its new president, Abdeen Jabara, a subway ad blitz by the ADC took place. Lifting a phrase from Nancy Reagan (used in the "war" on drugs), 350 ADC posters urged Metro riders to "just say no" to unconditional aid to Israel. One poster sported an Israeli soldier raising the butt end of his rifle over a cringing young Palestinian woman with the title, "Israel Putting Your Tax Dollars to Work." Though hit with intense criticism from some Jewish organizations, the DC Metro Board refused to censor the posters or throw them out. Another poster urging a two-state solution to the crisis reached an estimated 600,000 subway riders daily.

No one would have thought Sherman Oaks, California, had anything to do with the death of Palestinian infants during the intifada, but it did. Tear gas, liberally used by the Israeli Army on mosques, hospitals, and schools, had lethal effect on some infants, children, and the elderly; ADC secured a victory May 5 in getting TransTechnology Corporation of Sherman Oaks to stop shipment of its tear gas to Israel.

A sort of "Children's Crusade" in reverse, the first intifada captured the world's sympathy and drew many individuals to the area for a first-time first-hand look at what the Palestinians were facing. Of course, the IDF did its best to scrub the news and demonstrate how vicious were these kids with stones. ADC launched an

"Eyewitness Israel" project sending Americans from many fields—medicine, law, journalism, religion, human rights, education, and the US Congress—to monitor and take down notes on human rights abuses, as well as live with Palestinian families as they endured the crackdown. One such eyewitness was chased by Israeli soldiers who fired at him; he lived to run another day. Another reported witnessing a 10-year-old Palestinian boy shot for raising his hand in a "V." Some eyewitnesses unmasked the miserable conditions of Arab prisoners in south Lebanon's notorious Ansar III camp.

One of the more intriguing experiments in encouraging people-to-people alliances (the official US policy was still not to talk to the PLO) was ADC's taking to the occupied terrories under siege a group of mayors and their wives from Palestine, Texas; Palestine, Arkansas; and East Palestine, Ohio, as well as Hebron, Indiana; and Hebron, North Dakota. Most had had scant knowledge of the Middle East and admitted they viewed Palestinians as nothing more than terrorists before the trip. They came back changed.

Not all the consciousness raising, however, made it into the state department's yearly human rights report covering the occupied territories of Israel. In fact, reports of Israeli abuses during the intifada from the US consul general himself were deleted or whitewashed by the assistant secretary of state for human rights, Richard Schifter, who in a former life had been the founder of the Jewish Institute for National Security Affairs. Still, the 1988 state department report on human rights violations did state, "[Israeli] soldiers frequently used gunfire in situations that did not present mortal danger to troops, causing many avoidable deaths and injuries." Scrubbed or not, it was better than the norm.

Shortly after a unique ABC special, "*Nightline* from the Holy Land" that featured West Bank university administrator Dr. Hanan Mikhail-Ashrawi among the town meeting discussants, Ashrawi toured fourteen American cities and was warmly received. She addressed everyone from the Los Angeles World Affairs Council to several Jewish organizations. Ashrawi was very much the human—and articulate—face of the intifada to those abroad.

Novelist Gore Vidal traveled from Italy to address the 1988 ADC national convention. Worrying openly about an American empire gone wrong through client states in the Middle East such as Israel, Iraq, and Saudi Arabia that routinely abused human rights, Vidal was most concerned about "the fearful silence" in the states about Israel's suppression of the intifada and policy toward Palestinians in general.

On April 26, 1988, the Congressional Black Caucus held unprecedented hearings on the Palestinian uprising. Testimony came from the preeminent spokesperson for the Palestinian cause in the United States, Edward Said, as well as Ibrahim Abu-Lughod, Israeli

Knesset member and retired general Matti Peled, West Bank attorney Raja Shehadeh, SUNY professor Angela Gilliam, and Abdeen Jabara, who again brought up violations of the US Arms Export Control Act. The intifada hearings were among the first carried into American homes by the cable television station C-SPAN. These hearings led to high level discussions between Secretary of State George Schultz and Said and Abu-Lughod that ultimately opened diplomatic exchanges between the US and the PLO.

African-American concern for the Palestinian uprising worked its way into the unusual presidential campaign of Jesse Jackson, whose interest in the Middle East was not entirely new. In 1979, Jackson had visited Lebanon with other African-American leaders while it was being subjected to Israeli bombings and returned, he had said, a changed man. Now the founder of the Arab American Institute, Jim Zogby, was taken into his campaign as one of its directors, with the thought that maybe Arab-American pockets might be as deep as those of Jewish Americans. Jackson didn't get swamped by Arab-American contributions, though he did win an astounding victory in the Michigan primary. Michigan's sizable Arab-American population made a difference, as well as the barnstorming on Jackson's behalf by native Michiganian disc jockey Casey Kasem and his actress wife Jean. For only the second time in history, an Arab American (Zogby) got placed into a list of nominating speakers (for Jackson) at the 1988 Democratic National Convention in Detroit (Mary Rose Oakar had been one of the nominators of Jerry Brown in 1980).

In 1989, under the direction of lawyer Albert Mokhiber, ADC established a legal division that significantly increased its activities. These included a challenge to Israel's favored duty-free trade status under provisions of trade law that require protection of workers' rights, in this case, in the occupied territories. The tariff privileges were reviewed but not revoked in a spring 1989 decision by US Trade Representative Carla Hills. To help several hundred Palestinian Americans with issues like land confiscation, harrassment, and family unification denial, ADC opened a Jerusalem office, with local journalist Dauod Kuttab as its director. In another attempt to get a handle on Israel's lock on American special favors, six prominent Americans filed a 1989 complaint with the Federal Election Commission (FEC) that AIPAC and 27 other pro-Israel PACs routinely violate campaign finance laws. By September 1988, pro-Israel PACs had contributed $2.3 million to federal election campaigns. The six men who filed the complaint included former Undersecretary of State George Ball, former Illinois US Rep. Paul Findley, and three former US ambassadors. Release of AIPAC documents was anticipated as a bumper crop of evidence on how American elections are bought. But the complaint was rejected.

For years critics of the Palestinian national movement have decried the absence of a Palestianian "Martin Luther King"—a leader totally devoted to nonviolence. One of the ironies of this position is that at the height of the remarkably restrained first intifada, a Quaker-educated man who openly espoused nonviolence was deported by the Israelis from the West Bank. For a time, this man, Mubarak Awad, spoke across the United States, took American citizenship through marriage, then dropped out of sight. The British never threw Gandhi out of India.

But the intifada and its stones had hit home in the recesses of the American conscience. Soon American officials were actively engaging the PLO. In Algiers, the Palestine National Council had voted for a two-state solution and acceptance of Israel at the height of the intifada, a bending over backwards whose efficacy was impossible to deny. Kissinger's "no PLO talk" was finally breached. The breakthrough 1991 conference in Madrid that brought Israeli, PLO, Arab, and American officials together for the first time was launched by virtue of young brave hands of children far off. But before the herky-jerky, by turns exciting, dispiriting, and finally, hopeless Oslo peace process began, Saddam Hussein had ideas of empire, and the United States was only too willing to let him into the fanciful trap.

THE FIRST GULF WAR TRIGGERS HATE CRIMES

On July 25, 1990, Iraqi president Saddam Hussein met with US ambassador to Iraq April Glaspie. The subject of Kuwait came up; the Iraqis noted that Kuwait was slip-streaming oil from across its border with Iraq from Iraqi oil fields. Glaspie made vague reference to the United States "not taking sides" in intra-Arab disputes. Hussein, not surprisingly, took the neutrality as a green light to invade Kuwait and on August 2, that is exactly what he did.

Alarmed when Saddam marched right into Kuwait City, pillaged the place, and starting renaming streets with Iraqi patriot names, the first President Bush hit the tom-toms of war himself. There was, after all, a lot of oil at stake. As for Glaspie, she was whisked out of sight and out of government service.

Arab-Americans, like most Americans, were not interested in shedding American blood for oil; the prospect of liberating a corrupt sheikdom from a corrupt dictator was none too appealing. But most of the community's groups did condemn Iraq's violation of Kuwait's borders and spoke strongly in favor of United Nations resolutions calling for Saddam's expeditious withdrawal. The ADC in particular warned about insertion of American troops into the dispute and counseled that mediation by the Arab League might just solve the problem. The organization delivered a petition signed by 6,000 Arab

Americans to the Iraqi Embassy in Washington calling on Iraq to allow safe exit of all foreign nationals from Iraq and Kuwait immediately, but also to withdraw its forces from Kuwait.

Civilian casualties if the United States entered the fray were an urgent concern in an ADC letter that feared that "children and innocent civilians will face deprivation of basic necessities resulting in tragic consequences." The United States does not enter most frays timidly, but with the full brunt of its technological force. Civilians are inevitably hit. But not even ADC could have foreseen the death from bad water, lack of medicine, and illness that visited a half a million Iraqi children in the decade following the war, when Iraq endured crippling UN sanctions while it destroyed weapons of mass destruction.

Though at the last moment of the last withdrawal deadline King Hussein of Jordan appeared to have made a breakthrough with Saddam, and Arab League negotiating seemed to be paying off, President Bush had amassed such an impressive array of nations and armies on his side (including Syria and Turkey) that it seemed almost a shame not to use them. What a carnival! It's very hard to fold such tents without a high-wire act. The United States with its coalition forces began bombardment of Iraqi forces in Kuwait on January 16, 1991. Within a week of the start of the ground war (February 23), coalition forces had chased the hapless Saddam back into Iraq, stopping for the cease-fire about halfway up the country shy of Baghdad and the holy cities of Najaf and Karbala. In hindsight it was probably a wise decision, though many, even doves who did not want the invasion (including myself) thought the uprising of the Shi'ites and Kurds deserved support; we were in the country—we might as well finish the job. The job, as we now know too well from the second war in Iraq under the second Bush, is hopelessly complex and too expensive in lives and treasure to be worth it.

Many displaced Iraqis found themselves in refugee camps in Saudi Arabia. After two years in a dusty camp, Majid Aljaberi walked across the desert back into Iraq, only to discover his family property confiscated. He was arrested and told never to leave again, under pain of retribution on his relatives. But he did escape to Jordan. In the US, he had trouble getting work as a doctor, and changed his name to Mitch Freedman.

Another refugee from the 1991 war—and winner of a 2003 ADC essay contest about the ordeal—Leila Almallaki was only six at the time: "Hell urged its bitterness on the land. Black rain fell from the sky." After five years in a ramshackle camp in Saudi Arabia, Leila was resettled in Michigan.

By the time the smoke cleared from oil wells set on fire by Saddam and chemical dumps exploded by American shellfire (the source, many thought, of the mysterious Gulf War Syndrome that would afflict an estimated 15,000 GIs), 150,000 Iraqis and 246 US soldiers had died. (One-third of US soldiers by friendly fire). To pundits, it looked like a whopping success. It was certainly a slaughter. The Kuwaitis, of course, were grateful for their freedom.

But there were costs. In the midst of the conflict, MacArthur fellow and renowned environmentalist Gary Paul Nabhan hiked the southwest Arizona desert:

> I ponder those conflicts in the Middle East from my perspective as an Arab American... Here, in the late 1970s, the US military reputedly prepared for the ill-fated helicopter raid into Iran's arid turf to free American hostages, and more recently, it used this land to prepare its troops for Operation Desert Storm.

During the fighting Nabhan discovers from a Middle East geographer that the Nabhan tribe in Saudi Arabia was ascendant for two centuries in the Middle Ages, but what he really wants to know is the origin of human aggression, and thus he contemplates "dive bombing" hummingbirds. In his wonderful essay, "Hummingbirds and Human Aggression," he notes the struggle for water in the desert, when the Papagos took revenge only when Apaches and other migrants sucked up a year's supply of water. Plenty decreases aggression, in both hummingbird and man.

Startled by a soldier who shoos him from camping in a bombing range, Nabhan says of both Arizona and the Persian Gulf, "Scars left by military vehicles will be seen in the vegetation patterns and soils for a hundred to a thousand years." The Gulf war had left the desert in places "biologically sterile...[as] massive defense berms and count-less bomb craters interrupted watercourses." Over 9,000 tons of undetected explosives were left behind in desert areas by the US military, and carbon soot and acid rain from the Gulf oil fires were found as far away as the Himalayas and the Blue Nile "in unprecedented levels."

Nabhan concludes, palms open to the hummingbird in its fragile search for even a sip of food in a harsh world, giving off beauty as it goes:

> If Bush or Hussein had the mentality of a hummingbird, it would be clear to them that the resources crucial to our survival are no longer economically or ecologically defensible through territorial behavior. These resources are too diffuse, too globally interdependent, to be worth the risks both leaders have placed before us.[11]

Among those risks was a backlash against the Arab-American community at a level unseen before. With an American invasion force for the first time facing off against Arab troops, it did not matter that they were doing so to save "good Arabs" in Kuwait. What the man-on-the-street in Poughkeepsie saw was open season on any neighbor with a dark cast to his face. Many times they were of Arab origin; sometimes they were not, such as the Iranian-American family in Maryland attacked in its home. The doll, the song, the movie, the book over time take their toll.

Hate crimes against people of Arab origin (or thought to be so) hit record highs during the Gulf war. In 1990, ADC logged 39 hate crimes, only 4 prior to Iraq's invasion of Kuwait. But in 1991, 119 such hate crimes were recorded by ADC. This level of violence and threat to the community had never taken place before. They included, in 1991, four acts involving a bomb, five arsons, two shooting incidents, and twelve acts of physical assault. These figures did not include other kinds of intimidation, such as the upsurge in disc jockeys and talk show hosts on the Arab rampage (one announcer told his listeners to monitor the activities and movements of Arab American neighbors!). Neither were difficulties in obtaining a rental unit, harassment in airlines, or tasteless ads tallied (one tee-shirt popular at the time of the Gulf war had an Arab in the cross-hairs of a rifle with the slogan, "I'd fly 10,000 miles to smoke [military jargon for blast] a camel.") As always, some incidents were bizarre in their utter misidentification, but obvious in their hatred. For example, while America was freeing Kuwaitis, a Kuwaiti man delivering a pizza in San Francisco was attacked and beaten. In Baltimore, Maryland, five drunks shouted obscenities at a man, yelling "Filthy Arab! Arab pig!" He was a Polynesian Jew.

ADC thought that, "to a very limited extent" the unprecedented increase in hate crimes had to do with a "heightened awareness" on the Arab-American community's part and a willingness to report them, as well as a more sophisticated infrastructure at ADC to monitor the activities. But that wasn't the gist: "It is impossible to escape the conclusion that US entry into active hostilities with an Arab country resulted in a stunning escalation of hate crimes committed against Arab Americans and other persons of other ethnic origin who were mistaken for them."[12]

To its credit, the Anti-Defamation League of B'nai B'rith in a press release condemned attacks against Arab Americans as "unacceptable manifestations of bigotry." Unfortunately, on Israeli human rights abuses the ADL kept its powder dry.

Like all wars, the Gulf war was not tidy, and the stainless, spotless "smart" bombs somehow managed to kill and maim those its intelligent circuitry had supposedly been wired to save, or at least avoid. On February 13, 1991, 300 men, women, and children crammed into a Baghdad bomb shelter were blasted into body parts and blood by an American gunner far from the scene of the crime who will never be known or disciplined.

Whether palliative or true contrition, on Memorial Day weekend in 1991, President Bush gathered leaders of the Arab-American community and several prominent American writers to dedicate the first national monument to a member of the community on federal park land, in fact, the first such monument in the nation's capital to an American writer. It was the Kahlil Gibran Memorial. Certainly there were more worthy American writers to enstatue: Walt Whitman, Herman Melville, T.S. Eliot, Ernest Hemingway, to name a few. Even Mikhail Naimy might have been a better pick on literary grounds. But the community would take it as an honest, humanizing gesture at conciliation by the president.

At the 1991 dedication of the Gibran Memorial Garden, in Washington, DC, are left to right: poets Pablo Medina, Naomi Shihab Nye, and Reed Whittemore. Author's son Andy stands in front of the bronze bust of Gibran. (Gregory Orfalea)

Looking over the crowd, spotting Mike Baroody, who tirelessly championed the memorial throughout a battle with cancer he never mentioned to anyone, I thought of Gibran's great poem, "Defeat" in which he talks of defeat as his "bold companion," his "deathless courage," with whom he would "stand in the sun with a will/And we will be dangerous." It was a warning on that fall day. Did America understand the power, not to mention the anger, of the underdog that we were creating in the Arab world with our policies? One had hopes, at least then, that Bush would turn from his liberation of Kuwait and victory over Saddam to finally settle the Palestinian issue. Watching him wink at one of our sons as I held him up that day, I thought Bush might just finally right the primary festering wrong in US foreign policy. Hopes shined that day in marble brought from a great Druze manor in the Lebanon mountain, but slowly faded, as the marble itself faded and the Gibran Memorial grass grew tall and unkempt by the Park Service. One of the two giant cedars brought from Lebanon to shade Gibran along Massachusetts Avenue withered and died.

THE OSLO PEACE PROCESS

President Bush moved quickly after the Gulf war, in which American troops had "shielded Israel" from danger (that is, a hegemonic Iraq) to pressure the Israelis, at long last, to face their Palestinian neighbors and make peace. He had shed American blood, his most powerful card in this dangerous matter, and he declared he was not going backward to the status quo ante. He was going to make that blood count for something other than a free oil sheikdom.

Emboldened by the PLO's recognition of Israel in 1988 as well as the return of the Labor Party to power in Israel, Bush encouraged a back-channel PLO–Israel dialogue in Oslo under the auspices of Norway's foreign minister. Soon what became known as the "Oslo Accords" began to emerge, a framework, it was said, for all matters in dispute between the two parties—including the toughest issues, such as the final status of Jerusalem, the settlements, and the right of return of Palestinians. In 1991, barely had the cinders of the Gulf war settled when an extraordinary conference was held in Madrid under US auspices, strongly reinforced by the presence of Secretary of State James Baker, with representatives of the major players in the area, including Israel, Syria, Jordan, Egypt, Lebanon, and the PLO. It was a version of the Geneva Conference proposed in 1977 that had never materialized.

Bush made no bones about his intention to secure a deal and through Baker he threatened to cut off aid to Israel if it continued settling the territories during this critical phase of peace negotiations. Baker announced a four-month moratorium on issuing $10 billion in loan guarantees to Israel. It was later said that his son George W. believed his father's downfall in the 1992 election was due to this "get tough" policy with the Israelis in which hard-line Jewish–American coffers were emptied on Bill Clinton's table. In fact the aid was never cut off.

At first, negotiators for the Palestinians were linked to a Jordanian delegation. In January–February 1992 they toured the United States in care of the ADC after bilateral peace negotiations with the Israelis in Washington, DC. They visited Chicago, Cincinnati, Detroit, Los Angeles, Houston, Austin, Texas, Seattle, Miami, Phoenix, and Dallas. They spoke at universities, banquets, and were interviewed by the media. In Los Angeles, popular radio talk show host Michael Jackson queried Dr. Fayez Tarawneh of Jordan and Palestinian delegate Sami Keilani. For the first time in memory, the context of these contacts was positive and not adversarial or accusatory. The "peace fever" was spreading.

At the same time, attempts to "super-legitimize" Israeli settlements—which still had not stopped growing or spreading—took place, and Arab-American organizations and others jumped into the fray. For example, the University of New Haven was approached by an Israeli technical institute to establish an overseas campus in an Israeli settlement on the West Bank. Projected enrollment at this "Ha-Sharon" campus (an apochryphal name!) was 7,000. UNH was pummeled with protests organized by the Middle East Studies Association (MESA) with its 2,300 academics worldwide, as well as the Israeli Peace Now movement, the ADC, American churches, and the US state department. Even the *Chronicle of Higher Education*, hardly a journal that enters Middle East fires, editorialized against it. The scheme was dropped.

Extremists on both sides of the ledger, sensing the compromises real peace will always contain, struck in various ways. In December, 415 Palestinians were expelled into southern Lebanon. Shortly afterward four American citizens were arrested on the West Bank by Israel. The group were held incommunicado for nine days, denied bail or lawyer, and listened to supposed "confessions" (to "service in an illegal organization") in Hebrew, which they did not understand. After six months, one of them, Mohammed Jarad, was allowed to return to his hometown of Chicago, Illinois. Pressure from the state department eventually helped secure his release. But there was never any trial nor were any allegations substantiated—an Israeli harbinger of the Patriot Act.

As for the Arab hardline, a blow was struck closer to home. On February 26, 1993, members of a cell of terrorists centered around a New Jersey imam bombed the basement of the World Trade Center, killing six and leaving 1,000 injured. It was the first instance of mass killing by Arabs on American soil and it sent shock-waves throughout the nation, especially the Arab-American community, which now knew two stark facts: 1) their worst fears about an Arab attack on American soil over policies Arab Americans had long warned about were now realized, and 2) they could be targeted by bigots. In both cases, the community felt betrayed—by pathetic blood brothers and by callous fellow citizens. It was quietly terrifying.

Still, there was no mincing of words about what had happened. On March 5, the ADC hand-delivered a letter to President Clinton at the White House which expressed "grief and disgust" at the WTC bombing and noted that "several Arab-American businesses are tenants of the World Trade Center many of whom undoubtedly were among the victims." In a press release the day before, ADC President Albert Mokhiber cautioned:

> We urge the authorities not to draw any conclusions based on suspicion or unproved allegations. We urge the authorities to fully investigate this matter so that whoever is the culprit can be brought to justice. We see a danger in making quick arrests which result in a failure to pursue all the evidence and leads in such cases.

These were times when vigilance was round-the-clock: to keep the fragile, but real, moves toward peace on track and to stamp out escalation of prejudice or extremism. In August, when the Mississippi civil defense director led law enforcement officials in drills statewide against a mock terrorist group called "Arabs Against Americans," ADC objected. An apology from the state of Mississippi ensued and the drill was renamed "Anyone Against Americans." A minor victory, perhaps, but these were jittery times.

Sometimes the stereotyping wasn't so obvious or irony was put in play. For example, playing on the World Trade Center bombing, the July 26, 1993 issue of the *New Yorker* featured a sketch of boys at the beach building sand castles of the skyline of New York, while one boy dressed in Arab *kufiya* and dark glasses (with freckles) leaps toward the Twin Towers in sand to crush them. The other boys look up alarmed. Tina Brown, the *New Yorker's* editor, explained in a meeting with ADC officials in October that the cover tried to evoke the fears in America over the bombing and to demonstrate how quickly the stereotype could be appropriated by children. The ADC argued that the irony was too subtle, that most people would simply see Arabs as childish destroyers. In the December 27, 1993 issue, ADC president Albert Mokhiber's letter to the editor was published, warning that the cover didn't combat ethnic bigotry but might "actually enflame it." A tough call, but one I think ADC probably won by a nose. At the same time, the ADC asked the *New Yorker* to publish stories about the community. After a piece about an Arab American spraying a van of Jewish students with bullets and one about a Washington party for Arafat, the first essay on the community itself (Dearborn) was published in October 2001.[13]

ADC had better luck with *Aladdin*, a Disney cartoon movie based loosely on the *A Thousand and One Nights*. After five months of negotiation (and meetings with Mokhiber and Casey Kasem), the Disney studios agreed to cut out lines from a video release of the movie. These had to do with a faraway place where "they cut off your ear/If they don't like your face/It's barbaric, but hey, it's home." The *New York Times* editorialized its approval:

Understandably, Arab Americans are upset. They find it difficult enough that Saddam Hussein is the villain du jour and that terrorists from Arab countries have recently threatened New York. ...To characterize an entire region with this sort of tongue-in-cheek bigotry, especially in a movie aimed at children, borders on the barbaric.[14]

In spite of the confetti of the image wars, it seemed that newly-elected President Bill Clinton took quantum leaps toward peace by welcoming PLO Chairman Yasir Arafat to the White House and Washington, DC. NAAA's Randa Fahmy ushered Arafat around Capitol Hill, meeting the key chairmen of the foreign affairs and appropriations comittees. And then on September 13, 1993, Arafat and Israeli Prime Minister Yitzak Rabin signed the Declaration of Principles that so captivated the world. The handshake was genuine: Rabin extended his hand tentatively, almost afraid of what he was doing; then Arafat's extended further than halfway and pumped his partner's hand firmly, a ripple that Rabin felt and joined. It seemed in that moment a century of bitterness had finally begun to drain into the soil of the past. This was a new present, a new fact, that all the forces of hell would have to contend with.

Longtime activist Jim Zogby enthused, "a taboo was broken and a myth shattered." The taboo of "near religious proportions" was that of contacting, talking with, or recognizing the PLO. The myth was that the Palestinians were not really "a people," but rather "refugees," "strangers in the land of Israel" (in Biblical terms), or as Begin and Shamir had it "Arab inhabitants" of territories Israel claimed as Judea and Samaria. The multiple references to a distinct "Palestinian people," Zogby noted, "acknowledged for the first time the existence and legitimacy of a distinct national community of Palestinians." This would lead, most realized, to nationhood. The agreement, though not peace in itself, was "subtle, complex, comprehensive and masterfully constructed to allow for future accomodation" and for this reason was "eminently supportable."[15]

It was witnessed by hundreds of Arab- and Jewish-American leaders on the White House lawn, and feted later at a party at the nearby Marriott where Jews and Arabs who had long been antagonists on the issue were slapping each other on the back and toasting. I remember bumping into Leon Wieseltier of the *New Republic*; we rubbed our plastic cups in that all-too-short euphoria, as if the genie of peace might really emerge. John Cooley, one of the first American journalists to try and explain the Palestinians' cause to the American public as far back as the 1960s, stuck an ABC microphone in front of me and asked what I was thinking about. "All those who had lost their lives in this cause, especially people of peace like Fahd Kawasmeh," I said. Fahd was killed by his own. Cooley knew this and nodded; we both looked at the floor in the joyous din.

And then it happened. The minions of the night came forward. In 1995, during a peace rally in Tel Aviv, Rabin was shot dead by Yigal Amir, an associate of an ultra-right-wing settlement on the West Bank. The media, of course, did not refer to him as a terrorist.[16] Like Kawasmeh, Rabin was done in by his own. When Rabin fell, Oslo (however flawed it was) and the hope of peace itself fell with him. It hasn't gotten back up since.

In December 1997, for the first time in history a Muslim crescent-and-star was added to the White House Christmas tree on the Ellipse, alongside a lit-up Jewish menorah. Within days, the Morrocan-American artist who created the ten-foot wooden Muslim symbol discovered the star torn from the crescent, painted with a swastika and thrown alongside a nearby garbage can.[17] Perhaps it didn't fit.

OKLAHOMA CITY AND THE ANTI-TERRORISM ACT OF 1996

On April 19, 1995, an ex-Marine with a grudge against the US government named Timothy McVeigh exploded a truck bomb in front of the Murrah federal building in Oklahoma City, killing 168 people, including 19 children. At the time, it was perhaps the worst act of mass murder by an individual in US history. McVeigh's lineage was about as far from the Middle East as a Scottish-American can be. His grudge had nothing to do with Middle Eastern issues (he was taking vengeance, he said, for the federal government's crackdowns on ultra-right-wing survivalists in Idaho and a highly armed cult in Waco, Texas). Still, the Oklahoma City bombing unleashed a torrent of knee-jerk reactions against Arabs and Arab Americans and gave birth to a new anti-terrorist law aimed more at those of Arab origin than those of Scottish.

Before McVeigh and associates were arrested, the media was rife with speculation that the Oklahoma bombers might be, or even had to be, of Arab origin. Soon after the explosion, *USA Today* ran a headline, "Bomb Consistent with Mid-East Terror Tactics." A *New York Times* column was titled, "Beirut, Okla." On April 21, 1995, the *New York Post* ran a cartoon sporting three turbaned men, one burning the American flag in one hand while holding a bomb in the other, and all of them standing alongside the Statue of Liberty. An inscription on the Statue read, "Give us your tired, your poor, your huddled masses, your terrorists, your murderers, your slime, your evil cowards, your religious fanatics." The so-called terrorist experts were trotted out on the networks and CNN, scoping out the problem while lending their air of seriousness. In case we had any questions about the matter, one such luminary, Steven Emerson, set us straight on CBS just after the bombing, "This was done with the intent to inflict as many casualties as possible. That is a Middle Eastern trait."

ADC registered over 150 hate crimes against the Arab-American community in the eight months of 1995 following the Oklahoma City bombing, one of the more glaring examples of criminal mistaken identity in recent memory. A lesser, but still troubling, turbulence was registered by the Council on American Islamic Relations, which found 222 incidents of harassment of Muslim Americans within three days of Oklahoma City.

The misplaced backlash ranged from the tragic to the merely venal and bizarre. People in Oklahoma City threw a brick through a pregnant woman's window that traumatized her into a stillbirth. Another Oklahoma City resident and US citizen, Abraham Ahmed, was arrested in London on the way to visiting relatives in Jordan, strip-searched and interrogated, released, then detained again in Oklahoma, his family subjected to catcalls and thrown objects. Seven mosques were burned, including those in Springfield, IL; High Point, NC; and Hunstville, AL. A mosque near Atlanta was desecrated with satanic symbols. The front door of the home of a native of India in northern Virginia, mistaken for Arab, was spray-painted with "666" (a satanic cult number), with "F– you, Arab" painted on the driveway. At a New York airport, a police officer lost it, shouting profanities at an Arab-American couple (the wife wore the Muslim *hijab*); before the husband could move his car after removing luggage, the police officer hit him several times with a nightstick. Employment discrimination took an upsurge. The Arizona Ice Tea company reportedly fired 21 Arab-American salespeople after they complained about degrogatory remarks and the lack of flex-time for Muslim religious holidays.[18]

Within a year of the Oklahoma bombing, President Clinton signed the Antiterrorism and Effective Death Penalty Act of 1996. It revived long discredited aspects of repealed McCarran–Walter Act of 1952 wherein noncitizens could be arrested under "guilt by association" standards and deported without due process, legal representation, or even charges. Denial of political asylum benefits and sharp curtailments of habeas corpus were in the act. Secret evidence was once again enshrined as it had been during the McCarthy era. In the past, luminaries who had been associated with Communist or anarchist groups had been denied entry to even speak in the United States; the list is a distinguished one, including Charlie Chaplin, Nobel-prizewinning novelists Graham Greene and Gabriel Garcia Marquez, and actor Yves Montand. The 1996 Antiterrorist Act was not after luminaries, however. Within two years, 25 individuals were arrested and detained under the 1996 Act, most of them Arab, under vague associations with terrorist organizations. For whatever weeks or months people were held, virtually none of the arrests amounted to anything and all the detainees were released.

One effect was to subject anyone to arrest who supported armed struggle anywhere in the world or collected money for such causes. Under the new act, anyone attending a speech by Nelson Mandela and contributing to the coffers of his banned African National Council could easily have been rounded up. The same could hold true of tens of thousands of Irish-Americans who give to humanitarian causes run by the IRA. As one legal scholar put it, "People can be punished, the Act says, not for what they do or abet, but for supporting wholly lawful acts of disfavored groups... [it] contained some of the worst assaults on civil liberties in decades."[19]

The ADC testified before Congress that "the scope of the applicability of the provisions is so broad that it invites abuse and selective enforcement which we feel will be directed at the Arab American community, silencing protected speech and punishing lawful political activities."[20] In short, anyone expressing public sympathy with Palestinians, or shelling out dollars for gauze, medicine, and schools that would go to the West Bank and Gaza. The effect, even before September 11, was chilling.[21]

The case of Nasser Ahmad is representative. An Egyptian who lived with his wife and three children (all US citizens) and had been working as an electrical engineer in New York City since 1986, he was arrested in 1996 on the basis of secret evidence. Ahmad spent over three years in prison, charged with no crime. He was finally released in 1999 having done nothing worse than worship at the same mosque as Sheikh Omar Abdel Rahman, one of the 1993 World Trade Center conspirators. In other words, guilty by association.

ACCESS WHITE HOUSE OR AFFIRMATIVE ACTION?

In the mid-1990s, Arab Americans from older generations—not as susceptible, perhaps, to surveillance by the FBI or the vagaries of the new antiterrorist legislation—found themselves at the crossroads of two trends. On the one hand, the community was not only making its traditional strides in the business world and the professions, but burrowing in ever deeper into local, state, and national politics. They wanted, above all, to participate as Americans, with their Arabness subdued. On the other hand, Third Wave immigrant groups and their families saw real value in an effort by ADC president and lawyer Albert Mokhiber to seek minority status in order to secure government contracts in the special Small Business Administration 8(a) designation. In short, one part of the community was submerging its ethnicity to claim at least a toehold on the ladders of power. The other part was accentuating it more than ever to receive "favors" other minorities got. These trends were roughly identifiable with the workings of the AAI in the former case and the ADC in the latter.

In November 1995, the AAI held its tenth anniversary conference of 200 handpicked "leader" delegates, marked by an unusual roundtable discussion of Arab American political leaders with President Clinton and Vice President Gore, arranged by Gore's chief domestic policy advisor, Gregory Simon (a Lebanese American from Arkansas). Simon also led a panel on meeting community needs with declining funds with several locally elected officials of Arab origin, including Teresa Isaac, then vice-mayor of Lexington, KY; Lee Namey, the mayor of Wilkes-Barre, PA; and Rose Allan Tucker, Luzerne County (PA) commissioner. AAI's genius was to attach itself to political careers already in the works, and it established a sizable intra–Arab-American politico network that shared funders' lists and databases, put together the occasional lunch for candidates, tracked trends on the Hill, and generally played cheerleader for Arab Americans running for office, no matter the party. By 2000, it had founded a modest political action committee (PAC).

As for affirmative action, Mokhiber found himself in an uphill battle in his own community, the majority of whom appeared not to want special favors from the government and prided themselves in their native instincts for business. In fact, the US Small Business Administration listed Lebanese Americans second of all ethnic groups in the "rate of entrepreneurship"—the percentage of the community who start their own businesses. Only "Russian Americans" ranked higher.

Though more recent immigrants from the Arab world pushed hard for 8(a) status (with good reason, as Arab business owners with accents are more likely to be subjected to prejudice in the doling out of government contracts), the fact remained that the vast majority of Arab-American business owners were descendants of the First Wave immmigrants, and they saw the special favor of 8(a) and designation as a "protected minority" as unnecessary, at best, and even insulting. Why, they asked, did the people of Haggar Slacks, Kinko's Copies, Norma Kamali dresses, and Jacobs Engineering need a hand up?

The move for 8(a) status for Arab Americans was rejected. But some firms got special exemptions that qualified them for 8(a) in other ways, such as a Libyan-American owned company that filed for consideration as a socially disadvantaged firm utilizing, in part, the argument that if African-Americans got 8(a) contracts, well, then, Libya was in Africa. It also did not hurt coming from a country ruled by Muammar Qaddafi; for once, such an association was a blessing! A Palestinian-American contractor successfully showed the government that his background had hindered him economically.[22] Likewise, though most Jewish Americans have no interest in getting 8(a) status, or need for it, Hasidic Jewish diamond cutters in New York have gotten the special designation due to their unusual sect and the social disadvantages that obtain from it. Though it didn't open up wholesale government contracts to the community, a landmark 1987 Supreme Court decision over university tenure expanded the definition of "protected" classes in discrimination civil suits to include Arabs and Jews (see St. Francis College vs. al-Khazragi).

At about the same time as the 8(a) petition, Arab-American organizations approached the US Census Bureau with the idea that the 2000 Census contain, for the first time, an entry on the census form that would indicate the citizen was of Arab origin. The three million figure in this book is an estimate; there has never been such an entry, though there is for those of Hispanic, Asian, Native American, or African origin. Those of Middle Eastern origin are lumped in with "Caucasian," as are Jews of Middle Eastern or European origin.

On this issue, there was somewhat more interest across generations in the Arab-American community in getting the figure right. Still, the political groups took different tacts, with AAI wanting a broader "Middle Eastern" category (including those of Turkish, Armenian, and Iranian background, for example) and ADC arguing for a strictly "Arab" category. Such petitions are put forward by many groups. At the same time as it considered "Arab," the office that draws up the categories for the Census Bureau was considering the petition of Cape Verde Islanders for a little box on the form. Ultimately, due to "lack of unity in the community and lack of consciousness of the community in federal circles,"[23] the question was dropped. There was also a "new public mood with strong support in the new Congress that increasingly viewed racial or ethnic categories as symptoms of the disunity of America."[24] Instead, the 2000 Census form offered a voluntary ethnicity box for the first time, and 1.25 million Arab Americans checked it.

Even that partial reading brought out intriguing community statistics for the first time. According to the US Census Bureau, 40 percent of Arab Americans have college degrees, one-third higher than Americans-at-large. The average Arab-American income was $47,000 (higher than the $42,000 national average). Fully 17 percent of Arab Americans had post-graduate degrees, twice the national average. Clearly, education in this community was king.

This thirst for counting itself would come back to haunt Arab Americans. Packaging the new data on Arab Americans by population size, zip code, and country of origin, the Bureau of Census quietly shipped it off in the post-9/11 world to the US Customs Service and the Department of Homeland Security. In a rare joint protest statement by both ADC and AAI, the two organizations declared on August 13, 2004, "These actions are a violation of the public's trust in the Census Bureau, and a troubling reminder of one of our nation's darkest days when the sharing of similar information resulted in the internment of Japanese Americans during World War II." Be careful what you wish for.

THE DEATH OF OSLO AND THE SECOND INTIFADA

If only the Palestinians had had the luxury of a census debate! An official census form implies the existence of an independent state. It implies people have the freedom even to print and distribute such a form. By 2000, after seven years of Kafkaesque dickering, the Oslo peace process—crippled by Rabin's assassination and the coming to power, once again, of the Likud Party in Israel, which not only dragged its feet but cut off the Palestinians' legs—Oslo was nearly dead. All that was needed was for someone who never believed in it in the first place to push the drained body off a cliff.

The date usually given for the death of Oslo and the beginning of the second intifada is September 28, 2000. On that day, a man with a record of the massacres of innocents on his hands that stretches back half a century to Qibya in 1954, ascended the Temple Mount in Jerusalem. One is tempted to call the figure an Old Testament prophet, except in the Hebraic tradition, such figures as Isaiah, Jeremiah, and Ezekiel criticized ancient Israel for its wrongs. They were great moral forces, who preached virtues of justice and mercy in language that has inspired those fighting against oppression to this day. In 2000, the man ascending the Mount was a prophet pointed the wrong way. When Israel needed an Isaiah, it got Joshua.

Ariel Sharon—a man my own father warned me about just before his death two decades ago—took over the Temple Mount that day with his private military entourage and effectively closed all debate about Jerusalem belonging to two peoples. Cynically asserting the right of Jews to pray at the Wailing Wall (it had not been abridged), he shut off access for Muslims to the al-Aqsa mosque, one of Islam's holiest sites, the very place from which Mohammed is said to have journeyed to heaven on a horse. The next day the titular head of the country, Ehud Barak, sent nearly 1,000 troops to the Temple Mount to shore up the desecration by his political rival—head-shaking strange. But there was a lot of that and worse coming to the Middle East, and the United States, in the next two years.

The Israeli troops shot at least 4 demonstrating Palestinians dead on the Temple Mount that day and wounded 200. On September 30, the twelve-year-old Mohammed al-Durra, in a scene forgotten since our September 11 agony, but one to which that later disaster is inextricably linked, was shot and killed by Israeli troops. His father was also killed trying to cover him from a hailstorm of bullets. Television captured it all, and at the time, few Americans were not utterly revolted by it. Al-Durra's crime, it seems, was that he was near (but not one of) some rock-throwers and an Israeli settlement (Netzarim). The scene, it goes without saying, was replayed throughout the Arab and Muslim world. There was no apology played, or replayed.

Over the next few months, hundreds more Palestinians—unarmed, many children—were shot to death, often by Israeli snipers with long-range rifles and scopes not unlike the Bushmaster later used by the DC sniper in October 2002.[25] It was almost as if Sharon had put the starter flag down on these deadly volleys.

It's important to stress that in these first few months of the second intifada, the tactics of the first—demonstrations, stone-throwing, blockades of burning tires—were utilized. There was very little armed resistance at first. A UN inquiry in March 2001 said

> During these crucial days there was no evidence of Palestinian gunfire. The IDF (Israeli Army), operating behind fortifications with superior weaponry, endured not a single serious casualty as a result of Palestinian demonstrations and, further, their soldiers seemed to be in no life-threatening danger during the course of these events.[26]

What had changed was Israel's reaction to the uprising. If harsh before, now it was merciless. To add to the ignominy, on October 4, 2000, the American government approved an Israeli request for Apache helicopters with advanced attack equipment. Completely ignoring US arms export law, a US official said, "US weapons sales do not carry a stipulation that the weapons can't be used against civilians. We cannot second-guess an Israeli commander who calls in helicopter gunships."[27]

Someone deep in the caves of Afghanistan was taking notes. Though one of al-Qaeda's leaders captured by the United States in Pakistan has said the 9/11 attacks were five years in the planning, *The 9/11 Commission Report* reported that bin Laden, livid at Sharon's ascent at Temple Mount, ordered his lieutenants to move the date for the attacks on New York and Washington up a year, to that very moment in 2000. After vehement argument, they dissuaded him, citing lack of training.[28]

Few Arab Americans, or informed Americans of any sort, didn't instinctively link the atrocities meted on the United States on September 11 to those against unarmed Palestinians and their children a year before, or, for that matter, those on an uninterrupted line twenty years back to Israel's killing of 19,000 civilians in Lebanon. You don't need to think bin Laden was right or even sane to make the link, which he confirmed in his November 2004 pre-election message. Heinous in his opportunism? Absolutely. But Palestine is 50 percent of what he said from the start were his two reasons to topple the Twin Towers (the other was the presence of US troops in Saudi Arabia, his home country, and support for corrupt Arab regimes). What is truly frightening is nobody in power in the US government appears to have taken him at his word. With no serious American policy changes afoot on Palestine (save the oft-ignored Bush "road map"), but plenty of loopy anti-terrorist laws, bin Laden had no problem whipping recruits into white-hot anger by the unmitigated, unapologetic massacre of innocents. Grievances spanned decades; they were now on TV. They would soon be in Iraq.

How did this all happen? Let us take a closer look at how and why Oslo died.

Two eminent Palestinian-American authors who had active political lives in their community here and abroad are instructive on this matter: Columbia's Edward Said and Georgetown's Hisham Sharabi. Shortly after Oslo, Sharabi jumped into a reconciliation tour of Palestine and Israel with Israeli novelist Amos Oz, debating and discussing the prospects of peace "that suddenly and miraculously seemed to have descended upon us."[29] A stoic to the core, Sharabi was uncharacteristically excited and hopeful. But by 1996, three years after the Oslo accords, Sharabi had become disillusioned: "The negotiations were not about an honorable peace, but a cynical process designed to exact a humiliating surrender."[30]

Edward Said smelled a fish from the beginning:

> For the first time in the 20th century, an anti-colonial movement had not only discarded its own considerable achievements but made an agreement to cooperate with a military occupation before that occupation had ended, and before even the government of Israel had admitted that it was in effect a government of military occupation.[31]

Invited to the White House to witness the Arafat–Rabin signing by President Clinton, Said refused, saying the day should be one "of mourning."

Many Arab-American leaders, including James Zogby, enamored of the Oslo moment, thought Said's hold-out cynical and pessimistic in the extreme; Said's relations with Zogby, for one, broke down. But events (or non-events) evolved to the point that it is impossible to deny the truth of Said's warnings. Between 1993 and 2000, a period when peace was supposed to be not only in the air but in the ink, the settlement population of the West Bank and Gaza increased 85 percent—from 110,000 to 185,000. (This does not include the 150,000 settlers who have formed a human barrier behind East Jerusalem, cutting Palestinians there off from the rest of the West Bank. The total settlement population is about 350,000.) The rate of the increase was the fastest by far in any period since Israel took the land in 1967. The Palestinians could be pardoned for thinking that on the issue of settlements alone Oslo looked like a steroid for the outlaw. Many settlements continued to be populated not by Israeli crème de la crème but, like any outpost in the world (central Alaska, upper Idaho), by the fringe—including misfits toting machine guns. One had to believe that Israel during the 1990s was about as schizophrenic a society as exists. Even its leadership at one point, a prime minister-ship that was half Shimon Peres, half Netanyahu, was a hydra head.

Said wondered aloud if Oslo weren't "a gigantic fraud." All the while conditions for Palestinians worsened. As Harvard's Sara Roy (the child of Holocaust survivors) has shown with convincing detail and eloquence, the economy of the territories went into a severe, Orwellian tailspin throughout the decade.[32] The Israelis talked peace and brought pain. Since 1967, 10,000 Palestinian homes have been demolished; 3,000 of these destructions occurred since 2000. In the seven years after Oslo, the Israeli government confiscated approximately 35,000 acres of Arab land in the West Bank, much of it farmland and groves, worth $1 billion. Most of this land went to building the bypass roads to the expanding settlements. In one six-month period alone (October 2000 to April 2001), 181,000 trees—mostly olive trees, but also fruit and nut trees—were uprooted, destroying a traditional way of life many centuries in the making. In their place were box-like mobile homes or cement byways. And how strange those roads! Not even in the United States during the worst days of segregation and Jim Crow were blacks forbidden to walk or ride on public roads. The roads linking settlements are forbidden to Arabs. The United States is now irrefutably in the process of funding Israeli projects inimical to America's deepest values, projects that would be unconstitutional and unlawful in our own country.

Stateside, Arab Americans kept trying to plug the ever-leaking dike of such inequities, while supporting, however skeptically, the processing of peace. In 1998, through pressure from the ADC, Day's Inn, the large US cut-rate motel chain, closed one of its motels in Gush Katif, an Israel settlement in Gaza. Extensive media coverage of the issue was said to have temporarily dropped the company's stock by a point. Under similar protest, Ben and Jerry's Ice Cream company cancelled an agreement with an Israeli mineral water firm based on the Golan Heights, which had been seized from Syria in 1967. Such moves were not universally approved. When in September 1999, Burger King shut down an outlet in the large West Bank settlement of Maaleh Adumim, 73 US members of Congress, including a majority of the New York delegation, signed a letter chastizing Burger King for its "capitulation to pressure." One had to wonder if some of those New Yorkers were planning to summer on the West Bank and go duck hunting.

By April 2001, the unemployment rate in the occupied territories was about 39 percent; in Gaza itself, 60 percent of the population was out of work. These figures are duplicated in no other country in the world. They surpass the rate of unemployment at the peak of the Great Depression in the United States. By January 2001, close to 1 million people, or nearly one-third of Palestinians in the territories, were living below the poverty line. In only three months, by April, the number of poor doubled to 2 million, almost two-thirds of Palestinians. As Roy poignantly notes, "Hunger is now a fact of life for the majority of the people, as is the despair and rage that attend it. This appalling situation does not and will not affect Palestinians alone."[33] (One notes that the abysmal drop in the day-to-day living conditions coincided with Ariel Sharon's first trip to the White House where he was lauded by President Bush as "a man of peace." September 11 was only five months off.)

In the midst of this misery, Ehud Barak made one last-ditch effort to close a final peace with the Palestinians, variously termed "the deal of the century," "generous," and "an offer impossible to refuse." It was trumpeted that Barak was giving up 90 percent, even 94 percent, of the West Bank back to the Palestinians. It sounded good. Arab Americans, like everyone else, including President Clinton, heaped scorn on Arafat when he refused the golden goose in July 2000 at the second Camp David. How could he be so ungrateful?!

But soon, for anyone who read beyond the lock-step US press, it was obvious that Barak had offered nothing of the kind, and had been rigid on critical issues. Israeli journalists saw through it immediately. Within days, in her "The Camp David Fraud," Tanya Reinhart demonstrated in Israel's largest daily, *Yediot Ahronot*, that it was more like a 50–50 deal. The Israelis would annex 10 percent of the West Bank, but 40 percent was still to be "under debate."[34] Considering the patrolling of the Israeli army in the wide swath of the Jordan Valley that cuts off the West Bank from Jordan, the easements for the bypass roads, the thick seams of land that encompass the settlements (80 percent of which were to remain in place) and then chop the West Bank Palestinians into at least five completely disconnected population islands (Sara Roy says with real barriers in place beyond the map, it is more like 227 "tiny enclaves")—well, the 40 percent "under debate" gets swept up pretty quickly to Israel's side. As University of Chicago political science professor John Mearsheimer put it, "It is hard to imagine the Palestinians accepting such a state. Certainly no other nation in the world has such curtailed sovereignty."[35]

There were other assessments of the extremely convoluted "deal of the century" that was offered, but it was hard to turn up the miraculous 90 percent figure. Closely following the snake-like settlement paths Israel swept to itself into, out, and through the West Bank, Jan de Jong's extremely detailed maps for the Foundation for Middle East Peace in Washington, DC came up with no more than 60 percent of the West Bank in Palestinian hands. This is ratified by Mouin Rabbani, who summarized Ehud Barak's five "no's" announced "amid much fanfare" just before the second Camp David began: "no withdrawal to the June 4, 1967 boundaries; no dismantling of [all] settlements; no division of Jerusalem; no Arab army west of the Jordan River; and no return of Palestinian refugees."[36] For the most part, this red-line of Barak's held. It was all offered to Arafat as a take-it or leave-it proposition; he was not given the chance to counteroffer. It's no surprise he didn't think Israel or Clinton was serious and left.

Perhaps the best interpreters of the demise of the exceedingly tragic second Camp David are Rema Hammami and Salim Tamari. In their view, Israeli parsimony over three crucial areas wrecked the deal more than whether the amount of land to be returned was 60 or 90 percent. These issues are, in ascending importance: Palestinian refugees, Jerusalem, and the Israeli settlements.

The question of the return of Palestinian refugees is one that has dogged Israel since the very founding of the state in 1948. In 1962, President John Kennedy made a heartfelt effort to resettle the refugees, but was rebuked by Ben Gurion himself, who made no bones about the importance of shutting the refugees out: "Israel will regard this plan [of Kennedy's] as a more serious danger to her existence than all the threats of the Arab dictators and kings, then all the Arab armies... Israel will fight against this implementation down to the last man."[37] By the second Camp David in 2000, the Israelis did make an effort: the return of a few thousand refugees from Lebanon as "family reunification" spread over fifteen years, with an international fund for refugee compensation. This sounds reasonable. But consider: by this point four million Palestinians were living outside of historic Palestine, a half million in hovels in Lebanon alone. Lebanon was to be the only country from which "a few thousand" would be let into Israel stretched over a period so long that many would probably die first. No figure was mentioned for "compensation," just the promise of an amorphous "fund." After what Arafat had seen of promises since Oslo, this looked dubious. He would have to sign an "end of conflict" clause and renounce any further restitution claims. It was both too stark and indistinct. As Hammami and Tamari indicate, on that basis alone Arafat would have had to cut bait with the Palestinian diaspora. In retrospect, one thinks he might have done it if Israel had been more forthcoming on other issues, such as the settlements. But that was not at all the case; the vast majority were staying.

On Jerusalem, although Barak looked good saying at the outset each side could proclaim it a capital, on closer inspection Barak was not giving up East Jerusalem to Palestinian sovereignty. Certain Arab parts of the Old City got a kind of autonomy, but Israeli sovereignty would be retained. The most bizarre, and tortuous, offer was for the Temple Mount, or Haram al-Sharif, the holiest site for both Jews and Muslims in the Old City. Here Barak let Muslims control above ground, while Israel would control below ground. Inasmuch as Jewish extremists had barely been stopped from blowing up the al-Aqsa mosque from underground a few years back, this probably frightened Arafat as much as insulted him. But there were Jewish concerns, as well, for sacred items underground. So Jerusalem as an issue stalled underground.

Finally, the settlements. While Israel offered to take down 20 percent of them, fully 80 percent were staying. More importantly, the three settlement blocs Israel was to annex (Ariel, Etzion, and the Greater Jerusalem settlements, including Maale Adumim) broke the West Bank apart. It was hard enough to be separated from Gaza. The Palestinian state would look like a body in which the vital organs were detached from each other, dependent upon Israel for life-support. This violated the principle of "territorial integrity" that Clinton had promised Arafat at the very outset of the Oslo accords. In addition, as Hammami and Tamari point out, up to 100,000 Palestinians would be disenfranchised, entangled within the annexed settlement blocs. What would become of them? Would they be expelled? Would the Palestinian approach to settlement turn from a firm demand that they be completely dismantled, to acquiescing to 100,000 new Palestinians refugees? It was untenable.

On all three of these issues, Israel gave, but the giving was shy. Arafat had the opposite problem: he had given almost everything up at the start just to get a seat at the Oslo table, so he had little wiggle room at the end. It's interesting to note, as Clinton negotiator Robert Malley admitted later, that Arafat was willing to give up some of the Jewish neighborhoods of East Jerusalem. He was also willing to consider ways to limit the number of returning refugees to assuage Israeli security and demographic concerns. And, of course, he had been formally committed to the two-state solution and recognition of Israel's right to exist for over a dozen years. Nothing Arafat did at Camp David indicated he had gone back on that crucial promise, the firestorm of criticism to the contrary. Far from blaming Arafat for the breakdown, Malley gave him credit for significant concessions: "No other Arab party that has negotiated with Israel—not Anwar Sadat's Egypt, not King Hussein's Jordan, let alone Hafez al-Assad's Syria— ever came close to even considering such compromises."[38]

Perhaps the greatest tragedy about the second Camp David is that some months later, at Taba, without American interlocutors,

Egypt, Israeli and Palestinian negotiators went much further (returning a verifiable 85 percent of the West Bank to the Palestinians) and came very close to the final lineaments of a peace agreement. But by that time, Ariel Sharon had defeated Barak for the leadership of Israel. Taba was forgotten. And the second intifada in full, bloody swing.

Some months after Sharon's march to power on the Temple Mount the second intifada shifted from stone-throwing and road-blocking to armed rebellion. And worse. Two Israeli soldiers who lost their way in Ramallah were captured by a mob and lynched. The grisly photograph of a Palestinian covered in blood and smiling to the hoots of the mob made the front page of the *Washington Post* and matched, if not surpassed, the horror of the televised shooting of Mohammad al-Durra and his father. One was the premeditated shooting of civilians, the other the execution without trial of prisoners-of-war: both completely reprehensible and sickening.

Over three years' time, the second intifada lashed out at what it saw as a cynical "peace process" over a decade (and 35 years under the gun) that ended in nothing but Sharon's orgy of violence. The second uprising at first targeted the settlements, and then, to the dismay and anger of the Palestinians' most ardent supporters, civilians inside Israel proper. What Hammami and Tamari called "a battle against the settlements" was seen as as an assault on people armed to the teeth, with a "growing and conscious synergy between the army and the settlers."[39] But strapping plastic explosives to your belt and walking into a café or movie house or marketplace and obliterating people who may very well have been on your side was insanity, plain and simple.

From 2000 to 2003, over 100 suicide bombings took place, most of them by followers of two Islamic fundamentalist movements—Hamas and Islamic Jihad—but some by the al-Aqsa Martyrs Brigade (linked to Arafat's Fatah organization) and various independent nihilists. Four were done by young women. In many cases, Arabs were killed, as well as Jews. In one particularly heinous instance, on October 4, 2003, a young, beautiful Palestinian law student strapped a 22-pound bomb to her waist, strolled into a restaurant in Haifa patronized by Arabs and Jews for over four decades, and blew herself up, as well as nineteen others. Among the dead were four Arabs. The place had been, like Haifa itself, a model of inter-Jewish–Arab cooperation amidst the surrounding suspicion and hate.[40] The Council on American Islamic Relations (CAIR), based in Washington, DC, wasted no time in issuing a statement the day of the Haifa explosion, "CAIR condemns this vicious attack in the strongest possible terms. The bombing is particularly loathsome, coming as it did on the evening of the Jewish community's holiest day. We offer our condolences to the families of the victims and call for the swift apprehension of the perpetrators."

In early December 2001, two Palestinian suicide bombings in succession rocked Tel Aviv and Jerusalem, killing 26 people. Sharon's reaction to the various attacks was to bomb Syria for the first time in 26 years, to lay waste to the Palestinian Authority, and to seize back all of the West Bank, attacking cities with helicopter gun ships and imposing the worst collective punishment on Palestinians in the 35 years of occupation. Arafat, as usual, was blamed, and even though his police stations were destroyed, he was told to crack down on the fundamentalists. How he was supposed to do this with virtually no government left and under house arrest was an interesting question. With the conflict clearly shading toward religious fanaticism, it seemed as if the Palestinians had played into Sharon's—and bin Laden's—hands.

Between September 2000 and September 2003, 2,500 Palestinians were killed and 700 Israelis, close to a four to one ratio (versus twenty to one in the first intifada). Despairing of Oslo, was the Palestinian point to exact a higher proportion of Israeli civilian deaths, to make Israel, like some hapless bulldog, "finally let go" of the conquered territories, as my friend Max Holland thought? Or was it just more gas on the fire?

Despairing of this orgy of violence, Edward Said, in the year before his untimely death had found a balance in music. An excellent pianist and music critic himself, Said and Israeli conductor Daniel Berenboim had begun sponsoring seminars, duets, sestets, and other unlikely harmonies between Arab and Israeli musicians. It reminded me of Ann Patchett's miraculous novel *Bel Canto*, which reveals the stunning powers of music in the midst of a terrorist hostage taking, in which the Japanese business magnate and lover of opera finds happiness alongside his idol and fellow hostage, the world's greatest soprano. The magnate and his translator approach her to sing, "two small halves of courage making a brave whole."[41] Minuscule harmonies in the Middle East? Not a bad alternative given how many of the politicians and religious leaders had taken leave of sense.

In 1998, as Oslo unraveled, the ADC initiated the creation of a Palestinian quilt commemorating each of the 418 villages destroyed by Israel in 1948. It was unveiled on Capitol Hill and traveled throughout the country to college campuses, libraries, and community centers. As touching as this was, no one can find peace in that direction anymore. Even married couples find out soon enough that fixating on past hurt leads to present chaos. Another alternative to violence and looking back was looking forward with micro-rebuilding. The organizations Global Campaign to Rebuild Palestinian Homes based in Redwood City, California, with Salim Shawamreh and Donna Baranski-Walker, and Jeff Halper's Israeli

Committee Against House Demolitions have the right idea. Already 17 homes that were crushed have been built back, with 100 more Palestinians in line for the rebirth. Here an Israeli, American, and Arab American have joined forces that may rebuild a lot more than bricks and mortar.

Third, there is no avoiding the fact that the sooner the Palestinians can disarm Hamas and Islamic Jihad, the better. This probably won't start until the Israelis make tangible efforts to dismantle most of the settlements. Extremists like Sharon and Hamas don't give hope; either they must go or radically change. The United States could suspend aid to both Israel and the Palestinian Authority until the suicide bombing is forsworn and the settlements—both West Bank and Gaza—on their way out. (Or to both Egypt and Israel until the former democratizes and the latter gets off the Palestinians' backs.) None of this is likely to happen with a tepid Bush's "road map."

Fourth, every effort in the arts and education must be made to cut into and dismantle the evil stereotypes Americans have of Arabs and vice versa. (A 2005 survey of 200 books and pamphlets found at US mosques and Islamic centers, published by the Saudi royal family or government, were found to be filled with religious bigotry and contempt for US policies.[42]) In this sea of sludge, there is occasional fresh water—Whoopi Goldberg's television series with a wonderfully human, and funny, Muslim cabbie; Saudi Prince Alwaleed bin Talal's opening of a new center for American Studies at the American University of Beirut; the novels of Mona Simpson, Diana Abu Jaber, and Barbara Kingsolver; the children's books of Ella Marston; documentaries like "Caught in the Crossfire" in which a Yemeni-American New York policeman, Ahmed Nasser, jumps into the fray of 9/11 and walks his tough beat afterward.[43] The Levantine Center in Los Angeles run by Jordan Elgraby is a fine example of using the arts as a bridge to understanding.

US members of Congress who are true patriots might sign on to Res. 111 calling for a full investigation into the death by Israeli bulldozer of Rachel Corrie of Seattle, Washington, a 23-year-old American who was doing nothing more than standing up in front of a West Bank home when she was crushed and killed. As of August 2003, 42 Congressmen had signed on.

Lastly, though they have been tried and tried before, Arab-American and Jewish-American luminaries should gather with the intention of a issuing a joint statement calling for the dismantling of settlements and the armies of Hamas–Islamic Jihad. Top businessmen such as Philip Klutznik, Robert Abboud, and Joseph Jacobs joined forces in the 1980s, but failed. In more recent times, Lester Crown, Talat Othman, Newton Minow, and Cherif Bassiouni have released a two-page statement condemning the escalating and mindless violence.[44]

Principled Arab-American criticism of anti-Semitism, which is growing (just as anti-Arab sentiment grows), has never been more important to register. Chicago journalist Ray Hanania got it exactly right in a column, noting at first that the canard of labeling someone "anti-Semitic" is often used "to silence legitimate criticism of Israel." Hanania goes on:

> Sometimes, though, criticism of Israel has been anti-Semitic, and it should stop. As a Palestinian, I believe the conflict that divides Palestinians and Israelis is one involving two primary issues: land and politics. It is not about religion, and we should speak out against those who try to make it about religion... Anti-Semitism is immoral and based on religious bigotry.[45]

In a similar vein, when the director of a United Arab Emirates think tank made obvious anti-Semitic remarks about Jews being "the enemies of all nations" at a Cairo conference, Palestinian-American poet and scholar Sharif Elmusa, head of Middle East Studies at the American University of Cairo, condemned it in the *Los Angeles Times*: "I think this is an unfortunate development... [There are also] Christian fundamentalists who now think Islam is a religion of violence. We live in a poisonous atmosphere, here and there."[46] On the other hand, no good is done by B'nai B'rith's spying on Arab Americans and other groups (a 1999 ADC lawsuit shut down the intimidation)[47]; also, ADC's own endless listings of hate crimes, though necessary, have limited political returns. Paranoia is finally its own reward.

We need to cut the shackles of fear if we are to breathe again as Americans, as well as get off our high horse. It's instructive to take a close look at what one of the most fervent fanners of the flames of the war in Iraq, *Washington Post* columnist Jim Hoagland, had to say on the eve of September 11. He spoke in awe of "Israeli commandos [who] once journeyed to Beirut or Tunis to strike down Palestinian war chieftains," though today they don't have to travel far to "smite their adversaries with precision guided missiles on Israel's doorstep." Hoagland thought "the threat of a Middle East war, already minimized by Egypt's making peace with Israel and the disappearance of the Soviet Union, seems nonexistent today." Triumphant in his assessment, Hoagland asserted, "The Palestinian cause...is no longer a mobilizing force for a regional war...The Arab-Israeli conflict has shrunk back to its pre-1948 dimensions."[48]

Twelve days after Hoagland wrote this rosy, triumphalist assessment filled with biblical metaphors, the two tallest towers in New York were destroyed and the most impregnable fortress in the world breached. The Arab-Israeli conflict, far from shrinking, was here.

—NINE—

AFTER THE FLAMES: ARAB AMERICANS AND AMERICAN FEAR (2001–2005)

September 11 and the Patriot Act

On September 11, anyone in the United States not obviously black or white—anyone, in short, whose face was brown, hid it. Maybe only briefly. Maybe only to look away in a bus station, or down in a supermarket, or touching an open hand in line for a driver's license. That brown face—Italian, Hispanic, Sikh, Arab—knew not only anger at the hijackers, agony at the senseless slaughter, and determination that the killers be found and brought to justice (emotions nearly all Americans felt), but something different. Fear. And not just fear of fanatical Arabs.

Fear of being mistaken. Indeed, if brown hid you pleasantly before, if you managed to avoid the race riots between black and white and the attendant racial animosities, brown was not doing for you what it formerly did. Brown was now a kind of stripping. And if that particular brown face was Arab American, there were two more emotions that other Americans did not share on 9/11: a kind of shame and sense of betrayal.

For young Johnny Makhoul, born and raised in New Jersey, September 11 began as just another day at work as a stock and bond trader. At about 7:50 AM, he emerged from the subway at the World Trade Center, and walked to his office 100 yards away. Some traders were talking about Osama bin Laden, something that "didn't strike me as anything but pre-trading bullshitting."[1] At 8:46 AM, he heard a loud crash and wrote it off as "the air conditioner just turning on." But then he looked out the window:

> I saw people running and papers flying. From that window, we couldn't yet see the Trade Center. When we found out what had happened, everyone was panicking. First thoughts were it was a bomb, then we heard it was a plane... Our phones started ringing off the hook. About fifteen minutes later we heard another crash... Everyone started freaking out and we all walked down seventeen flights and left the building. People crying, laughing, kids playing

around not understanding what was happening. I was scared, but in awe. I looked up at these two monstrosities that I walked through twice a day just burning, with a ton of black smoke and two gaping holes in the sides.

Makhoul's sister Janine, who worked even closer to the WTC, told him the gruesome sight she had seen of people jumping. But after the second plane rammed into the south tower, he lost contact with her. Phones all went dead. He headed east in the smoke and the piñata-like confetti of documents that must have once seemed important. Miraculously, he found his sister waiting in line in the smoke for a pay phone, and the two of them headed uptown, away "from the mess and other landmarks we thought they may attack." They were going to go to Janine's apartment near the United Nations building, thought better of it, and went even further uptown before collapsing around 76th and Lexington at a friend's flat, crying, holding each other, astonished and grateful that "everyone we were close to was accounted for."

For some time, the smoke was "brutal" downtown and the traders wore surgical masks for months to protect from the stench and atomized toxins. "Even today," he says, "We are constantly reminded of 9/11." He had scouted his new apartment in Hoboken across the East River for the spectacular view of downtown and the towers. "We'll take it!" he and his roommate had exclaimed in August 2001. When they moved in that October, the towers were gone. "It was depressing," Makhoul admitted. "They are making progress now and I'm sure it will be similar to what it once was. But it will never be the same."

Little would be. The 3,100 people who died that day in New York, Virginia, and Pennsylvania constituted the second largest one-day death toll for violent attack in US history. (5,110 were killed in one day at the battle of Antietam in 1862.) For three days, almost no planes flew anywhere in the United States. In two weeks, 16 percent of all US scheduled flights were cut. The loss in revenue for an already ailing US industry was staggering.[2] Tourism, especially in Washington, DC, which also endured the anthrax scare, hit the floor. For months, attendance at the museums was down 25 percent, and even free ridership on the metro did not lure customers downtown.[3] Already festooned with barricades, cement barriers, and a closed Pennsylvania Avenue after a decade of attacks, September 11 made security and surveillance a cottage industry in the nation's capital. New guard huts, high fences, 24-hour cameras, roadblocks were everywhere. One columnist put it, "Our lovely capital is being held hostage to fear. Washington, a beautiful city, is becoming uglier by the day."[4]

Ugliness wasn't the worst of it by a long shot. A huge hole lay at the center of lower Manhattan, like an open heart surgery that extended for months, years. Said one columnist: "Instead of the city recovering, it still ails both physically and emotionally."[5] Two months after the attacks, a study of the American Medical Association found that 11 percent of New Yorkers were suffering from some form of post-traumatic stress disorder (PTSD) (compared to 3 percent of Washingtonians and 4 percent of the country overall).[6] Other studies showed depression rates double the norm in New York City (9.7 percent vs. 4.9 percent) and treatment admissions for substance abuse risen by 10–12 percent nationwide.[7] At Christmas 2001, there was no hot cider or bonfire at the national Christmas tree on the Mall; a nearby stage where music was usually played at night was empty and dark.

Some people with brown faces were not only looking aside or closing their eyes—they were leaving. Two-and-a-half years after September 11, nearly 10 percent (15,000 of 120,000) of the Pakistani community in Brooklyn had left the country for Canada, Europe or Pakistan itself.[8]

On the other hand, six of the firemen who risked their lives jumping into the flames and cinders to help rescue people in New York City were Arab American. It was not long before a telling figure was unearthed: 300 of the dead in the World Trade Center towers were Muslim, over 10 percent of the total. In fact, citizens of 80 nations had been killed. Among them was an American Muslim emergency medical technician who lost his life trying to save others. Two days after the tragedy, the chief imam of the Malcolm Shabazz Mosque in Harlem and the first Muslim chaplain of the New York City Police Department said in a sermon, "We, Muslims, Americans, stand today with a heavy weight on our shoulders that those who would dare do such dastardly acts claim our faith. They are no believers in God at all."[9]

The Arab-American response to the September 11 slaughter was immediate and principled. Ziad Asali, ADC's president, released an open letter to the American public:

> Make no mistake about it, this attack was aimed at all Americans without exception and the Arab-American community shared every bit of heartache and anguish that all Americans have been enduring. No matter who was responsible for this terrible crime, which no cause or ideology could possibly justify, Arab Americans will be no less moved, no less angry, and no less outraged than our fellow Americans. Clearly, the best answer to such a despicable attack is for all Americans to join hands and come together to support each other in our time of need. Arab Americans are among the most eager to do just that.[10]

AAI's September 11 press release expressed grief and asked for cool heads to reign:

Arab Americans, like all Americans, are transfixed by this tragedy. We have family and friends who worked in the World Trade Center. We mourn for those who lost their lives and those who were injured...We urge our fellow citizens not to rush to judgment and point fingers at their Arab American neighbors and colleagues who are suffering, like all Americans, from these despicable acts.

A joint statement of eight Arab–American national organizations, including the American Muslim Council (AMC) and American Muslim Alliance (AMA), said on September 12:

We condemn in no uncertain terms the horrifying attacks on the World Trade Center and the Pentagon on September 11. We are shocked and angered at such brutality...We firmly believe there can be no justification for such horrible acts. We join with the nation in calling for the perpetrators of this terrible crime to be brought swiftly to justice.[11]

But, as I have indicated, more was reverberating inside Arab Americans than outrage and a cry for vengeance. That was there. But there was also an undeniable sense of shame and betrayal. All nineteen of the suicide hijackers were Arab. One of the emergency rescue workers at the Pentagon, a Circassian Muslim woman, was told, "Your name sounds too Arabic," and denied the chance to go with the first wave of rescue. Yet she herself took off her "Allah" that she wore around her neck because she was that "disgusted" to learn of the hijackers' identity. Traumatized herself after helping soldiers with their third-degree burns, she confessed that she could no longer eat meat, "because of the sight and smell of the bodies." "I was made into an instantaneous vegetarian," she said.[12] After all the work the community had done in the States to convince people of the just cause and good sense of the vast majority of Arabs, a few crazies had confirmed the worst suspicions and prejudices of Americans. Now it would be open season.

Naomi Shihab Nye caught these emotions powerfully in a piece read on National Public Radio, directly addressing not the terrorists, but young people in the Arab world who might be thinking of doing the same thing, "would-be terrorists": "I am sorry I have to call you that, but I don't know how else to get your attention. I hate that word. Do you know how hard some of us have worked to get rid of that word, to deny its instant connection to the Middle East? And now look." You can almost feel Nye gulping air in her anguished repetitions, her insistence, as if she were holding some young Arab and shaking him by the shoulders:

Many people, thousands of people, perhaps even millions of people in the United States are very aware of the long unfairness of our country's policies regarding Israel and Palestine. We talk about this all the time. It exhausts us and we keep talking. We write letters to newspapers, to politicians, to each other. We speak out in public even when it is uncomfortable to do so, because that is our responsibility. Because I am Arab American, people always express these views to me, and I am amazed how many understand the intricate situation and have strong, caring feelings for Arabs and Palestinians even when they don't have to. Think of them, please: All those people who have been standing up for Arabs when they didn't have to... This tragedy could never help the Palestinians.

She took on fundamentalism:

Have you noticed how many roads there are? Sure you have. You must check out maps and highways and small alternate routes just like anyone else. There is no way everyone on earth could travel the same road, or believe in exactly the same religion. It would be too crowded; it would be dumb. I don't believe you want us all to be Muslims. My Palestinian grandmother lived to be 106 years old and did not read and write, but even she was smarter than that.

Nye concluded with an appeal to basic humanity in a young person with a grievance:

We will all die soon enough. Why not take the short time we have on this delicate planet and figure out some really interesting things we might do together? I promise you, God would be happier... Our hearts are broken: as yours may also feel broken in some ways, we can't understand, unless you tell us in words. Killing people won't tell us. We can't read that message. Find another way to live. Don't expect others to be like you. Read Rumi. Read Arabic poetry...Plant mint. Find a friend who is so different from you, you can't believe how much you have in common. Love them. Let them love you. Surprise people in gentle ways, as friends do. The rest of us will try harder too. Make our family proud.[13]

Some were already in action. Ali Taqi, a firefighter, drove all the way from Troy, Michigan, to New York City, along with seven other fireman, where they entered the smoking ruins and searched for victims.[14] Firefighter Ron Kuley, a child of Iraqi immigrants, fought the flames at the Pentagon and then hopped a helicopter north to fight them at the World Trade Center. Dr. Taufik Kassis treated many of the wounded at the Jersey City Medical Center. "It's important to speak out so people understand there is a huge difference between the terrorists who committed these attacks and other Muslims and Arabs or Arab Americans," he said.[15]

Americans returned the gestures. All across the country there was an outpouring of compassion and concern, not just for the victims and their families, but for Arab Americans and Muslims. For a week

303

after the attacks, Linda Jasper, an English teacher in Rockville, Maryland, stood guard with some friends all night long outside the Islamic Center of Maryland. Similarly, members of the Mennonite Church in Boise, ID, walked alongside Muslim women in *hijab* as they went to school or to pray. When the oldest mosque in Columbus, Ohio, was severely damaged by vandals, the First Congregational Church offered a temporary home for the Muslims to hold their services, as did a Columbus synagogue.[16]

Shortly after the September 11 attacks, Naomi Shihab Nye and I talked on the phone. Her father, Aziz, who had been an editor with the *Dallas Morning News* and now ran his own paper, the *Arab Star*, had said to her, "Why, Naomi? Why is no one asking why?" She said the first thought that came across her mind, after the shock and horror at the deaths, was "What can we do better?"

But before anyone would inspect the festering sores of American foreign policy, there was hell to pay here. On September 15, 2001, a Phoenix man on a shooting spree killed a Sikh while he was planting flowers at his gas station, shot and missed a Lebanese-American gas station clerk, and riddled the home of an Afghan with bullets. That same day a Christian Copt from Egypt was shot to death in his store in San Gabriel, CA. On October 2, a Yemeni father of eight was shot to death in his convenience store in Reedley, CA. On October 15, a Somali Muslim died of head wounds after he was slugged in the temple as he stood at a bus stop in Minneapolis. In places as disparate as Seattle and Tulsa, OK, taxi dispatchers received calls saying their Arab and Muslim drivers would be killed.[17]

As many as eleven people in the United States were killed due to backlash after September 11. ADC confirmed 700 violent incidents in the year after the terrorist attacks, most of them in the first three months. Nothing like this had happened before in American history; the figures were five times those during the 1991 Gulf war and three times those after the bombing at Oklahoma City. The FBI found anti-Muslim hate crimes for 2001 to be seventeen times higher than the year before (481 vs. 28). The Council on American Islamic Relations (CAIR) tabulated 1,717 incidents of backlash discrimination against Muslims in the six months following September 11. At least fifteen arsons, six of them at houses of worship, appeared to be September 11-related.[18]

The picture even a sampling of these incidents paints is not a pretty one. They spanned the entire country. On September 13, baseballs painted with "God Bless America" and "Freedom for all" shattered the windows of a Greek-American's café in Everett, MA. On September 14, an Arab-American resident of Atlanta, GA, heard this message left on her phone machine: "We know where you are and we can get you." That same day, in Lexington, KY, a man put up a sign in his neighborhood that read, "Arabs are Murderers." When the neighborhood association asked him to take it down, he refused. Two Arab Americans lived there. On September 15, 2001, a Pakistani-owned restaurant, Curry in a Hurry, was torched in Salt Lake City. On September 16, an auto repair shop in Houston owned by Pakistani-Americans was burned to the ground. On September 23, St. John's Assyrian American Church in Chicago was set on fire; many of its precious icons were destroyed. A street in north Baltimore was spray-painted with a message in large letters: "Kill All Arabs Now." Even as late as the next April, a man smashed into a mosque in Tallahassee, FL, with his pick-up truck.

Some near misses were just as frightening as the hits. On August 23, 2002, Robert Goldstein, a Florida podiatrist, was arrested in Tampa and charged with conspiring to bomb and destroy about 50 mosques across the state. The doctor's home contained rocket launchers, sniper rifles, Claymore mines, and twenty live bombs. (Goldstein was later convicted and sentenced to twelve years in prison.) In Los Angeles, two members of the Jewish Defense League (JDL)—Irving Rubin and Earl Leslie Krugel—were indicted for conspiring to bomb a mosque and the California office of Rep. Darrel Issa.[19]

For several weeks and months following September 11, relations at schools and universities across the country were especially strained. On September 12, a tennis coach in Ferndale, MI, told his team, "Palestinian children should be shot, killed." The next day, an Arab-American teacher in a Christian school in Philadelphia, PA, was replaced and asked not to return to school, as the principal said, "Because you're Arab." On September 14, a Brooklyn health teacher allegedly told her class that "Palestinian children all want to become terrorists." On September 18, an instructor at a Costa Mesa, CA, college lost it completely, accusing four Muslim students in class of being terrorists, Nazis, and murderers; he was placed on paid leave, but later reinstated. On October 1, an Arab-American engineer working in a Vienna, VA, public school was told by his supervisor to complete a daily log, outlining his activities for every fifteen minutes. No other school employee was asked to do this. On January 3, 2002, a non-Arab mother in Fairfax County, VA, reported that a librarian at their public middle school had removed Naomi Shihab Nye's teen novel, *Habibi*, from the shelves; an Israeli-American had accused the book of being racist. These are only a few of the dozens of reports that came in from worried and angry parents documented in ADC's massive 150-page report on hate crimes since September 11.

If there was one profession an Arab American might as well give up, it was being a pilot. After September 11, BankAir pilot Aziz Baroody was interrogated by his company "ruthlessly" as to whether his parents and friends were terrorists; he had to take a polygraph test. A graduate of the Citadel, Baroody "always wanted to be a pilot. It was my passion in life and purpose on earth."[20] In his two years with the firm, he had received several raises and was captain of a Lear jet. But shortly after the attacks, he heard his colleagues spew phrases like "Nuke all the Arabs"; they asked him, "You gonna fly a plane into a building?" By December 2001, he was fired and sued for damage to his aircraft, "something I didn't even do." Baroody launched his own employment suit through ADC lawyers.

The workplace for Arab Americans never was more perilous than after the attacks. Shortly after September 11, in Cupertino, CA, a Jordanian-American technician was fired from his job making computer circuit boards. His pre-September 11 ratings had all been positive. In Island Park, NY, a Kuwaiti-American employee of a laundromat was fired from her part-time job of three years. Her boss told her, "The customers, they're scared of you. They're scared you are going to put a bomb here." A Yemeni-American who had worked as a Detroit welder for fifteen years was fired; his boss said, "Go home, pray to your leader, I don't want to see your face." An Arab-American federal worker in Rockville, MD, had his computer seized and exhaustively searched.

Denials of service occurred everywhere. In the heartland of the country—Des Moines, Iowa—a Marriott hotel stopped a convention of Syrian-Lebanese Americans from being held. (Marriott later paid a fine and engaged in a training program to sensitize its employees about Arab Americans.)[21] In Warren, MI, an Arab-American woman was removed as a voting member of her condominium association. "Arabs Not Welcome" was posted outside a bar in Scottsdale, AZ. A New Jersey resident was told by a Dallas collection agency that either he make his car payments or he would be reported to the FBI as connected with the terrorist attacks. An Arab-American customer in an office supply shop in New York City was threatened with a throat-slitting for his accent. A mortgage applicant in Sunrise, FL, was told he was rejected because an underwriting manager thought him a terrorist, even though before September 11, the man had gotten a loan from the same company.[22]

In the year after September 11, ADC received at least 80 reports of illegal airline discrimination and denial of service to passengers. This disturbing pattern of airport profiling often occurred when some passenger complained of feeling "uncomfortable" with a fellow passenger on board or in a waiting area who looked Middle Eastern. In some cases, airline captains or stewardesses would give a passenger the hook purely over looks or accent. This inquisitional air had embarrassing, even absurd, outcomes. On Christmas Day of 2001, an Arab-American member of President Bush's Secret Service detail, traveling on a commercial flight, was pulled off the flight by airport police. On December 31, a woman in first class on Continental Airlines carried her poodle up and down the aisle three times before take-off, inspecting the human cargo. Within minutes, the plane captain was heard saying "brown skinned men are behaving suspiciously" in first class and three of them were removed, including an Arab American whose wife was an employee of Continental Airlines itself. One Pakistani-American was pulled off another Christmas flight on Northwest Airlines merely for looking "nervous" and "looking around" too much. Four men (one Arab American) were pulled off a Pittsburgh flight of US Airways at Washington Dulles Airport on October 5 when the stewardess found it odd that two of these dark men used the toilet without flushing![23] Lest anyone think this discrimination was not equal opportunity, according to the *San Francisco Chronicle* (September 28, 2001), a Jewish-American businessman with the wrong cast of skin was pulled aside by a ticket clerk at Chicago's O'Hare International Airport en route to Hartford, CT, and told the pilot didn't want him on the flight.

In spite of repeated efforts to get the US Department of Transportation (DoT) to issue guidelines for crews that would preempt such illegal plucking of certain passengers off flights for whatever willies they gave people, on June 4, 2002, ADC and the ACLU filed lawsuits against United Airlines, Continental, and American Airlines; ACLU filed a similar separate suit against Northwest Airlines. Two of the suits (American and United) have been settled; due partly to DoT intervention, United agreed to spend $1.5 million on racial sensitivity training. Still, because of 9/11, airline passengers are now color-coded—green, yellow, or red—based on so-called risk factors such as name, travel itinerary, home address, and traveling companions. Though most people get a green "pass," an estimated 8 percent get yellow (extra screening) and the 1–2 percent given red are refused boarding and face police questioning and possible arrest.[24] If your name is al-Bazz and you were born in Cairo, you're probably in for at least a yellow.

Not to be outdone in zealotry, Boston's celebrated T subway appeared to have inaugurated the first policy of random searches of bags carried by passengers in the nation. In July 2004, ADC joined the National Lawyers Guild in filing suit against the Massachusetts Bay Transportation Authority (MBTA) claiming that sweeping policy violates the Fourth Amendment to the US Constitution barring unreasonable searches and seizures.

At a time when spiritual leaders should have been reflective and calm, some seemed ready for the Crusades. Even a year after the attacks, Jerry Falwell could still say on the most popular news show on television, "I do believe Jesus set the example for love, as did Moses. And I think that Mohammed set an opposite example."[25] Franklin Graham, son of evangelist Billy Graham and a preacher himself, called Islam "a very evil and wicked religion" on network television.[26] On February 24, 2002, with plenty of time to reflect on it all, and read condemnations of the September 11 fanatics by Muslim leaders around the world, Rev. Pat Robertson told CNN, "Osama bin Laden is probably truer to Mohammed than some of the others."

Some political leaders did not help, particularly when they set themselves up as experts in comparative religion. Attorney General John Ashcroft was quoted in a syndicated column by Cal Thomas as saying, "Islam is a religion in which God requires you to send your son to die for him. Christianity is a faith in which God sends his son to die for you." Ashcroft said he was misquoted.[27] ADC met with Rep. John Cooksey (R-LA) after he said on Louisiana radio, "If I see someone come in that's got a diaper on his head, and a fan belt wrapped around that diaper on his head, that guy needs to be pulled over."[28] Rep. Howard Coble (R-NC) was unapologetic about his February 4, 2002, remarks on radio that agreed with the internment of Japanese in World War II; though he didn't think Arab Americans should necessarily be confined, he did agree with a caller that "some of these Arab Americans are probably intent on doing us harm." ADC sent him 5,000 signatures on a petition that he step down as chairman of the House Judiciary Subcommittee on Crime, Terrorism, and Homeland Security.[29]

The spillover from such attitudes toward Arabs and Muslims in general to those skewering Palestinians was all too swift. TV's *Hardball* host Chris Matthews was incredulous at the assertion by Rep. Dick Armey (R-TX) that the West Bank should be ethnically cleansed of its entire one million Arab population. Matthews repeatedly asked him if his position was that the occupied territories should be emptied of Palestinians. Armey said, "Yes." It was an endorsement of war crimes from the highest ranks of the US Congress. Armey's office later issued a weak retraction.[30] But what in Israel is called "the transfer solution" and has been planned by elements of the Likud Party for years was gaining ground in right-wing Republican circles. An editor at the *National Review* came out for explusion of the entire Palestinian population in the West Bank arguing, "Being Arabs they [Palestinians] are incapable of constructing a rational polity..."[31]

Wisdom, needless to say, was in short supply. Writing in New York's most popular daily newspaper, Zev Chafets blasted Arab Americans, accusing them en masse of "affinity for the worst elements in the Middle East [that] has been a hallmark of Arab-American political discourse for years."[32] Syndicated columnists Mona Charen and Richard Cohen became vehement supporters of ethnic profiling of those who resembled an Arab. Ann Coulter put it subtly: "We should invade their countries, kill their leaders, and convert them to Christianity."[33] Even the eminent and insightful military historian John Keegan got caught in the "clash of civilizations" fever with this astounding claim: "It is no good pretending that the peoples of the desert and the empty spaces exist on the same level of civilization as those who farm and manufacture. They do not. Their attitude to the West has always been that it is a world ripe for the picking."[34]

Sensing the outlines of a pogrom, President George W. Bush spoke out forcefully and with great sensitivity against discrimination. Meeting with Muslim leaders on September 17, 2001, at Washington's Islamic Center, he said,

> Like the good folks standing with me, the American people were appalled and outraged at last Tuesday's attacks. And so were Muslims all across the world...These acts of violence against innocents violate the fundamental tenets of the Islamic faith. And it's important for my fellow Americans to understand that. The face of terror is not the true faith of Islam...Women who cover their heads in this country must feel comfortable going outside their homes. Moms who wear cover must not be intimidated in America. That's not the American I know. That's not the America I value.

Within a day of the attacks, Senator Ted Kennedy (D–MA) called ADC's Asali and AAI's Zogby, both of whom had received death threats and threats against their families. There was more at play here than the fact that Kennedy's wife is Lebanese-American, or that he has been a longstanding champion of civil rights. Two of his brothers had lost their lives, essentially, to hate crimes. "Above all," he said in a press release that day, "We must guard against any acts of violence based on such bigotry. America's ideals are under attack, too, and we must do all we can to uphold them at this difficult time." Kennedy led the effort to create a Senate resolution warning of backlash against Arab Americans and urging clear heads and understanding.

Against the riptide of bigotry stood seawalls of goodness throughout the country, efforts by local governments, organizations, and individuals to shield Arab Americans from harm. Chicago Mayor Richard Daley declared November to be "Arab-American Heritage Month" and kicked off the event with 500 members of the community from around the Windy City. In Indiana, PA, posters and fliers in several languages were distributed all over town stating, "Our community is a hate-free zone." A Green Armband Project in Louisville, KY, paired escorts to Arab Americans and Muslim Americans afraid to move about freely. Political action organizations of Korean, South Asian, Japanese, and Mexican Americans announced support and held rallies. Hispanic leader Antonia Hernandez said, "Our communities, the Arab American and the Latino, would stand to suffer a great deal if any widespread xenophobic reaction is not checked." The Asian American Journalists Association reminded the media that "Arab Americans, along with all of us, are victims of this attack."[35]

One woman in Chicago undertook an amazing project. Anya Cordell set up the Campaign for Collateral Compassion, which asked the major September 11 charities to include victims of hate crimes backlash as beneficiaries. Six families who lost members in the September 11 attacks endorsed Cordell's project. Said Amber Amundsen, whose husband was killed at the Pentagon, "They, too, were victims of terrorism, just like those who died on September 11."[36] In a similarly generous, enlightened vein, the American Jewish World Service announced that it was providing funds to those hurt by the attacks with no health coverage; to organizations who aid undocumented workers cringing from the backlash; and to groups helping Arab Americans.

Courageous people in the entertainment and advertising industry stepped up to the plate. Actress Patricia Arquette, whose mother is Jewish and father Muslim, organized 50 actors and other celebrities for a public-service message campaign discouraging racist acts and hate crimes. Among her volunteers were actors Ben Stiller, Whoopi Goldberg, Benicio Del Toro, Lucy Liu, and Shannon Elizabeth (who is half Syro-Lebanese).[37] Likewise, the Ad Council collaborated with AAI to produce a striking ad picturing the Twin Towers as two tall messages under the title "Americans Stand United," which read, in part: "…[A] neighborhood mosque defaced by vandals. An Arab American shopkeeper in fear of reprisal. A scared Muslim child bullied because she is different. Hate is our enemy." The ad was printed in 10,000 newspapers, 1,300 magazines, and reached 64 million Americans as a spot on cable television.[38]

In an atmosphere of suspicion, bewilderment, and dread, while one branch of government was passing laws that put the Bill of Rights at risk, another was showing Arab Americans special compassion. In November 2001, the US Department of Health and Human Services' Substance Abuse and Mental Health Services Adminstration (SAMHSA) conducted a "listening session" in Rockville, MD, to get a sense of Arab-American mental health needs during this difficult time. One of the dozen or so attendants, Virginia social psychologist Salma Abugideiri said the chief questions on individuals' minds are: "How American am I? What does it mean to be an Arab?" Some noted the peculiar isolation of Christian Arab Americans, who feel estranged both from the Muslim world and from American political policies. Dr. Adnan Hammad from ACCESS in Detroit told of a friend who was greeted every morning at work after September 11 "Hi, Terrorist," but didn't confront anyone about it for fear of losing her job. A SAMHSA report on the unusual meeting said, "First-generation Arab Americans immigrated as refugees fleeing repressive regimes or war-torn countries. The events have caused a retraumatization for them in a country they had considered a haven."[39]

As the months after 9/11 stretched past four years without another horrific incident on American soil, tensions calmed some, and certain Arab American therapists and social workers, such as Lobna Ismail and Samira Hussein of suburban Maryland, helped sensitize police and other law enforcement officials to stereotypes in order avoid backlash in the future. In October 2003, Ismail addressed an audience of 150 FBI agents and police, dressed in traditional Muslim *hijab*.[40] After being victimized by hate crimes stretching back to the Gulf war, Samira Hussein[41] lobbied successfully for an Arab-American Day proclaimed by Montgomery County's executive Douglas Duncan, who enthusiastically attends each year.

Even as the community was buoyed and gratified by these gestures of kindness and support, the Patriot Act was giving people nervous pause. Passed with less than a half hour of debate by the Senate and signed into law on October 26, 2001, by President Bush, the 342-page USA Patriot Act had an imposing acronym constructed from the law's official title: The Uniting and Strengthening America by Providing Appropriate Tools Required to Intercept and Obstruct Terrorism Act. Much of the new legislation looked like common sense protection of citizens in a perilous time. While most Arab Americans, like most Americans, understood and even applauded the need for tighter security in crowded public places, especially at airports, and while they endured with general acceptance the

Police sergeant of Yemenite Jewish heritage on patrol in New York City, August 2001 (Mel Rosenthal)

mild indignity of being pulled out of line more often because of their last names or cast of face, certain parts of the Patriot Act worried them. They were not alone. Many began to wonder if the greatest victims of September 11 were the cherished freedoms enshrined in the Bill of Rights. One of the few dissenters in Congress, Rep. Dave Obey (D–WI) remarked bitterly, "Why should we care? It's only the Constitution."[42]

The Patriot Act took up where Clinton's 1996 Anti–Terrorism Act left off. Three of its most draconian measures deal with indefinite detention; searches, seizures and wiretapping; and guilt by association. No one really knows how many men of Middle Eastern origin were swooped up around the country into secret detention after September 11; the usual estimate is 1,200. ADC thought the figure closer to 2,000. Few outside law enforcement itself know where they have been held. Many waited months even to be allowed to retain an attorney or hear what charges were being leveled against them. It appears many, if not most, had expired visas—so they were held for fairly trivial reasons while more serious allegations (association with terrorism) were examined. Bail after a few days in jail for minor visa violations is usually under $2,500. Under the sweep, if bonds were even allowed, they went for $15,000. The Department of Justice has admitted to at least 600 secret hearings since September 11. Many people have been summarily deported with virtually no due process; on one occasion, 132 men were shipped off by plane to Pakistan and told not to come back.

The "Buffalo Six" case is less nuanced but more disturbing. In September 2002, five Yemenis, some of them students, were arrested in Buffalo, NY, and admitted in plea bargaining to being trained with weapons in Afghanistan. They are all serving sentences ranging from seven to ten years; a sixth was killed in Yemen by a Predator drone as he drove a car.[43] Are people trained in Idaho by white supremacists in the use of firearms liable to ten years in prison? Before they have done anything? How far does the law take us down the road of those who are "potentially dangerous"? Judging from the manic testimony of people on talk radio or late–night television shows such as Jerry Springer, maybe millions.

As of this writing, it appears only 73 of the detainees remain. Still, the government has refused to comply with an August 2, 2002, court order requiring basic information about those who were first rounded up and those who are left, such as their names. From reports of families pulled into the dragnet operation under the Patriot Act, ADC and Human Rights Watch began to collect profiles. Among them are the following:

A Pakistani student in Wiggens, MS, was pulled off an express bus headed to New York, found to have an expired visa, thrown into a jail cell where he was beaten up by hostile inmates and called "bin Laden." He sustained broken bones and loss of hearing in one ear.

An Egyptian national was picked up in Maryland two days after September 11 when a hotel clerk told police he "looked suspicious." He was held for two months before being deported for violating the terms of a previous visa stay.

Two Somali men were picked up in Texas while they were praying toward Mecca in a parking lot, roused by a "nervous bystander." They were arrested when a knife and an apparently altered driver's license was found in their car.

An Egyptian doctor was held for five months without counsel or any evidence of links to terrorism after New York City police saw him stopped by the side of the road looking at a map ten days after 9/11.

Most troubling was evidence of torture—not only in Iraq, but here, in the United States. Even as the scandal of American GIs beating and humiliating Arab prisoners at the Abu Ghraib complex in Baghdad came to light, stories emerged of similar treatment here, particularly at the Brooklyn, New York, Metropolitan Detention Center. A December 2003 Department of Justice Inspector General report detailed that the MDC torture, though not as severe as that at Abu Ghraib, bore striking similarities to it. Prisoners at the MDC (where 84 of 762 Muslims immigrants in the New York area were detained) were regularly stripped, sexually humiliated, subjected to prolonged sleep deprivation, slammed against walls, and beaten. Some were chained at both legs and told to run while guards stepped on the chains; some endured solitary confinement for months. One man, cleared of any ties to terrorism, spent about 24 days "in the hole" subjected to psychological torture using dogs. He said, "If this happened in Syria, Iraq, it's normal, but in America, it's different, really."[44]

Arab Americans, evidently, had little to fear from this dragnet; those picked up were generally foreign nationals. But the secrecy of it all was disturbing no matter what your background; the notion of being singled out by accent or ethnicity alarming. There were, after all, some 315,000 "absconders" in the country, people who are deportable for visa violations. Was it necessary to put Arabs at the head of the list? Some bent over backwards, giving law enforcement the benefit of the doubt during the time of tremendous fear that surrounded September 11. But two months later, Ashcroft issued orders that 5,000 men ages 18 to 33 who had come into the United States legally on non-immigrant visas from countries where al-Qaeda "has a terrorist presence or activity" since January 2000 be sought for interview. In March 2002, 3,000 more names were added. And then, fearing a terrorist spectacular (which never happened) in the election year of 2004, the FBI scoured the country, conducting 13,000 interviews almost entirely in the Muslim community (on October 21, the ACLU filed suit to obtain documents the FBI was withholding about these interviews).[45]

Inasmuch as the interview was voluntary it did not seem a horrific impingement on freedom, but where was this all going to end? Once you start a racial or religious profiling campaign of that magnitude, might it not matter, finally, whether you are a citizen or not? And how free is anyone, really, to turn down the FBI? One courageous police chief in Madison, WI, refused to conduct interviews "solely based on their country of origin, race, religion, or any other characteristics unless there is specific evidence linked to that person for a criminal act."[46] Another chief in Hillsboro, OR, ordered his officers to refuse compliance with any terrorism investigation that violates constitutional rights. Clearly, not all the citizenry were taking the Patriot Act lying down.

Still, the notion of what constitutes a criminal act expanded. In December 2003, Latinas at the National Countil of La Raza joined ADC and others in a lawsuit against the FBI after, for the first time in history, it expanded the FBI crime database (NCIC) to include violations of civil immigration laws. If you were a day late on your visa renewal, you were a criminal.

As for searches and seizures, under the Patriot Act it was now okay for the FBI to enter your home or office without notice, whether you are home or not, insert a "magic lantern" into your computer and allow far-off agents to download anything you had written, sent, or pulled up for reference. In May 2003, the Justice Department told Congress it had delayed notifying people of 47 searches and 15 seizures of their belongings.[47] The now infamous library searches were allowed: the FBI could go into libraries and bookstores to find out what a person read or bought; the connection to terrorism could be tenuous, at best. As Nat Hentoff has noted, a gag rule "unprecedented in American history"[48] forbids a librarian or bookstore owner from telling anyone, including the press, that these searches have occurred. One source told the *Washington Post* that FBI agents had contacted libraries 50 times in the past two years, but the actual number is unknown because it is classified. On July 30, 2003, ADC joined the ACLU and others filing suit against Section 215 of the Patriot Act—the part that allows such "library" searches.

Most troublesome of all was the "guilt by association" that pervaded the government's whole legal apparatus, a "Grand Inquisitor" approach to the threat of terrorism that had many people frightened, if not appalled. What constitutes "terrorism" or a "terrorist organization" is highly elastic under the Patriot Act; Section 411 of the act allows for detention and deportation of noncitizens for associations that might be utterly innocent. Being around vandalism or damage in a political rally can label one a "terrorist." Where was that sort of thing headed? A politically controversial speech merits jail? Someone gives a check for medicine for an overseas charity that helps Palestinians, and then you take him off into the woods?

The paranoia seemed at times to know no bounds. On August 3, 2004, a delegation of Iraqi leaders sponsored to come to this country by our own US state department was refused entrance to the Memphis (TN) City Hall. The City Council threatened to evacuate the building and send in bomb squads if the Iraqis set foot in the place.

If at first Arab Americans wondered if they might be immune to the storm of the Patriot Act, by 2002 they were thinking again. In December 2001, three sizable Muslim charities in the United States were effectively shut down—Benevolence International, Global Relief, and the Holy Land Foundation. Stung, the Muslim Public Affairs Council called for guidelines so American Muslims could fulfill their obligation to tithe (*zakat*) without fear: "Muslim charities are willing to adopt a policy of complete transparency. They are eager to show the government where their money comes from and what they use it for."[49]

Still, in mid-March 2002, fourteen American Muslim organizations were raided. No one was arrested and no offices closed, but federal agents entered homes at gunpoint, handcuffed residents during the raids, carted off boxes of material and destroyed some property, "all the while using affidavits which were 'secret and sealed' giving the victims no idea why these events happened, what was taken, and what they were hoping to find."[50]

In August 2002, the FBI announced it was closely monitoring money trails in small businesses owned by Arab Americans or Muslim Americans, "a chilling reminder of how widely the government's dragnet is being cast."[51] The intense scrutiny took itself even to the shadow of Disneyland. The South Brookhurst shopping district known as "Little Gaza" in Anaheim, California, has many Muslim-owned stores that, even in 2004, were being combed for "Islamic terrorists." One Syrian-born insurance company owner, Belal Dalati, watched with chagrin as police officers jotted down license plate numbers, asking to see vehicle registrations and green cards, and directing their binoculars to storefronts from unmarked cars. "It has been a very uncomfortable situation for a very long time," said Dalati. "Since 9/11, we don't feel like we're in America anymore. We understand that the FBI and police have to do their jobs to protect America. All we're asking is to treat us with respect and don't violate our rights."[52] Another businessman, Ahmad Alam, pressured to be an informant, was told by an officer that five of the butcher shops, restaurants, beauty salons, and offices in Little Gaza were "fronts for the militant group Hezbollah." It was a ridiculous claim, Delati explained. Hezbollah is a Shiʿite Muslim group; the Muslims of Anaheim are overwhelmingly Sunnis.

One Orwellian method of surveillance developed by the attorney general, so far held off from actual use, has lawmakers and others alarmed. The TIPS program (Terrorism Information and Prevention System) is an unabashed attempt to create an informer system in American society that could rival anything in the former Soviet Union. TIPS would ask certain types of workers with deep access to neighborhoods—letter carriers, service trucks, bus drivers, utility workers—to report to police about any "unusual events" or suspicious people. It was as close to Big Brother as the US had seen when, in spring 2002, the FBI issued an advisory that warned property owners, public housing officials, and landlords to monitor any signs of terrorists renting apartments. An imam at the Islamic Center of Southern California commented, "The community is really scared. Today it's apartments, tomorrow it's the neighborhood where people won't sell their houses to us."[53]

Closely related to this government sweep of Muslim charities, businesses, and communities was a microscopic scrutiny of the statements of Muslim professors by university administrators. One tenured professor of computer engineering at the University of South Florida was fired when it was determined two attendees at one of his conferences were involved in the 1993 World Trade Center bombing and with Islamic Jihad; Sami al-Arian denied knowing of these associations. Al-Arian, who is suing USF with the support of the faculty union and others, has been an outspoken supporter of the Palestinians and feels the real issue is academic freedom of speech. If the firing is sustained, he believed "every single tenured professor across the country could be terminated, especially Arabs." *Time* asked of a student senator who opposed al-Arian, "Should [he] someday become a college professor, how safe will he feel, after the al-Arian firing, to speak his mind?"[54] In February 2004, tenure was the least al-Arian was losing—he was indicted on several counts, including material support for terrorism, as the North American leader of Islamic Jihad and was put in solitary confinement. His trial began in July 2005.

To top all this off, in July 2002, a Bush-appointed member of the US Civil Rights Commission, Peter Kirsanow, indicated that another Arab terrorist strike on America could easily lead to internment of Arab Americans in camps. Though he didn't support such camps personally, in the event of another attack Kirsanow said "you can forget about civil rights" and that there would be "a groundswell of opinion" in the public for rounding up Arab Americans like the Japanese in World War II. "Not too many people will be crying in their beer if there are more detentions, more stops, more profiling," he said. Another Bush appointee on the commission, Jennifer Braceras, added fuel to the fire, "There's no constitutional right not to be inconvenienced or even embarrassed." When queried, a White House spokesman said the possibility of Arab internment camps had not been discussed by the president or his advisors.[55] Still, Arab Americans remained very concerned about Kirsanow's remarks in light of the 1987 Contingency Plan and the Japanese-American experience. Japanese Americans were on alert, too.[56]

WAR WITH AFGHANISTAN AND IRAQ

The hunt for bin Laden and his henchman in Afghanistan evolved into a full-scale war to topple the repressive Taliban regime. Arab Americans joined most Americans in supporting this effort, elusive as bin Laden himself turned out to be. (When asked if they supported "an all-out war against countries that harbor the terrorists who attacked America," 69 percent of Arab Americans agreed, according to a Zogby poll.) But it was with great dismay that they read about an Arab American taken into custody on that far-off battlefield.

Yaser Hamdi was not an Arab student whose visa had elapsed, but a young man born in the state of Louisiana. Yet he was afforded none of the normal rights afforded a US citizen under the Constitution, such as the right to counsel and the right to understand what he was being charged with; he was held incognito and indefinitely, apparently as an enemy combatant, in a Virginia navy brig for three years. Federal District Judge Robert Doumar was incredulous: "So the Constitution doesn't apply for Mr. Hamdi?"[57] After the Fourth Circuit Court of Appeals refused to set Hamdi free, an unprecedented violation of due process for an American citizen, dissenting judge Diana Gribbon Motz said, "[The ruling] marks the first time in our history that a federal court has approved the elimination of protections afforded a citizen by the Constitution solely on the basis of the executive's designation of that citizen as a enemy combatant, without testing the accuracy of that designation."[58] In June 2004 the US Supreme Court ruled that Hamdi and other detainees classified as enemy combatants could not be held indefinitely without charges. This led to an unusual "deal," wherein Hamdi was freed in October 2004 and sent to his family in Saudi Arabia after he agreed to renounce his US citizenship.[59]

In ensuing years, other arrests embarrassed and warned the community, increasing the fear of racial targeting and blanket blame. On February 23, 2005, a former Virginia high school valedictorian was indicted for plotting with al-Qaeda to kill the president. Ahmed Omar Abu Ali, 23, and an American citizen, was held in Saudi Arabia for two years, where his parents allege he was tortured.[60] In the midst of the Iraqi whirlwind with insurgent suicide bombers killing an average of 20 civilians a day, in 2005 three Iraqi Americans were arrested in Iraq "for engaging in suspicious activities," alleged involvement in kidnapping, and "having knowledge of planning associated with attacks on coalition forces." A Jordanian American was also arrested; he was thought to be close to Abu Musab Zarqawi.[61] It was truly unsettling that some in the community may have gone over the top, poisoned by hate. An already exposed community felt increasingly naked. It did not help that a non-Arab "American Taliban," grungy beard and all, was paraded before the public. John Walker Lindh had taken a Muslim name, in any case— "Abdul Hamid."[62]

Though most Arab Americans agreed with the Afghan campaign, there were troubling and costly mistakes. By December 2001, eight weeks into the Afghan war, 3,767 civilians were reported killed or wounded, and that was a conservative figure. Included in the bloody botches of not-so-smart US bombs was one that hit the UN office in Kabul on October 9, killing four UN employees and crippling mine removal operations. A week later, US planes bombed Red Cross buildings, apologized, and then a week after that, hit another Red Cross building in broad daylight, which "wrecked and set ablaze warehouses storing tons of food and blankets for civilians."[63] Perhaps the most embarrassing operation—well-intentioned, of course—was the air-dropping of 960,000 US food packets to an essentially starving population of 34 million. Tragically, inexplicably, they were colored bright yellow, the same color as cluster bombs dropped by US planes. Before too many children were blown up thinking a bomb was food, the Pentagon changed the food packet color to blue.[64]

The *coup de grace* after all this was that bin Laden, his sidekick Mullah Omar, and many other al-Qaeda faithful, appear to have escaped the spectacular cave bombings in Tora Bora, probably into Pakistan. But at least the United States had former Unocal Oil Company consultant Hamid Karzai to point to as a credible new leader of Afghanistan's rather delicate new democracy.

Over the invasion of Iraq, the Arab-American community was far more divided, reflecting misgivings in the public at large severe enough to make Iraq a major issue in the 2004 presidential election. Chaldean Americans and Iraqi Americans of Shi'ite background whose families had suffered from Saddam Hussein's repressive regime directly cheered the United States on. Once again, no one could possibly be against helping to bring democracy to a country in a region so hopelessly bereft of it. But at what cost ($87 billion was the President's price-tag in 2003—and in two years it doubled to $175 billion)? And for what purpose? Was Bush blurring the mission? Wasn't it al-Qaeda, stupid? And truly—were we safer? As Christopher Dickey has shown, what we spend every few days in Iraq ($100 million) would fund for a year tracking a real threat: nuclear weapons theft.[65] What was one to make of Bush's incredible January 29, 2002, State of the Union address in which he seemed to be creating antagonists from the shadows? If Iraq, Iran, and North Korea weren't implacable enemies before, now starring as an "axis of evil," they surely would be. Forget the fact that Iran had been one of the quickest Muslim nations to condemn the September 11 attacks and feed the US valuable intelligence on al-Qaeda. Forget that North Korea had been, for the first time in decades, toning down its nuclear rhetoric and, under Clinton, had been engaging America in direct talks. Discount completely the UN weapons inspection process in Iraq that had found nothing in its last years of real threat but bad water; it needed only a year to finish the job. Bush not only threatened to go it alone; he seemed to want to. There was something very Texan about all this—carpet-bagging Texan, to boot.

The word was that America had become a unilaterist nation, but what it really had become was an autocracy positing a war-without-end. Blind rage and a thirst for oil seemed to be substituting for foreign policy. For one thing, Saddam, as cruel as he was, seemed the wrong target. As the American poet Robert Hedin said, "Saddam is a convenient punching bag." Ten years before, bin Laden had offered the Saudis his own private army to route Saddam from Kuwait; there was no love lost between Saddam and Osama. No less a universally respected figure as Gen. Brent Scowcroft, head of Bush's Foreign Intelligence Advisory Board, tried to set the hawks straight: "There is scant evidence to tie Saddam to terrorist organizations, and even less to the September 11 attacks. Indeed, Saddam's goals have little in common with the terrorist who threatens us, and there is little incentive for him to make common cause with them."[66]

If nothing else, Bush's war on terrorism had proved the central point of his critics: it shouldn't have been prosecuted as a war. The chief criminal was still free. Full-scale wars create a lot of hubbub, smoke, new enemies, and tons of ways to escape, particularly in mountainous countries. Police manhunts—or commando raids—rely on stealth. They take a lot of patience and time, but they tend to work, especially if you have the population on your side. The full-scale military approach to curing the urge to terror in downtrodden societies can't work by itself; it may not even be the most effective weapon. Improving life conditions and eradicating unjust policies that destroy people's souls go a lot further than destroying a village, even a hostile one.

Had we walked into a civil war? The real war in Iraq seemed to start after we had declared victory. Appropriately enough, President Bush did so while "out at sea" on an American destroyer. Finding Saddam literally holed up in Tikrit was the easiest part of it all. Facing 20,000 mostly Sunni insurgent fighters whose attacks doubled from 2003 to 2004 was another thing entirely. And then there were brutal execution-style murders of Americans who were doing nothing more than trying to make things better for Iraqis. On May 13, 2004, ADC President Mary Rose Oakar condemned the murder of Nicholas Berg, an American civilian: "There is no possible rationalization for such appalling brutality. To showcase this horror on the Internet is simply beyond comprehension." On September 21, after Eugene Armstrong was beheaded, Oakar said in a press release, "These murders perpetuate the radicals' twisted agenda. The fact that the extremists invoke the name of God to suit their own purposes is repugnant to people of all faiths and creeds."

By the fall of 2004, the indicators in Iraq did not look good. Scholars from the Brookings Institution noted that though we were spending $5 billion a month in Iraq, electricity was available less than half the day to most households; the unemployment rate was 30 to 40 percent; and the crime rate "at least several times worse than that of America's worst neighborhoods."[67] These are all conditions worse than in the worst days of Saddam Hussein. Though most Iraqis are pleased to be free of him, a 2004 poll showed 80 percent of them having "lost faith" in the United States, viewing it more as an occupying rather than liberating force. By June 2005, a majority (52 percent) of Americans said that the Iraq war had *not* made the United States safer, and nearly two-thirds felt that the war was not worth fighting. Three-quarters of Americans called the number of US casualties (over 2,000 by October 2005) "unacceptable." At the end of June, 12,000 Iraqi civilians had also died.[68]

Perhaps it was time to let Iraqis "own" their own freedom, come what may. Citing the "Pottery Barn-theory" of international relations ("you break it, you own it"), columnist Michael Kinsley asked poignantly, "The question is whether at this point we're actually helping to tidy up, or only making a bigger mess."[69] On January 27, 2005, the *Los Angeles Times* became the first major American newspaper to editorialize for a pull-out from Iraq ("Which Way Out?"); the night before the much-touted Iraqi elections (January 29), Senator Ted Kennedy (D-MA) became the first US Senator to do so.

Poet Etel Adnan had advice on the eve of the Iraq campaign: "Before going to an all-out war which will inevitably send us all to some other world most of us are not eager to visit, let us look to our windows, look out, and discover the mysteries of the garden." After being abroad for two years, Adnan returned to America to witness a surprising takeover—of violets: "Those shy, timid, and modest purple flowers had overcome the cactuses... don't ever underestimate the 'weak' and don't do anything with small nations in the name of your own security because all you do is make room for the bigger sharks to move in. Mixed message, I agree."[70] If only Bush had looked at Adnan's garden.

Why had we ever gotten ourselves into Iraq? Many inside and outside the Arab-American community thought voices in the administration such as Richard Perle and Paul Wolfowitz had led the charge, in an effort to protect Israel. (It wasn't long before Perle was eyeing Syria as America's next target.) Crippling any Arab military or economic ascendancy is critical to Israel's maximalist territorial goals. In short, if the heat is on Saddam, it is not on Sharon.

Arab Americans generally hoped, at the very least, that Bush would put heat on both, or at least emerge from a victory in Iraq to hold Sharon's feet to the fire and finally secure peace and a Palestinian state. On May 9, 2003, in a speech at the University of South Carolina, Bush gave hope to the community and the world when he boldly affirmed his goal of such a state—the first president to do so: "If the Palestinian people take concrete steps to crack down on terror, continue on a path of peace, reform and democracy, they and all the world will see the flag of Palestine raised over a free and independent nation." Bush also insisted that "as progress is made toward peace, Israel must stop settlement activity in the occupied territories." It was followed by well-meaning, but oddly general remarks by Colin Powell to the ADC in the summer 2003, only the second time a standing Secretary of State addressed an Arab-American convention. (Warren Christopher had done it in 1992; James Baker did so after his tenure to the NAAA in 1995.)[71]

But they were only words. As for Bush's insistence on "progress" before settlements could be dismantled, from the Palestinian perspective, progress was supposed to have been made toward peace for a decade of the Oslo process, but settlements never stopped. They hadn't stopped before, during, or after Arafat's death in 2004. Twice Bush seemed to challenge Sharon—when Israelis first lay siege to Arafat's office in Ramallah, and when Israel dragged its feet in transferring tax revenue to the Palestinians. But both times, Bush got cold feet. There were murmurs in the press (far back in the *Washington Post*) of withholding US aid over settlements. But it came to nothing. Bush simply would not confront Sharon, leading more than Arab Americans to think that the United States was being dictated to by Israel.[72]

Though creative modes of opposing this state of affairs cropped up. Four orders of Catholic nuns joined the Berkeley-based Jewish Voices for Peace, drafting a resolution at a 2005 Caterpiller, Inc., shareholder meeting that ordered the company to investigate use of its tractors in bulldozing Palestinian homes. Several major Protestant denominations considered divesting from companies whose products are used by Israelis in the occupation.[73]

It was not easy to speak in public or in print about the possible motive (and recruitment tool) terrorists had in their pockets by unending, uncritical American largesse toward Israel. Edward Said called it "the last taboo":

> To call this quite literally the last taboo in American public life would not be an exaggeration. Abortion, homosexuality, the death penalty, even the sacrosanct military budget can be discussed with some freedom. The extermination of native Americans can be admitted, the morality of Hiroshima attacked, the national flag publicly committed to flames. But the systematic continuity of Israel's 52-year-old oppression and maltreatment of the Palestinians is virtually unmentionable, a narrative that has no permission to appear.[74]

If this were the case as the second intifada erupted, the silence was deeper, if not poison-tipped, after September 11. To be sure, bin Laden was cynically appropriating the Palestinian cause; he knew the galvanizing potential of that 50-year-old open wound in the Arab world. Arafat sensed the danger early on, and chastized bin Laden publicl: "I'm telling him [bin Laden] directly not to hide behind the Palestinian cause. [He] never helped us, he was working in another completely different area and against our interests."[75] But try as he might, Sharon was painting with a broad brush; he put that brush in Bush's hand, and he too, painted: Arafat = terrorism.

Meanwhile, a UN-commissioned "Arab Human Development Report" released in October 2003 showed the United States losing the race for hearts and minds in the Arab world in its scorched-earth policy toward terror: "The US-led war on terror has radicalized more Arabs angry both with the West and their autocratic rulers who are bent on curbing their political rights."[76]

Phyllis Bennis, a fellow at the Institute for Policy Studies, is one of the first and most compelling intellectuals to posit a different sort of struggle against terror than the Bush administration waged in Afghanistan and Iraq:

> The British journalist Robert Fisk wrote of "the crushed and humiliated people" in whose name the hijackers claimed to speak. Comprehending who those people are, and what role US policy might have in making or keeping them crushed and humiliated, would go very far in the effort to understanding why people support such horrific acts. And understanding that is a key step toward ensuring such events never happen again.

Bennis acknowledges what one commentator called "the jihad of the privileged,"[77] and its manipulations of the underclass, but she hacks away at the vines of cliché that have strangled public debate:

> The resentment is not aimed at America or Americans in some general sense. Contrary to Bush administration and media pundits, it is not democracy that is hated. In fact, it is America's support for regimes in the region that deny democracy to their people that fuels Arab anger. It is not even American power per se. Rather, it is the way that American power is used in the Middle East that has caused such enmity.

Admitting that the "complex web of illusions, religious zealotry, resentment, anger" that drove the nineteen hijackers to take so many innocents down with them finally may be unfathomable, Bennis insists this is besides the point. Those people can no longer hurt us; it is the masses of people who would follow them we need to address in revamping our policies to be fair not only to Israelis, but to Palestinians. She doesn't expect miracles or a squeaky clean world:

> This does not mean that if Western control of oil exploitation in Central Asia, and US support for the Israeli occupation of Palestine and for repressive and corrupt regimes elsewhere, were all to end overnight that there would never again be an act of terror. It does mean, however, that future anti-US terrorists would have to act in much greater isolation, without public support, without a popular base. In the long run that means that the threat of terrorism against American targets would be qualitatively reduced.[78]

No less an authority than John Lehman, member of the 9/11 Commission, agreed. In an October 2004 speech at Pitzer College in California, when asked if settling the Palestinian–Israeli conflict might take the oxygen out of al-Qaeda's recruitment, Lehman nodded and called "oxygen" the exact right metaphor.[79] The notion that political grievances might have political solutions through negotiations with al-Qaeda began to gain a hearing.[80] This was refreshing understanding from high quarters. And at least one respected commentator detected hints of a sea change in President Bush's own thinking in his 2005 State of the Union address: "Now Bush says that terrorists are actually the victims of tyranny."[81] It was a far cry from admitting any US role in tyranny of the past half-century in the Middle East, but it was intriguing and even hopeful. Hopeful, too, were commitments Bush made after a June 2005 meeting with Palestinian President Mahmoud Abbas that a "viable two-state solution must ensure contiguity of the West Bank."[82]

FRONT AND CENTER

Arab Americans found themselves in a newly visible and sought-after position. For many, their homelands were constantly in the news. The political system had its antennae up. Taking a page from George Bush, who warned against discriminating against Arab Americans in his 2000 presidential debate[83] with Albert Gore—helping him win Michigan in the razor-thin race—Democratic presidential hopefuls spoke in October 2003 at an AAI leadership conference in Detroit. This was a first for the community. Displaying some bravery, Senator Joseph Lieberman of Connecticut addressed the crowd. Though heckling over Sharon's West Bank wall was reported, the seven times the crowd applauded Lieberman were not.[84] About the wall, the Jewish-American senator said, "I regret the confiscations." He called for American handling over the governance of Iraq to "international hands" in 60 days, leading "quickly to Iraqi hands." Though he would not equate the destruction of 1,500 Palestinian homes that week in Gaza to terrorism, and though he voiced no criticism of Israeli settlements, insisting that Palestinians stop suicide bombings of civilians before anything else moves, he passionately promised

> with a fervor and intensity and sincerity, to do everything I can... to break the violence, to rebuild the trust and to do it so self-evidently in the interest of all the Palestinians and all the Israelis, which is to work our way to that two-state solution and to peace. That is my pledge.

That may have not seemed much, but in American politics, it was a jump. The only presidential candidate who had ever talked openly of two states before was Ralph Nader in 2000. To move from a marginal Arab-American candidate speaking of a Palestinian state to a Jewish-American presidential candidate doing so was, frankly, progress. At the same time, rousing standing applause at AAI was received by Howard Dean, who had called publicly for the dismantling of settlements (that, more than his much ballyhooed "scream," may have effected his demise).

It was hyperbole on the part of AAI to declare Arab Americans a community critical to the 2004 election. In fact, if anything, they migrated to Democratic candidate John Kerry, who lost. In the swing state of Florida, for example—the threshing floor of the entire 2000 election—Bush's share of the Arab-American vote went from 45 percent to 30 percent in 2004.[85] But one thing was for certain: after 100 years in the political shadows, Arab Americans were blinking in the light. There was peril in the light, but also promise. Respected *Washington Post* political commentator David Broder reflected on the 2004 candidates in Dearborn: "What happened here last weekend when about 300 Arab Americans from all parts of the country gathered in this Detroit suburb was another chapter in one of the unnoticed glories of American life—the entry of yet another immigrant group into the mainstream of the nation's politics."[86] Perhaps they and their Jewish-American fellows could press on power enough to focus attention on the root of the nation's sorest problem—its utter insecurity in the world. The root, strangely enough, was in the Holy Land.

In 2005, much discussion in the press and at high levels began at last to focus there. Would Sharon make his pledge to pull out of Gaza settlements a prelude to dismantling those on the West Bank? An advisor to six US secretaries of state said that Israel's very existence was at stake if Sharon did not proceed resolutely.[87] Could Mahmoud Abbas disarm Hamas and Islamic Jihad, or at least secure a complete halt of suicide bombings and other terror attacks? His outlawing firearm carrying in the territories was gutsy, a gun control effort one would like to see in the United States.[88] Would the Palestinians and Israelis dust off the Taba agreement and stand by it? Would the second-term president George Bush totally engage in shuttle diplomacy, or at least get someone who would, such as former president Jimmy Carter? Could Israelis and Palestinians finally arrive, as Israeli novelist David Grossman eloquently put it, "at a mutual acceptance of the other side's suffering"?[89]

As the new year turned, tidal waves of agony in Asia revealed how fleeting this life is. A light rain fell on Washington. Could a sense of mortality spur compassion? It was undeniably inspiring to see Iraqis voting at the end of January 2005 under threat of execution in Baghdad, and remarkable that Iraqi-Americans hopped a thirteen-van convoy from Seattle to drop a sheet of paper with their hope stamped on it into a slot in Irvine, California. Imagine plain old Americans being told they had to travel 1,200 miles to vote. We'd be a dictatorship in days! Still, before President Bush waxes too triumphant, it might do well to study the Algeria model and find credit outside the tracks of our tanks.

No, Iraq isn't the only democracy in the Arab world (and as of this writing, it is far from a viable one). There is a democracy in Lebanon, though fraught with problems. There is a representative parliament in Jordan. And early in 2004, what appeared to be a legitimate popular election (following a rigged one four years before) had taken hold in Algeria, once the bane of all moderates and a stridently revolutionary regime for decades after its bloody revolt against France. According to Walter Russell Mead, "[Abdelaziz] Bouteflika has lifted controls on the press and on the opposition...A brash and independent press criticizes the president daily...Visiting Americans enjoy a kind of celebrity status."[90] You won't find that in Iraq, even with the 2005 election in the bag. Why? Because in Algeria we are leading with our diplomats, our educators, and our dollars. In Iraq, we are still leading with the motley green of our troops. In Algeria, says Mead, they want sister cities with the United States, such as with Santa Monica, California (St. Monica, the mother of that great sinner, St. Augustine, was born in Algeria). In Iraq, two days before the election, 75 percent of the country were polled saying they wanted the US military to leave "either immediately or after an elected government is in place"[91] no matter how newly minted the voting booths. They want fresh vegetables and water, and they want to do it themselves.

As exultant as the President was, there were cold realities that the exhilarating moment could not mask. A heartwrenching *Los Angeles Times* photo of a solitary man voting in Ramadi (in the rebellious Sunni Triangle) at the long end of empty voting booths made one want to hug and cover him all at once. Though about 60 percent of the Iraqi electorate voted, only 2 percent of Mosul did, a city of 1.8 million Sunnis, Kurds, and Turkmen, and only 5 percent of Ramadi and Falluja. Nine suicide blasts and mortar attacks killed 44 Iraqis on election day (January 30, 2005). But they did not shut down the country. An all-too-rare victory for sanity and for courage.

There are other hard realities: in June 2004, a special US inspector general for Iraq found $9 billion in oil revenues unaccounted for; widespread graft and kickbacks are suspected—for us and our Iraqi "clients." That doesn't help our profile. Will the Shi'ites, who have garnered a majority of seats in the new legislature, resist the temptation to an Islamic state such as Iran's? And even if they do, can they bring in 40 percent of the country, the Sunnis, who have shunned the election? The fact remains, as our own CIA reported in December 2004, "Iraq has become a breeding ground for the next generation of 'professionalized' Islamic terrorists."[92] That was not the case before Bush went to war. I suspect bin Laden could hardly spell Zarqawi's name then, much less locate him. Of the 240,000 Iraqi Americans eligible to vote in the Iraqi election, only 11 percent did.

Still, who could deny—fourth rationale for the war or not—the wonder of Iraqis from Seattle kneeling at a rest stop in Eugene, Oregon, for the *zuhr*, the afternoon prayer? The satisfaction in seeing a long news feature on page one of a major daily newspaper divided by the five calls to Muslim prayer—*fajr* (morning), *zuhr* (afternoon), *asr* (late afternoon), *maghrib* (sunset), *ishq* (night)? In my reading, that is unprecedented evidence of an American journalist getting, for once, inside a culture and a mindset. And the keen adjustment that the journalist spots—arriving in Irvine, the *zuhr* is tossed aside in the elation to vote. As one Ghanem al-Nassar put it, "Which one is easier? You put your life on the line and someone crazy will blow [you] up, or drive 2,000 miles with your friends?"[93] Ah, the American at home on the road with the windows down!

In the ruins of 9/11, novelist Joyce Carol Oates spoke with great feeling, "Perhaps, unfairly, the future does not belong to those who only mourn."[94] Who could deny when the Kurd from Utah ran into the Shi'ite from Seattle in Irvine that they were undeterred by rain? Was anyone surprised that the boom boxes of Fayruz flew out, that each began to dance with his own flag—I mean Kurdish and Iraqi? And was it entirely unexpected that the two "stared at each other" before "they moved close together"[95] and danced in a circle slithering their flags like scarves along each others'cheeks? This was America, after all. Let's hope we get out of the way so that they can do such a dance in Iraq.

What Do Arab Americans Want?

People often ask what it is, beside a steaming plate of *kibbee* and a useful vote, Arab Americans really want. Recent polling of the community—virtually nonexistent before 2000—reveals some fascinating trends. For one thing, Arab Americans share surprisingly similar views about the Middle East as Jewish Americans.

In a June–July 2003 Zogby poll (the organization headed by James' brother, John) commissioned by Americans for Peace Now and AAI, both communities were overwhelmingly for a secure and independent Palestinian state (82 percent of Jewish Americans, 93 percent of Arab Americans). Though it is no surprise that 99.5 percent of Jewish Americans said Israel has a right to live, too, as a secure and independent state, 95 percent of Arab Americans agreed.

Adil Rikabi of Seattle, left, waves the Iraqi flag while Kamil Barzanji of Salt Lake City, right, holds the flag of Kurdistan in a dance of celebration after voting January 28, 2005 in Irvine, California (Los Angeles Times *photo by Don Bartletti*)

Clearly, the two-state solution is overwhelmingly favored by both Jewish and Arab citizens of America.

Should settlements at least be frozen? That modest idea is supported by a large portion of Jewish Americans (71 percent) and Arab Americans (80 percent). Far more Arab Americans favor ending Israel's military occupation of the West Bank and Gaza (84 percent) than Jewish Americans (59 percent). Perhaps in this poll some Jewish Americans were hesitant to go for a pull-out, thinking it meant "unconditional."

Getting more specific about the contours of a peace agreement, both communities were asked if they could agree to the elements of the 2000 Taba peace talks, the last time Palestinians and Israelis negotiators met. These include two states roughly along the June 4, 1967, border, evacuation of most settlements, a Palestinian right of return only inside the new Palestinian state, and Jerusalem as a shared capital. Fifty-nine percent of Jewish Americans agreed to this package, not quite as enthusiastic as the 85 percent of Arab Americans who did, but again, majorities of both communities.

As for President Bush's handling of the Arab–Israeli conflict to date, it comes up wanting. In fact, more Jewish Americans gave it thumbs down (69 percent) than Arab Americans (56 percent). In 2002, more Arab Americans were unhappy with Bush's overall Middle East policy (67 percent). Both of these figures show a sharp turn away from the president for a community that supported him by 8 percent more than they did Al Gore in the 2000 election.

James Zogby gives a shrewd analysis of the dovetailing of Arab American and Jewish Americans views toward peace, and where the roadblock is:

> There is in the United States a strong extremist anti-peace current that consists of some hard-line pro-Likud elements in the Jewish community, a substantial grouping of right-leaning fundamentalist Christians and other conservative anti-Arab hawks...When political leaders in either of the two parties cower from taking tough stands for peace and pander in support of Israeli policy, it is to these anti-peace forces and not to the American Jewish community, as a whole, that they are responding.[96]

Edward Tivnan, appealing to the Jewish community to stand up to "a tyranny of the minority" in its ranks, makes similar points in his important book, *The Lobby*.

The new polling of the Arab-American community is beginning to reveal its political leanings in other ways. The 2002 Zogby poll showed the community is more Democrat (39 percent) than Republican (31 percent); almost half (48 percent) feel the Middle East issue is "very" important in determining their vote; and the number of those who felt "reassured" by President Bush's conduct toward Arab Americans fell from a huge 90 percent right after 9/11 to 46 percent in October 2002.

Important to grasp inside these figures is that far more Democrat Arab Americans are born overseas (51 percent) than Republican Arab Americans (19 percent). More traditional, conservative Arab Americans come from the First Wave immigrants and their descendants, and tend to vote Republican, as opposed to Second Wavers and especially Third Wavers since 1967 who, like many immigrants, lean toward the Democrats.

In the 2000 presidential election, a sizable chunk of the Arab-American community voted for the first candidate ever from its ranks, Ralph Nader (14 percent). And though Clinton had overwhelming Arab-American favor in the 1996 election (52 percent vs. 32 percent for Republican Robert Dole), that did not transfer to Al Gore, who in 2000 got only 38 percent of the Arab American vote vs. 46 percent for George Bush. Bush's sensitive, ground-breaking remark about Arab-American civil rights in the debate with Gore had a big effect (an effect that apparently dissipated by his second term).

Having ancestors who were denied the franchise, Arab Americans have always been enthusiastic voters. AAI's voter registration campaigns among new immigrants continued that tradition; for the 2000 election, 89 percent of Arab Americans were registered to vote. Among ethnic groups, only Jewish Americans and African Americans have a higher percentage. In the 2002 mid-term election, the Arab American Leadership Council Political Action Committee (ALCPAC) distributed $150,000 in funds to 70 congressional candidates; 83 percent of them won their elections.[97] The amazing thing about this is of course not the dollar amount—minuscule compared to the NRA, AARP, and pro-Israel PACs. It is that it shows the distance Arab Americans had come in twenty years: their checks were not being returned or candidates demurring to speak to them. Arab-American support, in short, was no longer the kiss of death.

A major sea change in the community's demography was underway. Though the First Wave immigrants and their descendants were 90 percent Christian, the Second and Third Wavers were predominantly Muslim. By 2003, estimates showed about 23 percent of Arab Americans were Muslim (Catholics comprised 42 percent, Orthodox 23 percent, and Protestants 12 percent). The community of American Muslims (five to six million) was stepping up to the plate in the public forum in unprecedented numbers. According to a 2003 CAIR poll of all US Muslims, almost half (45 percent) increased their political activities since 9/11. Fifty-two percent say they have accelerated their interfaith activities. Far from hiding, 49 percent of Muslims say they are more public about their Muslim identity and 42 percent have increased donations to national Islamic organizations.

Even before these post-September 11 trends, Muslim visibility in American life led House Minority Leader Richard Gephardt (D-MO) to nominate Salam al-Marayati to the ten-member National Commission on Terrorism, which reviews national policy on preventing and punishing terrorism. Marayati had been an outspoken critic not only of Israeli policy, but of corruption and despotism in the Islamic world: "The problem in Muslim societies is rooted in authoritarianism, which burdens practically every community, mosque and family...When the Qu'ran, for example, stipulates 'There shall be no compulsion in religion' (2:256), there is no excuse for religious police patrolling Muslim streets."[98] Unfortunately, the Conference of Presidents of Major American Jewish Organizations hit hard on the nomination, and Gephardt got wobbly and withdrew it,[99] causing the *San Francisco Examiner* to editorialize, "American Jewish supporters of Israel do not help the Israeli cause by unfairly attacking the credentials of moderate Muslims to play a role in US affairs."[100] Al-Marayati rolled with the punches:

> Is this the place for us? Everyday the resounding answer is "Yes. This is home." Mormons had to do it; there was a bloody revolt. They were kicked out of Illinois and ended up in Utah. We are going through what is natural in the pluralism project that is America. As Arabs and Muslims succeed at being more mainstream, their threat to policy will bring more attacks.[101]

Much of this trend of American Muslims speaking out has to do with September 11, when the community realized it had to do so, and vociferously, to counter the al-Qaeda mentality; it could no longer keep its good works under the bushel of deference and humility. While 87 percent of US Muslims experienced bias or discrimination after September 11 (and 48 percent said their lives had changed for the worse), 79 percent also said they were the recipients of special kindnesses from friends and colleagues.

Even more sold than Arab Americans in general, in 2000 US Muslims voted for George Bush four times more than Al Gore (three times more than Ralph Nader). But by 2003, as with Arab Americans overall, American Muslims rated Bush a 3 on a scale of 1 to 10. They greatly favored Howard Dean (26 percent) over other 2004 Democratic presidential candidates (Dennis Kucinich was next with 11 percent); only 2 percent of US Muslims said in 2003 they would vote for Bush, an eighteen-fold drop in three years.[102]

Beyond politics, American Muslims are going through a transformative debate about Qu'ranic injunctions and adaptations to American culture. In no place is this debate more salient than in education and textbooks. There are between 200 and 600 Muslim religious day schools in the United States. Some Muslim educators are rewriting curricula "that infuses tenets of the religion into every lesson while providing a broad-minded worldview."[103] One eleventh-grade textbook, for example, says that the sign of the Day of Judgment will show Jews hiding behind trees fearing for their lives. Students themselves are speaking out about antiquated, if not hateful, passages. But literalism is trouble for all ancient religions. Al-Marayati draws attention to passages in the Old Testament and New Testament that are not exactly peaceful: "Now kill all the boys and all the women who have had sexual intercourse" (Numbers 31:17) and "Don't think I came to bring peace on earth! No rather, a sword." (Matthew 10:34). Yet, as he says, "it's Islam that is called the violent faith."[104]

It was often asked of the Arab world itself after September 11, "Why do they hate us?" and the pundits spewed forth all kinds of reasons—they hate our democracy, our freedom, our cars, our tattoos, Brittany Spears, you name it, they hate it. In fact, none of these things registered in a 2002 Zogby poll taken in ten countries, five Arab and eight Muslim. The poll was taken a month after a Gallup poll in early March of that year that basically painted the Islamic world as a pack of hounds baying at America; Gallup found many Arabs even denying Arab involvement in September 11.

John Zogby dug deeper, looking for attitudes toward American culture, politics, and business. In the five Arab countries surveyed—Egypt, Kuwait, Saudi Arabia, Lebanon, and the United Arab Emirates—clear majorities had a high regard for American science and technology, American democracy, entertainment and products, as well as American education (81 percent in Lebanon favored that, no surprise with a century-and-a-half of US investment in the American University of Beirut). The youngest polled were most enthusiastic about American education, as were those with Internet access. Results were mixed when Arabs were asked about their attitudes toward the American people. Large majorities of Kuwaitis and Lebanese were favorable (again, direct positive American involvement in the country has its effect), while as many as 47 percent of Egyptians and 51 percent of Saudis had a negative feeling about Americans.

The single overwhelming reason for antipathy toward the United States was not cultural license, or products, or freedom, or even people—but US policy in the Middle East, and specifically toward the Palestinians. Nine out of ten in every Arab nation polled gave the US low marks for its policy toward the Palestinians. Interestingly, those polled indicated that could change to a favorable stance. If American "were to apply pressure to ensure creation of the Palestinian state," Arabs would adjust their views of America upward accordingly: 69 percent of Egyptians said so, as did 79 percent of Saudi Arabians, 91 percent of Kuwaitis, 59 percent of Lebanese, and 67 percent of citizens of the Emirates. In short, as John Zogby put it, "They don't hate us, but the policy does appear to be taking its toll."[105]

Indeed it has. Since 9/11, the number of Arab students in the United States has declined by a significant 30 percent. Arab students may think well of us in most areas other than Palestine, but the Patriot Act, no doubt, has made many shy away and look elsewhere for their degrees. This is an ominous trend for the United States, which needs to build bridges to Arab youth like never before. Immigration trends, too, are worrisome. While Iraq had its highest one-year immigration figure to the United States in history in 2002 (5,196), that same year saw the highest one-year drop in immigration from Lebanon in a quarter century and from Jordan in half a century (each 14 percent less). Jordanian immigrants are largely Palestinian. Syrian immigration dropped 24 percent from 2001 to 2002; only once in 50 years had the drop been higher (right after the Israeli invasion of Lebanon). September 11 has to account for this precipitous drop: before the immigration numbers for all three countries to America had been climbing for at least fourteen years. In fact, the recent 14-year total (1989–2002) of immigrants from Syria, Lebanon, and Jordan is roughly equal to the previous 37-year total (1948–1985). Put another way, until September 11, immigration from three Levantine Arab countries that have always favored the United States as a new home, far from decreasing, had doubled its rate in the past decade-and-a-half despite US policy. But September 11 sharply reversed that trend. To what effect remains to be seen.

Ongoing Achievement

Though the past two decades in Arab-American life have been highly political and politicized—roughly from the breakthrough 1988 Madrid peace conference after the PLO officially recognized Israel through Oslo to the unprecedented 2003 address of presidential candidates to Arab Americans in Detroit—life went on. Fortunes were made and lost, couples married and broke up, babies were born and children died and old ones saw new light, too. Some reached personal heights, such as General John Abizaid in Iraq, or the Maloof brothers Joe and Gavin, who took their Sacramento Kings professional basketball team to the championship series in 2003. Yasser Seirawan, Syrian-American from Seattle, won the US chess championship three times. In 2004, Jennifer Shahade won the US women's chess championship. The largest retailer of American flags was Tony Ismail of Dallas. And in this best and worst of times, some went to jail for no political reason at all, because, to quote Philip Roth, of the human stain.

General Abizaid was not alone in his vocation: roughly 3,500 Arab Ameri-cans were on active duty with the US armed forces in 2005.

Though less than 1 percent of 2.6 million service men and women, they are both passionate about their calling and aware of being under close scrutiny. "I can't express in words how deep my commitment goes," attests Marine Master Sgt. Osama Shofani, a Palestinian American. Another, Army Sgt. Jamal Baadani, proudly makes it clear, "Just because I am angry over policies, don't ask me to take off the uniform."[106]

The community's achievements continued and in some cases accelerated. A closer look at three individuals gives a sense of the breadth of that achievement: the political ascendancy of Teresa Isaac,

mayor of Lexington, KY; the business and philanthropic efforts of Paul Orfalea, founder of Kinko's; and actor Tony Shalhoub, who won an Emmy in 2003 for his role in the television detective sitcom *Monk*.

In her youth, Teresa Isaac was named one of the 30 most prominent athletes in Kentucky, but it was exposure to the Appalachian poor of eastern Kentucky that would determine her life as a civil rights lawyer. Her grandparents had come from Lebanon at the end of the First Wave in the early twenties,

Jennifer Shahade, the 2004 US women's chess champion (Gwen Feldman)

settling in "bloody Harlan," a coal-mining community where black lung disease and short, brutal lives were the norm. The Isaacs, looking to give the community some escape, established a chain of seven movie theaters, one for each of the immigrant couple's children.

Teresa had an early feeling for the underdog. As a young lawyer, she sued a school system for not letting girls play sports, and won. As vice mayor of Lexington, she mediated disputes between Arab-

American grocery store owners and African-Americans, and helped calm tensions. In 2001, she ran for mayor of the Kentucky capital, and few at first gave her a chance to win. Not only were her campaign coffers tiny ($200,000) compared to her two opponents (who had $1.2 million and $800,000 each), this was a post-September 11 election. Isaac knew what had happened to Rep. Mary Rose Oakar's Cleveland mayoral campaign; way before September 11, and after, Oakar was attacked and her campaign never recovered.

Isaac, too, was attacked by bigots, who insinuated she was in league with terrorists and leafleted a synagogue to that effect. They pointed to her work monitoring the first elections for the Palestinian Authority during the Oslo process. But their efforts backfired. As she told the ADC convention in June 2003, "The Jewish community actually held a press conference defending me." Isaac's integrity won the day with 51 percent of the vote. Lexington is now the largest city in America with an Arab-American mayor. Isaac pointed to two things: "During my whole career, I had always shown how proud I was of being Arab American. And of my mother, who was a high school basketball referee. When you make a hard call, you can't take it back, but have to have the authority and courage to make it."[107]

Isaac's victory was part of a real surge of electoral initiative by the community. By 2005, there were Arab-American governors in Indiana (Mitch Daniels) and Maine (John Baldacci), a senator from New Hampshire (John Sununu), 3 congressmen, 20 state legislators, 6 mayors of sizable cities, and 37 elected to school boards, city councils, or county boards of supervisors.

Paul Orfalea, about whom I know a little something, is something else. Dubbed "the white sheep of the family" when we were kids, Paul took a lot of razzing from friends (and relatives, too), for his difficulties in school. He left or was thrown out of four schools, he once told me, before finally graduating from high school with "solid D's." Paul was dyslexic, but it wasn't diagnosed until late in his education. His parents, who loved and supported him, often threw up their arms at his antics, an acting out, no doubt, over his frustrations with pen, paper, and print. To this day, it is hard for him to read. He once entered my library at home and regarded the four walls of books wistfully, "Ah, a lifetime of reading!" I looked for the joke, because he is a joker, but there wasn't one. He meant me to feel the loss.

He took a merry revenge on his tormentors. If he wasn't going to read, he was going to copy what others read—literally. It came to him one day at the Univeristy of Southern California where he was barely scraping by (he'd matriculated there after community college) that one way he could help a business seminar would be to photocopy everyone else's papers. When the photocopy machine in the library broke down, sure, he got frustrated, but he also took mental note. Then in 1970, near

Dr. Michael DeBakey was named by US News and World Report *as one of the five most influencial Americans in the health field. He performed the first aorto-coronary artery bypass, and was the first to successfully use an artificial heart. At the height of his 60-year career as a surgeon, he averaged 500 coronary bypasses a year.* (Houston Chronicle)

the entrance to UC Santa Barbara, he borrowed $5,000 from his garment-manufacturing father Albert Orfalea to purchase a photocopier and placed it in a 100-square-foot former hamburger stand. Every day he'd wheel it out to a long line of students who came for copies cheaper than the library's. The rest is the history of Kinko's, a 1,200-store worldwide chain with 20,000 employees, at $2 billion the largest business services chain in the nation, and often named in *Fortune* magazine's list of 100 best companies to work for in America.

What drove Paul Orfalea to succeed? He cites family, a passion for business, and burning desire to prove himself—in that order. His father Al was a loving, laughing man and top garment manufacturer who appreciated a good nap and once cooked me eggs at 6 AM. His mother Virginia (Nahas), brought up in the little Arizona mining town of Bisbee, filled her son with her own dry wit and pearls of wisdom: "I really do think the timid ones get more out of life. They are always looked after. Well, I don't want to be timid," or "There's something so strong within us that you can't find it; you can't cut it and you can't operate on it," or "Don't ever get married close to your birthday because you get cheated out of a present."[108] An entrepreneurial tradition in the veins didn't hurt Paul: "I came from a Lebanese family where people didn't work for others. All my relatives had their own businesses. It was never part of my education to work for other people."[109]

At 57, he enjoys giving, speaking, and teaching. Now he has even taken to writing a book in which he reveals, among other things, that "in my family anger wasn't simply a sign of dysfunction but part and parcel of all the love.[110] Through the Orfalea Family Foundation, he and his wife Natalie have given over $45 million to higher education, including the largest donation to the California State college system ever (at Cal Poly San Luis Obispo, $15 million to endow the Orfalea College of Business, which sports a bronze plaque honoring his mother and father out front). Child development centers, early childhood health, and education have been key areas of interest to the foundation. After a gift of $8.5 million to the City College of San Francisco for several child-care centers, Natalie Orfalea noted, perhaps with September 11 in mind, the foundation's concern for the underprivileged: "We look at child care, at what kids learn, and we don't think it's going to have an impact on us. But if we don't put some time into this segment of society now, we're really going to be feeling it in the years to come."[111]

My cousin is a card, and loves cards, as did his mother, who died at the tables in Gardena. He even assigns poker to his students with the idea that "it's a great metaphor for life... It teaches [them] to manage their emotions, understand people and figure out probabilities."[112] I don't recall playing poker with Paul, but I do remember a great pick-up football game once against our brothers Dickie and Mark in a heavy LA rain just before we got married. I remember Paul yelling, "Go long! Go long!" A good metaphor for marriage. I'm still going. So is he.

Acting comes naturally for a community that has often had to mask itself, and actor Tony Shalhoub continues the tradition of Danny Thomas, Jamie Farr (whose last M★A★S★H show was the highest-rated television show ever), and F. Murray Abraham. Born in Green Bay, Wisconsin, in 1953, Shalhoub developed a passion for theater at age six when he joined a production of The King and I at his sister's high school. It was a bit part, but he bit. Shalhoub took a master's degree from the famed Yale Drama School and did four seasons with the American Repetory Theatre in Cambridge, MA, before heading to Broadway. There he was nominated for a Tony award for his role in *Conversations with My Father*, there he met and married actress Brook Adams.

In film, Shalhoub has had a knack for sprinkling humor into serious roles, as in *Men In Black*, and quirks that someone from an outsider ethnicity might discover in the comic roles. The detective he plays in the television series *Monk* is not only funny–he has obsessive compulsive disorder. There is sadness under the funny man always, and Shalhoub gives himself freely to this notion. There is pain in his performance in *The Siege*, one of the few humane roles for an Arab American in a movie dealing with terrorism. In 2003, he won his first Emmy for *Monk*, which he also produces for the cable USA Network.

Pinnacles in drama and film abound of late. Callie Khoury was the first Arab American to win an Academy Award for an original screenplay (*Thelma and Louise*). Salma Hayek starred in several acclaimed movies, including *Frida*, about Frida Kahlo, the wife of Mexican painter Diego Garcia. There's even a rap artist, Iron Sheik, who tours in the San Francisco Bay Area. If it is an especially anxious time to be an Arab American, work provides an ongoing haven. Anxiety, joy, love itself could pass, but for these folks, work is forever. Work is art.

To Be or Not to Be Arab American: A Look at the Literature

Diana Abu Jaber, at a 2003 bookstore reading in Washington, DC, for her novel *Crescent*, blurted out, "There's loneliness all over these people!" She was smiling and telling: the lovers in her novel are a lonely Iraqi professor in exile at UCLA and a cook in her thirties who was raised by her Arab uncle. Falling in love may be too powerful for what happens to them: leaning in love might be more like it. They are, after all, jacketed in that great invisible film known as America. Still, the writing is spirited and erotic: "Han's arms smell like bread and sleep; when he gathers her back, it is like being drawn into a world beneath the water." The troubled Iraqi remembers an early love in war-torn Iraq: "She can send him to a new place, away from the new president, as far away as the other side of the world, a place where he will no longer look at his brother and sister not sleeping, where he will not have to count his heartbeats, his breathing, the pulse in his eyelids."[113]

Is being an Arab American de facto lonely? Not to poet and storyteller Naomi Shihab Nye. In her poem, "For Lost and Found

Brothers" she proclaims, "we were born into a large family / our brothers cover the earth."[114] Somewhere between those poles of longing and belonging, of loneliness and connection, might hide the secret center of an American with Arab blood.

The problem of Arab-American identity, is, in many ways, the problem of American identity. We are all strangers to these shores, except for Native Americans, and even they came from Asia over the land bridge between Siberia and Alaska. America is the ultimate home of the wanderer. There is a lostness we cherish, see in strangers far from home, and a foundness we are constantly seeking.

But the identity of one on a search for self is compounded by an origin as complex, multi-ethnic, and multi-religious as the Arab world. When you come from Ireland to these shores, you could be Green or Orange, but that is pretty much it. But how does one get anything even close to a uniform Arab identity in America when, for example, one's ancestors could have been Muslim Berbers from Algeria, Christian Copts from Egypt, Druze from Lebanon, Black Catholic from Sudan, Antiochian Orthodox Palestinians, Shi'ite Iraqis, Kurdish Iraqis, Assyrian Christian Iraqis, Chaldean Catholic Iraqis, atheist Iraqis, Alawite Muslims from Syria, or, for that matter, Melkites who come from only one town in tiny Lebanon—Zahle? This is a universe where nearly everyone is a religion! But what better place from which to originate to enter the American maelstrom than the Arab world? America, Walt Whitman knew, was the land where each individual self was a song.

But how to find harmony? What constitutes it? Is it even achievable on this lonely orb in space? Must one emphasize identity to do so, or smother it? These questions transcend ethnicity, to be sure, but for those for whom ethnicity is either unavoidable or important, such existential questions cannot help but involve origins, skin color, customs, language, foods, values, soulful affinities. And in an Iraqi voting booth, such a question about identity could put your neck in a noose.

Philip Kayal notes the complex mutations of identity that have constituted someone negotiating American life with Arab insides:

> We did not automatically become a nationality or even hyphenated Americans. Rather, we went from being Asians to whites (a fascinating story in itself), Melkites, or Maronites, or Orthodox to being Catholics or Antiochians; or from being Aleppians, or Damascenes, or Turks to Syrians, then Lebanese, then Arabs (and for some, Phoenicians). We did this simultaneously while we both Americanized and communalized ourselves.

Just as Arab-American ethnic identity mutated and fractured over a century in America, America itself was changing, and that changed the community, too: "We are living in a highly urbanized and industrialized society that values private enterprise and personal success at the expense of the public good. We are responsible only for ourselves. This is not the prevailing motif of the Arab world, but it is to this world that we all have migrated."[115] While this is an exaggeration (one wonders, for example, how much public good the rulers of Egypt have brought about when hundreds of thousands, if not millions, of people in Cairo live quite literally in a cemetery), still the emphasis on self, and self-definition, over and above the group in America is generally not the way things are in the Arab world. The tensions released here from an ethic of self-abnegation to self-assertion are ongoing from the first step off the boat, or plane, or bramble on the border. They are tensions that can explode a family, if not a self.

Two of the earliest writers on these shores from the Arab world could not sustain the pace or contradictions. Both Amin Rihani and Mikhail Naimy, poets from Lebanon, returned there after many decades in America. In Rihani's poem, "I Dreamt I Was a Donkey Boy Again," a peddler in Central Park, New York, sees American women walking by, but he can neither sell to them nor talk to them as a man. And it isn't just the language barrier that stops him:

> He had tied my tongue, the goblin, and left me there alone.
> And in front of me, and toward me, and beside me
> Walked Allah's fairest cyclamens and anemones.
> I smell them, and the tears flow down my cheeks;
> I cannot even like the noon-day bulbul
> Whisper with my wings, salaam!

It is homesickness that keeps him from connecting: "O, let me sleep among the cyclamens /of my own land."[116] Who but a poet from the high Lebanon mountain would turn hard-bitten New York women into cyclamens and himself, a sorry peddler, into a songbird? No wonder Rihani fled! But not before he wrote of a self that could disappear in a Sufic dance: "Whirl, whirl, whirl / Till the world is the size of a pearl… Soar, soar, soar / Till the world is no more."[117]

Mikhail Naimy, though he fought in the US Army in World War I, found America, and New York in particular, a "horrible vortex." And although his hermetic personality took him back to the high mountain of Lebanon and a natural hermitage, he saw New Yorkers in another kind of isolation: "All of them are sentenced to live in dens inside dens inside dens. Some of these are caves, barns and basements, and some are palaces which shame those of the nobility, the princes, and kings. They are all sentenced to incessant motion, day and night."[118]

Rihani left the United States after a bitter divorce from an

American dancer, and Naimy after the death of his beloved friend, Kahlil Gibran. Both returned solitary to the Old World.

Not all those who stayed were happy roosting here. As Michael Suleiman notes, for the turn-of-the-century, impoverished critic Khalil Sakakini, life was too fast in the US. As early as 1908, long before McDonald's, Sakakini skewered fast food and that great American obsession, speed: "The American walks fast, talks fast, and eats fast... A person might even leave the restaurant with a bite still in his mouth!"[119]

Although early Syrian memoirists often sought to boost their roustabout credentials for American ingenuity (Salloum Rizk, Ibrahim Rihbany, George Hamid), by century's end, their children and grandchildren got closer to the hurtful marrow. Elmaz Abinader describes her grandfather fleeing war-torn Lebanon, "When Rachid is on the road, even with his son Boutros he feels loneliness that rings as hollow and deep as the caves of Gheta. He can't describe what he misses or longs for."[120] Even the irreverent, boisterous Anne Thomas Soffee catches an edge when she confesses the grain of truth that belly dancing is an excuse for "fat chicks to dress up. In the same way, one Yahoo with a big mouth and a small weenie makes the NRA look bad, or one Qurʿan-waving psycho ruins it for millions of peaceful Muslims, there are just enough tarted-up housewives in homemade *bedla* to perpetuate the stereotype among outsiders."[121]

Whatever the Arab part of the self might be (*kibbee*, cumin, anise, explosive temper, mild hand on child's head, tears, embraces, double and triple kisses, grim silence, handkerchief-wound-on-hand and twirled, hopeless politics, quick exits from a room, coffee ad infinitem, a fond wandering, a smelling of air, a sun-in-hand), and whatever American might be (free-for-all, fleas, frantic dancing, solemn pledges, baseball, football, muscles, jogging, blessed among the peoples of the world, goofy smiles, voracious desires, smart as a whip, tall everything from tales to buildings, love on the fly, families on the go, movies, willies), Naomi Shihab Nye was determined to get them fused and make a whole self. But it was no piece of cake: "When I think of the long history of the self /on its journey to becoming the whole self / I get tired." She sensed, as did Rihani, the way to get to it was to dance, but this did not send her back to the Arab world, but here: "Dance! The whole self was a current, a fragile cargo / a raft someone was paddling through the jungle, / and I was there, waving, and I would be there at the other end."[122] In short, the self was a journey that involved change. Without that journey, the self withered and died. It did not dance.

The self might disappear or mutate, but there were old, dark drags on it. What made William Peter Blatty, the only Arab-American author other than Gibran to sell over a million copies of one book, start his unique and shocking novel, *The Exorcist*, in Iraq? The whole book, excepting these few pages in the prologue, is set in Georgetown, and is based on a true exorcism there, recorded in the newspapers in the early 1950s when Blatty went to college at the Jesuit institution. But this parable of the palpable power of evil begins with the exorcist looking at an ancient Assyrian limestone statue in Nineveh of the demon Pazuzu. This is the priest who will confront the devil as he hisses from the body of a little American girl in Washington.

Blatty knew the Arab world better than most Arab Americans born in this country—he served with the US Information Agency in Lebanon for a time. What made him so haunted by evil? And pre-Islamic, pre-Christian evil, signs of darkness in the human leer thousands of years old? That crescent, after all, is more than fertile; those rivers all too often have been filled with blood.

I am not talking about stereotypes here, or Orientalism. The butchery of Nebuchadnezzar, the Hittite hordes who crushed innocents under the hooves of their horses, the killing of the firstborn by Herod, all of this ancient slaughter where civilization is said to have begun finds its contemporary counterparts in the near genocide of a million Armenians who were forced to walk into lakes and drown themselves by the Turks, the Lebanese starved by Turks and Europeans alike, not to mention locusts; the holocaust of six million Jews; the Palestinians massacred over and over again by people calling themselves religious, Christians even, pious Jews.

In the wake of ancient bloodshed, the biblical story of Hagar, a slave woman, didn't help matters, a story that relegated the Arabs to early illegitimate status, a people doomed to evil and violence who struggle to throw off their demons with the help of Moses or Christ or Mohammed. How the harpies sang at the ears of the first prophets! In the midst of the worst stages of the exorcism, when the fiend is spewing vomit and mucous and sacrilege at the two priests, Blatty finds a lesson in what often seems purposeless misery: "And yet even from this—from evil—will come good. In some way. In some way that we may never understand or see… Perhaps evil is the crucible of goodness… And perhaps even Satan—Satan, in spite of himself—somehow serves to work out the will of God."[123]

For poet Lawrence Joseph, there was solace in his craft: "Writing a poem does not stop the killing of innocent people, but it is an act of resistance."[124] In an stunning poem about the September 11 attacks (his flat is blocks from the World Trade Center), nightmarish images abound: "that woman staring into space, her dress / on fire… Hell the horrific / into the routine." It's almost as if language itself is melting in Joseph's tortured vision. True to his heritage, as an Arab Job he confronts the Deity: "Irreal is the word. I know of no / defense against those addicted to death. God. / My God. I thought it was over…" (from the poem "Unyieldingly Present").[125]

God runs through Arab speech, as Helen Thomas noted, almost as a verbal amulet. Evil is sleepless. To be an Arab-American writer is to draw on this ancient battle played out in contemporary landscape, perhaps, but never too far back in the consciousness. When Samuel Hazo reviews mothballed bombers and naval destroyers in his poem "The Toys," he confronts "Cain's rock and rocket." The poem ends, "In North America, the oldest skull's / a woman's brained from behind."[126]

In Palestinian-American memoir and poetry, of which there is a growing and fascinating literature, the evil, of course, is the disinheritance that began in 1948. For Edward Said, it was a jarring that gave him a feeling of being permanently "out of place." For poet Sharif Elmusa, brought up in a refugee camp outside Jericho, it was in the occupation army in Nablus:

> I go past the black machine guns
> Thinking how as a boy
> I caught black wasps
> and removed their stingers

In the same poem, "One Day in the Life of Nablus," Elmusa spots an "Office of Reconciliation" where a Samaritan rabbi sits on a couch "waiting, resigned to waiting." At the end Elmusa turns away from the settlements' "yellow lights" to assert "I want the kind breeze / the power of pears… ample love / that we may turn from this troubled page."[127]

Some, like Fawzi al-Asmar, took a while to come to America (after some time in an Israeli jail, smeared for things he didn't do and attitudes he didn't have, he finally gave up the ghost of Palestine in the 1970s, raising a family in Virginia). But as a young man, Fouzi tried desperately to cling to his home village of Lydda after it was ethnically cleansed of many of his neighbors by the Israelis. He even tried on Jewish habits to fit in. He describes with great poignancy how he was evicted from a kibbutz just before the onset of the 1967 war:

> "But Sarit, you asked me to come." She said that she had told all this to the Kibbutz Secretariat and yet they still insisted that I leave immediately and that if I did not leave immediately, they would come and remove me forcibly. I told her, "Don't be upset. This will pass too. In Arabic, we have a saying, 'A man is tested in time of trouble.'" I knew that perhaps they could not stand me, but I did not believe until this moment that they could hate me so. As I had no alternative, I got up and left. This was the victory of the kibbutz which preceded the victory of the 1967 war.[128]

Fawaz Turki also settled in Virginia after writing the electrifying *Disinherited*, which introduced Palestinian suffering and wandering to many Americans. In a wry poem, "Being a Good Americani," Turki takes a swipe at himself and other suburbanites: "I scolded my son for playing / with his genitals / ate french fries, / fought with my wife / and talked to her mother long distance." But in the middle of the night, with everyone else asleep, no longer secure that he has his life "figured out cold," Palestine and its olive trees come back: "and I pity myself / and the place I came from."[129]

Pity is the last thing on the mind of Palestinian-American poet Suheir Hammad, who in 2003 was part of a Tony-award winning Def Poetry Jam on Broadway revue: "Don't seduce yourself with my / otherness my hair wasn't put / on top of my head to entice you." Her eyes fluttering isn't a seduction, she says, "it's just / a blink."[130] Hammad seems determined to wrench essential humanity from those around her and counter the stereotype of the Arab seductress with almost scientific facts. Her assertiveness is an indication of a new boldness in Arab-American writing, and urgency. Let's set things straight, Hammad seems to say—then it will be harder to war.

Syrian American Mohja Kahf has spun a wonderful series of dramatic monologues of biblical and Qu'ranic figures thrown into present-day chaos. One is Asiya, the Muslim name of Moses' surrogate mother, who "…scans the faces of the passers-by / and the… oil stains under Pharoah's SUV." A neat satiric inversion has Pharoah in league with the neo-conservatives, and the poem ends with Asiya fed up by their talk as she "slips out / to the back porch and scans the riverbank / for a basket in the reeds" ("Asiya Is Waiting for a Sign"). In another visionary satire, "All Good," Kahf buries the hatchet between Sarah and Hagar: "Hagar pours a subtle, sweet / and heretofore unheard of wine / Sarah laughs again, more deeply / It's amazing how restored Abraham looks." The old violence? It's gone! The magic potion is "suffering… distilled in temperate hearts," transporting all "Here, Now, to her life, / and it is fine." Reading with such pleasure and delight, Kahf, for a second, takes us there.[131]

Fiction is taking off, aided by a publishing renaissance. Replications on American soil of the raucous warmth of the Arab family have finally begun to filter into Arab-American fiction in the past two decades. For the first time in over half a century, literary journals in English serving the Arab-American community surfaced in the 1990s in such places as Los Angeles (al-Jadid), Washington, DC (Jusoor), and most significantly in Minneapolis, with Mizna, which resembled the Syrian World in its scope and quality. The "felonious novel" Vance Bourjaily says he couldn't write because he didn't grow up in an Arab immigrant colony in America appears in the short stories of Joseph Geha set in the old Toledo, Ohio, community.

Geha has an eye for the outsider among outsiders, such as a mentally defective bum called Asfoori ("little bird") in "Monkey Business," who carries a sign for Yakoub's Yankee Café and Grille "stained dark from bobbing up and down against his chin." There's a great deal of death-in-life and life-out-of-death in his frantic, sad tale, even an aunt who tries to massage Asfoori back to life as he lies in his casket. That damned Lebanese "practicality" gets a good going over: "Cousin, every man pays for the love in his bed—that's life—but the practical man doesn't pay too much." Geha's ear for English tinged with Arabic is acute. Aunt Affi's "all right" is "awl ride." And it is telling—in the story "Everything, Everything" (its very title is a feverish Arab Americanism), when a great Jewish-like Lebanese mother asks her spinster daughter in a car, "Nat'ing?" the gap between generations is gaping: "Old women from the old country—they keep themselves helpless on purpose."[132] The "nothing" becomes everything they can't share—the daughter's passion for music, her heavy-set loneliness, cologne, and chocolate that spills on her mother's lap out of the glove compartment.

Most intriguing is the work of Arab-American novelists of split heritage or divorce, sometimes growing up on the edge or completely outside the Arab hearth, but with hankering desire to feel the original flame. Mona Simpson, whose father is Syrian, has written two novels of literary merit that follow a young American woman's odyssey searching for an Egyptian father who abandoned the family early on. The best of these, *The Lost Father*, takes a long time to warm up; there's a lot of quotidian confusion in the life of a typical 30-something single in New York City. But the last quarter of the book is riveting. With a clue or two, Mayan Atassi heads toward Egypt from New York, and speculates on the otherness she might contain:

> There weren't many Arabs in America. Not a popular minority. On all the forms you filled out where it gave some kind of advantage to minorities, they listed about seven different kinds with little boxes for you to check, and Arab was never a box. I guess they considered it just white. Or other. Being Arab was not something you'd want to right away admit, like being a Cherokee or Czech.[133]

Mayan, "suspicious of ethnics" because she isn't immediately identifiable as one (a disposition more present in the Arab American than not, I think), finally does find her Egyptian father working as a waiter in the farming town of Modesto, California. He is long remarried. It is a bittersweet encounter: "Disappearing was all you had to do to become somebody's god. And maybe being found was all it took to be mortal again."[134]

Underlying Mayan's search—Simpson's chief concern in the novel—is what it means to love. Intimately linked to this is her need to know why her father left, leaving her with a lifelong "unwanted" feeling. About the latter, her father (and a relative) try to explain it as two different cultures' views of raising a child. John Atassi tells her his ex-wife wouldn't let him kiss or touch her when Mayan cried as a baby. Mayan is totally confused, because for years her mother had said "my father left because I cried," that all he wanted to do was "to go out and go dancing." Conflicting views of the same phenomenon? Of child-rearing? But divorce is famous for this. Those who split each have their self-reinforcing reasons for why it happened, and prime among them can be disagreements over children.

Ultimately, neither Mayan nor her father can answer the searing question of why he left and worse, why he shrank from her. She realizes the frailty of humanity (her father has a young mistress in Modesto; he was a gambler), and accepts that although John Atassi was hardly someone to admire, he wasn't a terrible man, either. Finally finding her father does allow her to accept herself and far from denying or avoiding her ethnic background, by the end, "When people ask me, I say right away I'm half Arab."[135]

A self-professed "beginner" in matters of love, once all the American romanticism drains (she hunts down and beds a Cairo cabbie), she comes to a more realistic understanding of what love and devotion is, paradoxically, after exposing the frailties of her lost father:

> Over time he was still a man who had left his family and not tried to find us. I learned that people cannot be more or better than their lives. For one day they can. But everyday matters more. Love is only as good as days… Love can stun you still, I knew, but it was not that kind of bond. This was more fallen, of the earth, full of practicalities and chatter.

Real, yes, but also, if lasting, "always a surrender."[136]

Believe it or not, the same wisdom can be found in *The Exorcist*. Fr. Merrin, just before his heart finally gives out in the face of the demon, finds "possession" not so much in the grandiose killing of wars and murders, or the extraordinary taking over of the child he is dealing with, but "in the little things… the senseless, petty spites; the misunderstandings; the cruel and cutting word that leaps unbidden to the tongue between friends. Between lovers." The priest makes a case for durable love as a function of will and act, and not only, or primarily, feeling: "How many husbands and wives… must believe they have fallen out of love because their hearts no longer race at the sight of their beloveds!"[137]

Ah, for real love, and real Arabs! Two years after September 11, Diana Abu-Jaber wrote a marvelous portrait of her Jordanian immigrant father shouting at the television in Syracuse, trying to make sense of the bad reportage, al-Jazeera, the Iraq war. They get into an argument about whether Tony Shalhoub is Lebanese or Jordanian. She asks in exasperation, "What does it matter? You're practically cousins." Her father answer, "You see. That's the TV talking. Even you believe it. The TV says we're all the same. Nobody in America knows who the Arabs really are. Not even the Arabs."[138]

So who are the Arabs at core? More than what Gary David calls "the deficit model of ethnic identity" where you get "minus points" for being married to a non-Arab. By excessively opposing "Arab" and "American"—"being Arab American means never being fully one thing, but being less than either of the components." But as David shows, this is a false dichotomy and conclusion. For not all Arab Americans are torn apart, but "many more are very comfortable with the blending, epiphanies, and even contradictions of being always and forever brown."[139] Who is anyone? And wasn't that finally Abu-Jaber's point? We are all combinations, concoctions of history, and place, and climate, both like our parents and not.

To be an Arab American might be someone in touch with borders and border crossings in the self, someone who knows religion no more defines one than the clothes make the man. I found this out quite to my surprise when writing a kind of imaginative memoir of Daniel Pearl, the Jewish-American reporter who was assassinated in Pakistan by al-Qaeda. For no other reason than who he was.

And who was he? Well, he grew up not a mile from me in the San Fernando Valley. I imagined him riding his bike on streets I rode and touching the same old oak on Louise Avenue I touched:

> I do not know Daniel Pearl but I know him. And I know the people who killed him did not know him. Those who did this horrible thing do not know oranges or oaks, Encino or Tarzana; they do not know what America is or can be. They identified Daniel by one word only. Daniel never identified anyone with one word. Even that word they got wrong. Because Daniel was an Arab, a wandering Arab, and I am a skeptical Jew. I do not believe that God is the province of any one people, any one faith; any faith or people who kill in His name are allied with death and not life, not oaks and oranges, not olives and fig trees or grazing land or Kashmir or anywhere but darkness.[140]

To be an Arab American, a true one, is to be a true American, or better—a true human being. True, it may be riskier these days to stand up and be counted with an Arab spot on your soul. But once one has known the sun, the shade will never be the same. And wasn't that after all where all these ancestors came from? It wasn't ice. It was the glaring definition of the sun that poured on the poor human form and bid it do something besides eat and copulate and defecate and destroy. It said: Be a human being. You have something indelible and precious inside you. If you hoard it, it's worthless. Risk the other. Understand you are not alone in being misunderstood or persecuted or lonely. Go far to belong and to love. Even as far as America. Even further, if America is lost.

−TEN−

A CELEBRATION OF COMMUNITY

CENTER OF THE WORLD (WASHINGTON, DC)

I was at my windowless government office in Rockville, Maryland—eight stories up—when the secretary of our division appeared at my door, put her hand on its frame and said, "A plane has hit the World Trade Center." She was not looking at me, but at the door frame, as if suddenly questioning whether a door should have a frame. Or could have.

"That's too bad," I said, turning back to writing a series of brochures on substance abuse. But soon people were gathered in our conference room watching television. I watched the second plane hit the second tower, which fell before the first like sand.

Unreal City, T.S. Eliot called London and other cities that in "The Waste Land." It was 1917, during World War I, the first great unreality of history's most violent century. New York may have been unreal to those of us who watched the firestorm of the towers at the remove of television. Too real to those there. And then we were told we were hit.

The Pentagon, that is. The impregnable fortress across the Potomac, about eight miles from my office, where we gathered to greet my wife at the end of her Army ten-mile road race the year before, where we had gathered as a family to accept the Presidential Unit Citation with others of my father's forgotten battalion from World War II. The plane hit exactly that side of the Pentagon where we had been with General Shinseki, the army chief of staff. The army side of the Pentagon. With us that cold January day of the award was my cousin Dr. Nabeel "Nino" al-Anouf and his wife, Rabia, both Third Wave immigrants from Syria living in Delaware. It was a proud day; I was glad my cousins could be a part of it. They were as American as anyone else in the room, weren't they?

Nino phoned me and said, "We came to this country to be safe." And now it was clear no one was safe, not an Arab American, not a Finnish American. And most of all—not a Washingtonian or a New Yorker.

An alarm blared. A fourth plane seemed headed for the Capital. We were told to evacuate our government building in Rockville, unlikely a target as it might be. That sure upgraded its worth, I thought in a wicked moment. But then I realized: that fourth plane could hit one of our sons. Andy was attending high school only a block from the US Capitol. (Presumably, Matt was safe in his Hagerstown school, 50 miles away, and Luke in Rockville.)

For some moments, the threat became real to me. I frantically called the school. I couldn't get through. I reached my wife, who said she couldn't get through for an hour. I jumped in our car and headed toward the Capitol. A gigantic traffic jam on Military Road. No way. Had to turn around. Then the news that the fourth plane—the one aimed at the Capitol—was down in Pennsylvania. A selfish relief. After having been crowded into the school's basement with 900 other boys for many hours, our son Andy finally made it home in time for dinner. The next day he found out that one of the stewardesses who died in the plane that hit the Pentagon was the mother of one of his classmates. For a time, the classmate disappeared.

Over the weeks and months after the catastrophe, it became obvious that life in Washington was not going to be the same. The initial outrage turned into palpable fear, which itself mutated into a culture of surveillance I had never seen in this country. Over the past decade or so we had become accustomed in Washington to barricades going up around the Capitol and the state department and, after a plane flew into the White House, Pennsylvania Avenue between 16th and 17th Street was closed to vehicles. The simple pointing out from a car window of "Look, there's the White House" done on many occasions with many casual visitors to our city was deleted from our lives. Perhaps the word "casual" had exited the lexicon of the capital.

But that was nothing compared to the cameras after September 11. They cropped up on traffic lights, lamp poles, on billboards and fences and shop ceilings and in office corridors. There was a sense as the strange warm winter came that one was being watched in Washington, that there was no purely aimless stroll allowed in the city. Perhaps this is my imagining, but for a year there seemed no jets of water in our fountains. Only jets. Lots of them. Streaking by. And helicopters. Lots of them. Thwop-thwopping here and there. Few nights did not contain a cone of light searching our Chevy Chase neighborhood before it tried others. Perhaps there are more potential traitors in the upscale northwest of the city than in the hardscrabble ghetto, where a terrorist might run into a mugger.

Then as 2002 turned, we were hit with anthrax. No one knew where it came from, but suddenly the Friendship Heights post office, a mile from our house, was contaminated and sealed off. I made a bee-line for a medical supply house and came home with a large box of rubber gloves. For months we opened our mail outdoors with these gloves, discarded in an outdoor bucket. We directed our mail lady to put the mail on a certain wicker table, but NEVER to slide it through the mail slot. Who was sending this wretched powder to the capital? My friend's brother, who was investigating the source of the anthrax mailings, confessed to him, "We will never know."

Not long after the anthrax scare subsided and the rubber gloves came off, in October 2002 people in the District and its suburbs began to fall from anonymous gunshot. Within a three-week period, ten people in ten different spots around the city were shot and killed for no apparent reason. No robbery. No mugging. No kidnapping. It appeared pure target practice. One man was killed a block from my office while cutting grass, minutes after I had driven past the spot. Could I have been in the crosshairs? Where were the crosshairs? A woman was felled coming out of a store in Aspen Hill, not a mile from our home.

I found myself walking zigzag at night to my car in the parking lot at work, as if the sniper was anywhere and everywhere. The whole city began taking down license plate numbers of white vans, as police identified the getaway car (it turned out to be a blue Chevrolet Caprice). I called in at least five white van numbers myself. Sports events at all schools in the entire DC area were cancelled; this policy stretched to Frederick, Maryland, 50 miles north and to Richmond, Virginia, 50 miles south. One individual (or two as it turned out) had managed to frighten the center of the free world, the most guarded place on earth—more than an army, flotilla of warplanes, or set of guided missiles. We were protected by the greatest destructive force ever amassed by man, but we felt more vulnerable than a swimmer in a lagoon of piranhas. All we knew, and were reminded of nearly every day, subtly or not, by brilliant academic commentators, or raving maniacs on talk radio, was that these piranhas were probably Arabs. (A cooler head here and there recalled the Unabomber and Timothy McVeigh, homegrown Anglo nuts of the past decade.)

Nervous, not someone given to paranoia but feeling it slowly seep into my system, I remembered once being told that Eudora Welty, on hearing the radio report of the assassination of Martin Luther King, turned to her typewriter and, in a flurry, wrote a story from the point-of-view of the would-be assassin. It was quickly published and was partly responsible for leading the FBI to James Earl Ray, a southerner, the kind of person Eudora Welty knew all too well in her native Mississippi. Uncannily, Welty had written in her fiction a nearly exact profile of the killer.

I tried it. The police were getting nowhere and the "shooter" seemed to be getting bolder, leaving chilling messages, like "Your children are not safe anywhere at any time." Why not take a page from Welty, the master? It was, if nothing else, one way to work off nerves. So I wrote a short story, "Singing to the Choir," about a man of mixed race estranged from his wife who lives in the Washington, DC, area. The man has served some time in upstate Michigan, where Black Muslims convert him to Islam and imbue him with a hatred of American foreign policy, particularly in the Middle East, as well as historic inequities served to blacks. He is a veteran of the 1991 Gulf war, an expert marksman, and has fragged an officer in it, causing a dishonorable discharge that keeps him from getting a job. He comes to DC on a mission: to both frighten his wife and get back his children, and to be a one-man grim reaper for everything America is doing wrong in the world. He is not clinically crazy, perhaps, but crazy the way the terrorists who destroyed the World Trade Center were crazy: like a fox, filled with fanatic hatred that in some twisted way comes out to them holy. More than Jeremiah. Joshua smiting the Amorites.

I wrote the story in a fever of a day and sent it to the *Washington Post* and *Wall Street Journal*. The very next day John Allen Muhammed was caught with an accomplice, Lee Malvo, sleeping at a rest stop near Hagerstown, a place I often stopped on the way to visit our eldest son in school nearby. I did not divine a Malvo and Muhammed had been in Tacoma, Washington, not Michigan, and Muhammed wasn't dishonorably discharged (though he had been court-martialed), but most everything else was strangely accurate. My friend at the *Post* who was covering the sniper story and was struck by the resemblances said, "Maybe you missed your calling." "To be a great short story writer?" I asked hopefully. "A detective," he dropped. We shared a rare laugh at the end of a grim month in the Capital.

Almost nothing of the above had to have been written by an Arab American. The shock, anger, and fear that Washingtonians and New Yorkers felt, indeed Americans felt, foreigners with hearts felt, are plainly human. But I say "almost" because I'm not sure your run-of-the-mill American (not Arab, not Washingtonian) would have infused Muhammed with a twisted lethal grudge over the Middle East, nor perhaps would that American have identified the sniper with the righteous anger of Joshua. As it turns out, Muhammed's violence appears to have been somewhat copycat—he bought the used Caprice on September 11, 2002, and wrote on the receipt the actual time the first plane hit the World Trade Center.

What follows, however, is more to that point: how this Arab American and others live in the nation's capital, have lived, and, hardest of all, whether they will continue to do so. When a doctor friend of mine in Florida wrote asking, "What the hell is an Arab doing in Washington these days?" she wasn't being entirely humorous.

On a night in August 2003 when much of the power in

northwest Washington, DC, was blacked out by a bad thunder-and-lightning storm, I gathered seven Arab-American Washingtonians at the Parthenon Restaurant on Connecticut Avenue. The place was packed. People whose electric stoves were out were lined up outside. Luckily, I had reserved a table downstairs in the seldom-used basement. One by one, they came in from the storm.

They were an Antiochian Orthodox priest who has been pastor of a parish in suburban Maryland for over twenty years; a former US congresswoman from Cleveland, Ohio; a state department finance officer; a professor of Islamic studies at Georgetown University; the president of the local ADC chapter who works for a defense contractor; a Palestinian clinical psychologist; and a young Palestinian-American writer who was adopted and raised by the psychologist. Like many Washingtonians, most were not born in the capital, but had come for professional advancement or education or a case of "Potomac fever," that curious illness that can last a lifetime if not treated quickly. Some I knew well, some I knew not at all. All but one had been through September 11 in DC. That was the topic of our dinner discussion.

Fr. George Rados was first to arrive, the oldest in age and the youngest in spirit. Though I am Roman Catholic, when I first came to work in Washington in the late 1970s, I often joined an Orthodox friend of mine for liturgy at Fr. George's Sts. Peter and Paul Church, now in Potomac, Maryland. It was not difficult—my mother was raised Orthodox; I've never been far from icons and "ages of ages." Fr. George puts the lie to the Catholic obsession with priestly celibacy, that terribly thin argument (getting thinner, tragically, by the day) that celibate priests have more time to focus on their flock. Time, indeed! Fr. George and his wife raised five children (one would die tragically in a car accident), yet I know of no more tireless spiritual servant of the people.

Father George is an original every Sunday. He avoids the pulpit, often walking into the congregation. His homilies are peppered with history, literature, and science. One Sunday he addressed our culture's worship of the physical: "How beautiful is your body these days? Does it bother you that on television every lady is lovely and every man is macho? Ditto for movies, magazines, billboards. The heroes of history are more often persons who rise above physical afflictions." He pointed to the clubbed feet of Lord Byron and Sir Walter Scott, the blindness of Homer and Milton, those cripples Roosevelt and Pasteur.

Another Sunday he addressed the notion of wisdom: "It happens all the time. A smart fellow falls while a plodder with an ordinary IQ succeeds. There must be something beyond basic intellect that man-made measurements just can't gauge." He contrasted the brilliant Stephen A. Douglas to the log-splitting loser of their famous debates,

Abraham Lincoln: "All this is to say that intelligence is fine, but other qualities like enthusiasm, creativity, and common sense can count more. This strength beyond brains is wisdom."[1]

Born and raised in Canton, Ohio, where his Greek father and Syrian mother ran a café for factory workers, he chose the Antiochian rite over the Greek rite because the Greeks were more wary of his split heritage than the Syrians. Father George was also beat up as a boy for being Arab, and that may have settled it.[2]

One by one, they began to come in from the storm. As they settled down, jackets shaken of water, and water and wine-glasses poured, I asked them to describe where they were when September 11 occurred, their reactions to it, and its ripple effects in their lives. Their answers were as diverse and surprising as the Arab-American community itself.

In Charlotte, NC, George Saba, a native of Connecticut and a senior adviser to the chief financial officer of the state department, was in a car heading to teach a college management course and heard the news on the radio: "My immediate reaction was that this was not an accident. Being in the industry I am in, I was concerned that someone I knew might be affected. Many in the company, surprisingly enough, had decided to stay in their building nearby even after the second plane had hit. Some did leave. Luckily, no one I knew was hurt."[3]

Yvonne Haddad, a professor in the Center for Christian-Muslim Understanding at Georgetown University said, "I was at home. My sister called from Toronto and said, 'Are you watching TV?' I got a phone call from a former student who works with an intelligence agency. A week before he had come to see me and I had told him that what President Bush was saying and doing was going to bring a lot of problems and he asked 'Do you think they will hit us here?' and I had said, 'Yes.' So on the phone he said, 'Anything in particular?' And I said, no, it was just my hunch. That we had been so abusive, we had catered to Sharon so much, that what I had read in the Arab press showed people were livid. While I was talking to him, the [third] plane came [at the Pentagon], and he watched that, he was driving to the Pentagon and I lost touch with him.

"Two days later, I went on C-SPAN. The first reaction of our community was to hide and I had to ask my husband about doing it. I spoke for about an hour about our contributions as Arab Americans to United States history. That these people were not what these [hijackers] stood for. I got death threats. Quite a few. Hate mail. The university told me to keep a low profile or have a policeman outside my door, which I refused. My students at first were very empathetic toward Muslims and distinguished between Muslims and terrorists, but by the time we went to war in Afghanistan, with the war propaganda, they lost their empathy. They became very hostile toward Arabs and Muslims, [asking] why do we open our homes to them, our universities? Since then it's been very hard to get back to where we were prior to 9/11."[4]

A 25-year-old Palestinian-American DC native and graduate of Boston University, Hytham Abdul-Hadi, was getting his car washed. Someone at the car wash, who couldn't speak English well, told him about the tower crashes. Most of his friends in Washington are American: "We didn't talk much about it. We actually played football, sick of watching it on TV. A mix of a whole bunch of emotions. I couldn't concentrate on work at my company after that. We work with AID [Agency for International Development]. Automatically, it was the start of a new era. Everything is changed. I started to write this political black comedy about the Palestinian-Israeli conflict, 'Ramallah Rocks.'"[5]

Had Fr. George had any trouble from the federal government with his Middle East-related charity work? Suspicion that the monies might be going to "terrorism"? "No," he said. "I have never been questioned about our work. It goes through the Church."

Former sixteen-year Democratic US representative from Ohio Mary Rose Oakar, now the president of the Arab-American Anti-Discrimination Committee, was driving through Ohio, running for mayor of Cleveland, toward Columbus. An aide of hers gave her a play-by-play over a cell phone as she drove: "I thought he was exaggerating. I know a stewardess who does one of the Boston–Los Angeles flights regularly, one of the flights involved. I thought, oh my gosh, I wonder if Kathleen is on it. It turns out she was off that day. Her crew was on, however. Later, I stopped at a gas station. Columbus is 140 miles from Cleveland. I couldn't call anybody—all the phones were out. I finally got to the state capital of Ohio, but all the buildings were entirely locked. I turned around to Cleveland. One of my best friends lives in New York, Jane Campbell, I thought of her. My brother in New York saw the whole thing through a window and was really traumatized. I remember good ole Wolf Blitzer on CNN saying about Oklahoma, 'We think it's the Arabs' and it wasn't.

"In all the polls prior to September 11, I was way ahead [of mayorial race opposition]. It took a lot of energy out of me. It just flabbergasted me. I just felt so terrible. All the things I wanted to do for the city just dehydrated. Some of my opponents tried to use my meeting nineteen years before with Arafat once again against me. The polling went down after that… On a personal basis, you know, I'm glad I did not win. But I do think there is ethnic racism whenever any candidate runs for office who happens to be in any way Arab American. It's been there since the first day I ran for Congress, not so much for City Council when I won, but for Congress I was targeted.

"I think it was very devastating to me personally. I always represented a very ethnically diverse community in my sixteen years in Congress. It's interesting. I did a lot of immigration work as a congresswoman and the people who were more discriminated against than anyone were Middle Eastern and Irish. They thought the Irish were terrorists, too. As a Catholic, I grew up with the Irish and was sympathetic to their needs. I went to law school for a year in order to help these people. Then I got this call from ADC.

"Osama bin Laden set our people back a zillion years. More importantly, it brought out all the subconscious prejudice in the society; it made AIPAC much more powerful to portray our people as non-people and uncivilized. I mean we just heard they stopped a Lebanese woman from coming to this country to attend the vows of her son to become a priest! It's made me much more aware of the need to assist people of our common ancestry. It's worse now than ever before. Some of the people in the Bush Administration have a narrow vision and an agenda that perpetuates [prejudice] because of the 9/11 tragedy. They would want to do that anyway, but now they have an excuse. We have to work harder, no matter what role we are in, to eliminate the demonization of our people."[6]

Mona Hamoui, who works for the Mitre Corporation, a defense contractor in Virginia, remembered a coworker's comments after the Pentagon was hit: "I heard somebody say to me, 'We should just go over there and take those people out.' And I said, 'Who are those people?' He didn't say anything then. It was his natural assumption it was Arabs. Everytime something like this happens I feel anger. Just like Mary Rose says, it sets us back and we're having to defend ourselves in a way European-Americans never have to do, if [someone of that background] commits a crime. A lot of hurt, not feeling like I could really say anything. It was such a delicate time. I had this sense I had to defend who I was now. I felt myself getting more active, writing my senators, etc."

"Now with the word 'Arab,' I feel a twinge in my throat," she concluded.[7]

"We need more members at ADC to affect policy," Oakar said. "I went to get lists from the Orthodox church, no problem. The Muslim mosques, no problem. The Maronite priest, a problem. But later they grilled this priest for six hours at the airport on his way to Lebanon, absolutely frivolous. Way overboard. Now the priest says he's ready to give me the list. This blond-haired, blue-eyed Palestinian-American captain in the US air force who spoke at our convention was stopped at the airport and questioned. This is so obscene. It's worse than the McCarthy era."

"This boy in our church wanted to get married to a Russian Orthodox girl," Fr. George said. "After 9/11, his fiance began to get uptight and didn't trust him. She broke it off!"

Nuha Abudabbeh, a clinical and forensic psychologist, introduced herself.

"We could use you!" Oakar beamed. Table laughter.

Abudabbeh was downtown by the DC courts when told of the attack. Someone shouted "Don't go in the subway!" and pandemonium reigned. African-American coworkers, she said, related well to her anxiety, "their sentiments, their political ideology were the same. But guess who called the most to see if my relatives were okay? My Jewish friends. Which makes sense. It's minorities who build caring and love. Even some who were Zionists."[8]

During dinner our group spoke of the fallout in the weeks and months after 9/11 in their jobs, neighborhoods, communities, and relations, as well as experiences growing up Arab American. Mona Hamoui told about a child in her Virginia neighborhood who left his public school due to harassment as an Arab. Yvonne Haddad spoke about the citizenship muddle in the earliest years of Arab immigration to America, when Syrians were first thought to be Asians, and when a Massachusetts senator talked about "Lebanese trash." Fr. George said his parents went to Brazil at first because they were classified in the United States as Orientals. He mentioned with chagrin that as a young priest he had gone into a classroom in Montgomery County, Maryland, where the children were writing 'Happy Birthday, Israel' cards on Israel's Independence Day.

The subject turned to weaknesses in the Arab-American community, and even the so-called 'Arab psyche.' Abudabbeh said, "We have no interest in psychology, a field that is so significant not only on an individual level, but [look] how Jews have manipulated that field to their best interests. It's unbelievable how little our interest is in it."

I noted how difficult it was for my family to actually say my sister, a diagosed schizophrenic, was mentally ill. It was always, she was "down," "depressed," "not well."

"I'm not talking about psychology as treatment," Abudabbeh said. "I'm talking about it as a field—industrial psychology, political psychology. I think we basically are very superficial. I hate to say that. But that's my impression. Psychology is very deep, it is going inside. We are much more interested in outside activities. We like business, whatever makes money."

"It's changing with the current generation," Oakar said. "Journalists, artists."

"I think it's Americans in general," Hamoui said. "If a child wants to go into music, the parent says, 'What? How are you going to make a living?'"

"When people learned that I made good money as a psychologist, they said, Wow," Abudabbeh smiled. "They were suddenly interested in my field!"

I asked the group why they felt the 9/11 attacks happened. And were we getting to the roots of the problem in Afghanistan and Iraq?

"A world council could sit down and discuss the matter of terrorism, to find out what the bottom line is here about the causes, not just the effects," Fr. George said.

"It's narcissistic to assume that the terrorists want our liberty or are jealous of it," Abudabbeh said.

"Policy, policy, policy," said Haddad. "Our policy in Palestine, in Saudi Arabia. Wolfowitz and Company went into Iraq. As Bush said, 'I gave Sharon a present.' But our policies are still not being addressed."

"I don't think much has changed since 9/11," George Saba said. "I remember when I was a newspaper boy during the Six-Day War in 1967. It was portrayed as Good vs. Evil. It was about that time I started to recognize my ethnic background. I started to educate myself. You have to educate people. The public is not educated."

"The Christian right has never taken over our government before now," said Oakar. "The Jewish right has taken over Israel. I do think it is a little different today. The head of our Middle East policy is Elliott Abrams. He was off the wall in Central America [during the Reagan years]. The reason we have the policy we have is our people have not used their power."

"58,000 Muslims voted for Bush in Florida," said Haddad.

"Shame on Al Gore," Oakar said. "He took a pass on the issue in the debates and Bush didn't and it won him votes."

I noted that during the 2000 Presidential debates, Al Gore emphasized his support for Israel and then said, "As for the other side…" "Who is this 'other side?' I asked. "Don't we have a name, a face? Are we just some anonymous opponent?"

Oakar threw her hands up, "I can't believe Dick Cheney. He and the neo-conservatives talk about let's go into Syria, into Lebanon, the Gulf countries. If they ever do that, we have lost the Constitution of the United States. We have not protected the Israelis at all [with this policy]."

Where do we go from here? I asked.

Oakar recalled in the late 1980s being told that a camp was being built near New Orleans to intern Arab Americans and Iranian Americans. She and Rep. Nick Joe Rahall (D-WV) asked the FBI just before Operation Desert Storm to come to her office about it: "I asked the agent, who was Irish, 'How would you feel if they did this to the Irish [Americans] over the IRA?' He said, 'Oh, c'mon.' But they had the plans."

On the other hand, Oakar said, it was a good sign that seven Jewish groups worked with ADC to speak out against the appointment of neo-conservative Daniel Pipes to the US Institute of Peace. Some of them talked to her about civil disobedience, as in the days of South African apartheid.

"That's all we need," Oakar laughed. "Civil disobedience!"

The defeat of the attempt to halt Israeli settlements by Senator Adlai Stevenson in 1980 by cutting aid sent a bad message to others who would do such a thing, said Oakar, because Stevenson was, so to speak, hung out to dry. He lost his senate seat and later gubernatorial election. She mentioned that Rep. Jim Moran (D-VA) had caught hell in 2003 for opining that the invasion of Iraq was done largely to placate Israel. Moran was attacked as an anti-Semite. She said it would be terrible if Arab Americans abandoned Moran in his relection. "People contribute from all over the country against him." Oakar said. "One phone call and boom boom boom. Moran's opponent will get millions from some jerk who doesn't care about anything. Our people do not dig into their pockets, unfortunately. I wish that money was not a factor in any election. But it is."

"Richard Cohen of the *Washington Post* defended Moran," said Hamoui. "He said he wasn't anti-Semitic. He might have been insensitive."

"You know, after the UN Conference on Racism, when Colin Powell had to vote no because of Palestine, that happened right before September 11," Abdul-Hadi recalled.

"But we can never justify what Osama bin Laden did," Oakar asserted.

"We're not justifying it!" Haddad exclaimed.

"I do think that he's a selfish pig," Oakar put it. "If he really cared about the Palestinians, he never would have done what he did."

"But listen, he has been trained to think that way," Haddad said. "The US government trained him. The way you solve things is by killing people. He's their guy. They built up training camps [against Soviets]."

"I still can't conjure up what makes someone do what they did, the hatred, the world view with a very puristic Islamic thing," said Abudabbeh. "Some patients tell me, look at the naked stuff on TV, lesbians and gays, all of these things are unacceptable and incomprehensible to them."

"But I think it is very dangerous to say it's a cultural thing," Saba said. "Our culture vs. theirs. The issue is desperation. People that have no power, the Palestinians, for example, such a one-sided situation. You get rocks. You make a gun. Now a bomb."

"But the hijackers were not Palestinians," I said.

"I really think the first thing hijacked on 9/11 was the Palestinian cause," said Hamoui.

"If people in the Middle East just followed Martin Luther King, and went with nonviolence," said Oakar.

"We had Mubarak Awad," said Haddad.

"You need a real movement," said Oakar. "We need to exercise moderation in every way. It's easy for me to say… But look at this bureaucracy created by the Homeland Security. Our laws have changed; they have taken away our basic civil and human rights. No due process. What is happening to the Bill of Rights?"

"I had a very strange call last November by the FBI," said Abudabbeh. "I asked why they were asking all these questions. He mentioned me calling a certain hotel in Cambridge. He said the hijackers stayed at that hotel. Really? I said. It was a conference I was going to. How come a whole year has passed and you are calling me? I asked. It was obvious; it was any Arab-American name they were checking."

On that somber note, we went out into the steaming streets, and parted.

The Washington, DC, Arab American community—150,000 strong—has been, until September 11, a growing one, with lots of Third Wave immigration from Arab lands since 1967, including Palestinians, who number about 10,000. It is one of the ironies of immigrant history that one of the cities of choice for Palestinians in the United States is the very capital of the power that has kept their homeland from being free. Some are journalists who stayed, establishing families far beyond their initial expectations, such as Fawzi al-Asmar, who wrote the groundbreaking memoir, *To Be an Arab in Israel* and Ghassan Bishara of *al-Fajr*; some created businesses, such as Mama Ayesha's relatives, Khalil and Mohsen Aburish, who ran Bethany Travel Agency (after the West Bank town where lived Jesus's cousins, Mary and Martha), as well as a limousine service that ferried diplomats and American officials around the capital. And some, like builders Raymond and Edmund Howar, descend from an older Palestinian immigrant generation like their father A. Joseph Howar, who built the Islamic Center in 1949—the year cousin and restauranteur "Mama Ayesha" Howar arrived and the year he passed his business to his two sons.[9] The Islamic Center's stately minaret can be seen crossing the Taft Bridge over Rock Creek Park.

Some Palestinians, like Pakistanis, Ethiopians, Somalis, and other Africans, drive taxis. Cabdriver George Muhawi had seen close-up the loose grasp of history by Americans as he toured them around the city: "I mean, I've picked up so many people in my cab and as I drive along the Lincoln Memorial they will point to it and say, 'Is that Jefferson?' Typical Americans. It's not their fault; it's the system which does not enhance the knowledge of history, geography. It concentrates on creating the better machine which is a human being that goes along with the system as best it can."[10]

He decried the downward spiral of violence by both sides in his homeland: "Absolutely nothing is worth a drop of a human being's blood, because it is sacred." He risked his own every night he took his cab down the streets of the capital. I wonder now if he's still risking it. Thieves, after all, are nothing compared to white-collar hate.

In such a transient city as Washington, where people come and go every four years with the presidential elections (or every two years with congressional races), native Washingtonians are a special breed (I can testify, having married one), and though there aren't many left, Arab-American old-timers have contributed much to the city's remarkable history along the Potomac. There are Syro-Lebanese doctors William Driebe and Edward Soma; the Baroody family, whose father, William, founded the conservative think tank, the American Enterprise Institute, and whose sons worked in various Republican administrations. The Rizik family, which established a chic women's apparel store in the heart of the business and lobbying district at Connecticut and K Streets, goes back to the beginning of the 20th century. Then there is Buddia ("Bud") Rashid, ice cream scion of a 1,300-member clan in America, which drew people from 32 states to its annual family reunion in Washington in 1985.[11]

Sammy Abdullah Abbott, "the scourge of the mighty," was for five years the fiery socialist mayor of suburban Takoma Park, Maryland, making that town the first nuclear-free zone in America, believing, "If we can't do it here, there's no hope for the nation."[12]

Lawyer Richard Shadyac was, like Abbott, lured by power from humble origins (he grew up in Barre, Vermont, a part-Irish boy who served mill workers at his father's little market). But he landed in the gold, not nuclear-free, zone. Sporting large diamonds on his rings, a Lincoln Continental, and hair tightly coifed, the tall Shadyac had a gigantic laugh and something of the backroom Irish pol to his dark face. He seemed a tall version of James Cagney in the rapid-fire, restless tone of his voice. The manager of James Abourezk's Senate campaign in 1972, Shadyac asserted, "I invented the term 'Arab American'!"[13] He painted a scene of a DC coffee shop where he and Abourezk cooked up the catch-all phrase one night to sidestep the community's endless subsets. But watching the internecine battles and in-fighting in Arab-American political groups, Shadyac concluded glumly, "They all self-destruct."

The place that was perhaps the number one touchstone for an Arab American in the nation's capital was for nearly a century an institution for Georgetown residents of all stripes. Neam's Market, at the corner of P Street and Wisconsin Avenue, was founded in 1909 by two Lebanese brothers, one of whom had been a sponge diver in Tripoli before stowing away on a Brazil-bound steamer to escape the Ottoman Empire's "draft." Unfortunately, the market came to an inauspicious end in 2000, the victim of a dispute between the Neam family and recent Lebanese immigrants to whom they had leased the store.

But until then, how grand that humble little open air grocery by the streetcar tracks had become! Everyone from Franklin Roosevelt's son James to Elizabeth Taylor (who signed brown bags while buying a picnic lunch for fourth hubby Senator John Warner) came through Neam's door. The history of Washington and its politics over the 20th century could literally be seen between the parsley and cabbage at Neam's. When Ike wanted bib lettuce, no one had ever heard of it, but Neam's found it in Indiana and had it shipped. When Jimmy Carter sought something called Crutchfield's Hush Puppy Mix, the only place in Washington with the little cornmeal balls was Neam's. (The reader should not draw any conclusions about Carter's affinity for the Arab side of the ledger. The list of those who bought their bread at Neam's who wouldn't have known a Palestinian if he sneezed—much less offered him a tissue—is a long one, indeed.)

Once called by *Newsweek* "the most expensive market" in Washington, Neam's specialized in quality meats, blue lobsters lobbying in their tanks before a vote, caviar, strawberries year round (back when that was rare), two kinds of green turtle soup, 24 varieties of mustard, kidneys (not kidney beans—kidneys), quail, squab, you name it. Whatever you couldn't get at the chains, Neam's had. Veterans of two world wars and sixteen presidents got their vittles at Neam's. Mrs. Cornelius Vanderbuilt once ordered Russian caviar at $35 an ounce. And that was a deal! Nancy Kissinger tickled Henry's fancy with lobster. Gene Kelly danced among the rhubarb. Pearl Bailey crooned with the croutons. Bebe Rebozo reveled in the ratatouille. Johnson and Kennedy loved steaks. Jack Neam, one of the three store-working sons of Najeeb, remembered Kennedy whistling the theme from the *Bridge on the River Kwai*, picking out his Porterhouses as a senator in the 1950s.[14]

Even Art Buchwald celebrated Neam's in a well-loved column in 1978, putting these words in a satirized owner's mouth, "Consider this diamond-shaped pear an investment. In three days when it's ripe it will be worth three times what you paid for it."[15]

Delivered by his grandmother in the small residence atop the grocery store in 1921, Jack Neam grew up to stories of his father seeing a calf inside the gut of an Anaconda snake in Brazil and the old man braving a dinner of monkey. Perhaps that gave Père Neam a vision of a better world. It was also said that Najeeb had made it to Washington not only to link up with his brother, but because he came up to Texas on a boat with Teddy Roosevelt.

But it was not always life with the hoity-toity at Neam's. During the Depression, they had to throw away a lot of food going bad, every bunch of wilted lettuce. In 1939, Jack played guard and middle linebacker for Western High School's first city championship in football in 50 years, but his sorest memory is playing in 90-degree heat a Virginia team that had 110 players: "I played half the game and lost 12 pounds." To a grocer, everything is in weight. It's all scales.

Jack's father once literally "bet the store" on the second re-election of FDR in 1940 against Wendell Wilkie. He won $2 from a reporter.

About September 11, Jack's wife Laurice Neam "still gets teary-eyed."[16] She spoke at their Arlington home, with its lucky fig tree in front, not a mile from the famous cemetery. Apparently, one of their four children, a doctor who runs a ER unit at a Florida hospital, was called by the FBI and questioned during the anthrax scare. They had traced that Mohammed Atta, one of the hijackers, had gone to his ER room for "sores" that might have been related to anthrax. But that was not the case. They don't think the questioning had anything to do with their son's heritage.

Not after a century of Neam's. Not after their evenhanded scales.

Will Arabs stop coming to Washington, indeed, to this country? George Bush, after all, has declared his war on terror an unending one, which, the way he fights it, it is bound to be. Was the immigrant experience of my family and those I have interviewed over 25 years unique in this country, well on the road to dying out? I don't know. Time, and the wisdom or lack of it in our leaders, will tell. On October 22, 2004, the community breathed a collective sigh of relief when an amendment sponsored by Rep. Dave Weldon (R-FL) to shut off all visas to the United States for people of several Middle Eastern countries was mercifully dropped. Relief, yes, but why was such a thing in the air at all?

The thought of leaving the capital for good, even the country, to preserve life and limb of my family, not to mention sanity, is not a strange one to me. But that is not only an Arab-American thought.

I have spent half my life in the capital, some of it doing Middle East duty, but more as a college student, slaving in the government, and raising three wonderful sons with a beauteous native of the city. The venality, self-importance, and blithe insensitivities of the government company town that is Washington I have witnessed and lived to the point of disgust. The chance for real service to the public, for initiative, creativity, and vitality is thin, indeed. It is a town of millions of water carriers for a few mediocre individuals vaulted by dint of money and fate into the carousel of power. It was with the welcoming back of my soul that I accepted a position to teach college in my home state of California. And yet for all the professional frustration over this bureaucrat-mad, checkpoint, hashpoint, sieve-of-a-thousand-minds before anything is produced, usually dead-on-arrival-of-nonsense-or-incompetence capital, I have no personal regrets. There have been great familial pleasures along the Potomac, in Rock Creek Park, at myriad Little League fields. My brother forgot the ring at Dahlgren Chapel, to the roar of the crowd and my startled new wife. We toasted a comet with neighbors, heard many Messiahs at Christmas, had more than one brunch at Chadwick's with friends. We rolled Easter eggs at the White House with our little boys. Every New Year's, we walked or jogged with our DC Chevy Chase gang of friends to Hank Dietle's or the Irish Inn on the C&O Canal Towpath. When I was at Georgetown University I once bought a sandwich at the deli at Neam's, spending half my week's food allotment. It was delicious. A girlfriend once purchased steaks there for us. Delicious again. I saw shadows of flames from my perch in the Healy Tower lap against the Capitol dome after Martin Luther King was assassinated. It changed me, as much as 9/11, perhaps more. I saw Nixon take the oath of office in freezing weather. I walked many a street alone. I once looked up the white road of the Washington Monument thinking I would never be happy and a decade later flew a kite over the green there with three little boys, happy. Once, walking by the Capitol at night during the first Gulf war, I thought: What an amazing country this is, that I can do this and be so close to the source of power and not be stopped by some guard or barrier. The guards and the barriers came a decade later. Nothing I or any Arab American did or could do stopped that. The grayness of Washington seemed grayer; the hardness, harder. Everyone braces for an attack on the subways. Still, I have seen the cherry blossoms matt my sons' hair. Washington became my second home, swamp or no swamp, marble or not, riots or quiet, fear of Arabs or buzz of mosquitoes, humidity or torpidity, arrogance or flatulence, hope of peoples or bane, strange as only Washington can be, or familiar as my wife's hum.

Food You Can Trust (Detroit)

On a cool August night, two days before Labor Day and the reality of school, work, and fall itself, a nineteen-year-old woman in white voile *hijab* did something no Arab American in Detroit had ever done before. In front of home plate at Comerica Park, the Detroit Tigers' new baseball stadium, Amal Raychouni sang the "Star-Spangled Banner."

The Tigers went on to record their 100th loss of the 2003 season on the way to their worst season ever, one of the worst seasons in the history of baseball. But a few players did something rare for players—for someone other than themselves and something other than their sport, they clapped. They sensed a winner among the hometown losers. Her voice at "land of the freeee!" was like a bow on a rare violin. There was a tremble to it, as if that freedom were not assured. Maybe the ballplayers sensed the weight on the slender shoulders of Amal Raychouni. Heavier than a white voile headdress. Heavier than 100 losses. In the wake of the terrorist attacks of September 11 two years before, the weight of a community in danger of being not just mistaken or misunderstood. In 2003, with American troops shadow-boxing terror in Afghanistan and Iraq, another terrorist strike could find the community rounded up, like the Japanese in World War II, into bunkhouses.

A sophomore at the University of Michigan at Dearborn, Amal was a pre-med student majoring in history, as if history could teach you everything you need to know about the human body. For an Iraqi American, the daughter of immigrants from northern Iraq, maybe it was not so odd. History there had plenty to heap on a body.

"I don't care about people's ignorance," Amal said after her song, as she took a seat with other Arab Americans in a left field box suite next to the one labeled 'Ty Cobb.' "I just want to reach people where they are most human. Sometimes music can override all your thoughts."[17] I thought of Ty Cobb, that violent man, the greatest hitter in baseball history, whose name sits among the Tiger greats (Gehringer, Greenberg, Kaline) in a centerfield brick wall with no number. Cobb wore no number. Was it his uniqueness or embarrassment at his extraordinary violence that the Tigers never gave him a number? Politically unnumbered, so to speak, would Arab Americans be better numbered? Stamped? Easily called out?

It was "Arab-American Night" at Comerica Park, another first for major league baseball. Why Detroit? Motown has the largest, or second largest, population of Arab Americans in the country (an estimated 400,000). These include car-factory-working Yemenis in south Dearborn; Lebanese Christians and Shi'ites in Dearborn itself; Palestinians, many from Ramallah, in the suburb of Livonia; well off Iraqi Chaldeans in Livonia and Bloomfield, many of whom run about 2,000 "party stores" (Detroit parlance for convenience stores) in downtown Detroit.

Extrapolating from the 2000 census, Los Angeles has an estimated 340,000 Arab Americans, though by 2003, some thought it had passed Detroit as number one in Arab-American population. In any case, the Detroit community is far more concentrated. The seat of Henry Ford's birthplace and the headquarters of Ford Motor Company— Dearborn—is at least one-third (of the 100,000 population) Arab. And growing. Sixty percent of the children in Dearborn are of Arab origin. At least 92 percent of Fordham High School students are Arab American. No surprise, then, that in May 2005, the $15.3 million Arab American Museum opened in Dearborn, a city described as "a living, breathing extension of the museum."[18]

Within a week of the second anniversary of the attacks on New York, Washington, and Pennsylvania led by the fanatic al-Qaeda,

Arab-American Night at a ball field in Detroit could not escape the echoes of two-year-old dread. As if microscopic cinders from far-off New York were falling in the twilight of Comerica Park. What would these Arab Americans say to that? The small crowd of 7,000 fans, used to losing, listened.

The crowd at Comerica suddenly erupted, not for anything having to do with the Middle East. The Tiger catcher had led off the seventh inning with a triple, though the team was on its way to losing 5–2.

"One thing you can say for the Tigers," blue-eyed, tan Chaldean singer Steve Acho cut a small smile. "They never quit."[19] Maybe, the thought zings through the mind like a slider, Arab Americans, too. Even if Mike Makki, a Muslim from Dearborn, threw out the first ball to Detroit's catcher wildly outside in the dirt all the way to the backstop. No claps for that. Too close to home.

Among the eight people chosen to represent the community at home plate that night at Comerica Park were three Arab Muslims, all Americans, whose families originated in three different Arab countries: Lebanon, Iraq, and Egypt. Each in his own way registered the shock of 9/11 and the difficult task of dealing with aftershocks in an American city where Arabs were so conspicuous.

On September 11, Nasser Beydoun, the president of the Arab American Chamber of Commerce in Detroit, was at the banquet hall Burton Manor talking with its manager, Peter LaRosa, about a banquet contract, when he noticed on television the first of the Twin Towers falling. "I was devastated," he said. "I knew immediately there was only one person who could have done this—Osama bin Laden."[20] By 5 PM the day of the attacks, the Chamber had issued a press release: "In the strongest possible language, the 1,000-member Arab American Chamber of Commerce condemns the horrendous terrorist actions against the United States this morning."

The Chamber warned against collective punishment and hate crimes:

> As Americans, we must support all efforts to find the responsible parties and make them accountable. We urge our fellow citizens to withhold premature judgment until the responsible parties are found and not to point fingers at their Arab American neighbors and friends who are suffering like all Americans from these despicable acts.

The Chamber, with the social services agency ACCESS, spearheaded a blood drive for the victims in New York and Washington; a vigil was held in Dearborn; supportive statements by President Bush were circulated. As it turned out, no one in Beydoun's family was harassed, and there were surprisingly few hate crimes in Detroit. "Dearborn actually fared better than places with isolated pockets [of Arab Americans] because we are an old community," he said. "Most of us were born here in the United States." Beydoun counted 118 encouraging email responses to his press release, and five hate emails.

"Not a bad batting average," he said.

But the dark emails were chilling. One came in emphatic capital letters: "FUCKING DIE ARAB! YOU FUCKING ANIMAL NON HUMAN SMELLY ASS TOWEL HEAD. I HOPE YOU AND YOUR FAMILY DIE." Or, "I can't believe you exist. You will all be deported soon. Goodbye sand-niggers!"

A woman who traced her heritage back to the Mayflower era didn't mince words about who is fit and who isn't fit for these shores:

> I don't understand why you people are in America. I'm afraid you are trying to embed yourself so deeply in America that the next war will be a cival [sic] war in the USA. I want you all to go home. You are not the poor, tired, yearning to be free type Lady Liberty was talking about. I hate you all!!

A good batting average, yes, but the strike-outs may have been enough to lock the front entrance to the Chamber on Shaeffer Drive and hide the back entrance in a pharmacy. So confusing was access to the Chamber's offices, I finally gave up and called them from a pay phone on the street. When finally I was ushered upstairs, I found myself facing the toilet, then a long, dim corridor of old, poorly stained knotty pine. Ramshackle quarters. If this be the result of Arab oil largesse, I thought, the oil could be fit into a thimble.

Beydoun, 39, was born in Beirut to a Shi'ite Muslim family from Bint Jbeil in southern Lebanon. They immigrated before the Lebanese civil war—in 1969, a time when Lebanon's economy was supposedly booming. Nasser's father fled if not political collapse, certainly poverty, and worked for 30 years on the assembly line at Ford Motor Company. His son went to Wayne State University and got an MBA from the University of San Diego, before coming home to Detroit.

A tall father of two with a thick shock of hair who smiles little (though when he does the smile is deep), Beydoun credited the Jewish Community Council for "saying good things" just after September 11 that warned people against taking out their anger on the Arab population in Detroit. "We have a very good relationship with the Jewish leadership," he said.

A Republican himself, Beydoun credited George W. Bush, who visited the Dearborn community on April 28, 2003, with quelling prejudices. When Bush ticked off a long list of Iraqi leaders to admire from diverse backgrounds, he drew a swelling ovation, even if one Anglo protestor, as the president's motorcade left, yelled, "Hail to the thief!"[21]

Trying to explain why 9/11 occurred, Beydoun leaned back in his chair and looked out the fuzzy window to an overcast day in Dearborn. "I'm a believer in 'what goes around comes around,'" he said. "Our foreign policy is so screwed up. People don't respect us anymore around the world. I've traveled to some of our embassies and they are built like prisons. They are not warm and inviting."

Beydoun thought the United States hadn't fostered democracy since the 1940s. I mentioned Eastern Europe, but he countered that those countries had indigenous freedom movements, such as in Poland, that ultimately won out without our help. He ticked off a list of dictators we have supported: Pinochet, Somoza, Batista, the Shah, Mubarak. As for Iraq, he was skeptical: "It's not a benevolent act to install democracy. Right-wing hawks used false pretexts to get a counterbalance to Saudi oil and to placate Israel. This is a war that was not necessary. When you have no vision in your foreign policy, you get into wars you cannot get out of. Look what is happening now. Every time we build a power station, it is bombed." He thought getting the United Nations involved in policing and rebuilding Iraq was critical: "We can't afford to rebuild Iraq on our own."

Though Dearborn was not hit badly by backlash from 9/11, a local community leader, Rabih Haddad, was arrested in December 2001 without charges and his Islamic charity shut down, because it was "suspected of supporting and funding terrorist groups." For overstaying his visa, he was kept in jail for two years before being deported. Beydoun reflected: "That's a bunch of baloney that [Haddad] had a terrorist charity." When the media and agents swooped down on Dearborn after 9/11, he reminded them that "the terrorists were not part of our community and in fact the al-Qaeda training manual specifically tells its agents not to mix with the host population or the Arab-American community." Mentioning master Israeli spy Jonathan Pollard, he said, "There has never been an Arab American engaged in espionage in this whole country's history."

Whap. A home run over the centerfield fence by Chicago White Sox first baseman Frank Thomas, knocking in two players. Oddly, Tiger fans cheered. "At least it's a home run!" someone yelled from the bleachers. No way to unmask that the Tigers were rotten. Beydoun was not smiling.

What did Imam Hassan Qazwini think as he stood in front of home plate at Comerica Park? Home plate a good place for the knees? He adjusted his black turban, rubbed his scooping U-shaped beard, and put his hand over his heart at the sight of the American flag. The sound of Amal Raychouni's voice made him shudder. But for the life of him, he could not remember how a baseball game was won. All he knew was: the Detroit dugout didn't look too inviting.

Earlier in the day I had waited for Imam Qazwini at his mosque on Joy Road, a most un-joyous place. The street, along with Michigan and Woodward Avenues, makes Beirut look like a golf course. Shops with barricaded windows and doors, long stretches of vacant lots with refuse strewn among the weeds, liquor stores, body shops, a deadly quiet on Labor Day weekend. The destruction of the Detroit race riots of 1968 has never quite been erased from Joy Road. The largely poor African-American population tries bravely to assert joy with the Joy Club and the Mid-Joy Plaza.

In his poem "Then," Lawrence Joseph, an Arab-American poet born and raised in Detroit, attributes the genesis of his writing to the 1968 riots that apparently felled his father:

> You wouldn't have known
> it would take nine years
> before you'd realize the voice howling in you
> was born then.[22]

It was not the first time merchants in the ghetto took the brunt of black anger against privilege. In Los Angeles in 1992, Korean shopkeepers were targeted; in New York City in the 1980s, Jews and Italians in Bensonhurst took hits. In Joseph's case, it was a Lebanese store owner. Many, if not most, of those "party stores" were taken over by Iraqi Chaldeans in the past three decades. Though the violence has abated, it is never gone. From 1987 to 1997 alone, 70 Chaldean store owners and managers were shot to death during robberies in Detroit.[23] It is no comfort to say most, if not all of the killings, had nothing to do with the Middle East.

It was into this unpromising spot Hassan Qazwini came in 1997. Born in Iraq in 1964, educated in religious studies at the Iranian holy city of Qom, Qazwini first followed his imam father to California, where the elder Qazwini has a Muslim congregation in Southgate.

Imam Qazwini drove up in his Ford after a hard day of interviews with the national media. One of the two holiest sites in Shi'ite Islam—the Imam Ali mosque in al-Najaf, Iraq—had been car bombed the day before and over 100 people killed, including the revered moderate Ayatollah Mohammed Bakr al-Hakim, whose brother sits on the governing council appointed by US officials to guide Iraq to democratic rule.

Over the potholes, past the Rite Aid plastic bags fluttering in the impatiens bed, past the prayer hall (I am struck again at the austerity of the interior of small mosques—nothing on the white walls but sunlight from skylights cut around the dome), past the custodian who kindly served me coffee and dates, the imam led me into his office.

"It amazes me that the most powerful nation on earth with the most sophisticated weaponry cannot secure one mosque," he said. "I supported President Bush in removing Saddam Hussein from power. He was a cancer, a murderer. His invasion of Iran caused one million dead on both sides. But I am not very pleased with US policy post-Saddam. There is negligence. The American attitude in Iraq—" His voice trailed off. "They don't seem to care. The United States won the war, but is losing the post-war and not winning hearts and minds."[24]

I asked him where he was on September 11, 2001, and what he felt.

"I was here," he said. "I was appalled, of course, like everyone else, and very worried about outcomes. I hoped the perpetrators were not Muslims. The first victim when those few ignorant people who call themselves Muslims hijacked those planes was our faith."

Qazwini did not mince words about what Islam thinks about terrorism. Even if the US sided with Israel over the Palestinians and with "tyrannical regimes" creating "the ground for those terrorists" to grow, "this is not a justification for the actions of those people. They are no Muslims. Bin Laden is no different than Hitler. The car bomb yesterday at al-Najaf and the planes in New York and Washington—that is no faith in God. The Muslims are suffering from these people as much as the non-Muslims. Did you know that 300 Muslims were killed in the World Trade Center? That is 10 percent of the deaths on 9/11. These people are only using Islam as a cover."

"The overwhelming sense among Muslims has been to abhor these incidents," Imam Qazwini said. "You kill one innocent person, you are killing all of mankind."

"No quick ticket to heaven for a suicide bomber?" I asked.

"In all the monotheistic religions, human life has sanctity," he answered. "No one has the right to shed the blood of an innocent person. No Muslim can agree to kill innocent people by suicide bomber or not." Qazwini said he did not need to quote from the Qurʾan, but rather international law, to justify attacks by national resistance movements against the military forces of an occupier.

So shaken was Imam Qazwini by 9/11, he estimated he has spoken since at 150 churches, universities, and other public places to set American audiences straight about how appalled a Muslim would be by such attacks. He worries about "where we are heading with the Patriot Act" and wonders aloud if the fate of Arabs in America may become like the Japanese in World War II. The panegyrics of Billy Graham's son Franklin Graham against Islam after 9/11 he found "vicious, insulting, uneducated" and when he met with President Bush in November 2002 he asked him to say something against the fundamentalist Christian right. Though he didn't mention anyone by name, Bush did condemn such remarks and the hate campaigns they launch, to Qazwini's gratitude.

As for American culture, what is attractive to a Muslim and what not?

"I want our children to take the good from America, democracy, freedom, technology, organization," Imam Qazwini said. "Obviously, there is another side—unlimited freedom, lack of moral surveillance in the family or society, sexual liberalism."

And where did baseball stand?

"Oh, that's good!" Qazwini beamed as he pulled his Ford out onto Joy Road, where no one was playing in the streets.

As for the diminutive Ishmael Ahmed, the director of ACCESS, the chief social services agency for Arab Americans in Dearborn, he looked like a old shortstop, standing at Comerica Park, toeing the dirt. He had played his share of "pick-up" baseball as a kid. "I'm not a flag waver," he admitted. "'The Star-Spangled Banner' is a war song. I'd prefer 'American the Beautiful' for our anthem. But to have an Arab-American woman who is covered sing the national anthem, I was very proud. We can be part of America. We are part of America."

Born in downtown Brooklyn not far from my mother's birthplace, Ahmed was raised in Detroit by an Egyptian immigrant father and a mother whose parents homesteaded in South Dakota in the 1880s. His roots are proud. His grandmother Aliya Hassan was an early Egyptian patriot and helped plan Malcolm X's trip to Mecca. Ishmael himself served in Vietnam with the army, then later became active in the Vietnam Veterans Against the War, out of which grew the Arab Community Center for Economic and Social Services (ACCESS) in 1971.

ACCESS headquarters on Dix Avenue, not far from the River Rouge car factories and Wyandotte chemical plants, has been firebombed twice—once during the Arab oil boycott in 1973 and once during the 1979 Iranian hostage crisis. But not in 2001. Like Beydoun, Ahmed said, "By 9/11, this commuity had developed substantial roots and allies. Bill Ford [the chairman of Ford Motor Co.] called me on 9/11 and asked to meet with us immediately."[25] Ahmed himself is a member of the Democratic State Central Committee in Michigan, though he lost a bid to be on the Board of Directors of the University of Michigan.

For its first fifteen years, ACCESS was little more than a storefront, but it has grown exponentially since, said Ahmed. The organization has 500,000 contacts (one person in one day) per year in 70 programs. Its health clinic is "just short of a hospital" and it features mental health services, food programs, legal aid, community development projects, and cultural events. Led by cultural director Anan Ameri, ACCESS spearheaded the opening of the first Arab American Museum in the country in Dearborn.

Might there come a time, I wondered, when Arab immigration to the United States simply stops? When the price of coming here is too high, the surveillance too nerve-wracking (two of ACCESS's clients had been rounded up and held by the FBI), the stares too uncomfortable, the contradictions in US policy too glaring?

Ahmed didn't think so. "They're not going to go to Europe with its more homogeneous societies than here," he said. "As long as there is instability in the Middle East, they are going to want to go somewhere and we are still the favorite worldwide." Besides, he said, neat things happen when you combine the Arab with American. "Like my son's novel," he smiled. "It's called *Yo Scheherazade!*"

At the ball game, it was time for a seventh inning stretch. Ahmed, still working the crowd of the suite, nodded as if to say, "Stretch for me."

Stretching—his heart, his money, his time, his milk—comes naturally to Mike George, CEO of the largest privately owned dairy in Michigan and one of the largest in the Midwest, Melody Farms. George couldn't make it to Comerica Park, though he and fellow Chaldean Martin Manaa secured me a ticket, but he would have enjoyed the "Take Me Out to the Ballgame." Extracting music from the world (and milk from cows) gave him the firm's name. Before milk was homogenized, the cream used to sit on the top of the bottle. A dairy George bought out in the early 1960s called their new homogenized milk, "Melo-D." It rang in the ears of Mike George and his brother Sharkey as "melody." He confided, "Later I was told that of all words in the English language, the word 'melody' is one of the Top 10 that people like to say, just because it is so pretty."[26] Pretty prosperous, too. Melody Farms, which includes 100 flavors of ice cream, is worth $130 million. It may take a poet to know the beauty of language, but it takes a businessman to make it pay.

Mike George never knew his grandparents; they died young in Iraq early in the 20th century. His father, Tobia George Lossia, came in 1924 to Detroit from Telkaif in northern Iraq, a stronghold of Chaldeans, one of eighteen eastern Catholic rites. There are now about 80,000 Chaldeans in Detroit (four times the figure in 1980), about 20 percent of all Arab Americans there, with 30,000 in San Diego and 5,000 elsewhere. Worldwide, there are a half million Chaldeans, so a pretty sizable chunk of their heritage is breathing in Detroit.

Though the identification of "Chaldean" over Arab is sentimental (the Persians conquered Chaldea in 539 BCE and the Arabs took over in 636 CE), the clannishness of Chaldeans is legendary. Mike and Najat George have six sons, all but one of whom work in his businesses, and all of whom live within five miles of their parents with their own families.

When Mike George (much Americanized, the Lossia fell into

the water off Ellis Island, the Tobia became Tom) met me at the Ritz Carlton less than a mile from Henry Ford's birthplace, he immediately pulled out two long cigars. In these days of no indoor smoke, I marveled as he made one of the sitting rooms into a "Smoking Section" for two. The waitress did everything but serve us from a Model T.

Mike explained why the early immigrant Chaldeans took to peddling and grocery stores, while the earlier immigrant Arabs latched onto the Ford car factories: "The Arabs spoke Arabic among themselves at Ford, but the Chaldeans spoke Aramaic. They couldn't be understood at Ford by the whites or the Arabs. So they took to the road."[27]

Or the corner grocery. By the 1940s, there were 80 Chaldean families in Detroit and they were tight. "Any baptism or shower and the whole community came," said Mike George. "I called myself Syrian then. The Chaldean came later." The community has grown so large as to finally make for strangers and the great bugaboo of all ethnics—intermarriage.

"After 9/11, a crank caller yelled, 'You take our taxes, but you don't serve,'" Mike George said. "I couldn't tell him quickly enough 200 Detroit Chaldeans served in the armed forces as far back as World War II." George confirmed what I'd heard from Beydoun and Ahmed, that the backlash was not as bad as it had been during the Iran hostage crisis and the 1991 Gulf war. "This time, when we told the media we were Iraqi, they wanted to know more," he said. During the first war, however "two men dressed in Army fatigues shot at a Chaldean store owner, yelling "Bang, bang, you're dead, Arab."[28] At that time, during the invasion of Kuwait by Iraq, "People saw us as monsters," according to a cousin of Mike's, Tom George, who owns two groceries in the inner city. He said he spent "hundreds of hours" counteracting the impression that Chaldeans were Saddam Hussein's agents in Detroit.[29]

So sunk in were Chaldeans to party stores or groceries, with the post-World War II second and third wave immigration from Iraq, engineers and doctors entered the food business. Doctors also didn't want to wait the five years to get accredited to practice, said George.

Mike George started working at his father's small grocery store at 105 East Palmer at the age of eight. He swept the floor, hit the cash register. By twelve, he was learning how to cut meat and by fifteen he was his father's butcher. "I resented in a way I couldn't play sports," he confessed. But he had his own boys working in the milk business at twelve. "The harder group is my grandchildren," he smiled, painting the Ritz air with smoke. "This is a very sharp generation, always trying to figure out an angle. I'm trying to get 'em into the meat plant. They complain. Then I tell them, "Hey, try working in an ice cream freezer.

The meat plant looks good after that."[30]

The original George store burned down in the 1968 Detroit riots. "Crime has no color," said Mike. "Thieves are thieves." And somehow that brought us back to 9/11, a day, he said, "that brought our country a complete transition—nothing is going to be the same. Everyone overreacted a bit; government and people became paranoid. It's calmed down somewhat."

As an Iraqi American, what did he think of our current imbroglio in Iraq, with 150,000 troops subjected to almost daily car bomb attacks? "Our people in government don't make clear, precise, and truthful decisions," he believed. "But watch how things change once the people there get clean water and electricity and democracy."

As for the Israeli–Palestinian dispute, he felt, "The United States should have been more aggressive about this. This problem should have been solved long ago. We need to address this problem head on before the cancer spreads. Get people together and force a resolution." About cutting aid to Israel commensurate with its expenditures for settlements, he said "if necessary, yes, it should be done. Sometimes you need to show people death for them to accept sickness."

You don't have to go abroad to find an Arab souk. Try driving down Warren Avenue in Dearborn: The Al-Amer Restaurant (great *shish taouk!*), Nadia's Pharmacy, Pharoah's Café, Afrah Bakery, Al Jinan Halal Meat Market, Cedarlands Restaurant, Cedar Fruit Market, Harb Imports, Islamic Meat Market. Everywhere the English and Arabic script in tandem, like a stiff dancer with someone in love with twirls. Or turn on Shaeffer: Sheik Bakery, Ghada's Hair Salon, Ghandour's Pastries, Palm Springs Restaurant, Kabob Village. Come to a stop light. Listen. Some guy in a black Ford pulls up, windows down, blasting an *oud* on CD. Arab rap. At New Yasmine Bakery, I get out, buy some *baqlawa* and a strange looking *kunafa* with crumb topping instead of shredded wheat. As I leave, two women, a mother and daughter, approach, dressed in *hijab* and long flowered gowns in the hot August night. "*Shukran, kathiran,*" the mother says, smiling as I hold the door for them.

That's the first time in my life a total stranger said "thank you" to me in Arabic on a street in America. For a moment, the naturalness of it skewered me. And I was not middle-aged, hopelessly American, but a young man in Damascus. My grandfather before he set foot on a boat. August is August; the night is the night.

Food you can trust. We will serve only fresh and honest products. Now there's a post-9/11 bit of culture for you! Trustworthy food! No cyanide in the kebob, no arsenic in the *tabbouli*, no anthrax in the *kibba*. The owner of La Shish in Livonia is certainly not taking any chances of being mistaken for a terrorist. By the front door, a patriotic poem.

Before you get to your table, a large American flag. Only after do you notice the cherrywood-stained booths, the brass ornaments.

No matter. The *kibba* is delicious, the hummus superb, the bread hot and swollen, and the waiter, like all waiters, looking for other work.

I was taken to La Shish by two elder statesmen of the largest Antiochian Orthodox church in the United States, St. Mary's Basilica. They are Palestinians from Ramallah, that clannish West Bank town in which everyone can trace his ancestry to five original families of the Byzantine era. They are old friends, once teacher and student in the pre-Israel days at the American Quaker School. It is a wonder to watch their marvelous friendship, as if the friendship itself were a country.

For Palestinians, history is food. But not food you can trust. Ibrahim Hanania, 81, a distinguished man with solemn demeanor, came to the United States with his young family a month after the Israelis occupied the West Bank in 1967. Naim Kawwas, his old student, was already in Detroit and directed his teacher to come join them out of harm's way. And when Kawwas motions—quickly, with hands here and there and voice rat-a-tat-tat—you come. What a duo.

Hanania's father had come to the United States in 1913, peddling linens and tapestries to priests and churches in the New Haven, CT, area. When he returned to Palestine after the war, he set up a dry goods store in Jerusalem.

"We had Jewish employees," he remembered. "They would come out to Ramallah and visit us, bringing pastries. We had good Jewish friends at AUB [American University at Beirut]. One, Chaim Weinberg, was my roommate. He was like a brother to me."[31]

Hanania lived history like clothing. During World War II, while he was at school in Beirut, he noticed French Senegalese soldiers patrolling. Kawwas reminded him, "The Germans bombed halfway between Jericho and Jerusalem. They also bombed near Tel Aviv and Jaffa."

"And I remember Israeli planes hitting Ramallah," Hanania said quietly. This was during the 1948 war that scattered the Palestinians far and wide. "Nobody would have imagined what happened did happen," he said. "The Arabs were not united. We had refugees come to Ramallah by the thousands. I carried my daughter Leila, an infant then, downstairs. There was a lot of anxiety." Under Jordanian occupation, Ibrahim "had a good life" in Ramallah, where he ran a small Catholic school for 27 years and served on the city's municipal council. It was a culture shock of sorts coming to America in 1967 after the Israeli tanks had rolled into the town of his birth. He hoped to teach in America, but soon discovered, "If you tell a student to cut his hair, he will tell you, 'You are interfering with my constitutional freedom!' So I got stuck for seventeen years selling insurance. I forced myself to do it."

On September 11, 2001, Hanania was home in Livonia and, as always, got his daily phone call from Kawwas. But the news of hell was not far off this time.

"It was as if it were the end of the world," Hanania spoke. "I panicked, really. Whoever did that, I thought, was stupid, a crime, it was a big, big crime. If it were the Arabs who did it, they committed suicide. What could possibly be achieved?"

Here Kawwas, 79, jumps in: "We are all for fighting terrorism, God knows we are. One year later, we held a vigil here at St. Mary's with 1,000 people to condemn what had happened on 9/11—Christians, Muslims, and Jews. Senator Spencer Abraham (R–MI) was present, the mayor of Livonia. And you know what? Not two lines, not even a word, in the newspaper the next day. But for two Palestinians jumping around when it happened, you have all three networks. Why is that?"[32]

Kawwas shook his head, then went on, "You know, I wouldn't have said that two years ago. What did I lose from 9/11? I am afraid to speak."

When asked about the effects of 9/11 on Detroit he told the story of a Syrian who owned a restaurant in Bloomfield, where there is a large Jewish community. On 9/11, some woman was caught on television camera saying employees of the Syrian's restaurant were celebrating. The reporter later checked out the story and found out that it was false. But the calumny stuck, no one came to the restaurant, and the Syrian went broke.

Naim has a cousin, Jallil Jaber, who was injured as a marine on Iwo Jima; another was killed as an American GI in North Africa during Operation Torch in World War II. He ran down a list of several St. Mary's parishioners—all Palestinian-Americans—who fought for the United States in Vietnam and Korea. "Our people love and respect this country," he said.

"If the matter of Palestine is solved, there is great hope here. Especially for my children and grandchildren. This (America) is the country of their birth." Kawwas did not say what would happen if the Palestine issue is not solved.

But clearly, for these two old gentlemen, the world has changed utterly. There are now far more Christians from Ramallah in America than there are in Ramallah. Of a population of 75,000 in the West Bank town, only about 1,500 are Christian (they were once the clear majority). There are 30,000 Ramallans in the United States, nearly all Christian. With Jewish, Muslim, and even Christian fundamentalists butting horns in the occupied territories, anyone with a healthy heart wants out. The tank siege of Bethlehem by the Israelis in 2002 was extremely painful to Ibrahim and Naim, hardly putting Christians at ease in the Holy Land.

The old friends take me on a tour of the basilica of St. Mary's, spotless in its first year, wonderfully simple for its size. There are no stained glass windows, no cloying mosaics. The side windows are white-stenciled with symbols: a clutch of grapes, a dove of peace, an incensor, an open hand. Looking up at the dome with its skylights in the round, the feel is of a place where you could be quietly lifted up. Going below, the basement walls are lined by a series of remarkable 1885 photographs of the Holy Land, including the Garden of Gethsemane. They were taken by a German photographer who went off to war and never came back. They were stashed with a family in Ramallah who brought them to Detroit.

No electric lights. No settlements. No tanks. No soldiers. Just the broken walls of the Holy. That is the sight of their birthplace Ibrahim Hanania and Naim Kawwas will take when they, too, ascend, no doubt, hand in hand, toward the great banquet of food you can truly trust, up beyond these steps and the dome.

DANCE OVER THE DEATH HOME (BROOKLYN)

My mother was raised above a mortuary in Bay Ridge, Brooklyn. For many years the memory of it was painful to her, but, once in the sheet of sunlight that is California, she recalled the darkness, the funeral home lit by a flickering lamp, and the poverty in which her mother would rock a cradle with one foot and press the wrought iron pedal of a sewing machine with the other.

How did she spend Brooklyn teenage years in World War II? "We danced the Lindy over the dead," Mother's smile lit her white teeth, and she went for another cup of coffee for the ghost who is always coming to the home of an Arab for hospitality. That ghost may sit in the flesh of a neighbor, a Japanese gardener, even a housekeeper from El Salvador. For a day I was the ghost, a son taking the apricot jam and the muddy coffee, the Syrian bread and the yogurt. When I grew up in Los Angeles, you never put fruit in yogurt; you ate it sour as it was meant to be eaten.

Mother's actual birthplace on Henry Street is near Atlantic Avenue, the road in downtown Brooklyn from where so many of the original Arab Americans coursed in a widespread delta. A short walk from the two blocks of old Arab markets, restaurants, and record stores shows a most breathtaking vista of Manhattan from Brooklyn Heights. Antonios Bishallany, the first Lebanese immigrant, was buried in 1856 in Brooklyn's Greenwood Cemetery.

More than 150 years later, the original Brooklyn Arab-American community is dying. It is being replaced by a large influx of Greek immigrants, recent refugees from the escalating Palestinian–Israeli wars, and escapees from such impoverished Arab homelands as Yemen, which is not booming with oil riches. The old Brooklynite

Lebanese and Syrians are pulling up their pomegranate-colored Oriental rugs and moving to Englewood, NJ, the new seat of North America's Antiochian Orthodox bishop. As if reading the ill wind of change, the old Brooklynites established the first Arab-American home for the aged in America in 1982.

Something is being lost. My mother's life-out-of-death dance when she rattled the floor boards over the funeral home with her Lindy has always seemed typical of the Arab-American spirit to me. I sought out her Brooklyn before it, too, flickered and died, like the gas lamp near her home above the Home.

My first stop was Atlantic Avenue, the Baghdad of the East River, where frankincense and myrrh, olives, cheese, *tahini* (sesame seed oil), *halawa* (a sweet made of crushed sesame), bulgur wheat, and Arabic bread round and flat as a beret sustain a cultural tie to Arab-American households across the country. An Orthodox priest once told me, "When I was growing up in Canton, Ohio, one of the Malko Brothers would arrive from Atlantic Avenue in Brooklyn peddling hummus, olives, *baqlawa*. That's a pretty long milk run!"[33] Out in California I grew up on Sahadi desserts, condiments, Arab *mazza*, especially *halawa* (pronounced ha-ley-wee in Lebanese dialect), which has the texture of dried peanut butter. I used to think of it as a sweet chunk of the desert.

A. Sahadi & Co. sits opposite Malko Imports, both under tenements colored royal blue and purple. To walk into Sahadi's is to assault the nose with everything from pickled turnips to Izmir figs to olives soaked in brine. On a Saturday the place is tightly packed with customers of every race tasting twelve different kinds of olives. Charles Sahadi, whose great-uncle Abraham founded the company back in the 1890s, manned the old cash register that still rings a bell with a sale. The young bearded Sahadi, resembling a Vietnam veteran in his combat green fatigue shirt, pointed his finger. "Two pounds pistachio," he sang. "Two pounds it is. Who's next?"

He gave me a free piece of myrrh—which resembles hardened sludge—nothing like what you would expect the Wise Men to give the Christ child. "The Wise Men came all the way to Sahadi's to get this for Bethlehem?"

"Wise guy, huh?" he snickered, and told me to go see Rashid at the record store down the block.

Rashid kept an eye out for the purple-robed Muslim who was thumbing through records by Abdul Halim Hafez, Fayruz, and Umm Kulthum, an Egyptian singer who drew more Egyptians to her funeral—three million—than did either Sadat or Nasser.

Born in the southern Lebanon town of Marjayoun in 1908, Rashid—like many Arab immigrants at the time—came to America in 1920 on the heels of a brother who was fleeing conscription in the Turkish army. More than sixty years later, Rashid still had sharp memories of Ellis Island. One was the strange music that was piped through the speakers—opera—quite different from anything played with an ʿud or tabla (a tubular drum). Also, he fondly remembered a pitiful teenage Arab girl immigrant who panicked because she could not write in Arabic or English. Rashid taught her the first two lines of the Lord's Prayer as they waited for their medical exam. "She crossed herself and started reciting, 'Our Father, Who art in heaven...' and the immigration official was touched and let her go without lifting a pencil!" he laughed softly.

As a teenager in the '40s, Rose Awad Orfalea relaxes with friends in a Catskills Mountains rowboat. (Gary Awad)

From Ellis Island Rashid took a slow train to La Fayette, Illinois, where his brother was the only Arab in town. The small stream of dark-skinned Lebanese that got off the train in the Midwest that 1920s day caused a stir among the townspeople, who gawked out their windows. He later took a college degree, worked in the war industrial plants in Chicago, and finally came back to his port-of-entry and Brooklyn. For years, his store on Atlantic Avenue was the sole filter of Arab voices, which can hold a note in the air for minutes like a luminous eel. Umm Kulthum's first and last stand in America.

This man with his baggy gray suit pants, limp gray tie, and white hair flying in clouds off his head jumped from his desk to help a customer. He showed the poster that illustrates, in microscopic print, the entire Quʿran illuminated in gold. The wars have come and gone and will come again back home, but here, surrounded by Oriental clocks, brass urns, tapestries, books, and records, the old immigrant seemed quite at home squinting at the black Muslim, who was peddling beads.

"Plenty of quality work went into them," said the peddler in the ʿaba robe with a thin wire ring in his nose.

"I'm not worried about the work," Rashid mumbled, turning

the plastic, colored beads in his hand. "It's the material I'm worried about." And the ageless peddler cycle began anew. This time the Arab looked American, and the black looked Arab.

In the 1920s, one block from Sahadi's was a grocery store owned by Alex Habib. His young son, Philip, helped stock the shelves with canned goods, marking the prices with a black crayon. Philip would later sweat in a sheet metal factory in Brooklyn making metal boxes. He would also be the chief negotiator for the US in Vietnam, the Philippines, Nicaragua, and war-torn Beirut, shuttling inside the scream of Israeli howitzers, dive bombers, PLO katyshas (Soviet mortars), and the agony of the half-million trapped Beirutis.

One searches for boyhood preparations for such a pressure-cooker role. Habib actually grew up in the Jewish section of Brooklyn—Bensonhurst—and belonged to a street club called the Lone Eagles.

Before I finished blurting out that my mother lived in Brooklyn above a funeral parlor, Habib grabbed the phone and called his sister in Brooklyn: "Yeah, Violet. What are you tired of? What are you sick of? You're sick and tired? Accidents happen, Violet. What can you do? How the hell do I know from one month to the other! I've been away for six weeks."

Habib's hands flailed the air; his wolverine-like head dipped down and up, restless, twanging the words with Brooklynese ("month" becomes "monss"). "Listen, do you know a Rose Awad back in the old days?" he asked. "She lived above Cronin and Sons, I think. No? What's

Said Eldin, who came to the US from Egypt in 2000, owns Hot Bagels in Allentown, PA. (Mel Rosenthal)

that? Violet, you are a political innocent. The ALL is the Kata'ib. You just live your good, happy life. Okay. Eat! Eat! You're my Jewish mother—eat the *kibba*, the *mughliya* [powdered rice with spices]."[34]

It seemed that Habib's sister was attending—unsuspectingly—a meeting of an American Lebanese League (ALL), which was closely allied with the Lebanese right-wing Phalange. Habib hung up, saying that his sister's life back home and his were worlds apart and had been since he left Brooklyn at age seventeen for school in Idaho. He seemed a man caught in a whirlwind, who, for a second, was given a chance to step outside it. Typically, the step was taken toward family, the mainstay of the wandering, venturesome life of the Arab American. His sister, he said, speaks fluent Arabic: simple Arabic he understood and spoke.

Habib believed that "it took a long time for the Lebanese to come up the ladder of success in America. We lived in ghettos, were very clannish, and used to think of ourselves as second-class citizens. We're not." It took 35 years in the foreign service for an American of Arab background to be given a post in the Middle East. "In the old days of the foreign service they wouldn't send Greeks to Greece," he said. Habib himself served in Africa, as special negotiator at the Paris peace talks concerning Vietnam, and from 1976 to 1978 as undersecretary of state for political affairs. It was then that he was rocked by a series of heart attacks and resigned the post to recuperate at his home in San Francisco. But one year later, in 1979, he finally broke the "ethnic area barrier" as a presidential troubleshooter, trying to stave off an all-out war in Lebanon. On July 24, 1981, Habib negotiated a cease-fire that held for nine months. He also "got" the cease-fire (as he put it) in August 1982, after the Israeli invasion. When asked why the latter took 2½ months to "get," Habib went silent, the forehead furrowed, the raconteur-uncle gesticulations halted. "In this business, you don't try and look back on what you could have done," he mumbled. "That can kill you."

The smell of *za'tar* (a mixture of thyme, sumac, savory, and sesame) filled the air the spring morning Robert Thabit opened the door to the family home in Bay Ridge. He and his wife, Vivian, welcomed me immediately to the kitchen and bid me sit, take a round loaf of the bitter bread with *za'tar* seeds soaking in hot oil. That is a taste of the earth itself, hard to compare to anything in another cuisine. It speaks of our heritage—grainy, bitter, earthen, warm. An Arab saying: *Bread and thyme opens the mind. Za'tar* lines the walls of the mouth and the tongue with unspeakable loves and tragedies. When you are a child, you hate it. It can't match anything American: pizza, popcorn, Coke, cotton candy. You never know you're an adult until you discover you like *za'tar*.

"It was by and large a blissful community growing up amongst the Syrians in Brooklyn," said Thabit, a mild man with thinning gray hair and goatee belied by a boyish smile and shining eyes. "There wasn't much prejudice—I didn't notice any. As Arabs we were very well integrated into the society."[35]

New York has never been known to be a politically active seat for Arab Americans. Detroit, yes; Los Angeles, somewhat. But the boroughs of New York—never. The mere mention of organizing the Arab-American community politically brings frustration into Thabit's voice: "But frustation goes with the turf. Our people are unfortunately not doing enough... I would think that the fact that New York City is the bastion of Zionism would compel... look, there were 250,000 people in the streets in Israel protesting the war in Lebanon and Dr. Mehdi [New York activist for the Arab cause] gets what? Fifty? I think it's an insult."

From the Seventies block, in the cold spring air at his door that stiffened the threads of his Persian rugs, he pointed to the Eighties up the street. "Go see your Uncle Eddie," Thabit gestured. "He never got involved in politics—smart man! A sweet guy, your uncle." He closed the door on the za'tar.

For most of his life, Eddie Baloutine never got involved with moving, either. He lived in the same house in Bay Ridge in which his father, a Palestinian from Haifa, raised the family. It may have been one of the oldest homes in America continually inhabited by Palestinians.

A steady stream of people entered this old purplish-red brownstone from the backyard, where Eddie was spreading a newspaper at the breakfast table. He retired after 30 years in the baby-wear business. His partner, a Syrian Jew, later suffered paralysis, and Eddie visited him frequently. "We use to speak together in Arabic," he said to me after the coffee was poured. "Now I just wait for him to nod yes or no. We had a good business relationship and were friendly. We had him and his wife over a couple of times for dinner, but it was hard. They wanted strictly kosher meals. Don't get me on California, will you? I got beautiful pear trees out back. What do I need oranges for? What in hell are you writing about the Arabs for? It's all the same story here—they were good citizens, they prospered in business, and they didn't help each other."

"What was that?"

"Well, they're an independent people, what can I tell you."[38]

Eddie's father came to the United States at the turn of the century, another case of escaping Turkish conscription. He took a trip to Japan and soon was a middleman in the silk trade from Japan to the United States.

"What does Baloutine mean?"

"You mean 'Ballantine'?" he laughed. "That's what they always called me. Somebody from the *bilad* told me it comes from *balat tin* (concrete and mud). The guy who wets the cement. A cement wetter. That's what we were."

A jokester in the community, Eddie pillories California at the first chance. He had it in for all the Brooklynites (my mother's family being one branch) who escaped Brooklyn for California. He thinks Californians have their heads dried out by the sun, that they are forever tottering on extinction by earthquake, tidal wave, or free sex. His only story about the Arab–Israeli crisis hitting home to him in New York City concerned one Israel fundraising dinner to which he was invited, no one apparently aware of his origin. "One man would stand up and say, 'Mr. Chairman, last year I pledged $1,000 to Israel and this year I pledge $5,000!' and everyone would cheer," he told in animated voice. "The next guy was called Mr. Goldstein. 'Mr. Chairman,' he said, 'last year I gave $10,000 to Israel and this year I give the same amount!' Then they said, Eddie Baloutine. 'Mr. Chairman,' I said, 'I pledge to you this year exactly what I gave Israel last year.' Everybody cheered. They thought I'd donated a million!"

But this retired manufacturer of baby's clothes, who wouldn't call himself Arab or Palestinian ("Syrian is what they called us"), who labeled the Arab Americans as selfish, runs off twice a week to help a crippled girl on his block take whirlpool therapy. He also took me to St. Nicholas Home, the first Arab-American home for the aged in the United States. Eddie is one of the directors, as is Bob Thabit.

The old men were huddled in the cold along a stucco walk breathing vapor in cones outside St. Nicholas Home on Ovington Avenue, formerly the Bay Ridge Hospital. In 1978, the Arab community purchased the decrepit building and land for $2 million. By 2005, it housed seventy-five residents, many of whom are Arab in origin. Its success has been surprising, for the Syrian and Lebanese families cling to their elderly. The irony is that for many original immigrants, like Sadie Stonbely, St. Nicholas Home is a new sociological phenomenon—a place where the culture is completely integrated. There are Irish Catholics, Poles, Germans, and others.

Mrs. Stonbely, 85, born in Aleppo, Syria, became the first resident of the Brooklyn home. Sharp of mind, and clear of eye, she recalled her brother escaping a riot in which a man's head was decapitated in Tripoli, Lebanon. Shortly thereafter, Sadie and her family came to Ellis Island, where her eye was damaged for life from the poke of the trachoma examiner.[37]

The smell of age, a kind of powdered skin, clings to the home's faint, mint-colored walls. Handrails run everywhere. The chef, Raja Ramadan, saluted from the kitchen where he was fixing grape leaves, *safiha*, and *kibba*. Most American residents acquire a taste for Arabic food, and many non-Arabs have been known to smuggle extra bird's nest (*kunafa*) desserts to their rooms. Chef Ramadan loves the elderly; he left a job as head chef with the Biltmore Hotel in Manhattan, taking a salary cut.

Besides the distinction of being the first of its kind in the United States, St. Nicholas has another claim to uniqueness. "Here we have the very antithesis of the Middle East situation where they have been fighting for generations," explained Joe Atallah, the executive director of the home.[38] The Board of Directors contains Arab Americans from every Arab religious sect and is led by Richard Zarick. He sees the home as a community center eventually, with everything from a library to Arabic classes offered to help revive the dying Arab culture in Brooklyn. In a bad economy, too, the home has been an employment clearing house, even an apartment referral service.

"Let your light so shine," said Zarick, "that it will brighten the path for others." When asked about the apparent political torpidity of Brooklyn Arab Americans, Zarick drummed his fingers. "I believe you shine your light without killing your battery."[39]

Driving along the shore, Eddie Baloutine reminisced: "We used to use pearl buttons for bait to fish off Brooklyn pier." And then he sped up to get home in time to give therapy. He did not say the word "give."

Boxing had been a favorite sport of Eddie Baloutine in his youth; he had been in a few amateur fights himself. "You've got to go see Mustapha Hamsho," he urged. Hamsho, the one-time number-one contender for professional boxing's middleweight crown, lived in Brooklyn but hailed from Syria. His relatives lived next door to Eddie Baloutine, and my Christian uncle joked that he'd given the aggressive Muslim fighter a few tips.

Hamsho had been a ship painter from his native Latakia, Syria, when in 1974 he jumped ship in Providence, Rhode Island, to further a boxing career hampered in Syria, where there is no professional boxing. He explained, "I've been to other countries before. But America, to me, was the best place to live. It's where all people can live together—blacks, whites, Jews, and Arabs. There's no repression here. I like that."

Hamsho worked for awhile for his cousin Sammy Moustapha as a dishwasher in a Middle Eastern restaurant in Brooklyn. Sammy, a fight enthusiast, introduced him to the legendary promoter Paddy Flood. Soon the relentless left-handed puncher was in the ring, though he first fought under the pseudonym Mike "Rocky" Estafire to avoid immigration authorities, who would deport him as an illegal alien. Flood, who came up with the new name for Hamsho, said he "had a lot of fire in his workouts and resembled Sylvester Stallone." His cornerman of forty years' experience, Al Braverman, compared Hamsho to one of the greatest middleweights of all time, Harry Greb. "He's a real tough sonofabitch; a real take-'em-apart guy."[40]

Hamsho lost his first professional fight in 1976, against Pat Cuillo, who was 25 pounds heavier. But it was his only loss for seven years until a title bout with Marvelous Marvin Hagler in 1981, when the champion stopped the "slugging Syrian" on a TKO in twelve rounds of a bloody fight that left Hamsho's face raw; he took fifty stitches.[41]

In 1983, Hamsho opened a restaurant in Brooklyn's Atlantic Avenue Syrian colony, Hamsho's House. We met there, the fighter accompanied by a number of Syrian relatives and his personal advisor and confidant, Irish cop Jimmy Dennedy.

Palestinian girl on rollerblades, Bay Ridge, Brooklyn 1998 (Mel Rosenthal)

Arabic food and coffee were served. Hamsho, a handsome, broad-faced man of 157 pounds, trim and solid, said he wanted to give a fresh quality in food to people, like in Syria: "We don't have any alcohol in Latakia, all Muslim, you know. Life is really clear, everything fresh, we don't have a freezer. The fruit you eat there is of course different than here because everything there is natural. You don't put chemical stuff on food."[42]

His father drove a seven-horse cart like a taxi in Latakia. Myths about America were whispered to him early on—not gold in streets, but money thrown like rain: "One friend had come to the United States as a fighter and he said people were throwing money at him in the ring, almost a thousand dollars, like it was raining money! He told me in America if you want to work, to be somebody, you can be. Anything you want." When he arrived he found it lonely but a strange comfort that all immigrants were alike: "Everybody's a stranger here. Nobody's a real American."

In the 1967 war, Hamsho was fourteen, and he remembered being sent by his father up to the mountains to hide from air raids. Though patriotic, Hamsho was critical of the regime, "Assad is against his own people, you know. He is there by force, not by choice." He was revolted by the massacre by the government of its citizenry in Hama while quashing fundamentalist rebels. Hamsho himself is an Alawite Muslim, as is Assad. He felt sorrow over the destruction in Lebanon.

Still, he detailed incidents in which he has come against what he felt is discrimination here, especially with professional boxing's system of ratings. He recalled the boxing promoter Bob Arum stalling on setting up the championship fight with Hagler: "He says to my manager, 'You think that I'm going to help your fighter? He's an Arab. I'm a Jew. You think I'm going to let him do anything?'" Eddie Baloutine had told me he'd seen a Hamsho fight where the announcer referred to Hamsho as "that bad Arab." Only after the Hagler fight was his ability undeniable to the rating makers.

"I'm proud to be a Syrian," Hamsho said, glad that his fights were written up and viewed back in Syria. Though Hamsho is scrupulous about not talking religion or politics, Jimmy said, "They downplay him every chance they get. It's a stereotype right off the bat. It's not usually a direct ethnic slur, like that 'dopey Arab.' But if the opponent scores they say, 'Oh look at that, that was great.' If Mustapha scores they say, 'He's just a mauler.'"

Hamsho prayed five times a day at the New York mosque on Fifth Street, a devout Muslim. He did not find boxing to be as violent a sport as many have said, and he thought that most of the criticism came from nonboxers. Though he was mourning a boxing friend who had died the week before from a fight, he asserted that, if you keep in shape, you "will never get angry, or hurt."

We drove in his big, old Cadillac to a friend's house to watch a Hagler fight. Hamsho was riveted in front of the television, silently taking in all the moves he must parry. He did not know that in 1984 he would lose a rematch to Marvelous Marvin Hagler by a knockout in the third round, and that by the end of 1985 his boxing record would be 39-3-2, dropping his ranking to twelfth. But he continued to pray.

When a fellow Brooklynite of Hamsho's was baptised, the priest poured water over his head and pronounced his name, "Farid Mirʿi Ibrahim." Over the years, the Farid would turn to Fred, the Mirʿi to

Murray, and the Ibrahim to Abraham. And F. Murray Abraham, often taken for a Jew, would move from his native Pittsburgh, work at the Farah slacks plant in El Paso, Texas, and become a citizen of Brooklyn. He would also become the only Arab-American actor to win an Academy Award, as best actor for his role as Antonio Salieri, the composer jealous of Mozart, in *Amadeus.*

F. Murray Abraham is an Italian Arab American? It was a question on thousands of lips in the weeks after that night in 1985 when he held the Oscar high. Perhaps the Salieri role was fated. "Salieri's great compassion is what kills him," Abraham told me the night I met him in Baltimore. Anyone who has been on the outside—and what Semite hasn't?—can understand this.

I took a Syrian cousin of mine to a Baltimore Mozart concert, where Abraham gave dramatic readings. Dr. Nabeel al-Annouf had come from Damascus for advanced studies in surgery and pathology at Baltimore's Union Memorial Hospital, one of only a handful of Syrian students accepted in the United States that year. Nabeel, or Nino as we called him, had been a young boy when we visited Damascus in 1972; his father had been the one to spirit my own father on the midnight ride to find us in Lebanon. Nino himself was filled with curiosity and pride for Murray Abraham's feat; it was also his first classical symphony ever, one he had looked forward to all his life, having listened to many classical music tapes. After the stirring performance, Abraham was mobbed by autograph seekers, whom he handled with care and even brio.[43]

Alone with him in a black limousine going to a reception, I was very nervous. He was exhausted and said absently, "They don't know how much it takes out of you." I wondered if he was referring to the autograph hounds or the show. "It's all the show," he said. I tried to make small talk to break the silence, but he stopped me. "Please. Give me some time to rest."[44] And he leaned back, stretched out his legs, and closed his eyes. In a while his eyes fluttered open and he asked me to explain the purpose of my book. As the black car cruised through Baltimore, we began to exchange stories of our family life. He had had two brothers die as a result of military service, one in the US Army, the other a marine in Vietnam. Suddenly, I found myself telling him about my sister's decade-long struggle with psychological problems. He had this quality—to make even a stranger open, trusting. His voice softened, "I'm sorry. It affects you, doesn't it?" All I said was, "My parents," and he understood.

The reception was a happy affair—Baltimoreans are more relaxed, ebullient than the sometimes proper and sardonic Washingtonians. (Baltimore was appropriate: African Americans there in pony carts selling hard crabs used to be called "Ay-rabs.") When it came time to leave, Abraham tried to give the infant boy of our hosts his powder blue tie, one given him by Diana, Princess of Wales. The boy would not take it and turned away. Abraham stood there, chagrined, "It matches your suit. It matches your giggle!" But try as he might, the boy wouldn't take it. He stood there tie in hand, curiously like Salieri, his generosity turning sour.

Murray Abraham was born into the Syrian colony in Pittsburgh in 1940, his father from a village three days by oxcart from Damascus. He grew up to stories of his grandfather, who had made a recording with his lilting voice at the turn of the century, a remarkable feat for the time. "His voice would carry literally for miles and people would come when they heard him sing and sit in huge circles." As for the famine that rocked Syria and Lebanon during World War I, Abraham said his own father, Farid, had been the only male child to survive it and "the terrible attacks of the locusts." When growing up, he had heard stories of cannibalism from the dreaded time and his grandmother was so shaken by the experience of starvation she "simply wouldn't talk about it."

"My aunts spoke of the day-long search for grass and weeds to make soup," he recounted. "All of my uncles died during the famine. I wonder why the word 'holocaust' has come to mean something so specifically Jewish when in reality it is a horror that so many people have experienced: Armenians, Russians, Chinese, Japanese, Gypsies, American Indians. It is all a holocaust. And the lesson to be learned is that it must never again happen to anyone."

He and his wife had given his children Arab names, Jamili and Farid, who is nicknamed Mick. His reasons? "It was time. I think these things take care of themselves."

His mother is Italian, and growing up in Pittsburgh the co-mingling of Syrian and Italian halves of his family "seemed very natural to me." He was emphatic about what was most precious in life to him: "The family is the most important element in our society. There's no doubt in my mind about it. I believe in the extended family, too. I don't believe in the so-called nuclear family." He and his Irish-American wife had been married 23 years.

Would he have fought as his brother had in Vietnam? "Good question," he pondered. "I was a flower child, a product of the 1960s. I wouldn't have fought. But the men and women who did fight should get all the financial and medical and moral support we can give them. The same thing happened to those guys who were sent to Lebanon. What did Reagan prove?"

I wondered why he chose acting when the Syrian community pushed so many into business. "What you're talking about isn't strictly Syrians, Italians, or Lebanese. It's an old American thing—making a better life, money in the bank, something solid. But the fact is nothing is solid, especially in the current economy. Given the shaky nature of acting, I am more prepared than the average worker for this shaky economy."

He spoke enthusiastically of his testimony at a Senate subcommittee on behalf of the National Endowment for the Arts: "The hostage crisis was fermenting at the time and all I did was talk about the value of art in terms of international communications. Art can communicate when nothing else will."

Was he ever denied roles because of being of Syrian descent? "I'll never know. But at least 60 percent of the people for whom I've worked were Jews. And I intend to continue doing it. A lot of roles I've played have been Jewish, such as Teibele, the Jewish scholar, in *Teibele and Her Demon*, a great role. I also played the Rabbi of Prague in *The Golem*. I'm half Syrian, half Italian—of course I empathize with any Mediterranean people, especially Semites."[45]

Media coverage of the Middle East bothered him: "When Arabs are killed, they're suddenly 'a bunch of Arabs.' They have no name, no history. Why? Is it possible editors don't know that Arabs are human beings?" He called the siege of Beirut in 1982 "a pogrom against Arabs."

He continued: "My struggle has always been an individual one. I've never aligned myself with any group. I am primarily a man, a family man, an artist, and an American. And I have this heritage that goes back across the ocean. The more I know about myself through my heritage, I think, the more free that instinct will be."

As I drove back to Washington, I heard his words echo on the empty freeway: "Salieri is obsessed with flying, but he is earthbound."

THE SLAVE OF BALFOUR HOUSE (VICKSBURG)

It was Christmas Eve 1862. A ball saluting the Confederate Army stationed at Vicksburg was in full swing at the home of Dr. William T. Balfour. Known as the "Gibraltar of the Confederacy," Vicksburg's battlements were thought impregnable and its port on the lower Mississippi River the navel of an umbilical cord that tied the Confederacy together. If Richmond was the South's brains and Charleston its heart, Vicksburg was its solar plexus.

The Balfour House, designed in 1835 by a slave, shook—not from the whistle of parrot shells, but from the plucked strings of violin and cello and the dancers' booted feet. No one knew that a shadow-figure of the anonymous slave-architect was burned into an interior plank of an upstairs fireplace. Only a century later would the burnt silhouette be exposed when the Balfour House was restored by Phillip Weinberger in 1982. Likewise, no one heard the first gunboats of Gen. William Tecumseh Sherman rounding Milliken's Bend ten miles north of Vicksburg in preparation for the bloodiest siege of the War Between the States. During the 47-day siege, in which the city's population would come close to starving, they would take to living in caves.

I journeyed to Vicksburg to explore the legacy of another people who came to Vicksburg to escape starvation and who were also familiar with caves. They were the Lebanese, and they were said to own Vicksburg.

The Syro-Lebanese began to emigrate to Vicksburg as early as the 1880s, making it one of their earliest settlements in the country outside New York and Boston. The Lebanese on the high bluffs here apparently did better with the kudzu vines than their relatives did with each other in Lebanon. Their influence in both business and regional politics is disproportionate to their numbers; they are the largest ethnic community (700 of about 25,000) other than African Americans, followed by the Italians. Storefront names tell the story: Monsour, Abraham, Jabour, Nasif, Nassour, Baladi.

Why Vicksburg? Father Nicholas Saikley, longtime pastor of the one Eastern church in town, explained, "They came in from the port of New Orleans as well as Ellis Island. They sailed up river 175 miles and saw the town as a promontory. It appeared to be set just like El Munsif and Jbeil [Byblos], which overlook the Mediterranean twenty miles north of Beirut. They said, 'Hey, we're home!'"[46]

According to Father Saikley, my guardian angel for the week, 50 percent of the major businesses in Warren County, in which Vicksburg is located, are owned by Lebanese. Father Saikley had these facts out before he had sat down in the Old Southern Tea Room. He was quickly finagling with musician friends of mine to form a Vicksburg symphony orchestra. He owned an old black padre hat, called the ladies "Darlin'" and the men "Sweetheart." His movements were assured, nervously so. He said he couldn't sleep at night and so arose before dawn. He called me "sleepy" because I was ten minutes late for breakfast one morning.

"My father was a wetback from Ain Shaara, Syria, who came into the United States through Brownsville, Texas, using the backstroke," Father related. "I myself have a different form of backstroke." He scratched my neck and asked, "What can I do for you?"

"I want to know why the Syrians here are so prominent. I've seen prosperous everywhere from Los Angeles to Boston. But prominent— not much. They tend to be successful at business and blending."

"Well, I tell you, it may have to do with the fact that the early shopkeepers worked so damn hard. John Nosser's 86 years old and he's still putting in eight hours a day at his general store on Main Street. That's a slowdown for him. For years it was 5:00 AM to 11:00 PM."

"What about their attitudes toward the Middle East crisis?" I asked. "I should think the Lebanese could carry some weight here in that direction."

Peter Nosser, Vicksburg department store owner, is joined at home by the Reverend Nicholas Saikley, March 1984. (Gregory Orfalea)

Father Nick laughed and rolled up his carpeted forehead: "Our people here are too laid back on that one. In the 1967 war, I was able to collect all of $25 for the refugees. Our brethren on the other side of the Jordan and Mississippi rivers collected $100,000 in Vicksburg alone. I had my people at the Orthodox church saying, 'Oh, the poor Jews!' Many were agonized, many were silent, some confused. I tell you this—and don't mention her name—but one of my parishioners got a phone call after our Marines were killed in Beirut. The caller said, 'From now on, for every American boy that's killed in Lebanon, a Lebanese home is going to burn in Vicksburg.'"

The man who set the Mississippi state senate's record for longevity of service—36 years—visited me at my hotel that afternoon. Over the phone to Washington, DC, his voice had been a halting, collected one, cordial and honest. But there was a kind of groping in it. I found out why. Ellis Bodron was blind.

Accompanied by his wife, a striking blonde with shining blue eyes, Bodron in dark glasses and silver hair appeared a character right out of Faulkner or Carson McCullers. The Old Southern Tea Room was abustle. Senator Bodron was known throughout the state, as much a fixture as John Stennis, or Strom Thurmond in South Carolina. For twenty years chairman of the state's finance committee, Bodron held the second-most powerful position in Mississippi besides the governorship. Much of what he did and didn't do came down on him in 1982 when he lost his first election since 1947. As he said, "It's axiomatic that the people you annoy or offend remember you a hell

389

of a lot longer than the people that you favor or please."

His own manner was matter-of-fact and unflinching. When I asked why he got into politics—few Lebanese Americans do—he downplayed it: "The answer's going to disappoint you. I graduated from law school and I figured that'd be a good way to advertise that I was back in Vicksburg to practice law. There were four other lawyers running, too."[47]

A conservative Democrat, Bodron held the purse strings tightly in a state that never had enough money for services that other states took for granted. He felt, however, that his crowning achievement was the Education Reform Act of 1982, which established a statewide compulsory kindergarten and a reading aide program—a small revolution for a state whose education quality has been one of the lowest in America.

Country club politics came up. Bodron acknowledged that the Lebanese of Vicksburg were not always accepted and were in fact shut out of the country club until the late 1950s. The critical point was a complaint by a grocer, Pete Nosser, to the legislator.

"Nosser said, 'You know I don't care about belonging to any clubs but I've got daughters and primarily my sons-in-laws...' All of his sons-in-law were non-Arab but were excluded from clubs because of their marriage to his daughters. Now Pete Nosser had four large supermarkets and was very successful. I said to him, 'You buy a lot of things from a lot of different people—you're putting money in banks and you buy insurance. So don't [do it]. Determine who you buy from—a lot of them are influential at this club. You're in a position to correct the situation if you're not happy about it.' The situation began to change very shortly after that."

Bodrun grinned. "You know, history hasn't changed a whole lot. There ain't nothing more important than economics."

Now fully "integrated," the country club had an Arab-American president, Shouphie Habeeb, owner of the First Federal Savings and Loan; he was the first president since 1966 to bring the club into the black.

We discussed the turbulent times of school desegregation and racial confrontation in the South during the 1960s. Though a strong supporter of civil rights, Bodron believed that the growing number of black voters may have questioned his fiscal conservatism and hesitance to finance social programs other than his pet project of education.

"Intellectual integrity" was the key to sound politics, Bodron felt. Robert Taft, Winston Churchill, Barry Goldwater were examples of politicians he admired for putting honesty before everything and not bending to special interest pressure. In any case, Bodron was less than enthusiastic about the US Congress for which he had run once; his friends there convinced him "they don't really do a whole hell of a lot."

Middle Eastern politics never came up on the floor of the

Mississippi legislature in all his 36 years, Bodron said, though in states like New York, California, and Florida the issue often arises in assemblies. (The Santa Monica City Council, for instance, endorsed Israel's invasion of Lebanon on the urging of candidate Tom Hayden.) Bodron's views showed insight and knowledge: he felt "either the granting by Israel or the compelling of Israel to grant some territory which the Palestinians can call theirs... is an absolutely indispensable element to any permanent solution."

About the siege of Beirut, he stirred, "Well, hell, I had all the resentment of it that anybody could have. I understood the claims of self-defense and territorial protection were preposterous. And I communicated that to some of my friends in Congress."

During our discussion, the legislator emeritus wiped his eyes and snapped his wristwatch band. Two fingers were wrapped in gauze and a rubber splint. "He accidentally got his hand stuck in a car door this week," Mrs. Bodron shook her head. One of their two sons had been in a near-fatal car crash recently. It had been a difficult two years for the Bodrons. Yet you wouldn't know it by the man's generous allotment of time, his repeated calls to my hotel room to see how my work was going, and an offer to tour the State Capitol at Jackson.

When the couple left the Old Southern Tea Room, a marvelous thing happened. Jane Bodron took her husband's hands and looped them underneath her arms from behind. Bodron followed her as if they were doing a dance called the Locomotion out the room, his wife's blue eyes brimming with light.

It reminded me of an old Arab exclamation of love, *Ya'uyuni*, which means "My eyes."

Parrot shells and grapeshot bullets are still lodged in some walls of the eight antebellum homes restored in Vicksburg, scars of the siege. With nature victorious in forsythia and new leaves, I awoke early the next morning and ambled up Crawford Street. There I was drawn into the Roman-columned entry of the recently restored Balfour House. The wife of Dr. William T. Balfour, who had bought the house in 1850, was one of the few downtown residents who stayed home during the entire 47-day siege by the Union. She couldn't stand the mosquitoes in the caves where many townspeople hid. Emma Balfour kept one of the few extant diaries of the siege by a civilian. As I read it, while ascending the elegant winding staircase, I could not help but think of Beirut or, for that matter, Anne Frank.

In the massive master bedroom on the third floor lived in today by the Philip Weinberger family, Emma Balfour once tried to sleep, but couldn't with the shatter of shells falling "like hail." There she sewed, wrote, prepared bandages, and filled cartridges with powder. By the time of the surrender, ten thousand Confederate soldiers were too ill and ill-fed to lift a rifle. Supplies were completely exhausted. Nevertheless, Emma kept her humor: "I have quite a collection of shells which have fallen around us and if this goes on much longer I can build a pyramid."[48]

On the bed was a photo of a silhouette that riveted me. It was the burned image of the slave who designed the Balfour House, found inside the brickwork of the bedroom fireplace during restoration. There, kicking up his heels, was the anonymous signature of not just a house, but a whole people, a whole cause. It was the first hurrah of the oppressed, a watermark, a tattoo of a claimant to the new throne of freedom 30 years before it was proclaimed the cause by Abraham Lincoln, 100 years before the Voting Rights Act.

One Balfour stood proudly against the Union; another—Lord David Balfour in 1917—stood proudly for homeless Jews and pompously against the rooted inhabitants of the land.[49] But the Balfour I was growing to love was Emma, who spoke to me, as we descended her staircase, of the tragedy of war and the absurdity of brother fighting brother:

> (May 30, 1863) Conversations occur nightly between friends on the opposite sides. Two Missourian brothers held a conversation very friendly—one sent the other coffee and whiskey. Then they parted with an oath and an exclamation from one that he would "blow the other's head off tomorrow." How unnatural all this is.

After the light evaporated at the Balfour House, I took to the Old Southern Tea Room to meet an Arab judge. Justice John Ellis stood up, all six feet six inches of him, and said, "I knew you were a brother." Born in 1939, Ellis has done it all or had a crack at it all. As a senior at Ole Miss he was treasurer of the state's Young Democrats and handled John F. Kennedy's 1960 campaign here.

He was also elected commander of the University Grays, a fraternity established during the Civil War. At 28, he was elected district attorney of Warren County, taking over from a man who had served 33 years; Ellis won 70 percent of the vote. He became one of the few judges of Arab background in the United States, responsible for four counties, three which abut the Mississippi River.

Ellis ("Elia" in Arabic) presided over thousands of civil cases, lawsuits ranging from $10,000 to many millions, and criminal cases up to capital murder when a man was sentenced to the gas chamber. He attributed his career to two influences—John F. Kennedy and the African Americans of Vicksburg. "I wanted to be a banker," Ellis recalled in a slow, calm southern drawl. "But Kennedy showed me politics is a matter of working with people and their problems and not being selfish in the way you do it. I liked that."[50]

He hinted at an early bond between the Lebanese and African

Americans: "The blacks taught me something years ago. Their ancestors had come over from Africa before we Lebanese came in the 1880s. We had set up shops on the main streets of town, however, and they told me, 'Look, we helped your people get started because your people treated us fair.' They were still recalling from the old days of slavery and plantations. I've consistently won reelection by wide margins, so if there was prejudice against me you don't feel it. The blacks have felt closer to me from a political standpoint. They say, 'Well, look, you can understand us more when you administer justice because you've heard some racial comments against your people.'"

John Ellis was like the hero of the folk song about Big John—a Big, Big Man. Not portly, his limbs were meaty and his head large with dark hair coming down to a widow's peak on the brown forehead. The smile made him Smokey the Bear, with a gavel. Ducking under some scaffolding of workmen outside the courthouse, he stopped briefly to greet the men. They stayed their acetylene torches and raised their visors a second. He was well-liked and, maybe, well-feared.

One of many fond Ellis stories came out just before entering the new building as he looked over his shoulder at the Old Courthouse across the street; it is now a museum. "I used to play on the lawn of that place there, ballgames. And I would hear some hammering going on, some yelling inside the building. I thought it was a torture chamber! But of course it was the judge's gavel. Little did I know that one of the voices was the man I would defeat for D.A. when I grew up."

Judge Ellis was rooted, a tall cypress in the bogland. He loved the Mississippi basin and warmed to my thought that the townspeople of Vicksburg seemed to be the most natural on my trail southward. "As you get closer to the Mississippi River," he smiled, "you see the water changes people."

Raised Roman Catholic by the Brothers of the Sacred Heart, Ellis himself was not speared by prejudice. "A lot of black-headed fellows were at our school," he said, including black Irish and Italians. "But I didn't know there was any difference between Ay-rabs, Lebanese, and Eye-talians. I knew we ate *kibba* on Sunday. But my size—I'm probably larger than most Lebanese—no one was going to say anything to offend me. I was the one to protect them from the wolves." When he said "Ay-rab" he wasn't joking; that is the southern pronunciation.

"Dago" spread over both Lebanese and Italians in the early days. Ellis took pleasure in unwinding a yarn about a African American friend with political power in one of his districts whose nickname was "Dago." Before he was born, the man's mother bought such sundry items as thread, needles, and linens from a peddler she referred to as "the Dago man." This peddler had excellent prices and did not avoid the black neighborhoods. When she was pregnant with Ellis' friend, however, she couldn't catch up to the Dago man. One of her neighbors joked, "Don't worry, honey. You got the Dago man inside you!" Thus her son was nicknamed, "Dago." Possibly the peddler was not Italian, but Lebanese. Thus an Arab became an Italian who became an African!

Family records at the courthouse are combed by locals seeking heritage a century or so back. But Judge Ellis had traced his own family back to the 4th century CE. Originally the Jurige family south of Damascus, they fled to El Munsif in Lebanon due to religious intolerance. They were Orthodox Christians. Only recently had the family sold its last tract of land in El Munsif. The Ellis lineage traced itself right up to the Old Courthouse of Vicksburg—Ellis' father was born three blocks from it, Ellis two blocks away. It was almost as if law in America drew the Ellis clan close even as Lebanon moved into lawlessness.

"If the government is going to work to preserve civilization it has to have the loyalty of its subjects," he said, knocking his pipe on an ashtray like a gavel. "Otherwise you've got nothing but warlords, the rule of force. Every time there's a bullet fired, a person killed, it persists for generations. There are old scores to be settled. Italy had that problem—they called it the Mafia. I don't like to see the countryside of Lebanon blown apart... We have a similar problem here in the South. The whites cannot hold the blacks down economically, politically. If they do, they have a war. In this country we learned a lot since the civil rights days of the '60s. We need the blacks and the blacks need us. We have to get along with each other and learn how to cooperate. Over in Lebanon, they're gonna have to have a Civil Rights Act!"

The Judge cleared his throat, and refilled his pipe slowly. "When you get down to it, these politicians are here today, gone tomorrow. But Israel, Palestine, and Lebanon will still be there making history a hundred years from now. People have got to take a bigger view. I imagine if this government wanted to put the muzzle on Israel it could have. Whoever controls the purse strings is the one who should be able to dictate policy. We ought to be able to call the shots in Israel, without any ifs, ands, buts, or doubts about it. The president should be prepared to take any backlash. As long as the Jews or Christians are holding down the Muslims, you've got a brewing powder keg."

Judge Ellis brewed a pot of coffee instead, and we took a break. He took the cup and went to the great bay window of his large, mahogany-walled office, viewing the Old Courthouse through a grove of cypress and oak. He remembered the day World War II ended and wash tubs were beaten in the parade down Washington

Street for General Eisenhower. He recalled his pride in the medal-laden figure of GI Johnny Haddad, the community's hero (pronounced "Hay-dad" there), as well as the newly elected Lebanese legislator Ellis Bodron in the car with Ike.

Would Judge Ellis' Lebanese background inhibit a successful run for national office in Congress? "On the contrary, it would help. As I said, the blacks are the key. And they like us here."

Sadly, just before his sixtieth birthday in 1999, Judge Ellis died.

Peter Nosser's original introduction to the dream of America came in the form of a gift of chewing gum. The man who broke the race barrier at Vicksburg's country club told me of receiving a package of Wrigley's from the hand of a missionary-doctor in his village of El Munsif before World War I. It was different, sweeter. The 'ilki (chewing gum) the children were used to combined bukhur (incense) with beeswax.

"When I was that age I thought all of America was like that fellow who examined me on his lap and gave me that gum," Pete said, adjusting his thick-lensed glasses. "But here I was disappointed—a lot of people were not as kind as that man."[51] Searching for sweetness would be a theme in Pete's life. Docked at Le Havre for the final leg of his emigration in 1920, he went to a store. "I wanted to buy something sweet, having been used to figs and halawa in Lebanon," he said. "I picked out a tin with a label which seemed to be figs. I found out rather quickly that it was English peas. From then on I read the tin labels real well."

Pete Nosser was one of three octagenarian original Lebanese immigrants, all storekeepers, whom I met in steady succession. He recalled, as did his cousin, Johnny Nosser, witnessing an earthquake the day of the Armistice in 1918. Added to the horror was a plague of locusts, which Pete remembered: "All of a sudden it was like clouds settling on the ground. They were eight times as big as a grasshopper. As big as a finger. Anything green they ate. We would beat on a tin can to scare them—it was the only remedy." This coincided with my own grandmother's habit in California of hanging tin can lids by string in her fig trees to ward off marauding blue jays.

Born in 1902, Pete Nosser lived alone after his wife passed away. In spite of cataract surgery, his mind's eye was sharp. The fateful trip across the oceans in 1920, with twenty or thirty of his clan, came back to him. Packed in sailor's "cuts" on the ship from Beirut, they stopped and bought dates in Algiers, where they had no fear of thieves because "we had nothing to steal. Poverty made us leave. My father said there was nothing to do there [in El Munsif]." Lost in Vicksburg, he was directed to his family by a African American man.

"'What are you?' he asked me," recounted Pete. "I said, 'Syrian.' He said, 'I know a Syrian family.' And he led me to the woman who breast fed me in El Munsif! I ended up marrying her daughter," he smiled.

As with so many of the original Lebanese immigrants, religion filled Pete Nosser's fibers. Raising his silver-haired crown, he told of an interchange between Archbishop Anthony Bashir, who founded the parish in Vicksburg in 1906, and a skeptic, who once asked him, "Where is God?" According to Pete, the archbishop responded, "Some will ask questions to understand, others to irritate. I cannot show you the Good Lord. If you keep the commandments, you go to heaven. If there's no God, what have you lost?"

"Uncle Johnny" Nosser, at 86, was the reigning patriarch of the community in 1984 and much celebrated by the town. He had been written up a couple of times by the Vicksburg paper, "been put to sleep seventeen times—the Lord is good," caught bream at the corner of First and Washington streets during the 1927 flood, and worked like a dog eighteen hours a day at his 60-year-old store.

"They used to farm and I supplied horse collars, cow bells, harnesses for mules," Johnny announced, eyes a kilowatt of light. "Everything you need, I had. They couldn't find tire patches; I had 'em. 'Here ya go.' Nails of any description! Bolts, guns, chairs, iron pots for fried fish!"[52] He could have gone on forever and I would not have found out anything about him but what was in his store—an inventory that sounded like Walt Whitman's "Song of Myself."

Johnny Nosser was dressed impeccably when we met at the Orthodox church: chocolate sports coat, yellow cotton shirt, dark brown tie. There is no word for the veins on his long, spotted hands. They are runoff from the Mississippi and, maybe, the Dog River in Lebanon.

I asked him to name the best qualities of the Lebanese people. "That's easy," he said crisply, snapping a digit to the sky. "Number one, they pay for what they get. Number two, they care about their name if they was to be broke. Number three, they're religious. Number four, they love one another, they love everybody. And they pay their debts." But Lebanon was hardly peace loving.

"In the world—we need a lot of teaching," he called out. Then his voice settled, became humble. "I love to have peace in Lebanon. I'd love to have the government get together and be 50/50. I don't want our boys getting killed in Beirut. The Lebanese unfortunately couldn't help—their sons are getting killed, too, each day on the streets."

Johnny was only too happy in 1920 to arrive in America and forget the horrors he lived through during the Great War. First he tried working in a car factory in Cleveland making batteries. But the battery acid ruined his lungs. He took to a candy factory. Finally Vicksburg beckoned through some relatives.

He was an unabashed believer in miracles, having risen off the operating table so many times. Pittsburgh radio took his story and put it on the air. He had the form letter to prove it. But Johnny was nothing like a form letter. He knew the Palestinian case "is hard to sell."

He fairly jumped from his seat as if hit by an electric current: "You'll never see yesterday! Twenty years from today is closer than yesterday." And then the smile, as if he had just dropped the eight ball in the side pocket, a turn of the head, a pull of purplish cheek upward from the mouth, and the twinkling eye.

Haseeb Abraham, 82, who bought out the site where the first Coca Cola was bottled in America to expand his store, had a similar story to tell about the Old World. By 1917 in Bishmizeen, "everything was played out—six days would pass when we had nothing to eat at all."[53] The Turks forbid anyone to travel from the northern mountains to Tripoli to buy wheat. "Mother got us bran," said Haseeb, a short, armadillo-like man with a face of pinched magenta. "This was the chaff of the wheat. We had to take it with water—it wouldn't go down. We ate grass. Sixty-five percent of our village starved to death. We ate anything—dewberry, *khirsana* [wild grass], *tum* [a plant that looks like garlic] to live off it."

The key relationship between African Americans and Lebanese storeowners was explained further by Haseeb's daughter, Frances Abraham Thomas: "We worked with the black sharecroppers. They'd have a $100 mistake on their paychecks and we felt bad for them. We'd fix their errors and those of their employers so they wouldn't get taken again. When my mother passed away in 1983, I never saw blacks mourning the passing of a white like her."

For Mayme Farris, however, the view from the bridge on race and Lebanon was more complex—or perhaps less so. Mayme had the first formal marriage in St. George Orthodox Church in 1922. Her views were made all the more difficult by the strain it was for her to ease down her staircase, having broken her hip months before and rarely coming downstairs. Her view was this: the blacks were treated worse by the Union soldiers and carpetbaggers than by any men in Confederate gray; Michael Jackson ain't no good for blacks, making them avaricious and uppity; and Lebanon would do better if there were more Jews there.

Mayme Farris, one of the first girls born to the Vicksburg émigré colony, in 1902, was an old southern country gentlewoman—short, buxom, the beauty still present in her slender ankles. She was wise, sharp-witted, imbued with history, a bit prejudiced and very sympathetic. But she was all Lebanese, even if every phrase came out with a southern accent. Of the people I met in Vicksburg she was the most strongly anti-Muslim and pro-Christian Lebanese, even to the point of asking, incredulously, "You call the Druze Lebanese? I don't!" Father Saikley argued with her to no avail. "They're not Lebanese like I am."[54] You'd think she had been born in El Munsif!

Proud to nurture a family of writers, Mayme had a daughter teaching English in college and a grandson who published a short story in the *New Yorker* at the age of twenty, a remarkable feat. As for her own writing, done for the Vicksburg Historical Society and the early Syrian Progressive Aid Society, she said, "I couldn't work out, honey. I had to work at the kinsfolk." Still, she put word to work.

Mayme on love: "What they call love nowadays should be scratched out with a black marker."

Mayme on conforming: "I feel sorry for people that can't conform. Because I can. Not that I sanction what I am conforming to. But because I know who's talking to me is a human being and has his rights in the world."

Mayme on the lack of nationwide Lebanese political power: "You know as well as I that if you have a nice car and a nice home and you're going to give a little wine and dine you can get anybody. *Anybody.* That is the easiest thing in the world to do, a little wine and dine. But our people could not entertain; they entertained one another."

Mayme on intermarriage: "When our children intermarry [the spouses] become Lebanese pretty quick. Our heritage is so strong that our boys need not worry. [The spouses] are gonna come over."

Mayme on Muslims: "Why are the Muslims taking over our country? But they're more loyal to their faith than we are. In Beirut there's a mosque every other block, and they chant from the minaret, *Al-salah afdal min al-nawm*, 'Prayer is better than sleep.'"

Mayme on the solution to Lebanon's problems: "I hate for any Lebanese to hear me but if the Jews just had this country [Lebanon]. I wish they could let some Jews in there! We had it here, honey—Jews and Arabs—competition. Why, that's the salt of the earth!"

In her grandson James Hughes' short story, a character, Fig, tells his brother:

> People don't lose their lust for life. Anybody who says they've lost it never had it in the first place. I know dozens of people not even out of high school who spend all their time feeling sorry for themselves. They think they know what grief is all about, but all they're really into is self-pity. Why can't they get their grieving done and then get the hell on with business?[55]

The lust for life was in Mayme Farris' determined descent of her staircase, dressed up as if for the king. It was in the embroidered pillow of Byblos exhibited prominently on her fireplace mantel, as if the waters of that ancient seaport would boil. Hughes had written an epitaph for the whole Lebanese diaspora— "Get their grieving done and then get the hell on with business."

The last night of my visit to the city of crape myrtle, forsythia, and bluffs I looked out from Fort Hill, which, 120 years earlier, had anchored the Confederate left flank against the worst siege of an American city in the country's history.

The Lebanese had made a mark for themselves here, many years from one war and many miles from another. Their home country had been torn by a vicious civil war. They had left at the onset and in the wake of the first Great War of this century, opened shops in Vicksburg, been peacemakers between the defeated Johnny Reb and the blacks. Having starved, they sold food.

How much more horrid was the Lebanon civil war than our own? Over 150,000 Lebanese and Palestinians had died between 1975 and 1991; but more Americans had been killed in a shorter time between 1860 and 1865 in an era of rifles and no repeating weapons other than a few Gatling guns: 600,000. (The mortality rate of America's Civil War was 3 percent of the population; the Lebanese civil war death rate was similar—3.3 percent.) We have become conditioned in America to think that wars in other lands were somehow more bestial, that their place in the endless, bloody struggle for human dignity would suck us down.

In Vicksburg the Arabs had achieved unity where they hadn't in Lebanon. They had found peace after they had had none. It was not so unusual that the Lebanese built one of their most prominent roosts in America in the seat of the new country's worst civil war siege. They were planting mint in ashes—an old habit. Their success in Vicksburg was measured by how much good they could do for the downtrodden—a lesson still to be carried over in Lebanon itself.

Twenty years after the Union boys watched in unusual silence as Gen. John C. Pemberton surrendered to a grizzled U. S. Grant, the Lebanese began to come, were taken for Italians, opened stores for clothing and food, and wove the holes in the bills of the freed blacks; and the slave of the Balfour House slowly emerged from hiding. In the emergent spring, I thought of the words of Emma Balfour, in another spring when blossoms were threatened by shot, and how her humanity seemed larger in its respect for all creation than that of her illustrious namesake in Britain.

The moon rose like a silver button on a midnight breechcoat behind a obelisk of the Union Navy Memorial in honor of the sailors who braved the Confederate batteries. The wind drew its breath in and pulled the grass around to yearn. Now the waters below were silvery, the night air suffuse with flower and the graves sleeping. No, the river below Fort Hill was not strictly the Mississippi but the Yazoo River Diversion Canal. The Great River had grown tired of it all and, in a storm, moved.

Perhaps the Litani River or the Nahr El Kelb or the Jordan itself would have the same good taste. And let people live, come out from under the brick not as shadows but as free men speaking Arabic, or Hebrew, or joy.

THE MOSQUE AND THE PRAIRIE (ROSS, NORTH DAKOTA)

The largest grain elevator between Minot and Williston is in Ross, a town of fewer than fifty people in the northwest corner of North Dakota. In Ross, people love rain. You do not speak against the rain. Common expressions are "S'pose so," "Well, forevermore!" and "It'll have to do." To leave farming and work for anyone else is to "work out." The milk cows are patient. Saskatchewan is north about 30 miles, Montana mountains due west over the horizon. Teddy Roosevelt once shot bison south of here near Medora. Otherwise, the wind is the only constant. There is nothing much historical. Almost.

On a still summer day in 1978, with not a touch of tornado or cloud in the sky, after Omar Hamdan and others proposed it be torn down, the first Muslim mosque built in North America was bulldozed. It was in Ross. Omar Hamdan later poisoned gophers in the cemetery of his ancestors. It did not seem to follow. Hamdan was torn, like the rocky northern terrain he farms—"With used equipment," he said. "I never buy new." It was June. He had just turned the stubble—fallow farmed. He was also confused by more than a vanishing Syrian past. The US government announced that it would pay North Dakota farmers not to farm, in bushels of wheat.

"Now that would be just like when Chrysler went down," Hamdan looked at his Indian-red hand. "Just like paying Chrysler in automobiles. Wouldn't have made any sense, would it? It don't for us either. We don't need more wheat—we need markets."[56] Unsellable wheat choking the elevators, too much snow and no apricots, government money going for missiles instead of bellies, decades of women in short-shorts on Main Street of Stanley instead of veils—was this it? Maybe it was his wife, whose heritage is "everything... she doesn't know what all is in there," maybe the icy slough beyond the Muslim cemetery, but the group's proposition leveled the *jami'* on a hot summer day where the land is infinite as the sky. The actual bulldozing was done by twenty-year-old Hamed Juma, Jr. The twenty Syrians left in Ross and Stanley called it a desecration. One old woman named Nazira stood on the stoop of her trailer, took off her glasses, rubbed her blue eyes, and said, "It was like the death of my child."

Hamdan and Hamed Juma claimed ignorance when told of the

historicity of the Ross mosque, dedicated in 1930 at the height of the Great Depression to bolster the colony of Syrians. Others might have known we were worth something here—in the large concentrations of the 250,000 Arab-American Muslims, such as Detroit; in Michigan City, Indiana; and in Cedar Rapids, Iowa. We didn't, said Omar. The North Dakota Syrians hadn't held a service at the mosque for ten years. Most of the area's Muslims had turned Lutheran because of time and dwindling numbers. For a long while they had gathered themselves and their language like a cairn separated from the stony soil to the side of the wheat. But intermarriage and migration to Canada had broken down the identity of the group of eastern Mediterraneans in a blond sea.

Against the bitter purge stood the last fluent speaker of Arabic in the area, Shahati "Charlie" Juma, Hamed's uncle, a huge-fisted, raisin-skinned man with a tenacious shock of salt-and-pepper hair cut high above the ears as if in defiance. Charlie Juma shook the hand of every living thing in Stanley, population 1,300. His hand was a warm clamp; he wouldn't let go until he'd read your fortune, raised you on your toes for a laugh, or told you off. Knocking a Norseman's beer belly—a man who towered above him—Charlie quipped, "Hey Pete. You got two in there?"

Charlie was the first child born to the Ross Syrians, in 1903, on the Juma homestead. In 1899, his father, Hassan, gawked out the window of the Great Northern train, liked what he saw in Dakota, got out at Ross, walked down the railroad ties, and threw a painted stone to mark where he'd take his free 160 acres, thank you. Today Amtrak's Empire Builder line goes right through the original Juma homestead. There were few people in Ross back then. The Juma family grew with the town; Charlie's memory was the memory of Ross, the Norwegians, Syrians, Bohemians, the duck ponds, rattlers, and tornadoes.

A member of every civic board in Montrail County, from the Board of Education to the Grain Elevator Stockholders Association, farmer Charlie was loved by the people of the area. He walked down Main Street of Stanley like an old squat bear, holding people up with his paw and quip. Charlie was a North Dakota Sancho Panza. But when it came to his heritage, he was an olive tree thrashing in a field of flax. Lines on the bridge of his nose betrayed pain at the passing of an entire way of life. Ramadan in the fields. *Salli* (pray) with a rug in the wheat.

One sensed a showdown between Charlie Juma and Omar Hamdan. It would match a short, burly octagenarian with meaty hands ("I got 'em digging manure") and a wiry, handsome, brooding farmer who wore a cap with a hunter lifting a shotgun over the heads of two English setters.

Sally's Café was Charlie Juma's stage. It sported some of the holy icons of America's breadbasket on its walls. There were cheap copper paintings on black satin of the gods: three different John Waynes, Elvis Presley with the fat chin, various American Indians with their heads bowed on palominos, and way back in the café's rear, a plug-in painting of Jesus in the garden of Gethsemane, electric stars twinkling above His head. Charlie was joined under a bust of Wayne by a cousin, Laila Omar, and her husband, Clem. Laila worked at the bank. Though wearing a simple pullover and jeans, with her short black hair and bottomless brown eyes she was an exotic addition to Sally's.

The subject of prejudice came up—Laila confirmed that in the old days they were called Black Syrians, and there were fist fights. Everal McKinnon, a field worker for the Historical Data Project in Bismark who interviewed the Syrians in Ross, wrote in his report on 1939:

> Their homes, barns and other farm buildings are, in most cases, just shacks and look very much neglected. In most cases the barns look much better than the houses. They have exceptionally nice looking horses but only one out of ten of the men are able to drive and handle horses well, although they all have them.

Charlie, who was one of the few Syrians to speak to McKinnon in detail, was insulted by that section of his report. He didn't raise his voice, but his anger 45 years later was evident in a quick jab of words. McKinnon was wrong: our way with horses was just fine and our houses no different from anyone else's. And another of Charlie's nephews, Marshall Juma, was in 1983 the Midwest's number-one bareback bronco rider on the professional rodeo circuit.

"I think the Scandinavians have less prejudice than the Germans or Bohemians," Clem drawled. "My folks didn't impose prejudice on me—we're Swede. It's what you're taught at home in the final result."

Charlie butted in: "And you know, back in the old days there were no partialities between Christian and Muslim Syrians in Ross and Stanley. We had a few Christians. No partialities like they had down there in Williston."[57] Williston (pop. 13,000)—about 50 miles west of Ross—has a thriving Arab-American population of 150. They own real estate—the Habhabs, Josephs, Seebs. Another smaller community of Arab Americans is in nearby Bone Trail.

Strangely, none of the Muslims in the area had any idea what sect of Islam their ancestors were. Until the recent headlines of Sunni-Shiʿa struggles in Iraq and Iran and Lebanon, as well as the Arab–Israeli wars, Charlie admitted he didn't even know there was a difference. There was unity in the small community, and then the religion vanished. It never developed enough animosities and jealousies to bifurcate.

Coffee's poured by a girl with flaxen hair, meadow-blue eyes, and a sweat moustache. She rushed to cover all the outstretched cups of the farmers. The heat from grill and the bright street collided. Everyone sweated.

And the ruined mosque. "It's a *haram* [forbidden], a shame they tore it down," Laila's eyes flared. "I don't want to talk about it." She crushed her cigarette and looked knowingly at her husband. "Charlie and I weren't invited to the meeting." Her tone meant, the meeting didn't last long.

Later, Charlie mixed at the annual Grain Elevator Association meeting. He zigged like a bumblebee toward three ladies whose white hair had an aura of honey. "Gals," he proclaimed, "I'm a Finlander." They laughed and held tight to their plates of potatoes and gravy.

Charlie and visitor stood in line to get some food. Ahead was a glum lady with baggy arms: "There's a gal who's 75 who used to sit in front of me at grade school. She says I used to dip her pigtails in the inkwell!" Later, Charlie pointed out that the Ross schoolhouse had become yet another grain elevator. At the table the very picture of Lutheran suspicion and forebearance burst like a dandelion in a fast breeze when Charlie asked about her children. Her name was Mrs. Shroteek. Before leaving she bent over to shake the newcomer's hand and underlined, "We love Syrians. They work hard. I'm a Norwegian, you know. We're all together now and that's good."

Towheaded kids were getting antsy. More coffee. Seconds. Thirds. Charlie wanted to leave before the speeches started—he'd heard them all before anyway, and it was getting dimmer out. People waved good-bye as he passed. A giant farmer who traced his family back to Prague let out a hoot when he saw Charlie and went into a spiel about the price of wheat.

He stabbed Charlie with a finger in the chest as they shook hands. "You know, Charlie, I wonder what ever happened to that musique you all had? 'Member? Darndist tale I ever heard, a musique in North Dakota. What ever happened to that musique?"

There's no more music at the mew-zeek. Only the wind. Under the arc of a crescent moon and star—welded in steel tubing—Charlie struggled with the gate to the Muslim cemetery. The wind was blowing, the tall grass waving like the hair of a beautiful cousin who went away. Charlie clanked open the lock to the gate and silently moved on a field of poorly tended graves. Beyond, the cold slough rippled.

"That's where the *jami* was," he pointed to a large, dark patch of bending grass. A mermaid sank here, Charlie, the wind was saying. She had long green hair and came up from the Barada River that runs through Damascus. She followed up the Missouri River and sank. Her hair was not lime green like the rest. Dark green. The Syrians still pay a man fifty dollars a year to mow the turf of the cemetery. He must have been on strike.

The 1939 Historical Data Project account of the mosque went as follows:

> This basement church is 18 x 30 feet in size and rises four feet off the ground. The walls are built of cement and rock and the roof is temporary. It has four windows on each side and two on each end. The cash cost of the church was $400, and members did considerable work themselves. It was dedicated on October 31, 1930. Furnishings of the church consist of chairs, benches, a large rug, a coal heater and range. Members bring their own rugs for use in worshipping.

It never occurred to the writer to use any other word than "church" to describe the mosque.

The oldest grave in the little cemetery is marked by a white-painted cinder block, nothing more. Someone crudely scrawled in a two-foot strip of cement, SOLOMON HODGE, d. 1940. Hodge was the first Syrian peddler in the area and the only one to keep it up as a profession—a cheery man whose wife and kids in Syria were cut off from him all his life. Hodge's name may have been a twisting of "Hajj," indicating a family whose ancestors had made the *hajj* to Mecca.

Many of the graves had a crude hump of concrete on them, like a stifling coverlet, but no marker. Charlie pointed one out—his father's unmarked grave. No, the custom is not Islamic. He didn't know why it was done this way. Only two headstones in the cemetery had the star-cresent motif etched into them. On some graves the earth had buckled, as if the dead were restless. Grass had overgrown most and gopher holes abounded. No fresh flower on these graves.

Charlie called off the names as he walked: Osman, Omar. Juma, Hassan. Alex Asmel, d. 1941. A private in the 158th Infantry, 40th Division, a Muslim Arab American killed in World War II fighting for the United States. Belinda Osman Hudson: "She remarried a goddam drunk."

"Here's little Alex Hassan," Charlie nodded over a small stone the size of a common brick. "He died at the age of one. Richard Hassan was his father, but he died. He has relatives living in Detroit. But his older brothers there don't even know about him. I called them up and told them they had had a baby brother."

"Goddamit!" Charlie shouted, flinging a bear claw at the ground. "I'm the one that does all the dirty work! I make the calls. I get people together for the ʿId. When I die, who is going to remember Alex?"

The gate shut. The rain-filled clouds moved in a steel stencil of an Islamic moon. On the way back to Stanley, Charlie stopped in the well-kept Lutheran cemetery where the graves all have headstones, are equally spaced, where the grass is watered and cut, and flowers, fake or not, are present. He pointed out his wife, Mary's, grave and his own place beside her, waiting. But why was his own family's selected spot here and not out in Ross at the Muslim grounds? Without a blink he replied, "It's more livable."

The sun set on the old Juma homestead. Nine quarters in size (a quarter equals 160 acres) of barley, durum wheat, flax, and oats, as well as cattle, Charlie gave it all to his son, Charles Junior, who built a new house a mile up the road. The old Juma farmhouse is boarded up. For Charlie and many old farmers the days of the combine were over; the days of combining were not. They moved, like refugees from solitude, into town.

A proud stillness held the Juma spread. A 1940s Ford truck, purple as a hard-shelled beetle, leaned into a broken fence. A barn sagged down the middle as if it had been straddled too long by a heavy rider. It was brought in two huge pieces, Charlie explained, fingering his ear, in 1939 from 25 miles away. There was no timber long enough to move it in one section. It sagged from the weight of many snows and its own fault line. Old hay inside was spotted with oil along the floor from dead tools.

In North Dakota the life of a farm is often told in tornadoes. Those that hit, when they did, what they took with them. Farmers tell of tornadoes like you would mark the scars on the body to show where you have lived the most. Tornadoes according to Charlie: "It forms the cloud in the sky and comes down. It's a dark black cloud. And when it hits it's just like a snake, dips down and goes up, turning and jumping."

In 1950, there was a bad tornado in Ross. In 1962, Charlie and his wife were visiting a daughter in Texas. In the middle of the night the wife woke up in bed and said, "Something's happened to our farm. There's water, raining." The dream was prophetic—a twister had touched down on the Juma barn and pulled the top off like the cap from a bald man. The walls collapsed.

On the Fourth of July, 1979, a twister took the air-conditioner off the roof of his daughter Rosie's trailer house and twirled the kids, who were sleeping in a tent. "It scared the devil out of them," Charlie recounted. "Then it crossed the crick to the northwest of us and took two, three trailers down."

But the worst tornado of the century in the Dakotas struck twenty miles south of Ross at the Missouri River. It is a legend, dated 1935.

> It struck across the river at Charleston I guess… It took buildings all the way across the river. Just sucked the water out of the river so they could see the bare ground… [I]t took mail from Ernest Myers' farm clear up into Canada, about a hundred miles. They mailed the letter back to us from Canada.

Charlie Juma stands at the original Juma homestead in Ross, North Dakota
(Gregory Orfalea)

Did the Syrians—who surely would never have seen anything like them—react in any special way to tornadoes? "They would say—a gift of God, you know," Charlie mused. "It's the doings of God. It shows what power God has. Not Christ, not Jesus, not Mohammed, nobody but the good Lord. He dips down and He does what He wants."

The real loss for Charlie—beyond ancestral ways—was that of his first-born son, Hassan, who died at 39 in 1970. A wallet photo showed Hassan, winsome, fairer-skinned than the father, a Tyrone Power face. He said it many times in many places over a few days, but the most expression he allowed himself was: "Hassan's death was a letdown."

Up at the new spread, Charles Junior washed off some garden tools in front of his house. He's a burly, friendly fellow who once was knifed in a bar by a guy who teased him by swiping his cap. Charles Junior pursued, took the cap back. The fellow swung. Charles wrestled him with a bear hug and then felt a cold draft in his stomach. "He thought it was a bottle opener," Charlie recounted. But it was a knife. And guess who watched the entire battle, blood and all? Omar Hamdan, downing a tall one at the bar.

The next morning was Sunday—visiting time. Charlie driving. A Jeep sped by. "That fella is going like a house afire."

First there was Mrs. Andreeson on Main Street who told Charlie she met him many years ago. "You're a hundred years old?" He held her hand. She laughed.

A group of three women in their sixties was up ahead. Charlie used to give them rides to school in his horse-drawn sledge over the snow. Now they're in white shorts and thongs. "By God, girls, when are you gonna put your clothes on?" For a moment cackles turned to giggles and they went into Sally's Café with blushing wrinkles.

"Now I couldn't do that in Minot or Washington, DC, could I?" Charlie pronounced. "There's an advantage to being in a small town. You know just how to talk to everybody. You know what they like and what they dislike." Ah, the Levantine diplomat!

His daughter, Rosie, wanted us for dinner and Nazira—the oldest Arab woman in town—for supper. So at noon it was off to Rosie's. Aromas of *kusa* (zucchini), *kibba*, and *waraq ʿinab* (grape leaves) rose in a little kitchen surrounded by farms. Rosie is a widow; her only child, Will, wore a John Deere tractor hat. Like the rest of Charlie's children, she married a non-Arab. In fact, no surviving first- or second-generation Syrian in the two small towns was married to a Syrian.

Talk went around the table like a bottomless dish. The only restaurant in the area that served Arab food was in Williston. It was called the Viking! "Oh, the weddings," said Charlie, "were great for dancing the *dabka*." Omar Hamdan's father was especially good at dancing with a handkerchief wrapped in his palm. "He was light on his feet after he got drunk," Charlie dropped.

Screwing up her forehead and staring off out the window, Charlie's granddaughter Dawn came to the conclusion that she had never seen an Arab dance, and she noted, in all seriousness, "except, you know, *Fiddler on the Roof*." Astonishingly, no one corrected her. No one seemed to know that the famous play she referred to is about persecuted Jews in Russia.

Thank you's to Rosie as we left—she returned with the Nordic long o's in her slow cadenced speech, "Yoor very welcoom." Out front, what was this rusted old tub in the midst of Rosie's marigolds? It's used to scald pigs, she said. After that, the old Syrian farmers would clean out the bristle and dregs of pig and use the tub to soak *samid* for *kibba*. It may have been the only lamb around with an aftertaste of pork!

At Nazira Kurdi Omar's trailer the *kibba* was plain and the Syrian bread flaky and too thin, like the Norwegian, without substance. But she spouted flocks of language, birds with damaged wings, in broken Syrian and English and you had to love her. Born in Birey, Syria, in 1908 or 1912, she couldn't remember which, Nazira was delighted to have company since her seven children were all gone, one as far away as Anchorage, Alaska. She wore thick glasses, her face rubbery with deep rills.

Charlie respected Nazira and let her talk in the hopes her Arabic would spear some of the emotion flying out so fast. We were warned by Dawn that few people can understand Nazira, who never studied

English or Arabic and simply raised seven kids in a strange country. Her husband, *Allah yarhamu*, died young, a sickly man. Her birdlike voice was not loud, and many times she ended a thought with an "I don't know anyway."[58]

An innocent at 71 or 75, Nazira was the only remaining member of the Syrian community to refuse, on principle, to attend the Lutheran church. "There is no more mosque," she rubbed the welling of water from her eyes, "So I will go nowhere else." After many rounds of food drained of spice and piquancy by the long winters and her loneliness, Nazira pronounced with untypical clarity, "I want to be myself, not anybody else."

Omar knocked at Charlie's door, darkening the screen. The showdown at last. Omar's eyes were red and he did not take off his hunter's cap, but tipped it. Charlie smiled, did not shake his hand, rather faked a blow to Omar's belly. Play with tension behind it.

Perhaps Omar had been drinking, but it is also possible that the capillaries of his eyes were swollen from pollen or dust from fallow farming. Maybe he had not slept since he heard there was someone in town concerned about the history of the Syrians in Ross. Charlie's eyes, however, were as clear as crystal, the whites white as ivory. Omar was going to plug Charlie or Charlie was going to strangle Omar. This was it—the O.K. Corral. The prize was not a woman but the key to the corral of memory.

Small talk. The men tested each other. Omar, born in 1929, is the son of Abdul Karim Hamdan from Rafid, Syria, a town a few miles from Birey, from where most of the Syrians in the area originate. Omar is a Rafidi. A man already apart. Life in Rafid, as in Birey, was poor. "My father told me if a boy got a toy pistol over there it was as good as a Cadillac here," Omar murmured.

Omar mentioned the bind he was in with the government's payoff system of wheat for laying off work: "We give enough in taxes don't we? The government has to use all these taxes somehow, so they'll examine the sex life of flies in Argentina if they have to." He had it in for Argentina, which had been stealing a lot of North Dakota's international grain markets. He spoke without moving his long, brown hand, palm down, from the table.

Charlie put on coffee to break the silence after Omar spoke of the sex life of flies. He made a couple of calls to others and told them, Omar's here; no one else came. It seemed to be their first meeting in a long while. The coffee boiled over. Charlie's left eye was clear, but twitching a mile a minute. Omar's were red, looking downward. The coffee poured. "Yeah, seem to recall a lawnmower catching fire the last service out at the old mosque," he put forward in his low, dark voice. "Poured too much gas. Burned the thing to a crisp."

When was this? "1969, wasn't it, Charlie? The year before Hassan died, right?"

Charlie said something unintelligible.

The visitor asked him to explain why the mosque was destroyed. "Our information here is so slack that everybody around the world knows it was the first and we don't," he said, midstream in a thought. "So we put it underneath."

"Put it underneath, under the table," Charlie droned, caught by Omar's "we."

"Yeah, just sorta covered it up. It was kind of an eyesore for many years and of course there wasn't enough in the congregation to... you know, keep it up. So it looked kinda bad. Deteriorating. And the windows were boarded up. And the cellar was a sump hole."

Silence. Charlie's arms folded.

"I found out I was the most unpopular one of the whole works, see, after this came up. Now my uncle told me that his daughter had already read in one of the books that that was a historic church and he tried to tell me and I wouldn't listen. Now, I don't remember him trying to tell me that."

More silence. Like a call to prayer. There was no muezzin in the minaret then. There were so very few who could lead a service at all. Only the Dakota wind called to prayer on Friday.

"It's an awful strict religion," Omar continued. "That's why it's tough for kids to follow in a country where there is freedom. There's no way I'm going to send my kids to the religion I was brought up on. Heck, I'm not... in fact, if I was to say I was religious, it would be a disgrace to my religion, really. That's what kinda discouraged us a little bit... the fact that the religion was so strict and yet nobody really followed it."

Omar broke a sly smile, then went back to his studied expressionlessness.

This is where Charlie throws his haymaker, right? No. Because Omar began reciting the Qu'ran. Yes, he remembered a passage, a favorite: "Great God, the Savior of the World, Most Gracious and Most Merciful Master on the Day of Judgment. Thee We Do Worship and Thine Aid We Seek. Show Us the Straight Way... " As Omar recited, Charlie's eye stopped twitching. He was stunned.

"I didn't know about it being the first mosque in America," Omar admitted, with the first hint of remorse. "If I did maybe I wouldn't have let it happen."

"They dozed it," Charlie spoke quietly.

"If they're talkin' about building a new one, okay. That's fine, or maybe a historical plaque or something. But the way it was, with rats and gophers... "

"Omar," Charlie stood. "Who's gonna do this when I'm gone?"

On the table before him were piles of old photos of the Syrians in the Dakotas, articles for the North Dakota Historical Society, plaques and presentations in Arabic. He pleaded with Omar with emotions cooled by 80 years in the northern zone. There was no flailing of the hands. Only the eye twitching again. Strange. In a pang of sympathy, Charlie reached out to the prodigal son.

A quiet settled on the Juma house, bought by a retired farmer whose father came from Syria in 1899 and bowed his head to the east calling *Allahu akbar* in the wheat. It may be that Omar remembered that call, packed deeper inside him than anyone. Contrary to the obvious, the mosque was bulldozed not to slap Allah in the face but to hurt the community into realizing what its lassitude had done to its customs. Omar and Hamed Juma shocked the Muslims of Ross and Stanley. They were punishing them, and therefore themselves, for not praying five times a day and not keeping the faith, and not inculcating enough steel resolve to resist the tide of Norsehoostafests and the ever-loving English. Punishment for wanting the blue-eyed girl in the bathing suit of the movies and billboards that never stops coming at you in America. Perhaps Omar, in his heretical way, suffered from a hunger for meaning and righteousness. The violent act reducing the *jami'* to dust may have been an ardent act of faith.

As for Charlie, a more devout and temperate man whose father founded the mosque, he would be put to rest in the Lutheran cemetery. He fought the good fight, but because fate was against the Syrians in Ross, and the Lutheran church is here to stay and its grass is well trimmed, he sided with the inevitable. Why, after all, had he left his father's grave unmarked all these years? Was this devotion to the Muslim ways? He complained about gophers digging holes in the Muslim graves, but Omar—the recondite—was the one to poison them. And a quarter century later, it was Omar Hamdan who deposited funds from Sarah Omar to erect a monument on the site of the original mosque.

Just who felt the passing of an era more, who was the assimilationist and who the keeper of the flame, was not so easy to tell. But by 2005 there was only one active Syrian farmer left in Stanley-Ross. His children may read about mosques in books, or see a monument. But that is all. His name is Charles Juma, Jr. He drives a Winnebago and knows no Arabic.

A Porch in Pasadena (Los Angeles)

"We're gettin' old, honey." So my Thatee (grandmother), Matile Malouf Awad, said on a sunny spring day as she hoisted herself up the steps, grasping the wrought-iron handrails just installed by my cousin Dennis. And for the first time I realized that she was in the neighborhood of 75, though she walked swiftly each morning with her silky terrier, Mickey.

We entered the large L-shaped porch, a breezy alcove of legends where relatives and friends gathered in the years of my childhood, speaking of famine from the old land, dresses in the new, picking apricots that grew over the banisters. No screened-in porch, this blessed zone. This sweeping view on the corner of Bresee and Asbury streets sold the house to Jaddu Kamel Awad before he even walked into it. Was he to blame that the place only had two bedrooms for his four children and wife? A wide look at the world with the wind was more important.

And the porch? Heaven. An aroma of the afterlife. The sun is clear and bright. All the world a page of illuminated manuscript. I had finally come home in my long journey to the point I began— Los Angeles, the final point of the Arab community's own *hijra* in America, as it was for so many others. The old community sank its firmest roots in Pasadena under shade of pepper and eucalyptus trees, under the crest of the San Gabriel mountains, always hugging close to a mountain as if they were hunting not only the sun but also Mount Lebanon.

Here the world is good at core; the robins and jays and owls that feed here pay no heed to our wars or those of the Middle East. The spiked head of the bird-of-paradise gawks over the walkway; the first blossoms of apricot, resurrected from last night's rain—white with drops of magenta at the center—are praising the sun. The wind plays with the new leaves. Light cargoes of purple have touched the new leaves and the center of blossoms, as if nature herself demands a nip of wine in the veins of each reborn leaf.

Here Thatee planted a sumptuous garden of shrubs and flowers. The garden was a total contrast to the one of the old German lady next door. There, a plot of rectangles and squares, a perimeter of pansies surrounded that front yard like the chalk marks on a football field. Order! Flowers, attention! But in Thatee's Pasadena Lebanon, the ferns, onions, daffodils, hydrangeas, and lilacs lolled over their stucco borders and swallowed the flagstone walkway to the water spigot. Once arranged in an undulating pattern to hug the house, finally all became a tender chaos. The apricot trees would soon thrust pale orange clusters over the porch's banister. Beauty cared for enough to be allowed direction of its own. Inhale, traveler for roots. "The scent of your garments is like the scent of Lebanon... " Hers was a garden built of hunger.

If Haifa's hills recall San Francisco, if Beirut's steep mountain rise from the sea bears resemblance to Santa Barbara, the Middle East itself, as a beaten path of cultures in flux and conquest, could be

Emile Khouri in 1975 at the site of his architectural conception: Disneyland (Aramco World Magazine)

compared to another desert that "bloomed" with cloverleaf freeways, palms, and ivy—Los Angeles, Town of the Lost Angels.

This is a city whose very soul is in motion: a looping, intersecting, elongated concrete monument to the American Bedouin. Those with sun in the blood, Jews and Arabs, found plenty of beauty in the quaint county that was Los Angeles. It nearly doubled its population in the fifteen years after World War II. Since then both communities have burgeoned along with the city until today there are 550,000 Jewish and 340,000 Arab Americans in Los Angeles, often living as neighbors. Many, such as the fathers Blumberg and Orfalea, who lived facing each other in the San Fernando Valley, commuted 25 miles downtown to slave in the garment industry. The "rag," or *shmate*, business, in Los Angeles was a prototype of Arab–Jewish cooperation and competition, with the sons of Shem partners in making everything from lingerie to evening gowns.

Settling patterns are not easy to label in Los Angeles, which has the largest geographic area of any city in the country (464 square miles for the city proper, 4,083 square miles for Los Angeles County). Early Syrians picked Pasadena with its pepper and carob trees and huge porches. Recent Palestinian immigrants favor Orange County, the most conservative county in the state. One family established a "little Ramallah" in Fountain Valley with 300 members; they all live on a cul-de-sac and work in one family business, typically enough, a large clothing store. Many Arab-American garment manufacturers, lawyers, bankers, realtors, and construction firm owners live in the San Fernando and San Gabriel valleys. Out toward Riverside there is the Druze orange grower Amil Shab.

The Los Angeles Arab-American community may well be the wealthiest, per capita, in America. From only a few hundred people in the early 1920s, the community swelled from the East Coast migration after World War II to be the largest Arab American population outside Detroit. It would produce excellence in fields as diverse as furniture making (Sam Maloof)[59] and agriculture (Robert Andrews).[60] Of course, the community's share of television and movie stars have lived here, such as Danny Thomas, Jamie Farr, Vic Tayback.

One noteworthy Beverly Hills mansion houses the voice that has been called the "most familiar, listened to" in the world. Those vocal chords belong to an American Druze named Kamal Amin Kasem, otherwise known to millions of fans across the nation as disc jockey Casey Kasem. He is a small man, about five foot six, but there the smallness ends. Casey Kasem has been reaching higher than his grasp for years. He often has converted liability to achievement. His dream as a teenager was to be a baseball player, but when he ended up striking out like Casey at the Bat, he settled for the catchy nickname. Unable to break into the kind of acting roles he had wanted from early days studying with the likes of George C. Scott in Detroit, he reached further than most actors get—with his voice. He is heard on over 1,000 radio stations around the world with the progam America's Top 40, several thousand radio and television commercial spots for 175 different companies, over 2,000 individual cartoon episodes and, recently, in the flesh, on 150 television stations with his show, America's Top 40. He even reached high in his choice for a mate— second wife Jean Kasem is a striking, statuesque blonde actress.

Presidential politics were not beyond him, either. Kasem was so taken with Jesse Jackson's presentation in 1979 at Sammy Davis, Jr.'s, home, that he contributed a hefty sum to the minister's Operation PUSH. In 1980, he asked the Reverend Jackson to officiate at his wedding to Jean, to which Jackson graciously agreed. On June 3, 1984, at his mansion, Mille Fleurs, Kasem raised $60,000 for Jesse Jackson's landmark presidential campaign—at the time the second ever of an African American (Shirley Chisholm ran in 1972).

Kasem was no stranger to politics before his Jackson leap. A registered Republican, he had contributed $70,000 to his friend Mike Curb's successful campaign for California lieutenant-governor, and also hosted a fundraiser for Reagan and Bush in 1980. But something had changed in four years, "I don't think this is the time to go with a political party. It's the time to go with someone who says what I want to hear. Because I think we're just on the brink of Armageddon."[64] What he wanted to hear was something new about the Middle East, where the town of Armageddon (Megiddo, Israel) is located. He especially wanted to hear it after his ancestral Druze homeland in Lebanon was shelled by the USS *New Jersey* in 1983.

I met Casey Kasem after he had emceed an evening under a tent near the Capitol for the National Association of Arab Americans, hosting film actors Michael Ansara (*Broken Arrow*) and Vic Tayback (*Alice*). His wife, wearing a barebacked dress, had caught a cold on the chilly night, and Casey seemed on the verge of one. But he sat for three hours with me, gracious, thoughtful, soft-spoken, with that famous voice measuring its opinion in a tone that seemed lined with fur to take off the edges. One critic said of this million-dollar treble of Kasem's: "Slightly breathless, ever so polished, anxious to please. A salesman's voice. Most importantly, it is without regional accent, thereby coming to you from everywhere and nowhere at once. Call it Americaspeak."[62]

Kasem was born in Detroit in 1932, the son of a Druze immigrant grocer from al-Moukhtara, Lebanon, whose family name was actually Konsow. Amin Kasem's wedding to an American Druze girl from Carbondale, Pennsylvania, in his home village caused a controversy as the first "modern" wedding among the Druze in the mountains in 1929. Though Amin was illiterate himself, his wedding host wrote a monograph about the unusual event, transcribing some of Amin's own thoughts. Proud of his Druze identity (which, as a schismatic sect of Islam, believes in transmigration of souls, among other things), Amin Kasem had also been to America:

> My dear brethren, you know very well that the demands of time, place, and interests do not allow a person in my situation to marry but an educated, unveiled, and sociable lady to accompany me to this modern society—a lady who does not need a veil to endow her with virtue because virtue comes from within her. God guided me to Helen Safa. She has no need for a veil. She is modern and I am modern; she is unveiled and I believe in unveiling...You don't have to give me a reply for I am departing to the country of freedom where such an ado about nothing is never heard.[63]

His father's principled stance in marrying his mother affected Casey Kasem: "If I ever through my genes inherited anything from him I think it was sort of an innate sense of honesty and integrity that he must have inherited from somebody."[64]

In Detroit's large Arab community Kasem stuck to his own Druze group of about a hundred people. Fondly, he remembered the men separating from the women, sipping coffee, and carrying on verbal one-upsmanship: "The blacks call it 'the Dozens.' In other words, if you've got a question, I've got a dozen answers. Well, the Arabs had that going for them with poetry."

Kasem has acknowledged that the "familiarity" of his voice gives him, in a sense, great power: "Words are like weapons bouncing around in the brain of a vulnerable listener. I could be lethal if I weren't responsible."[65] Kasem surprised me by saying that when he started out he didn't particularly like any variety of music and didn't appreciate rock and roll until he learned to dance to it in 1958. He had never formed his own personal "Top Ten" but said that one tune he is sentimentally attached to is "With You I'm Born Again," by Bill

Preston, played at his wedding to Jean.

The dark-skinned Kasem said he always felt growing up that he was different, although he "was never led to feel anything but pride for my heritage and religion." He grew up in a neighborhood with Jews, and in the army a black man called him a Jew: "I didn't argue with him. I let him think that I was Jewish because I already had a feeling for the sensitivities of a minority group. I never did sit comfortably with ethnic jokes."

"I don't think there's a man or woman anywhere in the history of my career in broadcasting who would ever be able to say that they have ever heard me say anything negative about Jews. But they have heard me say that our foreign policy with regards to the Middle East is imbalanced, always has been, and that the rest of the world doesn't think like the United States does. So I think that's one of the reasons that I was able—perhaps like nobody in show business before—to back a man like Jesse Jackson in a community where there's half a million Jews. I think I got one nasty letter."

Kasem's left leg bounced as nervously as a drummer's while he probed his feelings about the Middle East. He plowed forward: "There is no time left. If people don't get involved, then we may all be incinerated. And the key to solving the nuclear problem is to eliminate the fuse where it is the shortest—the Middle East."

His solution was simple; he said: "The Israelis must realize they have to go back to the 1967 boundaries. Once the United States realizes that we're heading for a nuclear catastrophe if we don't solve the problems in the Middle East, I think they will have to force the Israelis, economically, to see in terms of justice." Kasem began, finally, to tire, but was certain that in time the Middle East equation would change: "A hundred years from today the Jews and the Arabs will be like the Germans, Japanese, and Americans today."

Many Los Angelenos, like Kasem, tend to be more politically involved in the Middle East problems than are their New York City counterparts. Some, such as the Mickools of Chatsworth, the Ajalats of La Canada, and the Awads of La Canada-Flintridge, reached out in adopting Lebanese orphans.[66]

I was on Thatee's porch another day—but a rainy one—when she came and urged me to come inside, that I would catch cold. When I pleaded with her that I was used to the misty cold after years in the East, she relented and brought me a blanket, with a bowl of *kibba má'a kishk* (meatball with bulgur and sour milk).

A call came from an aunt: I should really see Joe Jacobs since I was in Pasadena. The owner of the Jacobs Engineering Group, Inc., an émigré from the Brooklyn community in California like my mother's family, instantly agreed. I was lucky to catch him in the state, much less the country.

Dr. Joseph Jacobs, a Maronite born in Brooklyn in 1919, was just putting the finishing touches on what the World Bank has described as the finest manufacturing endeavor of its kind in the Middle East—the Arab Potash plant in Jordan. The old Palestine Potash company, built in 1928, had been destroyed during the 1948 war. Thirty-five years later, the son of a Lebanese immigrant peddler was helping to restore what, in a sense, had been wrecked by forces America had sided with. It was a project, he admitted, in which he had a deep emotional investment.

Jacobs was a marvelous combination of the straight-talking Brooklynite and the carefully wrought product of academia. He also had a knack for sales and management—his company is 35,000 employees strong, with sixty offices in over a dozen countries. Judging from the animated way he described his father's experience in America, dating back to arrival at Ellis Island in 1886, there was no doubt he felt gratitude for the perseverance of his forebear. His acceptance speech of an award from the respected engineering Newcomen Society both begins and ends with praise to his father.[67]

His father, Yusef Ibn Ya'qub, fled Beirut and "the oppression of the Ottoman Turks" after he strangled a Turkish officer in a fit of temper. Jacobs pointed to two traits his father imbued in him that he traced back to the Phoenicians—a knack for trading and standing by one's word. Ya'qub was changed to Jacobs at Ellis Island, and the immigrant soon traded his notions case for his own shop.

For a period during World War I, any American male who got up in the morning and stared at his unshaven mug in the mirror owed his deliverance to Yusef Ibn Ya'qub Jacobs, who had a virtual monopoly on the manufacture of straight razors when those imported from Germany were cut off by war.

What was ease for the consumer after the war—the invention of the safety razor—broke Yusef Jacobs; other attempts at business left him a casualty of the Depression, the son's voice choking at the memory. Yet Jacobs converted his father's fall and efforts to stand up—as did many firstborn Americans at the time—into a lesson. On his desk is a sign, "Babe Ruth Struck Out 1,330 Times." He also attributed something of his father's daring to cross the seas to his own restless compulsion to leave for California: "I guess what I sort of imprinted on my mind was that with a little courage, and a little guts, one can find new worlds to conquer and I guess it was a subtle psychological way of emulating my father."[68]

Jacobs married Violet Jabara, a relative of the famed ace pilot Jimmy Jabara, and for a while worked for Merck & Company in the development of new processes for making Vitamins B and C, as well as penicillin and DDT. A chance offer to work for a firm in

California had him traveling to San Francisco in 1944. It fit his own restlessness: "Otherwise I would have done what 95 percent of my close friends in those days did—that is, stay in the Lebanese-American community of Brooklyn."

Jacobs finally went out on his own, setting up Jacobs Engineering Company in Pasadena, and soon he was building plants for Southwest Potash (now AMAX) and Kaiser Aluminum. In 1974, the company was merged with the Pace Companies of Houston to form Jacobs Engineering Group, Inc., which today grosses $5 billion a year.

Jacobs identified a sociocultural reason for the lack of progress in the Middle East peace: "The Jews have never been victors. They have always been oppressed, so they didn't know how to handle victory. Very few countries have learned how to handle power; the Israelis haven't. And they threw away an opportunity in 1967. They could have secured a just and lasting peace, if they had reached down their hand and lifted up the Arabs and brushed them off." Instead, he said, the Israelis were trying to make the Arabs "negotiate from their knees" and showed no sensitivity to restoring some dignity to their defeat.

By the same token, he felt that Arab righteousness was leading nowhere: "There is an Arab trait that says, look, if I can have an argument with you and I can convince you logically that I am right, therefore I am right. And the whole world will recognize it. And we all have this tendency to say, 'Can't anyone see how we have been unjustly treated, driven out of our homes?' It's almost the same thing that happened to the Jews in Germany. Why doesn't the world have sympathy for us? And the fact of the matter is, the world couldn't care less. How the hell are we going to compete with the Jews who have done it for 2,000 years? The Jewish lobby is absolutely aces at playing at those guilt feelings."

Jacobs had friends in high places in the GOP, and he embodied the phrase "compassionate conservative" long before George W. Bush used it. The high-level gathering of Jewish and Arab-American businessmen that Najeeb Halaby had told me about, which included Occidental Petroleum's then president, Robert Abboud, was hosted privately by Jacobs at his home for a weekend. "I'm the perennial optimist," he said. "I keep hoping. People can't live with a garrison mentality forever, building up hatred on both sides."

Pink-faced, blond hair whitened, with blue eyes, Jacobs nodded bemusement that he was often taken for a Jew, especially with his last name. When asked if his Arab background had helped him in business, he retorted, "Surprisingly, in my dealings with the Arab world, it has hindered me more than helped." He referred to the endless waiting game that Gulf states would play with him—"a way of sort of getting back at Americans"—and he didn't deal with Saudi Arabia for that reason. At his project in Jordan, even, there were practices, like petty bribery at lower levels, that bothered him: "We won't tolerate it. It's hard being an American of Arab background to know that those things don't have to be that way and having to put up with that garbage." He also looked critically on the tendency of some Arabs not to delegate authority successfully, or to "talk a problem to death," lacking decisiveness. "We want to get on with it and get it done as Americans," he said.

In 2004, Jacobs died. In a eulogy distributed to the employees of his company, his successor CEO Noel Watson drew attention to Jacobs's own elucidation of his cherished principles: "pride without arrogance; professionalism without being hidebound; integrity without self-righteousness; daring without foolhardiness."

Los Angeles potato king Amean Haddad agreed with Jacobs about Lebanese thriving more after they'd taken to the road away from their drum-tight communities, though Haddad was speaking of Lebanon rather than Brooklyn: "Why they can't get along with their own in their own country, where they were born, has been a mystery. Because it shouldn't be—the first love is in the town in which you are born; therefore, it should accumulate love and interest and friendship. They cannot get rich in their own hometown, but they go to any country and they make success."[69] Haddad rubbed his bronzed forehead, leathered by decades out in the sun of the San Joaquin Valley where his workers dug up potatoes that supplied Safeway stores with half their stock. "That teaches me one thing, that they have it in them, but they are either afraid to hurt someone [of their own] in getting successful… I don't know what it is. I cannot give you the answer."

Born in 1902, Amean Haddad was one of the pillars of the original Los Angeles community, one of its oldest, most successful members, and one of the earliest to have come to California, in 1920. On arrival he worked as a butcher in Los Angeles, the same trade that allowed him to save enough money to come to America. Tired out, one ate a lot to sustain energy, and it was at a restaurant with his kid brother who wanted nothing but potatoes that Haddad realized everybody else was eating potatoes, too. "I want to be in a business everybody needs," he concluded, and soon he became a potato farmer, with fields in four western states, though he consolidated his farms to Oregon and Bakersfield. Haddad called his workers "quality people" and, like Haggar, preferred a family approach to the unions: "I'm a great believer in one thing. I like it to be open. And I'm a great believer in freedom. You can choose your friends and your business relations, but you can't choose your relatives."

Vital and active as an octogenarian can be, Haddad attributed this to his heritage and, of course, to potatoes. He then handed me his

Amean Haddad (front) inspects a water pump at one of his Bakersfield farms in 1945. (Amean and Wydea Haddad)

business card, a folded photo of a russet potato, a strain he helped develop. Inside the fold was a list of nutrients. A most unusual card—but perhaps not so much for one who had almost starved to death. I suddenly had a craving for french fries, but Amean Haddad reminded me that he does not sell to McDonald's and produces a potato only for boiling and baking.

Haddad told me a story close to his heart, an experience when at age nine he was taking water at a well with his grandfather in the desert between the Lebanon mountains and Syria. Because he had "a clean set of brains," he said the event had stuck in his mind:

> We saw dust from far away. Out of the dust came horseback riders. The leader was a man in middle age and the rest younger men, maybe 40 or 50 of them, to take on water. My grandfather became inquisitive. "Who may you be?" he asked. The man said he was Mohammed Assam, and the other riders were his sons. He was a Matawila [Lebanese Shi'ite Muslim]. My grandfather asked, "Do you love one more than the others?" The man replied, "Yes and no. I love the one more who is far away from us until he comes back, and I love the sick one more until he gets well.

The circle was closing. I sat on the porch again, shaded from the strong sunlight, gazing out at Thatee's thick grass, how it dipped in one place. It was there that Uncle Gary, when barely old enough to talk, felt the earth withdraw below him and found himself clinging to a precipice. The earth had fallen twenty feet into a cesspool. How little Gary had the gumption to hold onto the thick grass hovering at the top above a stinking black shaft is a mystery, as mysterious as why the Lebanese prosper only far away from home, as Amean Haddad had said. Gary has always held on; the community, too, has always held on, propelled by some gaping, stinking hole of the past. Gary's sensible crying finally roused Thatee, who rescued him, as she had rescued so many, instinctively. Did she see in a blurring second her younger brothers crying out before they expired from hunger? She fairly leapt from the porch. It was all written up in the *Pasadena Star News*. They filled the cesspool with boulders, but a slight dip remained, which I used to walk on as a child, testing it.

Testing… I lay back on the cool, faded pillows of the porch's couch and closed my eyes. What was it that joined the disparate lives of the three men I had just interviewed? It wasn't religion—Casey Kasem was a Druze; Joe Jacobs, a Maronite; Amean Haddad, an Orthodox. They were of different generations, Kasem and Jacobs firstborn Americans, Haddad a First Wave immigrant. Their chosen fields couldn't have been more different—radio broadcasting, chemical engineering, potato farming. They began their lives in America in three different cities: Detroit, Brooklyn, Los Angeles. Though Kasem and Jacobs were clearly haunted by the conflict in the Middle East, Haddad was not; he was the stoic. Perhaps he spoke for many of the First Wave when he related stories of a living hell that made the Arab–Israeli conflict pale. He had suffered everything a man can suffer and still survive in this world before there was ever a Palestine issue. About the only surface thing they shared was success, and an ancestral past traced to Lebanon.

Still, there were peddlers in all their backgrounds, though Kasem's father eventually set up a grocery, and Jacobs' a razor blade manufacturing plant, and Haddad himself a butcher shop and later potato farms. And they themselves in their various ways set out in early days to try to grasp what appeared beyond their grasp, to confront the unknown, Kasem bringing his voice to millions out of the milieu of a grocery store; Jacobs pulling away from the Depression and his dying father, to probe the atoms of chemicals; Haddad fleeing starvation only to dig relentlessly for potatoes that would feed America. Kasem and Jacobs were still not satisfied; they had reached back to the fire of the Middle East as if to an original scar, to try to heal it. Testiness, perhaps, they shared.

One could cite their obvious love of family and pride in heritage, too, except these accepted virtues of the Arab Americans were revealed on close inspection to be fraught with ambivalence. It was not Haddad's closeness to his parents that spurred him forward, but his absence from them. He had also drawn the line in dealing in business with his fellow Arabs, as if the well of feeling between them would drown them. Jacobs had admitted—as did many firstborn Americans—of being embarrassed by his family's "difference," trying himself to be American pure and simple; in later years, when he found himself restoring a factory destroyed in the first Arab–Israeli war, it was not so simple. The need to help was urgent; but the imprint of American pragmatism distanced him from certain things in Arab culture that he could not accept or understand. However courageous, Kasem's backing of Jesse Jackson and public criticism of US Mideast policy were, he admitted himself, recent phenomena.

Yet they spoke to me as if speaking for the first time about things that had lain heavily on their hearts for years, as if, in the context of a book with others of the community that spanned the country, they could participate in a kind of national voice. Though all prominent, it was as if each had a cache of secret sorrows held too long, too tightly, fighting off what for years had seemed a natural reticence to discuss controversy or adversity, that nefarious fear of ʿayb (shame) that Naff identified as part of the traditional Arab psyche. I could not say that my project brought something out in them that wasn't ready to come out. It had always been there, waiting, shared perhaps among friends and associates, but hesitant, perhaps, that there was no public forum that would or even should care.

All the immigrants and their children I had met and talked with rushed through my mind. Was there a quintessential Arab-American spirit? What could be culled as the nugget that would sidestep stereotype when in fact the community was as diverse as the human spirit itself?

In their candor, in their courage, these people who farmed in North Dakota or labored in Detroit's auto factories, voted in the halls of Congress or stitched together dresses, had shown that ultimately their relation to their heritage was one of ambivalence, of strong love, but of almost as strong puzzlement and even disdain. It seemed to me now—though my mind was barely clearing in the wind on Thatee's porch—that their virtues implied their faults, that each was the flip side of the other and had both lifted them up and held them back in America.

Cached in their ancient pride was a deference that had helped them assimilate so successfully in American society that they were rarely identifiable by ancestry (Italian? Spanish? Greek? Jewish?). Odd as it seems to assert today in the post-9/11 world, they had become the "new man" the American republic promised. At the same time, this "quick melt" had kept them politically distant from one another and the seats of power. They were not often complainers or critics even if their complaints or criticisms were legitimate. Their industriousness was born of want, or even, as the recent Palestinian and Lebanese immigrants showed, of futility. Their verve for life was the other side of temper, their gregariousness the other side of an acute sense of solitude brought on by—who knows?—millennia of life eked out in empty spaces, forbidding mountains, the clutch of empire, or now in a wary America they had long held dear. They cherished relatedness as one clings to green shoots in a desert. But their extraordinary love and nurturing of family had in some ways kept them isolated and resistant to change and the adjustments that love teaches. (Given the community's deep religious roots, some undoubtedly would say there are adjustments—to drugs, to free sex—love would do better not to teach.) In fact, America had magnified their individuality and their love of family—two at times opposing forces—with the result that both were reaching a critical mass in the community, mirroring a similar volatility in the society at large.

Though they were, as Vicksburg's Mayme Farris had put it, "clannish," and never learned to "wine and dine" the powerful, they had a native internationalism that often countered American provincialism. It was, after all, the stifling provincialism of those mountain Lebanese villages or West Bank towns under military occupation that made so many of them immigrate in the first place.

After all my travels, the central paradox of the Arab Americans still stood: they could be so exceptionally individual and yet so collectively anonymous. However fecund they found American values of self-reliance, with notable exceptions—Ralph Nader, the Monsour brothers of Pittsburgh, Sammie Abbott,[70] for example—they often stopped short of dissent. They took to Thoreau's pond, but not his jail.

No doubt, as I mentioned at the start, the heritage of the benevolent stranger, the protected one, that Abraham Rihbany had noted early in the century in Lebanon, had something to do with it. One was better off remaining a bit "strange," unidentifiable, elusive, for to be labeled in the feudalistic Middle East of the 19th century was inherit all of a sect's enemies. Better the "no partialities," as Charlie Juma had found in Ross, North Dakota, or Mama Ayesha's exclamation, "Everybody in America is my child!"

There were, to be sure, political reasons for their cloistering of culture, for their preference of the sideless stranger. Both in the Old Country, and in the new land at the start of a new century their names, or accents, or opinions, or memories could immediately link them to a world marked Terrorist. September 11 and the Patriot Act had turned the benevolent stranger more malevolent. It was one thing to be considered strange, a stranger; but it was quite another to be considered the embodiment of evil. Better to be a stranger, to stand back, to stand away.

Yet undeniably—Taxi Joe with his Rhode Island jay-bird laugh, Aziz Shihab with his midnight walk through Dallas, Bill Ezzy sewing up his tent holes in Alaska—they stood out. The barriers through which venerable journalist Helen Thomas rather naturally broke serve as prominent examples of something revealed to me time and again. They liked obstacles. And when you overcome obstacles, whether you like it or not, you stand out. They did not indulge in self-analysis the way Freud would define it. Yet they were curious, even driven, to speculate about the world outside. Self-knowledge often came to them through macrocosm, not infinitesimal self-scrutiny, but through the plentitude of experience. Their eyes were on the tapestry's whole, not the corner where the deer is bleeding to death. It made for survival, not art, at least as art had come to be known in America: a magnification of self to the point of burning.

But something inside them did burn, else why would so many have spoken to me with such little reserve? Perhaps the time had come. The self—after a hundred years in America—was ready to assert its presence as a self, and as something more. It did not surprise me at times that this brought exhaustion, even pain. The old fears of backlash, of losing Jewish customers or backing, of hatred, of judgment, of misjudgment were there. But what surprised me was that this assertion came with such gusts of freedom, or relief. The time had come for speaking as an American to Americans about what it was like to be in this remarkable, sad, hopeful, strange, disturbing land as part of a community with ancestral veins that could trace back to the cradle of civilization. They would risk not being strangers. Out of, what? Pride, self-assuredness, accomplishment, a sense of emergency, defeat, mortality, the pure passage of time. Or now, post-9/11, from outrage and an unabating anxiety. But if one was going to be pulled out anyway, invisibility was no longer an option. Better to pull yourself out and say, like Whitman: *Here I am.*

"Hurry, *ya'ayni*. We have to go see Auntie Hisson before Uncle Mike and Uncle Assad come!" It was Thatee's lilting voice breaking through my thoughts. The circle was closing. I got up to go down the street with her.

Hisson (Helen) Arbeely Dalool was for many years the closest surviving relative of the original Arab immigrant family to America (the Arbeelys) in 1878. Dr. Ibrahim Arbeely's wife had been at Auntie Hisson's son's wedding some years back, but they'd lost touch. There is some evidence that Ibrahim Arbeely is buried in Glendora.

Hisson came over on the boat to America with an aunt and uncle and settled on the legendary Washington Street near the wharf across from Ellis Island. Ibrahim Arbeely, who lived then in Washington, DC, was a frequent guest at her home. Arbeely even took little Hisson and other cousins to an orphanage in New York to sing for the children.

It seems that Hisson's visit to America was spurred by her husband-to-be's proposal to make her his bride; he sent the tickets for her trip, having only to wait for her to grow up! The aunt she came over with was detained in Marseilles with trachoma, and then was sent back to Syria. After a seasick journey when they put her in the captain's room, Hisson landed at Pawtucket, Rhode Island, on Christmas Day and was escorted to New York by her husband-to-be. "He used to take me shopping!" Hisson reminisced. "When I used to go with him, they would say, my father!"[71] Hisson's marriage to Khalil Dalool brought nine children into the world, seven still surviving when we talked.

Hisson and her husband ran the Courtland Hotel on Washington Street, and she worked cleaning out the rooms, changing the beds, the linens, for new immigrants and others. Later, they had another hotel on Midland Beach in Staten Island. She was, in fact, married at the Courtland Hotel by Father Nicholas Kherbawi, the legendary Orthodox priest of the Washington Street community.

In a romantic way, Hisson played a part in my grandmother Matile's young marriage to Kamel Awad, and she related a story I had heard many times growing up. Kamel actually lived with the Dalools in Brooklyn, and he petitioned Hisson for help when he fell in love with a beautiful fifteen-year-old who was the sister of his employer, Mike Malouf. Hisson hired the taxi that skirted Thatee away from the Maloufs to a train to Plainfield, New Jersey, to Mike's great anger. Hisson's brother-in-law Nageeb Dalool was the young couple's best man.

I piped up, recalling our trip to Arbeen in 1972, "Well, if it wasn't for Jaddu, I probably wouldn't even be writing this book."

"He got your momma!" Thatee sang from her tears.

Hisson visited California in 1946, disenchanted with the neighborhood where she kept furnished rooms on State Street in Brooklyn—it was getting run down and she had trouble collecting rent from the Puerto Ricans. By 1950, she had settled in Pasadena: "It's a cleaner life here. But people are distant; they are not as close as they are in New York. There we were like one happy family. In the summertime, sitting on the stoops."

Religion, as with many oldsters, was sunk in her bones as was the secret to longevity: "It's no secret, dear. It's all in the hands of the Lord. Every word in my mouth is nothing but the Lord."

Up the steps of Thatee's porch chugged Great-uncle Mike Malouf and his brother-in-law Assad Roum, the last immigrant patriarchs of our family, two pillars of the Los Angeles community, their faith in America as constant as Mike's unswerving allegiance to Buicks. He had stayed with Buick for decades, the three holes on the car's side growing narrower each year.

Mike Malouf, 80, ex-boxer, race-car driver, auto repairman, and realtor, was built solid, with a neck so thick it strained his collar. His handshake scared away many a young man and some older ones; even as we met he pulled me to the ground with his clasp, laughing silently, as was his fashion. Uncle Mike had the unnerving habit of grabbing you by the neck in what appeared to be an affectionate hold, only to pinch you like a vise. He made even my father yelp.

Uncle Assad Roum was a smaller man, with thick glasses and an endearing smile that caused his whole face to turn upward and his eyes to sparkle. His voice was not as strong as Mike's, but was tender. He greeted me with one of a thousand terms of Arab endearment, one special to him, however: "*Kifak ba'di* [How are you, part of me]?" We all moved into the dining room to feast under Thatee's large chandelier. And to talk.

Assad was orphaned before he was ten years old. His mother had contracted typhus in Arbeen, but she died in a freak accident when, bending dizzy over a well to take water with her medicine, she fell into it. She was dead when they pulled her out. "She musta died before she fell," Assad thought. As for his father, the end was no less apocalyptic. After his wife died, he had a nightmare where he, too, was approaching water, from a bridge, and lost his shoe in the stream. Later, during the fruit-picking season, he went to harvest apricots, olives, almonds, and walnuts at a big farm outside Arbeen. Assad watched his father being taunted by some workers as he knocked the almonds free with a long pole. But he lost his balance and fell and hit his head on the ground. "He gets down there, he talks nonsense," Assad ruminated.[72] His father soon after died in 1914.

After the war, Assad had a ticket to go to America and asked Kamel Awad if he'd like to come. "No," Grandfather said. But Assad, his cousin, convinced him to try his luck. If they had made it six miles from Arbeen to Damascus, why not go six thousand to New York? Their tickets cost two gold pounds each—about $15—to go from Damascus to New York and they boarded a steamship in Beirut. Along with them was an orphan girl, Mary Mazawi, raised by Muslims. Avoiding steerage, hoisting blankets, they slept on the poop deck. Assad described deadpan the Spanish- or Italian-speaking examining officer at Ellis Island:

"Kamel Awad. *Bono.* Mary Mazawi. *Bono.* Assad Roum. *No bono!*" Assad had to stay at Ellis Island until the eye inflammation he had from a cold subsided. He was comforted, however, by Dr. Salim Barbari, who had replaced the deceased Dr. Nageeb Arbeely as chief Arabic-speaking inspector at the island. When they arrived in New York, they met their distinguished ancestor Dr. Ibrahim Arbeely at the Courtland Hotel; he was to die within months.

Assad and Kamel moved across the Brooklyn Bridge to live with Auntie Hisson on 25th Street downtown and commuted to Bonnaz Embroidery on Harrison Street, run by Joseph Azar, doing pleating and stitching. Soon they saved enough money to buy five embroidery machines from a Syrian making kimonos and founded their first business in America, Pyramid Embroidery. Assad remembered with delight carrying his embroideries on the subway to deliver them. Slowly, by reading the newspaper, English seeped into the tongues. They made a card for their new business, located on 177 Court Street in Brooklyn. It was 1926.

But it was in that sweatshop hunched over embroidery machines that Jaddu's asthma worsened. He even took a trip back to Syria in the twenties to consult with doctors there. They urged him to return for good, that the dry, hot clime would help his breathing. He was in Damascus when my mother, Rose, was born on Henry Street above a candy store (later she would grow up above the funeral parlor). But Kamel was troubled by the turmoil in the country over the uprising against the French at the time and, missing his family and the life in America, came back, facing his asthma. Assad watched Kamel labor on the embroidery machine. "He used to get lotta attack. He's fainting on the machine, *ya haram*. Breathing harder!" The memory made Assad's eyes moist.

His deteriorating lungs and the Depression, devastating effects on their business, made Kamel begin thinking of going to California. Meanwhile, Assad and his three single brothers were beginning to hunger for the settled life. They had been cared for in America by their sister, Wardi (who later married Mike Malouf). In 1937, Assad went back to Syria after seventeen years in America, on an invitation from an uncle who wanted to match him up with his cousin Nora, who had been all of six years old when Assad had originally left Damascus. His relatives met him in Beirut, and he proudly showed them the cabins of the ship and let them be awed by something they had never seen. He was also welcomed by Ibrahim Arbeely's sister, who was teaching at AUB; she greeted him, "*Wayn al-ʿarus* [Where's the bride]?" Finally, the caravan of taxis left for Damascus.

Uncle Assad took out his handkerchief in describing his wife-to-be: "I love her very much on first sight. I first think I like her too because she was my first cousin. And other thing, she a beautiful lady, a wonderful girl. I got a life of my life! Forty-six years!" Sadly, Assad had recently become a widower.

On May 22, 1948, the Maloufs, Roums, and Awads packed into cars to head west. "We always say we wish we had come straight here to Los Angeles instead of New York," Assad raised his hands, elated.

"It used to be a most beautiful country," Assad reminisced about his life in America. "No fear, you safe. You used to leave, go on vacation, no problem. Today you can't trust yourself to walk on the streets at night. Even day time! That's the difference. You can't trust anybody today. There was a lady neighbor of mine who found a sick man in the car. It turned out to be a woman!"

Regarding the chaos in the Middle East and the Arab–Israeli war, Assad Roum could only contrast the enmity with the warm relations between Arab and Jew in the Syria of his youth: "We have Jews in Damascus; my brother Nick, he was mixing too much [honorifically "a lot"]. We invited about twenty Jewish girls from Damascus to Arbeen. They even ate Arab foods with us, not kosher. Musa Zaga, the Jewish shoe-maker, helped put this party together. We never think there was any division."

Mike Malouf wanted to know where I stayed in Brooklyn to do my interviews. Eddie Baloutine's house, but once at the Hotel Gregory, a real dive. Everybody laughed, but Mike said it was once the best hotel in Brooklyn. As a realtor who had thoroughly worked the Wilshire district between Vermont and Western in Los Angeles, he knew something about the deterioration: "I started real-estate work in the 1950s here near the Ambassador Hotel. All I used to smell is perfume, and I says, 'Gee, there are nice people living over there. We've got to buy this building. We go in there, check the building—oh, used to be glorious, beautiful!' Everybody gets beautiful linens, maid service, everything. Today, you walk over there, you get a doghouse."[73]

Deterioration wasn't the word for the Lebanon mountains closed tight by the blockade of Beirut harbor by the Allies during World War I. Uncle Mike lost three brothers to the war, two from starvation. He has often told me a story about how he hauled a chandelier they had bought from a monastery for two gold pounds up over the mountains for food, a story I turned into fiction.[74] But his memories about this tragic time seemed bottomless. This day he told me a number of incidents I had never heard before. He mentioned the devastation wrought in Lebanon by a six-foot-deep trench dug by the Turks from Beirut twenty-five miles to the Lebanon mountains: "If your house is in the way, down it goes. Don't mean nothing. You can't say nothing. If the trenches go that way, down it goes."

Mike got a job during the war with a Turkish captain, who asked him to take care of donkeys. The captain, a tall, imposing man, was wining and dining two young women in Beirut and gave Mike one gold pound to buy a bag of oats to feed the donkeys. "I saw one gold pound and I went crazy," he laughed. "I'm going to feed the *himar* oats? So I started getting some grass for him. And I kept the money and start going enjoying myself with the gold pound. Bought bananas, bought food. I wanna eat, not the *himar*! So on the way back the Turkish officer asked, 'Did you feed them good?' 'Sure,' I said. 'He ate very, very good.' On the way up the mountain, instead of him riding the *himar*, he had to push him to go up!"

Shortly after his brush with postwar "justice" (he was arrested for accidentally knifing a man with a tobacco shearing blade), Mike and his family arranged papers to come to America. "When I get on that ship, I look back at Beirut from the deck and I said, 'I never want to see this country again! The people, the country, and everything that's in it!'" he bellowed, as if reliving the humiliation and anger and sorrow. Thatee, of course, came with him.

I began to total up the reasons for my four grandparents coming to America: Matile Malouf came from starvation and war; Kamel Awad, from poverty; Aref Orfalea, from Homs, Syria, I had heard, for sheer opportunity; Nazera Jabaly, from Zahle, Lebanon, because her mother had abandoned the family. Starvation, poverty, opportunity, abandonment—these were the seeds that bloomed into the pungent flowers of my family in America.

It was a day of full spring; the sun could not have been higher, water lapped any more fervently by the roots. My father, out of work for five years following the demise of his million-dollar garment manufacturing business in the late 1970s, wanted to come with me that day to visit the Yemeni farmworkers in Delano. He volunteered to drive. I got off the porch, kissed Thatee goodbye, and entered his Mercury. It was the first trip we would take alone together since I was a boy commuting with him on summer days to the dress factory in downtown Los Angeles. It had been twenty years since we shared a front seat on a highway, and he would put on the news, turn it off, smoke, tell me about yardage, turnbacks, larcenous salesmen, and his brilliant new "line." Only now do I realize that in those summers I was my father's sounding board for such ideas as the granny dress.

Those hot days the freeway was always rush hour; we developed a bond in that sluggish traffic. Now, we were headed north on Route 5 in late morning, and the road was clear, the windows open. Dad as eager as I to meet the Yemenis. We could have driven to heaven!

The Yemenis laboring in the California farmlands are among the most recent Arab immigrants to America. Working from dawn to dusk (and often afterward, under a spotlight) harvesting the early asparagus, row crops, stone fruits, and grapes, they are in some ways the most unusual arrivals, as well.[75] Unique in that they are the only numbers of people from the Arabian Peninsula to settle in the United States, the Yemenis came for a reason that Saudi Arabians, for instance, would never have: poverty. Yemen is among the poorest countries in the world, separated from the oil kingdoms by a sharp mountain range and empty desert. Even after a decade of unexpected oil revenue, by 2004, 35 percent of the country was unemployed, industry and services accounted for less than 25 percent of jobs in Yemen, and the annual gross domestic product per capita was $800. Most work is subsistence farming for cotton and coffee. Average life expectancy for Yemen was 61 years, and only half of all Yemenis are literate.

Yemenis, astride the historic sealanes between the Mediterranean Sea and the Indian Ocean, have a tradition of wandering far from home, not unlike the Lebanese. It has been estimated that two-thirds of Yemeni males live outside Yemen. Unlike the Lebanese, however, the Yemenis tend to stay in transit—although a TWA representative in Los Angeles listed 100,000 airlifted from Yemen to California in the period 1965–1975; by 1983, Ahmed Shaibi, a Yemeni labor leader, estimated about 6,000 working in the San Joaquin Valley. Passage back and forth to Yemen is frequent, often occurring yearly after the harvests. Only a few have taken US citizenship.

My father and I pulled into Delano, a small farming town about 125 miles north of Los Angeles in the heart of the San Joaquin Valley. We were greeted at the spare office on the dusty main street of Delano by Ahmed Shaibi, a former grape picker, unionizer with Cesar Chavez, and then ADC representative for the Yemenis in the valley. Shaibi, a stout, friendly man in his thirties, introduced us to two other Yemeni workers, one disabled, Mike Shaw (once Mohammed E. Shaibi), and one out of work, Kassem Shaibi. Shaw wore the Arab *hatta* under his cap to shade his neck from the sun.

Ahmed came to the United States through New York eleven years before. He had been the unusual migrant who had been to college (in Southern Yemen), but he also sought economic opportunity and adventure. The very first day in California he was picking grapes at the Zaninovich farm: "It was very, very hard for me. I said if I stay in Yemen, was better."[76] When he saw the squalid conditions in the twelve Yemeni camps, Shaibi decided to join Chavez to help Yemenis. But in 1982, he left the UFW, disillusioned. "They are not pushing for the Yemenis as much," Ahmed said. "They are pushing for the Mexicans. I call that discrimination, and I talk to them about that and they blame it on the Yemeni workers. They said they didn't stand up for the union. I know they did when the union was very strong. But now they are scared from the UFW; they are scared from the growers." We toured the Yemeni camp in the fields, discovering blackened toilets, deckings of rotted wood in the showers, mold lining the dirty latrines and sleeping quarters.

One morning, hauling heavy crates of steel needles to tie up grape vines, Mike Shaw's back went out. His life for the next two years became a frustrating cycle of being denied workman's compensation and unemployment insurance. And Shaw himself was now persona non grata: "If you're injured more than one month, you're out," he said.[77]

Ahmed translated Kassem's Arabic: "Thirteen years ago with the Vietnam war he was sleeping in his motel room, not even looking for a job. The union went into his bedroom and woke him up [to work in the shipyards] because most of the young boys, they run away because they don't want to get to Vietnam. Right now he lost 90 days and he have a reason."[78] Father said, "They wanted him then, when they needed him. They won't accept him now." Ahmed and Kassem nodded their heads in agreement. Father took a drag off his cigarette. Mike Shaw adjusted his *hatta*.

We toured one of the Yemeni camps with Ahmed with his two unemployed friends. For a second I felt a flashback of having done this when viewing the Palestinian refugee camps a decade before with Dad; but these people had come by choice, and this squalor was in California.

Saying goodbye, my father thought it was "very important" that the Yemenis meet with the growers, too, to defuse the situtation of resentment, to table all matters. Ahmed Shaibi said that was a good idea. And they saluted us and waved, Mike Shaw's *hatta* rising in the dust our tires kicked up. I think they liked the fact that we were there, father and son, and interested in them. Yet our worlds seemed so far apart.

Were they? Driving down Main Street of Delano, I noticed Dad was slowing progress, as if he didn't want to leave. "Look at that!" he pointed, cutting an astonished grin. It was a Mode O'Day store, one he himself had opened up for the Malouf family chain when he worked for them in the late 1940s and early 1950s. The product of one young man's initiative 30 years before might today be selling dresses to a Yemeni for his Mexican girlfriend or his wife at home. He had planted a little seed before anyone in Delano even knew what a Yemeni was or he had thought of himself as "Arab American."

The incongruity of it all made him laugh softly to himself as we pulled onto the main highway, traveling south in a dusky light. He had gone on in 1952 to start his own dress manufacturing firm and, in the space of 25 years in that industry, reach its pinnacle, being named vice-president of the prestigious California Fashion Creators.

But he closed Mr. Aref of California in 1978 for a host of reasons—financial losses, attrition from bad salesmen, the recession, the inability to relocate his plant in cheaper overseas places like Hong Kong, not to mention his own nagging exhaustion with the grueling pace of a dress manufacturer who must restyle a product line five times a year.

I say he had been unemployed for five years, but this is not quite true. Father tried everything to seek a new path: starting a new company to computerize piece goods inventories, working for other manufacturers. Perhaps what was hardest to tolerate was suddenly not being one's own boss, and knowing that at age 60 with no college education—though with a wealth of management experience—his options were limited and closing by the day. He sent out hundreds of résumés, telling me he had never before used one. When I ghost-wrote one for him, he acquiesced silently.

I watched him sell his cars, his Harley Davidson motorcycle, trying to lose himself fixing things around the house. Mother for the first time in her life took work outside, at a menswear plant, at the University of Judaism. It was very painful to watch this vital man who was wounded fighting in World War II as a paratrooper, who had traveled the length of America establishing sales offices at merchandise marts, reduced to wandering, muttering incoherently to himself, in the front yard.

Perhaps he understood the Yemeni workers. I marveled later, going over the interviews, how he asked just the right questions with sincere interest and respect for them, a secret sharer of my project, steering me toward economy and perceptions I would have missed. I recalled as we drove in silence with the sun just touching the crag of the Sierras how generous he had been with his own workers. It always seemed he hired the kind of people who would have trouble finding work elsewhere: a black shipper with a cleft palate; two apprentice Mexican cutters who barely spoke English; a French designer with a hunchback; an Eastern European Jewish bookkeeper who was 70 and supporting his invalid brother; a Chinese picker.

And though he was demanding and had a temper, he treated them all with respect; many stayed on to the bitter end, not wanting to leave him. He was not physically debilitated like Mike Shaw. But he was out of work, too, and he was beginning to know what it

Aref Isper Orfalea, Sr., the original linen merchant in Cleveland, Ohio, stands in the late 1920s in his Avenue Gift Shop on Euclid Avenue. (Rose Orfalea)

meant to touch bottom with one's enthusiasm and ability unused, discarded. He was on disability—the disability of a multinational capitalist economy increasingly indifferent to the small businessman, to the needs of the aging, fixed on academic "credentials," the card of a man rather than his vital essence.

My father, more than anyone else in my family, also had felt the injustice of America's Middle East policy for years; his empathy was never more evident than when, after visiting the Palestinian refugee camp in Damascus, his stomach began to bleed. In 1973, he had helped take out a full-page ad in the *Los Angeles Times*, whose bold headline read, "Wake Up, Americans!" I had watched with admiration and bitterness his unanswered attempt to offer his formidable powers of salesmanship to the NAAA after his business went under.

I had often asked him whether he thought his outspokenness had harmed his dress business. I can't remember a categorical answer, though my mother ventured it may have. He had been partners with two Jewish Americans, both of whom became fast family friends and one of whom still celebrates Christmas with us and is considered very much a part of our family. I do know that one cousin who owned another dress firm and was more circumspect in his criticism of US Mideast policy had often chided Father for his direct, open opinions in "mixed" (i.e., Arab and Jewish) gatherings.

As we drove, I regarded the fine lines of my father's face, the high forehead, the long but not hooked nose, the carefully trimmed moustache, the handsome receding hairline. He wore a white pullover sweater. And I thought him in that second as ever-young, with not a hint of antipathy for a living thing in his soul.

When I ran out of money on my Arab-American odyssey, Dad was first to send me a check, though he had to take out a new mortgage on his house to do it. He felt that what I was doing was important, to give some voice to what had too long been voiceless, to help eradicate the distortions, the stereotypes that make it easy to hate. He told me that what I was doing was something he had wanted to do himself since he was a young man but had been prevented from doing with the onrush of family, business, the myriad responsibilities that pull one from the direct involvement in social injustices. He had looked forward to the book more, even, than to his own waning hope for success.

He would not live to read it. He did, however, humble himself to open a store of a photocopying chain and take it in two years into the black, designing it with the style of an artist. "I should have been an architect!" he once looked wistfully out a window. As his own father—the Syrian from Homs—had gone from being a Cleveland millionaire to operating a lathe after the Depression, he had fallen from designing dresses that were his and his alone, to photocopying. He did photocopy early parts of my manuscript. Is it my imagination alone that sees him there, feeding the paper, printing the shadow of his hand on my work?

We swerved off the road to have dinner and after the delicious, jovial meal over which we shared our hopes and dejections, I remember him pulling alongside a college girl in Ventura to ask directions, talking with her animatedly, and I had to laugh to myself. It was something I would have done! He raised his eyebrows driving away, shaking his head, ever the lover of beauty.

My father was an original. But he would have been the first to say: so is every human being. We entered the night road home, together, filled with the wind and the coming stars, all of a piece in a lost spring.

EPILOGUE

I am staring at my grandmother Matilda Awad's huge tapestry hanging at the entrance to the Arab American Museum. It is a sunburst.

How strange, yet fitting. There greeting all who come to this magnificent museum, newly dedicated in May 2005, is the handiwork of someone who could hardly read. Throw out the books. Throw out this book. Take a good close look at what the hands of this woman from high up in Lebanon made from others' scraps. Nothing wasted. Not a bit of cloth. Or bread.

I remember her snatching remnants of cloth from the factory floor in Pasadena, stuffing them in her apron. No one thought much of it. They were leftovers of leftovers—from the cutting tables where the dresses were shaped, and then from the men's ties made of what had already been overrun.

They should have been thrown out or burned. So much in the Middle East has ended that way. Those with all the color and no power.

She took to her Singer sewing machines these orphans of cloth. They would not cling to a woman's body nor knot around a man's neck. We thought absently she was just killing time. An old woman with nothing useful to do anymore, unable with osteoporosis even to pick her apricot trees. Whirrrrr went her machine in the kitchen. She sewed where she cooked. It was warm there. The men passed shaking their heads, out to the cool porch.

Look at it. The quilt is stitched of triangles of material, and the triangles overlap each other, many ends of men's ties already doubled in cloth, and now trebled, quadrupled, to a seeming infinity. God, it was too heavy to sleep under. Made thick like her pancakes. You felt crushed by beauty. It was gently folded and put in a closet for many years. We forgot it. Thatee died in 2000 and we forgot what she had made, never thought there was anything to it besides time.

Regard the center. A slit of darkness, triangles of dark brown and black and maroon. Moving outward, orange and white dominate, seem to burst with brightness from the dark core, from the place of the stab wound. Then at the border, the edge fades to dark again—maroon, brown, black.

It's the whole cycle of a human being's life stitched in discards. Did she plan that? Her son Eddie remembered her calling him asking for specific colors from the floor. All Thatee's pain was gathered in cloth: her two infant brothers breathing their last orange breaths in Shreen; her husband picking the last orange apricot, mildewed at the middle; the Brooklyn dentist who pulled all her teeth in her thirties;

the orange start of a day with all the children gone. Those who died before her are there in the dark middle: Kamel (1974); her brother Mike (1988) taking a turn in traffic to tend to a barking dog, hit from the blind side; Assad Roum lifted up on Transfiguration Day (August 6, 1993); Auntie Hisson hissing the oil on the skillet of God.

Thatee, I hear you. In these gorgeous remnants, you made a life that would last. You told us to forget no one, to discard no one, to leave nothing unjoined before the fire. I, too, bend toward age, and before your grand design. Your Singer still sings, the darkness still bursting, the orange rising in Dearborn above the mountain and the sea.

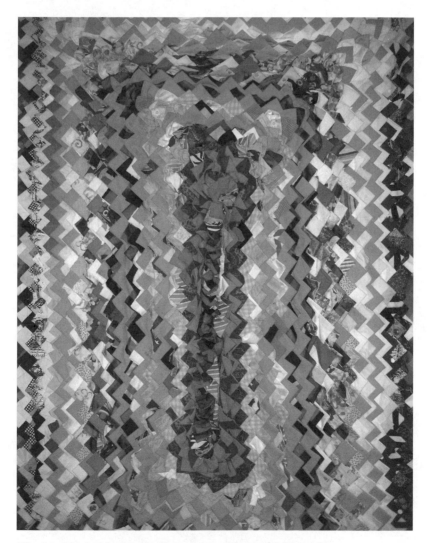

The Matilda Awad quilt (Arab American National Museum)

APPENDIXES

APPENDIX 1
Number of Arrivals in the United States from Turkey in Asia, by Sex, 1869–1898

Year	Males	Females	Total
1869	2	0	0
1870	0	0	0
1871	2	2	4
1872	0	0	0
1873	3	0	3
1874	2	4	6
1875	1	0	1
1876	5	3	8
1877	3	0	3
1878	—	—	—
1879	19	12	31
1880	1	3	4
1881	5	0	5
1882	0	0	0
1883	0	0	0
1884	0	0	0
1885	0	0	0
1886	14	1	15
1887	184	24	208
1888	230	43	273
1889	499	94	593
1890	841	285	1,126
1891	1,774	714	2.488
1892	—	—	—
1893	—	—	—
1894	—	—	—
1895	—	—	2,767
1896	2,915	1,224	4,139
1897	3,203	1,529	4,732
1898	2,651	1,624	4,275
Total	12,356	5,565	20,690

SOURCE: *International Migration Statistics*, Vol. 1, National Bureau of Economic Research, Inc., 1925. Table II-a "Distribution of Immigrant Aliens by Sex and Country of Origin," 1869–1898, pp. 418–431.
— Data not available

APPENDIX 2
Number of Arrivals from Syria in the United States by Sex, 1899–1932

Year	Males	Females	Total
1899	2,446	1,262	3,708
1900	1,813	1,107	2,920
1901	2,729	1,335	4,034
1902	3,337	1,645	4,932
1903	3,749	1,802	5,551
1904	2,480	1,173	3,653
1905	3,248	1,574	4,822
1906	4,100	1,724	5,824
1907	4,276	1,604	5,880
1908	3,926	1,594	5,520
1909	2,383	1,285	3,668
1910	4,148	2,169	6,317
1911	3,609	1,835	5,444
1912	3,646	1,879	5,525
1913	6,177	3,033	9,210
1914	6,391	2,632	9,023
1915	1,174	593	1,767
1916	474	202	676
1917	690	286	976
1918	143	67	210
1919	157	74	231
1920	1,915	1,132	3,047
1921	2,783	2,322	5,105
1922	685	649	1,334
1923	605	601	1,207
1924	801	794	1,595
1925	205	245	450
1926	184	304	488
1927	302	382	684
1928	226	387	613
1929	245	387	632
1930	249	388	637
1931	103	241	344
1932	114	170	284
Total	69,514	36,877	106,391

SOURCE: *International Migration Statistics*, Table X, pp. 432–443, for data to 1925. Data from 1925 on are found in *Annual Reports of Commissioner General of Immigration*, 1926 to 1933, Table(s) VIII, "Immigrant Aliens Admitted Fiscal Year Ending June 30 by Race or People, Sex and Age."

APPENDIX 3
Arab Immigration to the United States, 1948–1985

Year	Leb	Syr	Egy	Pal[a]	Jor[b]	Iraq	Alg	SA	Ku
1948	—	345	184	376	—	107	—	1	—
1949	19	331	165	234	4	100	—	2	—
1950	204	130	165	212	14	116	—	4	—
1951	220	131	169	210	74	109	—	2	—
1952	175	107	156	156	132	102	—	1	13
1953	261	124	168	118	186	125	36	—	—
1954	324	180	264	165	181	162	117	3	0
1955	276	155	214	140	271	159	112	5	3
1956	390	185	272	384	430	163	109	3	2
1957	411	198	332	475	519	180	166	7	2
1958	366	209	498	151	377	215	167	2	2
1959	438	234	1,177	247	360	238	122	9	1
1960	511	207	854	205	371	304	111	3	0
1961	498	191	452	173	485	256	112	11	0
1962	406	245	384	256	515	314	139	3	0
1963	448	226	760	196	556	426	233	11	0
1964	410	244	828	197	529	381	189	13	9
1965	430	255	1,429	170	532	279	206	6	1
1966	535	333	1,181	320	1,005	657	151	10	2
1967	752	555	1,703	421	1,183	1,071	105	14	14
1968	892	644	2,124	—	2,010	540	138	21	15
1969	1,313	904	3,411	—	2,617	1,208	79	25	30
1970	1,903	1,026	4,937	—	2,842	1,202	115	33	24
1971	1,867	951	3,643	—	2,588	1,231	102	48	35
1972	1,984	1,012	2,512	—	2,756	1,491	102	55	46
1973	1,977	1,128	2,274	—	2,450	1,039	96	50	61
1974	2,400	1,082	1,831	—	2,838	2,281	92	48	96
1975	2,075	1,222	1,707	—	2,578	2,796	72	51	142
1976	4,532	1,666	2,290	—	3,328	4,038	110	58	133
1977	5,685	1,676	2,328	—	2,875	2,811	89	55	160
1978	4,556	1,416	2,836	—	3,483	2,188	145	109	468
1979	4,634	1,528	3,241	—	3,360	2,871	140	93	303
1980	4,136	1,658	2,833	—	3,322	2,658	175	133	257
1981	3,955	2,127	3,366	—	2,825	2,535	184	159	317
1982	3,529	2,354	2,800	—	2,923	3,105	190	134	286
1983	2,941	1,683	2,600	—	2,718	2,343	201	170	344
1984	3,213	1,723	2,642	—	2,438	2,930	197	208	437
1985	3,385	1,518	2,802	—	2,998	1,951	202	228	503
Total	62,051	29,972	61,530	4,806	58,633	52,260	4,402	1,764	3,087

Total (1948–1985): 331,958

SOURCE: U.S. Immigration and Naturalization Service.
Note: Total Arab immigration to the United States, 1948–1985: 331,958. Data are based on country of birth of immigrant.
— Data not available.
[a] Beginning FY 1968, data for Palestine are included in Jordan.

Bah[c]	A.Pen[d]	UAE	Lib	Mor	Sud	Tun	SYem[e]	NYem[e]	Oman	Dji	Qat
—	—	—	—	103	—	—	—		—	—	—
—	—	—	—	118	—	—	—		—	—	—
—	—	—	—	95	—	—	10		—	—	—
—	—	—	—	111	—	—	20		—	—	—
13	—	—	—	77	—	—	62		—	—	—
4	—	—	11	132	2	41	132		—	—	—
0	—	0	43	186	13	118	20	87	0	6	0
2	—	0	83	215	14	123	19	59	1	0	1
5	—	0	150	259	20	131	25	64	1	1	1
8	—	0	132	280	40	149	40	52	0	1	1
3	—	0	101	295	44	144	36	58	0	4	0
2	—	0	122	344	30	154	20	69	1	0	1
—	11	—	82	355	68	152	17	87	2	1	—
—	11	—	118	276	43	129	15	102	0	3	—
—	13	—	85	274	27	144	11	106	0	0	—
—	6	—	97	282	30	97	10	106	1	0	—
—	13	—	79	303	57	151	29	103	1	2	—
—	23	—	11	280	47	93	55	89	0	0	—
—	21	—	4	298	68	116	79	130	0	1	—
—	7	—	4	457	57	78	32	127	1	0	—
—	19	—	10	442	56	142	20	138	1	0	—
—	17	—	8	589	47	112	20	361	0	1	—
—	12	—	15	475	64	107	48	515	9	1	—
—	19	—	11	391	51	80	38	564	2	0	—
—	27	—	10	421	41	112	94	920	5	3	—
—	29	—	5	445	65	84	139	121	2	1	—
9	—	3	14	455	43	67	113	561	7	1	11
21	—	3	10	390	38	93	97	227	0	1	8
13	—	7	76	516	60	82	60	682	8	3	23
8	—	13	65	401	48	78	48	376	9	3	13
14	—	11	86	461	71	86	126	258	15	5	11
22	—	30	111	486	77	90	174	203	24	2	5
39	—	32	163	465	83	92	261	160	20	2	16
28	—	24	165	512	65	98	347	230	18	8	22
22	—	40	196	445	78	99	179	305	13	7	13
25	—	31	221	479	128	91	239	268	15	6	19
29	—	76	106	506	199	97	7	324	7	2	17
43	—	92	242	570	271	92	3	432	7	8	28
302	232	361	2,736	12,344	198	3,423	2,427	8,982	170	76	191

[b] Ibid.

[c] For FY 1960–1973 Bahrein, Qatar, and United Arab Emirates are consolidated under Arabian Peninsula.

[d] Ibid.

[e] Total for both Yemens, 1948–1985 is 11, 6333; for 1948–1953, figures are for Yemen before the division.

APPENDIX 4
Arab Immigration to the US, 1986–2003

Year	Leb	Syr	Egy	Pal[a]	Jor	Iraq	Alg	SA	Ku
1986	3,994	1,604	2,989	——	3,081	1,523	183	275	496
1987	4,367	1,669	3,377	——	3,125	1,072	172	294	507
1988	4,910	2,183	3,016	——	3,232	1,022	199	338	599
1989	5,716	2,675	3,717	——	3,921	1,516	230	381	710
1990	5,634	2,972	4,117	——	4,449	1,756	302	518	691
1991	6,009	2,837	5,612	——	4,259	1,494	269	552	861
1992	5,838	2,940	3,576	——	4,036	4,111	407	584	989
1993	5,465	2,933	3,556	——	4,741	4,072	360	616	1,129
1994	4,319	2,426	3,392	——	3,990	6,025	364	668	1,065
1995	3,884	2,362	5,648	——	3,149	5,596	650	788	961
1996	4,382	3,072	6,186	——	4,445	5,481	1,059	1,164	1,202
1997	3,568	2,269	5,031	——	4,171	3,244	717	815	837
1998	3,290	2,840	4,831	——	3,255	2,220	804	703	749
1999	3,040	2,056	4,429	——	3,274	3,372	789	763	803
2000	3,674	2,374	4,461	——	3,909	5,132	907	1,063	1,018
2001	4,601	3,368	5,182	——	4,593	4,985	878	1,185	1,270
2002	3,966	2,567	4,875	——	3,980	5,196	1,031	1,018	1,063
2003	2,964	1,944	3,355	——	2,935	2,460	760	737	710
Total	79,521	45,091	77,340	——	69,045	60,077	10,081	12,462	15,660

Total (1986–2003): 470,869
Total (1948–2003): 802,827

a Beginning FY 1968, data for Palestine are included in Jordan
b Except for 1989–1990, figures are for a united Yemen

Bah	UAE	Lib	Mor	Sud	Tun	SYem[b]	NYem[b]	Oman	Dji	Qat
30	121	195	646	230	121		480	11	9	41
46	122	183	635	198	120		727	11	7	30
45	111	198	715	217	98		619	7	8	39
47	114	210	984	272	125	83	135	18	8	49
58	192	286	1,200	306	226	1,727	218	9	22	33
58	164	314	1,601	679	275		1,547	5	21	56
81	172	286	1,316	675	216		2,056	24	14	59
93	196	343	1,176	714	167		1,793	21	14	88
87	286	166	1,074	651	149		741	32	10	51
78	317	216	1,726	1,645	189		1,501	31	25	60
76	343	250	1,783	2,172	228		2,209	25	19	79
80	329	171	2,359	2,030	163		1,663	36	18	70
53	329	166	2,410	1,161	200		1,859	25	15	60
70	310	156	2,971	1,354	150		1,161	40	6	78
1,012	436	181	3,626	1,538	308		1,789	51	14	97
1,207	461	224	4,968	1,655	440		1,615	55	23	125
1,764	472	159	3,396	2,924	540		1,228	61	30	108
1,257	380	140	3,141	1,886	353		1,386	76	16	72
6,142	4,855	3,844	35,727	20,307	4,068		24,537	538	279	1,195

APPENDIX 5
Arab Eastern Rite Christian*, Muslim, and Druze US Population

	Members	Parishes	Priests
Antiochian Orthodox[a]	250,000	240	300
Coptic Orthodox[b]	250,000	70	100
Chaldean Catholic[c]	115,200	15	20
Maronite Catholic[d]	73,232	59	112
Melkite Catholic[e]	27,207	35	62
Syrian Catholic ("Syriacs")[f]	18,200	9	11
Syrian Orthodox ("Jacobite")[g]	20,000	18	16
Assyrian Orthodox[h]	20,000	2	2

		Mosques	Imams
Muslim[j]	750,000	500	—
Druze[k]	50,000	3	—

*There has been a significant attrition of original Eastern rite Christians to Roman Catholicism, Protestantism, or agnosticism/atheism.

[a] According to Father George Kevorkian at the Antiochian Archdiocese, Englewood, NJ. The Antiochian Orthodox Church is one of several Eastern Orthodox churches with a large Arab population that gradually gravitated to the doctrines and liturgy of Constantinople after the seat of Christendom broke off from Rome in 1054 CE. There is an increasing non-Arab U.S. membership.

[b] According to Bishop Serapion, head of the Los Angeles Coptic Diocese. The Copts derive almost exclusively from Egypt where they founded an early monastic movement. After the Council of Chalcedon (451 CE), most Copts broke with Rome by asserting the unity of Christ's divine and human nature (the Monophysite doctrine).

[c] Figures listed in the 2005 Catholic Directory, which are considered somewhat low due to traditional undercounting to lessen fees to the Archdiocese. The Chaldeans come from northern Iraq. Chaldean Catholicism is growing faster than any of the Eastern Catholic rites. For example, in 2004, there were 871 baptisms vs. 40 for Melkites.

[d] Figures listed in the 2005 Catholic Directory. Maronites find their origin in the priest and hermit Maron (350–410 CE) whose followers settled in Mount Lebanon and around the time of the Crusades came into union with Rome.

[e] Figures listed in the 2005 Catholic Directory. Melkites (sometimes called "Greek Catholics") derive their name from the Semitic word for "king" (*melek*); they follow the Byzantine liturgy after coming into union with Rome in 1724.

[f] Figures listed in the 2005 Catholic Directory. Syrian Catholics consider themselves the original Church of Antioch.

[g] Also known as the "Syriani" who originated in southeastern Turkey.

[h] According to Elias Hanna, 2005 chairman of the Assyrian American National Convention. Like the Syriani, they are Arabs from southeastern Turkey.

[i] Figure is an estimate from the Muslim Public Affairs Council and the Arab American Institute. There are an estimated 5 to 7 million Muslims in America, the vast majority being Black Muslims. Sunni Islam favors the traditions and successors of Mohammed's close friend, Abu Bakr; Sunnis make up 85 percent of Muslims. Shi'a Islam favors the traditions and successors of the prophet Mohammed's cousin and son-in-law Ali, and especially reveres Hussein, martyred during a rebellion against the ruling caliph in 680 CE.

[j] According to Emad Hosn of the American Druze Society. The Druze began as an Islamic reform movement in Cairo, Egypt, in the 11th century, and believe in a strict separation of church and state. There are no Druze mosques or imams so to speak. There are three "temples," with three more in development.

NOTES

Full source information is given in the Bibliography, page 463.

PREFACE

1 Josh Meyer, "Bin Laden, on Tape, Details September 11 Role," *Los Angeles Times* 30 October 2004.

2 Gregory Orfalea, *Before the Flames*, 219.

3 David Ignatius, "Achieving Real Victory Could Take Decades," *Washington Post* 26 December 2004.

1. GENERATIONS REUNITE IN ARBEEN, SYRIA

1 According to Sami's brother, Adeeb, under the Ottoman Turks, members of *bayt* Awad (the Awad family) were told to identify themselves as "Hanna" (John) because they were Christians. Awad could be either Muslim or Christian; Hanna only Christian. Apparently this last name persisted for the younger Awads of Arbeen.

2 See "Syria: A Lost Opportunity," in Seymour Hersh, *Chain of Command: The Road from 9/11 to Abu Ghraib* (New York: Harper Collins, 2004) 333–341.

3 Hitti, *Capital Cities of Islam* 61–64.

4 *The Orthodox Patriarchal Convent of Our Lady of Saydanaya.*

5 Fawaz Turki, "Beirut," in *Tel Zaater Was the Hill of Thyme* 19.

2. SEEDS TO THE WIND

1 See Charles Michael Boland's *They All Discovered America.* One enthusiast near Mechanicsburg was Joseph Ayoob, who authored "Were the Phoenicians the First to Discover America?," *Compiler* (Aliquippa, Pennsylvania, 1950).

2 Fell 236–306.

3 Mehdi 1.

4 Mehdi 60.

5 Makdisi, "Arab Adventurers in the New World." See also testimony of Larry Williams of Okracoke Island, North Carolina, in Gregory Orfalea and Libby Jackowski, "The Arab Americans," 23.

6 Herman Eilts, "Ahmad Bin Naaman's Mission to the United States in 1840."

7 Hooglund, *Taking Root* ii.

8 *First Immigrant* 23.

9 *First Immigrant* 30.

10 *First Immigrant* 31.

11 Lesley 159.

12 Jay J. Wagoner, *Early Arizona's Pre-History to the Civil War* 342 (cited in Issa Peters's paper delivered at the Philip K. Hitti Symposium).

13 Considine 31.

14 Edward Peplow, Jr., *The History of Arizona* 34. Cited in Peters.

15 Issawi 269; Kayal and Kayal 61.

16 Rizk 38.

17 Issawi 269.

18 Younis, *The Coming of the Arabic-Speaking People*, 2.

19 "The Maronite patriarch pronounced anathema on the missionaries and their converts. Maronites were 'not to visit or employ them or do them a favor, but

let them be avoided as a putrid member and a hellish dragon.' Native Christians who turned Protestant were persecuted. Their shops were boycotted, native teachers and ministers banished, men and women stoned in the streets, hung up by their thumbs, spat upon and struck in the face, tortured with bastinado and imprisoned without charge or trial" (David 70).

20 Fisk 30, 33–34

21 Fisk 46, 49.

22 Said, *Orientalism* 69.

23 Parsons 218; journals of Parsons and Fisk, Houghton Library, Harvard University (cited in Younis, "Salem and the Early Syrian Venture" 304).

24 Younis, *The Coming of the Arabic-Speaking People* 15–16.

25 Jessup 170.

26 Letter in Hayden 23.

27 Jessup 201.

28 I. M. Smilianskaya, "The Disintegration of Feudal Relations in Syria and Lebanon in the Middle of the 19th Century," Issawi 233.

29 *The Evangelist*, 19 December 1895 (cited in Younis, *The Coming of the Arabic-Speaking People* 90).

30 Bliss 212.

31 Shadid 25.

32 Younis, *The Coming of the Arabic-Speaking People* 120.

33 Hisson Arbeely Dalool, personal interview, 22 March 1983, Pasadena, California.

34 A French family-planning organization set figures in 1977 that had Lebanon with a 60 percent majority of Muslims. The breakdown of sects was 28 percent Shi'ite Muslims; 25 percent Maronite Catholics; 24 percent Sunni Muslims; 8 percent Druze; 15 percent other (mostly Eastern Orthodox and Melkite Catholics). If anything—with continuing Christian emigration—the Muslim majority is larger today.

35 Druze also live in the Hauran area in southern Syria, in Israel, and in the Israeli-occupied Golan Heights. There is a sprinkling of Palestinian Maronites.

36 Randal 38.

37 Randal 42.

38 Jessup 156.

39 Kayal and Kayal 62.

40 Hourani 301.

41 Sakir 1–17.

42 Quoted in Zelditch 10.

43 Hamid 16–17.

44 Rizk 17.

45 Assad Roum, personal interview, 23 March 1983, Pasadena, California.

46 Rihbany 74–75. There is an Arab proverb that expresses the opposite sentiment: "My brother and I against my cousin; my cousin and I against the stranger," which has been cited often to "explain" the incredible brutality of the Lebanese civil war. But I think it is not as convincing an explanation on close inspection as it seems (as with our own Civil War, brothers have found themselves on different sides of a battle) and certainly is not as operable in explaining the psychology of Arab immigrants as is Rihbany's thankful, "protected" strangers. In any case, another Arab proverb tends to support Rihbany: "Your friend who is near and not the brother who is far."

47 Issawi 207.

48 Issawi 207–208.

49 Abdeen Jabara, personal interview, 20 May 1983, Detroit, Michigan.

50 Najib Saliba, "Emigration from Syria," in Abraham and Abraham 32.

51 Spiegel 171.

52 Vance Boujaily, personal interview, 9 July 1983, Iowa City, Iowa.

53 Albert Rashid, personal interview, 2 February 1983, Brooklyn, New York.

54 Perkins 8.

55 Glubb 246.

56 Michael Malouf, personal interview, 22 March 1983, Pasadena, California.

57 Simon Rihbany, personal interview, 26 February 1983, West Roxbury, Massachusetts.

58 E. J. Dillon, "Turkey's Plight," *Contemporary Review*, July 1913: 123, 128 (cited in Kayal and Kayal 65).

59 Dr. Joseph Jacobs, personal interview, 4 April 1983, Pasadena, California.

60 Saliba, in Abraham and Abraham 37.

61 Rizk 37.

62 Matile Awad, personal interview, January 1983, Pasadena, California. Seventy years later, an Orthodox priest visited Shreen and was shocked to find its church gutted and its homes destroyed by the civil war (see Essey).

63 Hitti, *A Short History of Lebanon* 216–217.

64 Amean Haddad, personal interview, 24 March 1983, Encino, California.

65 Malouf interview.

66 Peter Nosser, personal interview, 15 March 1984, Vicksburg, Mississippi.

67 Saliba, in Abraham and Abraham 39.

68 Roum interview.

69 Helen Hatab Samhan, "Not Quite White: Race Classification and the Arab American Experience," Abu-Laban and Zeadey 216–218.

70 Brown and Roucik 286.

71 Rihbany 172, 175, 176.

72 Joseph Hamrah, personal interview, 8 August 1983, Houston, Texas.

73 Rihani 28.

74 Rizk 118.

75 Andrew Ghareeb, personal interview, 25 March 1985, Bethesda, Maryland.

76 Gary Awad, interview with Said Hanna, 1978, Pasadena, California.

77 "Five Recruited for Turkey."

78 Sadie Stonbely, personal interview, 18 February 1983, Brooklyn, New York.

79 Elias Joseph, personal interview, 1 March 1983, Woonsocket, Rhode Island.

80 Hitti, *The Syrians in America* 66. It is part of my mother's family folklore that Theodore Roosevelt—through Dr. Ibrahim Arbeely—interceded for the release of my great-grandfather from a Turkish prison (see "Deeb Awad," in *The Capital of Solitude*).

81 Stonbely interview.

82 Salloum Mokarzel, "History of the Syrians in New York."

83 Awad interview.

84 Stonbely interview.

85 Bourjaily interview.

86 Corsi 261–266.

87 Mokarzel, "History of the Syrians."

88 Edward Hall, *The Hidden Dimension*, quoted in Parillo 323.

89 Miller 51.

90 Orfalea, "There's a Wire Brush at My Bones," in *Crossing the Waters*, ed. Eric Hooglund.

91 Dalool interview.

92 Mrs. George Fauty, personal interview, 16 February 1983, Brooklyn, New York.

93 Ford, "Why I Wrote a Syrian Play."

94 Ford, *Anna Ascends*.

95 Hamod 19.

96 Mayor George Latimer, personal interview, 5 June 1983, St. Paul, Minnesota.

97 Casey Kasem, personal interview, 4 April 1985, Washington DC.

98 Philip Forzley, ed., "Autobiography of Bishara Khalil Forzley," (Immigration History and Research Center, University of Minnesota, 2 August 1953) 8.

99 Aliya Hassan, personal interview, 19 May 1983, Dearborn, Michigan.

100 Ellis Bodron, personal interview, 14 March 1984, Vicksburg, Mississippi.

101 Naff, *Becoming American* 183.

102 Naff, *Becoming American* 184.

103 Naff, *Becoming American* 164.

104 Thomas Nassif, personal interview, 23 February 1983, Washington, DC.

105 An important debunking of the thesis that a majority of early Syrians peddled was presented by Dr. Eric Hooglund in his introduction to the 1985 volume *Taking Root*. Hooglund and the ADC Research Institute tapped recently unsealed records of the US Census Bureau to discover that in ten communities in five states in 1900 and 1910 a majority of Syrian workers were listed as factory laborers. Though using those communities (most of which were northeastern) as a barometer to disprove the peddler theory is not entirely foolproof (one should note that peddlers by nature of their work were on the road and perhaps not as easily polled by Census officials), Hooglund's conclusion is compelling: "It is reasonable to say, however, that the 'Syrian peddler' idea is a stereotype... the experience of the early Arabs in America was as diverse as that of other ethnic groups who came in the great immigration wave during the generation leading up to World War I."

106 Joseph interview.

107 Katrina Thomas 6.

108 Hooglund, "From Down East to Near East: Ethnic Arabs in Waterville, Maine," in *Crossing the Waters*.

109 Sameer Y. Abraham, "Detroit's Arab-American Community: A Survey of Diversity and Commonality," in Abraham and Abraham 90.

110 Gorey, *Nader and the Power of Everyman* 166–167.

111 William Ezzy, personal interview, 3 March 1983, Alameda, California.

112 Orfalea and Jackowski.

113 George Fauty, personal interview, 16 February 1983, Brooklyn, New York.

114 Van Slyke 411; Alice E. Christgau, *The Laugh Peddler*, quoted in Naff, *Becoming American* 180–181.

115 Orfalea, "There's a Wire Brush."

116 Samra, "Rugby Update" 2. See also his "Early Beginnings of the Melkite Church in the US" 3.

117 Kayal and Kayal 122.

118 Father James Khoury, personal interview, 4 August 1983, San Antonio, Texas.

119 Macron.

120 See Andrzei Kulczycki and Arun Peter Lobo, "Patterns, Determinants, and Implications of Intermarriage among Arab Americans," *Journal of Marriage and Family* 64 (February 2002): 202–210.

121 Salloum Mokarzel, "Christian–Moslem Marriages," 14.

122 Naff, *Becoming American* 120.

123 Nelly Bitar, personal interview, 12 May 1983, Greentree, Pennsylvania.

124 Toby Smith 25.

125 Hitti, *The Syrians in America* 103.

126 Michael W. Suleiman, "Early Arab-Americans: The Search for Identity," in *Crossing the Waters*, ed. Hooglund.

127 Joseph interview.

128 Hawie 85–104.

129 Mikhail Naimy, "My Brother," in Orfalea and Sharif Elmusa.

130 In *History of Greene County* (cited in Makdisi, "The Moslems of America" 969–971).

131 Jabara interview.

132 Elkholy 17.

133 Abe Ayad, personal interview, 14 December 1983, San Francisco, California.

134 Hamod, "Lines to My Father," in *Dying with the Wrong Name* 7.

135 H. S. Hamod, personal interview, 25 February 1986, Washington, DC.

136 Stevenson 36–38.

137 Smith, "Arrows" 23.

138 Charles Juma, Sr., personal interview, 11 June 1983, Stanley, North Dakota.

139 Omar Hamdan, personal interview, 11 June 1983, Stanley, North Dakota.

3. TRANSPLANTING THE FIG TREE

1 Sam Kanaan, personal interview, 2 March 1983, West Roxbury, Massachusetts.

2 Shukri Khouri, personal interview, 12 September 1983, Chevy Chase, Maryland.

3 Peters.

4 Fauty interview.

5 Malouf interview.

6 Roum interview.

7 Joseph interview.

8 Spiegel, *That Haggar Man* 30.

9 John Nosser, personal interview, 15 March 1984, Vicksburg, Mississippi.

10 Faith Latimer, "Cultural Autobiography," unpublished paper, University of Minnesota, 13 May 1982.

11 "Relief Movements among US Syrians," *Syrian World* 6.2 (October 1931): 54–55.

12 Marlene Khoury Smith 156.

13 "Hunger" (14 March 1928), "A Solemn Vow" (8 April 28), "The Endless Race," (30 August 1928), *New York Times*.

14 "Hard Times," *Syrian World* 6.6 (February 1932): 44–45.

15 Marlene Khoury Smith 169.

16 "First American Jet Ace Dies as Car Overturns in Florida," *New York Times*, 18 November 1966.

17 Halaby 30–33.

18 "Flies 30 Missions, None of Crew Hurt," *Minneapolis Daily Times* 1 July 1944: 6.

19 Louis LaHood, *Wings in the Hands of the Lord*, 42, 46.

20 Bourjaily, *The End of My Life*, 183.

21 Bourjaily, *The End of My Life*, 28–29.

22 Danny Thomas, personal interview, 23 March 1983, Beverly Hills, California.

23 Danny Thomas, "The Vow," 4.

24 Papier.

25 Helen Thomas, personal interview, 1983, Washington, DC.

26 Papier 20.

27 Thomas, *Dateline: Washington*, 37.

28 Thomas, *Dateline* 87.

29 Ayesha Howar, personal interview, 6–7 July 1985, Washington, DC.

30 Halaby, *Crosswinds* 4.

31 Halaby 5.

32 Najeeb Halaby, personal interview, 25 March 1983, Washington, DC.

33 Halaby 317.

34 Queen Noor, *Leap of Faith* 24.

35 Bourjaily, "My Father's Life," *Esquire* March 1984.

36 Bourjaily interview.

37 Bourjaily, "My Father's Life."

38 Bourjaily, autobiographical entry, *Contemporary Authors Autobiography Series* 1:63–79.

39 Bourjaily, autobiographical entry.

40 Bourjaily, *Confessions of a Spent Youth* 239, 15, 273.

41 Evelyn Shakir, "Pretending to Be an Arab: Role-Playing in Vance Bourjaily's 'The Fractional Man,'" MELUS 9.1 (Spring 1982): 7–21.

4. THE PALESTINE DEBACLE

1 Alfred Farradj, personal interview, 10 March 1983, San Francisco, California.

2 See Elias II. Tuma, "The Palestinians in America," *The Link* 14.3 (July–August 1981): 1–14. Tuma cites estimates of the Palestine Institute of Statistics and *al-Fajr*, a West Bank daily newspaper, that the 1981 Palestinian-American population was 110, 200. Since immigration figures from the "Palestine" column abruptly (and bizarrely) disappear after 1967 [see Appendixes], it is difficult to tell from US immigration figures just who is Palestinian. It seems safe to assume, at the very least, that half the Arab immigrants from Lebanon, Syria, Iraq, and the Gulf states since 1967 were Palestinian, and that two-thirds of the Jordanian immigrants since 1967 were also Palestinian. This will more than account for the Arab American Institute estimate of 250,000 current Palestinian Americans.

3 Hisham Sharabi, personal interviews, 2 February, 10 March, 8 September 1983, Washington DC.

4 "Will the Palestinians Tolerate Such?"

5 Farradj interview.

6 Naim Halabi, personal interview, 18 April 1983, Foster City, California.

7 Khouri interview.

8 George Muhawi, personal interview, 18 September 1983, Kensington, Maryland.

9 See "Interview with Jonathan Kuttub," *Arab-American Affairs* 16 (Spring 1986): 120–127. Kuttub, with Mubarak Awad, the founder of the East Jerusalem-based Palestinian Center for Non-Violence. See also Mubarak Awad, "Nonviolent Resistance: A Strategy for the Occupied Territories."

10 Tillman 14.

11 Lilienthal 93.

12 Documents at the Truman Library in Independence, Missouri, reveal that Truman agreed to the meeting only after he was assured by acting Secretary of State James Webb that it would last only ten minutes. The Webb memo, signed by the president, leaves no doubt that the meeting was arranged solely for public relations purposes: "In view of the precarious state of our relations with the Arab countries, it would be advantageous if you could find time to receive the committee of the

Federation. It would be a simple courtesy call; publicity of the event by overseas news, radio and information agencies would have a favorable impact on the Arab world." An eleven-person delegation of Arab Americans met with Truman on the White House lawn October 3 and presented him with a seven-point program for peace in the Middle East. Summarizing it, Faris Malouf noted the desire that US foreign policy not "be influenced and affected by domestic considerations" and that a "generous and final" solution to the Arab refugee problem not "stretch over a period of years." The eleven in attendance were Malouf, Monsour Zanaty (National Federations president), Frank Maria, James Batal, George Barakat, Ellis Abide, Anthony Abraham, Mrs. Louis Nassif, Simon Rihbany, Rogers Bite, and Joseph Sado. A photograph that the *Federation Herald* ran of the event in its October 1951 issue is revealing. All but white-haired Simon Rihbany face a portly Faris Malouf, who, reading the document, faces not the president but Frank Maria. A brooding Truman stands back from the podium with the presidential seal, hands clasped, looking groundward.

13 Halabi interview.

14 See Aziz' return to the Jerusalem home in Nye's "One Village," in her collection *Never in a Hurry* 49–70.

15 Aziz Shihab, personal interview, 6 August 1983, Dallas, Texas.

16 Said, *The World, the Text, the Critic*, 4.

17 Edward Said, personal interview, 7 October 1983, New York, New York.

18 Said, *Out of Place*, 3.

19 See Said, *After the Last Sky*, 172.

20 Edward Said, "The Only Alternative," *Al-Ahram Weekly Online* 523: 1–7 March 2001.

21 Sharabi interview.

22 Hisham Sharabi, from *Embers and Ashes: Memoirs of an Arab Intellectual*, trans. by Issa Boullata, in *Post Gibran: New Arab American Writing*, ed. Munir Akash and Khaled Mattawa (Bethesda, MD: Jusoor, 1999) 360.

23 Sharabi 377.

24 Patricia Sullivan, "Arab Intellectual Hisham Sharabi, 77, Dies," *Washington Post* 16 January 2005.

25 Nabila Cronfel, personal interview, 3 August 1983, Houston, Texas.

26 Naomi Shihab Nye, "One Village," in *Never in a Hurry* 66–67.

27 George Bisharat, "History Prolongs Palestinian Family's Grief," *Arizona Republic* 16 May 2004.

28 Shahdan El Shazly, personal interview, 11 November 1983, Washington, DC.

29 Father Abdulahad Doumato, personal interview, 1 March 1983, Central Falls, Rhode Island.

5. THE THIRD WAVE

1 Kristine Ajrouch, "Family and Ethnic Identity in an Arab American Community," Suleiman, *Arabs in America* 132.

2 Baha Abu Laban and Sharon McIrvin Abu-Laban, "Arab-Canadian Youth in Immigrant Family Life," Suleiman, *Arabs in America* 148–149.

3 Estimates of the Assyrian community in the United States come from an interview with Aladin Khamis, president of the Assyrian American National Federation, 3 January 2005, Chicago, Illinois.

4 Sengstock 141.

5 Karim Alkadhi, personal interview, 10 August 1983, Houston, Texas.

6 Basim al-Khafaji, personal interview, August 5, 2005, Dearborn, Michigan.

7 Zuhair Allebban, personal interview, August 5, 2005, Dearborn, Michigan.

8 Mustapha Alsamarae, personal interview, August 5, 2005, Dearborn, Michigan.

9 See also Mary Beth Sheridan, "Educating Against Extremism," *Washington Post* 8 August 2005.

10 Swanson 13.

11 Morse.

12 Nabeel Abraham, "The Yemeni Immigrant Community of Detroit: Background, Emigration, and Community Life," in Abraham and Abraham 114.

13 Abraham 120–121, 126–128.

14 See Haiek 107–108.

15 Louise Cainkar, "The Deteriorating Ethnic Safety Net Among Arab Immigrants in Chicago," Suleiman, *Arabs in America* 192–206.

16 Joseph Haiek, personal interview, 22 March 1983, Glendale, California.

17 al-Asmar 57.

18 Bassam Idais, personal interview, 7 August 1983, San Antonio, Texas.

19 Diana Sahwani, personal interview, March 1983, Washington, DC.

20 Dr. Suheir Daoud, e-mail interview 12 October 2005, Claremont, CA.

21 State of Israel, Prime Minister's Office, Central Bureau of Statistics, *The Arab Population in Israel*, November 2002. Unless noted, other statistics in this passage derive from this document.

22 Dr. Suheir Daoud, "Palestinian Women in Politics in Israel: Obstacles and Challenges," unpublished paper, 2004.

23 Tony Khater, 25 July 1983, Washington DC.

24 ʿAlaʾ Drooby, personal interview, 2 August 1983, Houston, Texas.

25 ʿAlaʾ Drooby, personal interview, 11 January 2005, Houston, Texas.

6. THE POLITICAL AWAKENING

1 "US Arabs Block Terror," *New York Times*, 5 October 1972.

2 Jabara interview.

3 "The Civil Rights of Arab Americans," "The Special Measures," *AAUG Information Paper* 10 (January 1974).

4 Mowahid Shah, "The FBI and the Civil Rights of Arab Americans," *ADC Issue Paper* 5 (1981).

5 Kamal Boullata and Mirein Ghossein, eds., *The World of Rashid Hussein* (Detroit: AAUG, 1979) 98–100.

6 Boullata and Ghossein 112.

7 Jabara interview.

8 In 1967, Antiochian Archbishop Philip Saliba led a group of prelates to protest the Six-Day War in a meeting with President Lyndon Johnson.

9 Tillman 182.

10 Saba 18.

11 Michael Saba, personal interview, 20 August 2003

12 "How Much is Too Much?" *Counterpoint* 3 (NAAA) November 1978.

13 "An Interview with Sami Esmail," *The Link* (Americans for Middle East Understanding–AMEU) December 1978. See also the case of Elias Ayoub in "A Doctor and a Student: First Amendment Casualties," *Focus* 2.16–17 (1 September 1979); "Ayoub Wins Preliminary Victory," *Focus* 2.23 (1 December 1979). See also the case of Terre Fleener in "Terre Fleener: Human Rights Victim in US–Israel Tug-of-War," *Focus* 2.15 (1 August 1979).

14 "Ethnic Mudslinging in California," *Focus* 2.7 (1 April 1979).

15 "George Corey's Statement," *Focus* 2.8 (15 April 1979).

16 "PLO's Shafiq al-Hout Speaks at Middle East Institute," *Focus* 2.10 (15 May 1979).

17 "Up on the Hill and Around," *Focus* 2.7 (1 April 1979).

18 "Hisham Sharabi," *Voice* 6.3 (Summer 1979).

19 "Southern Lebanon:Vietnam Revisited?", *Focus* 2.15 (1 August 1979).

20 "House Members Hold Unusual 'Colloquy' Over Agonized Lebanon," *Focus* 2.18 (15 September 1979).

21 "Hatfield Offers Unprecedented 10% Cut in Arms for Israel Over Lebanon Strikes," *Focus* 2.20 (15 October 1979).

22 "ABSCAM is BADSCAM," *Focus* 3.4 (15 February 1980).

23 "Settle the Settlements Problem," *Focus* 3.5 (1 March 1980).

24 "McCloskey Conducts Settlements Colloquy in House," *Focus* 3.12 (15 June 1980).

25 "No Money for Settlements–Stevenson Offers Amendment," *Focus* 3.13 (1 July 1980).

26 "Howard Kurtz, "Arab Americans in New York Say Mayoral Nominees Spurn Support," *Washington Post* 16 October 1989.

27 Joseph Eger, "Is It Good for the Jews?", *Newsweek* 15 September 1980: 17.

28 Elizabeth Bumiller, "Abourezk's Arab Defense," *Washington Post* 3 July 1982.

29 See Shaheen's *Reel Bad Arabs*.

30 "The Other Anti-Semitism: The Arab as Scapegoat," *ADC Issues* 3 (1981).

31 "Investigation or Harrassment by the FBI?", *Minneapolis Tribune* 21 November 1980.

32 *ADC Report* 4 (February 1981).

33 *ADC Report* 4.

34 *ADC Report* 15 (November–December 1982).

35 *ADC Report* 8 (Summer 1981).

36 *ADC Report* 12 (March–April 1982).

37 *ADC Report* 12.

38 *ADC Report* 10 and 11 (January–February 1982).

39 *ADC Report* 12.

40 *ADC Report* 15.

41 James Bylin, *Bakersfield Californian*, 4 September 1981; Gordon Anderson, "Arab Americans to Get Help from National Group," *Bakersfield Californian*, 21 September 1981.

7. BACK TO LEBANON

1 See Robert Fisk, *Pity the Nation* and Randal, *Going All the Way*.

2 Chami 288–289.

3 See Dimbleby 85–94.

4 Gregory Orfalea, "Sifting the Ashes: Arab-American Activism During the 1982 Invasion of Lebanon," *Arab Studies Quarterly*, ed. by Michael Suleiman and Baha Abu-Laban, 11.2–3 (Spring/Summer 1989): 208.

5 Claudia Wright, "US Stepped Up Arms for Invasion," *New Statesman* 20 August 1982.

6 Orfalea, "Sifting," 212.

7 Orfalea, "Sifting," 215.

8 Orfalea, "Sifting," 215.

9 Josh Meyer, "Bin Laden, on Tape, Details September 11 Role," *Los Angeles*

Times 20 October 2004.

10 "Israeli Government Tries to Intimidate American Newspapers," *Focus* 5.22 (15 November 1982).

11 George Will, "Israel Should Show a Decent Respect," *Washington Post* 23 September 1982.

12 In David Shipler, *Arab and Jew: Wounded Spirits in the Promised Land* (New York: Penguin Books, 1986) 502.

13 Orfalea, "Sifting," 219.

14 Kahlil Jahshan, personal interview, 28 August 2003, Rockville, Maryland.

8. STUMBLING TOWARD PEACE

1 American-Arab Anti-Discrimination Committee, 1993 Activity Report, 16–17.

2 Gregory Orfalea, "Fiction Could Jolt Jews and Arabs into Coexistence," *National Catholic Reporter* 10 March 1989.

3 David Cole and James X. Dempsey, *Terrorism and the Constitution* (New York: The New Press, 2002) 37.

4 Cole and Dempsey 36.

5 Kathleen Moore, "A Closer Look at Anti-Terrorism Law: American-Arab Anti-Discrimination Committee v. Reno and the Construction of Aliens' Rights," Suleiman, *Arabs in America* 92.

6 Memorandum from Investigation Division, US Immigration and Naturalization Service, Alien Border Control Committee (ABC), Formation of Alien Border Control Committee, 27 June 1986.

7 Cole and Dempsey 40.

8 Jack Shaheen, *Reel Bad Arabs: How Hollywood Vilifies a People* (Northampton: Olive Branch Press, 2001) 262.

9 See Gregory Orfalea, "Literary Devolution: The Arab in the Post-World War II Novel in English," *Journal of Palestine Studies* 17.2 (Winter 1988).

10 Noam Chomsky, *The Fateful Triangle* (Cambridge, MA: South End Books, 1999) 473–474.

11 Gary Paul Nabhan, *Cultures of Habitat* (Washington, DC: Counterpoint, 1997) 112–132.

12 American-Arab Anti-Discrimination Committee, *1991 Report on Anti-Arab Hate Crimes, Political and Hate Violence Against Arab Americans,* February 1992.

13 Three *New Yorker* pieces touching on the community have appeared since September 11, 2001: "On the Sidelines," about how Ramadan is celebrated in the USA (24 December 2001), "Booklyn Boycott" by Ben McGrath, about an Arab American attempt to boycott the *New York Post* (22 July 2002); a piece on the NYC police force and Arab Americans (25 July 2005). Other than a piece by Edward Said, as far as I can tell no Arab-American author has published his original work in the *New Yorker* since 1993, and only 2 prior.

14 "It's Racist, But Hey, It's Disney," editorial, *New York Times* 14 July 1993.

15 James Zogby, "Making History," *San Diego Union* 19 September 1993.

16 *Religious Labels and the Rabin Assassination: A Survey of Three Major US Newspapers* (Los Angeles, CA: Muslim Public Affairs Council, 1995).

17 Hussein Ibish, ed. *1998–2000 Report on Hate Crimes and Discrimination against Arab Americans* (Washington, DC: ADC Research Institute, 2001) 11.

18 *1995 Report on Anti-Arab Racism: Hate Crimes, Discrimination, and Defamation of Arab Americans* (Washington, DC: ADC Research Institute, 1996).

19 Cole and Dempsey 117–118.

20 Testimony to the Senate Committee on the Judiciary, Subcommittee on Terrorism, Technology, and Government, 4 May 1995.

21 James Zogby, "Fighting Terrorism with Repression," *Washington Post* 27 March 1995.

22 Helen Hatab Samhan, in Suleiman, *Arabs in America* 219.

23 Marvin Wingfield, personal interview, June 2003, Washington, DC.

24 Samhan, in Suleiman, *Arabs in America* 223.

25 Michael Ruane and Sari Horowitz, the authors of the book *Sniper* about the DC sniper shooters, said at a book signing presentation in Washington, DC, that September 11, 2002, was the exact day John Muhammad and his accomplice Lee Malvo rented the Chevrolet Caprice in New Jersey that they bored with a gunsight hole in the trunk. Even more astonishing, Muhammad wrote the exact time that the first plane hit the World Trade Center that day on his receipt!

26 John Dugard (South Africa), Kamal Hossain (Bangladesh), and Richard Falk (USA), "Question of the Violation of Human Rights in the Occupied Territories, including Palestine, UN Economic and Social Council, Commission on Human Rights in Occupied Arab Territories, including Palestine," 6 March 2001. Quoted in Carey 15.

27 Dugard, Hossain, and Falk 7.

28 *The 9/11 Commission Report* 250.

29 Hisham Sharabi, "Framing the Final Phase," in *Beyond Rhetoric: Perspectives on a Negotiated Settlement in Palestine* (Washington, DC: The Center for Policy Analysis on Palestine, 1996) 1.

30 Sharabi 1.

31 Edward Said, *Peace and Its Discontents*, xxix.

32 Sarah Roy, "Decline and Disfigurement: The Palestinian Economy After Oslo," in Carey.

33 Roy 105.

34 Summarized in Edward Said, "Palestinians Under Siege," Carey 32.

35 John Mearsheimer, "The Impossible Partition," *New York Times* 11 January 2001.

36 Mouin Rabbani, "A Smorgasbord of Failure," Carey 78.

37 Edward Tivnan, *The Lobby: Jewish Political Power and American Foreign Policy* (New York: Simon and Schuster, 1987) 57–58.

38 Robert Malley, "Fictions about the Failure at Camp David," *New York Times* 8 July 2001.

39 Rema Hammami and Salim Tamari, "The Second Uprising: End or New Beginning?", *Journal of Palestine Studies*, 30.2 (Winter 2001) 5–25.

40 John Ward Anderson and Molly Moore, "For Two Families in Haifa, Three Generations of Victims," *Washington Post* October 6, 2003.

41 Ann Patchett, *Bel Canto* (New York: Harper Perennial, 2001) 91. In another gorgeous moment, one of the terrorists suggests to his commander that they should put a gun to the soprano's head to compel her to sing. The commander dissuades him, "Try first with a bird. Like our soprano, they have no capacity to understand authority. The bird doesn't know enough to be afraid and the person holding the gun will only end up looking like a lunatic."

42 See Anne Applebaum, "Think Again, Karen Hughes," *Washington Post* 27 July 2005.

43 Samuel Freedman, "Looking at Arab-American Lives, with Care, and One Eye Closed," *New York Times* September 2002.

44 Carol Martin, "Peace Is Somewhere in the Middle," *Chicago Tribune* 21 May 2003.

45 Ray Hanania, "Anti-Semitism Has No Place in Conflict with Israel," *Daily Herald* (Chicago) January 3, 2003.

46 Michael Slackman, "Arab Forum Assails Jews, 9/11 Propaganda," *Los Angeles Times* 31 August 2002.

47 *1998 Report on Hate Crimes.*

48 Jim Hoagland, "Now It's Personal," *Washington Post* 30 August 2001.

9. AFTER THE FLAMES

1 E-mail to author from Johnny Makhoul, New York, NY, 20 November 2003.

2 Chris Woodyard and Barbara Hanser, "Attacks' Fallout: Skies Less Crowded," *USA Today* September 27, 2001.

3 Carol Leaning and Raymond McCaffrey, "Freebies Fail to Lure Wary Public to Downtown," *Washington Post* 14 October 2001.

4 Fred Hiatt, "Sacrificed to Safety," *Washington Post* 17 December 2001.

5 Richard Cohen, "Wounded City," *Washington Post*, 16 October 2001.

6 William E. Schenger, PhD, et al, "Psychological Reactions to Terrorist Attacks," *The Journal of the American Medical Association* 7 August 2002: 581–588.

7 Jill Williams, "Depression, PTSD, Substance Abuse Increase in Wake of September 11 Attacks," National Institute on Drug Abuse, *NIDA Notes*, 17.4 (November 2002); "September 11 and Mass Trauma: Reaching for Alcohol and Drugs," Substance Abuse and Mental Health Services Administration, *Prevention Alert* 5.4 (22 February 2002).

8 Michael Powell, "An Exodus Grows in Brooklyn," *Washington Post* 29 May 2003.

9 Imam Izak E. Mu'ed Pasha, "Muslim Americans: A Prayer," in *From the Ashes: A Spiritual Response to the Attacks on America* (New York: Rodale, Inc., 2001) 150.

10 Ziad Asali, "America in Crisis: An Open Letter," *ADC Times* 21.4 (September 2001 Special Edition) 1.

11 Asali 2.

12 Nahidi Hadesh, personal interview, 9 September 2003. Falls Church, Virginia.

13 Naomi Shihab Nye, "To Any Would-Be Terrorists," in William Heyen, ed. *11 September 2001: American Writers Respond* (Silver Springs, MD: Etruscan Press, 2002) 287–291.

14 MSNBC, 15 September 2001.

15 Michael Lee, *Healing the Nation: The Arab American Experience After September 11* (Washington, DC: Arab American Institute, 2002) 3.

16 Dave Ghose, "Support Buoys City's Displaced Muslims," *Arab American News* 19–26 January 2002.

17 See "We Are Not the Enemy: Hate Crimes Against Arabs, Muslims and Those Perceived to be Arab or Muslim After September 11," *Human Rights Watch* 14.6, November 2002; also Hussein Ibish, ed., *Report on Hate Crimes and Discrimination Against Arab Americans: The Post-September 11 Backlash, September 11, 2001–October 11, 2002* (Washington, DC: American-Arab Anti-Discrimination Committee, 2003).

18 Ibish, "Report on Hate Crimes... Post-September 11."

19 Ibish, "Report on Hate Crimes... Post-September 11."

20 Aziz Baroody, speech, ADC convention, Arlington, Virginia, 12 April 2003.

21 Lee 7.

22 Ibish, "Report on Hate Crimes... Post-September 11," 87–91.

23 Ibish, "Report on Hate Crimes... Post-September 11," 21–30.

24 Sara Kehaulani Goo, "Fliers to be Rated for Risk Level," *Washington Post* 3

September 2003.

25 Rev. Jerry Falwell, *CBS Sixty Minutes* 6 October 2002.

26 Rev. Franklin Graham, *NBC Nightly News* 17 November 2001.

27 Ibish, "Report on Hate Crimes... Post-September 11," 128.

28 Ibish, "Report on Hate Crimes... Post-September 11," 128.

29 "ADC Reacts to Representative Coble's Remarks," *ADC Times* 21.10 (Pre-Convention 2003) 27.

30 "Dick Armey, *National Review*, Call for Ethnic Cleansing of Palestinians," *ADC Times* 21.7 (March–April 2002) 18.

31 "Dick Armey..." 18.

32 Zev Chafets, "Arab Americans Have to Choose," *New York Daily News* 16 September 2001.

33 Ann Coulter, "This is War," *National Review Online* 13 September 2001.

34 John Keegan, "Clash of Civilizations: The West Will Prevail," *San Diego Union-Tribune* 4 October 2001.

35 Lee 8–9.

36 Lee 8–9.

37 Ibish 136.

38 Lee 11–12; the poster is available at www.aaiusa.org.

39 Deborah Goodman, "Arab Americans and American Muslims Express Mental Health Needs," *SAMHSA News* X.11 (Winter 2002).

40 Mary Beth Sheridan, "Sensitizing Police Toward Muslims," *Washington Post* 6 October 2002.

41 See "Extraordinary...the Power of Individual Action," on Samira Hussein in *Rosie*, February 2002.

42 Cited in Hentoff 11.

43 Bill Powell, "Target America," *Time* 16 August 2004: 35.

44 Michelle Goldberg, "The Prisoner-Abuse Scandal at Home," *Salon.com* 19 May 2004.

45 David Kravets, "ACLU Seeks Data on FBI's Muslim Interviews," *Inland Valley Daily Bulletin* (CA) 22 October 2004.

46 Steven Elbow, "Madison Cop Won't Screen Muslims," *The Capital Times* (Madison, WI) 12 December 2001.

47 Amy Goldstein, "Fierce Fight Over Secrecy, Scope of Law," *Washington Post* 8 September 2003.

48 Hentoff 12.

49 Salam al-Marayati, "Indict Individuals, Not Charities," *New York Times* 11 October 2002.

50 Lee 20.

51 Lee 20.

52 H.G. Reza, "Anaheim Looks Into Muslims' Complaints," *Los Angeles Times* 13 September 2004.

53 "Arab Americans Wary of Warnings," *Detroit Free Press* 28 May 2002.

54 Tim Padgett and Rochelle Rinfor, "Fighting Words," *Time* 4 February 2002: 56.

55 Morak Warikoo, "Arabs in US Could Be Held, Official Warns," *Detroit Free Press* 20 July 2002.

56 See Irene Hirano, "History, Current Events, and a Network Link: The Japanese American Museum and the Arab American Community Center for Economic and Social Services," *Common Ground: The Japanese American Museum and the Culture of Collaboration* (Boulder: University of Colorado Press, 2005) 167–176.

57 Hentoff 12.

58 Hentoff 61.

59 "US-Freed 'Combatant' is Returned to Saudi Arabia," *Los Angeles Times* 12 October 2004.

60 John Hendren, "Man Indicted in Plot to Kill the President," *Los Angeles Times* 23 February 2005.

61 Josh White, "Five Americans Held by US Forces" *Washington Post* 7 July 2005.

62 See Mark Kuki's "My Heart Became Attached," *The Strange Odyssey of John Walker Lindh*. Dulles, VA: Potomac Books, 2003.

63 Elizabeth Becker and Eric Schmitt, "US Planes Bomb a Red Cross Site," *New York Times* 27 October 2001.

64 Bennis 143–149.

65 Chrisopher Dickey, "The Empire's New Clothes," *Newsweek*/MSNBC 24 June 2005.

66 Quoted in John Newhouse, *Imperial America: The Bush Assault on the World Order* (New York: Knopf, 2002) 47.

67 Michael O'Hanlon and Adriana Lins de Albuquerque, "Iraq—By the Numbers," *Los Angeles Times* 3 September 2004.

68 Dana Milbank and Claudia Dean, "Poll Finds Dimmer View of Iraq War," *Washington Post* 8 June 2005; Ellen Kickmayer, "Iraq Puts Civilian Toll at 12,000," *Washington Post* 3 June 2005. A Lancet/Johns Hopkins study of summer 2005 put the estimate much higher (100,000).

69 Michael Kinsley, "Destroying Iraq to Save It," *Los Angeles Times* 21 November 2004.

70 Etel Adnan, "The Politics of My Garden," in *Grantmakers in Arts Reader 15.3* (Fall 2004).

71 At the 1995 NAAA conference, which he thought "poorly attended," Edward Said thought Baker's main emphasis was on Israeli security: "If Palestinian autonomy does not improve Israeli security, there will be no Palestinian autonomy."

72 The usual motives for unswerving, even blind allegiance to Israel—great compassion if not guilt over the Holocaust, political campaign contributions, fealty to its "democracy"—no longer seems adequate to explain the suicidal danger we sustain in this "special relationship." Could it be much simpler, Machiavellian, terrifying? Israel has 400 nuclear bombs, a lot of leverage, after all.

73 Teresa Watanabe, "Jews Target Shareholders Effort," *Los Angeles Times* 13 April 2005.

74 Said, "America's Last Taboo," Carey 260.

75 Greg Myre, "Arafat: Bin Laden Exploits Palestinians," Associated Press 15 December 2002.

76 Suleiman al-Khalidi, "UN Report: US War on Terror Radicalizes Arabs," Reuters 20 October 2003.

77 David Ignatius, "Revolt of the Privileged, Muslim Style," *Washington Post* 27 July 2005.

78 Bennis 99–100.

79 Gregory Orfalea, "Snuffing the Fire of Radical Islam," *Los Angeles Times* 12 December 2004.

80 Allen Zerkin, "Is Al-Qaeda Asking to Negotiate?", *Los Angeles Times* 19 September 2005.

81 Michael Kinsley, "The Thinker," *Los Angeles Times* 6 February 2005.

82 Zbigniew Brzezinski and William Quandt, "From Bush, Mideast Words to Act On," *Washington Post* 17 June 2005.

83 Talat Othman of Chicago told me that he and Khalil Sahouri met Bush aide Karl Rove shortly before the 2000 presidential debate with Albert Gore. In a taxi, the Arab Americans suggested to Rove that "the best thing you could do is have Bush speak out against using secret evidence against Arab Americans, as it was unconstitutional." At the time, 28 people were being held on such secret evidence that had been allowed by Clinton's 1996 Anti-Terrorism law, among them 27 Arab Muslims, and one member of the IRA. Bush made his reference during the debates to his concern for the civil rights of all, including Arab Americans. It was so astounding to the community to hear its name referred to with concern that shortly afterwards, Muslim organizations banded together to endorse Bush.

84 Kathy Barks Hoffman, "Lieberman Heckled by Arab Americans," Associated Press 18 October 2003.

85 Peter Wallsten and John Glionna, "Arabs in Florida Angered by Bush," *Los Angeles Times* 4 October 2004.

86 David Broder, "Mobilizing Arab Americans," *Washington Post* 22 October 2003. See also David Broder, "Dean Greeted Warmly by Arab Americans," *Washington Post* 19 October 2003.

87 Aaron David Miller, "Why the Gaza Pullout Matters," *Los Angeles Times* 11 May 2005.

88 Laura King, "Abbas Acts to Get Guns Off the Streets," *Los Angeles Times* 28 January 2005.

89 David Grossman, "The Power of 'We're Sorry'," *Los Angeles Times* 8 February 2005.

90 Walter Russell Mead, "Algeria Unbound," (opinion) *Los Angeles Times* 25 April 2004.

91 Robert Scheer, "Now, US Must Get Out of Iraq's Way," *Los Angeles Times* 1 February, 2005.

92 Arianna Huffington, "So, Exactly What's Changed?", *Los Angeles Times* 2 February 2005.

93 Maria La Ganga, "They Drove 22 Hours for a Defining Moment," *Los Angeles Times* 30 January 2005.

94 Joyce Carol Oates, "Words Fail, Memory Blurs, Life Wins," *New York Times* 3 December 2001.

95 La Ganga.

96 James Zogby,"Arab Americans and American Jews Agree on Path of Peace," *Washington Watch*, Arab American Institute website 4 August 2003.

97 "Elections 2002: Arab Americans on the Move," Arab American Institute, Washington, DC 2003.

98 Salam al-Marayati and Maher Hathout, "The Tyranny of Brotherhood," *Los Angeles Times* 18 September 1994.

99 Laurie Goldstein, "Gephardt Bows to Jews' Anger Over Nominee," *New York Times* 9 July 1999.

100 "Anti-Muslim McCarthyism," editorial, *San Francisco Examiner* 11 July 1999.

101 Salam al-Marayati, personal interview, 28 January 2003, Los Angeles, California.

102 "Poll: US Muslims Increase Political Activity Since 9/11," press release, Council on American-Islamic Relations (CAIR), Washington, DC, 10 September

2003; "Poll: Majority of US Muslims Suffered Post-9/11 Backlash," CAIR press release, 21 August 2002.

103 Valerie Strauss and Emily Wax, "Where Two Worlds Collide," *Washington Post* 25 February 2002.

104 Salam al-Marayati, "Anti-Islam Rhetoric Undercuts Moderates," *Los Angeles Times* 11 December 2002.

105 Jim VanderHei, "Islam's Split-Screen View of the US," *Wall Street Journal* 11 April 2002; see also, "Arab Nation's 'Impressions of America' Poll, Zogby International, Utica, NY, April 19, 2002.

106 Lyric Wallwork Winik, "Why I Chose to Serve: The Challenge of Arab-Americans in the Military," *Parade* 17 April 2005.

107 Teresa Isaac, speech, ADC convention, Arlington, Virginia, June 2003.

108 Linda DeBlanco, *Poker, Cooking and Pearls of Wisdom: The Biography of Virginia Orfalea* (Santa Barbara, CA: Cottage Publishing, 1988) 58,73.

109 Sandra Leader, "Kinko's Founder Makes Giving His Main Business," *Los Angeles Times*, 3 June 2001.

110 Paul Orfalea, *Copy This! Lessons from a Hyperactive Dyslexic Who Turned a Bright Idea into One of America's Best Companies.* (New York, Workman Publishing Company, 2005) 100.

111 Stephanie Salter, "One Multimillionaire's Investment in the Future–Child Care," *San Francisco Chronicle* 3 October 2002.

112 Brian Deacon, "Copy This Man's Work Ethic," *Investor's Business Daily*.

113 Abu-Jaber, *Crescent*, 127; 16–17.

114 Nye, *Hugging the Jukebox*, 1.

115 Philip M. Kayal, "So, Who Are We? Who Am I?", Benson and Kayal 92–93.

116 Amin Rihani, "I Dreamt I Was a Donkey Boy Again," in Orfalea and Elmusa, eds., *Grape Leaves* 6.

117 Rihani, "A Chant of Mystics," in Orfalea and Elmusa 15.

118 Mikhail Naimy, cited in Suleiman, "Impressions of New York City by Early Arab Immigrants," *A Community of Many Worlds* 37.

119 Naimy 85.

120 Abinader, *Children of the Roojme*, 82.

121 Soffee 227.

122 Naomi Shihab Nye, *Different Ways to Pray* (Portland, OR: Breitenbush Publishers, 1980) 12.

123 William Peter Blatty, *The Exorcist* (New York: Bantam Books, 1971) 370.

124 Chris Hedges, "A Poet's Victory of Love over Evil," *International Herald Tribune* 10 April 2002.

125 Lawrence Joseph, *Into It* (New York: Farrar, Straus, and Giroux, 2005) 35–36.

126 Orfalea and Elmusa 119.

127 Sharif Elmusa, "One Day in the Life of Nablus," *Jusoor Special Issue: Culture, Creativity and Exile* (Bethesda, MD: Jusoor Books, 1996) 362.

128 Fouzi al-Asmar, *To Be an Arab in Israel* (Beirut, Lebanon: Institute of Palestine Studies, 1978) 126.

129 Orfalea and Elmusa 198–199.

130 Quoted in Danitia Smith, "Arab-American Writers, Uneasy in Two Worlds," *New York Times* 19 February 2003.

131 Mohja Kahf, unpublished poems read at the Radius of Arab American Writers (RAWI) Conference, "Kallimuna: Speak to Us!" Hunter College, New York, 3–5 June 2005.

132 Geha 22.

133 Mona Simpson, *The Lost Father*, 389.

134 Simpson 444.

135 Simpson 505.

136 Simpson 503.

137 Blatty 370.

138 Diana Abu-Jaber, "Reality TV," *Washington Post Magazine* 20 April 2003.

139 Gary David, "Rethinking Who is Arab American: Arab American Studies in the New Millenium," *al-Jadid* Summer 2003: 4–5.

140 Gregory Orfalea, "Valley Boys," *Michigan Quarterly Review* XLI.4 (Fall 2002).

10. A CELEBRATION OF COMMUNITY

1 Reverend George M. Rados, Saints Peter and Paul Antiochian Orthodox Church newsletters 46 (May 1984) and 47 (June 1984).

2 Father George Rados, personal interview, 22 February 1983, Washington, DC.

3 George Saba, personal interview, 26 August 2003, Washington, DC.

4 Yvonne Haddad, personal interview, 26 August 2003, Washington, DC.

5 Hytham Abul-Hadi, personal interview, 26 August 2003, Washington, DC.

6 Mary Rose Oakar, personal interview, 26 August 2003, Washington, DC.

7 Mona Hamoui, personal interview, 26 August 2003, Washington, DC.

8 Dr. Nuha Abudabbeh, personal interview, 26 August 2003, Washington, DC.

9 Philip Harsham, "One Arab's Immigration," *Aramco World Magazine*, March–April 1975: 14–15.

10 George Muhawi, personal interview, 18 September 1983, Kensington, Maryland.

11 Carla Hall, "The Rashids: It's All Relatives," *Washington Post* 8 July 1985.

12 Henry Allen, "What Makes Sammie Abbott So Angry?" *Washington Post* 22 September 1985.

13 Richard Shadyac, personal interview, 1983, Washington, DC.

14 Jack Neam, personal interview, 11 September 2003, Arlington, Virginia.

15 Art Buchwald, "A Pomegranate? Could We Have Your House As Collateral?" *Washington Post* 27 July 1978.

16 Laurice Neam, personal interview, 11 September 2003, Arlington, Virginia.

17 Amal Raychouni, personal interview, 30 August 2003, Detroit, Michigan.

18 Paul Bennett, "Arab-Americans Tell Their Story," *Wall Street Journal* 5 May 2005.

19 Steve Acho, personal interview, 30 August 2003, Detroit, Michigan.

20 Nasser Beydoun, personal interview, 29 August 2003, Dearborn, Michigan.

21 Alan Pinon, "Bush Meets with Local Iraqis in Dearborn," *Community Bridges*, a joint publication of the Press and Guide Newspapers and the Arab American Chamber of Commerce, May 2003.

22 Lawrence Joseph, *Shouting at No One*, University of Pittsburgh Press, 1983.

23 Jeffrey Ghannam, "Running the Store: Devotion Prevails," *Detroit Free Press* 18 August 1997.

24 Imam Hassan Qazwini, personal interview, 30 August 2003, Dearborn, Michigan.

25 Ishmael Ahmed, personal interview, 29 August 2003, Dearborn, Michigan.

26 Al Stark, "Rising to the Top," *Michigan: Detroit News (Sunday) Magazine*, 12 June 1988,

27 Mike George, personal interview, 29 August 2003, Dearborn, Michigan.

28 Amy Harmon, "No-Win Predicament of Iraqi Immigrant Merchants in Detroit," *Los Angeles Times* 16 March 1991.

29 Harmon.

30 See George grandchildren statements in *In Our Own Words*, privately printed 73-page book of testimonies to Mike George by family and friends, 21 September 2001.

31 Ibrahim Hanania, personal interview, 30 August 2003, Livonia, Michigan.

32 Naim Kawwas, personal interview, 30 August 2003, Livonia, Michigan.

33 Fr. George Rados, personal interview, 22 February 1983, Washington, DC.

34 Philip Habib, personal interview, 15 March 1983, Washington, DC.

35 Robert Thabit, personal interview, 20 February 1983, Brooklyn, New York.

36 Edward Baloutine, personal interview, 16 February 1983, Brooklyn, New York. In late 1985, Edward Baloutine followed the Bay Ridge colony's exodus to New Jersey, settling in Washington Township.

37 Stonbely interview.

38 Joseph Atallah, personal interview, 18 February 1983, Brooklyn, New York.

39 Richard Zarick, personal interview, 18 February 1983, Brooklyn, New York.

40 Joe Tintle, "Mustapha Hamsho: Syrian-Bred, American-Based," *Ring Magazine* December 1980: 35.

41 Mike Marley, "Hagler Lives Up to Tradition of Middleweight Champions," *New York Post* 3 October 1981.

42 Mustapha Hamsho, personal interview, 8 October 1983, Brooklyn, New York.

43 Alfred Hayes, "Abraham Perfect in BSO Narration," *Baltimore Sun* 11 July 1985.

44 F. Murray Abraham, personal interview, 10 July 1985, Baltimore, Maryland.

45 See "F. Murray Abraham's Class Act," *International Herald Tribune*, 4–5 October 1986: 20.

46 Father Nicolas Saikley, personal interview, 14 March 1984, Vicksburg, Mississippi.

47 Ellis Bodron, personal interview, 14 March 1984, Vicksburg, Mississippi.

48 Excerpts from Emma Balfour's 1893 diary in William Lovelace Foster and Kenneth Urquhart, eds. *Vicksburg: Southern City Under Siege*. Vicksburg: Historic N., 1980.

49 In 1917, in what came to be known as the Balfour Declaration, Lord David Balfour, the prime minister of Great Britain, wrote Lord Lionel Rothschild underscoring Britain's commitment to build a national home for the Jewish people, "it being clearly understood that nothing shall be done which may prejudice the civil and religious rights of the existing non-Jewish population." Later, Balfour dismissed his own guarantee to the 93 percent Arab population of Palestine. In a secret memorandum to the British cabinet, he wrote: "Zionism, be it right or wrong, good or bad, is rooted in age-long traditions, in present needs, in future hopes *of far profounder import* [italics mine] than the desires and prejudices of the 700,000 Arabs who now inhabit that ancient land." See David Hirst, *The Gun and the Olive Branch: The Roots of Violence in the Middle East*. London: Futura Publications, 1978: 41–42.

50 Judge John Ellis, personal interview, 15 March 1984, Vicksburg, Mississippi. Another judge of Lebanese background was Sen. George Mitchell of Maine, who distinguished himself in 1987 as a member of the US Senate investigatory committee on the Iran–Contra arms affair, and later chaired important commissions investigating the conflicts in Northern Ireland and Palestine.

51 P. Nosser interview.

52 J. Nosser interview.

53 Haseeb Abraham, personal interview, 15 March 1984, Vicksburg, Mississippi.

54 Mayme Farris, personal interview, 16 March 1984, Vicksburg, Mississippi.

55 James Hughes, "An Open House," *New Yorker*, October 1980.

56 Hamdan interview.

57 Juma, Sr. interview.

58 Nazira Kurdi Omar, personal interview, 12 June 1983, Stanley, North Dakota.

59 See Bevis Hillier, "California Craftsmen," *Los Angeles Times Home Magazine* 25 November 1984: 12–14. See also Sam Maloof, *Sam Maloof, Woodworker*.

60 See Mary Tahan, "Bob Andrews Heads Lettuce Kingdom While Scoring High in Community Services," *News Circle* 9.103 (January 1981): 23–29.

61 Merrill Shindler, "Jean and Casey Kasem Raise Pot of Gold for the Rainbow Coalition," *News Circle* 12.144 (June 1984): 32.

62 Nathan Pop, "Casey Kasem," *Boston Globe* 30 March 1985.

63 Milhem Safa, ed., "A Farewell Speech to My Brethren, the Druze," ms., Qara Qool al Druze, Lebanon, 22 January 1931.

64 Kasem interview.

65 Richard J. Piestschmann, "Casey's Quandary," *Los Angeles Magazine* 1 April 1983: 132.

66 Nicole Yorkin, "KNBC Newsman Helps Bring Couple Orphan Boy to LA," *Los Angeles Herald-Examiner* 1 December 1983.

67 Joseph J. Jacobs, *Jacobs Engineering Group, Inc.: A Story of Pride, Reputation, and Integrity*. Princeton, NJ: Newcomer Society, 1980.

68 Jacobs interview.

69 Haddad interview.

70 Sammie Abbott, the popular Marxist former mayor of Takoma Park, Maryland, helped prepare America's Abraham Lincoln Brigade that fought against fascists during the Spanish Civil War. See Henry Allen, "What Makes Sammie Abbott So Angry?" *Washington Post* 22 September 1985.

71 Dalool interview.

72 Roum interview.

73 Malouf interview.

74 Orfalea, "The Chandelier."

75 See Mary Bisharat, "Yemeni Migrant Workers," in *Arabs in America*, ed. Baha Abu-Laban and Faith T. Zeadey.

76 Ahmed Shaibi, personal interview, 5 April 1983, Delano, California.

77 Mike Shaw, personal interview, 5 April 1983, Delano, California.

78 Kassem Shaibi, personal interview, 5 April 1983, Delano, California.

BIBLIOGRAPHY

Abdul-Baki, Kathryn. *Ghost Songs*. Pueblo, CO: Pasasiggianta Press, 2000.

Abinader, Elmaz. *Children of the Roojme: A Family's Journey from Lebanon*. Madison, WI: University of Wisconsin Press, 1997.

Abraham, Nabeel, and Sameer Y. Abraham, eds. *Arabs in the New World: Studies on Arab American Communities*. Detroit: Wayne State University Center for Urban Ethnic Studies, 1983.

_____. and Andrew Shryrock, eds. *Arab Detroit*. Detroit: Wayne State University Press, 2000.

Abu-Jaber, Diana. *Arabian Jazz*. New York: Harcourt Brace, 1993.

_____. *Crescent*. New York: Norton, 2003.

Abu-Laban, Baha, and Faith T. Zeadey, eds. *Arabs in America: Myths and Realities*. Wilmette, IL: Medina University Press International, 1975.

Adnan, Etel. *In the Heart of the Heart of Another Country*. San Francisco: City Lights Books, 2005.

"Alex Odeh: First Victim of Terrorism against Arab-Americans in the United States." *News Circle* 14.160 (October 1985).

Allen, Henry. "What Makes Sammie Abbott So Angry?," *Washington Post*, 22 September 1985.

Ameri, Anan and Dawn Ramey, eds. *Arab American Encyclopedia*. Detroit: The Gale Group, 2000.

Anderson, Jack, and Dale Van Atta. "Israelis Harass Arab-American." *Washington Post*, 5 November 1986.

Apone, Carl. "Variety's Dapper Diplomat" [Joe Ferris]. *Pittsburgh Press*, 29 April 1962.

"Arab: An Inside Look at a Community under Siege." *Michigan Magazine of the Detroit News*, 6 April 1986.

The Arab-American Community: A Demographic Profile. New York: American-Arab Association for Commerce and Industry, 1980.

al-Asmar, Fouzi. *To Be an Arab in Israel*. Beirut: Institute of Palestine Studies, 1978.

Assali, Nicholas. *A Doctor's Life*. New York: Doubleday, 1979.

Aswad, Barbara. *Arabic-Speaking Communities in American Cities*. New York: Center for Migration Studies and the Association of Arab-American University Graduates, 1974.

Atiyeh, George, ed. *Arab and American Cultures*. Washington, DC: American Enterprise Institute for Public Policy Research, 1977.

Awad, Joseph. *The Neon Distances*. Francestown, NH: Golden Quill Press, 1980.

_____. *Big Bang: A Poem in Twelve Cantos*. Richmond, VA: The Poet's Press, 1999.

Awad, Mubarak. "Nonviolent Resistance: A Strategy for the Occupied Territories." *Journal of Palestine Studies* 13.4 (Summer 1984): 22–36.

Ayoob, Joseph. "Were the Phoenicians the First to Discover America?" *Compiler* (Aliquippa, PA), 1950.

Bache, Sami. "A Trip to the Interior of the Middle East." *In Greetings from Home*. Brooklyn, privately published, 4 July 1944.

Balfour, Emma. *Vicksburg, a City under Siege*. Vicksburg: Philip C. Weinberger [privately printed], 1983.

"Beirut Was Such a Marvelous City." *Village Voice*, 28 February 1984.

Benet, Lorenzo. "A Community Coming of Age: Arab-Americans in LA" *Daily News*, 12 May 1986.

Bengough, W. "The Syrian Colony." *Harper's Weekly*, 3 August 1895.

Bennis, Phyllis. *Before and After: US Foreign Policy and the September 11 Crisis.* Northampton: Olive Branch Press, 2003.

Benson, Kathleen, and Philip Kayal, eds. *A Community of Many Worlds: Arab Americans in New York City.* New York: The Museum of the City of New York/Syracuse University Press, 2002.

Benyon, E. D. "The Near East in Flint, Michigan: Assyrians and Druses and Their Antecedents." *Geographical Review* 24 (January 1944): 272–273.

Berger, Morroe. "America's Syrian Community." *Commentary* 25.4 (April 1958): 314–323.

Bishara, K. A. "The Contribution of the Syrian Immigrant to America." *Syrian World* 1.7 (January 1927): 16–18.

Blair, Clay. *Ridgeway's Paratroopers.* New York: Dial Press, 1985.

Blatty, William Peter. *I'll Tell Them I Remember You.* New York: W. W. Norton & Co., 1973.

_____. *The Exorcist.* New York: Harper Collins, 1972.

_____. *Which Way to Mecca, Jack?.* New York: B. Geis, 1960.

Bliss, Daniel. *Reminiscenses of Daniel Bliss.* New York: Fleming H. Revell Co., 1920.

Boland, Charles Michael. *They All Discovered America.* New York: Doubleday, 1961.

Boosahda, Elizabeth. *Arab American Faces and Voices: The Origins of an Immigrant Community.* Austin, TX: University of Texas Press, 2003.

Bourjaily, Vance. *Confessions of a Spent Youth.* New York: Arbor House, 1986 (reissue).

_____. *The End of My Life.* New York: Arbor House, 1984 (reissue).

_____, and Philip Bourjaily. *Fishing By Mail: The Outdoor Life of a Father and Son.* Boston: Atlantic Monthly Press, 1993.

_____. "My Father's Life." *Esquire*, March 1984.

_____. *Old Soldier.* New York: Dutton, 1990.

Brown, Francis, and Joseph Roucik, eds. *One America.* New York: Prentice-Hall, 1945.

Brown, Warren. "Detroit: Arabs' Mecca in the Midwest." *Washington Post*, 30 October 1978.

Buenker, John and Lorman Ratner, eds. *Multiculturalism in the United States: A Comparative Guide to Acculturation and Ethnicity.* Westport, CT: Greenwood Press, 2005.

Carey, Rowane, ed. *The New Intifada: Resisting Israel's Apartheid.* London: Verso Press, 2001.

Chami, Joseph. *Days of Tragedy.* Beirut: Shousan, 1978.

Charara, Hayan. *The Alchemist's Diary.* Brooklyn, NY: Hanging Loose Press, 2001.

Chessari, Joe. "Hagler Not Surprised at Hamsho's Win, Welcomes Rematch." *Dispatch* (Hudson/Bergen County, NJ), 27 July 1983.

Chomsky, Noam. *The Fateful Triangle.* Cambridge, MA: South End Books, 1999.

Clark, Brian. "Khalifa at the Bat." *Aramco World Magazine* 37.3 (May–June 1986): 6–13.

Cobban, Helena. *The Palestine Liberation Organization.* New York: Cambridge University Press, 1984.

Coll, Steven. "Down Home with the $10 Billion Barrister: Joe Jamail, a Law unto

Himself." *Washington Post*, 31 July 1986.

Considine, John. "Jeff Davis' Camels in Arizona." *Sunset*, May 1923.

Contemporary Authors Autobiography Series. Detroit: Gale Research Co., 1984.

Corning, Blair. "Meet San Antonio's King of the Forgotten." *San Antonio Express-News*, 28 November 1982.

Corsi, Edward. *The Shadow of Liberty.* New York: Macmillan, 1935.

Courtemanche, Dolores. "Worcester's Lebanese-Syrian Community: An Ethnic Success Story." *Sunday Telegram*, 14 September 1980.

Dallal, Shaw. *Scattered Like Seeds.* Syracuse, NY: Syracuse University Press, 1998.

David, Robert L. "American Influence in the Near East before 1861." *American Quarterly* 16.1 (Spring 1964) 70.

DeBakey, Michael E., and Lois DeBakey. "Relighting the Lamp of Excellence." *Forum on Medicine* 2.8 (August 1979): 523–528.

Demaret, Kent. "Heart Surgeon Michael DeBakey's Sisters Teach Doctors How to Cut Out That Confusing Jargon." *People Weekly* 17.4 (February 1, 1982): 89–90.

Dimbleby, Jonathan. *The Palestinians.* New York: Quartet Books, 1980.

Doche, Vivian. *Cedars by the Mississippi: The Lebanese-Americans in the Twin Cities.* San Francisco: R & E Research Associates, 1978.

Donahue, Jack. *Wildcatter: The Story of Michel T. Halbouty.* New York: McGraw-Hill, 1979.

Eilts, Herman. "Ahmad Bin Naaman's Mission to the United States in 1840." *Essex Institute Quarterly*, October 1962.

Eisenstein, Paul. "Detroit's Lebanese Achieve Harmony Homeland Lacks." *USA Today* 22 July 1983.

Elfin, David. "Khalifa: Potential Pirate from the Shore of Tripoli." *Washington Post* 10 July 1983.

Elkholy, Ahdo A. *The Arab Muslims in the United States: Religion and Assimilation.* New Haven, CT: College and University Press, 1966

Elon, Amos. *A Blood-Dimmed Tide.* New York: Columbia University Press, 1997.

Erian, Alicia. *Towelhead.* New York: Simon and Schuster, 2005.

Essey, Father Basil. "A Song of Hope." *The Word* 5 (May 1987): 9–11.

"F. Murray Abraham's Class Act." *International Herald Tribune*, October 4–5, 1986: 20.

"Factional War is Waged between Syrians in New York City." *New York Herald* 29 October 1905.

Fell, Barry. *Saga America.* New York: Times Books, 1980.

Ferris, George A. "Syrians' Future in America." *Syrian World* 3.11 (May 1929): 3–8.

Ferris, Joseph W. "Syrian Naturalization Questions in the United States: Certain Legal Aspects of Our Naturalization Laws." *Syrian World* 2.8 (February 1928): 3–11; 2.9 (March 1928): 18–24.

Findley, Paul. *They Dared to Speak Out.* Westport, CT: Lawrence Hill & Co., 1985.

"First American Jet Ace Dies as Car Overturns in Florida." *New York Times* 18 November 1966.

First Immigrant. Beirut: World Lebanese Cultural Union, 1972.

Fisk, Pliny. "The Holy Land an Interesting Field of Missionary Enterprise." *In Sermons of Rev. Messrs. Fisk & Parsons Just before Their Departure on the Palestine Mission.* Boston: Samuel T. Armstrong, 1819.

Fisk, Robert. *Pity the Nation: The Abduction of Lebanon.* Avalon Publishing Group, 2002.

"Five Recruited for Turkey—Story of the Arabs Now at Castle Gardens." *New York Daily Tribune* 24 May 1877.

"Flies 30 Missions, None of Crew Hurt." *Minneapolis Daily Times* 1 July 1944.

Ford, Henry Chapman. "Anna Ascends." *Syrian World* 2.1 (July 1927).

_____. "Why I Wrote a Syrian Play." *Syrian World* 2.1 (July 1927).

Foster, William Lovelace, and Kenneth Urquhart, eds. *Vicksburg: Southern City Under Siege.* Vicksburg, Historic N, 1980.

Franklin, Stephen. "Arab-Americans Organize for a Role in US Politics." *Philadelphia Inquirer,* 8 April 1984.

Friedman, Robert. *False Prophet: Rabbi Meir Kahane—From FBI Informant to Knesset Member.* Chicaco, IL: Chicago Review Press, 1992.

Geerhold, William. "The Mosque on Massachusetts Avenue." *Aramco World Magazine* 16 (May–June 1965): 20–21.

Geha, Joseph. *Through and Through: Toledo Stories.* St. Paul, MN: Graywolf Press, 1990.

"Ghetto Sights." *Cedar Rapids Evening Gazette,* 9 November 1897.

Gibran, Jean, and Kahlil Gibran. *Kahil Gibran: His Life and World.* New York: Avenel Books, 1981.

Gibran, Kahlil. "To Young Americans of Syrian Origin." *Syrian World* 1.1 (July 1926): 4–5.

Glubb, Sir John. *A Short History of the Arab Peoples.* New York: Stein and Day, 1969.

Goldberg, Merle. "Casbah in Brooklyn." *New York Magazine,* 14 July 1969: 62–65.

Gorey, Hays. *Nader and the Power of Everyman.* New York: Grosset and Dunlap, 1975.

Graff, Gary. "Oakland County's Arabs: Traditional, American." *Detroit Free Press,* 17 February 1983.

Haddad, Ameen. "The Return Home." *Federation Herald,* January 1953.

Haddad, Marian. *Somewhere between Mexico and a River Called Home.* Texas: Pecan Grove Press, 2004.

Hagopian, Elaine C., and Ann Paden, eds. *The Arab Americans: Studies in Assimilation.* Wilmette, IL: Medina University Press International, 1969.

Haiek, Joseph R., ed. *Arab American Almanac.* 5th ed. Glendale, Calif.: News Circle Publishing Co., 2003.

Hakim, A. "Conflicting Standards in the Syrian Home in America." *Syrian World* 6.3 (November 1931): 38–40.

Halaby, Lisa. *West of the Jordan.* Boston: Beacon Press, 2003.

Halaby, Najeeb. *Crosswinds.* New York: Doubleday, 1978.

Hall, Carla. "The Rashids: It's All Relatives." *Washington Post,* July 8, 1985.

Hall, Edward T. *The Hidden Dimension.* Garden City, NY: Doubleday, 1966.

Halsell, Grace. "Will the Arab Lobby Please Stand Up?." *Middle East* 98 (December 1982).

Hamid, George. *Circus.* New York: Sterling Publishing Co., 1953.

Hammad, Suheir. *Drops of This Story.* New York: Harlem River Press, 1996.

Hamod, Sam. *Dying with the Wrong Name.* New York: Anthe Publications, 1980.

Handal, Nathalie. *The Poetry of Arab Women: A Contemporary Anthology.* Northampton, MA: Interlink Books, 2001.

_____. *The Lives of Rain.* Northampton, MA: Interlink Books, 2005.

"Hard Times." *Syrian World* 6.6 (February 1932): 44–45.

Harsham, Philip. "Arabs in America." *Aramco World Magazine* 26.2 (March–April 1975).

_____. "Islam in Iowa." *Aramco World Magazine* 27 (November–December 1976): 30–36.

_____. "One Arab's America." *Aramco World Magazine* 26.2 (March–April 1975): 14–15.

Hawie, Ashad G. *The Rainbow Ends.* New York: T. Gaus' Sons, 1942.

Hayden, H. C., ed. *American Heroes in Mission Fields.* New York: American Tract Society, 1890.

Hayes, Alfred. "Abraham Perfect in BSO Narration." *Baltimore Sun,* 11 July 1985.

Hazo, Samuel. "A Poet's Journey: An American in the Land of His Ancestors." *Jubilee* (December 1965) 44–49.

_____. *Stills.* Syracuse: Syracuse University Press, 1997.

_____. *Thank a Bored Angel: Selected Poems.* New York: New Directions, 1983.

_____. *The Holy Surprise of Right Now.* Little Rock: University of Arkansas Prewss, 1996.

_____. *The Very Fall of the Sun.* New York: Pocket Books, 1979.

Hentoff, Nat. *The War on the Bill of Rights and the Gathering Resistance.* New York: Seven Stories Press, 2003.

Hillier, Bevis. "California Craftsmen." *Los Angeles Times Home Magazine,* 25 November 1984: 12–14.

Hitti, Philip K. *Capital Cities of Islam.* Minneapolis: University of Minnesota Press, 1973.

_____. *A Short History of Lebanon.* New York: St. Martin's Press, 1965.

_____. *Syria: A Short History.* London: Macmillan, 1959.

_____. *The Syrians in America.* New York: George Doran, 1924.

Al Hoda. *The Story of Lebanon and Its Emigrants.* New York: Al Hoda Press, 1968.

Hooglund, Eric, ed. *Crossing the Waters: Arabic-Speaking Immigrants to the United States before 1940.* Washington, DC: Smithsonian Institution Press, 1987.

_____. *Taking Root.* Washington, DC: American-Arab Anti-Discrimination Committee, 1985.

Houghton, Louise Seymour. "The Syrians in the United States." *Survey* 26.1–4 (1911): 480–495, 647–665, 786–802, 957–968.

Hourani, Albert. *A History of the Arab Peoples.* New York: Warner Books, 1991.

Howe, Russell Warren. "Arab-Americans Seen as Pro-Reagan." *Washington Times,* 31 August 1984.

Hughes, James. "An Open House." *New Yorker,* October 1980.

"The Hyaks and the Alkeks, among the Pioneer Grocerymen of Victoria." *In The Victoria Sesquicentennial Scrapbook, 1824–1974.* Victoria, Tex.: Advocate Printing, 1974.

"Interview with Jonathan Kuttub." *Arab-American Affairs* 16 (Spring 1986): 120–127.

Issawi, Charles, ed. *The Economic History of the Middle East, 1800–1914.* Chicago: University of Chicago Press/Midway Reprint, 1975.

Jaafari, Lafi Ibrahim. "The Brain Drain to the United States: The Migration of Jordanian and Palestinian Professionals and Students." *Journal of Palestine Studies* 3.1 (1971): 119–131.

Jacobs, Joseph J. *The Anatomy of an Entrepreneur: Family, Culture, and Ethics.* San Francisco: Institute of Contemporary Studies Press, 1991.

_____. *Jacobs Engineering Group, Inc.: A Story of Pride, Reputation, and Integrity.* Princeton, NJ: Newcomen Society, 1980.

_____. "Lebanon Reconstruction: Fantasy Amid Chaos." Paper delivered to a seminar at the Center for International Development, University of Maryland 23 July 1985.

Jessup, Henry. *Fifty-three Years in Syria.* New York: Fleming H. Revell Co., 1910.

Jiryis, Sabri. *The Arabs in Israel*. New York: Monthly Review Press, 1976.

Joseph, Lawrence. *Into It*. New York: Farrar, Strauss & Giroux, 2005.

_____. *Shouting at No One*. Pittsburgh: University of Pittsburgh Press, 1983.

Jubran, Zakia Makla. "The Makla Family History." Ms., Brooklyn, 1981.

Kadi, Joanna, ed. *Food for Our Grandmothers: Writings by Arab-American and Arab-Canadian Feminists*. Boston: South End Press, 1994.

Kahf, Mohja. *E-Mails from Scheherazad*. Gainesville, FL: University Press of Florida, 2003.

Karkabi, Barbara, and Rebecca Trounson. "Houston's Arab-Americas: Trying to Pull Together." *Houston Chronicle*, 18–20 January 1986.

Katibah, Habib Ibrahim. "Syrian Americans," in *One America*, ed. Francis J. Brown and Joseph S. Roucek. New York: Prentice-Hall, 1945.

_____, and Farhat Ziadeh. *Arabic-Speaking Americans*. New York: Institute of Arab American Affairs, 1941.

Kayal, Philip M. *An Arab-American Bibliographic Guide*. Belmont, MA: Association of Arab-American University Graduates, 1985.

_____, and Joseph M. Kayal. *The Syrian-Lebanese in America: A Study in Religion and Assimilation*. Boston: Twayne, 1975.

Khalidi, Rashid. *Palestinian Identity*. New York: Columbia University Press, 1997.

Khalidi, Walid. *Conflict and Violence in Lebanon*. Cambridge: Harvard University Press, 1979.

Kherbawi, Reverend Basil. *History of the United States and the History of the Syrian Immigration* (in Arabic). New York: Al-Dalil Press, 1913.

El-Khourie, H. A. "In Defense of the Semitic and the Syrian Especially." *Birmingham Ledger*, 20 September 1907.

Kimmerling, Baruch, and Joel S. Migdal. *Palestinians: The Making of a People*. New York: The Free Press, 1993.

Kinsley, Michael. "St. Ralph." *Washington Post*, 21 November 1985.

LaHood, Louis. *Wings in the Hands of the Lord: A World War II Journal*. Peoria, IL: Privately published, 1977.

Lamb, David. "US Arabs Close Ranks over Bias." *Los Angeles Times*, 13 March 1987: 1, 26, 27.

Lalami, Laila. *Hope and Other Dangerous Pursuits*. Chapel Hill, NC: Algonquin Books, 2005.

Latham, Scott. "No Slack Season for Haggar Chief." *Dallas Times-Herald*, 18 November 1976.

Lesley, Lewis Burt, ed. *Uncle Sam's Camels*. Cambridge: Harvard University Press, 1929.

Lilienthal, Alfred. *The Zionist Connection II: What Price Peace?*. Seal Beach, CA: Concord Books, 1983.

"The Lutemaker of Brooklyn" [Ernest Maliha]. *Aramco World Magazine* 9 (November 1958): 3–5.

McGarry, Charles. *Citizen Nader*. New York: Saturday Review Press, 1972.

Macron, Mary Haddad. *Arab-Americans and Their Communities of Cleveland*. Cleveland: Cleveland State University Ethnic Heritage Studies, 1979.

Madison, Christopher. "Arab-American Lobby Fights Rearguard Battle to Influence US Mideast Policy." *National Journal*, 31 August 1985: 1934–1939.

Makdisi, Nadim. "Arab Adventurers in the New World." *Yearbook 1965–66*. New York: Action Committee on Arab American Relations, 1966.

_____. "The Maronite in the Americas and in Atlanta." In *Golden Jubilee Book*. Atlanta: Atlanta Maronite Community, 1962.

_____. "The Moslems of America." *Christian Century* 76 (26 August 1959): 969–971.

Maloof, Sam. *Sam Maloof, Woodworker.* Tokyo: Kodan-sha, 1989.

Mansur, W. A. "Problems of Syrian Youth in America." *Syrian World* 2.6 (December 1927): 8–12; 2.7 (January 1928): 9–14.

Marley, Mike. "Hagler Lives Up to Tradition of Middleweight Champions." *New York Post,* 3 October 1981.

Mattawa, Khaled. *Ismailia Eclipse.* New York: Sheep Meadow Press, 1997.

_____ and Pauline Kaldas, eds. *Dinarzad's Children: An Anthology of Contemporary Arab American Fiction.* Little Rock, AK: University of Arkansas Press, 2004.

May, Clifford. "Lebanese in Africa: Tale of Success (and Anxiety)." *New York Times,* 9 July 1984.

Mehdi, Beverlee Turner. *The Arabs in America, 1492–1977: A Chronology and Fact Book.* Dobbs Ferry, NY: Oceana Publications, 1978.

Melhem, D. H. *Conversations with a Stone Mason.* New York: Ikon, Inc., 2003.

_____. *Rest in Love.* New York: Dovetail Press, 1975.

Melkites in America: A Dictionary and Informative Handbook. West Newton, MA: Melkite Exarchate, 1971.

Milbert, Neil. "Syrian Challenger Has Exotic Fight Credentials, Too." *Chicago Tribune,* 29 September 1981.

Miller, Lucius Hopkins. *Our Syrian Population: A Study of the Syrian Communities of Greater New York.* San Francisco: R. D. Reed, 1969 (reprint of the 1904 edition).

Moehinger, J. R. "Said's Style Is Convincing, Charisma Seen as Dangerous." *Yale Daily News,* 4 October 1983.

Mokarzel, Salloum. "Christian Muslem Marriages." *Syrian World* 2 (April 1928): 14.

_____. *The History of the Syrian American Immigrants in America, 1920–1921* (in Arabic). New York: Syrian American Press, n.d.

_____. "History of the Syrians in New York." *Syrian World* 2.5 (November 1927): 3–13.

_____. *A Picturesque Colony.* New York Tribune, 2 October 1892: 21.

Morse, Susan. "Dearborn Seamen Awarded $750,000 for Ship Accident." *Detroit Free Press,* 16 January 1977.

Moses, John G. *From Mt. Lebanon to the Mohawk Valley: The Story of Syro-Lebanese Americans of the Utica Area.* Utica, NY: Published by the author, 1981.

Murphy, Caryle. "Some Libyans Fear Qaddafi's Reach." *Washington Post,* 24 July 1985.

_____. "Tending Middle East Wounds, 12 Young Arabs Brought to US for Treatment." *Washington Post,* 5 March 1983.

Nabhan, Gary Paul. *Coming Home to Eat: The Pleasures and Politics of Local Foods.* New York: Norton, 2002.

_____. *Cultures of Habitat.* Washington, DC: Counterpoint, 1997.

_____. "Other Voices: Listening to a Broken World." *Orion,* May–June 2004.

Naff, Alixa. "Arabs." In *Harvard Encyclopedia of American Ethnic Groups,* ed. Stephen Thernstrom et al. Cambridge.: Belknap Press of Harvard University Press, 1980.

_____. *Becoming American: The Early Arab Immigrant Experience.* Carbondale, IL: Southern Illinois University Press, 1985.

Nasser, Eugene Paul. *A Walk Around the Block: Literary Texts and Social Contexts.* Utica, NY: Ethnic Heritage Studies Center, 1999.

_____. *Wind of the Land*. Detroit: Association of Arab-American University Graduates, 1979.

Neima, Dr. Theodore G. "An Epic Tale That Came Out of the Valley of Lebanon, a Biography of the Haddad Brothers." *News Circle* 10.117 (March 1982): 36–39.

The 9/11 Commission Report, New York: W. W. Norton & Co., 2004.

Noble, Alice. "Men's Clothing Store Only Sells American-Made Merchandise." *Chicago Tribune* 22 March 1981.

Noble, Frances Khirallah. *The Situe Stories*. Syracuse, NY: Syracuse University Press, 2000.

Noor, Queen. *Leap of Faith: Memoirs of an Unexpected Life*. New York: Miramax Books, 2003.

Nye, Naomi Shihab. *Habibi*. New York: Simon Pulse, 1999.

_____. *Hugging the Jukebox*. New York: Dutton, 1982.

_____. *Never in a Hurry: Essays on People and Places*. Columbia, SC: University of South Carolina Press, 1996.

_____. *19 Varieties of Gazelle: Poems of the Middle East*. New York: Greenwillow Press, 2002.

_____. "One Village." *Journal of Palestine Studies* 13.2 (January 1984): 31–47.

_____. *Words Under the Words: Selected Poems*. Portland, OR: Far Corner Books, 1995.

"Once Numerous Moslem Community Now Reduced to Half Dozen." *Minot [ND] Daily News,* 7 December 1968.

Orfalea, Gregory. *Before the Flames: A Quest for the History of Arab Americans*. Austin: University of Texas Press, 1988.

_____. *The Capital of Solitude*. Greenfield Center, NY: Ithaca House, 1988.

_____. "The Chandelier," in *Imagining America*. Wesley Brown and Amy Ling, eds. New York: Persea Books, 1991.

_____. *Messengers of the Lost Battalion: The Heroic 551st and the Turning of the Tide at the Battle of the Bulge*. New York: The Free Press, 1997.

_____. "Valley Boys." In *Jewish in America*. Sara Blair and Jonathan Freedman, eds. Ann Arbor: The University of Michigan Press, 2004.

_____, and Sharif Elmusa, eds. *Grape Leaves: A Century of Arab American Poetry*. Northampton, MA: Interlink, 2000.

_____, and Libby Jackowski. "The Arab Americans." *Aramco World Magazine* 37.5 (September–October 1986): 16–32.

_____, and Barbara Rosewicz, eds. *Up All Night: Practical Wisdom from Mothers and Fathers*. Mahwah, NJ: Paulist Press, 2004.

Orfalea, Paul and Ann Marsh. *Copy This!* New York: Workman Publishing Co., 2005.

The Orthodox Patriarchal Convent of Our Lady of Saydanaya. Jerusalem: Commercial Press, 1954.

Othman, Ibrahim. *Arabs in the United States: A Study of an Arab-American Community*. Amman, Jordan: Shashan and the University of Jordan, 1974.

Papier, Deborah. "Helen Thomas on the White House Beat." *Washington Times,* 5 December 1984.

Parrilo, Vincent A. *Strangers to These Shores*. New York: Macmillan, 1990.

Parsons, Levi. *Memoir of Levi Parsons, Late Missionary to Palestine*. Edited by Rev. Daniel O. Marton. Poultney, VT: 1924.

Perkins, Dr. Kenneth J. "Three Middle Eastern States Helped America Celebrate Its Centennial in Philadelphia." *Aramco World Magazine* 26.6 (November–December 1976).

Peters, Issa. "The Arabic-Speaking Community in Central Arizona before 1940."

Paper delivered at the Philip K. Hitti Symposium, Immigration History and Research Center, University of Minnesota, 4 June 1983.

Phelon, Craig. "Her Life Is a Festival All Year Long: A Day in the Life of Jo Ann Andera." *San Antonio Express News Sunday Magazine,* 31 July 1983.

Piestschmann, Richard J. "Casey's Quandary." *Los Angeles Magazine,* 1 April 1983: 132.

Pop, Nathan. "Casey Kasem." *Boston Globe,* 30 March 1985.

Al-Qazzaz, Ayad. *Transnational Links between Arab Community in the United States and the Arab World.* Sacramento: Cal Central Press, 1979.

Randal, Jonathan. *Going All the Way: Christian Warlords, Israeli Adventurers, and the War in Lebanon.* New York: Viking, 1983.

Reddy, Stan. "DeBakey." *Houston Chronicle (Texas Magazine),* 12 October 1980.

"Relief Movements among US Syrians." *Syrian World* 6.2 (October 1931): 54–55.

Rihani, Ameen. *The Book of Khalid.* New York: Dodd, Mead, 1911.

Rihbany, Abraham Mitry. *A Far Journey.* Boston: Houghton Mifflin, 1914.

Rizk, Salom. *Syrian Yankee.* Garden City, NY: Doubleday, 1943.

Rowe, Jonathan. "Nader Reconsidered." *Washington Monthly* March 1985: 12–21.

Roy, Sara. *The Gaza Strip: The Political Economy of Re-Development.* Washington, DC: Institute of Palestine Studies, 1995.

_____. in "Living with the Holocaust: the Journey of a Child of Holocaust Survivors," in *Prophets Outcast.* ed. Adam Shatz, New York: Nation Books, 2004.

Ruane, Michael and Sari Horwitz. *Sniper.* New York: Random House, 2004.

Saba, Michael. *The Armaggedon Network.* Vermont: Amana Books, 1984.

Sadd, Gladys Shibley. "First Generation Americans: A Stroll Down Memory Lane." *New Lebanese American Journal* 9.34 (6 December 1982): 8, 10.

Safa, Milhem, ed. "A Farewell Speech to My Brethren, the Druze." Ms., Qara Qool al Druze, Lebanon, 22 January 1931.

Said, Edward. *After the Last Sky.* New York: Pantheon, 1986.

_____. *Orientalism.* New York: Vintage Books, 1978.

_____. *Out of Place.* New York: Knopf, 2000.

_____. *Peace and Its Discontents.* New York: Vintage, 1996.

_____. *The World, the Text, the Critic.* Cambridge: Harvard University Press, 1983.

Sakir, Said Joseph. *The Original Eulogy of the Deceased Arbeely Family.* New York: Kowkab America, 1904. (In Arabic)

Salaita, Steven. *Terrifying Patriotism: How Anti-Arab Racism Justifies Empire and Threatens Democracy.* Monroe, ME: Common Courage Press, 2005.

Salamey, Margaret K. *Grandmother Told Me.* Utica, NY: Published by the author, 1982.

Samore, Lee T. "A Sociologistic Survey of the Lebanese Orthodox-Christian Community in Sioux City, Iowa." Paper delivered at the Philip K. Hitti Symposium, Immigration History and Research Center, University of Minnesota, 4 June 1983.

Samra, Father Nicholas. "Early Beginnings of the Melkite Church in the US" *Sophia* 13.2 (March–April 1983): 3.

_____. "Rugby Update." *Sophia* 13.6 (November–December 1983): 2.

Schmidt, Dana Adams. "Arab-Americans Gearing for Los Angeles Olympics." *Middle East Times,* 7–14 July 1984.

Scriber, Mary Jane. "DeBakey Keeps Ambitious Pace as He Nears 75." *Houston Post* 4 September 1983.

Selim, George Dimitri. *The Arabs in the United States: A Selected List of References.* Washington, DC: Library of Congress, 1983.

Sengstock, Mary C. *Chaldean Americans: Changing Conceptions of Ethnic Identity, 2nd ed.*. Staten Island, NY: Center for Migration Studies, 1998.

_____. *Chaldeans in Michigan*. Lansing: Michigan State University Press, 2005.

Shadid, Michael. *A Doctor for the People: The Autobiography of the Founder of America's First Cooperative Hospital*. New York: Vanguard Press, 1939.

Shaheen, Jack. "A Gathering of 4 Generations." *Pittsburgh Post Gazette,* 22 August 1983.

_____. *Reel Bad Arabs: How Hollywood Vilifies a People*. Northampton, MA: Olive Branch Press, 2001.

Shakir, Evelyn. *Bint Arab*. Westport, CT: Praeger, 1997.

_____. "Pretending to Be an Arab: Role-Playing in Vance Bourjaily's 'The Fractional Man,'" *MELUS* 9.1 (Spring 1982): 7–21.

_____. "Starting Anew: Arab-American Poetry." *Ethnic Forum* 7.1 (1983): 9–13.

Shatara, F. I. "Health Problems of the Syrians in the United States." *Syrian World* 1.3 (September 1926): 8-10.

Shihab, Aziz. *Sirhan*. San Antonio: Naylor Co., 1969.

_____. *A Taste of Palestine*. Texas: Corona Publishing Co., 1993.

Shindler, Merrill. "Jean and Casey Kasem Raise Pot of Gold for the Rainbow Coalition." *News Circle* 12.144 (June 1984): 32.

Shipler, David. *Arab and Jew: Wounded Spirits in the Promised Land*. New York: Penguin, 1987.

Smith, Marlene Khoury. "The Arabic-Speaking Communities in Rhode Island." In *Hidden Minorities: The Persistence of Ethnicity in American Life*, ed. Joan H. Rollins. Washington, DC: University Press of America, 1981.

Smith, Toby. "Arrows from Strong Bows." *New Mexico Magazine*, February 1982.

Soffee, Anne Thomas. *Snake Hips: Belly Dancing and How I Found Love*. Chicago: Chicago Review Press, 2002.

Spiegel, Joy. *That Haggar Man: A Biographical Portrait*. New York: Random House, 1978.

Stern, Zeida. *Ethnic New York*. New York: St. Martin's Press, 1980.

Stevenson, Kathy Jaber. "Modern Day Forty-Miners: The Druze of Southern California." *Our World* 1.2 (Winter 1985): 36–38.

Suleiman, Michael, ed. *Arabs in America: Building a New Future*. Philadelphia: Temple University Press, 1999.

_____. *Arabs in the Mind of America*. Brattleboro, VT: Amana Books, 1988.

Sullivan, Michael B. "Damascus in Brooklyn." *Aramco World Magazine* 17 (May–June 1961): 28–33.

Swanson, Jon. "Sojourners and Settlers in Yemen and America." Ms., 1985.

_____. *The Syrian and Lebanese Texans*. San Antonio: Institute of Texan Cultures, 1974.

"Syrians of Boston Present Symbolic Painting." *Syrian World* 6.8 (May 1932): 51.

Tahan, Mary. "Bob Andrews Heads Lettuce Kingdom While Scoring High in Community Services." *News Circle* 9.103 (January 1981): 23–29.

_____. "A Grateful Salute to the Haddads: Amean, Holline, Wydea, and Nazera." *News Circle* 10.117 (March 1982): 34–35.

Talhami, Shibley. *The Stakes: America and the Middle East*. Boulder, CO: Westview Press, 2002.

Tanber, George Joseph. "John's World: The Story of John Abood." *Toledo (Blade) Magazine,* January 18–24, 1987, pp. 6–12.

Tannous, Afif. "Acculturation of an Arab-Syrian Community in the Deep South." *American Sociological Review* 8 (June 1943): 264–271.

Thomas, Danny. "The Vow I Almost Forgot." *Guideposts* 36.3 (May 1981): 4.

Thomas, Helen. *Dateline: Washington.* New York: Macmillan, 1975.

_____. *Front Row at the White House: My Life and Times.* New York: Simon and Shuster, 2000.

Thomas, Katrina. "Festival in Fall River." *Aramco World Magazine* 27.6 (November–December 1976): 2–7.

Tillman, Seth. *The United States and the Middle East.* Bloomington: Indiana University Press, 1982.

Tintle, Joe. "Mustapha Hamsho: Syrian-Bred, American-Based." *Ring Magazine* December 1980: 35.

Tuma, Elias H. "The Palestinians in America." *The Link* 14.3 (July–August 1981):1–14.

Turki, Fawaz. *Exile's Return: The Making of a Palestinian American.* New York: Simon and Schuster, 1994.

_____. *Tel Zaatar Was the Hill of Thyme.* Washington, DC: Palestine Review Press, 1978.

Van Slyke, Lucille Baldwin. "The Peddler." *American Magazine,* 74 (August 1912): 411.

Viorst, Milton. "Building an Arab-American Lobby." *Washington Post Magazine,* 14 September 1980.

Wasfi, Atif A. *An Islamic-Lebanese Community in the USA: A Study in Cultural Anthropology.* Beirut: Beirut Arab University, 1971.

Wilbon, Michael. "Seikaly Is a Man of the World, a Babe on the Basketball Court." *Washington Post,* 22 February 1987.

"Will the Palestinians Tolerate Such?." *Al-Bayan,* November 16,1927. Translated in *Syrian World* 2.6 (December 1927).

Yorkin, Nicole. "KNBC Newsman Helps Bring Couple Orphan Boy to LA" *Los Angeles Herald-Examiner* 1 December 1983.

Younis, Adele. "The Arabs Who Followed Columbus." *Arab World* (New York) 12 March 1966: 13–14; August 1966: 14–15.

_____. Philip Kayal, ed. *The Coming of the Arabic-Speaking People to the United States.* New York: Center for Migration Studies, 1995.

_____. "Salem and the Early Syrian Venture." Essex Historical Collection, October 1966: 304.

Zelditch, Morris. "The Syrians in Pittsburgh." Master's thesis. University of Pennsylvania, 1936.

GLOSSARY

The Arabic words are given according to the Library of Congress transliteration system. That system uses literary, or classical, Arabic as a standard, which is the Arabic used in writing. Spoken Arabic has many dialects. Syro-Lebanese immigrants and their descendants rarely pronounce, for instance, an initial "q," or qaf, and tend to turn many "ah" endings into "ee." To give only one example: a Syrian or Lebanese would never ask for coffee by asking for *qahwah*, the classical written form, which is also what an Egyptian would say; he would ask for *ahwee*, or *ahwi*.

ʿaba: cloak, robe
ʿa biladna: to our country, or village
ʿadas: lentils
Adhraʾ: Blessed Mother, Virgin
Ahlan wa sahlan, ya akhi: Welcome, my
  brother.
ahwi: *See* qahwa.
Akbar minnak, walad: I'm older than
  you, kid.
ʿAla mahlak!: Take it easy!
Allahu Akbar: God is great.
Allah yirhamu: God rest his soul.
Allah yirhamu, dashshiruh: God rest his
  soul, let him be.
Allah yikhalliki: May God preserve you
  [fem.].
ʿammu: uncle
ʿaraq: licorice-flavored clear liquor;
  water turns it white
arjila: hubble-bubble, water pipe
Ashbal: "Tiger Cubs," military unit of
  youngsters
ʿayb: shame
ʿaysha: life (*li-ʿaysha*: to life)
aywa: yes

baba ghannuj: eggplant dip
bab: gate
balattin: concrete and mud
baqlawa: diamond-shaped sweet
basra: card game
battikh: watermelon
bayt: house or home
bayt al-hurriya: the house of freedom
bilad: home country
bilad al-kufr: land of unbelief
braak: *See* ibriq.
bakhur: incense
bumin: bums
burnus: cloak with hood

dabka: a circle dance
darabukka: bongo drum
dibs kharrub: bucket of carob syrup

ful: fava beans
fustuq halabi: pistachio

habibi: my love
hafla: party
hajj: pilgrimage
halawa: a sweet made of crushed sesame
haram: forbidden; pitiful
haram, al-himar: the poor ass
harb: war
harkasha: one who stirs things up
hatta: the cloth worn underneath the
  Arab headpiece fastener (*ʿigal*)
al-hawa al-asfar: yellow fever
hijab: Muslim headdress
hijra: flight to escape danger
himar: donkey
hummus: a spread/dip made from chickpeas
husrum: a kind of sour grape

ibriq: glass water jug
ʿilki: chewing gum
ʿigal: ropelike fastener for a kufiya

jaddu: grandfather
jamiʾ: mosque
jarad: locust

kaki: Japanese persimmon
kathiran: a lot
kashishi. See qashsha
khalas: It is finished
khirsana: wild grass
khubbayza: clover
khubz: bread
khokh: plum

474

khuri: Orthodox priest
kibba: meatball
kibba maʿa kishk: meatball with bulgur and sour milk
kibba naya: raw lamb
Kifak baʿdi?: How are you, part of me?
kufiya: headdress
kefta: meatball with bulgur
kull she: everything
kunafa: bird's nest (a sweet)
kusa: zucchini

la: no
laban: yogurt
labani: yogurt spread
lahm mashwi: grilled meat
lakin: but
lakinni: but I
lawajh Allah: for the face of God
layl: night
lubnan: white; Arabic for Lebanon
luz: almonds

Maʿalish?: What does it matter?
madjidy: Turkish dollar
Maktub: It is written.
Marhaban: Hello.
maʾzahr: orange water
mazza: hors d'oeuvre
mishmish Hindi: loquat
Mnerfaʿ al-mawta min al-qabr: We can raise the dead from the tomb; we can do anything.
muezzin: Muslim chanter who calls out the times for prayers
mughliya: powdered rice with spices, sugar, and nuts; made in celebration of newborns
murra: bitter
mutasarrif: ruler, governor; protectorate

al-Nakba: "The 1948 Catastrophe," Israel's war of independence
naʿnaʿ: mint
nashkur Allah: thanks to God
nastar: a fern
nilʿab waraq: play cards

qahwa: coffee
qamar al-din: pressed apricot (literally, moon of the religion)
qamh: wheat kernels, sweetened barley
qashsha: peddler's bag
qirfa: cinnamon
qishta: prickly custard apple
Qult, "Mat": I said, "He died."
quna: icon

rumman: pomegranates

safiha: meat pies
sahra: party
Al-salah afdal min al-nawm: Prayer is better than sleep.
Salamtik: Your [fem.] health
As-Salamu ʿalykum: Peace be with you, Greetings.
salli: pray [imperative]
samid: farina or semolina; a ring-shaped biscuit sprinkled with sesame seed
Sarit tibki, haram: She started to cry, sad to say.
sayidna: your eminence
shish taouk: chicken kebob
shu ismuh: what's his name
shukran: thank you
sunubar: pine nuts
suq: marketplace

tabbula: parsley and bulgur salad
tabla: tubular drum
tahina: sesame seed oil
taʿishin: frivolous ones
tarbush: fez
tawila: backgammon
tayo: Syriac for early Christians
tayta: grandmother
tadhkara: passport, identity card
thatee: See tayta.
thawra: revolution
tiz: buttocks
tum: garlic
tunbur: wagon

ʿud: musical instrument similar to a mandolin; oudist, one who plays an ʿud
ufaddilu: I prefer

wakil al-mughtaribin: native Yemeni lenders
Wallah: by God
waraq ʿinab: grape leaves
wasat: medium
Wayn al-ʿarus?: Where's the bride?
Wayn fatah?: Where are you opening?
Wiynu akhuki?: Where's your [fem.]
    brother?

ya Allah: my God
Ya ʿayni! Ya akhi: My eye! My brother!
ya ʿuyuni: my eyes
ya dini: my religion
Ya haram: What a shame.
Yallah!: Let's go!
Ya tiqburni: Bury me.

zaghrut: a woman's trilling cry of joy
zajal: folk poetry
zaʿtar: thyme
zayt: oil
zaytuna: an olive
zibib: raisins
zidra: stone bowl
zum: juice

INDEX OF NAMES

GENERAL INDEX

T

U